Handbook of Leadership and Administration for Special Education

This book brings together for the first time research informing leadership practice in special education from preschool through transition into post-secondary settings. It provides comprehensive coverage of 1) disability policy, 2) leadership knowledge, 3) school reform, and 4) effective educational leadership practices. Broader in scope than previous books, it provides in-depth analysis by prominent scholars from across the disciplines of both general and special education leadership. Coverage includes historical roots, policy and legal perspectives, and content that illustrates the use of collaborative learning in the administration of special education.

Comprehensive—This is the first book to integrate the knowledge bases of special education and educational leadership as these fields impact school improvement and the performance of students with disabilities.

Chapter Structure—Chapters provide a review of the knowledge base as well as recommendations for special education leadership and future research.

Multicultural Focus—Addressing special education leadership within the context of a multicultural society, chapters incorporate content related to the diversity of families, teachers, and students.

Expertise—Chapter authors have made significant contributions to the knowledge base in their specific areas of study such as educational policy, special education law and finance, school reform, organizational management, and instructional leadership.

This book is a reference volume for scholars, leaders, and policy makers and a textbook for graduate courses in special education, educational administration, and policy studies.

Jean B. Crockett (Ph.D. University of Virginia) is Professor and Director of the School of Special Education, School Psychology, and Early Childhood Studies at the University of Florida.

Bonnie S. Billingsley (Ed.D. Virginia Tech) is Professor and Chair of the Department of Specialized Education Services at the University of North Carolina at Greensboro.

Mary Lynn Boscardin (Ph.D. University of Illinois, at Urbana-Champaign) is Professor and Chair of the Department of Student Development at the University of Massachusetts Amherst.

Handbook of Leadership and Administration for Special Education

Edited by Jean B. Crockett,
Bonnie S. Billingsley,
and Mary Lynn Boscardin

Routledge
Taylor & Francis Group

NEW YORK AND LONDON

First published 2012
by Routledge
711 Third Avenue, New York, NY 10017

Simultaneously published in the UK
by Routledge
2 Park Square, Milton Park, Abingdon, Oxon OX14 4RN

Routledge is an imprint of the Taylor & Francis Group, an informa business

Library of Congress Cataloging in Publication Data
Handbook of leadership and administration for special education / [edited by] Jean B. Crockett, Bonnie Billingsley, Mary Lynn Boscardin.
    p. cm.
    Includes bibliographical references and index.
    1. Special education teachers—Handbooks, manuals, etc. 2. Educational leadership—United States.
    3. School management and organization. I. Crockett, Jean B. II. Billingsley, Bonnie S. III. Boscardin, Mary Lynn.
    LC3969.45.H35 2012
    371.9'043—dc23
    2011046130

ISBN: 978-0-415-87280-5 (hbk)
ISBN: 978-0-415-87281-2 (pbk)
ISBN: 978-0-203-83731-3 (ebk)

Typeset in Bembo and Stone Sans
by EvS Communication Networx, Inc.

SFI Certified Sourcing
www.sfiprogram.org
SFI-00453

Printed and bound in the United States of America
by Edwards Brothers, Inc.

Contents

Preface

Ensuring high quality special education is the responsibility of educators who lead increasingly diverse and inclusive schools. Although special education evolved in the 20th century to assume a prominent place in American schooling, concerns with legal and fiscal matters often dominated the professional literature, leaving other critical dimensions of leaders' work unaddressed or misunderstood. In the 21st century, current policies require that students with disabilities have opportunities to learn the same challenging content as their general education peers, which emphasizes the need for educational leaders to take a broad view of their work that considers the linkages of leadership, learning, and equity.

Balancing disability policy with other critical responsibilities, such as supporting effective instructional practices in schools, is difficult and requires a holistic picture of leadership that includes not only the legal and fiscal aspects of special education, but the core principles that guide the meaningful education of individuals with disabilities. We argue that leaders who are well informed about special education and educational administration are better positioned to (a) foster equity for students with disabilities, (b) encourage collaborative partnerships among professionals and parents, (c) support effective teaching practices, and (d) organize schools to enhance teachers' work and students' learning.

This handbook offers a review of the foundational knowledge that informs leadership and administrative practice related to special education. Thus, this volume is designed to meet the informational needs of influential stakeholders who share the responsibility of strengthening schools so that students with disabilities might achieve and participate as integral members of their communities. Counted among these stakeholders are policy makers and legislative leaders, agency and district administrators, school principals, teacher leaders, parents, and community members who need accessible, research-based information to guide their decisions.

We asked our contributors to synthesize critical research that informs leadership for special education from preschool through post-secondary transition with close attention to issues of disability policy, leadership knowledge, inclusive education, and evidence-based educational practices. We also asked authors to incorporate material related to cultural, gender, and linguistic diversity to address contemporary leadership issues within the context of a multi-cultural society.

We have organized the handbook into five sections, each of which addresses a critical aspect of special education leadership and administration. Some of the critical issues do not have a specific chapter devoted to them because they are addressed within many chapters. Readers should not assume that if a chapter is not dedicated to a topic, the handbook does not address it.

The first section addresses general topics related to leadership for learning. These chapters explain the importance of raising the performance of all students in the current era of accountability, historical and conceptual issues in leading and administrating special education, professional leadership standards, and the development of educational leaders. These topics provide the foundation for understanding the context and development of leadership for contemporary special education.

The second section addresses leadership from the perspective of special education policies and school reforms. Legal frameworks and funding methods for educating students with disabilities are explained in these chapters, and the special challenges posed by school choice and charter schools are also examined. This section closes with a critique of conventional policies and a call for strong democratic leadership concerned with issues of disability, difference, and justice.

The third section takes a broad view of collaborative leadership within a multi-cultural context, illustrating the involvement of leaders in creating inclusive and effective educational services for students with disabilities. These chapters examine research related to assuming a distributed perspective of leadership for special education, frameworks for leading systemic, inclusive change, home-school partnerships, building trust and responding to conflict, and reducing the disproportionate referral to and placement of culturally and linguistically diverse students in special education.

The fourth section is devoted to providing instructional leadership for special education and evaluating the educational outcomes for students. Effective instruction is central to ensuring an appropriate education and these chapters provide a foundation for leaders and administrators responsible for evaluating teachers. Two chapters are devoted to improving the quality and effectiveness of special education teaching. Other chapters in this section address effective leadership for special education from cradle to adulthood that fosters the use of evidence-based practices, school-wide positive behavior supports, early intervention for young children with and at risk for developing disabilities, and transition for older students to post-secondary settings.

Finally the fifth section addresses the challenges that leaders face every day in a policy context that emphasizes the use of a standards-based curriculum for educating all students, including students with disabilities. In this final chapter, the not-so-new standards-based reform movement is examined in relation to providing an equitable education for special education students. Perhaps the biggest challenge for educational leaders is reconciling the tensions and ambiguities between standards-based education and the individualized focus of special education policies.

We have attempted to address critical issues in providing leadership and administration for special education in 21st-century schools. As much as we tried, we know there is always more to say, but we hope this collection of writings by outstanding scholars will help to link research with the practice of leading and administering special education in contemporary schools.

We thank our chapter authors for working with us on this project. Their efforts were central to the compilation of research-based information about special education to guide the informed decisions of educational leaders. Their dedication to this project allows us to turn over the royalty earnings from this book into a fund providing an annual award for a researcher whose work has advanced the effective leadership and administration of special education.

Finally, we express appreciation for the encouragement and support of our editor at Routledge, Lane Akers, who suggested this project to us, supported us in the process, and encouraged us in our desire to contribute the proceeds from this volume toward the advancement of leadership for special education informed by the wisdom of practice and the power of educational research. Editorship was shared equally among the three editors, with each assuming leadership in different aspects of development.

JBC
BSB
MLB

Contributors

Leonard Baca, University of Colorado at Boulder

Bruce D. Baker, Rutgers University

Bonnie S. Billingsley, University of North Carolina at Greensboro

Mary Lynn Boscardin, University of Massachusetts Amherst

Mary T. Brownell, University of Florida

Bryan G. Cook, University of Hawaii at Manoa

Jake Cornett, SRI International

Jean B. Crockett, University of Florida

Robert Crow, Developmental Behavior Analysis, Gainesville, FL

Crystal D. Crowe, University of Florida

Donald D. Deshler, University of Kansas

Amy Eppolito, University of Colorado at Boulder

Preston C. Green, III, The Pennsylvania State University

Beth Harry, University of Miami

John J. Hoover, University of Colorado at Boulder

Robert H. Horner, University of Oregon

Jennifer J. Huber, Arizona State University

Antonis Katsiyannis, Clemson University

Janette K. Klingner, University of Colorado at Boulder

Elizabeth Kozleski, Arizona State University

Barbara J. Lake, Virginia Tech

Carl Lashley, University of North Carolina at Greensboro

Sheryl S. Lazarus, University of Minnesota

Timothy J. Lewis, University of Missouri

Margaret J. McLaughlin, University of Maryland

James McLeskey, University of Florida

Julie F. Mead, University of Wisconsin–Madison

Valerie L. Mazzotti, Western Carolina University

April L. Mustian, Illinois State University

Breda V. O'Keeffe, University of Utah

Barbara L. Pazey, University of Texas at Austin

Rachel F. Quenemoen, University of Minnesota

Matthew J. Ramsey, University of Kansas

Paul T. Sindelar, University of Florida

Thomas M. Skrtic, University of Kansas

Amy F. Smith, University of California at Davis

Garnett J. Smith, University of Hawaii at Manoa

Patricia A. Snyder, University of Florida

Art Stewart, Virginia Department of Education

George Sugai, University of Connecticut

David W. Test, University of North Carolina at Charlotte

Susan S. Thomas, Berkeley County School District, South Carolina

Martha L. Thurlow, University of Minnesota

Tracy G. Wilkinson, University of Maryland

James R. Yates, University of Texas at Austin

Mitchell L. Yell, University of South Carolina

Section I
The Context and Development of Leadership for Special Education
Introduction

Over the past 40 years children with disabilities, their parents, and the professionals who work with them have revolutionized schooling in developed countries around the globe. For most students, special education occurs in the context of schools and improving schools for the learning of all students is now the dominant concern of stakeholders. As a result much attention has been paid to the conditions in schools that help to explain student achievement, and much has been learned about educational leadership and the critical role it plays in improving schools.

The chapters in this section provide the foundation for understanding the context and development of leadership for contemporary special education. In the context of schools, leadership is defined as "the work of mobilizing and influencing others to articulate and achieve the school's shared intentions and goals" (Leithwood & Riehl, 2005, p. 14). By extension, leadership for special education, regardless of one's administrative title or professional role, ensures that these shared intentions and goals provide equitable access, appropriate expertise, and high quality programming that foster meaningful outcomes for students with disabilities.

Thurlow, Quenemoen, and Lazarus (Chapter 1) help to frame the chapters that follow by contextualizing the era in which students with disabilities are being educated. They point out that never before have the stakes seemed so high for school leaders. With the implementation of the 2001 reauthorization of the Elementary and Secondary Schools Act known as No Child Left Behind (NCLB), and many federal laws and regulations before and after it, school leaders are being and will be held accountable for the performance of all their students, including students with disabilities. In this era of accountability, the gap in performance of students with disabilities as a sub-group of the student population, presents a leadership challenge. Despite alternative accountability approaches, such as growth models and differentiated accountability, there remains a need for systematic efforts to improve their academic performance. The authors cite research-based evidence, emerging from schools where students with disabilities are performing at high levels, that can inform these improvement efforts. Based on the research, suggestions are provided for leaders at the district, school, and classroom levels.

Critical questions pertaining to the conceptual foundations of the leadership and administration of special education are addressed by Pazey and Yates (Chapter 2.) They trace the evolution of special education leadership over time, noting that the emergence of this role has not followed a linear progression, nor has it been without uncertainty, complexity, conflict, and stress on both individuals and systems responsible for ensuring services for students with disabilities. The authors examine previous strategies and models for providing services, and describe special education leadership as an emerging discipline today. Their discussion of the current context of special education leadership provides insight into the roles, responsibilities, potential conflicts, and changes leaders for special education are likely to face in the future. Forecasts are also made about the type of information, training and practice needs of leaders and administrators for special education in the 21st century.

Boscardin and Lashley (Chapter 3) note that the knowledge traditions and practices of special education have traditionally dominated the special education administration discourse. As inclusive practice and accountability continue to shape American education, they argue that special education and general education leaders will be challenged to join together to solve the problems of practice inherent in a diverse, complex, high-stakes educational environment. This chapter has three purposes: (a) to present the varied knowledge bases informing special and general education administration standards; (b) to present the national policy standards developed by the professional organizations representing special and general education administration; and (c) to introduce an expanded leadership framework to guide the work of aspiring to retiring leaders. These authors encourage readers to think of leadership standards as providing a vision and guidelines for policy that can be tailored to meet the professional needs of organizations and the individuals who lead them.

Concluding this section, Crockett (Chapter 4) examines the preparedness of educational leaders to support the equitable and effective education of students with disabilities and other diverse learners, and discusses approaches to developing the next generation of accomplished educational leaders for inclusive schools. In arguing for the improvement of leadership preparation and development, Crockett reviews research linking special education knowledge to leadership practices, and examines the ways special education knowledge and beliefs make a difference in providing opportunities to learn for a diversity of students. She also makes suggestions for strategies to strengthen leadership preparation, induction, and on-going support with knowledge and skills in leading special education that forge the linkage of leadership, learning, and equity.

References

Leithwood, K. A., & Riehl, C. (2005). What do we already know about educational leadership? In W. A. Firestone & C. Riehl (Eds.), *A new agenda for research in educational leadership* (pp. 12–27). New York: Teachers College Press.

Leadership for Student Performance in an Era of Accountability

Martha L. Thurlow, Rachel F. Quenemoen, and Sheryl S. Lazarus

NATIONAL CENTER ON EDUCATIONAL OUTCOMES, UNIVERSITY OF MINNESOTA

Educational leaders across the country have been bearing the burden for meeting accountability goals, whether they are setting accountability policies or implementing them. The goal of increasing the performance of students in general, and particularly increasing the performance of those students receiving special education services, seems to have been one of the greater challenges that educational leaders have faced. School leaders provide purpose and direction, shape culture and values, facilitate the development of a shared vision, formulate goals, and set priorities (Thomson, 1993). School leaders also are held accountable for student learning, so it is important to consider how to provide leadership that will improve student outcomes for all students, including students with disabilities.

Successful reform that leads to sustained change requires a continuous collaborative process that involves the entire school. To implement changes that lead to improved student performance, educational leaders must create a culture that values the learning of all students including students who are sometimes difficult to instruct and assess. An effective leader must help create a vision and culture that values all students and includes a "hunger to see improvement" (Kurland, Peretz, & Hertz-Lazarowitz, 2010; Thompson, Lazarus, Clapper, & Thurlow, 2006; Thomson, 1993).

This chapter addresses the opportunities and challenges that leaders face as special and general educators work together to design learning environments that support the achievement of grade-level content by all students, including students with disabilities. The purpose of this chapter is to describe the context of the current reform movement and highlight the policies that drive accountability for student performance, as well as recent policy initiatives that are meant to promote increased student achievement. We describe recent accountability models, including growth models and differentiated accountability, as well as explore state and district responses to accountability requirements. After exploring current progress in the participation and performance of students with disabilities, we identify and discuss the implications for leadership in the era of accountability.

Context and Policies

History and Background

For years, it has seemed that the philosophy of many educators has been that school reforms are fads that come and go, and that all one has to do is wait a few years, and the latest reform shall pass. In the 1980s, one such "fad" was born out of the Reagan administration's disinterest in a strong federal role in public education (U.S. Department of Education, 1998), and the slightly incongruous call to arms called "A Nation at Risk" that was based on work from a Commission established by Reagan's secretary of education (National Commission on Excellence in Education, 1983). At about the same time, a group of governors with a focused interest in educational reform had formed a coalition across party lines, geographic boundaries, and educational philosophies that pushed the limits of previous reform efforts (National Governors' Association, 1986). This reform—which eventually became known as standards-based reform—did not "pass" in a few years, and remains the dominant reform in place across the country (Shepard, Hannaway, & Baker, 2009).

We have achieved remarkable consensus on standards-based reform in this country over the decades since *A Nation at Risk* was released, across political parties and across social and economic boundaries. The basic premise of commitment to all students and accountability for all (see McDonnell, McLaughlin, & Morison, 1997) has sustained support. We may argue about how to carry these reforms out, but there appears to be agreement about the basic premise. Yet in special education for the past quarter century, there seemed to be a tendency to use the Individualized Education Program (IEP) process to define "how much lower the standard can be." Parents or advocates pushed back schools to ensure that the IEP process be used to identify the services, supports, and specialized instruction needed so that, the child did reach the standards required for successful futures.

The staying power of standards-based reform is not its only unique feature. Unlike most previous reform efforts, standards-based reform has been accompanied by federal laws and policies that require that all students—those with disabilities, poor students, and students of all ethnic groups—be included in the implementation of academic standards. Unlike most previous reform efforts, there was an emphasis on measuring outcomes to improve the results of public education systems, and not to sort students for promotion or placement. According to Goertz (2007):

> Accountability for the outcomes of schooling has shifted from students to schools and school districts, and the purposes of assessment have expanded from placing and promoting students to generating indicators of performance of the education system, motivating educators to change their instructional content and strategies, and aiding in instructional decisions about individual students.
>
> *(p. 10)*

Accountability Policies

Educational accountability has evolved over time. It has been implemented both for the process/procedures of education and for the results of education. The accountability models that have received the most attention in the past decade have been those that grew out of the Elementary and Secondary Education Act (ESEA), and that emphasized educational results. Yet, other models also have emerged, with states responding in a variety of ways to these accountability models.

Federal Laws and Regulations

ESEA was first enacted in 1965 to provide educational opportunities to children disadvantaged by poverty or ethnic status. The accountability mechanisms in this law were limited, primarily relying on school districts to keep track of the progress of their disadvantaged students in schools receiving Title I funds. Generally, progress was monitored by administering norm-referenced tests that showed improvements, regardless of how small the increases in performance were, or whether they related to the knowledge and skills that students were going to need to be successful in the next grade.

Because of concerns about the continued achievement gaps exhibited by disadvantaged students, the reauthorization of ESEA in 1994 (known as the Improving America's Schools Act—IASA) initiated the standards-based reform movement by requiring the progress of students receiving Title I services to be evaluated on the basis of state standards-based assessments in which all students in the state were to participate (Elmore & Rothman, 1999). "All students" was defined as including students with disabilities, as well as other groups of students. The accountability model for IASA was based on public reporting of the results of these state assessments. The results were to be disaggregated for several groups of students, including students with disabilities.

The 1997 reauthorization of IDEA built on the 1994 ESEA by adding requirements for the participation of students with disabilities in state assessments. It specifically required that students with disabilities participate in the regular state assessment, with accommodations as appropriate, and for those students with disabilities who were unable to participate in the regular state assessment, an alternate assessment was to be developed. IDEA 97 also promoted, for the first time, access to the general curriculum, as a goal for all students with disabilities (Nolet & McLaughlin, 2005). It also required that the results of students with disabilities on the regular assessment be reported to the public in the same detail and frequency as the results for other students. The underlying goal, as specified in the preamble to IDEA 97, was to ensure accountability for the educational results of students with disabilities:

> the implementation of this Act has been impeded by low expectations, and an insufficient focus on applying replicable research on proven methods of teaching and learning for children with disabilities.... Over 20 years of research and experience has demonstrated that the education of children with disabilities can be made more effective by—having high expectations for such children and ensuring their access in the general curriculum to the maximum extent possible.
>
> *(20 U.S.C. §§ 1400 et seq.)*

The reauthorization of ESEA in 2001, known as the No Child Left Behind Act (NCLB), lamented the lack of improvement in and accountability for student performance. Thus, with NCLB, standards and assessments continued as the key elements of Title I law, but now were bolstered by accountability requirements of adequate yearly progress (AYP). Specifically, states were required to define state content standards in reading/language arts and mathematics (and later, science), and to develop assessments aligned to those standards. All students were to be included in those assessments, including students with disabilities. Public reporting was required, as it had been in IASA, but in addition schools and districts had to meet AYP goals that the state set for them. Consequences were assigned to those schools and districts not meeting AYP overall or for any subgroup; these included graduated actions, such as requiring schools not meeting targets to allow students to transfer schools, provide supplemental educational services, plan for restructuring the school, and eventually, restructuring the school. Through regulation, alternate assessments for students with significant cognitive disabilities were allowed to be based on different achievement standards, and to count up to 1% of the total population of students as proficient on the alternate assessment based on alternate achievement standards for accountability purposes.

In 2004, IDEA was reauthorized with greater alignment to NCLB. Specifically, it reaffirmed the importance of access to the curriculum, standards, assessments, and accountability. In 2007, through regulation, both IDEA and NCLB provided for the participation of students in an optional alternate assessment—this one based on modified achievement standards. Students with disabilities, totaling up to 2% of the population of all students, could be considered proficient based on this assessment.

When it was time to reauthorize ESEA, there were calls for doing things differently. With a new administration in the White House, there was a push to identify and implement innovative assessment approaches, as well as a desire to rethink the accountability system. Funds to support innovative instructional and assessment systems were available to states. An accountability system that focused on the lowest performing schools emerged as well.

Alternative Accountability Models

Schools were challenged by the accountability requirements of NCLB. There were many complaints that students with disabilities were the main reason that schools did not meet AYP, even though evaluations demonstrated that this was not the case (Stullich, Eisner, McCrary, & Roney, 2006; Taylor, Stecher, O'Day, Naftel, & LeFloch, 2010). Regardless, as the time for reauthorization of ESEA drew near, there was increased discussion of how the accountability system should be changed (Commission on No Child Left Behind, 2007). These discussions included two approaches that had been pilot tested in several states—growth models and differentiated accountability.

Growth Models.

Growth Models. Parents and educators want to know that their students are making progress during the school year and across school years. Growth models were proposed as a means of documenting that students were gaining knowledge and skills even though they might not be crossing target thresholds, such as those between below proficient and proficient status. This was the argument underlying the push for growth models (Goldschmidt & Choi, 2007; Linn, 2005).

Growth models typically track the achievement of individual students from year to year, or even within the same year. As implemented in a pilot study in 2006, several requirements had to be met by the growth models that states proposed (U.S. Department of Education, 2006; see also Goldschmidt et al., 2005). These were presented as core principles reflecting NCLB requirements, and included: assumptions that the target continues to be that all students are proficient by 2013–14, and thus the trajectories must reflect that goal; expectations for growth cannot be based on student demographics or school characteristics; the growth model needed to produce separate accountability decisions for reading/English language arts and math; all students in the tested grades in all schools and districts need to be included in the growth model, including subgroups such as students with disabilities; all states approved must have peer-review-approved assessment systems in place; the growth model must be able to track individual students over time; the growth models for accountability were required to include student assessment participation rates and one additional indicator (e.g., attendance, high school graduation rate).

Ten states received approval to conduct pilot tests of growth models that met the criteria outlined by the seven core principles. And, by the end of 2008, all states were allowed to develop growth models (U.S. Department of Education, 2008). Still, the initial studies of eight of the states in the growth model pilot suggested these models did not dramatically increase the percentage of schools meeting AYP from other means of accountability (Hoffer, Hedberg, Brown,

Halverson, & McDonald, 2010). The interim study found that the growth models resulted in a range of percentages of all schools that made AYP uniquely by growth (from 0–1% of all schools in Alaska, Arizona, North Carolina, and Tennessee to 11% of all schools in Iowa). However, the study concluded that these models do add somewhat to the number of schools making AYP, especially among schools serving low-income populations, even when growth is defined with the principles of universal proficiency by 2014. These overall low additional schools identified as making AYP by growth also were affected by practices that exhausted all other pathways to determine AYP (e.g., confidence intervals, multi-year averaging), leaving far fewer schools where the pilot growth models were actually applied.

Differentiated Accountability.   In 2008, the U.S. Department of Education announced a pilot program for differentiated accountability. This program was designed to help states improve underperforming schools by allowing states to create ways to distinguish between schools needing dramatic interventions and those that are close to meeting goals. States eligible to participate in the pilot program were encouraged to think creatively about how to choose the schools that would receive intensive help, and the nature of that help. Priority for approval was given to states that had relatively high percentages of Title I schools identified for improvement and that applied significant interventions to the lowest performing schools earlier in the improvement process.

Nine core principles were defined for peer reviewers to evaluate proposed differentiated accountability pilots: the state makes AYP determinations and continues to hold schools accountability for all students reaching proficiency in reading/language arts and math by 2013–2014; the state must provide clear explanations of how AYP is calculated for schools and districts and how all students are included in the accountability process; although the state continues to identify schools and districts for improvement, identification labels (e.g., schools needing improvement, corrective action, restructuring) may be changed to reflect differentiated interventions; differentiation in identification of schools for improvement is to be based primarily on students' demonstration of proficiency in reading/language arts and math, and the methodology is to be technically and educationally sound, based on robust data analysis, and uniformly applied across the state; the state must consider the current status of schools and interventions already implemented when transitioning to a differentiated accountability model; the process for differentiation and the interventions used are to be data-driven, understandable, and transparent to the public; the state must require that all identified schools receiving Title I funds receive interventions and progress through interventions that increase in intensity over time; the model must include interventions that are educationally sound and designed to promote meaningful reform; the model must establish clear eligibility criteria for public school choice and supplemental educational services (SES) and an educationally sound model designed to result in increased numbers of students participating in choice and SES; and the model must establish a timeline for the lowest performing schools to receive the most substantive and comprehensive interventions.

Six states were approved to participate in the differentiated accountability pilot program. No evaluation report has been released to this date.

State and District Responses to Accountability

The responses of states and districts to accountability have been varied. States generally have supported the intents of the accountability provisions, as evident in this statement from the Council of Chief State School Officers (2010):

> We need dramatic and continuous improvement in student achievement for all learners, particularly poor and minority students, English language learners, and students with

disabilities. This will require bold leadership, a focus on innovation, and a new form of state-federal partnership. ESEA reauthorization represents a great opportunity for a new vision and approach to achieve educational excellence and equity. We need to move beyond the important yet narrow goal of *no child left behind* to a goal of *every child a graduate*—prepared with the knowledge and skills necessary to succeed in college and career as productive citizens of America's diverse interconnected society and a globally-interconnected world. States are committed to leading in education reform, with a real commitment to high standards for all students.

(p. 5)

Most resistance has come from school districts, where the challenges of closing the achievement gaps for all students including those with disabilities have been the greatest. Nevertheless, the Council of Great City Schools in 2004 publicly supported the goals in public testimony to Congress:

The Council of the Great City Schools supported the passage of *No Child Left Behind* and continues to support the Act today. We backed the bill knowing that it had numerous challenges for urban schools, multiple requirements, and some poorly calibrated provisions. But, we believed that the legislation set the right goals and targeted the resources on the right kids—those too often left behind.

(Casserly, 2004, Paragraph 4)

In fact, in 2008, the Council of the Great City Schools published its eighth report on "beating the odds" in urban schools districts. The report indicated that:

Beating the Odds VIII shows that the Great City Schools continue to make important gains in math and reading scores on state assessments. The study also presents evidence that gaps may be narrowing.

(Snipes, Horwitz, Soga, & Casserly, 2008, p. iii)

Student Performance

Due to the prevailing perception in some districts and schools that students with disabilities disproportionately contributed to schools and districts missing accountability targets, the evaluation of NCLB specifically reported on the effects of students with disabilities (and other subgroups) on performance results. Table 1.1 shows an Exhibit presented in the 2006 implementation evaluation of Title I (Stullich et al., 2006). It showed that contrary to the prevailing perception, students with disabilities often showed increases in the percentage who were proficient and above, often with higher numbers of states showing increases in performance for this subgroup compared to other subgroups.

In addition to examining the number of states in which students performed at or above proficient, the evaluation report also examined the extent to which the disability subgroup by itself was responsible for a school not meeting AYP criteria. Figure 1.1 presents the figure that showed the number of states missing AYP solely due to students with disabilities. This figure revealed that only 14% of schools that did not make AYP did so only because of the disability subgroup; in fact, 35% of these schools missed targets for "all students." These results are shaped in part by the use of various approaches to calculating AYP that resulted in masking of subgroup data when the numbers in a group are small. Similarly, the accountability requirements of ESEA and

Table 1.1   Exhibit in 2006 Title I Evaluation Report on NCLB

Exhibit E-2
Number of States Showing an Increase in the Percentage of 4th-Grade Students
Performing at or Above the State's Proficient Level from 2000-01 to 2002-03, by Student Subgroup

	Reading	*Mathematics*
All students	11 out of 23 states	17 out of 23 states
Low-income	12 out of 16 states	10 out of 10 states
Black	5 out of 7 states	5 out of 7 states
Hispanic	6 out of 7 states	5 out of 7 states
White	7 out of 7 states	7 out of 7 states
LEP	12 out of 20 states	15 out of 20 states
Migrant	11 out of 15 states	12 out of 16 states
Students with disabilities	14 out of 20 states	16 out of 20 states

Exhibit reads: The proportion of students performing at or above states' "proficient" levels in 4th-grade reading (or another nearby elementary grade) increased from 2000-01 to 2002-03 in 11 out of 23 states that had consistent trend data available.

Note: For states that did not consistently assess students in 4th-grade reading and mathematics from 2000–01 to 2002–03, this table is based on either 3rd-grade or 5th-grade results.
Source: Consolidated State Performance Reports (n = 23 states).
Source: From Stullich, Eisner, McCrary, & Roney, 2006, p. vi.

IDEA in some ways hid the progress that was made by students with disabilities, both in their participation in assessments and in their performance on these assessments (Simpson, Gong, & Marion, 2006).

Participation in Assessments

Students with disabilities had been excluded from state and district assessments for decades before NCLB and IDEA 1997 (Allington & McGill-Franzen, 1992, Kantrowitz & Springen, 1997; Zlatos, 1994). In 1990, most states included 10% or fewer of their students with disabilities in their assessments or had no idea of the participation rates (Shriner & Thurlow, 1993). By the mid-to-late 2000s, the participation rates across states were nearing 100%, with an average of 99% at the elementary school level, 98% at the middle school level, and 95% at the high school level (Altman, Thurlow, & Vang, 2010).

Performance Results

The performance of students with disabilities on state tests generally is lower than that of other subgroups (Albus, Thurlow, & Bremer, 2009). Nevertheless, performance results for this subgroup have increased over time (Altman, Thurlow, & Quenemoen, 2008; Thurlow, Quenemoen, Altman, Cuthbert, 2008) often more dramatically than the performance of other subgroups. This increase has been shown not only on state assessments, but also on the National Assessment of Educational Progress (NAEP) (see 2009 NAEP Reading Assessment results, http://nationsreportcard.gov/reading_2009/nat_g8.asp?subtab_id=Tab_6&tab_id=tab1#chart).

In summary, there are common misperceptions that students with disabilities are alone responsible for causing schools and districts to miss AYP, and misperceptions of the progress that has been made in the participation and performance of students with disabilities. Public school

Exhibit 28
AYP Targets Missed by Schools That Did Not Make Adequate Yearly Progress, 2005–06

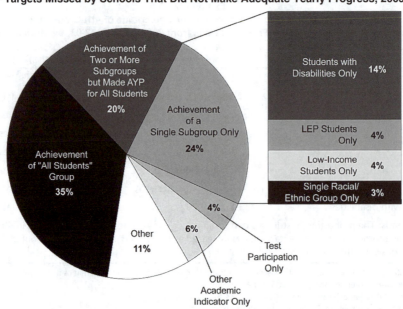

Exhibit reads: In 2005–06 testing, 35 percent of schools that did not make AYP missed targets for the achievement of the "all students" group in reading and/or mathematics.

Notes: The sum of the subcategories of the "Single Subgroup Only" category does not equal 24 percent due to rounding. Schools included in the "Achievement of the 'All Students' Group" and the "Achievement of Two or More Subgroups" segments of the graph may have also not made AYP for test participation or the other academic indicator. However, schools included in the "Achievement of a Single Subgroup Only" segment are those that did not make AYP for that factor alone and did not miss any other AYP targets. "Other" includes schools that did not make AYP for combinations of the achievement of a single subgroup, test participation, and/or the other academic indicator, or through a small school analysis.

Source: SSI-NCLB, National AYP and Identification database (based on data reported by 43 states for 20,463 schools that did not make AYP in these states).

Figure 1.1 Exhibit in 2010 Title I evaluation report on NCLB. From Taylor, Stecher, O'Day, Naftel, & Le Floch, 2010, p. 88.

leaders have an obligation to understand why these misperceptions exist and work to confront them. The next section discusses the implications these data have for leadership.

Implications for Leadership

A core activity of an instructional leader is to help guide the setting of the vision and mission of the organization and then link goals to the mission. Fostering an atmosphere where shared beliefs and the collaborative efforts of educators can create an environment that values all students is vital. According to Kurland et al. (2010), "it is important for a learning organization to have as a central tenet, a commitment to help people 'embrace' change," and "it does not happen automatically, but requires a commitment to building the necessary skills throughout the organization" (p. 10).

Given the challenges in changing business as usual in our schools, successful leadership to ensure success for all students requires both structures and values. Structures may include features such as a focused set of initiatives that are fully implemented in every classroom, elimination of competing agendas through systematic oversight and monitoring of agreed-upon practices, and district and building leadership teams that ensure consistent and committed implementation. Values include an articulation of individual and collective/organizational internal commitments and understandings to universal student success. When we work with states or districts in this context, we work to clarify how key stakeholders define the word "ALL" in "success for all." Sometimes, these beliefs are not consistent with a truly inclusive system, and that affects all actions and outcomes.

Although IEP teams may make decisions that lower standards instead of improving how the child learns, states, districts, and schools nonetheless are accountable for the performance of the student at grade level. School, district, and state leaders must work to refocus IEP team processes to ensure that students receive the services, supports, and specialized instruction necessary to achieve at high levels. Otherwise, we will continue to see competing agendas, cross purposes, and low achievement. Principled leadership requires backing this refocusing effort with high quality staff development, coaching, and resources, along with oversight and monitoring of implementation, so that all schools, all teachers, and all students are successful.

True reform requires leadership that works toward shifts in beliefs, attitudes, behaviors, practices, and policy. The literature on the effects of teacher expectations suggests students learn what we expect them to learn. Some students—with and without disabilities—may not achieve to the levels we hope even after high quality standards-based instruction. But we have no way to predict which ones will not (McGrew & Evans, 2004), so we have to teach them ALL well! If we test without teaching—or teach a separate curriculum—then we will not see achievement that will prepare students well for their futures. We will see more of the same low performance as in the past.

Tinkering on the edges of special education practice risks reverting to the status quo, scurrying back to educational comfort zones that feel safe for adults but that are very damaging to students. We are in revolutionary times in many ways—not for the faint of heart—a time that requires leadership, courage, and commitment, and a lot of hard work. And it requires open and honest discussion of competing agendas, and a willingness to go back to the drawing board to make things right. The preponderance of evidence is that the *system* is responsible for limited access to the general curriculum and the resulting achievement gap—not the student's disabilities, color, socioeconomic status, or other characteristics. Principled educational leaders—at the national, state, district, school, and classroom levels—will act on that evidence to ensure all students are successful.

We have observed dramatically increased participation in assessments and accountability systems, and a general trend toward increased achievement for students with disabilities since the advent of standards-based reform and accountability provisions. We also have observed pockets of excellence in schools and districts where students with disabilities are making rapid gains in achievement. Several researchers have documented practices in these schools and districts (Cortiella & Burnette, 2008; Donahue Institute, 2004; EDC, 2005; Hawkins, 2007; Silverman, Hazelwood, & Cronin, 2009). In a nutshell, what these studies found is that successful school and district leaders take systematic steps to ensure that all students are taught the challenging standards-based curriculum through effective instructional strategies, and all students are expected to learn it.

Factors Related to Improved Student Performance

One of the earliest studies to look at schools where the performance of students in special education increased more than expected was the Donahue Institute study, conducted in urban schools in Massachusetts. After using a quantitative approach to identify schools, researchers went into the schools using a qualitative approach (interviews and observations) to identify the practices in those schools with improved performance of students with disabilities. This study identified 11 factors as central to the success of urban districts and schools for special education students:

1. Pervasive emphasis on curriculum alignment with the state standards or frameworks[1]
2. Effective systems to support curriculum alignment.
3. Emphasis on inclusion and access to the curriculum.
4. Culture and practices that support high standards and student achievement.
5. Well disciplined academic and social environment.
6. Use of student assessment data to inform decision making.
7. Unified practice supported by targeted professional development.
8. Access to resources to support key initiatives.
9. Effective staff recruitment, retention, and deployment.
10. Flexible leaders and staff that work effectively in a dynamic environment.
11. Effective leadership that is essential to success.

These factors are consistent with other studies of effective schools for disadvantaged and minority status students but these studies did not focus specifically on students with disabilities (e.g., Ed Trust, 2005; Kannapel & Clements, 2005; Williams et al., 2005). It is encouraging to see that the same practices that ensure success for other students who have struggled with low achievement practices appear to be effective for students with disabilities.

EDC (2005) provided "portraits of excellence" of high schools where students with and without disabilities succeed. Starting from the data on state assessments to identify three high schools, and then interviewing school personnel and shadowing students (both those with and those without disabilities), the researchers identified practices that enabled students with disabilities to "access, participate in, and succeed in a rigorous, standards-based curriculum" (paragraph 7). Five characteristics of good high schools were identified:

•   Good high schools personalize learning for students with disabilities,
•   Good high schools promote teacher collaboration,
•   Good high schools support all students in reaching school and district standards,
•   Good high schools develop a particular focus or identity,
•   Good high schools promote strong leaders among their special education staff.

With regard to the last characteristic, the researchers noted the following:

> The special education staff at all three schools are multitalented leaders in the school community. They hold positions of authority, like assistant principalships, and they are strong advocates for young people with disabilities.
>
> *(paragraph 17)*

Although not looking at effectiveness specifically for students with disabilities, these points are in line with elements of high school improvement identified by the National High School Center (Harris, Cohen, & Flaherty, 2008).

A longitudinal study in Rhode Island (Hawkins, 2007) identified schools that despite their low rankings were raising the achievement of students with disabilities. Nearly one third of the state's 320 public schools "demonstrated significant improvement in closing the gap between the IEP subgroup and all students in either language arts or math" (p. 61). Using information from a survey of these schools, the researchers identified common characteristics across elementary, middle, and high school:

- Using inclusive strategies that engage students with special needs in general classrooms.
- Establishing common, high expectations for all learners, with a focus on achievement.
- Providing professional development to all staff members in research-based best practices.
- Employing a highly qualified staff that is trained, committed, and responsive to student needs.
- Having teams of teachers frequently analyze student work.
- Using multiple forms of assessment.
- Differentiating instructional practices to address student needs.
- Increasing instructional time in literacy.
- Involving parents in student learning.
- Creating safe learning environments that incorporate incentives for success. (p. 63)

The researchers concluded by noting:

> Successful schools had strong leadership and incorporated effective practices that promoted a responsive learning environment. Most important, they were committed to ensuring the success of each student.
>
> *(p. 63)*

Cortiella and Burnette (2008) studied five districts and schools where success with students with disabilities was achieved by "embracing change to tackle their challenges and by challenging themselves to change" (p. 3). The authors, who spoke to leaders in each school, noted that all of the schools:

- Included students with disabilities in general education classrooms,
- Used data to adjust instruction to each student's individual needs,
- Changed the ways that teachers work together,
- Restructured administrative organizations and procedures. (p. 4)

The Ohio Department of Education (Silverman et al., 2009) conducted follow-up studies on school districts where state assessment scores show strong gains in the achievement of students with disabilities over a period of four years. They conducted interviews and site visits to determine what factors contributed to the gains, and found common themes consistent with the Donahue Institute findings. Silverman et al. found that these successful districts shared key characteristics:

1. A focus on teaching and learning as the driver for all decisions.
2. An intentional culture shift away from a separate special education model to shared responsibility for all students, eliminating a culture of isolation.
3. Collaboration through structures and processes, including teacher-lead teams, to talk about data and inform instruction.
4. Leadership that starts at the district level and uses data to address issues, with monitoring of instructional practice, but shared leadership with principals, building staff, and teacher leaders.
5. Instructional practice that ensures access to general curriculum/grade-level content using research-based practices.

6. Assessment that includes use of common formative assessments.
7. Curriculum that is aligned, with use of power standards, pacing guides, curriculum calendars, and a relationship to formative assessment.

In short, these characteristics reflect a shift from a program-driven approach (e.g., special education, Title I, gifted) to a practice-driven approach where adults share responsibility for the success of all students through a focus on the consistent implementation of essential practices at all levels of the system. They reflect shared accountability, with individual and collective organizational commitments to the success of every student.

Conclusions

The characteristics of schools and districts where students with disabilities are achieving at higher levels reflect what we understand about leadership in a standards-based system. In the past, we have institutionalized parallel play in public schools, dividing up students by their characteristics or eligibility for support services—for example, special education, Title I, gifted—and defining the curriculum and outcomes differently depending on those characteristics. In the past, district, school, and classroom educators sometimes initiated agendas that reflected their individual view of what should be taught and who should be taught, sometimes resulting in competing goals and agendas throughout a district or even across the classrooms in one school. The words "aligned, coherent, and focused" have been watchwords of early standards-based reform, but the history that supported parallel play is difficult to overcome. It takes leaders at all levels of public education to chart a course to ensure that all students are successful, but it takes principled leadership to ensure that no educational kingdoms, no programmatic silos, no power structures, and no closed classroom doors get in the way of success. It is difficult to change the way we go about our business, but getting all of our students to a successful future requires it.

Note

1 This practice has been generalized to be more broadly applicable. Practice 1 identified in the Donahue Study was: Pervasive emphasis on curriculum alignment with the Massachusetts frameworks.

References

Albus, D., Thurlow, M., & Bremer, C. (2009). *Achieving transparency in the public reporting of 2006–2007 assessment results* (Technical Report 53). Minneapolis, MN: University of Minnesota, National Center on Educational Outcomes.

Allington, R., & McGill-Franzen, A. (1992). Unintended effects of reform in New York. *Educational Policy, 6*(4), 397–414.

Altman, J. R., Thurlow, M. L. & Quenemoen, R. (2008). *Trends in the participation and performance of students with disabilities* (NCEO Brief). Minneapolis, MN: University of Minnesota, National Center on Educational Outcomes.

Altman, J., Thurlow, M., & Vang, M. (2010). *Annual performance report: 2007–2008 state assessment data.* Minneapolis, MN: University of Minnesota, National Center on Educational Outcomes.

Casserly, M. (2004). Testimony on "No Child Left Behind: Raising Student Achievement in America's Big City Schools." Washington, DC: Council of Great City Schools. Retrieved from http://www.cgcs.org/pdfs/Testimony62404.pdf

Commission on No Child Left Behind. (2007). *Beyond NCLB: Fulfilling the promise to our nation's children.* Washington, DC: Aspen Institute.

Cortiella, C., & Burnette, J. (2008). *Challenging change: How schools and districts are improving the performance of special education students.* New York: National Center for Learning Disabilities.

Council of Chief State School Officers. (2010). *ESEA reauthorization principles and recommendations: A policy statement of the Council of Chief State School Officers.* Washington, DC: Author.

Donahue Institute. (2004). *A study of MCAS achievement and promising practices in urban special* education. Hadley, MA: University of Massachusetts Donahue Institute. Retrieved from http://www.donahue.umassp.edu/docs/exec_summary_field_rsrch_findings

EDC. (2005, Sept 1). *Inclusive schools: Portraits of excellent — three high schools were students with and without disabilities succeed.* Retrieved from http://www.edc.org/newsroom/articles/inclusive_schools_portraits_excellence

Ed Trust. (2005). *Gaining traction, gaining ground: How some high schools accelerate learning for struggling students.* Washington, DC: Education Trust. Retrieved from http://www2.edtrust.org/NR/rdonlyres/6226B581-83C3-4447-9CE7-31C5694B9EF6/0/GainingTractionGainingGround.pdf

Elmore, R., & Rothman, R. (1999). *Testing, teaching, and learning: A guide for states and school districts.* Washington, DC: National Academy Press.

Goertz, M. (2007). *Standards-based reform: Lessons from the past, directions for the future.* Paper presented at the Conference on the Uses of History to Inform and Improve Education Policy, Brown University, Providence, RI. Retrieved September 30, 2009, from http://www7.nationalacademies.org/cfe/Goertz%20Paper.pdf

Goldschmidt, P., & Choi, K. (2007). *The practical benefits of growth models for accountability and the limitations under NCLB* (CRESST Policy Brief 9). Los Angeles: University of California, National Center for Research on Evaluation, Standards, and Student Testing.

Goldschmidt, P., Roschewski, P., Choi, K., Auty, W., Hebbler, S., Blank, R., et al. (2005). *Policymakers' guide to growth models for school accountability: How do accountability models differ?* Washington, DC: Council of Chief State School Officers.

Harris, J. R., Cohen, P. L., & Flaherty, T. D. (2008). *Eight elements of high school improvement: A mapping framework.* Washington, DC: National High School Center. Retrieved from http://www.betterhighschools.com/pubs/documents/NHSCEight Elements7-25-08.pdf

Hawkins, V. J. (2007, February). Narrowing gaps for special-needs students. *Educational Leadership, 61*–63.

Hoffer, T. B., Hedberg, E. C., Brown, K. L., Halverson, M. L., & McDonald, S. K. (2010). *Interim report on the evaluation of the growth model pilot project.* Washington, DC: U.S. Department of Education, Office of Planning, Evaluation and Policy Development.

Kannapel, P. J., & Clements, S. K., with Taylor, D., & Hibpshman, T. (2005). *Inside the black box of high-performing, high poverty schools: A report from the Prichard committee for academic excellence.* Retrieved from http://www.prichardcommittee.org/Ford%20Study/FordReportJE.pdf

Kantrowitz, B., & Springen, K. (1997, Oct. 6). "Why Johnny Stayed Home." *Newsweek.*

Kurland, H., Peretz, H., & Hertz-Larazowitz, R. (2010). Leadership style and organizational learning; The mediate effect of school vision. *Journal of Educational Administration, 48*(1), 7–30.

Linn, R. L. (2005). *Test-based accountability in the era of No Child Left Behind* (CSE Rep. No. 651). Los Angeles: University of California, Center for Research on Evaluation, Standards, and Student Testing.

McDonnell, L. M., McLaughlin, M. J., & Morison, P. (Eds.). (1997). *Educating one & all: Students with disabilities and standards-based reform.* Washington, DC: National Academy Press.

McGrew, K. S., & Evans, J. (2004). *Expectations for students with cognitive disabilities: Is the cup half empty or half full? Can the cup flow over?* (Synthesis Report 55). Minneapolis, MN: University of Minnesota, National Center on Educational Outcomes.

National Commission on Excellence in Education. (1983). *A nation at risk: The imperative for educational reform.* Washington, DC: U.S. Government Printing Office.

National Governors' Association. (1986). *Time for results: The governors' 1991 report.* Washington, DC: Author.

Nolet, V., & McLaughlin, M. J. (2005). *Accessing the general curriculum: Including students with disabilities in standards-based reform* (2nd ed.). Thousand Oaks, CA: Corwin.

Shepard, L., Hannaway, J., & Baker, E. (2009). *Standards, assessments, and accountability* (Education Policy White Paper). Washington, DC: National Academy of Education. Retrieved September 25, 2009, from http://www.naeducation.org/Standards_Assessments_Accountability_White_Paper.pdf

Shriner, J. G., & Thurlow, M. L. (1993). *State special education outcomes 1992.* Minneapolis, MN: University of Minnesota, National Center on Educational Outcomes.

Silverman, S. K., Hazelwood, C., & Cronin, P. (2009). *Universal education: Principles and practices for advancing achievement of students with disabilities.* Columbus, OH: Ohio Department of Education.

Simpson, M., Gong, B., & Marion S. (2006). *Effect of minimum cell sizes and confidence interval sizes for special education subgroups on school-level AYP determinations* (Synthesis Report 61). Minneapolis, MN: University of Minnesota, National Center on Educational Outcomes.

Snipes, J., Horwitz, A., Soga, K., & Casserly, M. (2008). *Beating the odds: An analysis of student performance and achievement gaps on state assessments — Results from the 2006–2007 school year.* Washington, DC: Council of Great City Schools.

Stullich, S., Eisner, E., McCrary, J., & Roney, C. (2006). *National assessment of Title I Interim Report, Volume I: Implementation of Title I.* Washington, DC: Institute of Education Sciences.

Taylor, J., Stecher, B., O'Day, J., Naftel, S., & LeFloch, K. C. (2010). *State and local implementation of the No Child Left Behind Act, Volume IX: Accountability under NCLB: Final report.* Washington, DC: U.S. Department of Education, Office of Planning, Evaluation and Policy Development.

Thomson, S. D. (Ed.). (1993). *Principals for our changing schools: The knowledge and skill base.* Lancaster, PA: Technomic.

Thompson, S. J., Lazarus, S. S., Clapper, A. T., & Thurlow, M. L. (2006). Adequate yearly progress for students with disabilities: Competencies for teachers. *Teacher Education and Special Education, 29*(2), 137–147.

Thurlow, M., Quenemoen, R., Altman, J., & Cuthbert, M. (2008). *Trends in the participation and performance of students with disabilities* (Technical Report 50). Minneapolis, MN: University of Minnesota, National Center on Educational Outcomes.

U.S. Department of Education. (1998). *Changing federal strategies for supporting educational research, development, and statistics.* Washington, DC: Author. Retrieved September 30, 2009 from http://www.ed.gov/pubs/FedStrat/reagan.html

U.S. Department of Education. (2006). *No Child Left Behind growth models: Ensuring grade-level proficiency for all students by 2014.* Retrieved from http://www.ed.gov/admis/lead/acount/growthmodel/proficiency. pdf

U.S. Department of Education. (2008, Oct 29). Improving the academic achievement of the disadvantaged: Final regulations. *Federal Register, 73*(210), 64436–64513.

Williams, T., Kirst, M., Haertel, E., et al. (2005). *Similar students, different results: Why do some schools do better? A large-scale surbey of California elementary schools serving low-income students.* Mountain View, CA: EdSource. This report is available to download for free at: http://edsource.org/pub_abs_simstu05.cfm

Zlatos, B. (1994). Don't test, don't tell: Is "academic red-shirting" skewing the way we rank our schools? *American School Board Journal, 181*(11), 24–28.

2

Conceptual and Historical Foundations of Special Education Administration

Barbara L. Pazey and James R. Yates

THE UNIVERSITY OF TEXAS AT AUSTIN

More than 60 years ago, Berry (1941) stressed that the problems inherent in special education administration are similar to those in educational administration. The difference existed in the emphasis that was placed on the education of nondisabled children versus children with disabilities when changes in the social order occurred. Over 30 years later, the Education for All Handicapped Children Act (1975) mandated that public schools provide services for *all* "handicapped" students signaling that regular education had not made necessary "preparation to handle deviant children, despite the professed movement in education to adapt instruction to individual differences" (Vergason, Smith, & Wyatt, 1975, p. 99).

Despite the passing of time since Berry (1941) discerned similar administrative challenges regarding the need to structure learning for all students, and Vergason et al. (1975) described a lack of success in addressing the needs of students with disabilities, the question remains the same: What has been the response of educational policy makers and leadership? One could conclude that there is a conceptual and pragmatic need for the integration of these complementary disciplines to appropriately serve students with disabilities. However, the most accurate but not always obvious description of this nation's development of services for students with disabilities is separate, parallel, dual, segregated, and isolated. What evidence and insights are needed to understand the current state of educational leadership efforts to address the needs of students with disabilities? What will be required of educational leadership to increase the efficacy and efficiency of addressing the needs of this population of students? What will be the response of society and its institutions to these requirements? Will these complementary disciplines address the common and specialized knowledge, skills and experiences needed by educational leadership to serve students with disabilities?

For an understanding that leads to answering these questions related to special education administration, it is necessary to trace the history that created and supported separate, parallel, minimally integrated services to students with disabilities. Through this lens of history, deductions can be made to explain the current status of special education administration and project the future response of educational leadership to students with disabilities and their families.

History of Educational Access

Social attitudes have long influenced the educational opportunities of people with disabilities. The early Greeks, for example, utilized education as a mechanism to acculturate citizens and give them the tools needed to govern themselves. The definitive choice for an educated Greek citizen favored the strong over the weak (Woodruff, 2006). Individuals with physical impairments or with more obvious disabilities, however, were often misunderstood, viewed with superstition, or received inappropriate care and interventions. The intellectual capacity of an individual defined his or her assignment to a specific class (Ornstein & Levine, 2006). Consequentially, it was not uncommon for biases and prejudices to be held toward specific groups.

Early Christian teachings shed light on the discriminatory practices of the elite and challenged their favoritism toward the wealthy by addressing the needs of individuals traditionally forgotten or outcast by society. Advocacy for the needs of the poor, disenfranchised, and individuals with disabilities resulted in acts of healing for those with physical and mental infirmities and exorcism of evil spirits whose affliction exempted them from the ability to control their thoughts and behaviors. Although the religious reformation of the 16th and 17th centuries contributed to a concern for universal education, hierarchical views of class and the practice of providing access to education through a "dual-track system of schools" (Ornstein & Levine, 2006, p. 87) continued. During this period, individuals with disabilities encountered attitudes that were "callous, cruel, or dismissive" (Winzer, 2009, p. 2) and, regardless of the degree or type of disability, were categorically labeled as "idiot" (p. 2).

Development of Education Systems in the United States

In the 1800s, the ideas and influence of European educators, such as Pestalozzi, Rousseau, and Froebel, were brought to the United States. These concepts advocated for a more nurturing learning environment, individual approaches to learning, and hands-on, object-centered lessons (Ornstein & Levine, 2006; Osgood, 2007). The benefit of these methods had already been realized and used in the education of individuals with physical and other significant disabilities in some areas of Europe. During the 19th and early 20th centuries, the majority of American communities were rural, agrarian, and perceived to be homogenous in language and interests. A limited number of children attended school or left school by the age of 10 to work and support their family. Children with disabilities were less obvious and more likely to find acceptable and contributory activities in these rural settings.

French physician Edward Seguin (1907) applied an individualized approach in his work with individuals with developmental and cognitive disabilities, formerly defined as mental retardation, through motor and sensory learning, referred to as the "physiological method" (Osgood, 2007). Seguin's work, particularly with non-verbal assessments, has endured, but created a "scientific" means of sorting and categorizing individuals. Immigrants at Ellis Island were compartmentalized into functional categories, a practice that continued to be used until relatively recent times by diagnostic personnel in the determination of cognitive abilities of public school students. Procedures for categorizing and sorting students initiated similar practices that were used by schools as they began to address different educational needs of the student populations entering their schools. These procedures could be conceptualized as the beginning of "special" or different approaches for students in school. Immigration and migration from rural to urban areas, accompanied by increased industrialization, resulted in a mushroomed growth. This growth created a need for expanded educational opportunities as well as the need for schools to develop organizational structures that were capable of responding to the various student populations who were enrolling in schools. Policies geared to ensure social progress manifested through greater state and governmental control of education (Osgood). At the local level, questions emerged relevant to finding ways that schools could respond to the development of organizational structures and address the various social needs of diverse student groups.

Compulsory schooling provisions were first initiated in Massachusetts in 1852 (Simpson, 2004). Horace Mann and the state of Massachusetts led a movement to provide access to education for all through supervisory oversight of public schooling. According to Mann, public education would serve as a "great social equalizer" and provide children with the necessary skills and knowledge to "acquire better jobs and upward mobility" (Ornstein & Levine, p. 170). The creation of a required public education shed light on the importance of developing programs of education that would provide services for large numbers of students as well as a need for administrative leadership in serving the mass of students in the public schools.

Although one might consider the movement toward greater access and the concept of equality as a movement toward a system of education that encompassed all school-aged learners, universal education did not include individuals with disabilities or special education. The concept of providing such programs through a public education system was typically nonexistent. Most students who were limited by cognitive, physical, or behavioral impairments either stayed home, worked, or were housed in county-run institutions (Osgood, 2007). These "different" students were separated from ordinary school experiences by choice or placement, which eventually led to a dual system of education.

Progressive Education and the Creation of a Separate Education System

Progressive education served as a guidepost for reform. The common school was charged with the responsibility of enculturation through the promotion of a national identity and purpose. Although some progressive educators advocated for social reform through education, others, particularly administrators focused efforts on creating schools that were "more efficient and cost effective" (Ornstein & Levine, 2006, p. 113). Specific provisions for students with physical disabilities were offered primarily through the practice of institutionalization which served a dual purpose: to protect "disabled" children from the hazards and cruelty of society and to protect "normal" children from the potentially negative effects that association with "crippled," "feebleminded," and "incorrigible" children might incur (Osgood, 2007; Winzer, 2008, 2009). A general understanding of unequal or, at least, different services for individuals with disabilities was accepted by society and educational leadership. Leadership appeared to support or remain silent relative to these separated institutional approaches in addressing the needs of persons with disabilities.

In the late 1800s and into the early 1900s, legal action and social policies were designed to maintain control over the rights of individuals with disabilities. The eugenics movement led to institutionalization and involuntary sterilization of children and adults identified as "morons" and "unfit" due to "defective" health or mental characteristics and a fear that such groups would surpass the "normal" population of American citizens (O'Brien & Bundy, 2009). Eugenics was perceived as a control mechanism to limit heredity transmission of certain negative traits (Pfeiffer, 1994) that were linked to evils within society. Special education as separate classes emerged as a management tool, both practically and economically, for the public school system (Semmel, Gerber, & MacMillan, 1994). If eugenics was rejected as a drastic control mechanism, the separated "special class" provided a protective barrier supported by similar perceptions and values of "different" individuals in societies.

Identification and Placement of Individuals into Separate Education Programs

At the turn of the last century, the focus was on two kinds of disability: limited cognition or mental retardation, and a clearly overt physical disability. A deficit perspective dominated the thinking on disability: cognitive and physical disabilities were viewed as inherent in the individual. From these held views it was felt important to have techniques and procedures that could successfully identify these individuals.

The development of intelligence tests provided a "scientific" method for identification of differences. Individuals were identified as "deficient" due to their "feeble mindedness" and underwent a process of classification and sorting into specific groups or categorical levels of mental functioning ability. The French psychologist Alfred Binet with Theodore Simon (1916) initiated the era of modern intelligence testing. The Binet instrument was an accepted measure of the intellectual potential and ability of individuals and served as a sorting mechanism to differentiate between levels of ability and intelligence. With the 1916 revision of the instrument by Stanford professor Lewis Terman, the Stanford-Binet intelligence test provided the a mechanism for schools to sort students into categories of mental ability and, in turn, develop special programs to address these varying levels of "scientifically" determined intelligence.

Once deficient individuals were identified, they were separated according to disability and isolated from individuals who did not "possess" such deficiencies. During the early 1900s, individuals who were considered to be unfit for society were removed to institutions or placed in locked facilities. Administrators were assigned to manage and operate these institutions and the formalization of administrative practices evolved for operating and maintaining such institutions.

Students whose mental or physical condition interfered with their ability to learn were placed within "ungraded" classes, in contrast to the traditional, age-related structure of graded classrooms and schools. Students with low mental ability were placed in classrooms across several grade levels (Kobe, 2002). In some cases, the motive for providing special classes was a lesser alternative to losing the students to the street or a life of crime. In other cases, separate classes and instruction relieved "normal" students from being subject to "defective" students.

According to Kobe (2002), the initial framework for the education of students with disabilities began in a classroom within the New York City school system, taught by Elizabeth Farrell, under the leadership of William Maxwell, school superintendent. During that era, students who had educational needs that were different and beyond the scope of needs of other students were considered "atypical." Through an individualized and holistic approach to instruction, Farrell appealed to each student's learning needs with the use of materials that engaged students in hands-on activities and a theme-based curriculum that was related to the students' backgrounds and interests. By the early 1900s, the number of "ungraded" classes increased due, in part, to the benefit of maintaining separate classes to relieve the traditional classes of the "defective" student population (Kobe). These complex identification and assignment for instruction procedures that became a part of public schools demanded an administrator with special or unique skill and experience.

After justifying the existence of ungraded classes, superintendent Maxwell appointed Farrell as inspector of the ungraded class program, perhaps, the first special education administrator. Her administrative functions included classroom supervision and organization, oversight of admission, review and dismissal of students to the program, and approval of teachers assigned to ungraded classes (Hendick & MacMillan, 1989). Although separate instruction continued, Farrell recognized the importance of allowing students who benefited from individualized instruction in specific skills or topics the opportunity to learn in a classroom setting in which they could excel and demonstrate their understanding to others in both traditional and non-graded classes (Handrick & MacMillan, 1989; Kobe, 2002). As compulsory education laws stiffened and mandated education for all students up to 16 years of age, an increasing number of students with lower mental abilities were recommended for ungraded classes. To meet the various levels of ability as well as the varying chronological and mental age capacities of students, ungraded classes were differentiated based on the student's immediate or current identified need. Nevertheless, the assessment process and referral of students to certain programs were based more on "opinion and chance" (Kobe, p. 47).

Farrell began to refine and utilize systematic assessment procedures to assure that placement decisions would be more objective. Utilizing personnel from the disciplines of psychology, medicine, social services and education to determine whether the student would be served better in the ungraded classes or a different placement, the Psycho-Educational Clinic was formed in New York. If children were able to respond to treatment, they were able to remain in the "normal" classes. In addition, student placements were regularly reviewed to determine sufficient progress to justify transfer to "grade level," eligibility for institutional placement, or "aging out" of placement at 16 years.

Response to an Epidemic

In the early 1900s, children with contagious diseases such as tuberculosis were placed in "open air" or special day schools where they could be separated and sequestered from others while receiving rest, nourishment, and instruction (Safford & Safford, 1998). Individualized education was provided in these contexts, reducing physical demands on the students, while serving their diverse needs associated with chronic and significant health issues. However, this clinical model served as an alternative educational placement for students who would otherwise have been excluded from school; but, the education of the child was secondary to the perceived advantage of light, air, rest, and nourishment provided in more clinical settings.

Polio, which struck the United States in 1916, resurrected the concern for special and separate provisions of public school accommodations for "crippled children." The necessary adjustment "turned children's worlds upside down" (Altenbaugh, 2006, p. 210) due to the fact that those who contracted the disease were forced to move rapidly from a "normal" state to an "abnormal" or "disabled" state for which they were not prepared. The crippling effects of polio relegated children to wheelchairs and Iron Lungs and other specialized or modified equipment and facilities causing those within the education system to organize efforts to provide "special education" which responded to the physical and orthopedic needs of these children.

Architectural barriers and the lack of physical accommodations made access to school and integration into regular classrooms difficult. The realized need to service "crippled" children resulted in the erection and modification of physical facilities to house and service children with physical disabilities (Hollinshead, 1953; Hunt, 1966.) Teachers were trained and certified to deal with the orthopedic needs of children entering the schools in coordination with recommendations from medical authorities. Special desks, tables and chairs and instructional tools were designed to adjust to the ability and circumstances of physical needs of children with various physical disabilities (Wishik & Mackie, 1949). Mobilization efforts to treat and find a cure for polio (Altenbaugh, 2006; Oshinsky, 2005) eventually led to a vaccine in the 1950s, which virtually eliminated the disease among both children and adults. In responding to the watershed moment of finding a cure for the poliovirus, there was a flux of political sensitivities toward a special education system within the system of public education that had separate educational facilities and marginalized student populations, setting the stage for a social consciousness and collective action of integration.

Educational Administration Recognizes the Need for Special Education

At the advent of World War II and after surviving World War I and the Great Depression, the country turned toward a commitment to equality of educational opportunity and a democratic focus (Berry, 1941; Heck, 1944). Emphasis was placed on educating the "whole child" through instruction that accommodated individual differences and provided for the education of mentally and physically handicapped children. Special classes and schools were expected to address the problems inherent in transforming schools to child-centered organizations. By accepting "handicapped" children, equality was provided (Berry). Nevertheless, students with disabilities presented a more complex problem. Most programs for "special" students were situated in large urban areas and followed a medical model of identification and service provision and a vocationally based curriculum (Altenbaugh, 2006). Administrators viewed the shift from a traditional, curriculum-centered school to a child-centered education as problematic due to the changes required in the organization of school structures, supplies and materials, subject matter, instructional methodology, and personnel training.

After World War II, the field of special education expanded due, in part, to a greater societal "acceptance of individuals who deviate from the normal physically, mentally or emotionally" (Fourache, 1961, p. v) and collective efforts of parents of children with disabilities who advocated for their children's participation in public school and residential school programs. At the same time, racial integration, through *Brown v. Board of Education* (1954), provided the legal and philosophical basis for public schools to serve all students in a less segregated system of education. These racially motivated legal actions became a conceptual and legal foundation for a more integrated and socially responsible approach to the education of all students, including those with disabilities. However, the utilization in the south of private schools to avoid racial integration continued to support the concept that certain circumstances justify segregation of students. Nonetheless, *Brown v. Board of Education* (1954) opened the conversation to issues related to equal opportunity and access and individual differences. To obtain equal educational outcomes for students with disabilities required additional resources and resulted in different types of interventions which were not necessarily equal to those provided for the general student population. Typically, principals in traditional administrative preparation were trained to develop a common curriculum, provided through equal interventions or treatments. Therefore, they were unfamiliar with and unprepared to develop differentiated or "unequal" experiences for students with disabilities.

Outside the realm of K–12 administrative functions and the traditional model of school administration, there was a growing concern for leadership to have a fully developed knowledge base and accompanying skills related to mental hygiene and vocational education, highlighting the need for specially identified education administrators (Baker, 1944). These special education administrators were expected to be familiar with mental hygiene factors related to socially and emotionally deviant behaviors and to be knowledgeable of the available agencies capable of providing assistance or treatment for such behaviors. They were also expected to possess additional understanding of the various phases of development in relation to career-related interests and skills, vocational guidance and education, supported occupational activities, and the availability of courses such as shop and industrial arts, particularly for adolescents with physical disabilities. Through the interaction and consultation that occurred within and across these contexts, the role of special education administrator or supervisor emerged. These unique school leaders were given oversight of separate programs and services associated with the education of exceptional children. General education leaders, on the other hand, were responsible for negotiating space and other resources in conjunction with special education leaders and maintaining separate yet appropriate programs for special education.

Per-pupil costs for providing special education were determined to range from two to five times the costs of regular education (Baker, 1944). Some children with physical "handicaps" that made it "prohibitive" for them to participate in regular schools received medical treatment in separate facilities such as hospitals and convalescent homes. Separate, special education programs were provided for children with visual and auditory "handicaps," cerebral palsy, epilepsy, or cardiac conditions. Some states provided special subsidies to provide services to students with additional disabilities such as deaf/blindness. Greater consideration was given to children with physical disabilities than those with mental or social disabilities. According to Berry (1941), one of the major problems in providing for the education of exceptional children was the lack of universal federal assistance.

In the 1950s, the National Association for Retarded Children (ARC) lobbied Congress for the laws and financial support to develop strong programs for the population known then as mentally retarded (MR). In 1958, Public Law 85-926 (P.L. 85-926) was passed, which was designed to strengthen teaching and education for children and youth with intellectual disabilities. According to Mackie (1978), the law was instrumental in establishing a pathway for the involvement of federal government, particularly in regard to the provision of support for leadership preparation programs in special education and expanded benefits for training available for all areas of disability. Nevertheless, during the 1960s and early 1970s, states were selective in their decision to serve children with disabilities (Martin, Martin, & Terman, 1996).

Prior to the 1960s, students identified with disabilities were typically educated in self-contained classrooms for more fiscal efficiency. A resource distribution model of assigning certain levels of funding to separate classroom units, i.e., a designated number of students per unit, limited or reduced fiscal incentives to integrate classroom settings. Due to scarce resources, students were separated to meet the needs of low-achieving students and goals of special education: to "minimize the handicapping consequences of significant differences while supporting the effectiveness of regular classroom teaching" (Semmel et al., 1994, p. 483). In the meantime, parent advocacy groups for students with specific learning disabilities challenged the model of self-contained classrooms and supported a move to a more integrated service-delivery model. Variations in availability and "treatment" through special education coupled with the emergent political advocacy by parents created the need for administrators knowledgeable and supportive of the political activities of these parent groups and competent to manage the additional special program costs. But, there was less than universal acceptance of the need for this special administration support.

Despite the newly created demands and practices placed on the administration of special education, it was not until the 1960s that textbooks used to train school administrators began to mention an obligation to "handicapped youth" (McCleary & Hencley, 1965). Leo Connor (1961) provided the first handbook that dealt primarily with the problems inherent in special education as an effort to focus on the training of persons who directed societal institutions serving persons with disabilities. Although Connor's perspective and focus were derived from his position as Assistant Superintendent for the Lexington School for the Deaf, the content appears to contain little that is different from what one would find in textbooks for preparing general education leaders (i.e., personnel, budgeting, organizational management). On the other hand, based on his perspective as special education director for California's Los Angeles city schools, Willenberg (1970) stressed that administrators of special education must acquire functions that are unique and essential for providing exceptional children with specialized programs and services in performance of their leadership duties. Although administrative functions mirrored those of general education administrators, each function was described according to how public schools could serve students with disabilities more efficiently and effectively.

Specific functions of these general or special education administrators focused more on the management of organizations allowing for a more efficient provision of classes and services, whether for students with disabilities or for students viewed as "normal." What was becoming clear was the need to have knowledgeable administrators capable of addressing and managing the growing prevalence and complexities of programs and services for persons with disabilities.

Medical Model of Disability: Separate Educational Programs

Although the impact of the civil rights legislation challenged states and school districts to assume responsibility for all students, the practice of attributing disability conditions, physically or mentally, to medical conditions maintained the practice of providing segregated services for these students. The term "mental retardation" was used in a generic sense and included a wide range of factors of "subnormal intellectual development" (Dunn & Capobianco, 1959, p. 452). Demarcations in varying levels of mental ability were tied to intelligence quotient (IQ) scores, typically a score of below 75. As scores lowered, categorical definitions changed from "educable mentally retarded" to "trainable mentally retarded" to "custodial mentally retarded." Placement in classes was dependent on whether the individual student could perform to capacity, get along with peers, and refrain from placing a burden on the school, his/her parents, and the community. There was a desire to discover more precise diagnostic methods to create a more graduated system of designating different levels of disability. Individuals who did not "fit" the category of mental retardation were still designated as being deficient and lacking in ability to perform specific academic areas.

Screening procedures for tuberculosis and follow up studies of children with premature birth and other chronic health conditions based on student records within selected schools also identified potential defects and a need for additional classifications and segregation. There was effort to develop a "functional medical grading system" that could predict "social independence, educational possibilities, and employability" (Hunt, 1966, p. 165).

There was a developing concern, however, that something more than intellectual disabilities or overt physical conditions existed among some students. Perhaps such deficiencies in academic ability were attributed to neurological and sociological effects upon the individual. Neurologist Elizabeth Koppitz (1973) developed a set of tests to measure the short-term memory and sensory integration of male students, and used these in determining that learning difficulties and psychologically identified emotional disturbances caused them to perform below average on tasks required for reading and spelling such as integration, sequencing and recall of visual presentations, and oral or visual recall. The inability to perform at the same level as students identified as average was attributed to a minimal brain dysfunction (MBD) due to "immaturity and malfunction in short-term memory and intersensory integration" (p. 465). Although there was limited ability to locate brain dysfunctions, there was an emerging belief that language/learning disorders were caused by brain injury or abnormalities and were referenced as mild brain injuries (MBI). Subsequently, students with figure-ground perception problems, or who demonstrated difficulty with decoding and auditory discrimination functions were removed from regular class, separated and isolated from their peers to receive individualized instruction and intervention.

A Newly Coined Term: Learning Disability

When Samuel Kirk (Kirk, McCarthy, & Kirk,1968) and his colleagues at the Institute for Research for Exceptional Children at the University of Illinois developed the Illinois Test of Psycho-linguistic Abilities (ITPA), educators followed the assumption that the ITPA served as a valid diagnostic assessment in the identification of specific abilities of language development. Learning Disability (LD) was defined as "retardation, disorder, or delayed development in one or more of the processes of speech, language, reading, writing, arithmetic, or other school subject resulting from a psychological handicap caused by a possible cerebral dysfunction and/or emotional or behavioral disturbances" as opposed to "the result of mental retardation, sensory deprivation, or cultural and instructional factors" (Kirk, 1962, p. 263). Results obtained from the ITPA were assumed to lend practical value to schools in identifying learning disabilities that contributed to school failure, but the ITPA proved to be of limited value (Newcomer &

Hammill, 1975). This definition, however, brought many students with a broad range of school difficulties under the umbrella of special education broadening the need for special education administrators.

Political energy was shaping and challenging the lack of action by those in authority regarding the segregated placement of individuals with disabilities. These political actions began to have a trickle-down effect in the public schools and brought a response to designate persons with administrative responsibility for addressing the needs of students with disabilities and the parent advocacy groups supporting them. In 1963, Kirk addressed parents at an education conference and used the term "learning disability" which led to their adoption of the term and formation of a parent advocacy group (Hallahan & Mercer, n.d.), currently known as the Learning Disabilities Association of America (LDA). Their advocacy contributed to an examination of the efficacy of integrating students with learning disabilities into academic classes as opposed to the continuation of separate facilities for individuals with learning deficiencies.

Federal Involvement with Students with Disabilities

From 1948 to 1966, Dr. Romaine Mackie held the position of Chief for the Education of Exceptional Children and Youth. She was the only official in the federal Department of Health and Human Services assigned responsibility for children with disabilities, and during her tenure she developed and maintained national statistics on incidence and student enrollments in special education. Prior to this century, practically all care for persons with disabilities was for the affluent, provided in isolated private institutions (Mackie, 1965). When President John F. Kennedy was elected, he and his family voiced concerns regarding the placement of individuals in state institutions due, in part, to sensitivities toward their sister, Rose, who was identified as having intellectual disabilities. This national focus brought attention to special education, demonstrating "marked progress in providing educational opportunity for exceptional children" (Mackie, 1969, p. 27).

According to Mackie's (1969) data, pupil enrollments in special education programs increased by nearly 500% between 1948 and 1966 with growth five times faster than an increase of the school-age population during the same time frame. Despite the increased number of enrollments, in 1966 only 35% of the total number of children who required special education services were receiving services. It was clear that "a wide gap still exists between the number of children estimated to need some form of special education and the number who are receiving it.… America cannot afford to ignore the gap that remains" (pp. 5, 6). Mackie's report created the recognition of an important role for the federal government in services to students with disabilities. Samuel Kirk, a distinguished psychologist at the University of Illinois, was appointed by President Kennedy as the first Director of the newly formed Division of Handicapped Children and Youth within the U.S. Office of Education (Osgood, 2007), and this Division was eventually reorganized into the Bureau for the Education of the Handicapped (BEH). With these acts that formalized the federal role in the education of students with disabilities, legislation and funding for these students emerged. With policies and funding came responsibility and a need for leadership personnel with special administrative knowledge and skill related to serving students with disabilities.

Increased political energy and the legitimacy given to protests during the civil rights movement, the women's movement and student movement against the Vietnam War in the 1960s and early 1970s fueled further action from parent advocacy groups and national organizations representing service providers (Scotch, 1989). Together, they redefined the term "special education" to represent a "coalition of those seeking a broad legal right to a quality education" (Dorn, 2002, p. 317).

School principals who were accustomed to delegating their responsibility for students with disabilities to separate facilities and administrators of special education were faced with new challenges. Would they be able to utilize the expertise of special education administrators and specialist such as psychological services? Could they afford to delegate their responsibility to monitor the instruction and delivery of services to the expertise of special education personnel found in or outside of their school? Where would these students be placed or provided with physical space in the school? Would administrative and instructional personnel be able to handle the new demands placed on them to provide a quality education for these students? Would the parents of students with disabilities expect more attention and time? Was there an increased need for special training and collaboration of professionals in the schools? These were new considerations and concerns for the school principal and were not a typical part of general administration preparation or certification.

An Examination of Special Education Administration

The emergent questions and complexities of how to diagnose, identify, and create programs to serve students with disabilities created a need for leadership with unique knowledge, skill, and experience. However, a theory of special education administration at the federal, state, and local levels had yet to be developed (Willenberg, 1966). Professors of leadership preparation programs, and professionals in both special and general education administration, agreed on "traditional classifications of exceptional pupils identified with special education" (p. 136), yet differed in their positions concerning the specific classifications of exceptional students for whom special education departments within public schools should be responsible. Disagreement ranged from who should receive special education services, to how such services should be provided within the public schools, particularly for students with physical and intellectual disabilities.

Work within the academic community developed new conceptual frameworks for special education service delivery that allowed for a range of special placements. Reynolds (1962) called for students to receive special education services through a continuum of educational placements that ranged from "least restrictive" to "most restrictive" settings. Previously held beliefs about students identified as mildly mentally retarded and models of service delivery in "special classes" were criticized (Dunn, 1968; Lilly, 1970). Special educators were encouraged to function as consultants who worked with general education teachers, while special education placement supported students with more severe disabilities. Deno (1970) built on Reynold's continuum of service delivery model and offered a cascade of services model that offered a succession of program and placement alternatives. These models emphasized the provision of an individualized education and challenged administrators and government officials to move away from a categorical system of educational services toward a more integrated and child-focused approach. However, such models also brought complexity that supported the need for more informed educational leadership within schools. The special education administrator was often the school system's key leader in ensuring the inclusion of all students (Bakken, O'Brian, & Sheldon, 2007).

Instruction for students with disabilities moved toward arrangements that ranged from self-contained classroom instruction to "mainstreamed" regular-class instruction with resource support, while maintaining separate administrative functions for regular and special education. According to Hollingsworth (1974), comprehensive services for students with mild to severe or multiple disabilities entailed coordination between various school programs and non-school agencies, necessitating specialized expertise that was different from the typical skills of school site administrators. Although special education personnel training at colleges and universities existed, few programs provided specialized training in special education administration. There was a lack of specific curriculum in this area and there was ambiguity surrounding the role, functions, and expectations of a special education administrator. Until about 1965, development of leadership personnel in special education tended to follow a pattern of general academic preparation leading to the doctorate, with "little or any distinction drawn between programs leading to field administrative positions and those leading to the professorial role" (Yates, 1976, p 1). In fact, many administrators of special education stepped into their position without any previous administrative training or certification in education, and learned "on the job" (Hollingsworth, 1974, p. 19).

Meisgeier and King (1970) provided an initial effort to articulate the theoretical, political, and practical complexities of special education administration. Despite the need for a perspective related to a theoretical approach and organizational issues unique to the field, the authors noted a paucity of research pertaining to the organization, supervision, and administration of special education. Their summary of federal legislation and the emerging power of political action by "parent" groups supported their description of the need to specially prepare leaders and to link the complementary disciplines of general and special education leadership.

Sage (1976) reiterated this lack of special education leadership and presented a theoretical approach to special education administration. He attributed this lack to the historical tradition of special education to "deal with problems by themselves rather than as parts of the larger system" (p. 26) and the previously held perception of general education administration that special education was "'someone else's business'" (p. 26).

Federal Support for Special Education Administration

In 1966, a series of informal conversations between special education administration professors and the U.S. Office of Education led to funding in 1968 of a planning grant to develop improved preparation programs in special education administration. From this initial beginning in May of 1968, a national consortium was formalized with an Executive Committee of: Charles Meisgeier, University of Texas at Austin; Melton "Marty" Martinson, University of Oregon; Daniel Sage, Syracuse University; Godfrey Stevens, University of Pittsburgh; and a doctoral student representative, Robert Sloat, University of Texas at Austin. The Executive Committee developed and submitted a federal grant to the Office of Education that identified the University Council for Educational Administration (UCEA), a national agency devoted to the improvement of preparation programs for educational leaders, as the agency to facilitate the emerging goals of the consortium. At that time, UCEA member institutions housed almost all of the university preparation programs in existence that trained special education administrators. These UCEA institutions were publically dedicated to the development of "a systematic, ongoing staff development and education program utilizing multi-disciplinary approaches to problems of the field" (Yates, 1976, p. 2).

Similar to Mackie's call for action, the initial group of consortium members (University of Arizona, University of Cincinnati, Colorado State College, Columbia University, University of Connecticut, University of Illinois, Indiana University, University of Iowa, University of Kansas, University of Michigan, Michigan State University, University of Minnesota, University of Oregon, Pennsylvania State University, University of Pittsburgh, Syracuse University, and University of Texas at Austin), foresaw and anticipated a movement toward an integrated service delivery model and the demand for cooperation between special education and general education rather than the continuation of two separate systems. As stated by Yates (1976),

> If principals, superintendents and other general administrators were to be able to respond effectively to changes emerging in special education, such administrators would have to have had as part of their preparation information and understanding associated with special

education. Conversely, special education administrators, in order to furnish critical leadership needed by special education in the future, must be able to identify with the perspectives, values and concerns of the general education administrators.

(p. 5)

The outgrowth of this commitment to integrated educational leadership preparation was the conceptual frame for the formation of the General-Special Education Administration Consortium (GSEAC) in 1970. This small group of special education administration professors, committed to integrated preparation, articulated special education as the complementary discipline and, therefore, required the collaboration and commitment of general education leadership to be successful in leading programs that effectively serve students with disabilities. This was a powerful new set of ideas and models for systemic commitment to students with disabilities and their families. In fact, this small group of special education administration professors foresaw more than 40 years ago the significant changes in special education anticipated by very few individuals. They expressed a vision and articulated values and aspiration of goals that are today widely held and supported by law and policy (Boscardin, 2007). That small group of special education administration professors "saw clearly that special education was moving toward greater integration of education in general and that full and complete delivery of services needed by handicapped individuals within our emerging society demanded the closer cooperation at both the level of training and practice of special education and general education professors, students and practitioners" (Yates, 1976, p. 4).

Burrello and Sage (1979) developed a textbook for training special education administrators, while others (Nevin, 1979; Raske, 1979) focused upon competencies needed by general education administrators responsible for special education. These works emphasized special education as the complementary discipline, strengthening the rationale for collaboration and the integration of general and special education leadership preparation. In doing so, they precipitated a shift in focus from a functional and more specialized, technical expertise inherent in the discipline of special education, to a larger view of leadership characteristic within organizations. In addition, powerful simulation training materials were developed, e.g., Special Education Administration Simulation in Monroe City (SEASIM) (Martin & Yates, 1973), Special Education Administration Training Simulation (SEATS; Sage, 1972), State Education Agency Simulation Exercise (SEASE; Sage & Sontag, 1972). These materials provided professors and others preparing general and special education administrators with practical and flexible training materials for preparing leaders to respond to students with disabilities.

As the General Special Education Consortium (GSEAC) gained federal support, other national efforts were beginning to emerge that were linked to the conceptualization of an integration of general and special education complementary disciplines. In 1975, the Education for All Handicapped Children Act (EAHCA) created a federal commitment that all students should receive an appropriate education. The stipulation of "least restrictive environment" in the federal regulations of the EAHCA (also known as Public Law 94-142) signaled a change in conception and practice. Federal law now supported the integration of children with disabilities into school and society, and specified state and federal protocols for determining categories of disability, and processes for providing services for children and youth with disabilities within the public schools. This watershed legislation contributed to a recognized need to rethink ways in which children and youth with disabilities would be educated in schools and how districts would be administered in the context of the provision of such services. As stated by Mostert and Crockett (1999–2000), "from this point to the present, scholarship about children with special needs has been blended with public policy mandates as being central to civil rights and educational opportunity" (p. 140). For the first time, these requirements linked general and special education administration responsibilities. However, the complexity of this federal statute reinforced the need for educational leadership to be informed, skilled and experienced in developing, maintaining and supporting programs for students with disabilities. Clearly, school districts had a growing need for exceptionally well-trained special education administrators.

In the early 1970s, there was significant federal support for preparation programs through the Bureau for the Education of the Handicapped (BEH). Political energy was amassing for the successful passage of the federal law that assured national requirements to provide an appropriate education to all students with disabilities. Under the leadership of Edwin W. Martin, the BEH was concerned about the need for individual states to come into compliance with P.L. 94-142. This concern resulted in support to inform and train future general and special educational administrators. Many of the GSEAC consortium members secured federal support for special and general educational leadership personnel training. Often, these unique programs were supported by the conceptions articulated, training material developed, and professional development experiences provided by GSEAC through UCEA. The concept of boundary spanners across complementary disciplines brought professors and students together from Special Education and Educational Administration Departments, academic departments that are typically separate within universities. These federally supported preparation programs often created a "first time" experience of integrated efforts by these separate departments. Additionally, these concepts of integrated preparation reached to Washington, D.C. There was support within the Office of Education through a BEH funded national internship program, which shared doctoral students from the complementary disciplines during their clinical training.

State and Local School District Activity

Prior to the passage of P.L. 94-142 in 1975, a national survey of special education administrators who administered more than two programs and who spent at least half their time administering special education programs was conducted (Kohl & Marro, 1971). The results indicated that from state to state, certification requirements varied: few administrators held special education administration licenses and less than half held regular administration certificates. During this time, most of the states' legislation relevant to the provision of special education services provided incentives to school districts to designate a specific individual to administer special education programs for exceptional children. Smaller districts consolidated or formed cooperative units to provide specialized services for students in multi-district or multi-county configurations. At the time the study was conducted, the majority of special education administrators were males who had previously held the position of either school psychologist or instructor of children with mental retardation (Kohl & Marro). Their responsibilities were divided between direct services to students with special needs, clerical and managerial duties, and the supervision and coordination of instruction, curriculum, and program development. Central office demands limited their ability to distribute their time evenly to the tasks required.

In the mid-1970s, only 6 out of 50 states had certification requirements for special education administration. Due to the growth and complexities inherent in special education programs, and services for students with disabilities, there was need for special education administrators (Forgnone & Collings, 1975). The discussions and debates centered on whether there was the need for administrators to receive training in special education and educational administration with opportunities to participate in administrative practicum and internship experiences, or whether prior experience as a special education teacher or school psychologist was sufficient background to lead programs for students with disabilities.

Federal programs in the early and mid 1970s began to support professional training that focused upon issues of integrating students with disabilities into general education settings. For example, the U.S. Office of Education provided "Dean's Grants" to support leaders of colleges of education in the integration of faculty and the development of instructional materials that would facilitate the joint training of special education and general education professionals.

Innovations in state departments of education were also developed to entice school districts to integrate services for students with disabilities into general education programs. For example, the State of Texas Board of Education in February, 1970, approved an experimental program, "Plan A," for special education integration, philosophy, instruction, and staffing patterns (Descriptor, 1970). Plan A called for a movement away from self-contained special classes and for students with disabilities to enter the "normal stream of education." These efforts were conceptualized to reduce the isolation of special education classrooms and to respond to the "disproportional representation of poor, working class and racial and ethnic minority students in them" (McCall & Skrtic, 2009, p. 13). These early efforts were dependent upon critical mass of talented special education administrators such as Don Partridge, State Director of Special Education in Texas.

Politics and Special Education

As the relationship between general and special education progressed, terminology and interpretations relevant to the concept of the Least Restrictive Environment (LRE) continued to evolve. Prior to federal special education legislation, typically general and special education systems were separate and, in many cases, instruction and services for students with disabilities were provided solely through special education and in separated space or buildings. Although the EAHCA was designed to create an integrated system of education, initial attempts to implement the mandates codified by law resulted in the creation of two parallel, but separate educational systems. The conceptions of "mainstreaming" or "integration" served as a way of providing the opportunity for students to be educated with age-appropriate, nondisabled peers in peripheral regular education classes such as music, art, physical education, electives, and/or lunch.

At the national level, Madeleine C. Will (1986), Assistant Secretary of Education, initiated the Regular Education Initiative (REI), which stoked the fire of previous arguments for general educators to become more responsible for the education of students who have special needs in school (Davis, 1989). The REI called for the development of a partnership between regular and special education, which, for some, supported the argument to eliminate what were considered the negative effects of special education "labels" through the creation of a unified system of education. For others, this initiative introduced a mandate to place students in the regular education classroom, regardless of the severity or nature of their disability. In essence, Madeleine Will questioned the legitimacy of special education as a system of education separate and distinct from general education.

Philosophical arguments in favor of "mainstreaming" and "least restrictive alternatives" emerged from the newly defined concept of "normalization," which maintained that the normal conditions of daily life for mainstream society should be made available to individuals with disabilities (Jenkinson, 2002; Winzer, 1993). Segregated settings were viewed as counter-productive to normalization due to the adjustments necessary in making the necessary transition to a "normative community setting" (Jenkinson, p. 10). The regular school would serve as the most appropriate setting for educating students and, as a result, called for alternative service-delivery models and organizational structures (Hollingsworth, 1974).

Without question, these new conversations and political focus changed the landscape and philosophy of education as well as the roles and responsibilities of both special education administrators and educational administrators. Special education became the responsibility of every administrator. In addition to being knowledgeable about curriculum and instructional practices, additional competencies in fiscal management and planning and an understanding of school business management and special education law were required. To assist in the integration of special education into regular education, the placement of students with disabilities within the least restrictive environment, and the facilitation of working relationships between instructional and supervisory personnel in regular and special education, a new demand on building and district-level administrators to serve as advocates and change agents became apparent (Podemski, Price, Smith, & Marsh, 1984).

To respond to the mandate for restructuring and the call for a unified system of education, Sage and Burrello (1994) asserted that a philosophy of inclusion would necessitate a shift in thinking about the system of public education. General and special education administrators would need to work collaboratively toward the development of a shared vision and collegial model. In doing so, a new set of structural arrangements, instructional and administrative practices, and policies related to governance and decision-making, finance, technology, and accountability would need to be designed. They advocated for the use of a four-part framework to guide the process: (a) student participation in all aspects of school life; (b) professional and daily regularities in the work of teachers; (c) school decision-making and governance issues; and (d) the integration and coordination of community human, health, and social resources (p. 13). The principal was identified as the key person in facilitating such restructuring efforts as one who leads in the design and implementation of educational programs for every student in the school.

Increased and Conflicted Federal and State Policies for Inclusion

States and local school districts in the 1990s began to accept practices that brought students with disabilities more commonly into general education contexts. The majority of students with disabilities were spending 80% of the school day in general education classrooms. A sequence of descriptors evolved: "mainstreaming," "integration," "inclusion," all with different processes, policies, and practices depending upon which state, school district, or school was implementing them. These diverse practices brought concern and, at times, conflict among special education professionals and school policy makers, administrators, and union officials (McDonnell, McLaughlin, & Morison, 1997). Differences in perception of practice and requirements could be attributed to minimal professional preparation for serving students with disabilities, different perceptions of special education expertise, different expectations of resource allocation, and, in general, a confusion of law, policy, and practice.

These changes brought alterations in the role and expectations of behavior for special education administrators. Who was responsible for special education often was determined at specific points of concern. "Included" students with disabilities were general education's responsibility until there were problems or issues. At that moment, they were assumed to be the responsibility of special education and the solutions were to be effected by leadership from special education. No longer did the special education administrator have sole responsibility for developing services and personnel to serve students with disabilities. The special education administrator was in an unclear and confused position of determining when, how, and to what extent the responsibilities for students with disabilities were assigned to the special education administrator.

Special Education Administration in the Current Context

As the 21st century began, there was little relief from confusions about responsibility and practice to serve students with disabilities as federal law and policy were also conflicted. Reauthorization in 2001 of the Elementary and Secondary Education Act (ESEA), renamed as No Child Left Behind (NCLB), brought confusion for special education as components of the reauthorized act appeared to be in conflict with the 2004 reauthorized Individuals with Disabilities Education

Act (IDEA). For example, were NCLB requirements for "scientifically based" interventions developed from randomized studies applicable to small sample studies, which typically addressed interventions for students with disabilities? Was the requirement for standardized assessment for progress of "all" students applicable to students with severe cognitive disabilities?

The perception of NCLB bringing all students under its requirements, including those with disabilities, and the confusion of inclusion being defined as "total inclusion" led some school districts to assume there was no longer a need for a "special" education administrator. Indeed, some general administrators indicated that as much as 25% of their time was already assumed by issues of students with disabilities. However, increased responsibilities for special education did not result in increased training in these areas for general education administrators (Cusson, 2010). Of additional concern was that general education teachers had increasing responsibilities to students with disabilities; however, the content of teacher training programs did not address these instructional responsibilities in depth (Altobelli et al., 2009).

The reauthorized IDEA allowed a new model of identification of students with specific learning disabilities termed Response to Intervention (RTI). Although the specific application of RTI is authorized in the federal statute for students with disabilities, RTI conceptually and operationally is dependent upon general education (Fuchs, Fuchs, & Stecker, 2010). This specification of a general education responsibility and process to identify specific learning disabilities further dilutes the perception of need for a "special" education administrator. Interestingly, while the law placed RTI within the responsibility of general education, recent data indicate that professional educators perceive RTI to be a special education process and responsibility (Yates et al., 2010).

Special education administrators are often called upon to inhibit the tendency to find students eligible for special education who are culturally and linguistically diverse, and who may be experiencing achievement difficulties. Due to rapid and significant demographic changes in some states, a majority of students in public schools increasingly represent multicultural and linguistic diversity. This increase in students historically underserved or ineffectively served by schools creates confusion among general educators in determining difference from disability for this group of students (Artiles, Kozleski, Trent, Osher, & Ortiz, 2010). Additionally, there is the tendency of special educators to assume procedures are "color blind" and to explain away the disproportional representation of culturally and linguistically diverse students in special education with concepts of poverty (Hosp & Reschly, 2003). Although the increased representation of students from cultural and linguistic minorities has heightened the confusion between difference and disability, making these distinctions is not a new concern. The disproportional representation of minority students in special education was addressed in the 1980s by the National Research Council (NRC) (Heller, Holzman, & Messick, 1982), and these issues were recently addressed again by the NRC (Donovan & Cross, 2002). It is likely that special education administrators will continue to be called upon to develop system-wide responses in their school districts to this confusion of difference with disability, and the resulting disproportionality.

Special education administration is now at a crossroads, no longer solely responsible for the educational programs and services designed exclusively for students with disabilities. Special education administration is also regarded as a partner in the RTI process in providing quality interventions to an expanding number of general education students with instructional needs who are identified as "struggling learners." In short, the field is changing , and a recent force field analysis (Yates, 2010) identified three major forces currently impacting special education administration:

- Force #1: Movement for integration, desegregation and normalization of services for students with disabilities. Support for this force has been developing in uneven patterns, since the 1960s.

- Force #2: Linkages of general and special education complementary disciplines. The conceptual models of continuum of services and descriptions of general and specialized knowledge have forged the linkage of general and special education professional training and service delivery.
- Force #3: Societal commitment to all students. This force is supported by policy positions of equity; codification in law that requires nondiscrimination and access to appropriate services for all; political action by parents and other organizations; and new models of intervention such as RTI.

Other work (Sjostrom, 2009) has identified essential needs for special education administration:

- *Building and supporting special education administrator capacity* through enhanced specialized training experiences and opportunities;
- *Work that matters* in areas addressing comprehensive needs of students, using evidence based strategies, and positive behavioral interventions; and
- *System support* by promoting collaborations between general and special education.

The Future of Special Education Administration

The contemporary field of special education administration has evolved from past experiences, and the future of the field can be deduced from this history. In concluding this chapter, four future scenarios are presented in a simple, straightforward format to stimulate careful analysis, as well as to stimulate discussion and debate, that allows positions of advocacy to be formulated and insights to be developed.

Scenario #1: Diminished organizational visibility of special education reduces or eliminates the specific role and title designation of special education administrator. While there are forces in the context that would support this scenario; for example, a perception of general administration that all students are now the responsibility of general education, it could be argued that there are a variety of counter-balancing forces in the environment. For example, there are, and will continue to be in the school systems, students with disabilities who need special interventions and, therefore, special expertise in leadership to serve them.

Scenario #2: Increased organizational need for specialized expertise in leadership. There are increasing complexities to determining appropriate interventions that span complementary disciplines, organizational structures, professional expertise, accountability of success, and so forth. These complexities bring an awareness of the necessity of increased availability of special education administrators. The expectations for special education administrators in this complex environment supports increased vertical expertise in serving students with significant learning needs and horizontal expertise to successfully span the boundaries of the organization and disciplines represented in school organizations.

Scenario #3: Focused leadership to serve students with visible and/or severe disabilities. Given the increasing expectation and potential to serve students with high-incidence disabilities in general education, special education administrators may be directed toward roles and activities of leadership that are committed to the development and provision of appropriate services to students that have visible and/or severe disabilities within and beyond the general education context.

Scenario #4: Enhanced training across the complementary disciplines of general and special education administration. There is a rise in the development of integrated preparation or training of administrators that addresses the needs and complexities of an increasingly diverse population of students. Topics related to educating students with disabilities are a critical component included in training for all administrators so that there is leadership capable of bringing organizational changes needed to truly serve all students.

Change and forces bringing that change are historical and common in special education. Evolution of special education administration is descriptive of the continuous insertion of forces, most commonly external forces, that have had a powerful impact upon the discipline. It could be concluded that change *is the future* of special education administration. The question of importance is not *will* there be change, but *how* will special education administration determine and influence the directionality of change and do so in ways that will ultimately benefit students with disabilities and their families.

References

Altenbaugh, R. J. (2006). Where are the disabled in the history of education? The impact of polio on sites of learning. *History of Education, 35*(6), 705–730.

Altobelli, J., Bach, M., Cadle, S.; Cusson, M., Fugate, K., Langford, L., et al. (2009). *Necessary knowledge, skills and experiences for teachers serving students with high incidence disabilities: A Delphi study.* Austin, Texas: University of Texas at Austin, Department of Special Education, Project RISE.

Artiles, A. J., Kozleski, E. B., Trent, S. C., Osher, D., & Ortiz, A. (2010). Justifying and explaining disproportionality, 1968–2008: A critique of underlying views of culture. *Exceptional Children, 76*(3), 279–299.

Baker, H. (1944). Administration of special education. *Review of Educational Research, 14*(1), 209–216.

Bakken, J. P., O'Brian, M., & Sheldon, D. L. (2007). Changing roles and responsibilities of special education administrators. In F. Obiakor, A. Rotatori, & S. Burkhardt (Eds.), *Current perspectives in special education administration* (pp. 1–15). San Diego, CA: JAI Press.

Berry, C. S. (1941). General problems of philosophy and administration in the education of exceptional children. *Review of Educational Research, 11*(1), 253–260.

Binet, A., & Simon, T. (1916). *The development of intelligence in children: The Binet-Simon scale.* Publications of the Training School at Vineland, New Jersey, Department of Research; No. 11. E. S. Kite (Trans.). Baltimore, MD: Williams & Wilkins. Retrieved from http://books.google.com/books?id=jEQSAAAAYAAJ&printsec=frontcover&cd=1&source=gbs_ViewAPI#v=onepage&q&f=false

Boscardin, M. L. (2007). What is special about special education administration? *Exceptionality, 15*(3), 189–200.

Brown v. Board of Education, 347 U.S. 483 (1954).

Burrello, L. C., & Sage, D. D. (1979). *Leadership and change in special education.* Englewood Cliffs, NJ: Prentice-Hall.

Connor, L. E. (1961). *Administration of special education programs.* New York: Teachers College Press.

Cusson, M. (2010). *Current and emerging educational organization patterns for the delivery of services to students with disabilities: Implications for the preparation of school administrators.* (Unpublished doctoral dissertation). University of Texas at Austin, Austin, TX.

Davis, W. E. (1989) The regular education initiative debate: Its promises and problems. *Exceptional Children, 55*(5), 440–446.

Deno, E. (1970). Special education as developmental capital. *Exceptional Children, 37,* 229–237.

Descriptor (1970). New state plan, Austin, Texas: Special education instructional materials center. *The University of Texas at Austin, 4*(2), 1–2.

Donovan, M. S., & Cross, C. T. (Eds.). (2002*). Minority students in special and gifted education.* Washington, DC: National Academy Press.

Dorn, S. (2002). Public-private symbiosis in Nashville special education. *History of Education Quarterly, 42*(3), 368–394.

Dunn, L. M. (1968). Special education for the mildly retarded: Is much of it justifiable? *Exceptional Children, 35,* 5–22.

Dunn, L. M., & Capobianco, R. J. (1959). Mental retardation. *Review of Educational Research, 29*(5), 451–470.

Education for All Handicapped Children Act (1975), Pub. L. No. 94-142, 20 U.S.C. § 1400 et seq.

Education of Mentally Retarded Children Act (1958), Pub. L. No. 85-926.

Forgnone, C., & Collings, G.D. (1975). State certification-endorsement in special education administration. *Journal of Special Education, 9*(1), 5–9.

Fourache, M. H. (1961). Foreward. In L. E. Connor (Ed.), *Administration of special education programs* (pp. v–vi). New York: Teachers College Press.

Fuchs, D., Fuchs, L. S., & Stecker, P. M. (2010). The "blurring" of special education in a new continuum of general education. *Exceptional Children, 76*(3), 301–323.

Hallahan, D. P., & Mercer, C. D. (n.d.). *Learning disabilities: Historical perspectives.* Retrieved from http;//www.nrcld.org/resources/ldsummit/hallahan.pdf

Heck, A. O. (1944). General problems of philosophy and administration in the education of exceptional children. *Review of Educational Research, 14*(3), 201–208.

Handrick, I. G., & MacMillan, D. L. (1989). Selecting children for special education in New York City: William Maxwell, Elizabeth Farrell, and the development of ungraded classes, 1900–1920. *Journal of Special Education, 22*(4), 395–417.

Heller, K. A., Holtzman, W. H., & Messick, S. (Eds.) (1982). *Placing children in special education: A strategy for equity* Washington, DC: National Academy Press.

Hollingsworth, S. A. (1974). *Competency-based trainer programs: A generic model* (ED 145 644). Washington, DC: Bureau of Education for the Handicapped.

Hollinshead, M. T. (1953). The orthopedically handicapped. *Review of Educational Research, 23*(5), 492–507.

Hosp, J. L., & Reschly, D. J. (2003). Referral rates for intervention or assessment: A meta-analysis of racial differences. *The Journal of Special Education, 37*(2), 67–80.

Hunt, J. T. (1966). Crippling conditions and special health problems. *Review of Educational Research, 36*(1), 162–175.

Individuals With Disabilities Education Improvement Act (2004), Pub L. No. 108-446, 20 U.S.C. § 1400 *et seq.*

Jenkinson, J. C. (2002). *Mainstream or special? Educating students with disabilities* [NetLibrary version]. Retrieved from http://www.netlibrary.com.ezproxy.lib.utexas.edu/Details.aspx

Kirk, S. A. (1962). *Educating exceptional children.* Boston: Houghton Mifflin.

Kirk, S. A., McCarthy, J. J., & Kirk, W. D. (1968). *Illinois Test of Psycholinguistic Abilities.* Urbana: University of Illinois Press.

Kobe, K. (2002). *Elizabeth Farrell and the history of special education.* Arlington, VA: Council for Exceptional Children.

Kohl, J. W., & Marro, T. D. (1971). *A normative study of the administrative position in special education: Final report* (ED 058 679). Washington, DC: Bureau of Education for the Handicapped.

Koppitz, E. M. (1973). Visual aural digit span test performance of boys with emotional and learning problems. *Journal of Clinical Psychology, 29*(4), 463–466.

Lilly, M. S. (1970). Special education: A teapot in a tempest. *Exceptional Children, 37*(1), 43–48.

Mackie, R. P. (1965). Spotlighting advances in special education. *Exceptional Children, 32,* 77–81.

Mackie, R. P. (1969). *Special education in the United States: Statistics 1948–1966.* New York: Teachers College Press.

Mackie, R. P. (1978, June). *Organization and administration of special education in public schools in the United States* (ED 157 315). Paper presented at the World Congress on Future Special Education, Stirling, Scotland.

Martin, E. W., Martin, R., & Terman, D. L. (1996). The legislative and litigation history of special education. *The Future of Children, (6)*1, 25–39.

Martin, W. M., & Yates, J. R. (1973*). Special education administration simulation in Monroe City* (SEASIM). Columbus, Ohio: University Council for Educational Administration.

McCall, Z., & Skrtic, T. M. (2009). Intersectional needs politics: A policy frame for the wicked problem of disproportionality. *Multiple Voices for Ethnically Diverse Exceptional Learners, 11*(2), 3–23.

McCleary, L. E., & Hencley, S. P. (1965). *Secondary school administration.* New York: Dodd, Mead & Company.

McDonnell, L. M., McLaughlin, M. J., & Morison, P. (1997). *Educating one and all: Students with disabilities and standards-based reform.* Washington, DC: National Academy.

Meisgeier, C., & King, J.D. (1970). *The process of special education administration.* Scranton, PA: International Textbook Company.

Mostert, M. P., & Crockett, J. B. (1999–2000). Reclaiming the history of special education for more effective practice. *Exceptionality, 8*(2), 133–143.

Nevin, A. (1979) Special education administrator competencies required of the general education administrator. *Exceptional Children, 45*(5), 363–365.

Newcomer, P. L., & Hammill, D. D. (1975). ITPA and Academic Achievement: A Survey. *The Reading Teacher, 28*(8), 731–741.

No Child Left Behind Act (2001). Amendments to Title I of the Elementary and Secondary Education Act of 1965, 20 U.S.C. 6301 *et seq.*

O'Brien, G. V., & Bundy, M. E. (2009). Reaching beyond the "moron": Eugenic control of secondary disability groups. *Journal of Sociology and Social Welfare, 36*(4), 153–171.

Ornstein, A. C., & Levine, D. U. (2006). *Foundations of education* (5th ed). Boston: Houghton Mifflin.

Osgood, R. L. (2007). *The history of special education: A struggle for equality in American public schools* [EBL version]. Retrieved from http://www.utxa.eblib.com.ezproxy.lib.utexas.edu/patron/FullRecord.aspx?p=329171&userid=vaetfCZ67BQ7Y9zYmfEKKg%3d%3d&tstamp=1282259371&id=D3222324AD56973DBF1C894F1BF89E272B437E76

Oshinsky, D. M. (2005). *Polio: An American story.* New York: Oxford University Press.

Pfeiffer, D. (1994). Eugenics and disability discrimination. *Disability and Society, 9*(4), 481–499.

Podemski, R. S., Price, B. J., Smith, T. E. C., & Marsh, G. E. (1984). *Comprehensive administration of special education.* Rockville, MD: Aspen Systems Corporation.

Raske, D. E. (1979). The role of general school administrators responsible for special education programs. *Exceptional Children, 45*(8), 645–646.

Reynolds, M. (1962). A framework for considering some issues in special education, *Exceptional Children, 28,* 367–370.

Safford, P. L., & Safford, P. J. (1998). Visions of the special class. *Remedial and Special Education, 19*(4), 229–238.

Sage, D. (1972). The use of simulation in administration training (SEATS). Syracuse. NY: Syracuse University.

Sage, D. (1976). The planning period. In J. R. Yates (Ed.), *The integration of general and special education administration: Model, program and product development and evaluation* (pp. 12–29). Columbus, OH: UCEA.

Sage, D. D., & Burrello, L.C. (1994). *Leadership in educational reform: An administrator's guide to changes in special education.* Baltimore, MD: Paul H. Brookes.

Sage, D. D., & Sontag, E. (1972). *State Education Agency simulation exercise (SEASE).* Syracuse, NY: Syracuse University.

Scotch, R. K. (1989). Politics and policy in the history of the disability rights movement. *The Milbank Quarterly, 67*(Supplement 2), 380–400.

Seguin, E. (1907). *Idiocy and its treatment by the physiological method.* New York: Teacher's College, Columbia University. (Originally published 1866)

Semmel, M. I., Gerber, M. M., & MacMillan, D. L. (1994). Twenty-five years after Dunn's article: A legacy of policy analysis research in special education. *The Journal of Special Education 27*(4), 481–495.

Simpson, B. D. (2004, Nov. 29). The common school movement and compulsory education. *Mises Dailey.* Auburn, Alabama: Ludwig Von Mises Institute.

Sjostrom, C. (2009). *The future view of special education administration: A delphi study.* (Doctoral dissertation). Retrieved from UMI Number 3370204, ProQuest LLC, Ann Arbor, MI.

Vergason, G. A., Smith, F. V., & Wyatt, K. E. (1975). Questions for administrators about special education. *Theory into Practice, 14*(2), 99–104.

Will, M. (1986). Educating children with learning problems: A shared responsibility. *Exceptional Children, 52*(5), 411–415.

Willenberg, E. P. (1966). Organization, administration, and supervision of special education. *Review of Educational Research, 36*(1), 134–150.

Willenberg, E. P. (1970, March). Administration and supervision of special education. In G. Hensley & V. W. Patterson (Eds.), *Changing patterns of professional preparation and services in special education.* Selected papers of a working conference, Western Interstate Commission for Higher Education, Boulder, CO.

Winzer, M. A. (1993). *The history of special education: From isolation to integration* [NetLibrary version]. Retrieved from http://www.netlibrary.com.ezproxy.lib.utexas.edu/Details.aspx

Winzer, M. A. (2008). Confronting difference: an excursion through the history of special education. In L. Florian (Ed.), *The SAGE handbook of special education.* (pp. 20–33). London: SAGE.

Winzer, M. A. (2009). *From integration to inclusion: A history of special education in the 20th century.* Washington, DC: Gallaudet University Press.

Wishik, S. M., & Mackie, R. P. (1949). Adjustment of the school program for the physically handicapped child. *American Journal of Public Health, 39*(8) 992–998.

Woodruff, P. (2006). *First democracy: The challenge of an ancient idea.* New York: Oxford University Press.

Yates, J. R. (1976). History of the general-special education administration consortium. In J. R. Yates (Ed.), *The integration of general and special education administration: Model, program and product development and evaluation* (pp. 1–11). Columbus, Ohio: UCEA.

Yates, J. R. (2010). *Current forces impacting special education administration.* Manuscript in preparation.

Yates, J. R., Shelby, E., Blount, C.,., Fugate, K., Altobelli, J., Cadle, S., Sumbera, M., & Williams, J. (2010). *RTI's effect on changing roles in education.* Paper presented at the meeting of Council for Exceptional Children, Division for CEDS, San Antonio, Texas.

3

Expanding the Leadership Framework
An Alternate View of Professional Standards

Mary Lynn Boscardin

UNIVERSITY OF MASSACHUSETTS AMHERST

Carl Lashley

UNIVERSITY OF NORTH CAROLINA AT GREENSBORO

Over the past 15 years there has been a marked evolution of professional standards and their implementation in response to the various iterations of education reform. The contributions of researchers and scholars, professional organizations, practitioners, and other stakeholders to the identification and development of professional standards contributes to their universal application beyond that of preservice training. The utilitarian application of professional standards provides a disciplinary framework for better understanding the complex field of special education leadership and administration, thus, guiding and enriching the work lives of preservice, novice, and experienced educational leaders and administrators of special education.

Although standards have been used to combat low quality and extend opportunity (Porter, 1993), it is important that they not be used exclusively at the expense of higher levels of professional practice and accountability (Darling-Hammond, 1989). In this chapter, professional standards for leaders and administrators of special education will be elevated beyond a basic discussion. The context of the literature base supporting both general and special education administration in the broader context of leadership paradigms and policy reform efforts will serve as the basis for discussion. As Leithwood, Louis, Anderson, and Wahlstrom (2004) noted, "leadership is second only to classroom instruction among all school-related factors that contribute to what students learn at school" (p. 3).

Educational leadership standards are only one mechanism for helping us better understand how leadership influences instructional practices and student learning, yet they encompass many areas of the profession deserving further examination. The relationship among leadership and instructional practices, student learning, technology utilization in leadership roles, collaborative forms of leadership, capacity building, and the preparation and continued development of leaders for special education are just a few of the areas that will be explored in this chapter. Research linking various aspects of leadership in special education to all those aspects of education that influence student learning is gaining traction in contemporary leadership research (Boscardin, 2007; Leithwood et al., 2004). Understanding the premises and assumptions of special education leadership leads to interesting opportunities to cultivate collaboration between general and special education.

Considering Professional Leadership Titles and Roles

Without professional titles and roles, there would be little need for professional standards. Kern and Mayer (1970), Finkbinder (1981), and Whitworth and Hatley (1979) noted that one of the basic problems of the special education leadership position is the maze of various titles, labels, guidelines, and stipulations through which one understands the roles and functions of the position. Finkbinder noted that titles are an integral component to those assuming professional identities. Titles are symbolic, representing the ethos and culture that create the essence of the embodiment of a discipline or profession. Although most states use the title of director of special education or administrator of special education, there is some variation among the states requiring licensure/certification/endorsement.

Because of the confusion concerning the tasks associated with the role of administrators of special education and the knowledge base needed for leading and administrating special education programs (Finkbinder, 1981; Kern & Mayer, 1970; Whitworth & Hatley, 1985), the Council for Exceptional Children (2009) published *What Every Special Educator Must Know: Ethics, Standards, and Guidelines for Special Educators* in an effort to reconcile the national titular and professional standard ambiguities that dictate licensing requirements and standardize role expectations. Preservice training anchored by professional standards and a predictable course of study is another mechanism thought to aid in the development of professional identities. Schulman (2005) has referred to a predictable course of study for a profession, such as medicine or law, as *signature pedagogies*. It is Schulman's (2005) belief that signature pedagogies are another component that contributes to strong professional identities.

According to Billingsley (2005), professional teachers and administrators who complete accredited preservice programs that prepare them well in their disciplinary area, and who then work in educational environments that continue to support evidence-based practices, are more likely to remain in their chosen profession and be more effective. Administrators of special education with strong professional identities are considered to be essential to ensuring the delivery of high quality evidence-based special education programs in increasingly inclusive schools. These leaders are the standard bearers, those who set expectations of what it means to be a professional. Without this model of professionalism, there is a risk of continued role ambiguity and erosion challenging identities. Titles, notwithstanding, the disciplinary underpinnings of special education leadership and administration, represented in the form of standards, are the foundation of the field and model of professionalism for leaders of special education.

The Professionalization of Special Education Leaders

The development of special education leaders continues to be a dynamic process, characterized by ongoing revision and reconceptualization of models of professionalism as new research continues to inform the knowledge base. New ideas and leadership paradigms open the door for developing more far-reaching and comprehensive ways of thinking about leadership frameworks for special education as the field continues to expand. The form and function of leadership will change as new research emerges. For example, leadership recently has become more collaborative as it becomes distributive (Gronn, 2000; Mayrowetz & Smylie, 2004; Murphy, 2005; Spillane, Halverson, & Diamond, 2001, 2004), which in part is a function of a more democratic and pluralistic approach to leadership.

The examination of the research literature in the sections that follow provides an opportunity to examine the development and evolution of special education leadership competencies, and creates an opportunity for consideration of how the competencies might be more broadly incorporated throughout the career span of leaders and administrators of special education.

The Emergence of Skill-Based Special Education Administration Requirements

Initial interest in the skills special education administrators might need to carry out the responsibilities of their roles began to emerge as early as the early 1960s. At the 1962 annual meeting of the National Association of State Directors of Special Education (NASDSE), a committee was appointed to investigate (a) the training and experience expected of state directors and supervisors, and (b) the extent to which these expectations were being met in college and university programs accepting students under Public Law 85-926, which provided fellowships for advanced preparation of directors and supervisors.

Two years later, Milazzo and Blessing (1964) used P.L. 87-276, a law that emphasized the need for adequate preparation for administrators and coordinators of programs of special education in state and local school systems, as the basis for their investigation of the availability and content of training programs in institutions of higher education (IHEs) that included both colleges and universities. Affiliation with local, state, and national professional organizations related to special education was also an important aspect to being an administrator of special education (Milazzo & Blessing, 1964).

In a subsequent investigation, Brabandt (1969) found that none of the 98 veteran administrators responding to a questionnaire met the standards established by the Council for Exceptional Children or the requirements of the doctoral programs offered by the institutions of higher education. Most respondents had training as general educators or school psychologists, but were not specifically trained as administrators of special education. Despite institutions of higher education having programs accredited by CEC, only 2 of the 12 states participating in the study had certification requirements for administrators of special education, and 4 states had certification requirements for supervisors of special education. Only one state, as part of the certification process, met the CEC standards for administrators of special education. All 12 states required a general administrative credential.

Kern and Mayer (1970) and Marro and Kohl (1972) identified specific requirements that contributed most to the success of administrators of special education. However, many of the earlier studies did not investigate prior teaching experience (Prillaman & Richardson, 1985; Stile, Abernathy, & Pettibone 1986 Stile & Pettibone, 1980; Valesky & Hirth, 1992), practicum/internship requirements (Prillaman & Richardson, 1985; Stile et al., 1986; Stile & Pettibone, 1980; Valesky & Hirth, 1992), or continuing education requirements (Forgnone & Collings, 1975; Prillaman & Richardson, 1985; Stile et al. 1986; Stile & Pettibone, 1980; Valesky & Hirth, 1992).

Kern and Mayer (1970) and Finkbinder (1981) found that preservice training programs for special education administrators provided core administrative courses and field experiences delivered by special education faculty rather than following the practice of borrowing faculty from general education. Of the studies that did investigate specific requirements, these were in the form of course work, teaching experience, and degrees rather than specific competencies. The importance of previous teaching experience (Brabant, 1969; Milazzo & Blessing, 1964) and internships (Brabant, 1969; Finkbinder; Marro & Kohl, 1972; Milazzo & Blessing, 1964) to the training of administrators of special education was noted in these earlier studies. Other requirements included: a master's degree in special education, certification as a teacher in some area of special education, course work in educational foundations and educational administration, elective courses in psychology, guidance, and research methods, and practicum experiences (Kern &

Mayer, 1970). Brabant and Prillaman and Richardson (1985) suggested the need for: (a) a post-master's degree in administration which would include appropriate coursework in educational administration; (b) two or more years of teaching in special education; (c) an internship in special education administration; (d) cognate or support coursework in such related areas as personnel management, sociology, psychology, and organizational theory, and; (e) research experience.

The next set of researchers introduced the idea that prior teaching and practica might be important to developing effective administrators of special education. Brabant (1969), Kern and Mayer (1970), Forgnone and Collins (1975), and Whitworth and Hatley (1979) investigated prior teaching and practicum experience requirements. Kern and Mayer identified the need for extending training through professional development programs for inservice administrators of special education. Continuing education, a recent addition to credentialing requirements for administrators of special education since the passage of No Child Left Behind (NCLB, 2001), was used to build and maintain the professional leadership knowledge and skill capacity.

The Emergence of Knowledge-Based Special Education Administration Competencies

Special education leadership knowledge-based competencies began to emerge in concert with discrete course work and field-based requirements of the mid-1960s. Milazzo and Blessing (1964), using the input of university faculty, identified the following competencies in their research, though did not refer to them as such:

> (a) knowledge of federal, state, and local functions and responsibilities in special education; (b) supervisory and/or administrative experience; (c) an understanding of preservice and inservice educational activity; (d) community public relations experiences related to special education; and (e) involvement in direct services to one or more types of exceptional children.
>
> *(p. 133)*

It could be argued that these are not competencies applied to licensure candidates but requirements for program content and delivery. That is, they indicate program inputs rather than outcomes expected of candidates.

The following recommendations made by researchers for training administrators of special education are better aligned with competencies: (a) a common core that covers the broad aspects of exceptionality, such as child growth, development, and psychology of the exceptional child (Kern & Mayer, 1970; Marro & Kohl, 1972; Milazzo & Blessing, 1964; Prillaman & Richardson, 1985), and effective special education placement (Marro & Kohl, 1972); (b) curriculum and methods in an area of exceptionality (Milazzo & Blessing, 1964); (c) remediation of learning difficulties (Milazzo & Blessing, 1964); (d) internships in settings with normal children and in an area of exceptionality (Milazzo & Blessing, 1964); (e) advanced statistics and research design (Kern & Mayer, 1970; Milazzo & Blessing, 1964); (f) advanced seminars in special education (Milazzo & Blessing, 1964); (g) research and publications (Kern & Mayer, 1970; Milazzo & Blessing, 1964); and (h) electives (Milazzo & Blessing, 1964).

More advanced training recommendations included knowledge of: (a) general education administration (Kern & Mayer, 1970; Marro & Kohl, 1972; Milazzo & Blessing, 1964); (b) general education and supervision (Marro & Kohl, 1972; Milazzo & Blessing, 1964); (c) school law (Milazzo & Blessing, 1964); (d) school finance (Milazzo & Blessing, 1964); (e) administration and supervision in special education (Milazzo & Blessing, 1964); (f) personnel management (Prillaman & Richardson, 1985); (g) organizational theory (Prillaman & Richardson, 1985); and

(h) field work in special education (Milazzo & Blessing, 1964), in addition to a focused internship in administration and/or supervision of special education (Kern & Mayer, 1970; Milazzo & Blessing, 1964; Prillaman & Richardson, 1985).

None of the studies equated the acquisition of competencies with the knowledge, skills, and dispositions necessary for qualified leaders of special education. Instead, there appears to be a tacit assumption that the completion of a certain set of pre-specified requirements indicates that candidates have acquired the capacity to practice in the field. The expectation is with advances in the field, experiences that are paired with research-based knowledge will contribute to skill acquisition and induction into the field of special education leadership and administration in a way that cannot be achieved with course work alone. The development of evidenced based leadership practices provides a foundation that can be used to support improved instructional practices by teachers and educational achievement of students (Boscardin, 2007, 2004; Leithwood et al., 2004).

Influences of Policy on the Development of Professional Standards

Since the proliferation of school reform reports in the early 1980s, a sustained effort has been undertaken to fix, restructure, and rethink the American educational enterprise. The phrase *school reform* is a common reference to any proposal for change in public school policy and/or its operation. The connection to learning in the past has been limited to trying to better understand the connection between what teachers teach and what students learn (i.e., Educate America Act, 2000; No Child Left Behind, 2001; Teachers for the 21st Century, 1986; Tomorrow's Teachers, 1986).

In the 1970s, the first wave of top-down reform called for competency-based education, performance contracting, school-wide accountability, academic excellence, and legislated learning, an example of the latter being the federal publication entitled *What Works: Research about Teaching and Learning* (U.S. Department of Education, 1987). Barth (1990) regarded the top-down model as being too unwieldy and too complex for any one individual to address.

The second wave of educational reform was characterized by a bottom-up or grass-roots approach, with strong emphasis on processes, but not on outcomes. This wave of educational reform embraced the sharing of responsibilities and leadership in schools in order to infuse and develop a variety of leadership roles (Barth, 1990). Outcomes, while important, were not central to this second wave of reform.

The effective schools movement was marked by an implied causal relationship between school practices and student learning (Edmonds, 1983; Lezotte, 1981). During this era, researchers began to question the criteria used to determine school effectiveness. The criteria were in the form of standards that addressed leadership, teacher, and school traits and characteristics but were silent on student learning outcomes.

Era of Standards-Based Accountability Educational Reforms

The most recent era of educational reform, driven by a federal mandate referred to as the No Child Left Behind Act (NCLB, 2001), ushered in the era of accountability for student and teacher performance unlike no other educational reform movement. Expectations for student achievement and teacher performance are higher now than at any other time in history, and scientific research and public policy have become potent influences on the practices of educational leaders. How the link between leading and learning is established will depend much on how the field engages in the utilization of evidence-based practices, including the identification and use of scientifically-based instructional practices.

The purposes of NCLB (2001) and the Individuals with Disabilities Education Act (IDEA, 2004) are antithetical even though both laws have an achievement orientation as the centerpiece. NCLB addresses school large scale school improvement and IDEA mandates the development and provision of appropriate individualized educational programs for students with disabilities. In 2002 policy makers indicted the system used to implement special education for placing process over results and bureaucratic compliance above student achievement, excellence, academic, and social outcomes (President's Commission on Excellence in Special Education, 2002). In addition, the President's Commission cited a lack of highly qualified teachers and heralded the NCLB legislation as the "driving force behind IDEA reauthorization" (p. 7). However, two critical questions remain: Will better alignment between the *systems* of special and general education provide *students* with a greater opportunity to learn, or will blended systems result in diminished opportunities for students with disabilities to receive the individually appropriate instruction they need to grow into productive adulthood (Boscardin, 2005)?

IDEA 2004 builds on NCLB by emphasizing increased accountability for student performance at the classroom, school, and school district levels. The changes in IDEA 2004 are significant and include changes in the qualifications of instructional personnel and the approach to instruction itself. All special education teachers must be licensed in special education and meet the highly qualified teacher (HQT) requirements of NCLB. The use of instructional strategies and methods must be grounded in scientifically based research.

School Reform Limitations

School reforms initiated by NCLB (2001) and IDEA (2004) have led to increased accountability for ensuring high quality instruction, improving adequate yearly progress (AYP) for students with disabilities, and monitoring their progress in assessments. These emphases have significantly affected the duties, roles, and functions of all school administrators, including directors of special education programs. Administrators are also responsible for certifying that all students are taught by highly qualified teachers who use scientifically-based instructional practices, that students have access to and achieve in the general education curriculum, and that adequate resources support teaching and learning (Boscardin, 2004; DiPaola & Walther-Thomas, 2003).

These reform efforts for the most part have been silent on the role of leadership and its connection to student success. Yet, administrators are expected to interpret and put into place school reform efforts in a timely manner regardless of their own preparation to do so. When schools do not achieve their adequate yearly progress goals, the contribution of leadership to positive student performance is the first to be scrutinized. States now are on the cusp of considering new ways to evaluate the connection between leadership behaviors and student achievement (Leithwood et al., 2004; Waters, Marzano, & McNulty, 2003). The link between leadership behaviors and student achievement, as defined by Leithwood and colleagues, is inclusive of all student populations, although no specific reference is made in their research to students with disabilities.

These simultaneously occurring national policy initiatives require that special education administrators be well versed in the knowledge and skills that are brought to their practice from complementary disciplines. Becoming an effective special education leader for the 21st century requires that administrators work collaboratively with teachers, parents, other school administrators, and policymakers to bring resources, personnel, programs, and expertise together to solve problems of practice for all students.

Professional Leadership Standards for Administrators of Special Education

Professional standards provide a policy framework for the knowledge and skills thought to be important to the foundation of professional identities. National standards emanate from professional educator organizations with input from federal education agencies and university researchers. These national standards are then considered by states as they develop state licensure requirements. One way to assure that this standard is met is through the adoption of professional standards. The federal statute and the regulations of IDEA 2004 no longer refer to directors of special education and there is no specific reference as to what constitutes a highly qualified director of special education. One interpretation is that the federal government has left this decision to individual states.

The National Council for Accreditation of Teacher Education (NCATE), Teacher Education Accreditation Council (TEAC), Interstate New Teacher Assessment and Support Consortium (INTASC), Council for Exceptional Children Professional Standards Committee, and the National Policy Board for Educational Administration (NPBEA) have been interlinked and aligned to provide administrator education standards with a well-integrated set of expectations and outcomes upon which to base practice. For example, the Council for Exceptional Children's (CEC) Institutional and Program Requirements are aligned with INTASC and NCATE Standards to provide special educators with expectations and outcomes that are linked to those in general education. CEC and NCATE have joined together to develop special education administration leadership standards that provide guidelines for creating a vision, accountability mechanisms, flexibility, and options, with supported by disciplinary research.

Standards or domains are defined by knowledge, skills, and disposition statements or objectives. Some of these domains among the various accrediting organizations are well-aligned while others are organized differently. In this section, three sets of standards will be discussed; two sets of U.S. leadership standards, one for general education administrators and one for special education administrators, and one set of United Kingdom leadership standards for headteachers.

The Interstate School Leaders Licensure Consortium Standards

The National Council for Accreditation of Teacher Education (NCATE) and the Educational Leadership Constituent Council (ELCC) are two primary professional organizations responsible for the accreditation of administrator preparation programs, and thus the joint set of standards they have adopted play a crucial role in preparation program design and implementation. The ISLLC leadership standards for general education administrators have undergone several revisions since their inception. Like most standards, during their metamorphosis, the standards have been reoriented moving away from a process focus toward performance based measures.

The ISLLC 2008 standards provide the basis for evaluating the entry-level functions, as opposed to knowledge and skills, of educational administrators. In addition to guiding how practicing administrators should be evaluated as they progress toward expert performance, practice standards were establish to aid with the development of professional career plans and to guide the professional development of leaders as they progress toward expert performance (National Policy Board for Educational Administration,, 2008). The intent was for the ISLLC 2008 standards to have far-reaching applications, yet not be limited to governing accreditation of institutions of higher education (IHE). As stated in Educational Leadership Policy Standards: ISLLC 2008 published by the CSSO, policy standards serve as a "foundation, states can create a common language and bring consistency to education leadership policy at all levels so that there are clear expectation" (p. 5).

MCATE/ELCC and the National Policy Board for Educational Administration (NPBEA) have adopted the language of the Interstate School Leaders Licensure Consortium (ISLLC) standards. The six ISSLC standards include:

- Standard 1:   Setting a widely shared vision for learning;
- Standard 2:   Developing a school culture and instructional program conducive to student learning and staff professional growth;
- Standard 3:   Ensuring effective management of the organization, operation, and resources for a safe, efficient, and effective learning environment;
- Standard 4:   Collaborating with faculty and community members, responding to diverse community interests and needs, and mobilizing community resources;
- Standard 5:   Acting with integrity, fairness, and in an ethical manner; and
- Standard 6:   Understanding, responding to, and influencing the political, social, legal, and cultural contexts.

The Administrator of Special Education 2009 Standards

The Professional Standards for Administrators of Special Education developed by CEC with the sponsorship of the Council of Administrators of Special Education (CASE) identify the knowledge and skills that characterize competent leaders of special education. In this section, the differences between the 2003 and the 2009 Administrator of Special Education Standards will be dissected. The 2009 revalidation represents a major departure from the 2003 standards. Like the ISLLC 2008 standards, the 2009 CEC standards for administrators of special education were designed to set policy and vision, not prescribe a particular brand of leadership practice.

The 2003 Administrator of Special Education Standards were comprised of 7 of the 10 standards designed for first time licensees, otherwise known as an initial license candidates, and had very little to do with administration as they were primarily teacher focused. Three of the 10 standards (instructional strategies, learning environments and social interactions, and language) were deleted since they pertained to classroom instruction rather than leadership. Subsumed under the following seven remaining standards were 49 knowledge and skill statements (refer to the CEC Redbook, 2003):

- Standard 1:   Foundations (philosophical, historical, and legal)
- Standard 2:   Characteristics of Learners (human development, principles of learning)
- Standard 3:   Assessment, Diagnosis, and Evaluation
- Standard 4:   Instructional Content and Practice
- Standard 5:   Planning and Managing the Teaching and Learning Environment
- Standard 6:   Managing Student Behavior and Social Interactions
- Standard 7:   Communication and Collaborative Partnerships
- Standard 8:   Professionalism and Ethics

The new standards (CEC, 2009) differ significantly from the 2003 standards, in that, they are leadership focused and performance-based, in addition to having been elevated from the initial beginning level to the advanced professional level. Unlike the earlier standards that guided initial licensure and were more teacher-oriented, the language and approaches suggested by these advanced standards are grounded in the special education and general education administration knowledge traditions. The revised and validated performance-based standards for Special Education Administrators at the Advanced Level (2009) include 42 knowledge and skill statements (refer to the CEC 2009 Redbook) embedded within six standards that address the following:

- Standard 1:   Leadership & Policy
- Standard 2:   Program Development & Organization
- Standard 3:   Research & Inquiry
- Standard 4:   Evaluation

- Standard 5:   Professional Development & Ethical Practice
- Standard 6:   Collaboration

The national standards (CEC, 2009) describe the knowledge, skills, and dispositions needed for administrators of special education to effectively execute the functions of their jobs and they form the foundation for professional identities, as well as provide a framework for ongoing professional development. Before acquiring the advanced leadership competencies, leaders must demonstrate acquisition of initial knowledge and skills. While it may appear that instruction, assessment, diagnosis, evaluation, planning and management of the teaching and learning environment, and the management of student behavior and social interactions are overlooked; this is not the case, as these are still a part of initial licensing. Instead of being a single step process, leaders must now sequentially demonstrate initial then advanced sets of knowledge and skills to be an effective leader and administrator of special education.

Not all states that require endorsement/certification/ licensing as an administrator of special education fully incorporate the CEC administrator of special education standards into their state credentialing requirements. The standards that are least frequently included as state credentialing requirements are collaboration, and research and inquiry (Boscardin, Weir, & Kusek, 2010). This is understandable in a field that demands proficiency in laws and regulations, particularly laws that require strict procedural compliance, ongoing program evaluation, and annual accountability for student progress as measured by statewide assessments.

International Standards

International standards can be used to affirm and lend perspective to national practices in the United States. The National Standards for Headteachers (2004) in the United Kingdom influence the work of school administrators and headteachers. Headteachers roles are similar to those of administrators of special education, i.e., partially supportive and partially administrative. "The Standards embody three key principles, namely that the work of headteachers should be: learning-centred, focused on leadership, and reflect the highest possible professional standards" (National Standards for Headteachers, 2004). The UK Department for Education (2010) has also produced a companion document for headteachers and other administrators to provide additional support. Taken together, these documents provide guidelines for headteachers and other administrators as they lead programs for all children. Of particular note is that these standards are "used to identify the threshold levels of performance for the assessment framework within the National Professional Qualification for Headship" (National Standards for Headteachers, 2004, p. 5).

In the United Kingdom, teachers who aspire to be headteachers go through an extensive professional development and assessment regimen in order to qualify for a license. The standards include the following domains:

- Shaping the Future
- Leading, Learning, and Teaching
- Development of Self and Working with Others
- Managing the Organisation
- Securing Accountability
- Strengthening Community

These standard domains have much in common with the six ISLLC (2008) and CEC Administrator of Special Education (2009) domain areas. Differences occur with implementation. The United States has left the adoption of standards and accompanying assessments to individual states since education is constitutionally a state function. As such, some states have adopted the national standards and others have modified and adopted state specific standards for their practicing educators. Only four states require that prospective administrators of special education pass licensure exams (Boscardin et al., 2010).

Comparing and Contrasting Standards

Using the three sets of leadership standards presented in the previous sections, it is possible to visibly see the similarities and differences (see Table 3.1).

The revised and validated Administrator of Special Education at the Advanced Level (CEC, 2009), the Educational Leadership Policy Standards: ISLLC Standards (2008), and the National Standards for Headteachers (2004) are guided by six standard/domain areas. These sets of standards are strikingly similar in the areas of leadership and policy, program development and organization, professional development, ethical practice, and collaboration, yet differ noticeably in two domain areas, research and inquiry and accountability. Based on further review of the ISLLC standards, evaluation is addressed in two of the knowledge and skill statements rather than set apart as separate domains. Explicit or implicit mention of research and inquiry as they relate to educational administrative leadership is absent.

The standards use different and in some ways more explicit wording to capture the policy and leadership dimension. The use of shaping the future captures the dynamic nature of policy formation and leadership. Leading learning and teaching, development of self, and working with others captures the instructional leadership and professional development responsibilities. While strengthening community can be accomplished through varied methods, collaboration would seem to be the primary strategy. Accountability leaves no doubt regarding the outcome of evaluations, whereas that level of clarity is absent in the Administrator of Special Education and ISLLC standards.

The evolution of professional standards and their implementation comes mostly in response to the various iterations of education reform policies, in conjunction with the contributions of professional organizations, experts in the field, and multiple stakeholders. Through review and inclusion of related standards, it is possible to expand the knowledge base and practices so as

Table 3.1 Side by Side Comparison of the Special and General Education Administrative Standards

Administrators of Special Education at the Advanced Level (2009)	Educational Leadership Policy Standards: ISLLC (2008)	United Kingdom National Standards for Headteachers (2004)
Leadership & Policy	Effective Management Influencing Policy	Shaping the Future
Program Development & Organization	Shared Vision for Learning Developing a School Culture & Instructional Program	Leading Learning and Teaching Managing the Organisation
Research & Inquiry		
Evaluation	(Not a separate domain area but included in knowledge and skill statements)	
	Securing Accountability	
Professional Development & Ethical Practice	Ethical Practice	Development of Self and Working With Others
Collaboration	Collaboration	Strengthening Community

to enrich the professional lives of preservice, novice, and experienced educational leaders and administrators of special education and lead to improved learning outcomes for students.

Beyond the Standards: Contemporary Considerations for Special Education Leadership and Administration

The initial validation of the Administrator of Special Education (2009) standards commenced with a review of the literature (Boscardin et al., 2009). The evidence for each of the six domains is anchored within three sources: (a) theory or conceptual literature, (b) research literature, and/ or (c) practice literature. The theory/conceptual literature emphasize theories or philosophical reasoning derived from position papers, policy analyses, and descriptive reviews. The research literature is predicated on methodologies that address questions of cause and effect, and that researchers have independently replicated and found to be effective. The practice literature is derived from professional wisdom, promising practices, and model and lighthouse programs.

Researchers identified 42 new knowledge and skill statements that were supported by literature from one or more categories. While none of the statements from the 2003 Administrator of Special Education standards were retained in their entirety, certain conceptual aspects were represented in the new statements. The number of references associated with each of the domains appears in Table 3.2 (Boscardin et al., 2009, p. 74).

Although the theory/conceptual literature had the highest number of overall citations, the research literature did not differ significantly in the number of references. The practice literature consisted of the fewest citations. The majority of citations for leadership and policy and the professional development and ethical practice standards were found in the conceptual/theory literature. The research citations dominated the program development and organization, research and inquiry, evaluation, and collaboration standards. The practice references, for all but one standard, research and inquiry, was associated with the least number of citations. In many ways, this suggests a strong theory and research orientation in the field.

The earlier literature (Finkbinder, 1981; Kern & Mayer, 1970; Marro & Kohl, 1972; Milazzo & Blessing, 1964; Prillaman & Richardson, 1985; Stile et al., 1985; Stile & Pettibone, 1980; Valesky and Hirth, 1992; Whitworth & Hatley, 1985) and more recent reviews and investigations (Boscardin et al., 2009; Crockett, Becker, & Quinn, 2009; Leithwood et al., 2004; O'Brien, 2006; Waters et al., 2003) in concert with the various sets of standards reveal a broader context for envisioning special education leadership. The standards and literature base combine to challenge notions about how to best situate the leadership dimensions of special education at the domain level.

Table 3.2 Frequency of References by Standard

Standard	Literature/Theory-Based Evidence	Research-Based Evidence	Practice-Based Evidence
Leadership & Policy	95	41	33
Program Development & Organization	29	65	18
Research & Inquiry	10	20	11
Evaluation	27	31	16
Professional Development & Ethical Practice	53	36	24
Collaboration	15	17	8
TOTALS	**229**	**210**	**110**

Using the literature sources and standards cited in this chapter and the earlier work of Boscardin (2011), it is possible to identify and further expand domain areas for the leadership and administration of special education. The result is nine domain areas that include: (a) leadership, policy, and school reform; (b) economic and resource management; (c) context for leadership; (d) instructional leadership; (e) evaluation of educational programs and program outcomes; (f) research and inquiry; (g) professional development and human resources; (h) collaborative leadership; and (i) technology (see Table 3.3).

Table 3.3 Special Education Administration Leadership Domains by Focus and Source

Domain	Focus	Source
Context for Leadership	Building an inclusive vision, culture, order, discipline, & situational awareness, creating an environment that maximizes learning	Milazzo & Blessing (1964), Kern & Mayer (1970), Marro & Kohl (1972), Prillaman & Richardson (i985), Waters et al. (2003), Leithwood et al. (2004), O'Brien (2006), Boscardin, et al. (2009)
Leadership, Policy, & School Reform	Inspiring others, applying the laws & policies, managing organizational systems & processes, & engaging in meaningful strategic planning	Milazzo & Blessing (1964), Waters, et al. (2003), O'Brien (2006), Boscardin et al. (2009), and Crockett et al. (2009)
Economic Resource Management & Leadership	Creating fiscal equity, linking budgets to educational goals, managing systems & processes	Milazzo & Blessing (1964), Waters et al. (2003), O'Brien (2006), Boscardin et al. (2009), and Crockett et al. (2009)
Instructional Leadership	Pedagogical knowledge & application, building learning communities	Milazzo & Blessing (1964), Kern & Mayer (1970), Marro & Kohl (1972), Prillaman & Richardson (1985), Waters et al. (2003), Leithwood et al. (2004), O'Brien (2006), Boscardin et al. (2009), and Crockett et al. (2009)
Evaluation of Educational Programs & Program Outcomes	Assessment of learning outcomes, evaluation of program effectiveness, monitoring, decision-making, judgment	Milazzo & Blessing (1964), Waters et al. (2003), Leithwood et al. (2004), O'Brien (2006), Boscardin et al. (2009), Crockett et al. (2009)
Research & Inquiry	Publications, research design, data analysis	Brabant (1969), Milazzo & Blessing (1964), Kern & Mayer (1970), Boscardin et al. (2009)
Human Resource Development & Supervision	Professional values & ethics, commitment to ongoing personal & professional development, staff hiring, retention, supervision, & evaluation, intellectual stimulation, rewards, affirmation	Milazzo & Blessing (1964), Marro & Kohl (1972), Prillaman & Richardson (1985), Waters et al. (2003), Leithwood et al. (2004), O'Brien (2006), Boscardin et al. (2009), and Crockett et al. (2009)
Collaborative Leadership	Interpersonal, relationships, community building, communication	Milazzo & Blessing (1964), Waters et al. (2003), Leithwood et al. (2004), O'Brien (2006), Boscardin et al. (2009), and Crockett et al. (2009)
Technology & Information Systems	Data gathering and analysis, data warehousing, data sharing, technology assisted instruction, communication infra-structures	Crockett et al. (2009)

The nine domains noted in the above table each capture different, yet important, interdependent aspects of leadership. The leadership and policy foci capture the substantive and procedural aspects of leading. The foci of instructional leadership are on the important pedagogical components of leading that advance student learning and instruction. The foci of collaborative leadership are on the interpersonal, relational, community building complexities of leadership. Economic resource management and leadership represent an area of leading where the foci are on matters of equity, adequacy, efficiency, and access in relationship to providing instruction and promoting achievement, all of which are assessed through the evaluation of educational programs measured through program outcomes. With professional development serving as a catalyst for growing the organization, affirming values and ethical behaviors that contribute to personal and professional development and intellectual stimulation are critical and rely on research and inquiry capabilities. The domain not represented in the standards and literature, except for Crockett et al. (2009), is technology and information systems.

This leadership framework for leading and administering special education, while still emerging, demonstrates that there is an evolving body of knowledge that supports the disciplinary work of administrators of special education. Next steps would entail identifying how the discrete knowledge and skills associated with these special education leadership domains contribute to improved instruction and higher levels of achievement for students with disabilities (Boscardin, 2004; Leithwood et al., 2004).

As teaching, learning, and assessment systems that support the education of all students become more complex, all school leaders will be integral to designing, evaluating, and analyzing programs intended to support students with disabilities and their families. Leaders will be asked to create new, more effective solutions, and to work in innovative, collaborative ways to assure student achievement and success. As the leadership framework continues to expand by merging with the various sub-disciplines of educational leadership, possibilities for a shared leadership lexicon may emerge that better links visions with missions for educating students with disabilities.

Summary

The standards-based accountability reform movement has captured our imaginations about the possibilities for linking leading, teaching, and learning, connections that require further investigation. Evidence regarding what leaders of special education do makes a difference in the lives of students with disabilities and their families as pressures on resources mount, priorities and opportunities shift across career stages, and changes occur within systems. Standards are not singular in their purpose and function, rather, they serve multiple functions and act as a catalyst for identifying the knowledge and skills needed by leaders administering special education programs at varying career stages. While the development of national standards communicates the importance of leadership in special education, one would also hope that the professional standards communicate that special education leadership makes a difference.

As the roles of leaders evolve, one constant remains. Professional standards will continue to evolve and contribute to the development of the field of special education administration and leadership. What leaders of special education do to make a positive difference in the academic outcomes for students with disabilities and their families deserves deeper examination.

References

Barth, (1990). *Improving schools from within*. San Francisco, CA: Jossey-Bass.

Billingsley, B. (2005). *Cultivating and keeping committed special education teachers*. Thousand Oaks, CA: Corwin Press.

Boscardin, M. L. (2004). Transforming administration to support science in the schoolhouse for students with disabilities. *Journal of Learning Disabilities, 37,* 262–269.

Boscardin, M. L. (2005). The administrative role in transforming secondary schools to support inclusive evidence-based practices. *American Secondary Education Journal, 33*(3), 21–32.

Boscardin, M. L. (2007). What is special about special education administration? Considerations for school leadership. *Exceptionality, 15*, 189–200.

Boscardin, M. L. (2011). Using professional standards to inform leadership in special education. In J. M. Kauffman & D. P. Hallahan (Eds.), *Handbook of special education* (pp. 378–390). New York, NY: Taylor & Francis.

Boscardin, M. L., McCarthy, E., & Delgado, R. (2009). An integrated research-based approach to creating standards for special education leadership, *Journal of Special Education Leadership, 22*, 68–84.

Boscardin, M. L., Weir, K., & Kusek, C. (2010). A national study of state credentialing requirements for administrators of special education. *Journal of Special Education Leadership, 23*, 61-75.

Brabandt, Jr., E. W. (1969). *A comparative analysis of actual professional training, state credential requirements, and professional training requirements recommended by the Council for Exceptional Children for administrators of special education.* (Doctoral dissertation. Colorado State College) Ann Arbor, Mich. University Microfilms, 1969, No. 69–15.

Council for Exceptional Children. (2003). *What every special educator must know: Ethics, standards, and guidelines for special educators* (5th ed.). Arlington, VA: Author.

Council for Exceptional Children. (2009). *What every special educator must know: Ethics, standards, and guidelines for special educators* (6th ed.). Arlington, VA: Author.

Council of Chief State School Officers. (2008). *Educational leadership policy standards: ISLLC 2008.* Retrieved from http://www.npbea.org/projects.php

Crockett, J. B., Becker, M. K., & Quinn, D. (2009). Reviewing the knowledge base of special education leadership and administration. *Journal of Special Education Leadership, 22*, 55–67.

Darling-Hammond, L. (1989). Accountability for professional practice. *Teachers College Record, 91*(1), 59–80.

DiPaola, M. F., & Walther-Thomas, C. (2003). *Principals and special education: The critical role of school leaders.* (COPSSE Document No. IB-7). Gainesville: University of Florida, Center on Personnel Studies in Special Education.

Edmonds, R. R. (1983). Programs of school improvement: An overview. *Educational Leadership, 14*(4), 4–11.

The Education (Head Teachers' Qualifications) (England) (Revocation) Regulations, 2012 No. 18, Stautory Instruments. Retrieved January 22, 2012, from http://www.legislation.gov.uk/uksi/2012/18/

Finkbinder, R. L. (1981). Special education administration and supervision: The state of the art. *Journal of Special Education, 15*(4), 485–495.

Forgnone, C., & Collings, G. D. (1975). State certification endorsement in special education administration. *The Journal of Special Education, 9*, 5–9.

Gronn, P. (2000). Distributed leadership as a unit of analysis. *The Leadership Quarterly, 4*, 423–451.

Individuals with Disabilities Education Act, 20 U.S.C. § 1400 *et seq.* (2004).

Kern, W. H., & Mayer, J. F. (1970). Certification of directors of special education programs: The results of a national survey. *Contemporary Education, 42*, 126–128.

Leithwood, K., Louis, K. S., Anderson, S., & Wahlstrom, K. (2004). *How leadership influences student learning (executive summary)*, University of Minnesota and University of Toronto, commissioned by The Wallace Foundation (available at www.wallacefoundation.org).

Lezotte, L. W. (1981). Search for and description of characteristics of effective elementary schools: Lansing public schools. In R. R. Edmonds (Ed.), *A report on the research project: Search for effective schools* (pp. 6–15). East Lansing: Michigan State University.

Marro, T. D., & Kohl, J. S. (1972). Normative study of the administrative position in special education. *Exceptional Children, 39*(1), 5–14.

Mayrowetz, D., & Smylie, M. (2004). Work redesign that works for teachers. *Yearbook of the National Society for the Study of Education, 103*, 274–293.

Milazzo, T. C., & Blessing, K. R. (1964). The training of directors and supervisors of special education programs. *Exceptional Children, 31*, 129–141.

Murphy, J. (2005, September). Using the ISLLC standards for school leaders at the state level to strengthen school administration. *The State Education Standard*, 15–18.

No Child Left Behind Act, 20 U.S.C. 6301 *et seq.* (2001).

O'Brien, P. (2006). *"They know who I am" — Leadership capabilities in special education.* Sydney, New South Wales, Australia: Premiers Special education Scholarship sponsored by the Anika Foundation.

Porter, A. (1993). School delivery standards. *Educational Researcher, 22*(5), 24–30.

President's Commission on Excellence in Special Education. (2002). *A new era: Revitalizing special education for children and their families.* Jessup, MD: Ed Pubs.

Prillaman, D., & Richardson, R. (1985). State certification-endorsement requirements for special education administrators. *The Journal of Special Education, 19*(2), 231–236.

Schulman, L. (2005, February). *The signature pedagogies of the professions of law, medicine, engineering, and the clergy: Potential lessons for the education of teachers.* Paper delivered at the Math Science Partnership Workshop: "Teacher Education in Effective Teaching and Learning." National Research Council's Center for Education, Irvine, CA.

Spillane, J. P., Halverson, R., & Diamond, J. B. (2001). Investigation School leadership Practice: A distributed perspective. *Education Researcher, 30*(3), 23–28.

Spillane, J. P., Halverson, R., & Diamond, J. B. 2004. Towards a theory of leadership practice: A distributed perspective. *Journal of Curriculum Studies, 36*(1), 3-34.

Stephenson, W. (1953). *The study of behavior.* Chicago, IL: University of Chicago Press.

U.S. Department of Education (1987). *What works: Research about teaching and learning.* Washington, DC: U.S. Government Printing Office.

Stile, S., Abernathy, S., & Pettibone. T. (1986). Training and certification of special education administrators: A 5-year follow-up study. *Exceptional Children, 53,* 209–212.

Stile, S. W., & Pettibone, T. J. (1980). Training and certification of administrators in special education. *Exceptional Children, 46*(7), 530–533.

Valesky, T. C., & Hirth, M. A. (1992). Survey of the states: Special education knowledge requirements for school administrators. *Exceptional Children, 58*(5), 399–406.

Waters, J. T., Marzano, R. J., & McNulty, B. A. (2003). *Balanced leadership: What 30 years of research tells us about the effect of leadership on student achievement.* Aurora, CO: Mid-continent Research for Education and Learning.

Whitworth, J. E., & Hatley, R. V. (1979). Certification and special education leadership personnel: An analysis of state standards. *Journal of Special Education, 13*(3), 297–305.

4

Developing Educational Leaders for the Realities of Special Education in the 21st Century

Jean B. Crockett

UNIVERSITY OF FLORIDA

Educational leaders are influential, but often unprepared for the various roles that await them in leading schools inclusive of special needs learners (Garrison-Wade, Sobel, & Fulmer, 2007). Contemporary administrators are responsible for ensuring that every student with a disability receives appropriate services and supports from qualified teachers; that teachers develop the knowledge and skills to implement effective interventions; and that instructional leaders hold strong expectations for using these practices in schools that bolster the academic learning and social growth of students with wide-ranging needs (see Kozleski, Mainzer, & Deshler, 2000). Until recently though, school reform efforts had not made the inclusion of students with disabilities a priority, nor had they recognized the role of school administrators in supporting student achievement. Now, "in a climate of accountability and elevated expectations" (Boscardin, Weir, & Kusek, 2010, p. 62), there is interest in clarifying roles, responsibilities, and leadership development with newly revised professional standards for general and special education administrators (Boscardin, 2011), and redefined models of shared and sustainable leadership for improving schools and student learning (Murphy, 2006).

In today's schools the demand for administrators well prepared to lead special education exceeds the current supply (Boscardin et al., 2010). Some states have rigorous criteria clearly defining competencies and expectations for special education administrators, but many states have abandoned these criteria, electing to fill positions with candidates not trained in special education, but holding generic state leadership licensure. As a consequence of changing policies many administrators responsible for special education are learning about their roles and responsibilities from personal or professional experiences (Wakeman, Browder, Flowers, & Ahlgrim-Delzell, 2006). How they are prepared for their roles and responsibilities is of increasing importance to the lives of the children and families they serve.

In this chapter, the preparedness of educational leaders to assume administrative roles that support the equitable and effective education of students with disabilities and other diverse learners is examined along with various approaches to developing the next generation of accomplished educational leaders for inclusive schools. Reflections on the legacy of special education leadership preparation are offered before the complex roles of contemporary special education leaders are described. In arguing for the improvement of leadership preparation and development, research is reviewed linking special education knowledge to leadership practices. Reasons why special education knowledge and beliefs make a difference in providing opportunities to learn for a diversity of students are discussed next, and suggestions are made for strengthening leadership preparation, induction, and on-going support with knowledge and skills in leading special education that forge the linkage of leadership, learning, and equity.

This chapter proceeds from the perspective that students differ widely in how they learn, and that a disability represents a significant difference from what most children and youth can do, given their age, opportunities, and instruction (Kauffman & Hallahan, 2005). Even within the context of standards-based learning, educational leaders are responsible for ensuring the central concept of special education policy and practice, this is, recognizing and responding to individual learning needs of students with disabilities (Gerber, 2009). This chapter also proceeds from the perspective that administrative leadership is shaped by the interaction of (a) how clearly the purpose of special education policy is understood by those who implement it; (b) their beliefs and knowledge about effective instruction and the academic and social capabilities of students with disabilities; and (c) the cultural contexts that influence the ways in which special education is organized and delivered in schools (see Spillane, Reiser, & Reimer, 2002).

For these reasons, the development of accomplished educational leaders described in this chapter targets leadership skills that foster learning (i.e., setting a direction, developing people, and redesigning the organizational effort, Leithwood & Riehl, 2005), as well as content and dispositions specifically related to leading and administering special education that include (a) advocating for individually meaningful educational attainment, (b) encouraging collaboration among parents and professionals, (c) fostering effective instructional practices with a record of success for struggling learners, and (d) providing structures and resources to support a qualified workforce (Crockett, 2011). A conceptual model for guiding the development of educational leaders for special education is illustrated in Table 4.1.

Leadership Preparation and Special Education

Linking the administration of special education with the preparation of educational leaders is both a current problem and a perennial concern. In the middle of the 20th century Leo Connor (1966), a pioneer in the field of modern special education administration, raised concerns about the inadequacy of administrative training for special educators who knew little about leadership. At the beginning of the 21st century, however, concerns have shifted toward improving the preparation of educational leaders who need to know more, but know very little, about supporting students with disabilities and other diverse learners (U.S. Department of Education, 2010). A brief retrospective describes this shift in leadership preparation.

University preparation programs in special education administration and policy flourished before and after the passage of the Education for All Handicapped Children's Act (EAHCA) in 1975 directed by leaders that included Robert Henderson at the University of Illinois, Philip R. Jones at Virginia Tech, Daniel Sage at Syracuse University, and Leo Connor at Teachers College-Columbia University. During the academic year 1965–66, federal grants funded post-graduate training in special education administration at 4 universities; by 1971, more than 20 university programs were funded (Jones & Wilkerson, 1975). Additional impetus for innovation was provided in 1970, when another special education administrator, Edwin W. Martin, Director of the U.S. Office of Education's Bureau of Education for the Handicapped (BEH), awarded a planning grant to the University Council for Educational Administration (UCEA) to promote the integration of leadership preparation through the General-Special Education Administration Consortium (see Pazey & Yates, this volume).

Table 4.1 Conceptual Model to Guide the Development of Leadership for Special Education

I.	*Setting Direction:*
	1. *Developing leaders who advocate for individually meaningful educational attainment:* Instructional leaders for special education articulate a vision of educational access and accountability that begins with an analysis of teaching and learning that accounts for the unique educational needs of individual students with disabilities. This component prepares leaders to engage in practices that "(a) protect access to special education services, (b) recognize unique and shared characteristics of student with disabilities, and (c) promote more accurate and useful assessment and effective services" (Lloyd & Hallahan, 2007, p. 255).
II.	*Developing People:*
	2. *Developing leaders who encourage collaboration:* Instructional leaders for special education establish a collaborative culture by extending norms of trust, partnership, and academic press to all members of the educational community, and by engaging with parents of students with disabilities, and with professionals in specialized schools and service agencies that work with struggling youth and families. Collaborative cultures and supportive contexts play important roles in reinforcing the use of appropriate instructional practices (Hoy & Hoy, 2003).
	3. *Developing leaders who support effective instructional practices:* Instructional leaders for special education foster high expectations and support research-based teaching strategies with a record of success for special needs learners. This component prepares leaders to support special education teachers in providing specially designed instruction to students so they can access appropriate learning opportunities within and beyond the general education curriculum and classroom. Such practices include controlling for task difficulty; offering small interactive groups; providing direct and explicit instruction; teaching students to apply learning strategies; and teaching and monitoring specific academic, social, and functional skills.
III.	*Redesigning the Organizational Effort:*
	4. *Developing leaders who provide requisite structural supports and resources:* Instructional leaders for special education cultivate a qualified workforce able to mobilize organizational changes in ways that enhance learning for students with disabilities. This component prepares leaders to support the success of faculty and staff by providing professional development, adjusting schedules and personnel assignments, obtaining resources and materials, utilizing data, evaluating programs, and ensuring compliance with state and federal policies (Billingsley, 2011).

Adapted from J. B. Crockett (2011). Conceptual models for leading and administrating special education. In J. M. Kauffman and D. P. Hallahan (Eds.), *The handbook of special education.* NY: Taylor & Francis.

It was typical during these early years for special educators and general educators to follow separate pathways to leadership because administering programs for students with disabilities was traditionally confined to the supervision and management of separate classes, schools, and agencies. In 1966 Connor, a practitioner-scholar who held appointments at Teachers College while serving as the Executive Director of the Lexington Center for the Hearing Impaired in New York, synthesized the research to date identifying the knowledge and skills needed to lead specialized programs. His findings supported mandatory undergraduate or graduate level preparation as a special education teacher, as well as two or more years of experience working with students with disabilities for those who aspired to leading specialized programming. With the passage of the EAHCA in 1975, special education directors assumed new responsibilities for implementing the new federal law including the least restrictive environment (LRE) provisions, and the establishment of state and local policies to ensure a free appropriate public education (FAPE) to each special needs learner. As federal laws strengthened and public schools included more students with disabilities, leadership practices began to change.

Professional literature published in the 1970s suggests that preparing leaders for their roles and emerging responsibilities for administrating special education was a frequent topic as schools geared up for the creation of newly mandated special education programs (Crockett, Becker, & Quinn, 2009; Sage & Burrello, 1994). The qualities, attitudes, and competencies of administrators responsible for leading special education were emphasized in this decade along with new requirements for state certification and endorsement as a special education administrator. Several publications promoted *sensitivity training* for school principals and others administrating programs for students with disabilities (Burke & Sage, 1970; Jerrems, 1971). From 1980–1989 the development of *competencies* to guide the work of administrating special education was a frequent topic, as were coursework and professional experiences to enhance the special education knowledge and skills of school principals (see Davis, 1980; Rude & Sasso, 1988; Stile & Pettibone, 1980). With the results-oriented reforms of the 1990s and the mandates of the Individuals with Disabilities Education Act (IDEA) Amendments of 1997 to ensure access to the general education curriculum, leadership development shifted its focus to integrating special education content into programs preparing school principals with the beliefs, knowledge, skills, and reflective behaviors to lead learning for all students (see Sirotnik, & Kimball, 1994).

Leadership preparation addressing special education was the focus of multiple articles from 2000 to 2010, with more articles published on the topic than during any of the previous three decades. The content of these publications suggests renewed interest in the supply of and demand for knowledgeable administrators, and a sharper focus on equitable and high quality special education instruction. Frequently used terms in the recent literature include *leadership for social justice,* and the development of *democratic and effective leaders for inclusive schools* (Crockett et al., 2009).

In 2004 the federal special education law was renamed the *Individuals with Disabilities Education Improvement Act*, and the traditional administrative role of assuring compliance with its provisions remained critical. Administrators who oversee special education continue to provide leadership that fosters the use of effective practices for a diversity of learners, and the development of effective relationships with parents and external agencies (Hehir, 2005). What once were specialized administrative responsibilities are now subsumed within broader domains addressing the context for leadership; policy and school reform; economic resource management; evaluation of educational programs; research and inquiry; human resource development and supervision; collaborative leadership; and technology and information systems (Boscardin & Lashley, this volume). Questions continue to be raised, however, about how well administrators are prepared to address specialized concerns within these domains, and how special education knowledge influences the ways in which they perform their leadership roles.

Special Education Leadership Roles

In the first decade of the 21st century, more than 20,000 administrators hold the primary responsibility for administrating special education and related services in school districts and state agencies across the United States (U.S. Department of Education, 2010). Increasingly, they share this responsibility with building principals and other educational leaders in the nation's estimated 106,000 elementary and secondary schools. Over time administrative leadership roles have changed in response to cultural, political, and pedagogical conceptualizations of special education, and so has the emphasis on leadership preparation and development.

Traditional and Emerging Roles

Since the 1970s, the education of students with disabilities has been governed by public policy set by the U.S. Congress, and administrated through partnerships with state agencies and local school systems. Administrators working at federal, state, and local levels of the organizational structure traditionally used to implement special education are responsible for seeing that requirements of public policy are met (Meyen & Bui, 2007).

Federal Education Agencies.   The Office of Special Education and Rehabilitation Services (OSERS) is the division of the U.S. Department of Education that "supports programs that help educate children and youth with disabilities, provides for the rehabilitation of youth and adults with disabilities, and supports research to improve the lives of individuals with disabilities" (U.S. Department of Education, n.d.). Special education administrators at OSERS, and its affiliate Office of Special Education Programs, serve as a resource to Congress on legislative issues. These administrators also oversee compliance with federal laws, distribute federal funds to state and local education agencies, and provide leadership for grants that stimulate the personnel preparation of special education teachers and leaders.

State Education Agencies (SEA).   Special education administrators at the state level establish rules and regulations for approving local programs to educate special needs learners. These administrators serve as a resource to state legislators and provide leadership in statewide planning to ensure equal educational opportunities. Dispute resolution, coordinating services with families, providing in-service training, and overseeing compliance with state and federal rules also fall under their responsibilities.

Local Education Agencies (LEA).   Administrators in local school systems provide and ensure appropriate educational services for students with disabilities. Special education administrators with system-wide responsibilities, such as the local director of special education, and local supervisors and coordinators, are responsible for implementing programs that are both legally correct and educationally useful in meeting students' needs. They also address due process procedures, coordinate services with community agencies, and conduct in-service training for school district personnel, which often includes training for school principals designated by school boards as instructional leaders for their schools.

Every state department of education has a bureau and a state director dedicated to administrating special education, but local school systems have the primary responsibility for delivering educational services. Some states continue to use structures called Independent Education Units that serve to broker services between state and local levels. IEU administrators distribute state funds across several localities to provide services such as transportation, professional development, or highly specialized programs and equipment (Meyen & Bui, 2007).

The role of special education leaders across all levels of the educational system has changed significantly in recent years. Heightened accountability is now reflected in state performance plans and annual performance reports mandated by the IDEA 2004, and the requirement that schools and districts make Adequate Yearly Progress under the Elementary and Secondary Education Act (ESEA) reauthorized as the No Child Left Behind Act (NCLB) in 2001. To support the needs of diverse learners, several state agencies, including New York, Maryland, and Washington, D.C., restructured their organizations in ways that facilitate collaboration and stimulate initiatives such as Response to Intervention (RTI) that cut across units within departments of education. The result has reportedly fostered "closer formal connections between previously separate groups whose work was entwined with the work of special education" (NASDSE, 2009, p. 5).

At the local district level, some superintendents have promoted a culture of collaboration between general and special educators (Keller-Allen, 2009). Public policies have also prompted school principals to assume leadership for providing effective instruction to all students, and reshaped the role of local special education directors from compliance officers to system-wide instructional leaders (Boscardin, 2004; DiPaola, Tschannen-Moran, & Walther-Thomas, 2004). As organizational boundaries blur between general and special education, fewer states are continuing to require credentials for administrating special education, which stands in stark contrast to previous practices.

Credentialing Requirements

Studies of credentialing requirements prior to the 1975 passage of federal special education law focused on the training needs of special education administrators and the availability of suitable programs for their development at colleges and universities. Credentialing data from 1972 indicated that nationally only 32% of administrators held certificates in special education administration, and that only 40% had gained experience through internships. Three years later in 1975, data indicated that, although more than 20 university programs prepared personnel to fill increasing leadership positions in special education administration, only 6 states required competency based certification. Further, 23 states had no requirement for directors of special education to be credentialed as educational administrators. By the mid-1980s, however, 46 states offered university course work in special education administration, and 36 states required specialized certification or endorsements. In 20 states special education administrators were required to be certified in general education administration, and in 18 states the administration of special education was authorized as part of the general administration credential (Boscardin et al., 2010).

Within the past two decades, the use of specialized leadership credentials has decreased as special education has increasingly come to be viewed as a shared responsibility among all educators. In 2010, only 27 states required a license or certificate for a district special education director, and only 5 states offered endorsements in special education administration. In stark contrast to previous practices, only one state continued to require special education as part of the general education administration license. For some scholars these changes suggest an erosion of state licensing requirements for special education administrators, challenging professional identities and increasing role ambiguity for those charged with leading special education and for those charged with preparing them for leadership (see Boscardin et al., 2010).

Changes in Leadership Preparation

The system used to prepare aspiring general and special education administrators is also changing. Preparation programs, which customarily resided in universities, are being deregulated, and in some states (e.g., Michigan, South Dakota) administrator certification is no longer required for educational leaders (Murphy, Moorman, & McCarthy, 2008). An increasing number of states have opened additional pathways to leadership through alternative and nontraditional providers that offer a diverse set of options often free of constraints that bind university programs. Some states continue to require university leadership preparation but not necessarily from a college of education. In New Jersey, a degree in business or public administration would suffice. In other states, a degree from a college of education is still a requirement, but it could be a degree in special education, counseling, or curriculum and instruction rather than educational leadership.

Alternative models have emerged that ground leadership preparation in the work of professional associations rather than universities and, in some cases, transfer the responsibility of developing leaders to local school systems. Professional models include a voluntary national certificate for principals developed by the National Board for Professional Teaching Standards that targets core propositions about accomplished educational leaders (Maxwell, 2009). Alternatives also include entrepreneurial models guided by the mission of reformers, such as The New Leaders for New Schools program designed to prepare nontraditional candidates as administrators in large urban school systems, and the skills-based George W. Bush Institute, which has set a goal of preparing 50,000 school leaders by the year 2020 (Aarons, 2010).

With the emergence of alternative pathways to leadership, university preparation has come under the control of state departments of education, "placing demands on programs that would seem foreign to earlier generations of professors" (Murphy et al., 2008, p. 3). Universities are now required to base initial licensure programs on state or national professional leadership standards (most frequently the Interstate School Leaders Licensure Consortium [ISLLC] standards). States are also setting stringent outcome measures for university programs, and requiring students to complete licensure examinations.

These changes in credentialing and program requirements shift the emphasis from simply *preparing* educational leaders to ensuring their *readiness* to lead, equipped with the pedagogical background to move schools from "universal access to universal performance" (Flanery, in Aarons, 2010, p. 16). The complicated calculus of linking leadership to student outcomes is now at the center of American public policy, with funding priorities that support the preparation, training, and recruitment of high quality public school leaders.

Various Pathways to Leadership

Title II of the Elementary and Secondary Education Act (ESEA) provides grants to states to improve student achievement by improving the quality of teachers and school leaders through a variety of professional development activities (Yell, 2012). The federal blueprint for reauthorizing the ESEA specifically targets the development of transformational leaders by strengthening "traditional and alternative pathways into school leadership" (U.S. Department of Education, 2010, p. 18). Plans include competitive grants for the recruitment, preparation, and support of effective principals and leadership teams to turn around persistently low-performing schools. Grant priorities favor preparation programs with a record of preparing effective leaders, or those committed to tracking and assessing the effectiveness of their graduates. Priorities also include programs with substantial residency or field-based components, as well as induction supports for the success of new principals and other educational leaders. Competitive preparation programs must also address conditions such as staffing, budgets, instructional programs, and schedules that increase the likelihood graduates will be successful in improving student academic achievement and other outcomes at low-performing schools.

The ESEA reauthorization proposal is also designed "to recruit, prepare, place, and support the retention of effective state and district leaders, such as superintendents, chief academic officers, and human resource directors, who are able to lead transformational change in their states and districts" (U.S. Department of Education, 2010, p. 18). Although special education administrators are not specifically mentioned, the success of students with disabilities and English Language Learners is identified as a cross-cutting priority with the provisions of the IDEA and other school reforms. The proposed ESEA blueprint increases support for the inclusion and improved outcomes of students with disabilities by helping to ensure that:

1. teachers and leaders are better prepared to meet the needs of diverse learners,
2. assessments more accurately and appropriately measure the performance of students with disabilities,
3. more districts and schools implement high-quality, state- and locally-determined curricula and instructional supports that incorporate the principles of universal design for learning to meet all students' needs. (p. 20)

These policy priorities emphasize the importance of addressing issues related to special education and diverse learners as an essential component of the initial preparation and ongoing development of educational leaders. Regardless of whether conventional or alternative pathways to leadership are followed, thoughtful preparation, thorough induction, and ongoing professional learning are considered to be central to the preparedness of leaders who can support students with disabilities and other diverse learners (Burdette, 2010).

Preparing to Lead Special Education

The goals of leadership preparation are typically twofold: (a) to develop the skills and capacities of future educational leaders, and (b) to develop their aspirations to assume challenging and complex organizational roles (Orr, 2011). Available research suggests that some leadership skills and capacities are more effective than others in boosting student achievement and school improvement, and that "candidates 'preparation can positively influence leadership capacities and interests in career advancement" (p. 118). Although the evidence suggests that program content and delivery can influence what leadership candidates learn and do in practice, there is little research that examines their preparation for understanding how different children learn; improving the sensitivity of stakeholders to diversity and effectiveness in educating all students, including those with exceptional learning differences; redesigning the organization of schools to address teaching and learning; creating and maintaining an orderly learning environment; working closely with parents and collaborating with partners outside the school to support student learning (Crockett, 2002; Orr, 2011).

The need for initial leadership preparation and ongoing professional development in special education has been well established (Collins & White, 2001; Crockett, 2002; DiPaola et al., 2004; Garrison-Wade et al., 2007; Goor, Schwenn, & Boyer, 1997; Monteith, 2000; Sage & Burrello, 1994; Smith & Colon, 1998; Strahan, 1999; Valente, 2001; Valesky & Hirth, 1992). Unfortunately, research also suggests administrators continue to struggle with concepts of equity, and have limited knowledge about legal aspects or current trends in educating students with disabilities (Bays & Crockett, 2007; Crockett et al., 2009; Lyons & Algozzine, 2006; McHatton, Boyer, Shaunessy, & Terry, 2010; Powell & Hyle, 1997; Wakeman et al., 2006).

In an effort to improve the preparedness of educational leaders to support students with disabilities and other diverse learners the National Association of State Directors of Special Education (NASDSE) recently conducted a forum across networks of stakeholders to begin the process of defining challenges and identifying strategies to address them (Burdette, 2010). The administrators, teachers, parents, and scholars who participated in the forum defined the following challenges to the availability of well-prepared leaders:

1. Insufficient targeted leadership preparation to serve diverse populations.
2. Insufficient ongoing professional development (e.g., internship, mentoring, networking, leadership academies).
3. Insufficient alignment among principal preparation, evaluation, and professional standards with the knowledge needed to drive instruction for students with diverse needs.
4. Insufficient knowledge among principals about current trends in special education.
5. Insufficient skills in how to lead from the middle—leading teachers and working with central office personnel.
6. Insufficient sensitivity to issues encountered in education by diverse populations of students and families.

Also listed among the challenges in school districts, but more indirectly than directly related to leadership preparation, was the frequent practice of assigning the least prepared leaders to schools with the most diverse student populations. In the following section the development of educational leaders is examined from the perspective of what they need to know about special education, why it matters, and what can be done to strengthen their initial preparation, induction, and on-going support.

What Leaders Need to Know about Special Education

In the context of inclusive reforms and high accountability educational leaders are better positioned to address issues related to students with disabilities when they understand what special education is and why it is needed (see Kauffman & Hallahan, 2005), as well as what their roles are in providing its delivery (Bartlett, Etscheidt, & Weisentein, 2007; Crockett, 2002). Research addressing administrative practices related to special education includes descriptions of (a) the attitudes of leaders toward the inclusion of students with disabilities (Barnett & Monda-Amaya, 1998; Cook, Semmel, & Gerber, 1999; Praisner, 2003); (b) knowledge of special education law (Davidson & Algozzine, 2002); (c) knowledge and capacity to ensure the delivery of effective special education (Bays & Crockett, 2007; Crockett, Myers, Griffith, & Hollandsworth, 2007; Goor et al., 1997; McLaughlin, 2009); and ways to create supportive and inclusive learning environments (Burch, Theoharris, & Rauscher, 2010; Salisbury & McGregor, 2002).

Typically, educational leadership development has focused on administrative skills in managing budgets and complying with minimum requirements to meet diverse learning needs (e.g., representing the LEA in the Individualized Education Program [IEP] process). This approach, however, leaves current administrators underprepared to understand, create, and lead the kind of restructuring that data suggest helps transform comprehensive school reforms into improvements in teaching and learning (Burch et al., 2010).

Students with disabilities and English language learners are currently and historically underserved populations, and what leaders know and believe about their education can influence student achievement and school improvement (Burch et al., 2010). Current policies and inclusive reforms demand comprehensive knowledge and its application to real-world problems requiring administrators to recognize and respond to students' unusual learning needs, as well as to be mindful of equitable policies and effective practices to support their success. In a qualitative study of the practices of nine elementary principals leading comprehensive school reforms, Burch et al. noted that those who were most successful were knowledgeable about ways to restructure service delivery in ways that "maximize human and financial resources for schools' most vulnerable students" (p. 355).

In a survey assessing the special education knowledge of a random sample of 1,000 administrators from all 50 states and the District of Columbia, Wakeman and her colleagues (2006) reported that knowledgeable school leaders were more actively involved with special education programming; "in other words, principals who reported knowing more, also reported doing more" (p. 167). Practices and leadership behaviors linked to greater knowledge about special education include (a) reflecting purposefully on practical experiences, (b) increasing understanding about disability-related needs, (c) providing resources for effective instructional practices, and (d) participating in decisions about programs and services (Wakeman et al., 2006).

Why Knowledge and Beliefs Matter

Leaders with more knowledge and experience with special education are more inclined to reflect on situations in their schools and to consider the implications of their leadership practices for students with disabilities and their teachers (Burch et al., 2010; Wakeman, et al., 2006). Knowledgeable leaders reported meeting regularly with special education teachers to better understand distinctive features of different disabilities and successful ways to teach students. Knowledge of laws, and of the educational needs of students with disabilities, is also linked with leadership that supports special educators with resources. In other words, "principals who understand what teachers need to teach and *why* they need it, are more apt to provide resources to meet the instructional needs of the students" (Wakeman et al., emphasis in original, p. 167) Greater knowledge is also linked to greater participation by school leaders in decisions about programs and services to ensure special needs learners have meaningful access to the general education curriculum.

Improving Leadership Preparation and Development

Although leadership supporting successful learning for all students is a high priority, little is known about the content, organization, and structure of exemplary administrative preparation programs (Murphy & Vriesenga, 2006). Instead, research conducted over the past decade, cites persistent weaknesses in many university-based leadership preparation programs that include (a) low admission standards; (b) outmoded curricula that inadequately reflects the needs of schools, districts and increasingly diverse students, including students with disabilities; (c) weak links between theory and practice; (d) few faculty with field experience as leaders; and (e) poorly designed internships (see Murphy et al., 2008; Wallace Foundation, 2008). Little research has been done to determine the effectiveness of various preparation models, and there is little agreement regarding the outcome measures to use in assessing their worth (Murphy & Vriesenga; Orr, 2009). In short, "there is limited research evidence to inform which preparation approaches most effectively influence what graduates learn, their post-preparation career progress, and their leadership practices" (Orr, 2011, p. 116). Although there is emerging evidence of support for the evaluation of general educational administrative preparation programs (see Pounder, 2011), there is little evidence of how institutes, professional associations, and universities intend to address the challenges specific to leading special education.

Little is known about exemplary opportunities for administrators to prepare for their roles in providing leadership for special education. Rigorous scholarship addressing this topic is scant with few empirically anchored investigations of administrator preparation. The literature base is dominated by theoretical or interpretive commentaries and narrative descriptions highlighting perceived and reported weaknesses in programs preparing leaders to address special education policy and practice. The empirical support for this knowledge base was derived primarily from surveys, case studies, and qualitative narratives. Little is known about how students are recruited and selected to participate in educational leadership preparation or development programs, how they are instructed, or how their progress is monitored or addressed. Little is also known about the organization of administrative preparation programs, how they address special education issues, or the qualities of the faculty members who educate prospective school leaders for their contemporary roles (Crockett et al., 2009).

There is evidence, however, of a substantial investment in the university preparation of special education administrators provided through the U.S. Department of Education's Office of Special Education Programs (OSEP). Currently more than 100 graduate students are pursuing degrees in special education administration as participants in federally funded projects (see OSEPs Discretionary Grants Public Database for currently active projects addressing special education administration at http://publicddb.tadnet.org, retrieved January 23, 2011).

Federally supported leadership preparation for special education administration has been available since the 1970s, and has been a priority area for funding over the past 11 years (Boscardin et al., 2010). Most often this training is provided at the doctoral level with graduates assuming executive administrative positions in federal and state education departments, and local school districts. Projects preparing aspiring leaders at the masters degree level are less frequent, but have broad impact because more students can be prepared for initial leadership practice in a two-year, rather than four-year program of study. Rigorous monitoring is now associated with each leadership project and students who are funded are required to register with a national database to ensure they meet the service obligation of working for two years in a field related to the leadership training for every year of funding received as a participant in the federal project.

OSEP funded projects are designed to build the capacity of educational leaders to support special education by stimulating interactions across university programs. Although students funded with OSEP dollars have traditionally been required to earn degrees in special education, their curriculum is typically taught by university faculty in the disciplines of special education and educational administration, and guided by the professional standards endorsed by both fields (i.e., CEC's Advanced Standards for Special Education Administrators, and the ISLLC Standards).

Conclusions: Preparing Accomplished Educational Leaders

The reality of 21st-century educational leadership is that those who lead special education at the federal, state, and local school district levels are responsible for serving and supporting exceptional learners and their families in ways that are both educationally productive and legally correct (see http://www.casecec.org/about/ retrieved July 30, 2009). The practice of providing administrative leadership for special education is moving from a compliance-driven model to an instructional model focused on equitable educational attainment. As a result, leadership to that end is distributed across multiple personnel with a diversity of expertise, raising important questions such as (a) who is responsible for special education at different levels within a school system, and (b) to what extent do leadership practices and professional preparation support successful learning for students with disabilities, and other diverse learners (Billingsley, this volume; Crockett, 2007; Snyder et al., this volume).

Improving the quality of leadership preparation is now viewed as a primary approach to improving student achievement, and current policies stress the need for programs to emphasize research-based leadership practices associated with school improvement (Orr, 2011). With regard to leadership that improves the achievement of special education students, Boscardin (2007) suggested "the underlying premise is that administrators who are able to incorporate evidence-based leadership practices will be best positioned to affect improved, equitable, and just educational opportunities for students who have disabilities" (p. 2).

Preparing Accomplished Leaders for Special Education

Administrators accomplished in leading special education have traditionally been viewed as experts in implementing disability-related policies and ensuring that teachers use effective instructional practices. With regard to preparing accomplished educational leaders, more needs to be known about newly appointed administrators of special education and their initial preparation, recruitment, induction, and retention. More also needs to be known about the ways they use technology to communicate and disseminate information, and to monitor evidence and make decisions about student progress (see Miller & Baker, 2009). More research is needed that addresses how aspiring and developing leaders learn about special education and how they are provided with on-going technical assistance. More also needs to be known about the impact of including special education topics in leadership licensure requirements and principal preparation programs. Above all, more research is needed to demonstrate the effect of principals who use research-based leadership practices and who encourage teachers to use evidence-based instructional practices, on the achievement of special education students (see Wakeman et al., 2006).

The challenge of developing accomplished leaders for special education may be best met by future research that examines the relationship between quality program features and graduate outcomes in the form of relevant, "on-the-job" leadership behaviors affecting students with disabilities and their teachers.

Addressing the Leadership Development Challenge

The evidence suggests that programs to prepare accomplished educational leaders with knowledge and skills in administer special education should be different from the majority of existing programs. Key findings from recent research on leadership preparation suggest that certain features enhance graduates' reported learning outcomes.

- Preparation programs should be highly selective, focused on improving instruction, closely tied to the needs of districts, and provide internships with hands-on leadership experiences that align with relevant coursework (see Angelle & Bilton, 2009; Murphy et al., 2008; Pounder, 2011).
- Training in leadership, including leadership for educating students with disabilities and other diverse learners, should be on-going with high-quality induction and professional development to promote career-long growth in line with the evolving needs of schools and districts, and issues relevant to leading special education (Burdette, 2010; Crockett, 2011; Murphy et al., 2008; Pounder, 2011.
- Leadership development can make a real difference, but it can also be expensive. Resources should be targeted to quality programs that demonstrate linkages between leadership preparation and effective leadership practices that enhance equitable educational opportunities for all students (Murphy et al., 2008).
- Training needs to be coordinated with, and connected to the realities of, the schools and districts that graduates will eventually lead (Murphy et al., 2008).
- States, districts, and universities should align with professional leadership standards that put learning, including the learning of students with disabilities, in a prominent position (Boscardin & Lashley, this volume; Murphy et al., 2008).
- Policies regarding leadership standards, training, and working conditions should all align so they drive toward the same objective of preparing accomplished personnel who are both prepared and supported to provide leadership for the learning of students with disabilities, and other diverse learners (Billingsley, this volume; McLaughlin, Smith, & Wilkinson, this volume; Murphy et al., 2008).

Evidence also suggests that how leadership is framed in professional preparation and development, and how learning experiences are designed to provide opportunities for participants to engage in active, experiential, and reflective activities, positively influences leadership knowledge (Burch et al., 2010; Orr, 2011). Pounder (2011) in reviewing learning outcomes across high-quality programs noted that graduates reported acquiring "a greater understanding of the complexity of educational leadership and the interrelatedness of educational issues, strategies and outcomes" (p. 263); greater facility in using data to solve problems and inform decisions; stronger collaborative and team-building skills; and deeper knowledge about instructional and organizational leadership, and practices to improve the climate and context of schools. These outcomes could make a positive difference for students with diverse and exceptional learning needs and their teachers by linking together the triad of leadership, learning, and equity.

Finally, addressing the leadership development challenge means (a) confronting the difficult working conditions in high-needs schools that face many new administrators, such as insufficient instructional time, and unavailable or inadequate use of data, and (b) finding more accurate ways of evaluating leadership performance—especially leadership performance that improves the teaching and learning environment for students with disabilities and other diverse learners. The effective administration of special education in contemporary schools is judged less by procedural precision, and more by the impact of leadership practices that set the context for meaningful student outcomes. Consequently, the central issue in developing educational leaders for the 21st century is not *whether* to address special education content, but rather *how* to provide relevant, research-based information and assess effective special education leadership practices across traditional and alternative pathways.

References

Aarons, D. I. (2010). Initiative aims to refashion training path for principals. *Education Week, 30*(6), 1, 16.

Angelle, P., & Bilton, L. M. (2009). Confronting the unknown: Principal preparation training in issues related to special education. *Journal of Scholarship and Practice, 5*, 5–9.

Bartlett, L. D., Etscheidt, S., & Weisenstein, G. R. (2007). *Special education law and practice in public schools.* Upper Saddle River, NJ: Pearson.

Barnett, C., & Monda-Amaya, L. E. (1998). Principals' knowledge of and attitudes toward inclusion. *Remedial and Special Education, 19*, 181–192.

Bays, D. A., & Crockett, J. B. (2007). Investigating instructional leadership for special education. *Exceptionality. 15*, 143–161.

Billingsley, B. S. (2011). Factors influencing special education teacher quality and effectiveness. In J. M. Kauffman & D. P. Hallahan (Eds.), *Handbook of special education* (pp. 391–405). New York, NY: Taylor & Francis.

Boscardin, M. L. (2004). Transforming administration to support science in the schoolhouse for students with disabilities. *The Journal of Learning Disabilities, 37*, 262–269.

Boscardin, M. L. (2007). What is special about special education administration? Considerations for school leadership. *Exceptionality, 15*, 189–200.

Boscardin, M. L. (2011). Using professional standards to inform leadership in special education. In J. M. Kauffman & D. P. Hallahan (Eds.), *Handbook of special education* (pp. 378–390). New York, NY: Taylor & Francis.

Boscardin, M. L., Weir, K., & Kusek, C. (2010). A national study of state credentialing requirements for administrators of special education. *Journal of Special Education Leadership, 23*, 61–75.

Burch, P., Theoharris, G., & Rauscher E. (2010). Class size reduction in practice. *Educational Policy 24*(2), 330–358.

Burdette, P. (2010). *Principal preparedness to support students with disabilities and other diverse learners.* Alexandria, VA: National Association of State Directors of Special Education.

Burke, P. J., & Sage, D. D., (1970). The unorthodox use of a simulation instrument. *Simulation and Games, 1*, 155–171.

Collins, L., & White, G. P. (2001, April). *Leading inclusive programs for all special education students: A pre-service training program for principals.* Paper presented at the annual meeting of the American Educational Research Association, Seattle, WA. (ERIC Document Reproduction Service No. ED456604)

Connor, L. E. (1966). Preparation programs for special education administrators. *Exceptional Children, 33*, 161–166.

Cook, B. G., Semmel, M. I., & Gerber, M. (1999). Attitudes of principals and special education teachers toward the inclusion of students with mild disabilities: Critical differences of opinion. *Remedial and Special Education, 20*, 199–207.

Crockett, J. B. (2002). Special education's role in preparing responsive leaders for inclusive schools. *Remedial and Special Education, 23*, 157–168.

Crockett, J. B. (2007). The changing landscape of special education administration. *Exceptionality, 15*(3), 139–142.

Crockett, J. B. (2011). Conceptual models for leading and administrating special education. In J. M. Kauffman & D. P. Hallahan (Eds.), *Handbook of special education* (pp. 351–362). New York, NY: Taylor & Francis.

Crockett, J. B., Becker, M. K., & Quinn, D. (2009). Reviewing the knowledge base of special education leadership and administration: 1970–2009. *Journal of Special Education Leadership, 22*, 55–67.

Crockett, J. B., Myers, S., Griffin, A., & Hollandsworth, B. (2007). The unintended side effects of inclusion for students with learning disabilities: The perspectives of school administrators. *Learning Disabilities: A Multidisciplinary Journal, 14*(3), 155-166.

Davidson, D., & Algozzine, R. (2002). Administrators' perceptions of special education law. *Journal of Special Education Leadership, 15*, 43–48.

Davis, W. E. (1980). An analysis of principals' formal training in special education. *Education, 101*, 89–94.

DiPaola, M. F., Tschannen-Moran, M., & Walther-Thomas, C. (2004). School principals and specation: Creating the context for academic success. *Focus on Exceptional Children, 37*, 1–10.

Garrison-Wade, D., Sobel, D., & Fulmer, C. L. (2007). Inclusive leadership: Preparing principals for the role that awaits them. *Educational Leadership and Administration, 19*, 117–132.

Gerber, M. M. (2009). *Special education: Our future role and needed policy supports. Keynote Panel Session, OSEP Project Directors Conference, Washington, D. C., July 20.*

Goor, M. B., Schwenn, J. O., & Boyer, L. (1997). Preparing principals for leadership in special education. *Intervention in School and Clinic, 32,* 133 141.

Hehir, T. (2005). *New directions in special education: Eliminating ableism in policy and practice.* Cambridge, MA: Harvard Educational Press.

Hoy, A. W., & Hoy, W. K. (2003). *Instructional leadership: A learning-centered guide.* Boston, MA: Allyn & Bacon.

Jerrems, R. L. (1971). Sensitivity training, the affective dimension of inservice training. Sensitivity training and the school administrator: A special section, part IV. *National Elementary Principal, 50*, 63–69.

Jones, P. R., & Wilkerson, W. R. (1975). Preparing special education administrators. *Theory into Practice, XIV* (2) 105–109.

Keller-Allen, C. (2009). *Superintendent leadership: Promoting general and special education collaboration.* National Association of State Directors of Special Education. Retrieved December 27, 2010, from http://projectforum.org/docs/SuperintendentLeadership-PromotingGeneralandSpEdCollaboration.pdf

Kauffman, J. M., & Hallahan, D. P. (2005). *Special education: What it is and why we need it.* Boston, MA: Pearson Education.

Kozleski, E., Mainzer, R., & Deshler, D. (2000). *Bright futures for exceptional learners: An action agenda to achieve quality conditions for teaching and learning.* Reston, VA: Council for Exceptional Children.

Leithwood, K. A., & Riehl, C. (2005). What do we already know about educational leadership? In W. A. Firestone & C. Riehl (Eds.), *A new agenda for research in educational leadership* (pp. 12–27). New York, NY: Teachers College Press.

Lloyd, J. W., & Hallahan, D. P. (2007). Advocacy and reform of special education. In J. B. Crockett, M. M., Gerber, & T. J. Landrum (Eds.), *Achieving the radical reform of special education: Essays in honor of James M. Kauffman* (pp. 245-263). Mahwah, NJ: Erlbaum.

Lyons, J. E., & Algozzine, B. (2006). Perceptions of the impact of accountability on the role of principals. *Education Policy Analysis Archives, 14*, 1–16.

McHatton, P. A., Boyer, N. R., Shaunessy, E., & Terry, P. M. (2010). Principals' perceptions of preparation and practice in gifted and special education content: Are we doing enough? *Journal of Research on Leadership Education, 5*, 1–22.

McLaughlin, M. (2009). *What every principal needs to know about special education.* Thousand Oaks, CA: Corwin Press.

Maxwell, L. A. (2009). Principals' certificate on horizon. *Education Week, 29*(15), 1, 11.

Meyen, E. L., & Bui, Y. N. (2007). *Exceptional children in today's schools.* Denver, CO: Love.

Miller, M., & Baker, P. (2009). What are the needs of beginning special education administrators? *In Case, 50*(6), 6–10.

Monteith, D. S. (2000). Professional development for administrators in special education: Evaluation of a program for underrepresented personnel. *Teacher Education and Special Education, 23*(4), 281–289.

Murphy, J. (2006). *Preparing school leaders: Defining a research and action agenda.* Lanham, MD: Rowman & Littlefield Education.

Murphy, J., Moorman, H. N., & McCarthy, M. (2008). A framework for rebuilding initial certification and preparation programs in educational leadership: Lessons from whole-state reform initiatives. *Teachers College Record, 110*, 2172–2203.

Murphy, J., & Vriesenga, M. (2006). Research on school leadership preparation in the United States: An analysis. *School Leadership & Management, 26*, 183–195.

National Association of State Directors of Special Education (NASDSE). (2009). *Staffing patterns of five state special education units.* Retrieved December 27, 2010, from http://www.projectforum.org/docs/StaffingPatternsofFiveStateSpecialEducationUnits.pdf

Orr, M. T. (2009). Program evaluation in leadership preparation and related fields. In M. D. Young & G. Crow (Eds.), *Handbook of research on the education of school leaders* (pp. 457–498). New York, NY: Routledge.

Orr, M. T. (2011). Pipeline to preparation to advancement: Graduates' experiences in, through, and beyond leadership preparation. *Educational Administration Quarterly, 47*, 114–172.

Pounder, D. G. (2011). Leader preparation special issue: Implications for policy, practice, and research. *Educational Administration Quarterly, 47*, 258–267.

Powell, D., & Hyle, A. E. (1997). Principals and school reform: Barriers to inclusion in three secondary schools. *Journal of School Leadership, 7*, 301–326.

Praisner, C. L. (2003). Attitudes of elementary school principals toward the inclusion of students with disabilities. *Exceptional Children, 69*, 35–45.

Rude, H. A., & Sasso, G. M. (1988) Colorado special education administrative competencies. *Teacher Education and Special Education, 11,* 139–143.

Sage, D. D., & Burrello, L. C. (1994). *Leadership in educational reform: An administrator's guide to changes in special education.* Baltimore: Paul H. Brookes.

Salisbury, C., & McGregor, G. (2002). The administrative climate and context of inclusive elementary schools. *Exceptional Children, 68,* 259–274.

Sirotnik, K. A., & Kimball, K. (1994). The unspecial place of special education in programs that prepare school administrators. *Journal of School Leadership, 4,* 598–630.

Smith, J. O., & Colon, R. J. (1998). Legal responsibilities toward students with disabilities: What every administrator should know. *NASSP Bulletin, 82,* 40–53.

Spillane, J. P., Reiser, B. J., & Reimer, T. (2002). Policy implementation and cognition: Reframing and refocusing implementation research. *Review of Educational Research, 72,* 387–431.

Stile, S. W., & Pettibone, T. J. (1980). Training and certification of administrators in special education. *Exceptional Children, 46,* 530–533.

Strahan, R. D. (1999). Building leadership and legal strategies. In L. W. Hughes (Ed.), *The principal as leader* (2nd ed., pp. 291–322). Upper Saddle River, NJ: Prentice Hall.

U.S. Department of Education. (2010). *ESEA Blueprint for Reform,* Washington, D.C: Office of Planning, Evaluation and Policy Development.

U.S. Department of Education. (n.d.). Office of Special Education and Rehabilitation Services (OSERS). Retrieved April 20, 2011, from http://www2.ed.gov/about/offices/list/osers/index.html

Valente, W. D. (2001). *Law in the schools* (5th ed.). Upper Saddle River, NJ: Prentice Hall.

Valesky, T. C., & Hirth, M.A. (1992). Survey of the states: Special education knowledge requirements for school administrators. *Exceptional Children, 58,* 399–406.

Wakeman, S. Y., Browder, D. M., Flowers, C., & Ahlgrim-Delzell, L. (2006). Principals' knowledge of fundamental and current issues in special education. *NASSP Bulletin, 90,* 153–174.

Wallace Foundation (2008*). Becoming a leader: Preparing school principals for today's schools.* Retrieved February 19, 2011, from http://www.wallacefoundation.org

Yell, M. L. (2012). *The law and special education.* Upper Saddle River, NJ: Pearson.

Section II

Leadership, Policy, and School Reform

Introduction

Throughout U.S. history schools have been pressured to respond to various educational reform initiatives and legislative mandates. In this section, the effects of various policies on the shaping of leadership for special education are explored as they intertwine with legislative reform efforts, legal and fiscal policies, and school choice. The intent of the educational policy initiatives and reform movements has been to change practices in schools to strengthen and ensure students with disabilities receive a free appropriate public education (FAPE). The chapters in this section explore how leadership, policy, and school reforms relate to equity, democracy, and student learning.

Yell, Thomas, and Katsiyannis (Chapter 5) discuss how legal frameworks are designed to prepare children with disabilities for further educational opportunities, employment, and independent living. The purpose of the Individuals with Disabilities Education Improvement Act of 2004 (IDEA 2004) is to ensure that all children with disabilities receive a FAPE. IDEA 2004 is the latest of several reauthorizations of the *Education for All Handicapped Children Act of 1975* (EAHCA). Unlike previous reauthorizations, IDEA 2004 was developed with an emphasis to complement the academic requirements of the Elementary and Secondary Education Act, reauthorized in 2001 as the No Child Left Behind Act (NCLB). Yell shows how simply meeting legal mandates is not enough in an era of accountability. Children with disabilities are ensured services that meet their individual needs under their Individualized Education Program (IEP).

Baker, Green, and Ramsey (Chapter 6) focus on the role of state school finance litigation emphasizing state constitutional obligations to provide funding to local public school districts in order to first, balance differences in local fiscal capacity to provide educational services, and second, to target resources to student populations with greater needs. Highlighted is the noticeable absence of the cost of producing adequate educational outcomes, or the cost of closing achievement gaps between children with mild to moderate disabilities. The authors' goal is to extrapolate leadership responsibilities in financing the education of students with disabilities from specific state school finance cases in which courts have articulated a strong state obligation to provide differentiated funding toward achieving equal educational opportunity, despite the expanded federal role in financing special education programs under the American Recovery and Reinvestment Act of 2009.

Mead and Green (Chapter 7) explore how the IDEA's requirements for the delivery of special education in exchange for federal funding affect the assurance of the Least Restrictive Environment (LRE) provision in relation to two types of issues for children with disabilities and their parents, (a) access and (b) appropriate programming. Mead and Green consider school choice options as a way of potentially serving a variety of purposes. As various forms of publicly funded parental choice options have developed across the country, how to include children with disabilities in those programs has become a major concern. As with all programming for children with disabilities, the requirements for participation in school choice programs are grounded in three federal laws including the IDEA, Section 504 of the Rehabilitation Act of 1973, and the Americans with Disabilities Act (ADA).

Skrtic (Chapter 8) argues that the law's provisions, and their judicial and institutional interpretation, undercut democratic solutions to special education problems like segregation and disproportionality. In his analysis Skrtic illustrates how bureaucratic mandates, regardless of good intentions, interrupt the "egalitarian and democratic impulses" of laws such as the IDEA. Skrtic argues that challenges to legal mandates supporting the education of students with disabilities launched by parents and schools have evolved into narrow technical challenges to diagnoses and accommodations, thereby transforming a law that was premised on democratic reform into a bureaucratic process. Skrtic contends that this is an unintended consequence of the IDEA and calls for substantial reconceptualization of special education leadership.

5

Special Education Law for Leaders and Administrators of Special Education

Mitchell L. Yell

UNIVERSITY OF SOUTH CAROLINA

Susan S. Thomas

BERKELEY COUNTY SCHOOL DISTRICT, SOUTH CAROLINA

Antonis Katsiyannis

CLEMSON UNIVERSITY

The effective implementation and supervision of special education programs requires that special education administrators possess (a) a thorough understanding of special education laws and (b) the ability to implement programs in a manner that is consistent with these laws. In this chapter we briefly review the primary federal law that is of special importance to special education administrators: the Individuals with Disabilities Education Act (IDEA). We also provide guidance to administrators in developing and implementing special education programs that are educationally appropriate and legally sound, with an emphasis on avoiding legal errors. Prior to examining the laws and their importance, we turn to a discussion of the various aspects of law and how they affect the administration of special education programs.

Special Education Law

Special education law is made up of federal and state laws, regulations, and litigation (i.e., hearings, state level rulings, and court cases). Additionally, the practice of special education is also influenced by administrative policies and guidance from the United States Department of Education. Understanding these laws, regulations, litigation, and guidance from the federal government will help special educator administrators understand how they may provide effective and legally sound special education services to students with disabilities. We next briefly discuss the various aspects of special education law.

The Federal Government and Special Education

The American system is a federal system, which means that the government of the United States is comprised of a union of states joined under a central federal government (Yell, 2012). The

United States Constitution delineates the nature of this arrangement in the 10th Amendment. The federal government has only those powers that are granted to it in the Constitution and the states have all powers not specifically granted to the federal government. Because the Constitution does not contain any provisions regarding education, therefore, this area is a power reserved to the states. Nonetheless, federal involvement has been an important factor in the progress and growth of education.

One method by which the federal government has become involved in education is by providing assistance to the states through categorical grants. The purposes of the categorical grants have been to provide supplementary assistance to the state systems of education and to shape educational policy in the states. States have the option of accepting or rejecting the categorical grants offered by the federal government. If state officials accept the categorical grants, they must abide by the federal guidelines for the use of these funds. An example of a federal categorical grant is the IDEA.

Federal and State Laws

In 1975 President Gerald Ford signed the Education for All Handicapped Children Act into (EAHCA). This law, which was renamed the Individuals with Disabilities Education Act in 1990, offered federal funding to states in exchange for the states providing educational services to specified categories of students with disabilities. Moreover, the educational services offered to students with disabilities in public schools in the state had to be provided in conformity with the requirements of the EAHCA.

To receive federal funding each state was required to submit a state plan to the Bureau of Education for the Handicapped in the Department of Health, Education, and Welfare.[1] The purpose of the plan was to describe the state's policies and procedures to educate students with disabilities in accordance with the procedures in the EAHCA. Although prior to the enactment of the EAHCA some states had laws requiring that public schools provide special education services to students, soon after the enactment of the law all 50 states had passed such laws. Some states provided greater protections and rights for students with disabilities than did the federal law; however, states could not provide fewer protections and rights.

Both the federal laws and state laws are of critical importance to special education administrators. This is because public school special education programs must adhere to the strictures of these federal and state laws. Table 5.1 contains a list of websites that present the full text of the IDEA statute and websites where administrators can locate the special education laws in their respective states.

Federal and State Regulations

When Congress passes a law, it delegates authority to the appropriate administrative agency to promulgate or create specific regulations to implement these laws. The federal administrative agency that created the regulations implementing the EAHCA was the United States Department of Education. States also have administrative agencies that promulgate regulations that implement the state laws. Both federal and state regulations supply specifics to the general con-

Table 5.1 Websites with the Complete Text of the IDEA and State Law Websites

Website	URL
Building the Legacy: IDEA 2004	http://idea.ed.gov/download/statute.html
State Education Statutes by State	http://topics.law.cornell.edu/wex/table_education

Table 5.2   Websites with the Complete Text of the IDEA Regulations and State Regulations Websites

Website	URL
Building the Legacy: IDEA 2004	http://idea.ed.gov/download/finalregulations.pdf
State Education Regulations by State	http://www.law.cornell.edu/states/listing.html

tent of the law and provide procedures by which the law can be enforced. In a sense regulations are the rules that govern the implementation of special education and have the force of law. A violation of a regulation, therefore, is as serious as a violation of the law. As such, special education administrators should have a thorough understanding of federal and state regulations.

Table 5.2[2] contains websites with the regulations that implement the IDEA and websites in which administrators can locate the special education laws in their respective states.

Litigation

Litigation refers to the process of bringing a lawsuit or legal action to a court to resolve a legal matter or question. When the rulings of a judge or judges are published, these decisions form a body of case law, which is quite different from statutes or regulations. Courts exist at both the federal and state level. However, the large majority of cases regarding special education are heard at the federal level. Therefore, we will limit our discussion to federal litigation.

The American legal system relies heavily on the value of these court decisions and the legal precedents they establish. Because only a small fraction of cases results in published rulings, these few cases take on a great deal of importance. If a judicial decision is not published, it typically has no precedential value (i.e., the ruling does not establish a legal rule or authority for future cases). Special education has been the subject of much litigation, therefore, there is a body of case law that affects the practice of special education. The results of these decisions can be very important to special education administrators. To make the understanding of case law somewhat more difficult, the level of a court and the jurisdiction in which a ruling was issued will make a judicial ruling more or less important to a particular school district.

There are three levels in the federal court system (and in most state courts). The lowest level of federal court is the federal district court. There are close to 100 district courts in the federal judicial system. The geographic distribution of the district courts is based on state boundaries, with all states having between one and four district courts. In special education cases, judges at the district court level hear appeals of decisions made by due process hearing officers or state level review boards. Thus, the role of the district court judge is to rule on whether the hearing officer or officers correctly applied the law to the facts of the case. Whereas court rulings in special education litigation at the federal district court level can provide administrators with useful information, the only federal court decisions that represent the law, and therefore must be followed, are published federal district court decisions in the home state or jurisdiction in which the special education administrator works.

The rulings of district court judges can be appealed to a higher court. The next level of courts in the federal system is the United State Circuit Courts of Appeal or appellate courts. These courts hear appeals from the District Courts. The appellate court judges determine whether the judgment at the District Court should be affirmed, reversed, or modified. Decisions of the appellate court develop case law through the creation of precedents.

There are 13 appellate circuits in the United States. The first through eleventh Circuits cover three or more states each, a twelfth covers the District of Columbia, and the thirteenth, called the *Federal Circuit,* hears appeals from throughout the country on specialized matters (e.g., patents). The courts of appeal hear cases from district courts in their jurisdictions (e.g., an appeal of a

Table 5.3 Circuit Courts

1st	2nd	3rd	4th	5th	6th	7th	8th	9th	10th	11th	DC	Fed
ME	CT	DE	MD	LA	KY	IL	AR	AK	CO	AL	DC	
MA	NY	NJ	NC	MS	OH	IN	IA	AZ	KS	GA		
NH	VT	PA	SC	TX	MI	WS	MN	CA	NM	FL		
RI			VA		TN		MO	HI	OK			
			WV				NE	ID	UT			
							ND	MT	WY			
							SD	NV				
								OR				
								WA				

District Court ruling in Texas would be heard by the U.S. Court of Appeals for the Fifth Circuit, which covers Louisiana, Mississippi, and Texas). These decisions become controlling authority in the court's jurisdiction; that means lower courts in that jurisdiction must follow the decision of the higher court. Therefore, a decision out of the 4th circuit, which covers, Maryland, South Carolina, North Carolina, Virginia, and West Virginia, does not have the force of law in the seventh circuit, which covers Kentucky, Michigan, Ohio, and Tennessee. It is important, therefore, that special education administrators know which circuit in which they work and attend most closely to decisions from the Circuit Court of Appeals that has jurisdiction over their state. Table 5.3 is a list of the jurisdictions of the U.S. Circuit Courts of Appeals.

The highest court in the United States is the Supreme Court. The Supreme Court hears appeals of Circuit court decisions to determine if the law has been applied correctly. The Supreme Court hears only a fraction of the cases that are appealed to it; nonetheless, the decisions from the Supreme Court are binding on all lower courts and must be followed throughout the United States. Of course, it is important that administrators understand and follow all rulings from the U.S. Supreme Court.

Due Process Hearings

The IDEA contains procedural safeguards that school district's must afford to parents of students with disabilities. These safeguards include the right to request a due process hearing when school district personnel and a student's parents cannot agree on a child's special education identification, program, or placement. The purpose of the due process hearing is to allow an impartial third party, the due process hearing officer, to hear both sides of a dispute, examine the issues in dispute, apply the law to the specific situation, and issue a ruling that settles the dispute[3].

The IDEA permits states to adopt either a one-tier or two-tier hearing procedure. In a one-tier system the state educational agency (SEA) is responsible for the conducting the due process hearing. An appeal of the state-level hearing decision goes directly to court. In a two-tier system the school district (also called the local educational agency or LEA) is responsible for conducting the due process hearing. If the hearing officer's decision is appealed it goes to the second tier, which is a hearing at the SEA level. This decision can then be appealed to a state or federal court

The rulings in either LEA or SEA hearings are binding on both parties, however, they do not have precedential value. Nevertheless, rulings in hearings at the SEA level can be very important within the state in which the hearings are held. This is because if the SEA rulings are in your state they will give you an indication of how the SEA may rule in similar cases. Unfortunately, these decisions can be very difficult to find. Many states, however, are beginning to post the opinions in LEA and SEA hearings online.

Policy Letters from the U.S Department of Education

The United States Department of Education is comprised of a number of offices, including the Office of Special Education and Rehabilitative Service (OSERS). The Office of Special Education Programs (OSEP) is located within OSERS. Both OSERS and OSEP provide leadership and fiscal resources to assist states and local school districts to educate students with disabilities. One way that OSERS and OSEP accomplish this is by developing, communicating, and disseminating federal policy interpretations on special education through policy letters, guidance documents, and memos. Although these decisions do not have the force of law they may be cited in hearings or court cases because they do have some legal authority. They are also very important to special education administrators because they do give official guidance regarding numerous issues in special education law. We next begin our discussion of the IDEA.

The Individuals with Disabilities Education Act

The most important law in special education is the IDEA. The purpose of the law is to ensure that all eligible students with disabilities in public schools are provided with a free appropriate public education (FAPE), which consists of special education and related services that are designed to meet students' unique educational needs. Some scholars have divided Part B into six major principles (Turnbull, Turnbull, Stowe, & Huerta 2010). Although this is a useful structure for purposes of discussion, neither the IDEA's statutory language nor the U.S. Department of Education recognizes the division of the law into these six principles. These six principles are zero reject, protection in evaluation, free appropriate public education, least restrictive environment, procedural safeguards, and parent participation. Table 5.4 contains a brief explanation of these six principles. We next turn to an examination of the principle of FAPE.

Free Appropriate Public Education

Students who are eligible for special education under the IDEA have the right to receive a FAPE, consisting of special education and related services that (a) are provided at public expense, under public supervision and direction, and without charge; (b) meet the standards of the SEA; (d) include preschool, elementary school, or secondary school education in the child's state; and

Table 5.4 Six Principles of IDEA

Principle	Description
Zero Reject	School districts must locate, identify, and provide special education services to all eligible students with disabilities
Protection in Evaluation	School districts must conduct full and individualized assessments of students with disabilities before initially providing special education services
Free Appropriate Public Education	School districts must provide special education and related services at public expense, that meet the standards of the SEA, and are provided in conformity with students' IEPs
Least Restrictive Environment	School districts must ensure that to the maximum extent appropriate students with disabilities are to be educated with students who do not have disabilities.
Procedural Safeguards	School districts must adopt or develop procedures developed to ensure that students and their parents are involved in the special education process.
Parental Participation	Parents must be meaningfully involved in IEP development (i.e., assessment, programming, and placement).

(e) are provided in conformity with an individualized education program (IEP) that meets the requirements of the IDEA (IDEA, 20 U.S.C. § 1401(a)(18)).

When writing the original IDEA, the Congressional writers of the bill understood that it would be impossible to define a FAPE in such a way that the actual substantive educational requirements were listed, so instead they defined a FAPE primarily in accordance with the procedures necessary to ensure that parents and school personnel would collaborate to develop a program of special education and related services that would meet the unique educational needs of individual students. The IDEA, therefore, was specific in setting forth the procedures by which parents and school personnel, working together, would create programs that would provide an appropriate education.

Procedural Safeguards

The IDEA's procedural safeguards require that school personnel (a) provide notice to parents anytime their child's education program was discussed so they could participate in the discussions in a meaningful way, (b) invite parents to participate in meetings to develop their child's educational program, (c) secure parental consent prior to initiating evaluations of their child or placing their child in a special education program, (d) allow parents the opportunity to examine their child's educational records, and (e) permit parents to obtain an independent educational evaluation at public expense if the parents disagreed with the school's evaluation. Furthermore, when parents and school personnel cannot agree on a child's evaluation, programming, or placement, the parents can parents request mediation, an impartial due process hearing, and even file a suit in federal or state court to resolve (IDEA Regulations, 34 C.F.R. § 300.500-515).

The purpose of the procedural safeguards is to ensure parental participation and consultation throughout the special education process. The writers of the EAHCA believed that requiring meaningful collaboration between parents and school personnel and providing protections for parents when collaboration did not occur, would help to ensure that a FAPE would be developed and implemented for all students in special education.

Board of Education v. Rowley, 1982

In *Board of Education of the Hendrick Hudson Central School District v. Rowley* (hereafter *Rowley*) the Supreme Court interpreted the FAPE requirement of the EAHCA. The decision in *Rowley* has been the most important and influential court ruling in the history of special education, and it is very important that special education administrators understand the ramifications of this case.

The high court's decision in *Rowley* was announced on June 29, 1982. The majority opinion, written by Justice Rehnquist, noted that to meet the FAPE requirements of the EAHCA school districts had to provide personalized instruction with sufficient support services to permit a child with a disability to benefit educationally, which in the *Rowley* case had been satisfied.

According to the Court, the EAHCA required that special education services be provided at public expense, meet state standards, and comport with the student's IEP. If this instruction allowed the child to benefit from educational services and met the other requirements of the law, the student was receiving a FAPE. The court noted that any substantive standard prescribing the level of education to be accorded students with disabilities was absent from the language of the IDEA and that Congress had sought primarily to make public education available to children with disabilities rather than to guarantee any particular level of education.

The Supreme Court also formulated a two-part test that courts should use in ruling on FAPE cases. The *Rowley* two-part test has become the standard by which hearing officers and courts will judge FAPE cases. Because approximately 80% to 85% of all due process and SEA hearings involve FAPE, the specifics of this test are extremely important for special educators to understand if they are to ensure that the special education programs in their districts confer FAPE on IDEA eligible students with disabilities (Gerl, 2011). If the two parts of the *Rowley* test are met, a school has complied with FAPE requirements of the IDEA. We next examine the two-part *Rowley* Test.

The Rowley *Test: Part One*

The first part of the *Rowley* test requires that the court determine if the school district complied with the procedures set forth in the IDEA? This is, in essence, a procedural litmus test. In the *Rowley* case, the Supreme Court found that the school district had complied with the procedures of the law. This part of the *Rowley* test does require that school districts must follow the procedural requirements of the law. When a court determines that a school district has not adhered to the procedural requirement of the IDEA, therefore, the court could rule that the district had denied a student a FAPE.

Despite the fact that school districts are required to comply with IDEA's procedural requirements, procedural flaws do not automatically require a finding of a denial of a FAPE. The Individuals with Disabilities Education Improvement Act of 2004 (IDEA 2004) clarified the relative importance of the procedural requirements of the special education law. According to the IDEA 2004, when a school district commits a procedural violation of the law, it is only a denial of FAPE, and therefore a violation of the IDEA, when the infraction (a) impedes the student's right to a FAPE, (b) impedes the parents' right to meaningful participation in the special education, and (c) causes a deprivation of educational benefit (IDEA, 20 U.S.C. § 115(f)(3)(E)(ii)). It is likely that when school district personnel commit procedural errors that result in a denial of FAPE or exclude parents from meaningful participation, the district would likely be found in violation of the IDEA. Even though minor procedural errors may not arise to a violation of the IDEA, it is very important that special education administrators ensure that school personnel carefully adhere to the procedures of the law when developing a student's special education program.

The Rowley *Test: Part Two*

In the majority opinion *of Rowley,* Justice Rehnquist wrote that Congress' "intent ... was more to open the door of public education to handicapped children on appropriate terms than to guarantee any particular level of education once inside" (*Rowley,* p. 192). Justice Rehnquist further wrote, however, that the special education services provided to a student had to be "sufficient to confer some educational benefit upon the handicapped child ... But in seeking to provide such access to public education, Congress did not impose upon the States any greater substantive educational standard than would be necessary to make such access meaningful ..." (*Rowley,* p. 200). Justice Rehnquist also ruled that students with disabilities did not have a right to the best possible education or an education that allowed them to achieve their maximum potential.

In a 1993 decision in *Doe v. Board of Education of Tullahoma Schools,* the U.S. Court of Appeals for the Third Circuit used an interesting metaphor to drive this point home. According to the court, the IDEA does not require school districts to provide the educational equivalent of a Cadillac to every eligible student with disabilities, but school districts are required to provide the educational equivalent of a serviceable Chevrolet to every student.

Clearly, because of its substantive nature (i.e., is the IEP calculated to confer educational benefit) part two of the *Rowley* test is a more difficult question for hearing officers and judges. To answer this question a court has to determine what constitutes educational benefit for a student. The early post-*Rowley* courts tended to agree that the school district had provided a FAPE as long as the student obtained some educational benefit (Osborne, 1992). In these early rulings, the courts seemingly regarded IEPs as appropriate even if the benefit to a student was minimal. Other court decisions regarding FAPE, however, have required that school districts provide special education programs that conferred *meaningful* educational, and that a minimal or trivial benefit would not be sufficient to provide a FAPE.

In an important post-*Rowley* ruling the U.S. Court of Appeals for the Fourth Circuit, in *Hall v. Vance County Board of Education* (1985), held that the *Rowley* decision required courts to examine the IEP to determine what substantive standards meet the second principle of the *Rowley* test. The court cited *Rowley* as stating that this could only be accomplished on a case-by-case basis. In *Hall*, the appellate court upheld a district court's ruling that the plaintiff, who had a learning disability, had made no educational progress in the special education program. Additionally, because the IEP was inadequate (i.e., conferred no educational benefit), the school district had to reimburse the parents for private school tuition. The court noted that it was not sufficient for a school district special education program to offer educational programs that produced only trivial academic advancement.

In two other cases in which circuit courts addressed the second part of the *Rowley* test, the standard was also held to require more than trivial benefit. In *J.C. v. Central Regional School District* (1996), the U.S. Court of Appeals for the Third Circuit ruled that school districts must provide a special education program that leads to more than a *de minimus* or trivial education. In this case, the IEP developed for a student with severe disabilities failed to address important educational needs and the student had made little or no progress, and actually regressed in some areas. Thus, the IEP did not confer meaningful benefit.

In *Polk v. Central Susquehanna Intermediate Unit 16* (1988), the U.S. Court of Appeals for the Third Circuit discussed the *Rowley* decision and the IDEA's requirement to provide a "meaningful" education. The Third Circuit court noted that Amy Rowley did very well in her general education class. Because of this, the Supreme Court was able to avoid the substantive second principle of the *Rowley* test and concentrate on the procedural principle. In the case before the Third Circuit Court, however, the court had to address how much benefit was required to meet the "meaningful" standard in educating the plaintiff, Christopher Polk. Similarly in *Cypress-Fairbanks ISD v. Michael F.* (1997), the U.S. Court of Appeals of the 5th Circuit held that the second prong of the *Rowley* test requires an IEP that produces progress and that the educational benefit must be meaningful.

The Importance of the Rowley *decision*

According to the Supreme Court ruling in the *Rowley* decision, when the EAHCA was passed in 1975, Congress intended that the law open the doors of public education for students with disabilities rather than requiring the best possible education. The two part *Rowley* test became the standard that lower courts, due process hearing officers, and state review boards to use to rule in litigation involving FAPE issues. Because the hearing officers' and judges' rulings in such cases will involve application of he *Rowley* test, it is a good tool by which administrators can assess the educational services provided in their special education programs. When administrators evaluate their special education programs, therefore, they should ask themselves the following questions related to the *Rowley* ruling:

• Do the programs comply with the procedures set forth in the IDEA and in state law?
• Are students' parents meaningfully involved in developing their programs of special education?
• Are the IEPs developed resonable calculated to provide meaningful educational benefit?

Table 5.5   Supreme Court Cases

Case	Decision
School Committee of the Town of Burlington v. Department of Education, 471 U.S. 359 (1985)	Parents are entitled to reimbursement for costs associated with unilateral placements in a private facility if the court determines that such placement, rather than the proposed IEP, is appropriate.
Florence County School District Four v. Shannon Carter, 510 U.S. 7 (1993)	Parents' failure to select a state approved program in favor of an unapproved option does not bar reimbursement if the court determines that such placement, rather than the proposed IEP, is appropriate
Forest Grove v. T.A., 557 U. S. ____ (2009).	Parents are entitled to reimbursement if the court determines that such placement, rather than the proposed IEP, is appropriate regardless of whether the child previously received special education services from the district (the child was yet to found eligible for services under IDEA).

• Do special education teachers collect data that show that their students are benefiting from their special education programs?

It is important that administrators understand that the responsibility to make FAPE available rests with the school district in which the child resides. If the school district fails to develop a special education program that confers a FAPE and the parents then obtain appropriate services such as a private school placement, either a due process hearing officer or a court may require that a school district reimburse the parents for expenses incurred as a result of the district failing to prvide a FAPE. The U.S. Supreme Court has also issued rulings in a number of cases involving the remedies that courts may issue in cases in which a school district has not provided a FAPE. These decisions are listed in Table 5.5.

In addition to the Supreme Court decisions there have been many rulings regarding the remedies that hearing officers and courts may award to parents when they prevail in lawsuits against school districts that had failed to provide a FAPE. Hearing officers and courts have broad authority to fashion relief in such cases. Previous litigation has awarded parents tuition reimbursement, compensatory education, and attorneys' fees (Yell, 2012).

FAPE and the IDEA Reauthorizations of 1997 and 2004

Clearly, the law has been dramatically successful in the original goal of providing access to public education for students with disabilities. When the IDEA was authorized in 1997 and again in 2004, however, the writers of the law believed that the promise of the IDEA had not been fulfilled for too many children with disabilities (House of Representatives Report, 1997). The underlying theme of IDEA 1997 and IDEA 2004, therefore, was to improve the effectiveness of special education by requiring demonstrable improvements in the educational achievement of students with disabilities. Indeed, a quality education for each student with disabilities became the new goal of IDEA in 1997 (Eyer, 1998) and in 2004 (Huefner, 2008). As Eyers wrote "The IDEA can no longer be fairly perceived as a statute which merely affords children access to education. Today, the IDEA is designed to improve the effectiveness of special education and increase the benefits afforded to children with disabilities to the extent such benefits are necessary to achieve measurable progress" (Eyer, 1998, p. 16). Moreover, in the 2004 reauthorization the Congressional Report emphasized "improving educational results for children with disabilities is an essential element of our national policy of ensuring equality of opportunity, full participation, independent living, and economic self-sufficiency for individuals with disabilities" (IDEA, 20 U.S.C. § 1400[c][1]).

In an article in 2008, Huefner noted that

> The purpose of the (IDEA) is no longer to provide a "basic floor of opportunity." The expectation of academic and functional progress calls for more than a floor. Although IDEA does not expect, let alone guarantee any certain standard of achievement, it expects meaningful or substantive progress both toward general curriculum goals and the student's unique educational goals (such as social/behavioral, physical, functional, and developmental goals) resulting from the disability.
>
> *(p. 378)*

When considering cases involving the FAPE standard, courts must rely on the statutory definition of FAPE and the Supreme Court's decision in *Rowley*. The definition of FAPE has remained unchanged since 1975 and *Rowley* still remains the Supreme Court's most important decision regarding FAPE (Blau, 2007; Crockett & Yell, 2008; Daniel & Meinhardt, 2007; Zirkel, 2008). Despite the large gap between the *Rowley* minimalistic standard and the new requirements of the law, until there is a substantive statutory reauthorization of FAPE or judicial redefinition of FAPE, probably by the U.S. Supreme Court, this gap will only continue to grow. Blau (2007) suggested that in future reauthorizations Congress should define FAPE in terms of a special education that requires a quantifiable measure of meaningful and adequate progress toward a student's goals. Until these changes occur, courts will continue to wrestle with the meaning of a FAPE and what constitutes educational benefit. Nonetheless, until that time special education administrators should ensure that their IEP team members understand that a FAPE requires that a student's IEP confer meaningful educational benefit.

The key to providing a FAPE is for school personnel to develop and implement a program of individualized special education instruction, based on a full and individualized assessment of a student, which is tailored to confer meaningful educational benefit to the student (Yell, 2012). To ensure that each student covered by the IDEA receives a FAPE, Congress required that school-based teams develop an IEP. This process, which provides the students with a FAPE, consists of specially designed instruction and services provided at public expense. The IEP is at the center of many, perhaps most, IDEA disputes, especially those over reimbursement for private school placements (Bateman, 2011). According to Bateman (2011) the IEP is the primary evidence of the appropriateness of the child's educational program—its development, implementation and efficacy. Moreover, Bateman observed that generally the IEP is accepted in legal proceedings as an accurate depiction of a student's special education program, and unless there is evidence of implementation failures, the IEP is the primary basis for finding whether FAPE was delivered. We next examine the process for developing a student's IEP.

The Individualized Education Program Development Process

Developing a student's special education program is a collaborative process between a student's parents and a team of school-based personnel, and, in some cases, the student. In fact, the most basic of all IDEA requirements related to IEPs is that the parents are full and equal participants with the district in IEP development (Bateman, 2011). The IEP is the written document of a student's special education program that is developed through this collaborative process.

The special education process begins with a full and individualized assessment of a student's academic and functional needs. The second step of the special education process is developing a student's IEP. The IEP describes a student's educational needs and details the special education and related services that will be provided to the student. The IEP also contains a student's goals and how his or her educational progress will be measured. Students' IEPs must also address their

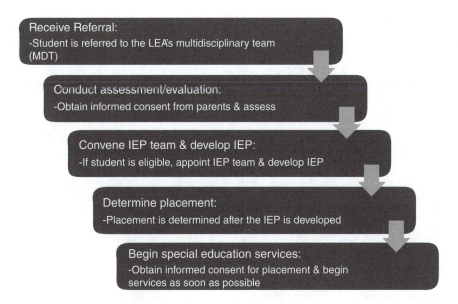

Figure 5.1 The IEP development process

involvement and participation in the general education curriculum. Finally, IEP teams usually determine a student's placement, although the IDEA does not require that an IEP team make placement decisions. Figure 5.1 depicts this process. We next discuss the development a student's individualized program of special education.

Conducting the Assessment/Evaluation

The IEP process begins with a full and individualized assessment or evaluation of a student's educational needs. According to Bateman (2011), if we think of the IEP as a house, the assessment/evaluation is the foundation. She goes on to observe that the IEP must stand solidly on a foundation of current, accurate evaluations of the student's level of performance in academic and functional areas. Essentially the assessment/evaluation must reveal all of a student's academic and functional needs upon which the IEP will be developed. If the assessment is incomplete or inaccurate, the rest of the IEP will likely be inaccurate. A U.S. District Court judge in *Kirby v. Cabell County Board of Education* (2006) aptly stated the importance of the assessment to ensuring that a student will receive a FAPE:

> If the IEP fails to assess the 'child's present levels of academic achievement and functional performance' the IEP does not comply with [IDEA]. This deficiency goes to the heart of the IEP; the child's level of academic achievement and functional performance is the foundation on which the IEP must be built. Without a clear identification of [the child's] present levels, the IEP cannot set measurable goals, evaluate the child's progress and determine which educational and related services are needed.
>
> *(p. 694)*

Thus, because the initial assessment/evaluation is the keystone of students' IEPs conducting the assessment/evaluation is a very important part of providing FAPE. The following are suggestions that special education administrators and supervisors should take to ensure that assessments are conducted that provide a sound basis for a student's IEP.

- School-based teams must assess all suspected areas of academic or functional needs. Because a student's parents have an important role in their child's assessment, their opinions and views regarding his or her needs must receive full consideration by the team.
- The assessment/evaluation must thoroughly assess a student's instructional and functional needs so that instruction can be planned. Too often the assessment just involves norm-referenced tests that are used to determine eligibility (Reschly, 2000). This is inappropriate and will not result in the types of information necessary to plan a student's IEP. Norm-referenced tests can give the team clues to help indicate students' needs as compared to the student's peers, however, more fine-grained assessments using procedures such as curriculum-based assessment, curriculum-based measurement, direct observation, and functional behavioral assessment will be much more useful to the team in determining the students' presents levels of performance and skill deficits in areas in which they need individualized instruction.
- Include professionals on the team with expertise in assessment/evaluation. Often a school psychologist who specializes in assessment will be included on the team. However, depending on students suspected needs, a person with specialized assessment expertise may also be needed on the team (e.g., persons with expertise in conducting functional behavioral assessments, assistive technology assessments, transition assessments).
- Consider the assessment information as the baseline upon which students' IEP goals will be measured. The assessment is the path to good goals and subsequent monitoring of student progress.

Developing the IEP

Developing students' IEPs refers to the process of creating a students individualized program. The IEP is the document that formalizes this process and, as such, is the blueprint of a student's FAPE. The IDEA mandates the process and procedures for developing the IEP. We next briefly review these procedures.

IEP Team Participants

The IDEA requires that certain persons comprise the IEP team. Other school-based personnel are permitted, but not required, to attend the IEP meeting. Table 5.6 lists and describes the required members of students' IEP teams who collaborate to create their program of special education.

Having the appropriate IEP team members at IEP meetings is very important. In fact, Lake (2007) observed that very few procedural errors will foil a school district's ability to provide a FAPE as will failing to ensure that the composition of the IEP team is in line with the requirements of the IDEA. Courts and due process hearing officers have invalidated IEPs when the required participants were not involved in the process and their absence affected the document's development (Yell, 2012). A state review officer stressed the importance of having a properly constituted IEP team in *Board of Education of the Monroe-Woodbury Central School District* (1999). In his ruling, the officer ruled that an IEP prepared by an invalidly composed IEP team was a "nullity" and was, therefore, illegal. It is likely that hearing officers and courts will conclude that the IEP developed by an improperly constituted IEP team will likewise be defective and will not provide FAPE (Lake, 2007). The following are suggestions for special education administrators will help ensure that IEP teams are comprised of appropriate members.

- Ensure that LEA representatives understand the importance of including all required members on IEP teams.

Table 5.6   IEP Team Members

IEP team members	Description
* The parents of the student	Either one or both parents
* General education teacher of the student	At least one of the student's general education teachers
* Special education teacher of the student	At least one of the student's special education teacher
* LEA representative	Must be (a) qualified to provide or supervise special education, (b) knowledgeable about the general education curriculum, and (c) knowledgeable about the availability of LEA resources
* Individual who can interpret the instructional implications of the assessment/evaluation	May be another person already on the IEP team
Others who have knowledge of special expertise regarding the student, including related services personnel	At the parent's or the LEA's discretion
Whenever appropriate, the student	The student must be invited to the IEP team if transition services are considered

* Required members

- Ensure that at least one of the student's general education teachers is a participant and is meaningfully involved on the IEP team. The general education teacher should be the teacher who has primarily responsible for implementing a student's IEP.
- Ensure that the LEA representative is qualified to provide, or supervision the provision of, special education and that he or she is knowledgeable about the general education curriculum and resources available to the school district.
- Include the student on the team when transition services are being discussed. According to the IDEA, transition services must be included in the first IEP that is developed after a student turns 16. However, school districts should be aware of their state's requirements for including transition services in students' IEPs because some states mandate that transition services begin at a younger age (e.g., South Carolina requires that transition services be included in the IEP of students at 13 years of age).

Parental Participation in IEP Meetings.

The IDEA requires that school districts ensure that parents are full and equal participants by (a) providing adequate notice of the meetings; (b) scheduling the meeting at a mutually agreed upon time and place; (c) informing the parents of the purpose, time, and place of the meetings and who will attend by district request; and (d) informing the parents of their right to bring others of their choice with knowledge or special expertise regarding a student to the meeting (IDEA Regulations, 34 C.F.R. § 300.322). One of the most serious errors that school districts can make is failing to ensure that a student's parents are *meaningful participants in the IEP process.* In fact, allowing parents to participate fully in the special education process is so important that failing to do so is one of the two procedural grounds by which a due process hearing officer may rule that a school district has denied a student a FAPE, this violating the IDEA (IDEA Regulations, 34 C.F.R. § 300.513(a)(2)).

Bateman (2011) asserted that courts more vigorously protect parental participation than any of the IDEA's procedural rights. For example, in *Amanda J. v. Clark County School District,* (2001), the U.S. Court of Appeals for the Ninth Circuit held that interference with parental participation in the development of an IEP undermines the very essence of the IDEA.

In the 2007 Supreme Court ruling in *Winkleman v. Parma City School District,* Justice Kennedy stressed the critical importance of parental participation throughout the special education process in his majority opinion. In this decision, the unanimous high court held that "We conclude IDEA grants independent, enforceable rights. These rights, which are not limited to certain procedural and reimbursement-related matters, encompass the entitlement to a free appropriate public education for the parents' child" (p. 2005). The high court thus ruled that the IDEA mandates that (a) parents must be meaningfully involved in the development of their child's IEP, (b) parents have enforceable rights under the law, and (c) parental participation in the special education process is crucial to ensuring that children with disabilities receive a FAPE (Yell & Crockett, 2011).

The IEP, therefore, is a process by which parents and school district personnel determine a student's IEP and the placement where the special education services will be delivered. Unfortunately, school districts have often determined the content of a student's IEP and his or her placement outside of the IEP process. This practice, which has been called predetermination, is a serious violation of the IDEA, and could result in a ruling that a school district had denied a student a FAPE (Lake, 2007; Slater, 2010). Predetermination occurs when an IEP team essentially develops a student's IEP prior to an IEP meeting, thereby making "full and meaningful" parental participation a ruse. When IEP team members make definitive statements about what the school will and will not consider putting the IEP, it is a strong indication that predetermination has occurred (e.g., "We always …" or "We never …").

On the other hand, it is permissible for IEP team members to hold informal preparatory meetings and even to come to an IEP meeting with a draft IEP. In such cases, it is crucial that a student's parents understand that the draft IEP is only a draft and is subject to changes during the IEP meeting. In fact, it is advisable that a draft IEP have the words "DRAFT" printed on the IEP. As the judge in the case *Doyle v. Arlington* (1992) colorfully wrote, "School Officials must come to the IEP table with an open mind. But this does not mean they should come … with a blank mind (p. 156).

Clearly, the IEP team must carefully consider all suggestions made by a student's parents in order to avoid accusations of predetermination. In addition to being a legal requirement, however, meaningful parental involvement is also a best practice in special education programs (Iovannone, Dunlap, Huber, & Kincaid, 2003). As noted in a 2004 report by the Southeastern Educational Development Laboratory, "the evidence is consistent, positive, and convincing: families have a major influence on their children's achievement in school and through life. When schools, families, and community groups work together to support learning, children tend to do better in school, stay in school longer, and like school more" (Henderson & Mapp, 2002, p. 1).

The following are suggestions that will help special education administrators ensure that their school district personnel adhere to the IEP team requirements of the IDEA.

- Schedule IEP meeting with parents at a mutually agreeable time and place. Keep thorough records of attempts to arrange IEP meetings. If neither parent can attend, the district may use other methods to ensure parent participation, including alternative meeting arrangements (e.g., teleconference). The IEP meeting may be held without the parents if the school district has documentation (e.g., record of telephone calls, emails, and home visits) that attempts at including the parents were unsuccessful.

- Ensure that parents fully understand the purposes of all special education meetings and are encouraged to contribute. Special education administrators may want to consider appointing a school district staff member, perhaps a school counselor, to assist parents to understand their rights and responsibilities in the special education process.

- Ensure that IEP team members come to all IEP meetings prepared but not with their minds made up.

- Document parental participation at IEP meetings. A school district participant should take thorough notes during IEP meeting. In these notes parents' contributions should be recorded, as are subsequent discussions of these contributions during the meeting. The meeting notes should be reviewed with participants in the meeting to ensure accuracy. This will help ensure that parents are meaningful participants in the IEP process.

- Document efforts (e.g., telephone calls, emails, mail, home visits) to obtain parental consent. This will be especially important if a school district is unable to convince a student's parents to participate in IEP meetings.
- Provide a student's parents with frequent and regular communication regarding their child's special education program, including reports of the student's progress.

Excusing IEP Team Members.   When the IDEA was reauthorized in 2004, important exceptions to the general rules regarding mandatory attendance at IEP meetings were added to the law. First, a member of an IEP team whose area of curriculum or related service is not being modified or discussed may be excused from the IEP meeting if the parent and school district "agree that the attendance of such member is not necessary" (IDEA, 20 U.S.C. § 1414(d)(I)(C)(i)). Second, a member of an IEP team may be excused from attending all or part of a meeting even when his or her area of curriculum or related services is being modified or discussed as long as (a) the parents provide informed consent of the excusal in writing and (b) the excused team members submits written input to the team regarding the development of the IEP (IDEA, 20 U.S.C. § 1414(d)(I)(C)(i)). These excusal provisions were added to the IDEA to provide flexibility to school districts and parents in scheduling IEP meetings. Unfortunately these provisions have created potential problems that special education administrators need to avoid. According to Lake (2007), the greatest pitfall is the temptation to routinely or unilaterally excuse IEP team members, especially general education teachers, from team meetings. According to the U.S Department of Education a school district that routinely excuses IEP team members will not be in compliance with the IDEA (71 Federal Register 46,674, 2006). Another potential pitfall may occur when school districts fail to get agreement or informed written consent from a student's parents to excuse members (Lake, 2007). The following are suggestions that will help special education administrators ensure that they do not run afoul of the excusal provisions of the IDEA.

- Provide training for LEA representatives and IEP members on the excusal provisions of the IDEA (including the importance of not overusing excusal procedures).
- Ensure that LEA representatives understand the importance of including all required members on IEP teams, especially general education teachers
- Ensure that parents understand that they have to provide consent for excusal and if they do not grant consent all required members must be in attendance at an IEP meeting.
- Develop a parental agreement form for excusing IEP team members whose areas will not be discussed.
- Develop a parental consent form for excusing IEP team members whose areas are being discussed. This form must meet the informed consent requirements of the IDEA: The (a) parents must be fully informed in their native language or mode of communication; (b) parents understand and agree in writing to the activities, which are fully described; and (c) parents understanding that the granting of consent is voluntary and can be revoked
- Develop a form for excused team members whose areas will be discussed to provide written input to the IEP team. This form should include recommendations to the team and must be available to the team before the meeting.

Content of the IEP

Students' IEPs must be developed, reviewed, and revised in an IEP meeting. The IDEA requires that, at a minimum, eight components be present in the IEP. States and local agencies, however,

Table 5.7 Required Components of IEPs

IEP components required for all students	IEP components required for some students
• Present levels of academic achievement & functional performance	Transition goals & services for students aged 16 (or younger if required by a state or determined appropriate by an IEP Team
• Measurable annual goals	For students who take alternate state assessments, a description of benchmarks or short term objectives
• Description of how progress will be measured & when progress reported to parents	If students take a state alternate assessment, a statement of why they cannot participate in the regular assessment & what assessment they will take
• Statement of special education and other services based on peer-reviewed research	For students whose behavior impedes their learning the team must consider positive behavioral interventions & supports
• An explanation of the extent, if any, that a student will not participate with nondisabled students in the general education classroom	IEP teams must consider whether a student needs assistive technology devices & services
• A statement of accommodations need on state and districtwide assessments	Additional special factors if required-Limited English proficiency, blind/visually impaired, deaf/hard of hearing
• Projected dates, frequency, location, & duration of services	

may require additional elements. The required components of IEPs are listed and described in Table 5.7.

It is crucial that these elements be discussed at the IEP meeting and included in the IEP document. Courts have determined that when these components are missing from a student's IEP and adversely affect a student's special education program, the resulting IEP is invalid (e.g., *Big Beaver Falls Area School District v. Jackson*, 1993).

These components reveal four questions that are at the heart of the IEP process. Special education administrators must ensure that their IEP teams focus on answering these questions. The questions are:

1. What are the student's unique educational needs that must be considered in developing the individualized program?
2. What measurable goals will enable the student to achieve meaningful educational benefit?
3. What services will the school district provide to the student to address each of his or her educational needs?
4. How will the team monitor the student's progress to determine if the instructional program is effective?

In the following section we briefly describe the four components of the IEP that specifically answer these key questions.

Present Levels of Academic Achievement and Functional Performance. The present levels of academic achievement and functional performance (PLAAFP) are determined from the full and individualized assessment of a student's unique educational needs. The PLAAFPs include accurate information that serves as the keystone of the IEP. The information is the baseline data from which the IEP team can determine the annual goals and measure a student's progress. A hearing officer wrote of the importance of the present levels information in his opinion in Board of Education of the Rhinebeck Central School District (2003). The officer had ruled two years of a school district's IEPs were deficient because they "lacked adequate objective data by which to measure the student's present levels of performance in reading and language arts. The lack of objective data resulted in an inadequate basis upon which to measure (the student's) progress in those areas and to develop meaningful, measurable goals" (p. 148).

The U.S. Department of Education's question and answer document on IEPs aptly described the relationship between the present levels and other aspects of the IEP as follows:

> There should be a direct relationship between the present levels of performance and the other components of the IEP. Thus, if the statement describes a problem with the child's reading level and points to a deficiency in reading skills, the problem should be addressed under both goals and specific special education and related services provided to the child"
>
> *(Question and Answer, 2007, p. 36)*

Measurable Annual Goals.   Since the enactment of the EAHCA in 1975, annual goals have been required in all students' IEPs. Annual goals are projections the team makes regarding the progress of the student in one school year. When the IEP team develops the annual goals, they must consider the student's past achievement and current level of performance (Bateman & Linden, 2006).

In the reauthorization of the IDEA in 1997, the requirement was changed from "annual goals" to "measurable annual goals." After 1997, the IEP goals still focus on remediation of academic or nonacademic problems and are based on the student's current level of educational performance but now they had to be measurable. Moreover, when IEP teams fail to include measurable goals for each area of student need that failure can render an IEP inappropriate, and thus violate the FAPE provisions of the IDEA (Bateman, 2007; Bateman & Linden, 2006; Yell & Crockett, 2011). Unfortunately, only a fraction of IEPs contain goals that are actually measurable (Bateman, 2007, 2011). When the goals are not measurable, an IEP will likely not provide a FAPE, which may violate the IDEA (Bateman & Linden, 2006). Similarly, when goals are not measured, an IEP will not provide a FAPE, which may violate the IDEA (Bateman & Linden, 2006). Developing measurable annual goals and then measuring them, therefore, is critical to planning and implementing FAPE.

The importance of including measurable annual goals in the IEP was shown in the opinion of the following due process hearing. A hearing officer in New Mexico found that a school district's IEP did not provide FAPE when the

> Student's annual goals and objectives in each IEP simply do not contain objective criteria which permit measurement of Student's progress.... A goal of 'increasing' reading comprehension skills or 'improving decoding skills' is not a measurable goal.... Even if [present levels of performance] were clearly stated, an open-ended statement that Student will 'improve' does not meet the requirement ... for a 'measurable' goal. The addition of a percentage of accuracy is not helpful where the IEP fails to define a starting point, an ending point, the curriculum in which Student will achieve 80 to 85% accuracy, or a procedure for pre and post-testing.
>
> *(Rio Rancho Public Schools, 2003, p. 563)*

Bateman (2011) asserted that too few IEP team members and special education teachers know how to write measurable goals and too few goal writers intend that anyone will actually measure the progress the student has made, which makes IEP goals meaningless and useless. It is

- Bateman, B.D. (2007). *From Gobbledygook to clearly written annual IEP goals.* Verona WI: Attainment Company

- Johnston, T.C. (2010). *Data without tears: How to write measurable educational goals and collect meaningful data.* Champaign, IL: Research Press

- Kosinsky, C. (2008). *IEP goals that make a difference: An administrator's guide to improving the process.* Horsham, PA: LRP Publications

- Mager, R.F. (1998). *Preparing instructional objectives: A critical tool in the development of effective instruction.* Atlanta, GA: Center for Effective Performance

Figure 5.2   Guides to writing measurable goals

important that IEP team members, especially special education teachers and school psychologists understand how they to write measurable goals. Figure 5.2 contains four guides to writing measurable goals.

In the IDEA reauthorization of 2004, Congress eliminated the requirement that IEPs must include short-term objectives (STOs), except for special education students who are assessed on state/district tests using alternate assessments and alternate standards. However, states have the option of continuing to require that IEPs of all special education students include STOs. The requirements regarding annual goals and objectives are identical except for the length of time anticipated for accomplishment. For example, STOs can be similar to the goals, but written in shorter time frames. For example, use the same basic goal but write it for 9 weeks rather than 1 year. Short-term objectives can also be written in the form of a task analysis. Therefore, the STOs represent progressive and sequential steps that a student must accomplish in order that he or she reaches the goal.

It is also important that IEP team members develop annual goals that are ambitious, but reasonable. If a hearing officer or court determines that if a student achieves the goals in his or her IEP but the goals were trivial in the first place, it becomes much more likely that the IEP will be found to be deficient. Special education administrators do not need to be concerned that a student's goals are too ambitious as long as the LEA has made good faith efforts in providing special education services and have the data to prove that a student made educational progress.

Special Education Services.   All students' IEPs must include a statement of the specific educational services, related services, and supplementary aids and services to be provided by the school. The purpose of the statements is to clarify the services that the school will provide to help a student (a) progress toward his or her annual goals, and (b) be involved in and progress in the general education curriculum. The IDEA's definition of special education is "specially designed instruction to meet the unique needs of a student with a disability (IDEA Regulations, 34 C.F.R. § 300.39(a)(2006). Specially designed instruction is further defined as "adapting the content, methodology or delivery of instruction (IDEA Regulations, 34 C.F.R. § 300.39(b)(3)(2006).

In IDEA 2004, Congress added the requirement that IEPs must include "a statement of the special education and related services and supplementary aids and services, based on peer-reviewed research to the extent practicable (IDEA, 20 U.S.C. § 1414(d)(1)(A)(i)(IV)). This requirement applies to the (a) selection and provision of special education methodology; (b) selection and provision of related services, which are services that are required to assist a student to benefit from special education; and (c) selection and provision of aids, services and supports provided in regular education settings. The U.S. Department of Education declined to define the term "peer-reviewed research"; rather the Department did note that phrase was adopted from the following criteria that school districts could use to identifying scientifically-based research (SBR) from the Elementary and Secondary Education Act (ESEA): "research that has been accepted by a *peer-reviewed* journal or approved by a panel of independent experts through a comparably rigorous, objective, and scientific review)Elementary and Secondary Education Act, 20 U.S.C. § 1208(6)(B)). In the final regulations to the IDEA issued on August 14, 2006, the U.S. Department of Education defined "peer-reviewed research" in the commentary as generally referring "to research that is reviewed by qualified and independent reviewers to ensure that the quality of the information meets the standards of the field before the research is published" (71 *Fed. Reg.* 46664). According to Etscheidt and Curran (2010), the legislative history of the IDEA 2004 and the definition and commentary on the peer-reviewed research requirement reveals that the intent of this section of the law was to ensure that IEP teams' selection of educational approaches reflect sound practices which have been validated empirically whenever possible. Table 5.8 includes a number of legitimate websites that include information on PRR.

Table 5.8 Websites with Peer-Reviewed Research

Center & URL	Description
Doing What Works: Research-Based Education Practices Online (http://dww.ed.gov/)	U.S. Department of Education website that provides information to help educators to practical tools to improve classroom instruction.
Center on Positive Behavioral Interventions and Supports (PBIS) http://www.pbis.org/	The Technical Assistance Center on Positive Behavioral Interventions and Supports is devoted to giving schools information and technical assistance for identifying, adapting, and sustaining effective school-wide disciplinary practices.
National Center on Response to Intervention (NCRTI) http://www.rti4success.org/	The National Center on Response to Intervention (RTI) mission is to provide technical assistance to states and districts and build the capacity of states to assist districts in implementing proven models for RTI.
National Dissemination Center for Children with Disabilities (NICHCY) www.nichcy.org	A central source of information on infants, toddlers, children, and youth with disabilities. Includes information on law and PRR.
National Dropout Prevention Center for Students with Disabilities (NDPC-SD) http://www.ndpc-sd.org/	National Dropout Prevention Center for Students with Disabilities is committed to providing technical assistance in designing, selecting and implementing effective, evidence-based interventions to address dropout among students with disabilities.
National Early Childhood Technical Assistance Center (NECTAC) http://www.nectac.org/	The National Early Childhood Technical Assistance Center is dedicated to improving service systems and outcomes for children with disabilities and their families in all 50 states and 10 jurisdictions
National Professional Development Center on Autism Spectrum Disorders http://autismpdc.fpg.unc.edu/	The National Professional Development Center on Autism Spectrum Disorders seeks to promote the use of evidence-based practice for children and adolescents with autism spectrum disorders.
National Secondary Transition Technical Assistance Center (NSTTAC) http://www.nsttac.org/	The National Secondary Transition Technical Assistance Center (NSTTAC) is dedicated to ensuring full implementation of the IDEA and helping youth with disabilities and their families achieve desired post-school outcomes.
Promising Practices Network www.promsingpractices.net	This center offers research-based information on what works to improve the lives of children and families.
What Works Clearinghouse http://ies.ed.gov/ncee/wwc/	The What Works Clearinghouse is an initiative of the U.S. Department of Education's Institute of Education Sciences. It is a central source of scientific evidence for what works in education.

In the first reported due process hearing on the PRR requirement, *Waukee Community School District*, 2007, a school district was ruled to have violated the FAPE requirement of the IDEA. The hearing officer ruled that a preponderance of evidence revealed that the school districts interventions were not based on PRR to the extent practicable. In another due process hearing that involved the PRR requirement, *Rocklin Unified School District* (2007), a hearing officer ruled in favor of a school district when they provided evidence in the form of PRR for the educational procedures that they used. Zirkel (2008) analyzed the limited litigation on the PRR requirement of the IDEA and came to the following three conclusions regarding these cases: (a) the *Rowley* standard will continue as the substantive measure of a program's appropriateness; (b) if a program is reasonably calculated to confer educational benefit and has been crafted based on PRR to the extent practicable, choice of methodology is the discretion of the school district; and (c) a program based on PRR must be implemented in a manner consistent with how the PRR intended that the intervention be implemented.

According to the U.S. Department of Education, the statement of services must be unambiguous so that the school's commitment of resources is clear to parents and other members of the team (IDEA Regulations, 34 C.F.R. § Appendix C to Part 300, number 51). According to Bateman and Linden (2006), this crucial component of the IEP too often consists of only checkmarks on the face sheet of the IEP, however, a review of scores of IEP rulings have shown that a much broader and detailed explanation of the services is required.

A statement of program modifications or supports for school personnel must be included in this section of the IEP. These modifications and supports are "aids, services, and other supports that are provided in regular education classes or other education-related settings to enable children with disabilities to be educated with nondisabled children to the maximum extent appropriate" (IDEA, 20 U.S.C. § 1401(25)).

Measuring Student Progress. "Progress monitoring is a scientifically based practice that is used to assess students' academic and functional performance and evaluate the effectiveness of instruction" (National Center on Progress Monitoring, n.d). The IEP must include a statement of how a student's progress toward the annual goals will be measured. This requirement is a response to the movement toward greater accountability in education, and its purpose is to inform parents and educators of how a student's progress toward his or her annual goals will be measured (Yell, 2012). The statement must also describe how a student's parents will be regularly informed about their child's progress toward the annual goals. Parents of students with disabilities must be informed about their child's progress as regularly as are parents of children without disabilities (e.g., through regular report cards).

There is probably less substantive compliance with this component of the IEP than any other (Yell, 2012). Appropriate evaluation of a student's progress toward meeting IEP goals and objectives is essential because without monitoring it will be impossible to determine if the student's program is working. If the goals and objectives of the IEP cannot be measured or evaluated, the IEP will not appropriately address the student's needs, which may result in the denial of FAPE. The importance of progress monitoring was described as follows in the decision in *Escambia County Public School System*: "Periodic review of progress on the goals and objectives provides the disabled student's teacher with supportive data needed to make a determination of the success of the intervention ..." (p. 248). How much progress a student makes has also been a factor in court's determination of whether FAPE was provided. In early cases, attention focused on whether the IEP, as written, was reasonably calculated to enable the student to receive educational benefit, following *Rowley*, however, recently courts have also examined the actual progress that students have made in their special education programs (Bateman, 2011). For example, in *Cranston School District v. Q.D.* (2008), the court ruled that a school district had failed to provide

FAPE because a student had not made academic gains. Similarly, the school district denied FAPE in *Taylor v. Sandusky* (2005). In this case a student failed to make progress toward his goals on his third grade IEP. The IEP team made matters worse by using the same IEP for the student when he was in the fourth grade. In *Draper v. Atlanta Independent School System* (2007) a district was found to have violated FAPE, and the student was awarded a private placement, when a student failed to make progress toward his goals. On the other hand, in *M.P. v. South Brunswick Board of Education* (2008), the court found that a school district had provided FAPE despite having a flawed IEP because the data collected by a special education teacher showed that the student had made meaningful academic progress. The decisions in these cases show that when a student doesn't make meaningful progress, or an IEP team fails to collect data regarding student progress, it is possible that a school district could be found in violation of the FAPE mandate of the IDEA. However, when an IEP collects legitimate data, and the data shows that a student has made progress, the school district has clearly provided FAPE.

IEP teams must make decisions regarding the nature of the data that will be collected and analyzed. Anecdotal data and other subjective procedures are not appropriate for monitoring progress, and should not be the basis of a progress monitoring system (Yell & Drasgow, 2000). The most appropriate progress monitoring systems are those in which objective numerical data are collected, graphed, analyzed., and used to make instructional decisions (Yell, 2012). Two examples of such systems are curriculum-based measurement (Deno, 1985) and applied behavior analysis (Alberto & Troutman, 2009).

A Federal District Court in Virginia addressed the importance of data collection in *County School Board of Henrico County, Virginia v. R.T.* (2006). The parents of a young child with autism, R.T., placed their son in a private school because he had failed to make progress in the school district's program. The boy's teacher and other school district personnel countered that R.T. had made progress in the school's program. The court, however, did not find the testimony credible because the evidence of R.T.'s progress was based only on anecdotal information and no data had been collected. The Court wrote, "(the teacher's) assessment of R.T. is entitled to little weight because it is based on anecdotal, rather than systematic, data collection" (p. 685). In *Board of Education of the Rhinebeck Central School District* a school district's IEP was invalid because no legitimate data were collected to show student progress. In fact, the student's goals were measured by teacher observation. According to the decision "although *subjective* teacher observation provides valuable information, *teacher observation is not an adequate method of monitoring student progress*" and "Without supporting data, teacher observation is *opinion which cannot be verified*" (italics added, p. 148).

Following are suggestions that will help special education administrators ensure that their IEPs teams develop programs that are educationally appropriate and legally correct:

- Ensure that IEPs teams include members with expertise in conducting formal assessments for determining eligibility and informal assessments, direct observations, curriculum-based assessments, curriculum-based measurement, and criterion-referenced testing for determining instructional programming.
- Ensure that when needed IEP teams have available to them persons with specialized expertise in areas such as assistive technology, functional behavioral assessment, positive behavior support, progress monitoring, etc.
- Provide training for IEP team members, especially special education teachers and school psychologists, in writing measurable annual goals.
- Ensure that special education teachers understand the importance of basing special education services on peer-reviewed research.
- Provide regular training to special education teachers in research-based procedures that appear in peer-reviewed journals or are approved by an independent panel of experts.

- Provide training for special education teachers in research-based progress monitoring and ensure that such practices are actually occurring.
- Frequently and systematically evaluate IEPs developed in by school IEP teams. The purposes of such evaluations should be to target problem areas in IEPs and develop training programs for team members and special education teachers so that they will have the skills to remedy these problems.

Determining Placement

Determining the placement of a student in special education should be a relatively straightforward process because it has essentially remained unchanged since the original passage of the EAHCA in 1975. A placement team, which includes a student's parents, reviews the student's IEP and determines the least restrictive environment in which his or her special education can be implemented and a FAPE can be provided.

Placement decisions must be based on a student's IEP (IDEA Regulations, 34 C.F.R. § 300.116(b)(2006). Although the placement decision is not actually a part of the IEP process, usually the IEP team determines a student's placement. The IDEA requires that a placement team, consisting of a student's parents, persons knowledgeable about the child, the meaning of the evaluation data and the placement options, determine a student's placement. Bateman (2011) asserted that the practice of having the IEP team determine placement is acceptable because parents are participating members of both the placement and the IEP team.

Perhaps the three most important requirements in determining students' placement are as follows. First the placement decision can only be made after the IEP is written. This is because the team needs to have a basis for determining where a student's unique educational needs can best be met, and this basis is his or her IEP. Case law has been abundantly clear on this point: A school district cannot assign placement before the education program is developed (Bateman, 2011; Lake, 2007). Some legal authorities have used the term "shoehorning" to describe the clearly illegal practice of placing a student in a program and then developing his or her IEP (i.e., goals and services) to fit the program (Lake, 2007; Slater, 2010).

Second, a student's placement must be individually determined based on his or her needs. IEP teams cannot place students in programs based on factors such as the students' category of disability, severity of disability, the availability of special education or related services, availability of space, or administrative convenience (71 Federal Register, 46,588; 2006). Whereas these factors may be considered they cannot be the sole determining factor in determining placement (Lake, 2007).

Third, students' placements must be made in accordance with the IDEA's principle of least restrictive environment (LRE). According to this principle (a) to the maximum extent appropriate students with disabilities should be educated with students who are not disabled, and (b) removal may occur only when education in the general education classroom with supplementary aides and services cannot be achieved satisfactorily. The IDEA, therefore, prefers general education placement but allows for more restrictive placements when attempts to maintain a student in general education by providing supplementary services has not been successful. Thus, IEP team members must make good-faith efforts, which should be documented, to educate a student in the least restrictive environment before proposing a more restrictive placement. When it is apparent that a student is not making academic progress in a particular placement, it is important the IEP team consider a placement in which a student will progress.

Unfortunately, placement has been an issue that has engendered a considerable amount of litigation (Slater, 2010). This is because school districts' often make procedural and substantive errors in determining a student's placement. We offer the following suggestions to assist special education administrators to ensure that their IEP teams or placement teachers correctly determine appropriate placements for students with disabilities.

- Ensure that IEPs team members develop students' IEPs prior to determining placement.
- Ensure that a student's parents are on the team that determines their son or daughter's educational placement.
- Ensure that a student's IEP or placement team determines his or her placement based on the student's individual needs and not on the student's category of disability or severity of disability. Similarly, do not substitute a policy of full inclusion for the consideration of a student's individual needs.
- Ensure that IEP teams make diligent, good faith efforts to educate students with disabilities in general education settings with supplementary aids and services. Monitor a student's progress and if a student is not succeeding in a placement, the IEP or placement team should meet to consider placement in a more appropriate, and sometimes more restrictive, setting.
- Ensure that when a decision is made to place a student in a more restrictive setting that the team thoroughly documents the decision-making process, including that they followed the continuum of alternative placements in a step-by-step manner. Additionally, in such situations the team should make all efforts to include opportunities for students with disabilities to be included in integrated settings.
- Ensure that placement and IEP teams avoid predetermining a student's placement.

Implementing the IEP

Following the development of a student's IEP it is the responsibility of the school district to implement the IEP as written. When implementing an IEP, it is important that administrators understand that in this respect the IEP is similar to a contractual obligation. That is, the school district is promising, in writing, to provide specific educational services to a particular student in order to ensure that the student receives a FAPE (Lake, 2007). The IEP is not a guarantee of performance but it is a guarantee of resources and services.

A number of cases have examined situations in which school districts have not implemented the IEP entirely as written. The primary issue in such cases is how perfect the implementation must be in order to comply with IDEA (Bateman, 2011). The U.S. Courts of Appeals for the 5th, 8th, and 9th Circuits have held that a school district's failure to implement an IEP must involve a significant or material failure to implement an IEP to arise to a violation of the IDEA and that a minor discrepancy between the IEP services listed and the actual services offered would not be a violation of the IDEA (*Houston Independent Sch. Dist. v. Bobby R.*, 2000; *Neosho R-V Sch. Dist. v. Clark*, 2003; *Van Duyn v Baker School District FJ*, 2007). Table 5.9 contains examples of significant failures to implement an IEP, which lead to a court ruling the district had violated the IDEA by not providing a FAPE.

Special education administrators should note that in cases such as *Houston Independent Sch. Dist. v. Bobby R.* (see Table 5.9) a ruling out of the 5th circuit in 2000, a school district did not violate the IDEA despite not implementing a student's IEP as entirely as written because the district was able to prove that their program had resulting in the student making meaningful educational progress. Moreover the 9th circuit in the Van Duyn ruling held that a court may consider a student's progress or lack thereof in determining the nature of a failure to implement an IEP (i.e., whether the error was substantial or minor). It is important that special education administrators ensure that all the services and resources included in a student's IEP are implemented.

The IDEA also requires that students' IEPs must be reviewed at least annually to determine whether the annual goals are being achieved (IDEA Regulations, 34 C.F.R. § 300.324 (b)(i)).

Table 5.9 Examples of LEAs Denying FAPE because of Inadequacies in Implementing IEPs

LEA Denied FAPE	
An LEA provided 3 hours per weeks of math instruction instead of the 8 to 10 hours listed in a student's IEP (*Van Duyn v. Baser Sch. Dist.*, 2007)	A student's special education teacher was unqualified, had no teaching certification, had no special education experience, and was unable to implement his IEP (*Damian J. v. School District of Philadelphia*, 2008)
An LEA failed to provide a behavior intervention plan as required by a student's IEP (*Nesho R-V. Sch. District v. Clark*, 2003)	An LEA discontinued a student's after school instruction even though it was written in the IEP (*Student with a Disability*, 2010)
An LEA provided 11 hours a week of reading instruction instead of 20 hours as required in a student's IEP (*Grossman Union High School Association*, 2006).	An assistive technology device that was required for FAPE was not included in an IEP (*Miami Dade County Sch. Bd.*, 2010)
An LEA failed to provide reading instruction of 20 hours per week for 5 months (*Anchorage SD v. Parents of M.P.*, 2006)	An LEA failed to provide an assistive technology device that was included in an IEP (*Lyon County Sch. Dist.*, 2010)
An LEA provided special education support services for only 74 of 97 days (*NYC Dept. of Ed*, 2006)	Although a student's IEP included a behavior information plan, many of the student's teachers didn't know about it and other teachers were misinformed about its contents (*Jefferson County Public School*, 2004)
A student's IEP called for a 1:1 aide but the aide was frequently pulled to perform other duties (*DB v. District of Columbia*, 2010)	An LEA failed to initiate behavioral interventions for 10 months after an IEP was developed (*Student with a Disability*, 2010)

Moreover if the review shows that the student is not progressing the IEP team must revise the IEP as appropriate to address the lack of expected progress toward the goals (IDEA Regulations, 34 C.F.R. § 300.324 (b)(ii)).

Special Education Administrators and the Law

Developing, implementing, and supervising special education programs requires a thorough knowledge of all aspects of special education law and an understanding of the relative importance of the different types of law and policy. Table 5.10 depicts sources of information that administrators may use to get information on special education law. Additionally, the Building the Legacy website (first entry in the table) contains excellent training materials on the IDEA developed by the National Dissemination Center for Children with Disabilities.

The following suggestions are offered to assist special education administrators in their important work.

Keep Abreast of Developments in Special Education Law

Special education administrators must stay current on developments in special education. The IDEA goes through a process called reauthorization every 4 to 6 years. Often the law is amended during the reauthorization process, which can mean significant changes in requirements of the IDEA and the IDEA regulations. Court rulings, especially those from the United States Supreme Court and the Circuit of Appeals in a special education administrator's judicial circuit, need to be monitored. To stay current with legal developments, special education administrators should attend conferences in which such information is presented. Additionally, administrators should

Table 5.10   Information on Special Education Law

Resource	URL
IDEA 2004 Training Materials (Building the legacy)	http://nichcy.org/laws/idea/legacy
Council of Administrators of Special Education (CASE)	www.casecec.org/
Developments in Special Education Law (Written by H. Jeffrey Marcus)	http://blog.jeffmarcuslaw.com/
Council of Exceptional Children	www.cec.sped.org
Office of Special Education's IDEA Website: Building the Legacy	http://idea.ed.gov/
Special Education Law Blog (Written by Charles Fox)	specialedlaw.blogs.com
Special Education Law Blog (Written by Jim Gerl)	Specialeducationlawblog.blogspot.com
Special Ed Connection (LRP, fee-based service)	www.specialedconnection.com
The Law and Special Education	www.ed.sc.edu/spedlaw/lawpage.htm
The Law and Special Education Blog (Witten by Mitchell Yell)	http://spedlaw.wordpress.com

consider becoming members of the Council of Administrators of Special Education (CASE). The Council is a division of the International Council of Exceptional Children (CEC).

It is also vital that special education administrators understand that federal and in-state laws and regulations are extremely important and must be strictly followed. With respect to litigation, the most important decisions for special education administrators will be rulings from the federal district and appellate courts with legal authority in their jurisdictions (i.e., the geographical territory over which the court has legal control). Decisions from courts in other jurisdictions may exert persuasive authority (i.e., courts that are not legally bound to follow a higher court's ruling because it is not in their jurisdiction but the judge or judges find the decisions so legally compelling that they adhere to the decisions when developing their legal position) but the decisions do not create precedence and are not legally binding. Decisions from the U.S. Supreme Court are always legally binding and must be understood by administrators.

Ensure that Faculty and Staff Understand Their Responsibilities Under the IDEA.

Because mistakes that are made during the special education process can result in school district liability, it is extremely important that principals and IEP team members understand their responsibilities and duties under the IDEA. Additionally, because the law is always evolving, special education teachers should be especially aware of developments in the law. For example, the IDEA is reauthorized, and often amended, every 4 or 5 years, so teachers should keep current in these developments in special education law. Additionally, litigation may result in important developments and should be followed. Special education administrators may ensure that principals and special education teachers keep current by providing relevant and meaningful professional development activities. Special education teachers should also be supported and encouraged to attend professional conferences in their fields, where such responsibilities are discussed.

Involve Parents in Meaningful Collaboration with School district Personnel in Developing Their Children's Special Education Programs

The IDEA requires that a student's parents are involved in all aspects of the special education process (e.g., assessment, IEP development, placement). Failing to include parents as meaningful partners in this process is a violation of the IDEA and could lead to a ruling that a school district did not provide a FAPE. Special education administrators need to inform IEP teams of the importance of parental involvement. When parents are difficult to convince to become involved, or they deliberately choose not to become involved, IEP teams must thoroughly document all efforts to encourage their involvement (e.g., documentation by phone records, emails, and home visits). Special education administrators should consider appointing staff members in their schools who are not directly engaged in the IEP process (e.g., counselors) to act as liaisons to parents who become involved in the special education process.

Ensure that LEA Personnel Develop Educationally Meaningful and Legally Sound IEPs

The IEP is the heart and soul of the IDEA. The primary responsibility of special education administrators is to ensure that IEP teams in the schools under their supervision have the skills and knowledge to develop special education programs that confer meaningful educational benefit and thus provide FAPE to all eligible students with disabilities. Administrators must ensure that IEP teams include members with expertise in (a) conducting assessments that provide relevant information for educationally planning, (b) writing measurable annual goals that are ambitious, (c) planning programming using empirically validate procedures, (d) monitoring student progress, and (e) analyzing progress monitoring data. When IEP teams develop ambitious goals and special education teachers use research-proven practices in their instruction, monitor student progress, and react in accordance with the information from the data, it is increases the likelihood that students will make meaningful educational progress, thus meeting the FAPE requirement of the IDEA.

Summary

It has been over 36 years since the passage of the IDEA. During this time the law has changed from an emphasis on access to public education to an emphasis on quality and accountability. During these years the responsibilities of special education administrators has also changed considerably. To successfully discharge their responsibilities, it is important that administrators understand the IDEA and how they may ensure that principals, faculty, and staff develop special education programs that provide a FAPE for all eligible students with disabilities. Because the IEP is the heart and soul of a FAPE, it is crucial that school-based teams working together with students' parents collaboratively develop IEPs that confer meaningful educational benefit. In this chapter we have highlighted the greatest areas of difficulty that schools have in special education programming and offered strategies and suggestions to assist school district personnel to develop IEPs that are educationally meaningful and legally sound.

Notes

1 In 1979 the Department of Education was created from the Department of Health, Education, and Welfare (HEW) and HEW became the Department of Health and Human Services
2 State regulations can be difficult to locate. The source in Table 5.2 contains links to the each states government website
3 Excellent information on the IDEA's dispute resolution system can be found at the website of the Center for Dispute Resolution in Special Education (CADRE: www.directservice.org/CADRE). The Office of Special Education Programs (OSEP) in the United States Department of Education funds the CADRE center.

References

Alberto, P. A., & Troutman, A. C. (2009). *Applied Behavior Analysis for Teachers* (8th ed.). Upper Saddle River, NJ: Pearson/Merrill Education.

Amanda J. v. Clark County Sch. Dist., 260 F.3d 1106 (9th Cir. 2001).

Bateman, B. D. (2007). *From gobbledygook to clearly written IEP goals*. Verona, WI: Attainment Co.

Bateman, B. D. (2011). Individual education programs for children with disabilities. In J. M. Kauffman & D. P. Hallahan (Eds.), *Handbook of special education* (pp. 91–106). New York: Routledge.

Big Beaver Falls Area School District v. Jackson, 624 A.2d 806 (PA Commonwealth, 1993)

Blau, A. (2007). The IDEIA and the right to an "appropriate" education. B.Y.U. *Education and Law Journal*, 1–24.

Board of Education of the Rhinebeck Central School District, 39 IDELR 148, 2003.

Board of Education of Hendrick Hudson Sch. Dist. v. Rowley, 458 U.S. 176 (1982).

Board of Education of the Arlington Central Sch. Dist., 42 IDELR 226 (SEA N.Y. 2004).

Board of Education of Monroe-Woodbury Central Sch. Dist., 31 IDELR 121 (SEA NY 1999).

County School Board of Henrico County, Virginia v. R.T., 433 F.Supp.2d 657 (E.D. VA 2006).

Cranston School District v. Q. D., 51 IDELR 41 (D. R.I. 2008).

Crockett, J. B., & Yell, M. L. (2008). Without data all we have are assumptions: Revisiting the meaning of a free appropriate public education. *Journal of Law and Education*, 37, 381–392.

Cypress-Fairbanks ISD v. Michael F., 118 F.3d. 245 (5th Cir. 1997).

Daniel, P. T. K., & Meinhardt, J. (2007). Valuing the Education of Students with Disabilities: Has Government Legislation Caused a Reinterpretation of Free Appropriate Public Education? *Education Law Reporter*, 222, 519–522.

DB v. District of Columbia, 720 F. Supp. 2d 83, D DC 2010

Deno, S. L. (1985). Curriculum-based measurement: The emerging alternative. *Exceptional Children*, 52, 219–232.

Doe v. Board of Education of Tullahoma Schools, 9 F.3d. 455 (6th Cir. 1993).

Doyle v. Arlington, 806 F.Supp. 1253 (E.D. VA 1992).

Draper v. Atlanta Independent School System, 47 IDELR 260 (N.D. Ga. 2007).

Elementary and Secondary Education Act, 20 U.S.C. § 1208(6)(B)

Escambia County Public School System, 42 IDELR 248 (SEA NY 2004).

Etscheidt, S., & Curran, C. M. (2010). Reauthorization of the Individuals With Disabilities Education Improvement Act (IDEA 2004): The peer-reviewed research requirement. *Journal of Disability Policy Studies*, 21, 29–39.

Eyer, T. (1998). Greater Expectations: How the 1997 IDEA amendments raise the basic floor of opportunity for children with disabilities, *Education Law Reporter*, 126, 1, 17.

Federal Register, 71, 46,588-46,674 (2006).

Gerl, J. (2011, June). *Special education law update: Judicial and administrative decisions*. Presentation for the South Carolina Hearing Officers, Columbia, SC.

Grossmont Union High School Association, 47 IDELR 144 (SEA Cal. 2006).

Hall v. Vance County Board of Education, 774 F.2d. 629 (4th Cir. 1985). (1985)

Henderson, A. T., & Mapp, K. L. (2002). *A new wave of evidence: The impact of school, family, and community connections on students' achievement*. Austin, TX: National Center of Family & Community Connections with Schools: Southwest Educational Development Laboratory.

House of Representatives Report, 105-95 at 83-84, May 13, 1997.

Houston Independent School District v. Bobby R., 200 F.3d 341 (5th Cir. 2000)

Huefner, D. F. (2008). Understanding the FAPE requirements under IDEA. *Journal of Law and Education*, 37, 367–380.

In re Student with a Disability, 47 IDELR 119 (SEA Alaska 2006).

Individuals with Disabilities Education Act (IDEA) of 2004, 20 U.S.C. § 1401 et seq.

Individuals with Disabilities Education Act Regulations of 2006, 34 C.F.R. § 300.1 et seq.

Individuals with Disabilities Education Improvement Act of 2004, Pub. L. No. 108, §446, 118 Stat. 2647 (2004)

Iovannone R., Dunlap G., Huber H., & Kincaid D. (2003). Effective Educational Practices for Students with Autism Spectrum Disorders. *Focus on Autism and Other Developmental Disabilities*, 18, 150–165.

J.C. v. Central Regional School District, 23 IDELR 1181 (3rd. Cir. 1996).

Jefferson County (KY) Public Schools, 43 IDELR 144 (OCR 2004).

Kirby v. Cabell County Board of Education, 46 IDELR § 156 (S.D. W. VA 2006).

Lake, S. E. (2007). Slippery slope! The IEP missteps every IEP team must know—And how to avoid them. Horsham, PA: LRP Publications.

Lyon County Sch. District, 110 LRP 73249, SEA NV 2010

M.P. v. South Brunswick Bd. of Educ., 51 IDELR 219 (D.N. J. 2008).

Maroni v. Pemi-Baker Regional School District, 343, F.3d 247 (1st Cir. 2003).

Miami Dade County School Board, 110 LRP 38102 SEA FL 2010

National Center on Progress Monitoring. (n.d.). Retrieved June 24, 2010, from http://www.studentprogress.org

Neosho R-V Sch. Dist. v. Clark, 315 F.3d 1022 (8th Cir. 2003)

Osborne, A. G. (1992). Legal standards for an appropriate education in the post-Rowley era. *Exceptional Children*, 58, 488–494.

Polk v. Central Susquehanna Intermediate Unit 16, 853 F.2d 171 (3rd Cir. 1988)

Questions and answers on individual education programs, evaluations and reevaluations. 47 IDELR §166 (OSERS, 2007).

Reschly, D. (2000). Assessment and eligibility determination in the Individuals with Disabilities Education Act of 1997. In C. Telzrow & M. Tankersley (Eds.), *IDEA Amendments of 1997: Practice guidelines for school-based teams* (pp. 65–104). Bethesda, MD: National Association of School Psychologists.

Rio Rancho Pub. Sch., 40 IDELR 140 (SEA N.M. 2003).

Slater, A. E. (2010). *Placement under the IDEA: Avoiding predetermination and other legal pitfalls.* Horsham, PA: LRP Publication.

Student with a Disability, 110 LRP 20100, SEA NY 2010

Student with a Disability, 110 LRP 22976, SEA NY 2010

Taylor v. Sandusky, 43 IDELR 4 (D. Md. 2005).

Turnbull, H. R. Turnbull, A .P., Stowe, M., & Huerta, N. (2007). *Free appropriate public education: The law and students with disabilities.* Denver, CO: Love Publishing.

Van Duyn v Baker School District FJ, 481 F.3d 770, (9th Cir. 2007)

Winkleman v. Parma City School District, 550 U.S. 516 (2007).

Yell, M. L. (2012). *The law and special education* (3rd ed.). Upper Saddle River, NJ: Pearson/Merrill Education.

Yell, M. L., & Crockett, J. B. (2011). Free appropriate public education. In J. M. Kauffman & D. P. Hallahan (Eds.), *Handbook of special education* (pp. 91–106). New York: Routledge.

Yell, M. L., & Drasgow, E. (2000). Litigating a free appropriate education: The Lovaas hearings and cases. *Journal of Special Education, 33,* 205–214.

Zirkel, P. A. (2008). Have the Amendments to the Individuals with Disabilities Education Act Razed *Rowley* and Raised the Substantive Standard for "Free Appropriate Public Education"? *Journal of the National Association of Administrative Law Judiciary, 28,* 396–418.

6

Financing Education for Children with Special Needs

Bruce D. Baker

RUTGERS UNIVERSITY

Preston C. Green, III

THE PENNSYLVANIA STATE UNIVERSITY

Matthew J. Ramsey

UNIVERSITY OF KANSAS

With the passage of PL 94-142, the Education for all Handicapped Children Act, now the Individual with Disabilities Education Act (IDEA), in 1975, states and local school districts were mandated to provide a free and appropriate public education (FAPE) to all children with disabilities.

Localized multi-disciplinary teams were charged with developing programs of education to meet the obligation of FAPE without regard to the cost of these services, thus creating a fiscal burden shared by federal, state and local educational authorities. While disability advocates continued to apply pressure for more and better services to students with disabilities, means to fund these services in a balanced manner created significant challenges for policy makers. More than 35 years later we find the field continuing to grapple with funding issues in the context of an equitable and adequate educational good for all students.

This chapter provides a review of general conceptions of equity and adequacy in school finance and within the context of special education funding. Further development of both regular education and special education law, reauthorizations of the Elementary and Secondary Education Act (ESEA), No Child Left Behind Act (NCLB), and IDEA and how they influence service delivery are explored. Additionally, we outline the conceptualization of financing public educations systems as a state responsibility. Next, we discuss approaches to determining the additional expenditures on special education and additional costs of providing special education services and review the evidence on special education spending and cost. Finally, we review state policies for financing special education programs and the literature on various features of those policies.

Conceptions of Equity and Adequacy

In this section, we review general concepts of school funding equity, equal educational opportunity and educational adequacy. Authors in school finance often attempt to separate too quickly from the relevant broader context, the position of children with one or more classified disabilities from the system as a whole and from the conceptual frameworks of equity and adequacy. To some extent, as we will discuss later in this chapter, this choice is driven by the separate federal legal framework governing special education, versus those governing the system as a whole.

Equity can be viewed either in terms of fiscal inputs alone, in terms of programs and services provided with those financial inputs, or in terms of outcomes attainable with specific inputs, programs and services. Further, equity can be, but is not by definition, linked to educational adequacy where the level of outcomes attainable with given inputs, programs and services is characterized as "adequate" or not. Finally, while it should go without saying, generalized conceptions of equity and adequacy are applicable across all children.

Equity of Nominal Fiscal Inputs

Equity of nominal fiscal inputs to schooling concerns only whether or not schools and school districts have access to equal dollar inputs—equal revenues and/or expenditures per pupil— regardless of their location or of other attributes of the district or children they serve. On the one hand, evaluating equity of nominal fiscal inputs is convenient and straightforward because nominal dollar values are readily available.

But, it has become clear over time that this approach does not adequately characterize either the programs and services available to children across settings and locations or the outcomes attainable. For example, in geographically and economically diverse states such as Illinois, New York, Texas, or California the costs of putting comparable quality teachers in front of classrooms filled with 20 children each can vary widely from one end of the state to another.[1] Further, it would clearly be inappropriate to provide the same level of financial resources for children having severe disabilities as for the "average" child in a school district, because the appropriate programs and services required for children with disabilities may have substantially different costs.

Equity of Programs and Services

An alternative perspective on equity is that each child, school, and school district should be provided sufficient fiscal inputs in order to be able to provide equal, or the same programs and services to children. That is, to provide a specific quantity and quality of teachers, quality of classroom space, materials, supplies and equipment regardless of where in the state a child attends school and regardless of the attributes of children who attend any given school. This approach can be a significant step forward over evaluating fiscal inputs alone.

Clearly, it is more relevant to determine that each child across a state has access to similarly qualified teachers and his or her own box of crayons, etc., whether that box of crayons costs $1.00 in one location or $1.25 per box in another or whether the salary required for hiring the teacher is $45,000 in one location or $65,000 in another. But this approach assumes only that each child should receive the same programs and services, regardless of any differences there might be in: (a) the individual needs of students in order to achieve desired outcomes, (b) the collective needs of the student population in order to achieve desired outcomes, or (c) the setting within which the resources must be provided in order to achieve desired outcomes. Regarding setting, for example, it may be infeasible to organize children into symmetrical classes of 20 each per grade level in remote rural locations. Setting alone may constrain the equal provision of programs and services.

Equity of programs and services requires only that students—regardless of their individual differences—have access to the same programs and services. But, in the case of children with disabilities, there may exist specific additional programs, services, and related services that would more appropriately meet their needs.

Equal Educational Opportunity

Differentiating programs and services across children requires that we address two key questions: Who is in need of differential programs and services? And how different should those programs and services be? Equal educational opportunity concerns not merely the equal provision of programs and services (inputs), but rather, the provision of programs and services which provide all children across the state equal opportunity to achieve comparable educational outcomes. This differs from an equal provision of inputs—programs and services—because equal educational opportunity acknowledges that the costs of achieving specific educational outcomes vary not only as a function of the different prices of inputs, but also as a function of the different sets of inputs that may be needed for one group of children versus another, educated in one type of setting versus another.

Under an equal educational opportunity framework, all children are assumed equal regardless of race, language proficiency, poverty status, or disability status. As such, our expectations of educational outcomes should be common across all children. That is, the "equity object" in question is the outcome expectation, which should be accessible to each and every child. The cost of attaining the equity object—educational outcomes—for each child varies by location, setting, and child.

While some factors more strongly affect the cost of attaining outcomes, the various factors that influence cost interact in important ways, leading to an overall relative cost of equal opportunity to achieve outcomes for each child in each setting. Ignoring these differences in costs when providing financial inputs to schools leads to disparity across children in the ability to attain, and ultimately in the attainment itself, of equitable educational outcomes. Even "equal" nominal financial inputs across substantively different settings and children leads to unequal opportunities.

While the pure conception of equal educational opportunity requires differentiation of inputs, programs and services to the extent necessary to achieve equal educational outcomes, practical applications often accept the logic of equal educational opportunity but otherwise fall short on full provision of equal opportunity. For example, financing for special education programs or programs for children with limited English language proficiency may on average be greater than for the hypothetical "average" child, but rarely if ever are such resources scaled up to the point that equal outcomes are attainable.

Educational Adequacy

Educational adequacy concerns the level of educational outcomes that should be attainable either by all children in a state in the aggregate or by children according to their individual needs and school setting. In the aggregate, a state's education system could be deemed adequate merely on the basis that a sufficient number of students overall achieve an adequate educational outcome—for example, 80% of all students, statewide scoring proficient or higher on state assessments. That is, adequacy in isolation means only that a sufficient number of students perform sufficiently well, regardless of who may or may not be left out and regardless of the extent that some children far exceed the "adequacy" threshold. In fact, such an adequacy standard could be achieved while leaving behind the vast majority of children with disabilities. Significant equity concerns may arise when statewide adequacy is the exclusive focus.

At the intersection of *educational adequacy* and *equal opportunity* lies the notion that all children, regardless of their individual differences or where they attend school in a state are deserving of *equal opportunity* to achieve *adequate* educational outcomes. This notion is an extension of *equal educational opportunity* as explained above. Where *equal educational opportunity* provides that each child have equal opportunity to achieve any given set of outcomes, *equal opportunity* linked with *adequacy* provides that each child have equal opportunity to achieve a specific set of adequate educational outcomes.

Caught Between IDEA and NCLB

Here we provide a brief synopsis of position of children with disabilities—in terms of legal frameworks for understanding equal educational opportunities—under the *due process* oriented IDEA framework and under the outcomes oriented NCLB. Albeit an oversimplified delineation (as framed here), differing perspectives regarding rights to access least restrictive environments and free and appropriate education versus obligations to close outcome gaps between subgroups lead to very different assumptions regarding financial obligation of states and local public school districts. These assumptions are further complicated by a recent string of case law which potentially increases state and local school district financial obligation to support costs of private placements.

The NCLB's purpose is "to ensure that all children have a fair, equal, and significant opportunity to obtain a high-quality education and reach, at a minimum, proficiency on challenging State academic achievement standards and state academic assessments."[2] One of the goals of NCLB is to meet "the educational needs of low-achieving children in our Nation's highest-poverty schools."[3] The Act also provides as one of its goals the closure of "the achievement gap between high- and low-performing children, especially the achievement gaps between minority and nonminority students, and between disadvantaged children and their more advantaged peers."[4]

IDEA's purpose is "to ensure that all children with disabilities have available to them a free appropriate public education that emphasizes special education and related services designed to meet their unique needs and prepare them for further education, employment, and independent living."[5] The statute also seeks to protect the rights of students of disabilities and their parents.[6] The statute also tries to "assist States, localities, educational service agencies, and Federal agencies to provide for the education of all children with disabilities."[7]

IDEA and NCLB have ostensibly different and conflicting goals. IDEA requires school districts to provide students with a basic floor of education as defined by the Individual Education Plan (IEP). The educational goals are based upon the student's ability as determined by the student's multi-disciplinary team. By contrast, NCLB provides a framework in which all children must be provided equal educational opportunity. Congress and the Department of Education have attempted to harmonize IDEA with NCLB (Huefner, 2008). The 2004 authorization of IDEA requires all IEP's to maintain "present levels of *academic* achievement and the *academic* achievement goals," regardless of the disability.[8]

In an apparent attempt to overcome the conflict between NCLB and IDEA, the 2004 reauthorization of IDEA also requires that children with disabilities participate in state assessments promulgated under NCLB, but with accommodations where appropriate. NCLB regulations "acknowledge the need for flexibility when assessing children with disabilities and now specify three kinds of alternative assessments of reading and math flexibility."[9] IDEA 2004 also contains "parallel alternate assessment provisions in IEP requirements and elsewhere in the statute."[10] While assessments of children with disabilities may influence school or district accountability status under NCLB, the extent and type of accommodations required for some children may significantly compromise the reliability and meaningfulness of those assessments as a true measure of "adequate" educational outcomes for children with disabilities. In our view, this attempted link between NCLB and IDEA frameworks falls well short of fully integrated the legal frameworks of equity and adequacy for children with disabilities and the general population of which they are a part.

School Finance: A State Responsibility

While IDEA and NCLB provide conflicting federal statutory guidelines, most concerns over school funding equity and adequacy are governed under state constitutions as interpreted by state courts, and as acted upon by state legislatures. State school funding formulas, including components of those formulas pertaining to special education are primarily the responsibility of the states. In this section, we explain how the financing of equal educational opportunity has evolved over time to become primarily a state responsibility. We focus on the role of state school finance litigation emphasizing state constitutional obligations to provide funding to local public school districts in order to first, balance differences in local fiscal capacity to provide educational services, and second to target resources to student populations with greater needs. We end this section with a discussion of specific state school finance cases in which courts have articulated a strong state obligation to provide differentiated funding toward achieving equal educational opportunity.

Overview of Waves of Litigation

Many scholars describe school finance litigation as occurring in three major waves. The first wave, in the late 1960s and early 1970s, entailed challenges to school funding equity in federal court and was based on the Equal Protection Clause of the 14th Amendment to the U.S. Constitution. It ended abruptly with the Supreme Court's ruling in *San Antonio Independent School District v. Rodriguez* in 1973 (411 U.S. 1 (1973)). The Court decided that education is not a fundamental right under the U.S. Constitution and that wealth is not a "suspect classification." Upon making these determinations, the Court then determined that differences in financial resources that result from differences in local wealth and property taxation do not violate equal protection. This ruling does not, however, protect states against federal equal protection challenges to other forms of differences in school funding (Green & Baker, 2002).

The second wave, which emerged concurrently with the first, focused on state constitutions rather than the federal constitution. Plaintiff groups argued that disparities in funding across school districts—largely resulting from differences in property tax revenues—ran afoul of state equal protection and education clauses. This approach had limited success, with courts in six states overturning their school finance formulas while 13 other state formulas were upheld (Baker, Green, & Richards, 2008, p. 86). The beginning of the third wave, which was also based on state constitutional provisions, is usually marked by the 1989 Kentucky Supreme Court's decision in *Rose v. Council for Better Education*. That case shifted the focus toward "adequate" education funding, where adequacy was defined in terms of funding sufficient to produce adequate student outcomes. *Rose* was followed by several successful third wave challenges throughout the 1990s and early 2000s.

Nevertheless, the successes of the 1990s have given way to some judicial reluctance to engage (Welner & Gebhardt, 2011). From 2007 through 2009, there were some signs of a waning of political will on the part of some state courts to rule against state legislatures or to maintain oversight of school funding as part of existing remedial processes. State courts in Arizona (*Espinoza v. State*, 2008), Oklahoma (*Oklahoma Education Association v. State*, 2007), Missouri (*Committee for Educational Equality v. State of Missouri*, 2009) Nebraska (*Nebraska Coalition for Educational Equity and Adequacy v. Heineman*, 2007), South Dakota (*Davis v. State of South Dakota, 2009*), and New Jersey (*Abbott v. Burke*, 2009) upheld as constitutional their states' existing state school funding formulas, rejecting claims by plaintiffs that those funding systems deprive poor and minority children of much-needed resources. While the degree of funding inequities and inadequacies varies widely in these six states, the overall sense from the decisions rendered in these cases was one of judicial retreat and deference to the politics of legislative decision making.

One might expect such judicial timidity to have increased following the sharp economic downturn that began in mid-2008 and placed increased scrutiny on state budgets and expenditures across the board, and on elementary and secondary education spending in particular. However, three decisions handed down in late 2009 and early 2010 suggest that the earlier trend toward retreat has not continued. In *Lobato v. State* (2009), the Colorado Supreme Court held an adequacy challenge to be justiciable and sent the case back to the trial court. In *McCleary v. State* (2010), the trial court in the Washington found that state's finance system unconstitutional because it is "not correlated to what it actually costs to operate this State's public schools" (p. 53, para. 220). And in *Connecticut Coalition for Justice in Education Funding, Inc. v. Rell* (2010), the Connecticut Supreme Court decided that the issue of whether education funding legislation makes "suitable provision" for education is justiciable.

Recent Special Education Cases with Significant Financial Implications

A handful of recent cases have raised new questions regarding the financial obligations of local public school districts to provide financing for services for children with disabilities. In *Forest Grove School District v. T.A.* (129 S.Ct. 2484, 2009), the Supreme Court held that IDEA authorized reimbursement of private-education tuition where the school district had failed to provide that child with FAPE and the private education was appropriate. The Court found in this manner even though the school district had not provided the child with special services. By finding that the child was ineligible for special-education services and refusing to provide him with an IEP, the district failed to offer him FAPE as required by the statute.

The Potential Influence of IDEA on State School Finance Systems

While *Forest Grove* in particular may place pressure on local school districts to pay the high cost associated with out-of-district placements, the case does not necessarily place any increased burden on states to ensure that local public school districts have the available resources to cover those costs. One case currently progressing through the federal courts attempts to press the Commonwealth of Pennsylvania to alter its special education funding formula to ensure that poorer districts with very high concentrations of children with disabilities have sufficient resources to comply with IDEA.[11] According to Weber (20010):

> One court has upheld a claim that the Pennsylvania funding formula, which requires the state to allocate special education funds based on a school district's overall average daily membership, rather than on the district's special education needs or ability to provide appropriate education (combined with the guarantee that the district not receive less special education money than in year before and a mechanism for funding tuition for approved private schools separately) violated due process rights, section 504, and the Equal Educational Opportunity Act and caused the plaintiffs, who were parents of special education students in the district, injury in fact.
>
> *(p. 34)*

This particular case hinges on an argument that the Pennsylvania special education finance formula, and the way in which the formula built on top of disparities in general education funding, leads to substantially unequal opportunities across Pennsylvania school districts with regard to providing individualized educational programs compliant with IDEA.

Understanding Costs and Additional Expenditures

In order to advocate that opportunities for children with disabilities should not only be equal across children with disabilities, but should also be adequate with respect to desired educational outcomes and appropriate programs and services, one would need reasonably precise estimates of the costs of achieving adequate educational outcomes and/or providing appropriate programs and services. In this section we evaluate the knowledge base regarding the additional costs of providing services to children with disabilities. We link cost conceptions back to equal educational opportunity conceptions, noting that cost analysis, per se, for children with disabilities has traditionally taken either of two approaches—estimation of the average expenditures of average existing programs and services for children with disabilities in general and by need and placement, and more recently, estimation of hypothetically "adequate" staffing and non-staffing resources for providing statutorily compliant special education programs and services. Notably absent in cost analysis of special education programs and services are analysis of the cost of producing adequate educational outcomes, or closing achievement gaps between children with mild to moderate disabilities and other children.

Measuring Education Costs

Evaluating educational opportunity and educational adequacy requires estimating the costs of achieving adequate educational outcomes across varied settings and children. There exist two general categories of methods for determine the differences in costs of providing equal educational opportunity:

Input-oriented: The first involves prescribing the resource inputs necessary for providing basic educational services and special educational services. Inputs required for service delivery may either be prescribed by panels of local constituents, practitioners and experts, or by outside expert consultants. This approach leads to estimates of the differential costs of recommended educational services for different settings and children, the intent being that the differential services (and resulting cost differentials) recommended will aid in the attainment of common educational outcomes.

Outcome-oriented: A more direct approach involves estimating a model of the statistical relationships among existing spending levels (education cost function), existing outcome levels and various factors that influence the ways in which current spending is associated with current outcomes. That is, to use existing data to tease out underlying differences in costs of producing specific levels of education outcomes across settings and children.

Ideally, if one wished to estimate the costs of providing children with disabilities the opportunity to achieve defined, measured outcome levels, one would need sufficient data on children with varied levels of disabilities meeting the defined outcome standards, and sufficient data on expenditures on those children. That is, to conduct outcome oriented analyses, one needs sufficiently detailed outcome data and sufficiently accurate spending data, as well as all relevant information on students' individual needs. Such analyses can prove problematic for estimating costs of achieving common outcomes for children requiring substantial accommodations on the assessments that measure those outcomes. Several outcome based models of education costs do include estimates of the additional spending associated with achieving common outcomes for children with disabilities, but there has been little attempt as of yet to evaluate the consistency of those findings. Further, most such analyses include either a single measure of the percent of children classified, or a bifurcated measure indicating high-cost-low-incidence, and low-cost-high-incidence disabilities.

More commonly, studies of additional costs for special education students evaluate either: (a) existing spending on existing programs and services, regardless of outcomes achieved; or (b) the summed input costs of recommended resources for providing programs and services (Baker et al., 2008). Studies of expenditures on existing programs and services generally do not evaluate whether those existing programs and services produce adequate educational outcomes, or whether those programs and services would be considered adequate or appropriate. Rather, such studies merely characterize the average of "what is" (Baker et al., 2008).

Alternatively, some studies of educational costs attempt to estimate the costs of implementing programs and services that should be adequate, or appropriate, or a hypothetical "what should be." But, these studies rarely follow up on evaluating whether the programs and services produce adequate student outcomes. Alternatively, one could attempt to identify high quality existing programs and service delivery models that produce adequate student outcomes for children with one or more specific disabilities, and determine the costs of providing those programs and/or service delivery models.

Historical Efforts to Evaluate Special Education Costs and Spending

Over the decades following initial adoption of IDEA (as P.L. 94-142), there have been a handful of national studies of special education spending. Most recently, the Special Education Expenditures Project (SEEP), conducted by the Center for Special Education Finance (CSEF), run by the American Institutes for Research (AIR), studied past special education expenditures, in order to identify the "additional expenditures" on special education students in the late 1990s and early 2000s.

Findings of the SEEP studies published in 2002 included:

- The total spending to provide a combination of regular and special education services to students with disabilities amounted to $77.3 billion, or an average of $12,474 per student. Students with disabilities for other special needs programs (e.g., Title I, ELL, or gifted and talented students) received an additional $1 billion, bringing the per-student amount to $12,639.
- The additional expenditure to educate the average student with a disability is estimated to be $5,918 per student. This is the difference between the total expenditure per student eligible for special education services ($12,474) and the total expenditure per regular education student ($6,556).
- Based on 1999–2000 school year data, the total expenditure to educate the average student with disabilities is an estimated *1.90 times* that expended to educate the typical regular education student with no special needs. This ratio has actually declined since 1985, when Moore, Strang, Schwartz, and Braddock (1988) estimated it to be 2.28 (Chambers, Parrish, & Harr, 2002).

That is, the average additional expense per special education child has remained somewhat consistent, declining slightly, at about twice the average expense per "regular" education child. The authors of SEEP explain that they have evaluated the "additional expenditures" associated with special education rather than "excess costs," the language of earlier special education spending studies (Chambers et al., 2002. As discussed previously, additional expenditures are merely the amount that public schools have spent, historically, on special education students. Additional expenditures are not costs, because no specific quality of service exists, and because no outcome standard is associated with the spending patterns (other than the average of current practice).

In the aggregate, the SEEP studies determined that local education agencies received $3.7 billion in federal IDEA funding in 1999–2000, accounting for 10.2% of the additional total expenditure on special education students (or $605 per special education student), and about 7.5% of total special education spending. If Medicaid funds are included, federal funding covers 12% of the total additional expenditure on special education students (i.e., 10.2% from IDEA and 1.8% from Medicaid) (Chambers et al., 2002).

Chambers (1999) offers a more fine-grained approach to resource-cost analysis in special education involving five dimensions: (a) type of environment (departmentalized, non-departmentalized[12]); (b) grade levels; (c) service prototype (regular classroom, outside the regular classroom, or separate facility); (d) primary disability; and (e) student need (extent of curricular, behavioral, or medical–physical adaptations necessary to provide instructional services).

Using data on existing special education services in Massachusetts in the 1990s, Chambers conducted an analysis of additional expenditures of special education services at the intersections of the various dimension listed previously. Chambers found that on average, expenditures on a special education student in a non–departmentalized setting was 2.17 times that for educating the regular education student; in a departmentalized setting, the spending was 1.21 times regular education spending; and in an external assignment, the spending was 8.38 times regular education spending.

Chambers (1999) found that additional spending for students in grades 4–8 in non–departmentalized settings were 3% above (1.03 times) spending for grades 1–3 in non–departmentalized settings. In addition, the ratio of base expenditures for a student with disabilities compared to a regular education student was 1.24 for non–departmentalized settings. Finally, students requiring minor curricular adaptation had additional spending 17% above (1.17 times) those requiring no curricular adaptation. Multiplying the weights across the dimensions, we find that this student has additional spending toward his or her education of 1.49 ($1.03 \times 1.24 \times 1.17 = 1.49$).

Special Education Costs in the Context of Educational Adequacy Studies

Over the past decade and a half, there has been an increasing trend of state legislatures and interest groups contracting external consultants to conduct cost studies in order to determine the costs of providing all children in a given state with a constitutionally adequate education. These studies have generally been conducted under either of two scenarios. First, state legislatures have contracted outside firms to assist them in estimating the costs of providing an education system that meets state constitutional standards for educational adequacy. In some cases, state legislatures have undertaken this activity seemingly preemptively or at least with previous school funding litigation well in the rear view mirror, but in other cases legislatures have undertaken this activity while under judicial oversight or during the remedy phase of litigation. Alternatively, many similar studies have been sponsored by individuals or groups staging legal challenges over funding equity and adequacy against states (see Baker, 2006). Much has been written about the variability in findings across these studies, especially in regard to the underlying basic costs of educational adequacy across states (Baker, 2006). However, little has been written about the often deeply buried findings of these studies regarding special education programs and costs.

Table 6.1 lists a series of studies all using a method known as Professional Judgment Analysis, each of these studies is also addressed by Baker, Taylor, and Vedlitz (2005). As discussed above, a professional judgment study relies on the knowledge and wisdom of panels of selected experts to propose a set of schooling inputs (human resources, physical resources, time) that would be

Table 6.1 Findings from State Level Resource Cost Studies of Education Costs (through 2008)

State Study	Study Method	Author	Data (estimate) Year	Base (0 Additional Needs)	Adj. Basic Cost	Sped Mild	Sped Moderate	Sped Severe	Sped Overall
Colorado PJ	PJ	Augenblick & Colleagues	2002	$6,815	$6,113				1.11
Colorado PJ2	PJ	Augenblick & Colleagues	2005	$7,237	$5,965	0.94	1.80	5.23	
Connecticut PJ	PJ	Augenblick & Colleagues	2004	$9,207	$6,823	1.12	1.45	3.32	
Kansas PJ	PJ	Augenblick & Colleagues	2001	$5,811	$6,172				2.08
Maryland PJ	PJ	Augenblick & Colleagues	2000	$6,612	$5,967				1.17
Minnesota PJ	PJ	Augenblick & Colleagues	2005	$5,938	$4,857				1.00
Missouri PJ	PJ	Augenblick & Colleagues	2002	$7,832	$7,542				1.23
Montana PJ	PJ	Augenblick & Colleagues	2002	$6,004	$6,999				1.20
Montana PJ	PJ	APA	2007	$9,030	$9,025	0.77	1.32	2.93	
Nebraska PJ	PJ	Augenblick & Colleagues	2001	$5,845	$6,376				1.57
Nevada PJ	PJ	Augenblick & Colleagues	2004	$7,229	$5,883	0.90			
New Jersey PJ	PJ	Augenblick & Colleagues	2005	$8,016	$5,610		1.42	4.08	
North Dakota PJ	PJ	Augenblick & Colleagues	2002	$6,005	$6,570	1.08			
Pennsylvania	PJ	Augenblick & Colleagues	2006	$8,003	$6,427				1.30
South Dakota	PJ	APA	2004	$6,362	$6,790	1.33			
Tennessee PJ	PJ	Augenblick & Colleagues	2003	$6,207	$5,785	0.48	1.00	3.45	

sufficient for achieving adequate educational outcomes. To a large extent, these proposals are hypothetical and, to at least some extent, the proposed resources draw on the actual experiences and actual resources that inform those on Table 6.1. Nonetheless, this approach is somewhat different from prior SEEP studies which looked only at actual programs and services and spending on them.

Table 6.1 shows the underlying basic cost—cost per pupil for a child with no additional special needs from each study, and the additional costs—or cost weights derived from each study for special education. Only some of these studies endeavored to determine different weights based on severity of need. None is as precise as the late 1990s exercise undertaken by Chambers (1999). Overall weights tend to be somewhat greater than 100% above basic costs, consistent with previous studies of actual spending. These weights appear somewhat higher, which might be explained by panelists recommending desired, adequate resource levels rather than current averages. But, the comparisons between average expenditure studies and these estimates are imperfect. Average expenditure studies express the special education marginal spending as a ratio to the average cost of non-special education children and not to the minimum, as done in Table 6.1. The ratio to the minimum cost will necessarily appear higher than the ratio to the average expense.

On review of these various studies, one concern we raise is that most appear not to dedicate sufficient space to discussing the rationale for their proposed service delivery configurations for special education. Rather, the studies report the panelists' final determinations and may include a handful of footnotes to selective studies on special education. It is difficult to evaluate the "reasonableness" of the proposed staffing configurations for special education with respect to the likelihood of improving outcomes for children with disabilities.

State School Finance Formulas & Children with Special Needs

As explained herein, it is ultimately a state responsibility to ensure that general and special education funding is adequate and equitably distributed across school districts, schools and children statewide. Despite decades of promises, federal funds provide only modest support. Local districts ultimately bear the burden of complying with IDEA, regardless of state support. Here, we review basic approaches used by states in their school funding formulas for providing differentiated funding—or not—across local public school districts in order to meet the needs of children with disabilities—to provide them with equal educational opportunity. Five basic mechanisms are used to deliver special education funding to local school districts, as described by Ahearn (2010).

- Weighted Pupil: "Funding (either a series of multiples of the general education amount or tiered dollar amounts) allocated per special education student that varies by disability, type of placement, or student need." Or "Funding (either a single multiple of the general education amount or a fixed dollar amount) allocated per special education student" (p. 3).
- Resource Based: "Funding based on payment for a certain number of specific education resources (e.g., teachers or classroom units), usually determined by prescribed staff/student ratios that may vary by disability, type of placement or student need" (p. 3).
- Percentage Reimbursement: "Funding based on a percentage of allowable, actual expenditures" (p. 3).
- Census-Based: "A fixed dollar amount per total enrollment or Average Daily Membership" (ADM) (p. 3).
- Block Grant: Funding based on base-year or prior year allocations, revenues, and/or enrollment (p. 3).

In the late 1980s and early 1990s, concerns emerged over the growth in special education populations and special education spending, along with concerns that specific funding mechanisms which increased funding in relation to classified headcounts (such as weighted funding) might lead to inappropriate growth in classification rates. In some cases, state policymakers responded by adopting "census-based" funding models which distribute an equal share of funds to all districts based on an assumed fixed share of the student population qualifying for special education programs.

Funding Formula Type—Fiscal, Classification and Placement Effects

There exists a modest body of research on the effects of these alternative funding mechanisms on the provision of special education programming and classification of children with disabilities. A handful of studies have validated underlying concerns addressed by census based financing that local public school districts are in fact responsive to financial incentives for identification and service of children with disabilities and further that capitation of the fiscal incentive, by methods such as census-based financing can limit increased identification. For example, Cullen (2003) notes: "My central estimates imply that fiscal incentives can explain nearly 40% of the recent growth in student disability rates in Texas. The magnitude of the institutional response varies by district size and enrollment concentration, student race/ethnicity and the level of fiscal constraint." (p. 1557). Lipscomb (2009) notes that Dhuey and Lipscomb (2009) find evidence of a strong association between states adopting capitation systems for special education from 1991–92 to 2003–04 and a post-reform decline in their learning disability rates that averaged about 7%. In addition, Kwak (2008 cited in Lipscomb, 2009) concludes that finance reform in California decreased the state's special education enrollment rate.

Cullen (2003) also points to distributional effects of fiscal incentives, explaining that districts with greater Black populations in Texas were more responsive (increasing special education identification rates) to state aid for special education and districts receiving low state aid were more likely to attempt to increase aid through special education. In short, fiscal incentives created by headcount-sensitive special education aid may lead not only to greater overall growth in special education populations but also to disparate distributions of identified students in relation to district conditions. That is, fiscal incentives may explain a portion of the unevenness of special education populations across districts within states, specifically increased identification of speech impairments in the elementary grades and learning disabilities in the secondary grades.

The above mentioned studies, however, do not endeavor to determine whether the incentivized identification rates are closer to or further from actual underlying rates of special educational needs among student populations clustered in districts, which is a difficult if not implausible empirical task. Rather, the implicit assumption is that any incentivized increase in identification leads to identification rates that are further from true need. Further, any correction by capitation necessarily leads to identification rates closer to true need. This may be far from true if incentives are created in areas where children with disabilities were previously underserved or if strict capitation policies provide insufficient resources to very high need districts lacking sufficient alternative revenues sources to accommodate those needs.

Other studies, framed as evaluation studies of state special education finance programs, have focused on the virtues of census-based funding such as flexibility in use of resources provided via census-based block grants and the potential for greater inclusion of special education students in general education programs. Chambers, Parrish, and Hikido (1996) evaluate the Massachusetts census-based finance formula, and, while the study explored special education revenues and expenditures across district grade range types and by specific services provided, the study did not evaluate the equity effects of distributing census-based grants across districts by shares of actual students served, nor did the study address variations in rates of actual students served or whether overall rates and variation in rates across districts have changed substantively since implementing census based funding.

Few studies have attempted to address head-on, the primary concern associated with census-based funding, expressed by Parrish and Harr (2005) as follows: "Concerns in regard to possible identification and placement incentives would be neutralized by adoption of a census-based system. However, this approach leads to other concerns, e.g., the possible incentive to under-identify and under-serve special education students (p. 10, note 3)

The California studies conducted for the state by Parrish and colleagues (Parrish, Kaleba, Gerber, & McKaughli, 1998; Parrish, Harr, Kidron, Brock, & Anand, 2003) began to address this issue for a limited subset of special education students—those with higher cost, more severe disabilities. Reiterating the concern above, Parrish and colleagues (1998) note: "A potential problem associated with population-based systems, however, is that they appear to be based on the assumption of an equal prevalence of students requiring special education. That is, one possible rationale for having districts or states of the same size receive the same amount of special education funding is the assumption that incidence rates for students with disabilities are approximately the same across jurisdictions. The purpose of this study is to test this assumption, and if found to be false, to recommend appropriate adjustments to the new AB 602 funding system" (pp. vi–vii).

Parrish et al. (1998) found that "severe and/or high cost students are *not* randomly distributed throughout the state. These findings were consistent and clear, regardless of the definition of severity used" (pp. vi–vii). This finding was reiterated in a follow-up study 5 years later. Both studies eventually proposed statistical methods based on census data to provide adjusted special education enrollment counts to be used for financing services for more severely disabled students. No attempt was made to evaluate whether similar methods might be appropriate for students with less severe disabilities and no attempt was made to discern whether these students also vary in concentration across districts at rates greater than chance alone. Parrish (2000b), however, explains that around the same time, New York State had developed a census based funding formula which included a poverty-based adjustment for special education populations including lower severity, higher incidence students.

A Pennsylvania study conducted by the Pennsylvania Department of Education (PDE) endeavored to determine the underlying causes of wide variations in special education identification rates across districts in that state several years after implementing a census-based funding formula which was intended to curb such variation. The study audited the identification practices of districts identified as having disproportionately high and disproportionately low special education identification rates. The study found that "High incidence school districts were reported to be disproportionately poor, with high rates of student/family mobility, and community based social services which attract and hold families likely to have students at-risk" (PDE, 2000, p. 6).

The report found demographic measures including poverty and racial composition to explain significant amounts of the variation in incidence rates across districts (PDE 2000, see statistical analysis in report appendix). That is, the report found that even several years after special education had been de-incentivized in Pennsylvania, factors such as poverty remained associated with special education identification rates. Perhaps more importantly, however, the study found no differences in the identification practices of higher and lower incidence districts, specifically that "all districts generally adhered to the processes and procedures outlined in law, and districts with high incidence rates used virtually the same procedures and processes as districts with low incidence rates" (p. 6).

In many states, disability incidence rates measured by identification practices of school district officials range from as low as 5% in some districts to nearly 30% in others, even in states that have maintained census-based finance formulas for decades. The majority of identified students in these districts are students with speech impairments, specific learning disabilities and behavioral disorders. Census-based school finance formulas assume that the true underlying distribution is even across districts, in sharp contrast with existing distributions that result from district identification practices. Few attempts have been made to reconcile district identification practices with the census-based assumption, or to validate the census-based assumption disregarding district practices.

Parrish (2000a), like the PDE study, points to a correlation between district poverty rates, minority concentrations and special education identification rates. But, authors of studies revealing such patterns are tentative about suggesting that race and poverty are associated with true prevalence of disabilities, rather ascribing the relationship to biases in district identification procedures. If these patterns do represent bias rather than actual need, it would be appropriate to implement policies to curb the bias. However, there may exist real connections between poverty and learning disability rates. For example, numerous studies have indicated a strong relationship between low birth weight and learning disabilities (Litt, Taylor, Klein, & Hack, 2005), and further a connection between low birth weight and socio-economic status.

The PDE (2000) study also indicates a likelihood of parents of children with disabilities to locate themselves in communities with more comprehensive services for children with disabilities. The availability of such services and migration patterns of parents of children with disabilities might explain a portion of remaining variation in district identification rates in states that are geographically diverse. Yet, little strong empirical research addresses the geographic distribution of families of children with disabilities and mobility patterns of families upon having a child identified as having a disability.

A study of Pennsylvania and New Jersey by Baker and Ramsey (2010) shows that children with disabilities tend to be spatially clustered by locations within states. That is, incidence rates vary widely by location in a state and school district incidence rates are associated with census data on disabilities in the general population. Baker and Ramsey use U.S. Census American Community Survey Data to explore family self-reported disability status by city location within states and broad region across states and then correlate those data to district classification rates. While the relationship between census self-reports and district classification rates was fuzzy, the geographic variations in disability rates were undeniable. As a result, Baker and Ramsey show that adopting the assumption of census based financing can lead to severe inequities in the distribution of special education aid.

Finally, Baker (2003) indicates that districts in states using percentage reimbursement programs for special education generally have more funding available to use on their core instructional programs. That is, special education is less of a drain on general education funds in states that use percentage reimbursement (Baker, 2003). This finding is likely not so much a function of the funding mechanism itself, and more likely associated with the level of support provided for special education in states using this approach during the time period investigated.

Encroachment

A concern related to growth in classification rates is whether the rapid growth rate in special education costs has adversely affected, or *encroached* upon, available resources for the general population (Lankford & Wyckoff, 1999). That is, if total education revenues grow more slowly than special education spending, regular education resources will decline. Lankford and Wyckoff find that when total revenues are constrained, perhaps by overall economic conditions or by local fiscal capacity, encroachment of regular education funds increases or is higher.

That is, because local districts are obligated to comply with IDEA regardless of the level of state or federal support they receive, local fiscal capacity plays a significant role in determining the extent that districts can raise additional revenues to cover special education costs, or must reshuffle existing resources. Because fiscal capacity varies, and general education resource levels vary, the extent of encroachment also varies. Murphy and Picus (1996) similarly find:

> ... encroachment in California varies in terms of both expenditures per pupil and in terms of the percentage of the general fund that the encroachment represents. As a result, this system could result in a loss of equity, potentially damaging the state's claim that it has achieved the level of equity demanded in the *Serrano* lawsuit.
>
> *(p. 386)*

The National Research Council (NRC; 1999) report, *Making Money Matter: Financing America's Schools*, suggests that while the problem of encroachment may exist, it may be more productive to address whether the current "entitlement and categorical approach to educating children with disabilities best serves their learning needs," rather than to continue pitting one student population against another for access to finite resources (p. 222). The NRC recommends more integrated approaches to placement, improving the capacity of schools to accommodate students in integrated environments, improving accountability for special education student's outcomes, and providing schools and parents greater control over the use of public funds to accomplish these tasks (1999).

Interestingly, however, few if any researchers have questioned whether general education expenditures might constrain or encroach upon special education expenditures under tight budgetary conditions or the presence of severe budget cuts, coupled with general accountability pressures such as avoidance of being identified as a *failing school* under NCLB. Finance formulas driving special education support through general aid formulas may allow for greater reshuffling of resources away from children with disabilities, especially when left in the hands of local majority politics as seemingly recommended by Ladd and Hansen (1999).

Table 6.2 summarizes funding approaches used across states, based largely on recent work by Ahearn (2010) and the Education Commission on the States. One notable finding in the Ahearn report is that states seem to be moving away from census based financing of special education. This may be occurring because most states adopting the approach also included safety valves to accommodate "exceptions" to the rule—exceptions to the assumption of even distribution of children with disabilities. As Baker and Ramsey (2010) point out, these exceptions quickly become the rule. Despite continued concerns over head-count based methods, most states continue to use some form of weighting system to drive special education funding to local school districts.

The Future of Special Education Finance

Researchers and policymakers need to carefully consider the continued desire to categorize the problem and to determine costs and aid formulas only with respect to current categories and current classification schemes. The continued either/or mentality regarding financing of general and special education programs may inhibit progress, as it arguably has in the past. IDEA 2004 specifically refers to Response to Intervention (RtI) as a model for consideration in the identification of students with disabilities. As RtI continues to be adopted, we might expect to see identification rates drop as more students are served through regular education interventions and not identified as special education students. This service delivery model could significantly change the face of special education services and costs associated with the services.

Despite all of the public attention on special education costs and all of the interest in education cost analysis and determining the costs of adequate educational programs and services,

Bruce D. Baker, Preston C. Green, III, and Matthew J. Ramsey

Table 6.2 Summary of Funding Approaches

Formula Type	States	Strengths	Weaknesses
Weighted Pupil (varied weights)	Arizona, Colorado, Florida, Georgia, Indiana, Iowa, Kentucky, New Mexico, Ohio, Oklahoma, South Carolina, Texas	Ability to target additional resources to districts serving children in need, and to vary those resources by need levels.	May influence not only aggregate identification rates, but severity of classifications. Even more problematic if separate weights tied to placement type. (see Parrish et al., 1994, 2000)
Weighted Pupil (single weight, or flat grant per SE pupil)	Louisiana, Maine, New Hampshire, New York, North Carolina, Oregon, Washington	Simplicity. Ability to target additional aid to districts serving greater shares of children in need.	Insensitive to differences in concentration of disabilities by severity.
Resource Based	Delaware, Kansas, Mississippi, Nevada, Tennessee, Virginia	Ability to target additional aid to districts serving greater shares of children in need.	If based on fixed sum (typical), may lead to spreading resources to thin across districts/ services/children
Percentage Reimbursement	Michigan, Minnesota, Nebraska, Wisconsin, Wyoming	Less encroachment (Baker, 2003) Ability to target additional aid to districts serving greater shares of children in need.	Potentially cumbersome compliance procedures of accounting for allowable expenses. If based on fixed sum (typical), may lead to spreading resources to thin across districts/ services/children
Census-Based	Alabama, California, Idaho, Massachusetts, Montana, New Jersey, Pennsylvania	Reduces incentive to mis-classify or over-classify (Parrish, 1994)	Potential to deprive districts with uncontrollably high disability rates of necessary resources (Baker and Ramsey, 2010)
Combination of Above Elements (perhaps as multiple Tiers)	Alaska, Illinois, Maryland, South Dakota, Vermont		
No separate special education formula	Arkansas, Connecticut, Hawaii, Missouri*, North Dakota, Rhode Island, West Virginia		

* misclassified by ECS. Formula includes single weight (.75) for each special education student above fixed percent of enrollment. http://www.projectforum.org/docs/FinancingSpecialEducation-StateFundingFormulas.pdf

surprisingly little has been done in recent years to advance the art of determining the costs of special education programs and services or advancing the design of state school finance systems to ensure that districts can cover these costs. Indeed, we should still be concerned with the incentives provided under alternative state funding models and we should seek to better understand the relationship between funding approaches, classification of children and quality of services provided. As noted herein, some progress had been made in this regard nearly a decade ago with attempts to identify factors outside of district control that may serve as predictors of incidence rates.

But, if we are going to design better funding mechanisms to drive resources to districts, schools, and children, we also need a clearer picture of the service delivery models we intend to support and the outcome levels we expect. Researchers and advocates should explore ways to intersect the high quality research on special educational additional expenditures from the 1990s with research on adequate programming—not just current average programming. One option is to identify large enough numbers, within and across states of school and district programs, that truly generate adequate educational outcomes for children with disabilities, both in an IDEA and in an NCLB sense. If we can identify such programs and/or service delivery models, it would behoove us to dig deeply to better understand the cost structure of these approaches, that is, determine not the average expenditure of the existing average—but the average expenditure (and underlying structure) of that which is truly adequate (or excellent). If such programs simply do not exist, perhaps due to current resource constraints, it may be time to try harder and accept the reality that we may actually need to spend more to achieve our desired goals.

Notes

1 Taylor and Fowler (2006) note: "In California, New York, Texas, West Virginia, Pennsylvania, Virginia, Illinois, and New Mexico, the education dollar can stretch at least 40 percent further in one part of the state than in another." (p. v) Clearly, children's access to a comparable quantity of comparable quality teachers is a more relevant equity concern than dollar inputs alone. Evaluation of nominal fiscal inputs may still be of some value, however. If it can be shown that even nominal fiscal inputs are disparately distributed and that those locations and children having fewer nominal fiscal inputs face higher costs of true equity, then it can be inferred that the actual disparities are even greater than the measured nominal disparities.

2 20 U.S.C. § 6301. Schools accepting Title I funding are required to comply with the NCLB. *See* 20 U.S.C. § 6311.

3 20 U.S.C. § 6301(2) (2008).

4 Id. § 6301(3).

5 20 U.S.C. § 1400(d)(1)(A) (2010).

6 Id. § 1400(d)(1)(b).

7 Id. § 1400(d)(1)(C).

8 Id. (emphasis in the original).

9 Id.

10 Id.

11 C.G. v. Pa. Dep't of Educ., 547 F. Supp. 2d 422 (M.D. Pa. 2008), *on reconsideration*, No. CIV.A. 1:06-CV-1523, 2008 WL 4820474 (M.D. Pa. Nov 03, 2008) (holding that general-education student plaintiff lacked standing).

12 Departmentalized by subject area as within high schools.

References

Ahern, E. (2010) Financing special education: State funding formulas. National Association of State Directors of Special Education Programs. Retrieved from http://www.projectforum.org

Baker, B. D. (2003). State policy influences on the internal allocation of school district resources: Evidence from the common core of data. *Journal of Education Finance, 29*(1) 1–24

Baker, B. D. (2006). Evaluating the reliability, validity, and usefulness of education cost studies. *Journal of Education Finance, 32*(2), 170-201.

Baker, B. D., Green, P. C., & Richards, C. E. (2008). *Financing education systems.* New York: Merrill-Prentice Hall.

Baker, B. D., & Ramsey, M. J. (2010). What we don't know can't hurt us: Equity consequences of financing special education on the untested assumption of uniform needs. *Journal of Education Finance, 35*(3) 245–275.

Baker, B. D., Taylor, L. L., & Vedlitz, A. (2005). Measuring educational adequacy in public schools. Working Paper #580. Bush School of Government & Public Service. Texas A&M University. Retrieved from http://bush.tamu.edu/research/workingpapers/ltaylor/measuring_edu_adequacy_in_public_schools.pdf

Chambers, J. G.. (1999). Patterns of expenditures on students with disabilities: A methodological and empirical analysis. In T. B. Parrish, J. G. Chambers, & C. M. Guarino (Eds.), *Funding special education: Nineteenth annual yearbook of the American Education Finance Association* (pp. 89–123). Thousand Oaks, CA: Corwin Press.

Chambers, J. G., Parrish, T. B., & Brock, L. (2000). New Jersey Special Education Expenditures Project (NJ SEEP). Washington, DC: American Institutes for Research, Center for Special Education Finance.

Chambers, J. G., Parrish, T., & Harr, J. J. (2002). *What are we spending on special education services in the United States, 1999–2000?* Palo Alto, CA: American Institutes for Research. Retrieved from http://www.seep.org

Chambers, J. G., Parrish, T. B., & Hikido, C. (1996). *Special education expenditures and revenues in a census-based funding system: A case study in the Commonwealth of Massachusetts.* Washington, DC: American Institutes for Research, Center for Special Education Finance.

Cullen, J. B. (2003). The impact of fiscal incentives on student disability rates. *Journal of Public Economics*, 87, 1557–1589.

Dhuey, E., & Lipscomb, S. (2009). *The effects of fiscal incentives in special education: Evidence from capitation finance reforms* (working paper). Sacramento: Public Policy Institute of California.

Green, P. C., & Baker, B. D. (2002). Circumventing Rodriguez: Can plaintiffs use the Equal Protection Clause to challenge school finance disparities caused by inequitable state distribution policies? *Texas Forum on Civil Liberties and Civil Rights*, 7(2) 141–165.

Huefner, D. S. (2008). Updating the FAPE standard under IDEA. *Journal of Law & Education*, 37, 367, 372.

Lankford, H., & Wyckoff, J. (1999). The allocation of resources to special education and regular instruction in New York State. In Parrish et al. (Eds.), *Funding special education* (pp. 147–175). Thousand Oaks, CA: Corwin Press.

Lipscomb, S. (2009). *Students with disabilities in California's special education program.* Sacramento: Public Policy Institute of California.

Litt, J., Taylor, H. G., Klein, N., & Hack, M. (2005). Learning disabilities in children with very low birthweight: Prevalence, neuropsychological correlates and treatment. *Journal of Learning Disabilities*, 38(2), 130–141.

Moore, M. T., Strang, E. W., Schwartz, M., & Braddock, M. (1988). *Patterns in special education service delivery and cost.* Washington, DC: Decision Resources Corp. (ERIC Document Reproduction Service No. ED 303 027)

Murphy, J., & Picus, L. O. (1996). Special program encroachment on school district general funds in California: Implications for Serrano equalization. *Journal of Education Finance*, 21(3), 366–386.

National Research Council. (1999). *Making money matter: Financing America's schools. Committee on Education Finance.* H. F. Ladd & J. Hansen (Eds.), Commission on Behavioral and Social Sciences and Education. Washington, DC: National Academy Press.

Parrish, T. (2000a). *Disparities in the identification, funding and provision of special education.* Submitted to the Civil Rights Project for the Conference on Minority Issues in Special Education in Public Schools.

Parrish, T. B. (2000b) Restructuring Special Education Funding in New York to Promote the Objective of High Learning Standards for All Students. *Economics of Education Review*, 19, 431–445.

Parrish, T., Gerber, M., Kaleba, D., & Brock, L. (2000). *Adjusting special education aid for severity: The case of census-based funding in California.* Palo Alto, CA: Center for Special Education Finance, American Institutes for Research.

Parrish, T. B., & Harr, J. (2005). Reconsidering special education funding in Georgia. Washington, D.C., American Institutes for Research. Retrieved from http://csef.air.org/publications/related/AIR%20Georgia%20Report.pdf

Parrish, T. B., Harr, J., Kidron, Y., Brock, L., & Anand, P. (2003). Study of the Incidence Adjustment in the Special Education Funding Model: Final Report. American Institutes for Research. Submitted to the California Department of Education.

Parrish, T. B., & Hikido, C. S. (1998). *Inequalities in public school district revenues.* NCES 98–210. Washington, DC: National Center for Education Statistics.

Parrish, T. B., Kaleba, D., Gerber, M., & McLaughlin, M. (1998). Special education: Study of incidence of disabilities: Final report. American Institutes for Research. Submitted to the California Department of Education.

Pennsylvania Department of Education. (2000). *A report on special education Incidence rates.* Harrisburg, PA: Author.

Weber, M. C. (2010). Special education form the (damp) ground up: Children with disabilities in a charter school-dependent education system. 11 *Loyola Journal of Public Interest Law* 217

Welner, K. G., & Gebhardt, K. (forthcoming). School finance: When state courts refuse to engage. In P. First (Ed.), *Policy for American schools.* New York: Rowman & Littlefield.

7

Special Education and School Choice
A Special Leadership Challenge

Julie F. Mead

UNIVERSITY OF WISCONSIN–MADISON

Preston C. Green, III

THE PENNSYLVANIA STATE UNIVERSITY

As various forms of publicly funded parental choice options have developed across the country, policy makers and school leaders have had to consider how to include children with disabilities in those programs. As with all programming for children with disabilities, the requirements for such participation are grounded in three federal laws; Section 504 of the Rehabilitation Act of 1973, the Americans with Disabilities Act (ADA), and the Individuals with Disabilities Education Act (IDEA). Both Section 504 and the ADA prohibit discrimination on the basis of disability. IDEA sets out detailed requirements for the delivery of special education in exchange for federal funding. Ensuring that children with disabilities have meaningful opportunities to participate in publicly funded parental choice programs in a manner that complies with these federal guarantees presents a special challenge to school leaders.

School choice programs may serve a variety of purposes, from racial integration to program innovation to school reform achieved through competition. Programs may also simply permit parental choice for its own sake, adopting the position that there is value in allowing parents to select schools rather than assigning children to them through an administrative process. The common element in each type of choice program is that parents select from a menu of school options for their child, rather than being assigned to a school by virtue of residential attendance zones. Listed in roughly the chronological order they developed (Mead, 2008b), Table 7.1 lists the types of publicly funded school choice programs and their descriptions.

In general, the application of the legal principles from Section 504, the ADA, and the IDEA to school choice programs raises two types of issues for children with disabilities and their parents, (a) access and (b) appropriate programming (Mead, 2008b). Issues of access relate to the extent parents of students with disabilities enjoy the same choices as parents of students without disabilities. Since it would violate Section 504 and the ADA to limit participation solely on the student's status as disabled or nondisabled, publicly funded school choice programs must avoid discrimination and ensure that children with disabilities may participate. Issues related to appropriate programming involve what happens after access to the school of choice is achieved. As will

Table 7.1 Forms of Publicly Funded School Choice

	Description	Relationship to Local Education Agencies (LEAs)
Intradistrict Open Enrollment Programs	These programs allow students to request placement at schools within a given school district regardless of the location of the family residence. Intradistrict programs may also include magnet schools, those schools with distinctive curricula, as options.	Transfers within an LEA
Interdistrict Open Enrollment Programs	These plans typically take two forms. The oldest form permits city-suburban transfers within a metropolitan area. The second form is statewide open enrollment which allows parents to enroll their children in one district while residing in another.	Transfers between LEAs
Charter Schools:	Voluntary enrollment public schools developed through an authorizing process. Charter schools receive some relief from state regulations in exchange for accountability by means of a charter contract (Green & Mead, 2004).	Transfers to a charter school may be within or between LEAs depending on state law and charter school type.
Voucher Programs:	Publicly funded voucher programs allow parents to enroll their children in private schools at public expense.	Exit LEAs for private system

be discussed further below, issues related to programming involve legal responsibility for service delivery (which entity serves as the LEA), the availability of appropriate programming, and compliance with the legal directive to educate children with disabilities with their non-disabled peers "to the maximum extent appropriate" (IDEA, 20 U.S.C. §1412(a)(5)).

As numerous researchers have explained, there is an underlying policy tension between parental choice and procedural aspects of federal disability law (Ahearn, Lange, Rhim, & McLaughlin, 2001; McKinney, 1992; Mead, 1995, 2008a,b). Parental choice programs vest authority in the parents to select where a child goes to school. As a way to ensure that a child's right to equal opportunity is protected, federal law requires that decisions about the programming and placement of children with disabilities be determined through a team process that includes school personnel and parents. Parents have a voice in that process, but may not dictate placement. Therein lies the tension.

Questions around this tension have arisen in every type of choice program. As Mead (2008b) explained, through a series of administrative rulings and letters from various offices in the United States Department of Education, four reasonably clear principles provide guidance for leaders involved in choice programs with regard to children with disabilities:

1. All publicly funded choice programs must be accessible to children with disabilities (Letter to Bina, 1991; Letter to Bocketti, 1999; Letter to Evans, 1991; Letter to Gloecker, 2000; Letter to Lunar, 1991).
2. Parents and children cannot be required to waive needed services in order to participate in the choice program (Chattanooga Public School District, 1993; Fallbrook Union Elementary School District, 1990; San Francisco Unified School District, 1990).

3. A student's right to "free appropriate public education" must be preserved in any choice program delivered in public schools (Letter to Bina, 1991; Letter to Bocketti, 1999; Letter to Evans, 1991; Letter to Gloecker, 2000; Letter to Lunar, 1991).

4. States need to determine which entity (the sending district, receiving school or district, a combination, or some other entity) will serve as the responsible "local education agency" for purposes of IDEA (Letter to Bocketti, 1999; Letter to Gloecker, 2000; San Francisco Unified School District, 1990)

What follows is an exploration of the issues of access and appropriate programming captured by these four directives in relationship to each type of school choice. This chapter concludes with lessons for school leaders who may be involved in school choice programs in one form or another.

Intradistrict Open Enrollment Programs

In special education terms, intradistrict choice programs may be the least complicated form of publicly funded choice available. To explain why this statement is so, it is first necessary to understand how responsibility for special education delivery is determined under federal law. As will become clear in the discussions of the other forms of choice, the legal entity responsible for ensuring that the child receives a free appropriate public education is at the heart of issues of both access and appropriate programming.

Recall that at its base, IDEA is a funding statute. As such, funding and responsibility are inextricably tied together. IDEA funding flows first to the state education agency (SEA) and states then promise that funds will be used to ensure that each child with a disability has available a free appropriate public education (FAPE) (20 U.S.C. 1412(a)). To accomplish this obligation, the SEA also promises that each local education agency (LEA) will implement the law to ensure the result (20 U.S.C. 1413(a)(1)). So the funds flow from the SEA to the LEA, but the LEA is the entity responsible for evaluation, development of the Individualized Education Program (IEP), and program delivery. In short, states guarantee that LEAs will deliver, but it is the LEA that interacts with parents and is responsible for all programming decisions.

Intradistrict choice programs are the least complex simply because they exist within a single LEA. Therefore, the responsible entity for ensuring both access and appropriate programming is the same and the child that elects to choose is doing so within a single system. Figure 7.1 illustrates this relationship.

Public School District as LEA

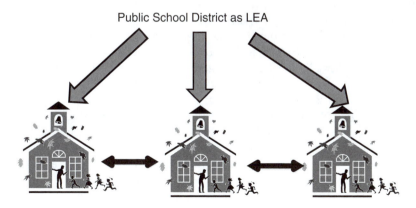

Transfer within schools operated by same LEA

Figure 7.1   *Intra*-district open enrollment and LEA status: Transfer within schools operated by same LEA

Two decisions by the Office for Civil Rights (OCR) in the early 1990s put school districts on notice that intradistrict choice programs needed to provide access to children with disabilities. In both San Francisco (1990) and Chattanooga (1993), officials had created alternative and magnet school offerings that did not provide any special educational services. In San Francisco, parents had to sign a form upon enrollment acknowledging that no special education services were available in the alternative schools. In essence, parents were effectively required to waive special education services. Parents in Chattanooga were not permitted to enroll their child in the district's magnet school unless the child had "the capacity to function without special education services other than speech, hearing, and vision services." This policy created a categorical barrier to participation in the Chattanooga's magnet schools for many children with disabilities. Because both districts conditioned choice on a student's disability status by limiting available appropriate programming, OCR found both districts had engaged in discriminatory conduct in violation of Section 504 (Chattanooga Public School District, 1993; San Francisco Unified School District, 1990).

What both these decisions also illustrate is the relationship between service delivery patterns and access to school choice. If school officials decide that some services are "unavailable" in a particular magnet or choice school, they have effectively excluded any child who needs those services from those schools and the choice program. Accordingly, in order to operate a choice program free from discrimination on the basis of disability, it is important that officials examine service delivery plans in order to provide meaningful opportunities for the participation of children with a broad spectrum of needs in the choice plans (Mead, 1995).

Interdistrict Open Enrollment Programs

Interdistrict choice programs, those that permit children who reside in one district to enroll in another district, exist in 42 of the 50 states (Education Commission of the States, 2010). Some of the programs involve transfer between urban and suburban districts of metropolitan areas, while others allow transfer statewide. The latter are typically called statewide open enrollment programs.

Once again guidance from the U.S. Department of Education in the early 1990s provides instruction. First, OCR investigated a complaint against a California district participating in the state's open enrollment program (Fallbrook Union Elementary School District, 1990). While the district opened its doors to students generally, officials excluded students with disabilities from participation. The district justified their policy on the basis of cost, citing the additional monies associated with the provision of special education. OCR found the justification unpersuasive and concluded that the district's policy was discriminatory in violation of Section 504.

Likewise, a series of letters from the U.S. Department of Education further elucidate the relationship between interdistrict choice programs and special education. IDEA contains a provision that requires that a local educational agency (LEA) ensure FAPE for each child residing within it geographical borders (20 U.S.C. §1413(a)(1)). But in a system that permits the transfer between LEAs, which LEA is responsible for the child with a disability who participates in the open enrollment program? In response to state inquiries on this very issue, the Office of Special Education Programs recommended that the obligation to provide FAPE be transferred from the resident or sending district to the enrolling or receiving district (Letter to Nebraska Department of Education, 1990; Letter to Tatel, 1990). In other words, once the child enrolled in the new district, the obligation to ensure that the child received appropriate programming would likewise shift from the district where the child lived to the district where the child attended school. Figure 7.2 illustrates this relationship.

The federal office noted, however, that states had the discretion to determine how the interdistrict choice program would operate as long as states "ensure that the rights guaranteed to

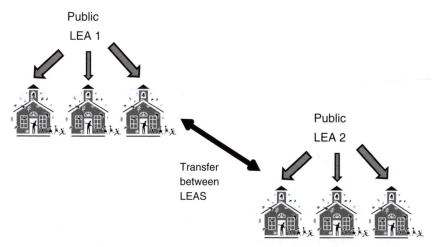

Figure 7.2 *Inter*-district open enrollment and LEA status: Transfer between LEAs

children with handicaps and their parents by the EHA-B [now IDEA] and Section 504 are not diminished by virtue of the child's participation in the [choice] program" (Letter to Nebraska Department of Education, 1990, p. 555). Accordingly it is very important for school leaders to understand what system has been codified by state officials for responsibility for students who need special education and wish to participate in the statewide open enrollment program. Does the obligation to provide FAPE stay with the resident school district? Does the obligation shift to the receiving district? Is the obligation somehow shared? For example, the receiving district may be obligated to serve, while the sending district retains some of the financial obligations for the costs of that service. Whatever policies have been put in place, officials must ensure that the child does not have to trade FAPE in order to participate in choice.

Charter Schools

Charter schools are another form of parental choice that exists in 40 states, the District of Columbia, and Puerto Rico. Charter schools enroll students on a voluntary basis only, depending completely on parents who elect to send their children there, rather than having any children assigned to attend. Depending on the state, charter schools may be authorized by school districts, universities, city governments, non-profit organizations, or special state charter school boards. In all states, regardless of the charter authorizer, charter schools are public schools that are relieved from some state (and sometimes local school district) regulations in exchange for compliance with a specific charter contract (Green & Mead, 2004). While the exact nature of charter schools and the state and local requirements that bind them varies widely from state to state, as public schools they all must comply with federal law, including Section 504, the ADA, and the IDEA. As such, it is imperative that charter schools provide meaningful programmatic access to children with disabilities, just as traditional public schools must provide that access (Lake, 2010).

In the same way that other types of parental school choice must consider how programming affects access, charter schools also have wrestled with establishing programs that provide non-discriminatory admission to children with disabilities. In this instance, where states adopt charter school statutes, at least in part, to spur innovation and try new educational approaches, the requirement to consider how programming decisions may create barriers to participation is especially relevant. Researchers at the National Association of State Directors of Special Education (NASDSE) have documented this problem (Ahearn et al., 2001). They have noted that some charter schools create programs and then "counsel out" the parents of children with disabilities because the school is not a good "fit." Of course, whether such a practice is discriminatory under Section 504 and the ADA depends on whether children with and without disabilities are treated similarly or whether only children with disabilities are counseled that the school would not fit their needs. Charter schools in some, but not all states, are permitted to establish non-discriminatory admissions requirements (e.g., artistic ability for a school for the arts), but must ensure that otherwise qualified children with disabilities are permitted to enroll. One way to think about the issue of non-discriminatory access is to consider that charter schools may innovate around curriculum and organization, but need to ensure that the program is ready to serve the entire range of the public that may have an interest in what they have to offer.

Perhaps one of the most complicated issues, however, is determining what entity serves as the LEA and is therefore responsible for ensuring that the charter school provides FAPE for each child with a disability once enrolled (Ahearn et al., 2001; Lake, 2010; Mead, 2002). Just as states creating statewide open enrollment programs have some discretion in determining whether a sending or receiving district is responsible under the IDEA when parents exercise the option to transfer their child, so, too, state legislatures have available to them more than one approach as they craft their charter school statutes to ensure each child with a disability enrolled in charter schools receives FAPE. The IDEA's statute and regulations outline three types of charter schools for IDEA purposes: (a) charter schools that are independent and serve as their own LEA; (b) charter schools that are part of another LEA; (c) charter schools that are neither independent LEAs, nor part of LEAs (20 U.S.C. 1413(a)(5); 34 C.F.R. §300.209). Figure 7.3 illustrates the first two types of charter schools' LEA status.

Green and Mead (2004) documented the variation charter school states have adopted in regard to charter schools and LEA status. Sixteen states designate the charter school as the LEA, while another 16 states name the school district as the LEA. In the latter case the school district is also often the entity that authorized the charter school. Five states have established systems where charter schools of both LEA types exist: (a) where the entity authorizing the charter school determines the responsible LEA as part of the chartering process; (b) or the type of authorizer (school district or other) dictates whether the school is its own LEA or part of another; (c) or the charter school elects or petitions to be independent or part of a system for the purposes of the IDEA. Three states require the school district where the child resides to retain the obligation to

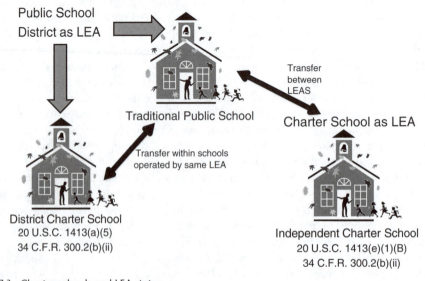

Figure 7.3 Charter schools and LEA status

ensure FAPE, regardless of where the charter school is located or how it was authorized. Finally, one state establishes a system of shared responsibility between the charter school and the authorizing school district.

If this variation was not complicated enough, examining the state statute is just the first step to determining the responsible LEA for each charter school. In addition to examining statutory provisions, it is also necessary to examine the school's charter contract. For example, the state's statute may establish the charter school as independently responsible, but permit the authorizing school district to serve as the LEA for IDEA purposes if the authorizer and the charter school agree to such an arrangement in the charter contract.

As is apparent, there is considerable difference from state to state and even from charter school to charter school within a state with regard to the LEA status of charter schools. However, it is imperative to note that while variance on the approach for assigning LEA responsibility under IDEA is permitted, the regulations make clear that "[c]hildren with disabilities who attend public charter schools and their parents retain all rights under [the IDEA]"(34 C.F.R. §300.209(a)).

Of course determining legal responsibility for ensuring children's rights marks only the starting point for charter school leaders. Then, as with any public school, begins the process of providing equitable opportunities for all enrolled children, including children with disabilities. To that end, Green and Mead (2004) lay out seven directives to guide charter school operators and leaders.

They should:

1. Familiarize themselves with IDEA and its requirements;
2. Determine whether, under state law, the school will be an LEA for the purposes of special education;
3. Consider whether any contract provisions are needed to make explicit the various responsibilities of the school and its authorizer, particularly if the authorizer is the school's LEA;
4. Adopt policies and procedures for compliance with IDEA's requirements;
5. Prepare materials to inform parents of their rights under IDEA;
6. Consider how the school will acquire the necessary expertise to evaluate and serve children with disabilities during the charter school design or development phase;
7. Train all staff concerning their role in IDEA implementation (Green & Mead, 2004, p. 157).

Virtual Charter Schools

Virtual charter schools raise a particular set of issues with respect to special education delivery. Again NASDSE has provided leadership on considering these special issues (Rhim & Kowal, 2008). Virtual charter schools, also know as cyber charters, on-line charters, or technology based charters, have raised a number of unique issues for children with and without disabilities (Rhim & Kowal, 2008). These schools are characterized by the use of internet web-based computer technology as the primary means of instructional delivery, whether synchronous or asynchronous. Moving beyond issues of attractiveness to parents and general admission issues, the question becomes, what does special education look like when the school has no "bricks and mortar"? First as noted above, it is important for virtual charter school operators to ensure their programs are accessible. In terms of technology, that accessibility requires attention to principles of universal design for learning which address both how individuals receive instruction and express their understanding (http://www.cast.org/ as cited in Rhim & Kowal, 2008). Following universal design principles seeks to ensure the maximum accessibility for persons with disabilities, regardless of type, by providing multiple pathways to engage content (visual, auditory, etc.) as well as multiple ways to demonstrate comprehension and mastery.

In addition to access issues, virtual charter schools must also plan for logistical issues that may be encountered in service delivery. For example, children enrolled in a virtual school and the teachers that serve them may be separated by hundreds of miles. As such, it may be necessary for virtual charter school operators to contract with local service providers in order to deliver necessary special education services (e.g., physical therapy) if that service can not be delivered through technological means. The logistics of conducting IEP meetings must be coordinated, whether face-to-face or technologically in order to satisfy IDEA requirements. Finally, virtual charters raise the issue of socialization for students, given that the students may spend the majority of their instructional time in their homes, rather than in a "class" and interaction is mediated through the computer. Considering how to ensure that students with disabilities develop appropriate social skills when that is part of the IEP may require additional creativity and cooperation between school officials and parents, with consideration given to community resources. As Rhim and Kowal (2008) explain:

> Non-academic needs can be a challenge for virtual charter schools, especially for virtual schools serving students dispersed across a large geographic area. Nevertheless, if the IEP team determines that a child with a disability needs to improve social or other skills, the virtual school is required to provide these services. Examples of these services may be field trips or social functions that require the student to interact appropriately with peers. Virtual schools personnel may organize regular picnics, gathering at local parks, or attendance at cultural events in the community.
>
> *(p. 26)*

Charter Schools Designed for Children with Disabilities

Another special type of charter school that requires attention is the charter school specifically designed for children with disabilities. Similar to the variation documented above with respect to LEA type, state charter school statutes sometimes prohibit, sometimes permit, and sometimes specifically authorize the development of these specially designed charter schools (Mead, 2008a). A study commissioned by NASDE found 71 charter schools designed for children with disabilities operating in 13 states and the District of Columbia (Mead, 2008a). These schools fell into three types: (a) schools explicitly designed to serve a particular disability population (e.g., children who are deaf, children who have autism, etc.); (b) schools explicitly designed to serve children with any disability; or (c) schools explicitly designed to serve children with disabilities by creating what may be called "model inclusion schools" (p. 10). While the first two categories serve student populations that are predominantly or exclusively comprised of children with disabilities, the latter category seeks to enroll children of all abilities, though a particular design feature of the school is to better serve children with disabilities through best practices integrating them with non-disabled peers.

The first question raised by these schools is whether state and federal law permits charter schools that serve children with disabilities exclusively. In other words: "May these charter schools admit only children with disabilities or must the schools accept children without disabilities?" (Mead, 2008a, p.13). The answer to that question is a complex legal one that requires attention to federal and state anti-discrimination laws. Many states have concluded that the schools must enroll any interested child, even though the school's curriculum is designed to serve a particular population. While Section 504 and the ADA prohibit the denial of benefits on the basis of disability, some may argue that the laws were not meant to apply to situations where a program is designed to provide special opportunities to persons with disabilities. Another reasonable interpretation, however, is that these federal non-discrimination statutes are designed to ensure that benefits are not conditioned on disability status and therefore would consider exclusive admissions policies discriminatory. In addition to these federal provisions, state charter and non-discrimination statutes may also be implicated.

Naturally, then, these schools raise policy questions at the heart of longstanding concerns about how children with disabilities should be educated (Crockett & Kaufman, 1999) as they draw particular attention to the central policy tension between parental choice and the IDEA's principle that children should be educated in the least restrictive environment (LRE). IDEA's LRE provision requires that:

> To the maximum extent appropriate, children with disabilities, including children in public or private institutions or other care facilities, are educated with children who are not disabled, and special classes, separate schooling, or other removal of children with disabilities from the regular educational environment occurs only when the nature or severity of the disability of a child is such that education in regular classes with the use of supplementary aids and services cannot be achieved satisfactorily.
>
> *(20 U.S.C. §1412(a)(5))*

This language clearly establishes the statutory right of children with disabilities to be educated with children who are not disabled and makes clear that child centered rationales related to the nature and severity of the child's disability should justify any other arrangement. That said, determining the LRE for particular child is a function of the IEP Team, which includes the parents.

Given this language, an important question arises in the application of this principle in the context of charter schools designed for children with disabilities. What if parents prefer a more specialized and separate learning environment than the "nature and severity" of the child's needs would suggest? Can parental choice essentially trump the LRE provision? Interestingly, guidance on this question can be found in letters written in response to officials at a state school for the blind in the context of statewide open enrollment. When Indiana adopted statewide open enrollment, officials from the state's residential school for the blind wondered how to reconcile parental choices with IEP team placement procedures. The letter asked whether parents could elect enrollment at the segregated state school under open enrollment. The Office for Special Education Programs made clear that all provisions of what is now the IDEA must be respected and cautioned that it would be inconsistent with federal law to permit any choice program to operate that "specifically provides that parent preference is the sole criterion for placement of children," and that "parent preference cannot override the decision of the child's [IEP] team" (Letter to Bina, 1991; see also Letter to Evans 1991; Letter to Lunar, 1991).

Commentary published with the posting of the most recent IDEA regulations in 2006 suggests the U.S. Department of Education remains committed to this interpretation of the LRE provision in parental choice environments. When initially proposed after the reauthorization of IDEA in 2004, the regulatory provision guiding placement decisions included the phrase "unless parents agree otherwise." After reviewing comments made about the proposed regulations, federal officials deleted that phrase from the final regulations, explaining:

> Several commenters stated that including the phrase undermines the statutory requirement for children with disabilities to be placed in the LRE based on their IEPs and allows more restrictive placements based on parental choice. Many commenters interpreted this phrase to mean that placement is a matter of parental choice even in public school settings and stated that a child's LRE rights should not be overridden by parental choice … A parent has always had this option [sending the child to a charter, magnet, or other specialized

school option]; *a parent who chooses this option for the child does not violate the LRE mandate as long as the child is educated with his or her peers without disabilities to the maximum extent appropriate*. However, we agree that this phrase is unnecessary, confusing, and may be misunderstood to mean that parents have a right to veto the placement decision made by the group of individuals ... We have removed the phrase "unless the parent agrees otherwise."

(71 Fed. Reg. 46587-46588, emphasis added)

As noted then, regardless of context, IDEA requires full compliance with all its provisions, even the LRE principle that since the law's first adoption as the Education for all Handicapped Children Act in 1975 has required that children with disabilities be educated with typical peers "to the maximum extent appropriate." So to the extent parental choices are consistent with IDEA, they must be honored, but the language also suggests that parental choices inconsistent with the principles laid out in the law, including the LRE provision, may not be honored by school authorities.

In addition to the central LRE question above, specially designed charter schools raise other policy questions, including: How do specially designed charter schools provide access to the "general curriculum"? When a school's population is voluntary, do schools have an incentive to enroll students in the environment even if their needs do not suggest such specialized services are necessary? What, if any, special issues of oversight, either by charter authorizers or SEAs, are needed to ensure specially designed charters operate in a manner consistent with IDEA? Operational or logistical questions are also raised. When should IEPs be reviewed in the admissions process? How can schools provide avenues for interaction with non-disabled peers? What if the child's skills develop such that the child no longer needs a separated setting to gain meaningful benefit from the instruction? Mead (2008a) explores these questions and the ambiguity surrounding them, concluding:

> While this study provides a glimpse into why and how these schools operate, more research is necessary in order to fully understand their development and operation.... [T]hese schools involve a situation that arguably illustrates in the starkest terms the policy tension between parental choice and group decision-making [under the IDEA].... While the numbers of such schools are decidedly small when compared to all charter schools and even smaller when viewed as part of all public educational options, if their numbers continue to expand, policymakers, particularly those at the federal level, may need to address directly whether and how such schools can achieve their aims while genuinely espousing the principles of that have characterized our national policy on the education of children with disabilities since the mid 1970s.
>
> *(p. 22)*

Voucher Programs

Voucher programs in the United States remain few, numbering less than 10 across the country (NSBA, 2011; CER, 2011). Like charter schools, some voucher programs have been designed to serve children generally and others to serve children with disabilities specifically. The earliest publicly funded voucher programs in Milwaukee, Wisconsin, and Cleveland, Ohio, exemplify the first type—general voucher programs that provide public funds to support eligible children (those who meet family poverty criteria in these instances) enrolled by their parents in private schools. For these programs, where parents and students exit the public school system, issues of access differ from those described for the other school choice programs reviewed above. For when children with disabilities exit public schools, they lose some of the rights established by the IDEA and Section 504. As will be discussed below, IDEA has specific rules for children placed by their parents in private schools (20 U.S.C. §1412(a)(10)). Section 504 only applies to schools that receive federal funds (29 U.S.C. §794). Since most private schools do not, Section 504 does not apply to private schools.

That is not to suggest, however, that private schools may discriminate on the basis of disability. All private schools, whether participating in voucher programs or not, must abide by the dictates of the ADA. The ADA requires that private schools operate their programs without discrimination (42 U.S.C. 12101 *et seq.*). In practice, non-discrimination means that while private schools may not categorically exclude children with disabilities who otherwise qualify for the services provided, they need not provide special education or special services in the manner expected of public schools. Accordingly, private schools must reasonably accommodate a child with a disability, but if the child requires more than accommodations to succeed, the school has no obligation to provide those services or accept the child as a student (28 C.F.R. §35.130).

IDEA, too, has different application for children in private schools. While the IDEA does require local educational agencies to serve children with disabilities in private schools, those children only have a right to equitable participation in IDEA funded activities (20 U.S.C. §1412(a)(10)). To obtain their full right to FAPE, the child must remain in a public school. While FAPE is an individual entitlement to a level of meaningfully beneficial programming, equitable participation is a group entitlement. That is, local educational agencies are only required to expend federal funds in the same proportion as the number of children with disabilities enrolled in private schools within its boundaries.

For example, imagine that a local school district had identified a total of 200 children with disabilities within its borders, with 190 of those children enrolled in various public schools, while 10 of those children were enrolled by their parents in private schools. Then the district would be required to spend 5% of *federal* IDEA funds on services for children with disabilities enrolled in private schools. Unless state law specifies otherwise, there is no requirement to expend any *state* or *local* funds to serve children in private schools. The process enunciated by IDEA to determine those services requires consultation with private school officials, but does not require that every service available in public schools be likewise made available in private schools (20 U.S.C. §1412(a)(10)(i)(II)). So a child may be eligible for a variety of services within a public school setting, but may only receive some of those services if enrolled by their parents in private schools. In addition, the services funded under equitable participation may be delivered at the private school, or the students may be required to come to a public setting to receive the offered services (20 U.S.C. §1412(a)(10)(i)(III)). In essence, when parents enroll their child in a private school, whether through a voucher process or not, the child's right to FAPE does not follow the child as it does when enrolled in any of the public choice programs described above. Figure 7.4 illustrates these concepts.

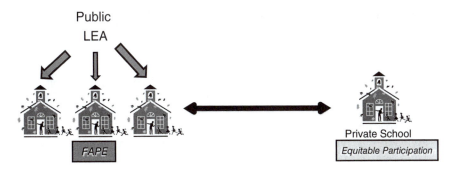

Transfer from LEA to Private school

Figure 7.4 Voucher programs and LEA status

There is also a difference in the application of the laws in special education voucher programs. Four states, Florida, Georgia, Ohio, and Utah, have created special education voucher programs. In each of these programs, parents unhappy with the special education program in the public school setting may use a voucher to transfer to a public or private school of their choice to receive the programming desired. The most generous of these programs is Ohio's Autism Scholarship Program, which provides up to $20,000 per year to cover the costs of programming for children identified as having autism (Ohio Department of Education, 2010). In all cases, students have to have been enrolled in the public school and served under an IEP the previous year. States also typically set requirements for the private schools participating in the program to ensure that the private schools meet minimum quality standards.

While parents who participate in general voucher programs trade FAPE for equitable partici- pation and may lose access to special educational opportunities, parents who participate in special education voucher programs are specifically choosing to transfer to obtain preferred program- ming. As such it could be argued that they have greater control over the specialized program- ming received by their child—including the inclusiveness or segregated nature of the setting. The policy issues regarding programs that may result in more segregated learning environments than the LRE provisions of IDEA contemplate (described in the charter school section) would also apply to these special voucher programs. Is it good public policy to permit more options for parents to obtain education that separates children from their non-disabled peers? However, the legal context of the two situations is different because of the transfer between systems.

In this instance and in contrast to the discussion of specially designed charter schools above, the parents are exiting the public system. Exercising parental choice to enroll a child in a charter school transfers the child from one public school program to another. As such the child retains all rights under IDEA, including the LRE placement provisions. Parents who exercise their options in the special education voucher programs, as do parents in all private school voucher programs, move to another system with different rules. Arguably in this setting, parental choice may essen- tially trump more general public policy initiatives that encourage the placement of children with disabilities in the same educational settings as their non-disabled peers.

These programs also seem to presume that the parents' choice will be as or more effective than the program the child is exiting. That is a question that should be tested empirically.

School leaders working in private schools have a number of considerations. First and foremost will be the decision of whether to participate in available public voucher programs and the atten- dant advantages and disadvantages for the school of that participation. In addition, as with other forms of choice, fully comprehending the statutory context of the choice program is important in order to know what is expected of participating schools. Finally, private school leaders would benefit from developing good relationships with public school leaders in order to meaningfully participate with LEAs through the consultative process required by IDEA in defining what "equitable participation" will mean in that locality.

Conclusion

Special education, by the nature of the procedural requirements developed to guide its delivery, is complex in all systems. As the foregoing discussion has outlined, adding an element of parental choice to the process further complicates the issues. It also raises a number of questions that go to the heart of what we, as the body politic, value. Further research is needed both to understand how these programs operate and whether children with disabilities are meaningfully served by them, both in terms of access and in terms of effective use of public resources.

Current school leaders, of course, do not have the luxury of waiting for the research com- munity to provide those understandings as they have the responsibility to implement the parental choice systems that exist now. Throughout this chapter, suggestions have been made relative to each form of choice. What is common to serving children with disabilities in all school choice contexts can be summarized in two primary directives.

First, know the law. Knowing the law means understanding both special education law and the statutes that apply to the particular form of parental choice at issue (e.g., the charter school law, the statewide open enrollment law). Leaders who know the law have developed a firm grasp of both state and federal provisions in order to understand what they may or may not do; what they must or must not do. Only by fully understanding the system in which a leader operates can she or he take full advantage of their discretion to ensure students with disabilities have their interests served.

Second, plan ahead. Children with disabilities can only be meaningfully included in publicly funded parental programs when leaders consider in advance (a) how access will be guaranteed, (b) how the requisite expertise will be obtained, and (c) how quality programming will be delivered. While some of that planning clearly falls to legislators and state education officials who develop the programs, school level planning is also needed to create structures sufficiently robust to serve the needs of all children and families who exercise the choices available to them with public funding.

Parental school choice programs in the form of intradistrict open enrollment, interdistrict open enrollment, charter schools, and voucher programs have become part of our public educational landscape. For any initiative adopted as part of what defines "public education," the challenge to school leaders is to make certain the programs they direct fully address the needs of all the families that form that "public," including those that consist of children with special educational needs arising from disabilities. That goal is the special leadership challenge to integrating special education and school choice.

References

Ahearn, E., Lange, C., Rhim, L., & McLaughlin, M. (2001). *Project Search: Special education as requirements in charter schools, final report of a research study*. Alexandria, VA: National Association of State Directors of Special Education.

Center for Education Reform (CER). (2010). Choice options state by state. Retrieved January 7, 2011, from http://www.edreform.com/published_pdf/Choice_Options_State_by_State.pdf

Chattanooga Public School District, 20 IDELR 999 (OCR 1993).

Crockett, J., & Kauffman, J. (1999). *The least restrictive environment: Its origins and interpretations in special education*. Mahwah, NJ: Erlbaum.

Education Commission of the States. (2010). *Open enrollment: 50-state report*. Denver, CO. Retrieved January 7, 2011, from http://mb2.ecs.org/reports/Report.aspx?id=268

Fallbrook Union Elementary School District, 16 IDELR 754 (OCR 1990).

Green, P. C. & Mead, J. F. (2004). *Charter schools and the law: Establishing new legal relationships*. Norwood, MA: Christopher Gordon.

Lake, R. (Ed.). (2010). *Unique schools serving unique students: Charter schools and children with special needs*. Seattle, WA: Center on Reinventing Public Education.

Letter to Bina, 18 IDELR 582 (OSEP 1991).

Letter to Bocketti, 32 IDELR 225 (OCR 1999).

Letter to Evans, 17 IDELR 836 (OSEP 1991).

Letter to Gloecker, 33 IDELR 222 (OSEP 2000).

Letter to Lunar, 17 IDELR 834 (OSEP 1991).

Letter to Nebraska Department of Education, 16 EHLR 554 (OSERS 1990).

Letter to Tatel, 16 EHLR 349 (OSERS, OCR 1990).

McKinney, J. (1992). Special education and parental choice: An oxymoron in the making. *West's Education Law Reporter, 76*, 667–677.

Mead, J. F. (1995). Including students with disabilities in parental choice programs: The challenge of meaningful choice." *West's Education Law Reporter, 10*(2), 463–496.

Mead, J. F. (2002). Determining charter schools' responsibilities for children with disabilities: A guide through the legal labyrinth. *Boston University Public Interest Law Journal, 11*(2-3), 167–189.

Mead, J. F. (2008a). *Charter schools designed for children with disabilities: An initial examination of issues and questions raised.* Alexandria, VA: National Association of State Directors of Special Education. Retrieved from http://www.uscharterschools.org/cs/spedp/print/uscs_docs/spedp/reports.htm

Mead, J. F. (2008b). *How legislation and litigation shape school choice.* East Lansing, MI: Great Lakes Center for Education Research & Practice. Retrieved from http://www.greatlakescenter.org/School_Choice.php

National School Boards Association (NSBA), Voucher Strategy Center. (2011). Retrieved January 7, 2011. from http://www.nsba.org/MainMenu/Advocacy/FederalLaws/SchoolVouchers/VoucherStrategyCenter.aspx

Ohio Department of Education. (2010). Autism Scholarship Program: Questions and answers 2010–2011, Retrieved January 7, 2011, from http://www.ode.state.oh.us/GD/Templates/Pages/ODE/ODEDetail.aspx?Page=3&TopicRelationID=1540&Content=96835

Rhim, L. M., & Kowal, J. (2008). *Demystifying special education in virtual charter schools.* Alexandria, VA: National Association of State Directors of Special Education. http://www.uscharterschools.org/specialedprimers/download/special_report_rhim.pdf

San Francisco Unified School District, 16 IDELR 824 (OCR 1990).

8

Disability, Difference, and Justice
Strong Democratic Leadership for Undemocratic Times

Thomas M. Skrtic

UNIVERSITY OF KANSAS

In *Distinguishing Disability: Parents, Privilege, and Special Education*, Colin Ong-Dean (2009) argues that the egalitarian and democratic impulses that produced the Education for All Handicapped Children Act of 1975 (EAHCA) were undercut by the statute's legal and institutional interpretation and by the design of its parent participation and procedural due process provisions. As a result, rather than democratic solutions to the recognized special education problems of ineffective instruction, exclusion, and racial/ethnic and social class bias, the EAHCA—and its progeny, the Individuals with Disabilities Education Act (IDEA)—merely enabled individual parents to mount narrow technical challenges to the their child's diagnosis, needs, and accommodations. Beyond muting broader social concerns about the special education system, by reducing its problems to isolated cases the IDEA created "an individualized and competitive environment" (Ong-Dean, 2009, p. 14) that favors privileged parents, thereby turning a law premised on democratic reform into yet another instrument of racial/ethnic and class injustice (see Skrtic, 2010). This and other unintended consequences of the IDEA, alone and in conjunction with the No Child Left Behind Act of 2001 (NCLB), forms the moral and political backdrop of special education leadership today, an institutional context whose transformation, I believe, should be the aim and focus of leadership development in education and special education.

The chapter is presented in five parts, starting with a brief institutional history of the IDEA tracing how its initial egalitarian and democratic impulses and reform strategies were compromised by the design of the statute and its legal and institutional interpretation. Then, because understanding how these impulses and reform strategies were compromised requires understanding the institutional context they were meant to change, the second part introduces four examples of institutional analysis that are used in the third part to critically review the implementation of key elements of special education reform under the IDEA, a review that shows how the IDEA perpetuates injustices it was meant to eliminate while introducing and sustaining new ones. Relating this review to the initial egalitarian and democratic conception of the IDEA, the fourth part proposes policy and organizational changes to actualize the aims and reform strategies envisioned by the social movement that produced the statute, including democratic approaches to school organization and educational reform, professionalism, and leadership, all of which both require and contribute to a transformation of liberal democracy itself. Given the fundamental nature of the proposed institutional changes, the conclusion places them in historical perspective to underscore their social significance and the educational and social costs of the existing state of affairs.

A Brief Institutional History of the IDEA

In Senate hearings held prior to its passage, proponents of the EAHCA—parents of children with disabilities, disability advocates and activists, policy experts, and federal legislators—described what they saw as its value and potential. In 3,500 pages of recorded testimony, it is clear that the statute was a product of "egalitarian and democratic impulses ... target[ing] multiple forms of exclusion and inequality ... [and aimed at creating] democratic solutions to the problems of special education" (Ong-Dean, 2009, pp. 13–14). Proponents argued that broad social goals of equality and inclusion would be achieved by EAHCA provisions that resolved the special education problems of ineffective instruction, exclusion, and race and class bias (Dunn, 1968; Mercer, 1973). Although courts subsequently interpreted these provisions "in ways that had little to do with social reform, proponents were hopeful that the law would not be a narrow one" (Ong-Dean, 2009, p. 21).

The provisions in question, of course, are those that operationalize what became the grounding principles of the EAHCA and IDEA—zero-reject, nondiscriminatory evaluation, appropriate education, least restrictive environment, parent participation, and procedural due process (Turnbull, Stowe, & Huerta, 2007). The first four govern the processes school districts are to follow in order to "confer on each IDEA-covered student the benefit of a free appropriate education in the least restrictive environment," while the last two are procedural safeguards that covered students and their parents use "to hold the [school district] accountable for complying with the first four principles and to be partners with the schools in the student's education" (Turnbull et al., p. 44). The procedural safeguards were considered essential because Congress knew that "it was asking the same professionals who had excluded [children with disabilities] in the past to now ensure their right to an appropriate education" (Kuriloff, 1985, p. 90). In this regard, Congress believed that the process to be followed in developing an individualized educational plan (IEP) was "'a way to provide parent involvement and protection to assure that appropriate services are provided to a [child with disability].' Although it did not explicitly so state, Congress clearly assumed that educators would not on their own maximize the educational potential of each child" (Clune & Van Pelt, 1985, p. 13).

Beyond their value in maximizing the potential of individual children, however, disability advocates and members of Congress saw parent participation and due process rights as essential to achieving systemic reform of special education, which they saw as essential if its recognized problems were to be resolved and the broader social goals of equality and inclusion were to be advanced. Although Congressional framers assumed that due process procedures would be "relatively informal, inexpensive, and quick" (Clune & Van Pelt, 1985, p. 13), they saw the hearings as substantively oriented, thereby resulting in "more systematic pressure on school systems" to improve special education practice, ultimately putting students with disabilities "on an educational par with [nondisabled] students, and lead[ing] to uniformity of treatment among [students with disabilities]" (p. 13). Toward the end of resolving problems at the system level, disability advocates wanted the "results in individual cases [to] be followed across the board, producing a general pattern of compliance" (pp. 13–14). In an important article reprinted in the hearings record, Kirp, Buss, and Kuriloff (1974) envisioned such a precedent-based due process hearing system as open to the public, with nonprofit advocacy organizations representing the collective interests of children with disabilities and their families, thus leading to continuous improvement of special education nationwide through the diffusion of common norms of practice. With regard to disproportionate representation, parent participation and due process rights were valued more highly than the statute's nondiscriminatory evaluation provision. Oliver Hurley, an

African American special education professor and leading critic of racial bias in special education, made no mention of the nondiscriminatory evaluation provision in his testimony, while claiming that parent participation and due process rights would "'substantially help' to alleviate the problem of minority overrepresentation" (Ong-Dean, 2009, p. 24). Kirp et al. (1974) agreed, arguing that such a system would alleviate the disproportionate representation problem because "the reasons for each [student] classification would be out in the open. If the reasons were invalid, they would be exposed, and the resulting public disapproval would force adjustments in a salutary direction" (p. 121).

Although "democratization of decision making" (Ong-Dean, 2009, p. 24) through parent participation and due process rights was essential to systemic reform, the design, judicial interpretation, and implementation of these components of the law ultimately undermined this possibility and thus the aim of improved special education practice and the broader goals of social equality and inclusion. Rather than the envisioned precedent-based system of open hearings and collective advocacy leading to improved practice through systemic reform, actual due process hearings are private affairs "centered on the student's 'individualized' educational plan" (p. 25), thus subverting joint action and systemic reform.[1] As a result, rather than advancing appropriate education and inclusion of children with disabilities, eliminating racial/ethnic and class inequalities, and allowing parents to be active participants in institutional decision making, the EAHCA "mainly enabled parents to raise individualized, technical disputes over their children's disability diagnoses and needs" (Ong-Dean, 2009, p. 10). Moreover, rather than advancing social equality and inclusion in society, judicial interpretation of these and other components of the statute has rendered it "less a basis for social reform and more a call for improved technical management of individual cases" (p. 31).[2]

Although the EAHCA was a product of egalitarian and democratic impulses, it has resulted in a system that bears little resemblance to the one envisioned by the statute's proponents. A subsequent section on its implementation will show how and why that system fails to resolve the special education problems that the statute was enacted to address and, with regard to Ong-Dean's (2009) claims, how and why it both mutes public concern for those problems and creates an environment that favors privileged parents and thereby perpetuates special education's racial/ethnic and class inequalities. As such, the claim that the IDEA confers substantive rights on children with disabilities and their parents is only true in a formal sense. These rights are not fully enforceable in public education, the institutional context that the statute seeks to change, in part because of the nature of that context, but also because its procedural safeguard provisions subvert systemic special education reform and thus the kinds of changes necessary to actualize its substantive provisions. In preparation for this analysis and a discussion of policy and organizational changes for transforming the system, the following section presents an analytic framework for understanding the nature and effects of the institutional context whose transformation should be the aim and focus of special education leadership development.

Rights, Needs, and Institutionalized Organizations

These problems—disjunction between conferred and actualized rights, diminished concern for presenting problems, and preservation and extension of inequalities—are not unique to disability rights. They are central concerns in the critique of liberal legal consciousness, the framework that underwrites the IDEA and other disability and civil rights legislation, which holds that, as a political strategy, legal rights discourse, or "rights talk," is both indeterminate and legitimating. It is indeterminate in eliminating injustice because the value of a right is determined by the structure and political commitments of its institutional context, not the right itself. It is legitimating because, by appearing to confer rights in such contexts, it relieves pressure for reform, in effect continuing and justifying the injustices the rights were to eliminate (Crenshaw,

1988, p. 1351; Kelman, 1987). In response to this "post-rights" critique, however, legal scholars of color defended rights talk as a political strategy, both crediting it for rights achieved in the civil rights movement and, recognizing the indeterminate and legitimating effects of the idiom, also calling for a "jurisprudence of reconstruction" (Harris, 1994, p. 744) to fully actualize those rights by reconstructing them to reflect the real needs and political commitments of communities of color (Crenshaw, 1988; Crenshaw, Gotanda, Peller, & Thomas, 1995; Williams, 1991).

Today, the disability rights movement is in a position similar to the broader civil rights movement.[3] It has used the rights idiom successfully to establish disability rights for children and families, but the actualization of those rights is at best indeterminate, institutionally mediated, and disempowering, especially for children and families subject to intersecting race, class, and disability injustices (Connor, 2008; McCall & Skrtic, 2009). In terms of a direction for remedial action, the one proposed by civil rights scholars has merit, as far as it goes; that is, while recognizing what has been achieved using the rights idiom, the current indeterminate and legitimating rights of the IDEA must be reconstructed to reflect the real needs of children with disabilities and their families and the political commitments of the disability community. However, reconstructing disability rights requires more than a reconstruction of rights in the IDEA. It also requires overcoming two additional problems, a conceptual problem discussed below, and a political problem introduced below and addressed more fully in the concluding section.

Conceptual Problem

The conceptual problem is that understanding the indeterminacy of the IDEA requires theorizing the institutional context in which reconstructed disability rights are to be adjudicated. In turn, this requires general recognition of the role of institutions in creating just conditions for the realization of rights, as well as specific consideration of what such conditions would entail and how they would be achieved and sustained. Moreover, such a theorization also would require clarity about what injustice is in these contexts, what it entails and how it is enacted and sustained. Perhaps the most exemplary scholarship on these aspects of the indeterminacy problem has been done by political philosophers Iris Marion Young (1990) and Nancy Fraser (1989, 2008) and legal scholar Martha Minow (1990).

Indeterminate Rights and Institutionalized Injustice. Although Young (1990) accepted John Rawls's (1971) distributive theory of justice with regard to distribution of material goods (primarily income and wealth), she criticized it for misrepresenting nonmaterial goods—including rights, opportunities, and self-respect—which, she argued, are not things; they are *relationships* based on processes that are mediated by social institutions. As such, social institutions are implicated in the construction, oppression, and domination of difference and Young is concerned with theorizing the scope and substance of "institutionalized injustice" (p. 327). In this regard, she argued that we cannot know what justice requires in particular social situations until we listen, albeit critically, to individuals and groups who are suffering various forms of institutionalized injustice (also see Young, 2000; Fraser & Honneth, 2003).

Minow (1990) criticizes rights analysis for too often resulting in incremental reforms that leave institutional sources of injustice intact. As an alternative to an exclusively rights-focused approach to justice, Minow proposed a "social-relations approach to the legal treatment of difference" (1990, p. 172) which, like Young's (1990) relational interpretation of rights, locates "rights *in* relationship" (p. 282). In addition, like Young (1990, 2000) and Fraser (1989, 2008), her social relations approach treats existing social institutions as a source of the problem of difference rather than as a neutral background, analyzing difference in terms of "the relationships that construct it" (1990, p. 112). In this regard, she links the source of such unjust institutional arrangements to early 20th-century progressive reformers, commending them for advancing policies to care for and protect dependent and vulnerable citizens, while criticizing the institutions they created to actualize these policies for failing to include the voices of their intended beneficiaries, for lacking "genuine democracy, through which people would share decisions about their collective future" (p. 264). Thus, like Young, Minow argues that we cannot know what justice requires unless those who are suffering institutionalized injustice have a voice and role in the ongoing process of its elimination.

Indeterminate Rights and Needs Politics. Young (2000) and Minow (1990) address the conceptual problem by theorizing the nature of rights and injustice in social institutions. Fraser (1989) addresses it by theorizing how injustice is enacted in these institutions, focusing on the political and institutional processes for making and adjudicating the needs–claims that rights are established to recognize and satisfy. This requires an understanding of the political career of such claims in liberal welfare state societies, for which Fraser introduces the concept of "needs talk" (p. 161), a political idiom involving disputes about people's needs and whether and how government should provide for them. Arguing that needs talk is the dominant form of political discourse in such societies, co-existing with talk about rights and interests, she is concerned with the barriers and opportunities it poses for social movements that want to make these political cultures more just and equitable. Her research is an institutional analysis of power in which "needs politics" is the medium of struggle among unequal groups, a process through which the relationship between oppression and activism is enacted in social institutions (see McCall & Skrtic, 2009; Skrtic, 2000).

Key among Fraser's (1989) insights on needs politics are two axes of needs struggle. The first is the struggle between what she calls "oppositional" and "reprivatization" discourses (p. 171). Oppositional discourses are those of social movements that attempt to "politicize" their needs by reinterpreting them in ways that make them a matter of public concern and provision, such as the one that produced the EAHCA (McCall & Skrtic, 2009; Skrtic, 2000). Reprivatization discourses arise in resistance to oppositional discourses. They reflect entrenched need interpretations of those who oppose state provision for reinterpreted needs and thus try to "depoliticize them" (p. 172) or keep government from accepting responsibility for them by arguing that they should be met by the family or, for those who can afford it, through services purchased in the private marketplace. Moreover, oppositional discourses are about more than reinterpreting needs. By politicizing their needs, members of oppositional discourses contest their subordinate identities and invent new discursive forms and vehicles for interpreting and disseminating their alternative need interpretations.[4] As such, oppositional needs talk is "a moment in the self-constitution of new collective [political] agents" (p. 171).

The second, largely veiled, axis of needs struggle pits successful oppositional discourses against expert discourses in government human service agencies. As the vehicle for translating state-recognized needs into objects of state intervention, expert discourses emerge when politicized needs become candidates for state provision. The central issue here, Fraser (1989) explains, is politics versus administration. Administratively, expert discourses translate successfully-reinterpreted oppositional needs into "administrable needs" (p. 174) by recasting them in terms that tacitly presuppose the prerogatives of the service agency and its professionals, typically redefining them as needs already covered by an existing service or program, or by one that can be established with the least increment of disruption to the system. Politically, expert discourses simultaneously recast members of successful oppositional movements as individual "cases," thereby turning political activists into "individualized victims" (p. 176). As such, expert discourses are also depoliticizing. In the end, those who collectively secured the political status of their needs are atomized and pathologized, recast as individual victims rather than members of a political movement, thereby positioning them as passive recipients of predefined services rather than agents involved in interpreting their needs and shaping their life.

Legitimation and Institutional Theory.   If our inherited social institutions are unjust, and rights analysis only leads to incremental reforms that leave institutional sources of injustice intact, how have these institutions survived for so long? Our ability to answer such questions was advanced considerably with the advent of institutional theory, which is concerned with institutionalization processes in organizations and their effects on the way organizations respond to their social environments. With regard to the former, it emphasizes the formation of taken-for-granted institutional rules, myths, and beliefs that guide thought and action in organizations (Powell & DiMaggio, 1991) and, with regard to the latter, the effects of these institutional processes on the structural characteristics of organizations (Meyer & Rowan, 1977; Scott & Meyer, 1987) and the nature of organizational change (Meyer, 1979; Zucker, 1981, 1988).

Institutional theory posits that schools' survival depends on their ability to maintain legitimacy and stability (Powell & DiMaggio, 1991). To maintain legitimacy, they must be responsive to the often conflicting demands and constraints of four environmental entities—the social state (and its governmental agencies, regulatory structures, laws, and courts), the education profession, influential interest groups, and public opinion generally (DiMaggio & Powel, 1983; Scott, 1987)—which they do by reproducing or imitating organizational structures, activities, and routines to respond to legal and regulatory requirements and cultural expectations, model similar organizations perceived to be more legitimate or successful, and/or conform to the expectations of the profession (Powell & DiMaggio, 1991, p. 66). Over time, the resulting structures, activities, and routines become calcified because imitation involves conformity, habit, and ritualized activity rather than reflective strategic choice, leading to unquestioned acceptance of institutionalized structures, classifications, and practices (DiMaggio, 1988; Tolbert & Zucker, 1983).

As such, schools define and structure their activities around functions—such as general education and special education—that reflect institutionalized or "ritual" classifications of students, personnel, and programs rather than technical assessments of effectiveness and efficiency (Meyer & Rowan, 1978, 1983; Powell & DiMaggio, 1991). Although ritualization fosters stability in schools, it also makes it more difficult for them to change in response to evolving regulatory requirements and cultural expectations, and especially to more punctuated change mandates like the IDEA that require substantially different structures and activities. Schools cope with these threats to legitimacy by using "ceremonial activity" (Meyer & Rowan, 1978, p. 355) and "decoupling" (p. 357) devices to signal the environment that they have changed when in fact they remain largely the same (Meyer, 1979; Zucker, 1981). Indeed, as discussed below, special education generally and IDEA implementation in particular are archetypical cases of such symbolic change in public education (see, Skrtic, 1991b, 1995; Skrtic & McCall, 2010).[5]

Political Problem

The political problem is that actualizing reconstructed disability rights in liberal welfare state societies requires more than restructuring the social institutions in which those rights and needs-claims are adjudicated. The necessary institutional restructuring—including the material and ideational or cultural structure of social service organizations—will require restructuring liberal democracy itself, not by rejecting the liberal tradition, but rather by drawing upon the "developmental" strain of liberalism within it. The political problem is discussed more fully in the concluding section, but first I want to use the institutional analyses introduced above to highlight problems with the design and implementation of the IDEA, problems that question the sense of justice that its provisions are presumed to extend to covered students and their families.

Relational Analysis of IDEA Implementation

In this section IDEA's substantive and procedural safeguard principles are considered from the perspective of the institutional analysis of rights, needs, and schools.[6] Based on this analysis, the next section is a proposal for resolving these problems by returning to the initial democratic reform strategies proposed for the EAHCA.

Appropriate Education

With regard to the principle of appropriate education, the IEP for most IDEA-covered students is largely symbolic. From its introduction in the 1970s, it has served more to signal compliance with the appropriate education provision than actually specify and guide a needs-based individualized education (Pretti-Frontczak & Bricker, 2000; Skrtic, 1991b; Smith, 1990; Smith & Kotering, 1997; Ysseldyke et al., 1983). Already by the early 1980s, questions of IEP quality and utility had given way to concern for "reducing the cost and time necessary to complete [them]" (Smith, 1990, p. 11), and eventually to development of computerized IEPs that did so by "using formulas and following rules, rather than ... individualized [planning]" (1990, pp. 10–11). Moreover, despite concerns about the alignment of IDEA with the standards-based accountability model of NCLB narrowing the curriculum for students with disabilities (Wehmeyer & Schalock, 2001) and standardizing their instruction (Skrtic, Harris, & Shriner, 2005), by 1999 states already had begun using "standards-based IEPs" to align instructional goals for students with disabilities with general education curriculum standards (Ahrens, 2006, p. 4), and today two-thirds have instituted or are implementing them (Ahrens, 2010). Whereas "IDEA and good practice dictate that, for a student's education to be appropriate, it must be individually tailored to fit that student" (Turnbull et al., 2007, p. 161), standards-based IEPs are premised on students' attainment of state "academic standards for [their] enrolled grade" (Ahrens, 2010, p. 2).[7] Although the goal of increasing the academic achievement of students with disabilities is laudable, like symbolic IEP implementation, an over-emphasis on academic achievement defined narrowly as attainment of state standards contradicts the statute's original emphasis on appropriate *individualized* education, turning the principle of individualization into standardization of curriculum and instruction.

Beyond standardization of the IEP, the appropriate education principle has been further eroded by a deterioration of the organizational conditions of its implementation under standards-based reform. Implementing the appropriate education principle always has been difficult because the bureaucratic organization of schools virtually precludes the kind of general-special educator collaboration necessary to implement an IEP (Skrtic, 1991b). Today, the standards-based framework of NCLB/IDEA is making schools even more bureaucratic, and thus less collaborative, because of NCLB's extreme bureaucratic approach to outcomes-based accountability (O'Day, 2002), the very approach that William Spady, architect of outcomes-based education, cautioned against at the start of the standards-based reform movement. Spady (Spady & Marshall, 1991, p. 68) called this approach the "traditional model" of outcomes-based reform, which he rejected because its primary reform strategy, curriculum alignment, retains and extends the existing bureaucratic structure of schools (also see Champlin, 1991).[8]

Least Restrictive Environment (LRE)

Although the IDEA contains a regulatory preference for inclusive placements, the LRE principle is a rebuttable presumption; placement in a general educational classroom "is not an absolute right but is secondary to the primary purpose of [appropriate] education" (Turnbull, 1993, p. 159). The value of LRE placements for included and mainstream students is recognized, but the statute gives an appropriate education precedence over a least restrictive one, an ordering of principles consistently upheld by the courts (Douvanis & Hulsey, 2002; Thomas & Rapport, 1998).

From the perspective of institutional theory, schools use separate, decoupled classrooms and programs to signal compliance with environmental demands while minimizing disruption to their institutionalized structures, classifications, and practices, thereby helping them maintain stability and legitimacy simultaneously (Meyer & Rowan, 1977, 1978). The segregated special classroom is a key example of this form of decoupling. It was created in the early 20th century to separate and contain student diversity resulting from compulsory attendance legislation (Lazerson, 1983; Sarason & Doris, 1979; Tropea, 1987), thereby maintaining the stability and legitimacy of schools by signaling compliance with the demand for universal public education (Skrtic, 1991b, 1995). Criticism of these classrooms as racially biased, instructionally ineffective, and psychologically and socially damaging (e.g., Dunn, 1968; Mercer, 1973) added force to EAHCA proponents' campaign against exclusion, but the ambiguity created by the statute's dual commitment to the principles of appropriate education and LRE often is exploited in schools by using arguments for the former to defeat the latter. "After all," Minow (1985) explained, the LRE principle was devised "to combat [the] very reluctance of the classroom teacher to deal with the unusual or more difficult child" (p. 178), and the ambiguity created by IDEA's commitment to both principles permits "the incentives of teachers … to give content to the law" (p. 178).

Moreover, consideration of inclusive placements in schools often locates the problem of difference in the student to be included, "while making the unimpaired students—and the classroom designed for them—the norm" (Minow, 1990, p. 84). However, applying the curriculum principles of "universal design for learning" (UDL) to such classrooms, Minow provides a counterexample in which a teacher includes a student with a profound hearing impairment by teaching all her students sign language and then teaching in sign and spoken language simultaneously, thereby "treat[ing] the problem of difference as embedded in the relationships among all the students … [using] an approach that [works] to the educational benefit of every student in the classroom" (p. 84; also see Minow, 2008). Among the advantages of such a relational approach to difference and inclusion, Minow notes that rather than making the trait of hearing impairment "signify stigma or isolation," it responds to that trait "as an issue for the entire community" (p. 84). Conversely, by focusing on the individual child, individualized planning "tends to ignore the child's relationships with others and the construction of difference in those relationships" (p. 86). Moreover, an individualized plan would not have conceived of a class of students fluent in sign language because it would "leave in place the existing classroom methods … [and expect the included student to] adjust to the existing educational structure" (p. 86). This illustration disrupts the relative merit of the two IDEA principles, "in effect making the LRE principle as primary as that of appropriate education and relegating the conventional regular classroom to a rebuttable presumption" (Skrtic & Kent, in press).

Nondiscriminatory Evaluation

The statute's nondiscriminatory evaluation principle addresses the most obdurate problem in special education—the disproportionate identification and placement of poor, working class, and racial/ethnic minority students in special education.[9] Drawing upon the civil rights movement and the decision, as well as on the early research on the disproportionate representation problem noted above, disability advocates and EAHCA proponents conceptualized the nondiscriminatory evaluation (NDE) principle to address "the risks of misclassification and labeling in creating stigma and low self-esteem, and the abusive use of separate classes to perpetuate discrimination against racial and ethnic minorities" (Minow, 1985, p. 168). Although NDE provisions require nondiscriminatory classification and placement decisions, disproportionate representation of economically disadvantaged and racial/ethnic minority students both in special education and, especially for African American students, in more restrictive special education placements has continued largely unabated over the history of the IDEA (National Research Council [NRC], 1982; NRC, 2002; Skiba, Poloni-Staudinger, Gallini, Simmons, & Feggins-Azziz, 2006; Skiba, et al., 2008).

Disproportionate representation was formally recognized as a policy problem over the course of the 1960s when, in the context of resistance to the *Brown* decision, including various forms of "resegregation within desegregated schools" (Bell, 1980, p. 531), the disproportionate identification of African American students as "educable mentally retarded" attracted increasing attention (e.g., Dunn, 1968; Christophos & Renz, 1969). Although Bell didn't link special education to this form of resistance, others have implicated it in the resegregation process (e.g., Ferri & Connors, 2005; Skrtic, 1991b). From an institutional perspective, disproportionate representation can be understood as another form of decoupling in which schools use an existing decoupling device—selected special education programs—to maintain their legitimacy and stability while failing to meet the needs of disproportionate numbers of African American students in purportedly desegregated schools (Skrtic, 2003). This is possible because, like complying with IEP provisions, compliance with those of NDE is ceremonialized within team evaluation processes (Skrtic, 2003; Skrtic & McCall, 2010). Ultimately, ceremonial compliance legitimates IDEA identification and placement processes by making them and their decisions seem lawful, principled, and objective, thus justifying continued abusive use of special education to perpetuate racial/ethnic and social class discrimination.

Procedural Safeguards

In addition to problems implementing IDEA's substantive provisions, its procedural safeguard provisions themselves have become a barrier to resolving special education problems in two interrelated ways. First, implementation of the parent participation and procedural due process provisions atomizes the oppositional discourse that produced the law by individualizing activism within IEP meetings and due process hearings focused on individual children and families. Rather than collective agents of a political movement, "the law requires parents to advocate for their children individually in direct, solitary encounters with expert discourses in schools and school districts" (McCall & Skrtic, 2009, p. 14), encounters in which they are at a distinct disadvantage (Mehan, Hertweck, & Meihls, 1986), especially if they are poor, working class, and/ or members of a racial, ethnic, or linguistic minority group (Harry, Klingner, & Hart, 2005; Kalyanpur, Harry, & Skrtic, 2000; Ong-Dean, 2009).

Second, the design and legal interpretation of these provisions undercut the egalitarian and democratic motivations of the social movement that fought for and won the law (Ong-Dean, 2009). In the end, rather than democratic solutions to recognized special education problems, the law merely enables individual parents to mount "individualized, technical disputes" (p. 10) over their child's disability diagnosis and accommodations. In addition to muting broader social concerns about special education problems, reducing them to isolated cases of individual children and families creates the individualized and competitive environment characterized by Ong-Dean, which from a needs politics perspective, has "supplanted the solidarity of collective agents involved in a political movement and institutionalized a class divide in the special education process" (McCall & Skrtic, 2009, p. 14).

Although these provisions atomize advocacy the degree to which parents are reduced to passive cases in the special education process depends on their economic and cultural capital, with privileged parents—those who are "white, middle- to high-income, English-speaking, professional, and college educated" (Ong-Dean, 2009, p. 3)—in the most advantageous position in terms of advocating for their children. In terms of needs politics, privileged parents have greater access to the discursive resources necessary to press their needs claims with experts in

IEP meetings, which puts them in a better position to act as agents in interpreting their children's needs and shaping their life conditions (McCall & Skrtic, 2009). As far as challenging IEP decisions, cultural and economic capital also affect the nature and distribution of due process hearing requests and cases, both of which are more prevalent in wealthier school districts where the challenges put forth "presuppose a fair degree of parental privilege" (Ong-Dean, 2009, p. 132). Moreover, because privileged parents are in a far better position to use IEP and due process procedures to secure better educational outcomes for their children, the IDEA's individualized and competitive environment "perpetuate[s] the hierarchies from which their own privileges come" (p. 3).

Finally, in terms of disproportionate representation, the concept of cultural and economic capital enhances our understanding of the social cost of a biased IEP process. That is, the bias favoring privilege puts poor, working class, and racial/ethnic minority parents at a disadvantage relative to professionals and more privileged parents in resisting inappropriate disability diagnoses, accommodations, and placements for their children or, when called for, recognizing and claiming the most advantageous ones for them (McCall & Skrtic, 2009). As such, the unfair influence of economic and cultural capital in special education perpetuates the disproportionality problem, while the parent participation and procedural due process provisions of the IDEA legitimate their unjust outcomes, thereby muting broader social concern for the long-standing disproportionality problem and perpetuating the racial-ethnic and social class hierarchies that sustain it. Moreover, this is not merely an implementation problem; this injustice is built into the structure of the law itself, into the very procedural safeguards that were intended to ensure schools' compliance with the principles of appropriate education, least restrictive environment, and nondiscriminatory evaluation.

Proposal[10]

This section is a proposal for addressing past and current special education injustices by recovering the democratic reform strategies envisioned by the social movement that produced the EAHCA. Base on the above institutional analysis of IDEA provisions, it considers policy and organizational changes necessary to resolve these injustices in ways that actualize the principles of the IDEA and the egalitarian and democratic impulses that produced it, including redesigning special education policy to reconstitute IDEA's procedural safeguards as a mechanism of systemic reform, restructuring schools according to the principles of UDL, and transforming the professional culture of education. These changes are meant to transform schools into more just institutions by giving the individuals and groups who are suffering these injustices a voice and role in their elimination, thereby reconstructing disability rights in terms of the real needs of the disability community. The first two changes are taken up in this section. The third is introduced here and elaborated in the concluding section, which addresses the political problem introduced above by placing these changes and their broader social significance in historical perspective.

Redesigning Special Education Policy

The system created by the parent participation and due process provisions that were enacted is quite different from the one envisioned in the early 1970s. Rather than a precedent-based system of open hearings and collective advocacy, it is individualized, competitive, and virtually closed,[11] which atomizes advocacy and depoliticizes activism, thereby precluding systemic reform and leaving historical injustices unresolved while creating and perpetuating new ones. Because there is little hope of justly resolving these inequities with these procedural safeguard provisions in their current form, they need to be redesigned along the lines proposed by EAHCA proponents prior to the statute's enactment. The goal with regard to procedural due process would be to give students and parents who are suffering special education injustices a voice and role in their elimination by creating an open, substantively-oriented and deliberative precedent-based hearing system, one premised on collective advocacy for children and families and broad application of findings and corrective actions to all like cases, first, in the school, district, and state, and ultimately, as state precedent builds, to all like cases in the nation (see below). With regard to parent participation, the goal would be to create an open, deliberative IEP process with collective advocacy to protect the interests of all students and families—especially those currently most disadvantaged in solitary encounters with professionals—and to equalize assess to the best student accommodations and outcomes.

The envisioned deliberative process is much like that of the social planning model used in frame analysis or "frame-reflective inquiry" (Schön & Rein, 1994, p. 50) to resolve "wicked" policy problems in which it is "the very formulation of the problem that is problematic" (Blanco, 1994, p. 22). It emerged as an alternative to the rational model of policy analysis, which is premised on *instrumental* reasoning and its positivist conception of progress and cost-benefit approach to policy choice, and thus, like positivism itself, is best suited to narrowly defined, single-aim problems rather than ambiguous ones (Anderson, 1993; Lindblom, 1991). Policy scholars working from the frame analysis perspective are largely Deweyan or classical pragmatists (Kaufman-Osborn, 1985). They reject an exclusively rational approach to policy analysis in favor of social planning because, as a dialogical process grounded in *practical* reasoning, it engages alternative interpretations of social problems, learning from opposing views while attempting to understand them and their respective preferred solutions critically (Richardson, 2002). Moreover, in terms of policy choice, social planning, like classical pragmatism, is politically deliberative, judging alternative frames and solutions and selecting among or integrating them on the basis of their social consequences, particularly their contribution to the realization of the democratic ideals of liberty, equality, and especially community or participation, because reform through social planning requires equal participation in the deliberative process (Dewey, 1989/1931, 1981/1917, 1991/1939; Kaufman-Osborn, 1985).[12]

Applying the social planning model to IDEA's procedural safeguard provisions would mean that interpretations of children's needs and accommodations would be judged and selected or integrated in terms of their educational and social consequences for children and families, as well as for their contribution to the practical realization of democratic ideals in schools and communities. Confidentiality understandably will be an issue in some cases but, like using appropriate education arguments to defeat LRE placements, it should not be used to argue against collective advocacy, especially since parents currently can invite representatives of advocacy groups to IEP meetings, opt for open due process hearings, and access redacted hearing decisions. As such, instituting collective advocacy under a social planning model is more a matter of increasing awareness of its potential rather than changing policy. Moreover, the trade-offs between confidentiality and collective advocacy and repoliticized activism are substantial, including reinvigorating the democratic impulses of the social movement that fought for the EAHCA and IDEA and empowering parents and disability advocates to move schools, through systemic reform, in the direction envisioned in the spirit of the statute, producing a general pattern of compliance and continuous improvement of special education practice, gradually reducing the need for due process hearings. Ultimately, such a process would alter the structural dynamics of needs politics in schools by eliminating parents' solitary encounters with expert discourses, which would help to demystify institutional justifications for oppressive practices and thereby positively influence the lived experiences and individual consciousness of IDEA-covered and overrepresented children and their parents.

Restructuring Schools

If we are to resolve long-standing and emergent special education policy problems through such a deliberative process, an essential direction of systemic reform is replacing the current professional bureaucracy structure of schools. This structure, and the institutional processes that sustain and legitimate it, are both the source of special education's most intractable problems, including that of disproportionate representation, and the reason a function like special education emerged in public education (Skrtic, 1991b, 2003). Like all professional bureaucracies, schools divide and coordinate their work through specialization and professionalization, respectively. A specialized division of labor is premised on matching students with like needs to teachers with presumed corresponding repertoires of practices, and professionalization achieves coordination by standardizing the repertoires of the teachers in these specializations through professional education. As such, schools are performance organizations, largely non-adaptable structures in which teachers apply standard instructional practices to students with needs to which the practices have been matched. Although there is some room for adaptation, teachers working in professional bureaucracies do not invent new practices for students with unfamiliar needs (see Simon, 1977; Weick, 1976). In principle, when teachers encounter assigned students whose needs fall outside the standard practices in their repertoires, they must force the student's needs artificially into an available practice, or the student must be sent to a different specialist whose repertoire presumably contains the matching practice (Mintzberg, 1979). Rather than adapt to diversity by having classroom teachers develop new applicable practices, historically schools have screened out diversity by removing it from regular classrooms and containing it in decoupled programs like special education (Skrtic, 1991a).[13]

This type of decoupling is possible in schools because together specialization and professionalization create a cellular or "loosely coupled" interdependence among teachers and programs (Mintzberg, 1979; Weick, 1976), which historically has allowed schools to change "by accretion, by adding new rooms to the structure, thereby enabling educators to absorb demands for change without much damage to vested educational interests" (Tyack & Hansot, 1981, p. 21). That is, given their inherent non-adaptability, schools resist change by signaling the public that it has occurred when it hasn't (Meyer & Rowan, 1977; Zucker, 1981), and the segregated special education classroom is a key example of this form of decoupling (Skrtic, 1991b). Created to contain diversity in schools resulting from compulsory attendance legislation (Sarason & Doris, 1979; Tropea, 1987), these classrooms served as a legitimating device, signaling that schools had complied with the demand for universal public education while, at the same time, permitting them to maintain their conventional organizational structures, activities, and routines. The disproportional representation of poor, working class, and racial/ethnic minority students in special education is another form of decoupling in which, following *Brown,* schools used an existing decoupling device—the special education system—to signal compliance and thus maintain legitimacy while failing to meet the needs of disproportionate numbers of these students in the regular classrooms of desegregated schools (Skrtic, 1995, 2003).

The only way to eliminate unjust decoupling practices in schools is to eliminate the structural features that make such practices possible and the institutional incentives that sustain them by restructuring schools as learning organizations (Argyris & Schön, 1978), the non-bureaucratic organizational configuration known historically as "adhocracy" (Bennis & Slater, 1964). Professional bureaucracies are *performance* organizations engaged in convergent thinking aimed at perfection, whereas adhocracies are *problem solving* organizations engaged in divergent thinking aimed at innovation (Mintzberg, 1979, 1989). They are premised on innovation rather than standardization, on the invention of unique, customized products and services through processes of organizational learning based on collaboration, mutual adjustment, and deliberative discourse among workers and between them and their clients and customers. As adhocracies, schools would divide their labor through collaboration or interdisciplinary team work and coordinate it through mutual adjustment or reflective deconstruction and reconstruction of team members' respective conventional theories and practices. Together, these structural contingencies yield a deliberative form of interdependence premised on collaborative problem solving among professionals, parents and other community stakeholders and, when appropriate, students (Skrtic, 1991b, 1995). Again, this arrangement follows the social planning model in that teams would consider alternative interpretations of children's needs and associated practices, deliberatively judging and selecting or integrating them in terms of their educational and social consequences for children and families, and their democratic consequences for schools and communities.

As such, adhocracy is both the means and end of the reform process. It is required for the deliberative IEP and due process system as a means of systemic reform, and it is the structure for schools that would resolve special education's most intractable problems, those identified in the 1960s and 1970s, targeted for elimination by IDEA's substantive principles, but still with us today. In principle, social and educational outcomes would improve considerably in adhocratic schools because instruction is tailored to each student's actual needs, virtually removing the need for segregated placements, thereby minimizing labeling and eliminating the institutional incentives for restrictive placements and disproportionate representation.

In the same way that Minow (1990) applied the curriculum principles of UDL to a general education classroom, Hehir (2005) argued for applying them to school organization itself, creating what he called "universally designed schools" (p. 109). For Hehir, these are schools that "allow disabled students to access education naturally," schools in which "the needs that arise out of their disability become situated more within the environment in which they are functioning than within themselves" (p. 109), much like Minow (1990) treated needs that arose from a hearing impairment in her universally designed classroom. Hehir based his case for applying UDL principles to school organization on two organizational analyses: my analysis of school organization and special education reform (Skrtic, 1991b), key aspects of which are presented above, and Richard Elmore's (2004) analysis of school organization and standards-based reform which, according to Hehir, is a call for "fundamental changes in the institutional practice and structure of public schools" (p. 109) in the interest of improving educational performance under NCLB.[14]

Noting that my analysis "predated the application of the term 'universal design' to schooling" (Hehir, 2005, p. 106), Hehir explained that nonetheless, in proposing the adhocratic structure for schools, it "clearly advocates the [organizational] principles that would create the conditions under which children with disabilities and other diverse learners would be able to access schooling in a natural and effective manner" (pp. 106–107). Based on examples of effective inclusive schools in Boston that follow these adhocratic principles, he reported that, with respect to educating students with disabilities, they "almost always implement nonstandard approaches that require problem solving from a variety of people with different perspectives and backgrounds, including parents" (p. 107). Such schools, he explained, have "moved away from traditional structures and provide many opportunities for professionals to work together in classrooms to improve curriculum and instruction" (p. 109). Moreover, Hehir pointed to mounting evidence that good, inclusive urban schools that extend these organizational principles beyond students with disabilities to all students are "among the best-performing schools in urban districts" (p. 107).

Reconstructing Professionalism

Because the adhocratic restructuring of public education described above is meaningless without a parallel reconstruction of professional culture, another essential requirement of systemic reform is a transformation of education's technocratic form of professionalism into the alternative model of professionalism advanced by Dewey and other early twentieth century pragmatist progressives (Dewey, 1988a/1929–1930, 1988b/1927). This type of civic (Sullivan, 2005) or democratic (Dzur, 2008) professionalism is premised on the capacities and sensibilities of the strong democrat, the practical reasoning of classical pragmatism, and the traditional idea of a profession as a calling to serve the common good (see Skrtic, 2000, 2005). As democratic professionals, educators would work collaboratively and deliberatively with students, parents, and community stakeholders to identify child, family, and community needs, then adjust their conventional theories and practices to address those needs in empowering ways. Once again, these professionals would be following the social planning model of classical pragmatism, a deliberative mode of inquiry in which alternative interpretations of needs, accommodations, and associated practices are judged and selected or integrated in terms of their educational and social consequences for children and families, and their contribution to the realization of democratic ideals in schools, communities, and society at large.

To avoid a change in form but not substance, the availability of a non-bureaucratic structure for schooling is necessary but not sufficient. Taking full advantage of the adhocracy configuration requires a corresponding transformation of professional culture. Moreover, in addition to civic professional teachers, systemic reform also requires a new civic or democratic culture of leadership in schools and, ultimately, the emergence of a strong developmentally liberal democracy. Given the fundamental nature of these proposed changes, the next section places them in historical perspective to highlight both their broader social significance and the social and political costs of the status quo.

Strong Democratic Leadership

As we know, Minow (1990) credited early 20th-century progressives for their enlightened reforms to serve dependent and vulnerable citizens while criticizing them for the type of social institutions they created to do so. These institutions were problematic she argued because, by avoiding the kind of participatory processes that could have challenged their institutional biases, they imposed their interests on the people they claimed to serve, ultimately perpetuating and legitimating the injustices they suffered while expanding bureaucratic power. As such, Minow concludes that the oppressive institutional arrangements that she criticizes are a legacy of American progressivism. However, this view of progressivism captures only one of its tracks of reform, the one informed by what I will refer to below as "managerial liberalism." The second, politically less powerful track was informed by the "developmental" strain of liberalism advanced by progressives that Minow clearly admires—John Dewey, Jane Addams, and George Herbert Mead. Whatever shortcomings and naiveté we may find among these early developmental liberals, for the most part they respected cultural differences, defended communicative reciprocity across them, and argued for strong democracy (Furner, 1993; Kent, 2000, 2007; Muncy, 1991).[15]

Historically, we have ascribed three related but incompatible purposes to public education—democratic equality, social mobility, and social efficiency (Labaree, 1997). Democratic equality is concerned with preparing all of our young "with equal care" (p. 17) for effective citizenship, as well as with minimizing inequality in society to permit equal participation in the political process. Social mobility involves giving some students an advantage over others in the competition for social positions, which turns education into a commodity, thereby making schooling increasingly stratified and unequal. Social efficiency is concerned with allocating students to particular social positions, which requires schooling to mirror the stratified and unequal structure of the market economy. Because both of these purposes involve advantaging some individuals and groups over others in school and society, they increase social inequality and ultimately undermine the purpose of democratic equality.

This incompatibility of educational purposes reflects the basic tension at the core of all liberal democracies—the tension between democracy and capitalism, between the ideal of political equality and the reality of social inequality—which must be balanced in social institutions like education that serve both masters (Labaree, 1997). However, the possibility of achieving this balance becomes increasingly remote when one or more purposes dominate the others, which in turn depends on which of three competing political philosophies is dominant in society—market liberalism, developmental liberalism, or managerial liberalism—each of which represent a fundamentally different approach to balancing the tension between democracy and capitalism (Ryan, 1972; Macpherson, 1977).

Emerging in the first half of the nineteenth century, market liberalism is the classical form of liberal political economy. Market liberals argue for minimal government, expansion of free markets, and laissez faire economic and social policies, which yields a weak form of democracy in which citizens are mere competitors for political and economic goods and government is little more than a protector of economic markets and private rights (Held, 1996; Macpherson, 1977). Democracy in this view is weak, largely amounting to occasional voting for self-selected political elites, a non-participatory model that insists on a restricted role for citizens (and democracy itself) to prevent government interference in the economy (Foner, 1998; Ryan, 1972). Beginning in the 1980s, an extreme form of market liberalism, labeled *neoliberalism* by its critics (see below), became dominant in American political culture (Harvey, 2005; Mirowski & Plehwe, 2009), inordinately influencing the way we think and talk about public education, justify its existence (or elimination), and attempt to reform it (Engel, 2000; Henig, 1994). The dominance of neoliberalism largely explains why educational reform from *A Nation at Risk* (1983) through NCLB has elevated the purposes of social efficiency and social mobility to the virtual exclusion of democratic equality (Skrtic, 2005).[16]

Developmental liberalism and managerial liberalism emerged in the early twentieth century as two new strains of liberalism at the core of American progressivism, both of which opposed the economic and social dislocations of unregulated capitalism under market liberalism (Foner, 1998; Kloppenberg, 1986).[17] Although both strains were egalitarian in ways that market liberals have never been, the egalitarianism of developmental liberalism, unlike that of the managerial strain, was premised on active citizenship and a stronger conception of democracy that extended participation beyond the machinery of government into the larger society, including into public education (Gutmann, 1980). As such, developmental liberalism emphasizes the educational purpose of democratic equality because it views political participation itself as a primary social good, a reciprocal process of self and social improvement through which citizens progressively improve society and their capacities for democratic deliberation by engaging in collaborative social planning in and around social institutions (Hanson, 1985; Macpherson, 1977). Deweyan developmental liberals share a commitment to this type of strong democracy in which all social institutions become sites of political development through participatory social planning (Barber, 1984). In this sense, Dewey considered schools to be doubly educational, sites of democratic training for the young and of political development for citizens and professionals, which in turn required the kind of civic professionalism noted above, as well as what he called "democratic administration" (1981/1937, p. 225) or leadership in engaging citizens and professionals in deliberative problem solving aimed at improving education's responsiveness to the educational *and* social needs of students, families, and communities by balancing public education's purposes, values, and interests (Dewey, 1976/1899, 1980/1916).

During the progressive era, Dewey and other developmental progressives promoted democratic administration and civic professionalism as an antidote to market liberalism and weak democracy. Unfortunately, their vision lost out to the technocratic progressivism of managerial liberalism, which is the rightful target of Minow's (1990) criticism; the oppressive social institutions that she and Fraser (2008; Fraser & Honneth, 2003) and Young (1990, 2000) reject are the legacy of managerial liberalism, not progressivism. Inspired by positivism, utilitarianism, technocratic professionalization, and empirical social science, managerial liberals argued for an expanded government capacity to regulate the economy and distribute social services premised on the promise of technocratic efficiency through science and bureaucratic administration (Dewey, 1988b/1927; Price, 1974; Ryan, 1972). Although they opposed market liberalism, managerial liberals are weak democrats because, like market liberals, they favor limited citizen participation in politics, in their case to insulate the expert discourses of public bureaucracies from lay citizen interference. Prominent among early 20th century managerial liberals were the "administrative progressives" (Tyack, 1990, p. 177; Tyack & Hansot, 1982), the first generation of university-trained school superintendents and their professors who institutionalized bureaucracy and technocratic administration in public education, creating by the 1950s a "closed system" characterized by "the increasing ability of school officials to ignore parents, reformers, and others outside the system" (Katz, 1987, p. 109; Tyack, 1990).[18]

Of course, this is the closed, tracked system that was called it into question first by the *Brown* decision in 1954 and then by the oppositional civil and disability rights movements, in which activists attacked IQ testing and tracking and demanded democratic equality, including a role for parents and community stakeholders in educational decision making. Although with passage of the Elementary and Secondary Education Act of 1965 (ESEA) and the EAHCA in 1975 activists appeared to have cracked the closed system, as we have seen, their victory was hollow, in part, because of the closed system's ability to resist meaningful change through symbolized and ceremonialized compliance with their most fundamental requirements, including both statutes' parent and citizen participation requirements (Skrtic, 1995, 2003). Moreover, given the historical pattern of reform by accretion, what the activists got was new forms of tracking, an array of new ritualized programs merely added to and decoupled within largely unchanged institutionalized bureaucracies (Skrtic, 1991b; Tyack & Hansot, 1982; Wise, 1979).

More ominously, the activists' victory was hollowed out further by the ideological hijacking of both laws by standards-based reform, beginning with publication of *A Nation at Risk* (1983) and culminating in the 2001 reauthorization of the ESEA as NCLB and the 1997 and 2004 authorizations of IDEA. As a result, today both statutes are premised on the market fundamentalism of neoliberalism, under which test scores have become a type of bottom line for schools, creating a market-like rationality in the historically non-market institution of public education, including competition among schools, performance bonuses and penalties, and privatizing and outsourcing. As a result, in education as in other social institutions under the grip of neoliberalism, government is recast as a relationship between market and customers, and efficiency and productivity have become the sole value of public administration, eclipsing the strong democratic values of responsiveness and participation (Denhardt & Denhardt, 2003; Engel, 2000), the very values upon which the original ESEA and EAHCA were premised. Beyond threatening the well-being of their intended beneficiaries, the neoliberal orientation of NCLB and IDEA further elevate the educational purposes of social mobility and social efficiency over that of democratic equality, thus extending and further ensconcing weak democracy (Skrtic, 2005; also see Apple, 2001; Loxley & Thomas, 2001).

We can begin the process of intervening in this untenable situation by changing our approach to outcomes-based reform. As an alternative to NCLB/IDEA's extreme form of traditional standards-based reform that merely extends bureaucracy, Spady (Spady & Marshall, 1991, p. 68) recommended a "transformational" model of outcomes-based reform, which begins with a deliberative discourse among school and community stakeholders aimed at reaching consensus on broad school outcomes leading to desirable social conditions of life for students as future citizens. At this point, "districts set their existing curriculum frameworks aside" (p. 70), allowing their curriculum, instructional practices, and organizational structure to evolve in support of educational outcomes leading to the agreed-upon preferred future for students and communities. Of course, I am proposing the social planning model for the initial and ongoing deliberative discourse among school and community stakeholders and adhocracy as the desired structured for schooling, the only structure that is consistent with the substantive and procedural safeguard principles of the IDEA and, as universally designed schooling, capable of making education naturally equitable and excellent for all students and families, communities, and the country as a whole.

The advantage of the transformational approach as the way to such a system is that, beyond holding schools accountable for important educational and social outcomes for all students, it brings deliberative politics into education and, more importantly, focuses it precisely on the purposes of education and the type of schooling necessary to achieve them in a balanced way. Achieving and sustaining this type of deliberative engagement among citizens and professionals in public education requires the kind of democratic administration that John Dewey called for at the start of the 20th century, that is, leadership in making schools doubly educational by creating and sustaining the material and cultural conditions for ongoing deliberative social planning in which alternative interpretations of needs, accommodations, and associated practices and structures are judged and selected or integrated in terms of their educational and social consequences for every child and family, and their contribution to the realization of democratic ideals in schools, communities, and the nation. Preparing and supporting such strong democratic leaders in public education should be the focus and mission of higher education leadership preparation programs, especially in special education since strong, deliberative democracy is the best defense against all forms of injustice in school and society.

Notes

1 Technically, parents can request an open due process hearings but few do, and though redacted hearing decisions are accessible to the public, they typically are not used by parents individually or collectively through advocacy groups in the precedent-setting way envisioned by pre-1975 EAHCA proponents. Moreover, the courts, especially since the Supreme Court decision in *Hendrick Hudson School District v. Rowley*, "now review due process hearing decisions primarily to question their legal reasoning ... while deferring to the hearing officer's findings of fact" (Ong-Dean, 2009, pp. 114–115).

2 Movement in this direction has been advanced considerably by the *Rowley* decision, since which federal courts have been less inclined to entertain challenges to school authority like those in earlier antidiscrimination cases like *Pennsylvania Association for Retarded Children v. Pennsylvania (PARC)* and *Mills v. Board of Education*. Now, such challenges largely are confined to due process hearings where "disputes are individualized and highly technical ... [thus limiting] the impact they can have on other cases" (p. 33) and thus systemic reform. However, see Weber (1990) and Yudof (1984) on lower court resistance to Rowley.

3 "Disability rights movement" here refers both to the larger social movement of the 1960s and 1970s that ran parallel to the women's and civil rights movements and over time won legislation like Section 504 and the Americans with Disabilities Act, as well as that portion of it led by U.S.-based parents and parent and professional groups that lobbied for the EAHCA.

4 All of these things, of course, were done by the social movement that produced the EAHCA (see Skrtic, 2000).

5 The fact that such changes may be largely ceremonial does not make them necessarily inconsequential (Powell & DiMaggio, 1991; Ritti & Goldner, 1979). See note 13.

6 For more comprehensive institutional analyses of public education, special education, and IDEA implementation, including each of the implementation problems highlighted in this section, see Skrtic (1991a,b, 1995, 2003) and Skrtic and McCall (2010).

7 Other indications of a move away from individualization in the 2004 IDEA reauthorization are elimination of IEP "benchmarks and short-terms objectives" except for covered students who take alternate assessments, and creation of a15-state paperwork reduction experiment which arguably will weaken oversight of IEP implementation.

8 The negative effects of this model of reform are apparent in the deteriorating conditions of special education practice since 1997. For a review, see Skrtic (2005) and Skrtic, Harris, and Shriner (2005).

9 The IDEA only addresses disproportionate representation on the basis of race and ethnicity, but research shows it is a more complex phenomenon involving multiple, intersecting factors also including social class, gender, age, language, and geography (Artiles, 2004; McCall & Skrtic, 2010; Skiba, Poloni-Staudinger, Simmons, Feggins-Azziz, & Chung, 2005).

10 This section based on McCall and Skrtic (2009).

11 See note 1.

12 Whereas positivist inquiry attempts to *justify* social knowledge, practices, and institutions by showing that they correspond to a true representation of the world, the goal of classical pragmatism is to *reform* social knowledge, practices, and institutions by reconciling them with moral ideals (Bernstein, 1971, 1991; Kloppenberg, 1986). See Kaufman-Osborn (1985) on the misinterpretation of Deweyan pragmatism in the policy sciences as social engineering rather than social planning.

13 Although special education functions as a decoupling device in this respect, the programs it provides for students who are forced out of regular classrooms can benefit them. Moreover, because professionals become advocates for their functions in organizations, they can alter power relations over the long run which can benefit them and their function, thus possibly better serving the client group assigned to their function (see Ritti & Goldner, 1979).

14 According to Hehir, central to Elmore's approach to such school improvement is the concept of "distributive leadership" (2005, p. 108) or the ability to guide instructional improvement by distributing responsibility for it across all school professionals (also see Elmore, 2000, 2002; Spillane, Halverson, & Diamond, 2001). Although the concept of distributed leadership is relevant to the proposed adhocratic restructuring of schools, in the sense that leadership in both cases is collaborative and distributed throughout the organization, it falls far short of the model of deliberative social planning described above and its requisite "civic professionalism" and "strong democratic leadership" discussed below. Whereas distributed leadership is concerned with distributing leadership in instructional improvement among professionals in schools, the latter engages professionals *and* parents and citizens generally in educational *and* social improvement. Moreover, the principal improvement goal of such professionals and leaders, democratic equality, is undermined by reform approaches like distributed leadership. See note 16.

15 For a more extensive critique of Minnow's criticism of progressive era reformers, see Skrtic and Kent (in press), and for an extended argument for this interpretation of progressivism, see Kent (2007), Skrtic and Kent (in press), and note 17.

16 As opposed to the more democratic or "developmentally liberal" school restructuring proposals of the late 1980s which sought excellence and equity simultaneously through adhocratic-like reforms (e.g., McNeil, 1986; Oakes, 1985), the corporate or neoliberal restructuring models of the 1990s—epitomized by Comer's (Comer, Ben-Avie, Haynes, & Joyner 1999; Comer, Joyner, & Ben-Avie 2004) School Development Program, Levin's (1987) Accelerated Schools, Sizer's (1984) Essential Schools—also are premised on decentralization and collaboration but use them not to pursue democratic purposes but to "maximize efficiency [and] productivity" (Engel, 2000, p. 124). Although such models can be democratic in rhetoric, a closer look reveals the opposite because they are based on "the undemocratic theory and practice of the market economy" (p. 125). Distributed leadership (Elmore, 2004; Spillane et al., 2001) is a more recent neoliberal reform strategy. For more on the structure and culture of what I am calling developmentally liberal restructured schools, see Skrtic (1995, 2005), McCall and Skrtic (2009), and Skrtic and McCall (2010).

17 While at the core of American progressivism, these two strains of liberalism do not exhaust its internal complexity as an intellectual and political phenomenon. Nevertheless, the fundamental cleavage between managerial and developmental liberals and its significance is widely recognized (see Foner, 1998; Greenstone; 1993; Hanson, 1985; Kloppenberg, 1986; Price, 1974).

18 On similar negative effects of managerial liberalism in public administration, see Denhardt and Denhardt (2003).

References

Ahrens, E. (2006). *Standards-based IEPs: Implementation in selected states.* Alexandria, VA: National Association of State Directors of Special Education.

Ahrens, E. (2010). *Standards-based IEPs: Implementation update.* Alexandria, VA: National Association of State Directors of Special Education.

Anderson, C. W. (1993). *Prescribing the life of the mind: An essay on the purpose of the university, the aims of liberal education, the competence of citizens, and the cultivation of practical reason.* Madison: University of Wisconsin Press.

Apple, M. W. (2001). *Educating the "Right" way: Markets, standards, God, and inequality.* New York: RoutledgeFalmer.

Argyris, C., & Schön, D. A. (1978). *Organizational learning: A theory of action perspective.* Reading, MA: Addison-Wesley.

Artiles, A. J. (2004). The end of innocence: Historiography and representation in the discursive practices of LD. *Journal of Learning Disabilities, 37,* 55–555.

Barber, B. R. (1984). *Strong democracy: Participatory politics for a new age.* Berkeley: University of California Press.

Bell, D. (1980). *Brown vs. Board of Education* and the interest-convergence principle. *Harvard Law Review, 93,* 51–533.

Bennis, W. G., & Slater, P. L. (1964). *The temporary society.* New York: Harper and Row.

Bernstein, R. J. (1971). *Praxis and action: Contemporary philosophies of human activity* Philadelphia: University of Pennsylvania Press.

Bernstein, R. J. (1991). *The new constellation: The ethical-political horizons of modernity/postmodernity.* Cambridge, UK: Polity Press.

Blanco, H. (1994). *How to think about social problems: American pragmatism and the idea of planning.* Westport, CT: Greenwood Press.

Brown v. Board of Education (1954). 347 U.S. 483, 74 S. Ct. 686, 98 L. Ed. 873.

Campbell, J. (1992). *The community reconstructs: The meaning of pragmatic social thought* Champaign: University of Illinois Press.

Champlin, J. (1991). Taking stock and moving on. *Journal of the National Center for Outcomes Based Education, 1,* 5–8.

Christophos, F., & Renz, P. (1969). A critical examination of special education programs. *Journal of Special Education, 3*(4), 371–380.

Clune, W. H., & Van Pelt, M. H. (1985). A political method of evaluating the Education for All Handicapped Children Act of 1975 and the several gaps of gap analysis. *Law and Contemporary Problems, 48*(1), 7–62.

Comer, J. P., Ben-Avie, M., Haynes, N. M., & Joyner, E. T. (Eds.). (1999). *Child by child: The Comer process for change in education.* New York: Teachers College Press.

Comer, J. P., Joyner, E. T., & Ben-Avie, M. (Eds.). (2004). *The field guide to Comer schools in action.* Thousand Oaks, CA: Corwin Press.

Connor, D. J. (2008). *Urban narratives: Portraits in progress: Life at the intersection of learning disability, race, and social class.* New York: Peter Lang.

Crenshaw, K. W. (1988). Race, reform, and retrenchment: Transformation and legitimation in antidiscrimination law. *Harvard Law Review, 101*(7), 1331–1387.

Crenshaw, K., Gotanda, N., Peller, G., & Thomas, K. (1995). Introduction. In K. Crenshaw, N. Gotanda, G. Peller, & K. Thomas (Eds.), *Critical race theory: The key writings that formed the movement* (pp. xi–xxxii). New York: New Press.

Denhardt, J. V., & Denhardt, R. B. (2003). *The new public service: Serving, not steering.* Armonk, NY: M. E. Sharpe.

Dewey, J. (1976). *The school and society.* In J. A. Boydston (Ed.), *John Dewey: The middle works, 1899–1924* (Vol. 1, pp. 1–109). Carbondale: Southern Illinois University Press. (Original work published 1899)

Dewey, J. (1980). *Democracy and education.* In J. A. Boydston (Ed.), *John Dewey: The Middle Works, 1899–1924* (Vol. 9, pp. 1–370). Carbondale, IL: Southern Illinois University Press. (Original work published 1916)

Dewey, J. (1981). Democracy and educational administration. In J. A. Boydston (Ed.), *John Dewey: The later works, 1925–1953* (Vol. 11, pp. 217–225). Carbondale: Southern Illinois University Press. (Original work published 1937)

Dewey, J. (1981). The need for a recovery of philosophy. In J. J. McDermott, *The philosophy of John Dewey* (pp. 58–97). Chicago: University of Chicago Press. (Original work published 1917)

Dewey, J. (1988a). Individualism, old and new. In J. A. Boydston (Ed.), *John Dewey: The later works, 1925–1953* (Vol. 5: 1929–1930, pp. 41–123). Carbondale: Southern Illinois University Press. (Original work published 1929–1930)

Dewey, J. (1988b). The public and its problems. In J. A. Boydston (Ed.), *John Dewey: The later works, 1925–1953* (Vol. 2: 1925–1927 (pp. 235–372). Carbondale: Southern Illinois University Press. (Original work published 1927)

Dewey, J. (1989). The development of American pragmatism. In H. S. Thayer (Ed.), *Pragmatism: The classic writings* (pp. 23–40). Indianapolis, IN: Hackett. (Original work published 1931)

Dewey, J. (1991). Creative democracy—The task before us. In J. A. Boydston (Ed.), *John Dewey: The later Works, 1925–1953* (Vol. 14, pp. 224–230). Carbondale: Southern Illinois University Press. (Original work published 1939)

DiMaggio, P. J. (1988). Interest and agency in institutional theory. In L. G. Zucker (Ed.), *Institutional patterns and organizations: Culture and environment* (pp. 3–22). Cambridge, MA: Ballinger.

DiMaggio, P. J., & Powell, W. W. (1983). The iron cage revisited: Institutional isomorphism and collective rationality in organizational fields. *American Sociological Review, 48,* 147–160.

Douvanis, G., & Hulse, D. (2002). *The least restrictive environment mandate: How has it been defined by the courts?* Arlington, VA: The ERIC Clearinghouse on Disabilities and Gifted Education.

Dunn, L. M. (1968). Special education for the mildly retarded—Is much of it justifiable? *Exceptional Children, 35*(1), 5–22.

Dzur, A. W. (2008). *Democratic professionalism: Citizen participation and the reconstruction of professional ethics, identity, and practice.* University Park, PA: The Pennsylvania State University Press.

Education for All Handicapped Children Act of 1975. Public Law 94-142.

Elementary and Secondary Education Act of 1965. Public Law 89-10.

Elmore, R. (2000). *Building a new structure for school leadership.* Washington, DC: The Albert Shanker Institute.

Elmore, R. (2002). Hard questions about practice. *Educational Leadership, 59*(8), 22–25.

Elmore, R. F. (2004). *School reform from the inside out: Policy, practice, and performance.* Cambridge, MA: Harvard Education Press.

Engel, M. (2000). *The struggle for control of public education: Market ideology vs. democratic values.* Philadelphia: Temple University Press.

Ferri, B. A., & Connor, D. J. (2005). In the shadow of *Brown*: Special education and overrepresentation of students of color. *Remedial and Special Education, 26,* 93–100.

Foner, E. (1998). *The story of American freedom.* New York: W. W. Norton.

Fraser, N. (1989). Struggle over needs: Outline of a socialist-feminist critical theory of late capitalist political culture. In *Unruly practices: Power, discourse, and gender in contemporary social theory* (pp. 161–187). Minneapolis: University of Minnesota Press.

Fraser, N. (2008), Prioritizing justice as participatory parity: A reply to Kompridis and Forst. In K. Olson (Ed.), *Adding insult to injury* (pp. 327–346). London: Verso.

Fraser, N., & Honneth, A. (2003). *Redistribution or recognition: A political-philosophical exchange.* London: Verso.

Furner, M. O. (1993). The Republican tradition and the New Liberalism: Social investigation, state building, and social learning in the Gilded Age. In M. J. Lacey & M. O. Furner (Eds.), *The state and social investigation in Britain and the United States* (pp. 171–241). New York: Woodrow Wilson Center Press.

Gilhool, T. K. (1989). The right to an effective education: From *Brown* to P. L. 94–142 and beyond. In D. K. Lipsky & A. Gartner (Eds.), *Beyond separate education: Quality education for all* (pp. 243–253). Baltimore, MD: Paul H. Brookes.

Greenstone, J. D. (1993). *The Lincoln persuasion: Remaking American liberalism.* Princeton, NJ: Princeton University Press.

Gutmann, A. (1980). *Liberal equality.* Cambridge, UK: Cambridge University Press.

Harris, A. P. (1994). Foreword: The jurisprudence of reconstruction. *California Law Review, 82*(4), 741-785.

Harry, B., & Klingner, J. (2006). *Why are so many minority students in special education?* New York: Teachers College Press.

Harry, B., Klingner, J. K., & Hart, J. (2005). African American families under fire: Ethnographic views of family strengths. *Remedial and Special Education, 26*(2), 101–112.

Harvey, D. (2005). *A brief history of neoliberalism.* Oxford: Oxford University Press.

Hehir, T. (2005). *New directions in special education: Eliminating ableism in policy and practice.* Cambridge, MA: Harvard Education Press.

Held, D. (1996). *Models of democracy* (2nd ed.). Stanford, CA: Stanford University Press.

Henig, J. R. (1994). *Rethinking school choice: Limits of the market metaphor.* Princeton, NJ: Princeton University Press.

Individuals with Disabilities Education Act Amendments of 1997. Public Law 105-17.

Individuals with Disabilities Education Improvement Act of 2004. Public Law 108-446.

Kalyanpur, M., Harry, B., & Skrtic, T. (2000). Equity and advocacy expectations of culturally diverse families' participation in special education. *International Journal of Disability, Development and Education, 47*(2), 119–136.

Katz, M. B. (1987). *Reconstructing American education.* Cambridge, MA: Harvard University Press.

Kaufman-Osborn, T. V. (1985). Pragmatism, policy science, and the state. *American Journal of Political Science, 29*(4), 827–849.

Kelman, M., (1987). *A guide to critical legal studies.* Cambridge, MA: Harvard University Press.

Kent, J. R. (2000). Dewey and the project of critical social theory. *Social Thought and Research, 23*(1&2), 1–43.

Kent, J. R. (2007). Review essay: Is American liberalism singular or plural? *American Studies, 48*(4), 129–45.

Kirp, D., Buss, W., & Kuriloff, P. (1974). Legal reform of special education: Empirical studies and procedural proposals. *California Law Review, 62*(1), 40–155.

Kloppenberg, J. T. (1986). *Uncertain victory: Social democracy and progressivism in European and American thought, 1870–1920.* New York: Oxford University Press.

Kuriloff, P. J. (1985). Is justice served by due process? Affecting the outcome of special education hearings in Pennsylvania. *Law and Contemporary Problems, 48*(1), 89–118.

Labaree, D. F. (1997). *How to succeed in school without really learning: The credentials race in American education.* New Haven, CT: Yale University Press.

Lazerson, M. (1983). The origins of special education. In J. G. Chambers & W. T. Hartman (Eds.), *Special education policies: Their history, implementation, and finance* (pp. 15–47). Philadelphia: Temple University Press.

Levin, H. M. (1987). Accelerated schools for disadvantaged students. *Educational Leadership, 44*(6), 19–21.

Lindblom, C. E. (1991). *Inquiry and change: The troubled attempt to understand and shape society.* New Haven, CT: Yale University Press.

Loxley, A., & Thomas, G. (2001). Neo-conservatives, neo-liberals, the New Left and inclusion: Stirring the pot. *Cambridge Journal of Education, 31*(3), 291–301

Macpherson, C. B. (1977). *The life and times of liberal democracy.* Oxford, UK: Oxford University Press.

McCall, Z., & Skrtic, T. M. (2009). Intersectional needs politics: A policy frame for the wicked problem of disproportionality. *Multiple Voices for Ethnically Diverse Exceptional Learners, 11*(2), 3–23.

McNeil, L. M. (1986). *Contradictions of control: School structure and school knowledge.* New York: Methuem/Routledge & Kegan Paul.

Mehan, H., Hertweck, A., & Meihls, J. L. (1986). *Handicapping the handicapped: Decision making in students' educational careers.* Stanford, CA: Stanford University Press.

Mercer, J. (1973). *Labeling the mentally retarded: Clinical and social system perspectives on mental retardation.* Berkeley: University of California Press.

Meyer, M. W. (1979). Organizational structure as signaling. *Pacific Sociological Review, 22*(4), 481–500.

Meyer, J. W., & Rowan, B. (1977). Institutionalized organizations: Formal structure as myth and ceremony. *American Journal of Sociology, 83*, 340–363.

Meyer, J. W., & Rowan, B. (1978). The structure of educational organizations. In M. W. Meyer (Ed.), *Environments and organizations* (pp. 78-109). San Francisco: Jossey-Bass.

Meyer, J. W., & Rowan, B. (1983). The structure of educational organizations. In J. W. Meyer & W. R. Scott (Eds.), *Organizational environments: Ritual and rationality* (pp. 71-78). Beverly Hills, CA: Sage.

Minow, M. (1985). Learning to live with the dilemma of difference: Bilingual and special education. *Law and Contemporary Problems, 48*(2), 157–211.

Minow, M. (1990). *Making all the difference: Inclusion, exclusion, and American law.* Ithaca, NY: Cornell University Press.

Minow, M. (2008). Accommodating integration, *University of Pennsylvania Law Review, 57*(1), 1–10.

Mintzberg, H. (1979). *The structuring of organizations.* Englewood Cliffs, NJ: Prentice-Hall.

Mintzberg, H. (1989). *Mintzberg on management: Inside our strange world of organizations.* New York: The Free Press.

Mirowski, P., & Plehwe, D. (2009). *The road from Mont Pelerin.* Cambridge, MA: Harvard University Press.

Muncy. R. (1991). *Creating a female dominion in American reform: 1890–1935.* Oxford, UK: Oxford University Press.

National Research Council. (1982). *Placing children in special education: A strategy for equity.* Panel on Selection and Placement of Students in Programs for the Mentally Retarded, Committee on Child Development Research and Public Policy, K. A. Heller, W. H. Holtzman, & S. Messick (Eds.), Commission on Behavioral and Social Sciences and Education. Washington, DC: National Academy Press.

National Research Council. (2002). *Minority students in special and gifted education.* Committee on Minority Representation in Special Education, M. S. Donovan & C. T. Cross (Eds.), Division of Behavioral and Social Sciences and Education. Washington DC: National Academy Press.

National Commission on Excellence in Education. (1983). *A nation at risk: The imperative for educational reform.* Washington, DC: Government Printing Office.

No Child Left Behind Act of 2001. Public Law 107-110.

Oakes, J. (1985). *Keeping track: How schools structure inequality.* New Haven, CT: Yale University Press.

O'Day, J. A. (2002). Complexity, accountability, and school improvement. *Harvard Educational Review, 72*(3), 293–329.

Ong-Dean, C. (2009). *Distinguishing disability: Parents, privilege, and special education.* Chicago: The University of Chicago Press.

Powell, W. W., & DiMaggio, P. J. (1991). *The new institutionalism in organizational analysis.* Chicago: University of Chicago Press.

Pretti-Frontczak, K., & Bricker, D. (2000). Enhancing the quality of Individualized Education Plan (IEP) goals and objectives. *Journal of Early Intervention, 23*(2), 92–105.

Price, D. F. (1974). Community and control: Critical democratic theory in the Progressive period. *American Political Science Review, 68*, 1663–1678.

Rawls, J. (1971). *A theory of justice.* Cambridge, MA: Belknap Press.

Reynolds, M. C., Wang, M. C., & Walberg, H. J. (1987). The necessary restructuring of special and general education. *Exceptional Children, 53*(5), 391–398.

Richardson, H. S. (2002). *Democratic autonomy: Public reasoning about the ends of policy.* Oxford: Oxford University Press.

Ritti, R. R., & Goldner, F. H. (1979). Professional pluralism in an industrial organization. *Management Science, 16*, 233–246.

Ryan, A. (1972). Two concepts of politics and democracy: James & John Stuart Mill. In M. Fleisher (Ed.), *Machiavelli and the nature of political thought* (pp. 76–113). New York: Atheneum.

Sarason, S. B., & Doris, J. (1979). *Educational handicap, public policy, and social history.* New York: The Free Press.

Schön, D. A., & Rein, M. (1994). *Frame reflection: Toward the resolution of intractable policy controversies.* New York: Basi.

Scott, W. R. (1987). The adolescence of institutional theory. *Administrative Science Quarterly, 32*, 493–511.

Scott, W. R., & Meyer, J. W. (1987). Environmental linkages and organizational complexity: Public and private schools. In H. M. Levin & T. James (Eds.), *Comparing public and private schools* (pp. 128–160). New York: Fulmer Press.

Simon, H. A. (1977). *The new science of management decision.* Englewood Cliffs, NJ: Prentice-Hall.

Sizer, T. (1984). *Horace's compromise: The dilemma of the American high school.* Boston: Houghton Mifflin.

Skiba, R. J., Poloni-Staudinger, L., Gallini, S., Simmons, A. B., & Feggins-Azziz, R. (2006). Disparate access: The disproportionality of African American students with disabilities across educational environments. *Exceptional Children, 72*, 411–424.

Skiba, R. J., Poloni-Staudinger, L., Simmons, A. B., Feggins-Azziz, L. R., & Chung, C. G. (2005). Unproven links: Can poverty explain ethnic disproportionality in special education? *The Journal of Special Education, 39*(3), 130–144.

Skiba, R. J., Simmons, A. B., Ritter, S., Gibb, A. C., Rausch, M. K., Cuadrado, J., & Chung, C. (2008). Achieving equity in special education: History, status, and current challenges. *Exceptional Children, 74*, 264–288.

Skrtic, T. M. (1991a). *Behind special education: A critical analysis of professional culture and school organization.* Denver, CO: Love Publishing.

Skrtic, T. M. (1991b). The special education paradox: Equity as the way to excellence. *Harvard Educational Review, 61*(2), 148–206.

Skrtic, T. M. (1995). Special education and student disability as organizational pathologies: Toward a metatheory of school organization and change. In T. Skrtic (Ed.), *Disability and democracy: Reconstructing (special) education for postmodernity* (pp. 190–232). New York: Teachers College Press.

Skrtic, T. M. (2000, July). *Civic professionalism and the struggle over needs.* Paper presented at the annual Leadership Project Directors' Conference, Office of Special Education Programs, U.S. Department of Education, Washington, DC.

Skrtic, T. M. (2003). An organizational analysis of the overrepresentation of poor and minority students in special education. *Multiple Voices for Ethnically Diverse Exceptional Learners, 6*(1), 41–57.

Skrtic, T. M. (2005). A political economy of learning disabilities. *Learning Disabilities Quarterly, 28*(2), 149–155.

Skrtic, T. M. (2010). Review of *Distinguishing disability: Parents, privilege, and special education,* by Colin Ong-Dean. *Contemporary Sociology, 39*(2), 188–190.

Skrtic, T. M., Harris, K. R., & Shriner, J. G. (Eds.) (2005). The context of special education practice today. In T. Skrtic, K. Harris, & J. Shriner (Eds.), *Special education policy and practice: Accountability, instruction, and social challenges* (pp. 1–18). Denver, CO: Love Publishing.

Skrtic, T. M., & Kent, J. R. (in press). Rights, capabilities, and disability needs politics: Institutional barriers to social justice. In A. Kanter & B. Ferri (Eds.), *Righting educational wrongs: Disability studies in law and education.* Syracure, NY: Syracuse University Press.

Skrtic, T. M., & McCall, Z. (2010). Ideology, institutions, and equity: Comments on Christine Sleeter's *Why Is There Learning Disabilities? Disability Studies Quarterly.*

Smith, S. W. (1990). Individualized education programs (IEPs) in special education: From intent to acquiescence. *Exceptional Children 57*(1), 6–14.

Smith, S. W., & Kotering, L. (1997). Using computers to generate IEPs: Rethinking the process. *Journal of Special Education Technology 13*(2), 81–90.

Spady W., & Marshall, K. (1991). Beyond traditional outcome-based education. *Educational Leadership, 49,* 67–72.

Spillane, J. P., Halverson, R., & Diamond, J. B. (2001). Investigating school leadership practice: A distributed perspective. *Educational Researcher, 30*(3), 23–28.

Sullivan, W. M. (2005). *Work and integrity: The crisis and promise of professionalism in America* (2nd ed.). San Francisco, CA: Jossey-Bass.

Thomas, S. B., & Rapport, M. J. K. (1998). Least restrictive environment: Understanding the direction of the courts. *Journal of Special Education, 32*(2), 66–78.

Tolbert, P. S., & Zucker, L. G. (1983). Institutional sources of change in the formal structure of organizations: The diffusion of civil service reforms, 1880–1935. *Administrative Science Quarterly, 23,* 22–39.

Tropea, J. L. (1987). Bureaucratic order and special children: Urban schools, 1890s-1940s. *History of Education Quarterly, 27*(1), 29–53.

Turnbull, H. R. (1993). *Free appropriate public education: The law and children with disabilities.* Denver: Love Publishing.

Turnbull, H. R., Stowe, M. J., & Huerta, N. E. (2007). *Free appropriate public education: The law and children with disabilities* (7th ed.). Denver, CO: Love Publishing.

Tyack, D. (1990). Restructuring" in historical perspective: Tinkering toward utopia. *Teachers College Record, 92*(2), 170–191.

Tyack, D., & Hansot, E. (1981). Conflict and consensus in American public education. *Daedalus, 110*(3), 1–25.

Weber, M. C. (1990). The transformation of the Education of the Handicapped Act: A study in the interpretation of radical statutes. *UC Davis Law Review, 24*(1), 349–436.

Wehmeyer, M. L., & Schalock, R. L. (2001). Self-determination and quality of life: Implications for special education services and supports. *Focus on Exceptional Children, 33,* 1–16.

Weick, K. E. (1976). Educational organizations as loosely coupled systems. *Administrative Science Quarterly, 21*(1), 1–19.

Williams, P. J. (1991). *The alchemy of race and rights: Diary of a law professor.* Cambridge, MA: Harvard University Press.

Wise, A. E. (1979). *Legislated learning: The bureaucratization of the American classroom.* Berkeley: University of California Press.

Young, I. M. (1990). *Justice and the politics of difference.* Princeton, NJ: Princeton University Press.

Young, I. M. (2000). *Inclusion and democracy.* Oxford, UK: Oxford University Press.

Ysseldyke, J., Thurlow, M., Graden, J., Wesson, C., Algozzine, B., & Deno, S. (1983). Generalizations from five years of research on assessment and decision making: The University of Minnesota Institute. *Exceptional Education Quarterly, 4*(1), 75–93.

Yudof, M. G. (1984). Education for the handicapped: *Rowley* in perspective. *American Journal of Education, 92*(2), 163–177.

Zucker, L. G. (1981). Institutional structure and organizational processes: The role of evaluation units in schools. In A. Bank & R. C. Williams (Eds.), *Evaluation and Decision Making,* (CSE Monograph Series, No. 10). Los Angeles: UCLA Center for the Study of Evaluation.

Zucker, L. G. (1988). Where do institutional patterns come from? Organizations as actors in social systems. In L. G. Zucker (Ed.), *Institutional patterns and organizations: Culture and environment* (pp. 23–49). Cambridge, MA: Ballinger.

Section III

Collaborative Leadership for Special Education in Multicultural Contexts
Introduction

In this section a broad focus on collaborative leadership is emphasized, illustrating the involvement of leaders within and across educational systems in creating inclusive and effective educational services for students with disabilities. In the professional literature on contemporary schools, there are many and varied references to collaborative forms of leadership, including discussions about distributed leadership, shared decision-making, professional learning communities, and teacher leadership (Fullan, 2007; Leithwood, Harris, & Hopkins 2008; Spillane, 2006). For students who struggle in schools, collaborative forms of leadership are especially important to support the interactions necessary among stakeholders to address the needs of students with complex educational needs. Administrators, general and special educators, support personnel, and families need to share their understanding of students' needs, make individual decisions about services, and use their knowledge, skills, and resources to create instructional environments that support positive student outcomes. A second theme that is addressed across most of the chapters is the need for leaders to work collaboratively to assure that educational programs are responsive to the needs of students who differ across their racial, cultural, language, and socioeconomic backgrounds.

In the first chapter of this section, Kozleski and Huber (Chapter 9) focus on systemic change, providing a big picture of the varied systems (i.e., federal, state, district, school, and practitioner) and the interactions across systems that are necessary to create programs that are responsive to all students. They discuss the importance of systemic leadership, the relevance of history and context, the importance of sociocultural lenses, and the nature of cultural responsivity. More specifically, they discuss The Systemic Change Framework, providing a visual representation of the varying levels of effort that that are needed to influence student achievement and learning in schools. They emphasize that the delivery of special education services should be "a seamless system of supports and services" delivered within general education. At the end of the chapter, they outline how systems change can be accomplished and outline specific principles for leaders to consider in the development of an equitable and culturally responsive general education system.

In the next chapter, Billingsley (Chapter 10) reviews key research studies in the leadership literature on including students with disabilities in general education settings. The expectation today is that students with disabilities not only have opportunities to learn in the contexts of general education schools and classrooms, but also to achieve the standards set for all students (Individuals with Disabilities Education Act, 2004; No Child Left Behind Act, 2002). Billingsley used two frameworks to consider research findings on leadership for inclusive schools. In the first, a distributed perspective of leadership for inclusive change considers both the collective impact and the unique contributions of leaders from both outside and inside the school, including those from State Education Agencies, Institutions of Higher Education, and districts, as well as principals, teachers and parents. She considers the activities of leadership for inclusive school reform across the three phases of the change process described by Fullan (2007) including: (a) initiation and adoption; (b) implementation or the initial experiences of trying to put a reform into practice; and (c) institutionalization, which is the extent to which change is integrated into the system or disappears. While the initiation of inclusion usually came from outside the school, "buy-in" and ownership at the school level were critical for implementing and sustaining change. Billingsley considers the future of inclusive change and provides eight recommendations for leaders of inclusive change efforts.

In a chapter on collaborative decision-making in multi-cultural contexts, Hoover, Eppolito, Klingner, and Baca (Chapter 11) address a topic of long-standing interest to special education, how to gather and use academic performance data in the identification and education of students with disabilities. They examine special education decision-making research and practices with particular emphasis on issues encountered, associated findings, and implications for school and problem-solving team leadership, particularly as these relate to cultural and linguistically diverse learners. They begin by comparing historical and contemporary perspectives on special education decision-making, moving to the current emphasis on response to intervention (RTI). They specifically consider the promise of RTI in reducing the disproportionate referral to and placement of culturally and linguistically diverse students in special education. Hoover and colleagues then consider the role of administrative leadership in collaborative decision-making, pointing out the cornerstone of administrative support in successful teams. They recommend a flexible, proactive approach to RTI decision-making and outline specific questions for school leaders as they guide collaborative decision-making in multi-lingual and multi-cultural schools.

In addressing leadership to encourage family collaboration, Harry (Chapter 12) examines the differing roles of leaders across three specific contexts, including Early Intervention, Pre-School, and School-age services and considers the differences and challenges facing administrators in community-based versus building-based programs. She begins the chapter with a discussion of legal mandates for involving parents in providing special education services and raises the question of whether the law can truly legislate collaborative practice. She organizes her review around two main questions, what is the meaning of collaboration and why is it so difficult to achieve. She then considers what constitutes leadership for collaboration in the field and identifies challenges leaders face in different service delivery contexts (i.e., Early Intervention, Pre-school and School-age services), noting challenges facing administrators in community-based versus building-based programs. At the end of her chapter, she addresses challenges of collaboration with families of diverse cultural and social backgrounds, especially in light of the disproportionate placement of students of color in high-incidence disability categories and restrictive placements.

In the final chapter of this section, Lake and Stewart (Chapter 13) address the importance of negotiating conflict in special education. Due to the high financial and emotional costs of parent-school conflict, it is important for leaders to understand the specific complexities that give rise to these conflicts, and to develop an understanding of processes to prevent and address these disagreements. However, the authors point out that parents, special educators, and school administrators have little preparation in understanding and responding to conflict. Lake and Stewart review the foundation and progression of special education conflict resolution as well as varied types of resolution. Factors that contribute to conflict are identified and discussed, and considerations for responding effectively to parent-school conflict are suggested. The authors emphasize specific actions that district leaders can take to build trust and resolve conflicts early.

References

Fullan, M. (2007). *The new meaning of education change* (3rd ed.). New York: Teachers College Press.

Individuals with Disabilities Education Improvement Act, 20 U.S.C. §1401 et seq. (2004)

Leithwood, K., Harris, A., & Hopkins, D. (2008). Seven strong claims about successful school leadership. *School Leadership and Management, 28*(1), 27–42.

No Child Left Behind Act, 20 U.S.C. §6301 et seq. (2002).

Spillane, J. P. (2006). *Distributed leadership*. San Francisco, CA: Jossey-Bass.

9

System-Wide Leadership for Culturally-Responsive Education

Elizabeth Kozleski and Jennifer J. Huber

ARIZONA STATE UNIVERSITY

Where organizations, causes, and communities exist, information must be networked, a common purpose developed, strategic activities designed, sustainability addressed, continuous improvement embedded, and milestones celebrated. Along the way, community members must gauge the distance between where they are and where they want to be in order to select the most robust strategies for whatever success is deemed to be. The funds of knowledge and the talents that exist within the community need to be engaged so that the community or organization takes on a life of its own beyond individual careers and aspirations. Leadership is needed to support and facilitate engagement in moving forward, identifying outcomes, and examining the processes used to achieve outcomes (Heifitz, 1994). In this chapter, we make a case for leadership as a cultural activity fraught with the complexities of informal and formal authority, challenged by social networks for change, and intersected by fractals of race, class, gender, and power.

Individuals and coalitions of individuals provide leadership to any number of agendas such as sustaining and protecting fragile systems to helping the young understand and embrace existing roles and distribution of labor to redesigning regulatory, political, information, and/or structural environments. Whatever the mission of an organization, it is a cultural arena in which notions of leadership are expressions of the culture itself. This is true of both the public and private sectors, whether the arena is government, medicine, finance, social services, entertainment, or education. In contemporary U.S society, legendary leaders are rife: Steve Jobs, Chief Executive Officer (CEO) of Apple, Phil Jackson, coach of the professional basketball organization, the Los Angeles Lakers, Joel Klein, Chancellor of the New York City Public Schools, Colin Powell, former four-star General in the U.S Army and U.S. Secretary of State, and Jack Welsh, CEO of General Electric. Yet, each of these leaders, as well as the many other leaders who head large organizations, exemplifies very different styles and perspectives on how to lead organizations.

However unique or stylized their leadership might be, they lead organizations that also have particular trajectories and cultures. For instance, Apple is known best for its advances in technology and its organization would be recognizable to other individuals in the technology industry because the rhythms and patterns of its product cycles and its organizational units are more like other technology organizations than say, the rhythms and patterns of an athletic organization like the Los Angeles Lakers. Recognizing that variations in leadership within categories of industry exist (e.g., the *Wall Street Journal* versus the *New York Times*), organizations and institutions have rhythms and cycles that are specific to particular typologies of industry. The nature of the labor within each industry, the customers that the industry services, the demands of modernization and globalization, and the flow of capital have great influence on the culture of particular kinds of industries. So, leadership from individuals is tempered, reciprocated, and shaped by the demands of the institution or organization that is being led. And within that, the nature of governance and the distribution of resources also produce different kinds of leadership. Thus, leadership itself springs not solely from a particular person but it is tempered and mediated by context and opportunity in response to particular circumstances. These notions of negotiated and mediated effort are captured in the work of Cole, Gallegos, and many others in the Laboratory of Human Comparative Cognition (Cole, Engeström, & Vasquez, 1997).

In this chapter, we explore notions of leadership that are specific to providing leadership in educational settings. Because of the seismic shift that is happening demographically in the United States, educational leaders need to understand how to capitalize on the great assets that are available within their organizations because of the cultural histories, as well as negotiated and institutional cultures that educators, families, and students have experienced and anticipate receiving. Further, notions of time and space complicate this work of leaders since education exists in our individual and collective understanding both in terms of physical and conceptual spaces (Artiles, 2003). What we call and conceptualize as school now is also shifting rapidly with the advent of knowledge networks, online education, and other forms of digitally mediated learning. But more covert and less visible are the second spaces in which internalized, mental models of power, authority, privilege and rules govern external actions and reactions to daily practice (Artiles, 2003). While school system superintendents might conceptualize the role of principals as instructional leaders, share that vision, and set up policies that support and enhance the capacity of principals to engage that role, principals in buildings may have very different mental models of their role and work (Kozleski & Smith, 2009). While they may be compliant with the mandates and edicts of the current administration, school leaders also find ways to manifest their own role conceptions and respond to their interpretations of the needs of the communities they serve. Culturally responsive leadership requires a deep understanding of the ways in these concepts of conceptual space interact and complicate what is often essentialized in reform policies and mandates. Since classrooms and schools are nested in larger educational systems like school districts, state and federal educational agencies and are interdependent, it is vital that we understand leadership from a *sociocultural* and *systemic* perspective so that educational organizations build their capacity for responsivity to the changing needs of their students and families. In the following sections, we explore (a) why systemic leadership is critical, (b) the relevance of history and context, (c) the importance of sociocultural lenses, and (d) the nature of cultural responsivity. By the end of the chapter, readers will understand how systems change can be accomplished through systemic, culturally responsive leadership.

Why Systemic Leadership is Critical

Systemic improvement is predicated on deep understanding of sociocultural, historical, and psychological perspectives (Kozleski & Smith, 2009). Human systems like organizations and institutions function as a result of specific practice that is organized into rituals, routines, and cycles of activity. Thus, social reproduction can be said to be part of the cultural work of systems but systems have a dynamic of their own that is constantly negotiated and mediated. Smaller activity cycles influence how larger cycles operate and vice versa (Ferguson, Kozleski, & Smith, 2003). The people within these activity arenas respond and act producing activity that accomplishes particular outcomes or goals (Engeström, 1999). Thus, systems may be said to be reciprocal and responsive to the people, practices, and policies that exist within these activity arenas (Klingner et al., 2005).

Educational systems engage these same processes. Smaller units like student/teacher interactions are influenced by curriculum, classroom policies and intentions while curricular implementation, classroom policies, routines, and intentions are influenced by the kinds of teacher/ student interactions that operate in any given context. Classrooms as activity arenas are influenced by and impact school organization and culture. Schools are nested within districts, within states, and within federal mandates. Each of these levels is engaged in a reciprocal dance within and between levels. And, rather than one level being impacted only by its adjacent levels, each level is engaged in reciprocal interactions with all other levels. Boundaries are breached through boundary encounters such as classroom walk throughs performed by district administrators (Cobb & McClain, 2006), visits from other school teams, or site monitoring visits made in classrooms by state department representatives. Boundary objects like individualized educational plans (IEPs) or standardized test scores that are presumed to have the same meaning across boundaries are, in fact, objects that are constructed and interpreted in very different ways making policy implementation complex and unpredictable (Cobb & McClain, 2006). Thus, policy and practice travel, not in linear paths as policy is often assumed to travel, but in non-linear networks that complicate the diffusion of innovation (Kozleski, 2004).

Described in depth by Kozleski and Smith (2009), the Systemic Change Framework (Ferguson et al., 2003) offers a way of understanding these nested relationships. The framework helps to organize thinking about educational systems and it reminds us that relationships between levels within the framework operate simultaneously and porously so that reciprocity can exist between any level within the framework. Thus, classroom teachers may respond to and inform federal policy and vice versa even as they are also impacted by and impact their individual schools. Systems, like those that we observe in nature such as the human body or the earth's atmosphere, are impacted and change in response to multiple stimuli. Thinking systemically requires understanding that these complex, dynamic relationships are in play at all times. Thinking and acting unilaterally at one layer of the system creates the possibility that systems will resist change and maintain stasis because other layers operate with their own sets of rules and rhythms that may resist the changes being instituted.

The Systemic Change Framework

The Systemic Change Framework (Ferguson et al., 2003; Shanklin et al,, 2003) visually represents the varying levels of effort that combine to impact student achievement and learning in urban schools (see Figure 9.1). Because of our focus on inclusive education, the framework was designed to bring together the work of practitioners into a unified system of teaching and learning in which the learning contexts for students are organized in ways that engage the students at the margins, such as those with disabilities, as well as those in mainstream. In doing this work, researchers at the National Institute for Urban School Improvement (NIUSI) sought to reduce the number of students inappropriately placed in special education and enhance general education curricular frameworks and assessments so that learning can be individualized within the context of classroom communities. NIUSI began with a unified framework to reduce the boundaries that are often observed between the work of special and general educators.

The Systemic Change Framework provides a common language among school professionals whose specialization often creates barriers to common interests. Further, since these elements describe the work of teaching for students with and without disabilities, schools were able to integrate inclusive practices with other reform goals to form a coherent approach to change and renew educational processes. Five levels of the framework are interconnected, represented by shared borders between levels. The Systemic Change Framework was used to assess district and school needs for professional learning as well as a scaffold for guiding the planning of school improvement efforts. The framework owes much to Bronfenbrenner's nested ecological model (1979). Students comprise the microsystem, bringing their cultural histories into classrooms and other school environments, participating in the construction of the dynamic cultures that are

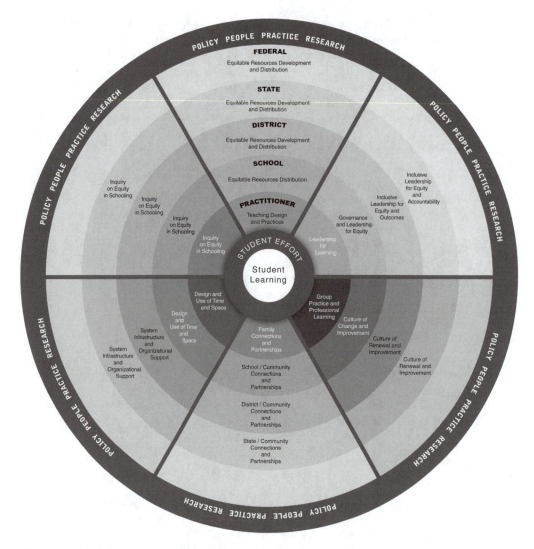

Figure 9.1 The Systemic Change Framework

constructed within classrooms (Gallego, Cole, & LCHC, 2001). Teachers and their professional worlds are actively engaged in shaping and organizing these cultural contexts through an amalgam of their individual and collective cultural histories that have been shaped by professional, personal, and community exchanges. Schools, where teachers and students create these worlds together form the mesosystems in which overlapping cultures collide, collaborate and negotiate participation, values, and outcomes. Beyond schools, lie the regulatory constraints imposed by school systems acting as intermediaries between local communities and state and federal policy.

Students.   Most observers would agree that students are at the heart of schooling, conceptualized not by their individual set of psychological characteristics, but by the interplay between those characteristics, the cultural histories that serve as vehicles through which students view and interact with the world, and the participatory demands of the classroom itself (Cole, 1996). As Rogoff (2003) writes,

In the emerging sociocultural perspective, culture is not an entity that influences individuals. Instead, people contribute to the creation of cultural processes and cultural processes contribute to the creation of people. Thus, individual and cultural processes are *mutually* constituting rather than defined separately for each other.

(p 51)

Students expend effort as they seek to make meaning of schooling experiences. This effort recognizes the dynamic nature of learning as a cultural practice that is inhibited or accelerated by individual and institutional responses (Sternberg, 2007). Therefore, the inner circle of the Systemic Change Framework represents student learning and student effort.

Practitioners. The next layer consists of professional elements that affect student effort and learning. How learning environments are established and maintained rests on the technical and relational skills, intellectual creativity and curiosity, and cultural perspectives of teachers and other practitioners. These efforts were organized into five dimensions: (a) learning standards, (b) teaching design and practices, (c) family participation in teaching and learning, (d) group practice, and (e) learning assessment. Through everyday negotiation based on the interplay among students, families, and practitioners, these elements are reconfigured and shaped into idiosyncratic activity arenas called classrooms.

Schools. The next layer of the Systemic Change Framework contains school-level elements. It is here that structures and processes are established to frame and support the work of educators and students. Six dimensions categorize activity at this level: (a) governance and leadership, (b) structure and use of time, (c) resource development and allocation, (d) school/community relations, (e) culture of change and improvement, and (f) physical environment and facilities. In all cases, schools are influenced by the activity arenas of the student and practitioner levels and by the mandates and structures of the districts in which they reside. Yet, schools also influence these other arenas by the ways in which administrators connect practitioners, reach out to families, use and distribute resources and structure time, meetings, and agendas.

School Districts. The next level identifies the systemic elements at the district-level. At this level, seven elements emerge, and each of these is conceived as important to the district's efforts for supporting what schools do: student services, inquiry on schools and schooling, organizational supports, resource development and allocation, systemic infrastructure, culture of renewal and improvement, and district/community partnerships. State law, regulation, and technical assistance shape the work of school systems as does the education policies of the U.S. Department of Education.

This nested view of schooling and the work of urban students and educators guided practice during the 11 years that NIUSI was funded. In the systems that we partnered with, work focused on bringing coherence to the district, school, and classroom levels of practice. In doing so, a set of tools shaped the structural, cultural, and learning work of school organizations.

Understanding the Role of Power

Even when coherence in vision and in the tools of reform exist, educational systems are not closed (Hartley, 2009). They respond and react to macro-contexts and histories such as political, economic, legal, and social forces and structures (Anyon, 2005). And, in a systemic view, these outside forces can disturb any level of the system compounding the problem of coherence within the system between individual agency (how students, families, teachers, and school leaders construct their individual roles and responsibilities) and the institutional assumptions about the role and purpose of education and its processes. The degrees of freedom for individual agency are signified by the formal and informal uses of power and influence that people are able to barter, garner and confer (Erikson, 2010). Accordingly, the politics of power and cultural privilege weigh heavily within activity arenas yet are often masked or unrecognized. What is stressed and omitted from the socialization of teachers, educational leaders, and researchers suggests what the dominant cultural assumptions are (Apple, 1996). So, for example, when Arzubiaga, Artiles, King, and Murri (2008) identify the *lack* of research and scholarly discourse in special education about the ethnic, racial, class, gender, and linguistic differences, they name a silence that both identifies what is considered important and what is peripheral to study and know. Socialization about what is important to know and do informs choices of what to study next and what practices to adopt. Thus, structures built into systems bolster some ideas without being transparent about what is omitted. Similarly, educational leaders learn what the dominant discourse and problem spaces are and are socialized to organize their effort and their skills development on those issues. Careers and individual agency can be built on the ability to read emerging trends and gain traction by promoting particular ideas and policies.

A powerful policy change like No Child Left Behind (NCLB) passed in the United States in 2002 touched all levels of the education system, although the policy was imposed unilaterally (e.g., from the top down). NCLB reified particular problem spaces, used the language of objectivity to bolster the credibility of its solutions, and mined notions of justice that hid the concepts of normalcy that pervaded its measurement system (Waitoller, 2010). Students and families, educators, schools, school districts, state education agencies, and the federal departments that monitored and tracked performance all shifted their patterns and rituals in response to the law (Kozol, 2005). In some cases, policy and local practice were congruent. But in many cases, after initial disruptions and gridlock, local practitioners and leaders learned to game the law as well as contest it so that they were able to continue local practices while conforming to the rules and regulations that regulated the flow of financial support (Hatch, 2002). Changing systems is complex work and shifts in policy and regulation at one level can be powerful but not sufficient to create fundamental transformation (Fullan, 2008). Where fundamental transformation is needed to change the daily work of educators and students in the light of emerging knowledge and the multifaceted challenges of a post-modern world, systemic leadership is needed to change practice at multiple levels of the system simultaneously (Ferguson et al., 2003).

The appropriation of the notion of complex adaptive systems from the biological sciences to the social sciences signals growing understanding that change and transformation are processes that describe intricate, interactive, dynamic exchanges in which human, material, and geographies of time and space intersect and influence one another creating what is referred to as complex adaptive systems (Lichtenstein et al., 2006). Complexity theory offers a way of identifying and understanding leverage points that offer the greatest potential for sustained and robust improvement (Bar-Yam, 2005). For systemic change to occur, leaders within systems need to understand their work through three lenses: the technical, the contextual, and the critical (Van Manen, 1990). These lenses help to shape the skills that are needed to move the work forward (i.e., technical), create the contexts and structures that allow the cultural work of school to flourish (i.e., contextual), and leverage equity by understanding whose needs are being served and for what purpose (i.e., critical). By understanding who is privileged and who is marginalized by specific policies and decisions, systems leaders can begin to address and redress the built in equity traps that exist within systems (McKenzie & Scheurich, 2004). In order for a new generation of students to learn in complex ways, we need leadership practice that recognizes the complexity of human systems, the underlying importance of cultural practices, and a deep understanding of how history and context shapes activity.

The Relevance of History and Context

Schools are in many respects a microcosm of the communities in which they are located. Consider the ways in which schools in Eufala, Alabama, and Kalispell, Montana, are organized, engage their students, and produce learning results. The students are different; they use language and connect with one another in context and culture bound ways. They represent and express a range of cultural historical contexts and psychological characteristics that are borne out of specific, cultural, socioeconomic and political circumstances that produce with and between group differences (Cole, 1996). The teachers also differ because of the unique combinations of age, experience, heritage, and education that they bring and the ways in which those heritages combine and define new cultures within classrooms and school buildings.

Kalispell was not incorporated until 1892 although White ranchers came to the valley as early as the 1850s when the Native Americans who lived there were forced to move onto reservation land. The legacy of this segregation may impact the relatively high risk (2.05 in the 2007–08 academic year) that students from Native American backgrounds have for being identified for specific disability categories in special education (National Center for Culturally Responsive Educational Systems [NCCREST], 2008). In contrast, in Eufala, Alabama, established approximately 20 years earlier, also moved three Indian tribes to northern Florida about 1832, experienced the impact of the Civil War, and was the center of a long tradition of cotton farming that employed African Americans as slaves before the Civil War and as low-paid labor afterwards. In the 20th century both these towns of relatively similar size have continued to respond to both global and local contexts. Both communities were impacted by the two World Wars, the Korean, Vietnam, and Middle Eastern conflicts. But Montanans dealt with the impacts of the ebb and flow of mining, ranching, hunting, and tourism industries while Eufala was impacted by Jim Crow laws, the loss of the textile industries, and the African American diaspora to north industrial cities. Legal segregation ended in the 1960s, dismantling a complex, powerful system of African American schooling that supported the development and continuation of generations of educators (Walker, 1996).

These local contexts shape the values and beliefs of children who are socialized in the schools and some of whom become educators themselves passing on both tradition and assumptions about what school is supposed look and feel like. Thus, success and failure, risk and promise, belonging and rejection are negotiated within the institution of school, mediated by professional knowledge but also by the conferred practices of previous generations. Unless challenging the status quo and the assumptions that undergird common practice is a norm, schooling practices and customs are likely to be unexamined.

Yet, a social reproduction lens is not sufficient to understand the differences that exist in these two educational systems (Artiles, 2003). While states and local districts in which schools operate constrain and focus effort through the existing regulatory environment, contemporary transactions are also steeped in the history of local politics, churches, commerce, and civic activities. Power and authority are exercised in particular ways because of these histories within and outside schools. The constant interplay between historical referents to the ways that things have been and current practice is important because interplay is captured and instantiated in what is passed on to generations of students and the expectations that the communities have for their children and the graduates of their schools. This happens locally because people interact and respond with one another based on their unique cultural and psychological characteristics creating a unique context. Thus, people, policies, and practices conspire, by their very co-existence, to create specific and unique contexts in which schooling is practiced (Klingner et al., 2005). Equilibrium is achieved through the ebb and flow of power and identity politics which influence the confluence of people, policies, and practices. To lose sight of the dynamic complexity of schools and school systems as sites of cultural practice, is to lose sight of what we must understand in order to transform schools from sites of cultural reproduction to generative sites for equity, democracy, and the development of creative, intellectual and social capital.

The Importance of a Sociocultural Activity Lens

In a country filled with local contextual complexity, the institution of public schooling has had great staying power. Its sustainability and resistance to change has been a strength because it has created a social pattern in most communities in the United States that includes a formal system of educating youth. It has also been one of the pillars of institutionalizing power and privilege for some groups and ways of being while it has simultaneously been an agent of exclusion and repression for other groups. The question that culturally responsive leaders must grapple with is leadership for what and for whom. Engaging this question must be undertaken within the complex political climate of school funding and governance, understanding that school and district leaders are employees of school districts and hence, elected school boards whose values and agendas may differ from that of the professional educator.

Cultural historical activity theory (Cole, 1996) provides a theoretical framework for understanding the focus of leadership as well as its functions. Cultural historical activity theory helps us to integrate anthropological/sociological views of social organizations and psychological and cognitive models. School communities can ask questions and devise strategies for change and renewal that draw from both traditions to act in ways that recognize the whole community, understand the division of labor, identify the organizational outcomes for work, make rules for engagement explicit, engage the participants, and use tools and participant structures to mediate the work. This way of recognizing key elements of activity is called cultural historical activity theory (CHAT) (Cole, 1996). Using CHAT helps participants understand the current structure of interaction and activity as well as understand the gaps between what currently exists and what might be imagined outcomes. The distance between the current and imagined activity arena can be viewed as what Vygotsky called the zone of proximal development (Engeström, 1999). Engaging classroom communities, school communities, and districts in examining their work requires that the participants engage with information and data about the current status of their arena and then facilitate careful analysis of what emerges so that the myths and conventional wisdom about why things occur as they do are troubled and reassembled so that the participants can better understand the hidden and obvious forces at work.

Approaching systems change from the perspective of examining the current situation from multiple sets of data, help participants understand the underlying complexity, the ongoing nature of cultural mediation, and the areas in which group assumptions have created blindspots or contradictions in what is intended and what is experienced. This section has explored foundations of systemic leadership: the relevance of history and context and the importance of a sociocultural activity lens. In the next section, we highlight the critical importance of a culturally responsive stance to education and educational systems.

Foregrounding Culture in Systemic Educational Change

A variety of critical theorists have suggested that the use of the achievement gap as a centerpiece in educational reform separates groups of students by examining deficits in academic performance between White and their peers by racial/ethnic, language, and ability categories (Artiles, Kozleski, Trent, Osher, & Ortiz, 2010). This view of troubling the status quo by examining differences between groups privileges some kinds of knowledge and ways of knowing over others, ignores the rich tapestry of indigenous and migrant knowledge that many students from minority backgrounds may have, and telegraphs to educators what counts and is to be valued in our educational institutions (Brayboy, 2005). Perhaps even more troubling, focusing educational policy on reducing between group achievement gaps sanctions monolithic views of cultural groups that reduces our understanding of culture to a static variable. What the achievement gap conversation masks are the ways in which hidden codes for behaving, using language, and valuing some kinds of knowing are mediated daily by institutional and individual cultural practices that open passages for some and close them for others. In a constant dance, cultural practices are negotiated and reinforced in practice, thus creating culture in action (Erickson, 2010).

While the path to college is based on banking particular kinds of knowledge and using it to demonstrate competence, practical and indigenous ways of knowing offer great insight and have ecological and social significance. In 2000, Professor Geneva Gay wrote that culturally responsive teaching connects students' cultural knowledge, prior experiences, and performance styles to academic knowledge and intellectual tools in ways that legitimize what students already know (Gay, 2000). By embracing the sociocultural realities and histories of students through what is taught and how, culturally responsive teachers negotiate intellectual and social cultures with their students that reflect the communities where both teachers and students develop and grow (Lee, 2007). To do this requires that teachers transcend their own cultural biases and preferences to establish and develop patterns for learning and communicating that engage and sustain student participation and achievement. They also must negotiate and mediate the social, political, and intellectual traditions that are embedded in the institution of school itself. Thus, cultural responsivity means simultaneously negotiating and mediating three cultural spaces: (a) the cultures and embedded assumptions that teachers and students bring to school, (b) the way that meaning and value is constructed in the classroom, and (c) the institutional boundaries, constraints, and affordances (Gallego, Cole, & LCHC, 2001; Rogoff, 2003). Becoming culturally responsive means that educators (teachers and leaders) as well as students have to negotiate cultural practices and routines that occupy their figurative (mental) and physical spaces.

Organizational Learning as Cultural Work

Organizations' learning occurs when organizations make shifts in their understanding of their roles, their agendas, and/or their outcomes, and organization actions are coherent with these changes. Something new that has been introduced into the cultural practices of the organization has replaced older patterns and beliefs. Both individual and collective shifts must occur for this to happen. Engeström (1999) observes that this kind of learning requires both internal mental shifts and externalized behaviors that reflect those shifts. Individuals within organizations appropriate novel concepts, create new adapted processes, innovate and routinize new practices in a way that cannot be traced to a single genesis but rather to a collective synergy.

Educators play a critical role in mediating the social and academic curriculum of schools. While acknowledging what students already know, educators connect the curriculum with frameworks and models for thinking and organizing knowledge that are embedded within disciplines such as literacy, mathematics, social studies, and the sciences (Lee, 2007). Culturally responsive educators realize that absorbing academic knowledge involves making transparent the nature of content maps. That is, content maps themselves project a particular view of events and what information is important. Further, since knowledge is been constructed and conveyed to foreground some perspectives, other perspectives may be lost or dismissed. Science, religion, philosophy, mathematics, and history as well as other disciplines and fields offer distinctive within and between discipline ways of knowing, establishing credibility for what is known, and determining the value of particular kinds of knowledge.

Pedagogies for Institutional Learning and Change

In construction, scaffolds are used to elevate laborers and provide support during work on tall structures such as skyscraper windows. Without a scaffold, the work would not be accomplished. Likewise, to become culturally responsive educational systems requires scaffolds that educational leaders can use to transform their system. These scaffolds are technical as educators get to know themselves and their students, contextual in that they are situationally dependent and require a deep understanding of the historical and cultural legacies of educational contexts, and critical as they mean all educators must deeply reflect, critique, and act to move their systems forward toward greater cultural responsivity.

The Role of Individual and Collective Identity

The technical work of educators often becomes the focus of change because it is observable and measurable. For this reason, one of the most important elements of technical work is often over-looked: the central role of identity. Identities are the active internalization of the dialogic self that is displayed through behavior (Holland & Lachicotte, 2007). Although identities are products of social interactions in context, the internalized meanings that are attributed to social experiences provide motivation for action. Experiences are internally processed and explained. Individuals may be said to author their own identities in this way. Educators display their self-authored identity to students, peers, and leaders and, depending on responses, shift and adjust their identities.

Engaging the Difficult Questions

While comprehensive school reform initiatives flowered in the 1990s, few of those initiatives focused on bringing special education services into the mix. And, fewer still focused per se on urban schools. The U.S. Department of Education's Office of Special Education Programs (OSEP) funded a technical assistance center, called the National Institute for Urban School Improvement (NIUSI) designed to target assistance to urban school systems across the country to improve access to general education for students with disabilities. NIUSI's mission was to build the capacity of urban schools and systems to serve students in inclusive classrooms and schools. This was complicated because two separate, special education dialogues were being engaged: (a) disproportionality with its perspectives on the troubling numbers of children from culturally and linguistically diverse backgrounds being inappropriately placed in special education, and (b) inclusive education with its focus on social justice and pushing students with disabilities into the general education system (Artiles, 2003). An important question being raised was "inclusion into what?" since general education was also producing poor outcomes for students of color (Erikson, 1996).

As has been noted in other studies, despite growing consensus around definitions, inclusive education models and practices have little similarity from context to context beyond surface markers (Kozleski, Artiles, Fletcher, & Engelbrecht, 2009). This is shaped in part by the significant heterogeneity of the sociocultural contexts in which the idea of inclusive education is enacted (Artiles & Kozleski, 2007). Similarly to the ways in which disproportionality seems to play out against regional differences, so inclusive education has experienced different levels of engagement depending on state and local context. There has been little discourse about the impact of these local and regional differences on principles, policies, or practices of inclusive education. Further, the impact of these universal mandates on how families and children from indigenous and minority cultures and experiences negotiated schooling remained unexamined.

In 1997, when NIUSI was initially funded, most urban school systems in the country served students with disabilities in clustered programs that pulled students with disabilities out of their home schools and bused them to center programs for students with disabilities. Clustering of students meant that districts could provide onsite specialized services such as physical and occupational therapies, speech/language, mental health support, and other specialized therapies. This practice was widespread throughout the country despite relatively poor results for students in terms of meeting curriculum standards, social networking, and opportunities for participation in school activities. In New York City, for example, District 75 was designed to offer such services as a separate system and did so for about 22,000 students in the city.

In spite of data from the first National Longitudinal Transition Study (Blackorby & Wagner, 1996), small qualitative studies, and examples of inclusive education systems in a few parts of the country that demonstrated the widespread benefits of inclusive education, special education services were conceptualized and delivered apart (for the most part) for students with disabilities. Data from the 1997–98 school year, reported by state to the U.S. Department of Education, showed that, of the six million students who are identified with disabilities in schools, approximately 48% were educated in general education classrooms. However, in urban school systems, this percentage was as low as 10% of the special education population.

In a comparison between the 1996–1997 and 2006–2007 academic years, in three disability categories used in federal statute to identify students with disabilities (learning disability, emotional disturbance, and mental retardation), the number of states that reported serving more than 50% of their students in general education for 80% or more of the time increased for students with learning disabilities (from 24 states to 33 states) and for students with emotional disabilities (from three states to seven states) (see NIUSI data maps online at www.urbanschools.org). In fact, students with mental retardation (MR) labels experienced greater segregation in the 2006–2007 school year; only one state reported serving students with MR in general education settings more than 80% of the time. This comparison is somewhat compromised by changes in the ways in which data are reported to the U.S. Department of Education. In the 1996–1997 academic year, states were reporting percentages of students served in special education classrooms less than 21% of the time while in 2006–2007, states were reporting the percentage of students served in general education more than 80% of the time. However, it does suggest that some states are progressing in some categories while the vast majority of states have remained relatively static in the ways in which they provide special education services.

The Special Education Elementary Longitudinal Study (SEELS), a study of over 11,000 school-age students funded by the OSEP, suggests that continued concern about where a student with disabilities is educated is important. The SEELS data indicate that overall, students with disabilities who spend more time in general education classrooms tend to be absent less, perform closer to grade level than their peers in pull-out settings, and have higher achievement test scores (Blackorby et al., 2005). This finding was corroborated by the second National Longitudinal Transition Study (NLTS-2) which found that, although secondary students with disabilities who take more general education classes have lower GPAs than their peers in pull-out academic settings, they score closer to grade level than their peers in math and science even when disability classification is taken into consideration (Wagner, Newman, Cameto, Levine, & Marder, 2003). In spite of these findings, as the OSEP study of State and Local Implementation and Impact of IDEA (SLIIDEA) indicates, progress towards more and more robust, effective instruction in the general education environment seems to be hampered by a lack of systemic, sustained programmatic attention to teacher education, professional learning, the use of data driven decision-making, and school capacity development (Schiller, O'Reilly, & Fiore, 2006). In a longitudinal evaluation of progress in seven school systems Schiller et al. (2006) found that the majority of the systems they studied relied on the individual expertise of teachers rather than district-level policy tools related to issuing guidelines, allocating resources, and supporting professional development and training.

How Systems Persist and Sustain the Status Quo

The special education system that exists in the United States is a product of federal law, intended to protect the rights of students who have disabilities and to ensure that they have access to a free, appropriate education. At the time that it was first signed into law in 1975, it was estimated that there were almost eight million children with disabilities who could gain access to public education in the United States. As of the 24th Report to Congress on what is now called the Individuals with Disabilities Law, six million students identified as having disabilities are enrolled in public education and, about half of them attend school most of the day with their general education peers. So, federal policy has changed the landscape of services for students with disabilities. However, it has also ensured protections through a process of assessing, identifying, categorizing, and placing students in services based on several problematic assumptions:

1. Disability resides within the individual;
2. Categories of disability applied by practitioners in local contexts distinguish between groups of students identified as learning disabled or emotionally disturbed in spite of evidence to the contrary;
3. The categories are useful in predicting what students with one label may need in terms of supports and services as opposed to what students with another label may need;
4. Educational professionals must have specialized knowledge to support learners who have disability labels and students with disabilities cannot progress intellectually, academically, or socially without a special educator present;
5. As a result of assessment for identification, multidisciplinary teams provide sound, practical, and appropriate advice to classroom and special education teachers to design effective learning environments.

By troubling these propositions, many schools and school leaders have found ways to support and extend the learning of students who might be considered as having a disability without limiting their learning approaches to remediation. Further, by implementing tiered approaches to instruction that are built on frequent assessments of learning and adjustments to teaching strategies, educators have begun to worry less about labeling what's wrong with students and moved towards understanding differentiated and personalized approaches to learning. Finally, while specialists who understand deeply how children learn and how to shift pedagogies to support learner development and mastery are needed in every school, learning can be supported by many kinds of educators in consultation and collaboration with specialists. Finally, with more emphasis on progress monitoring and response to intervention, initial special education assessments can be more complete blueprints for teaching and learning in the future. These shifts in assumptions (such as those above) about students with special educational needs have enabled school and district leaders to shift their investments in building the capacity of systems to serve all students.

If we conceptualize schooling as an enculturating process, then the frictions between student and organizational cultures can be viewed as spaces where the school and its staff need to assess their own cultural perspectives to understand how they might change institutional patterns, structures, and practices so that students do not have to fit in but school becomes a place where the institution learns to fit its students. As Artiles and Kozleski (2007) wrote:

> Hence, inclusive schools must not ignore the ubiquity of enduring legacies of racial oppression and stratification in U.S. society. Any version of inclusive education that ignores this fact cannot have legitimacy and authenticity in the eyes of minority students and their families. Second, inclusive education research and practice should take into account the

complex processes of identity formation and change that take place in the life of communities of practice. Similarly, the work individuals do to forge identities that signal membership in these communities is not always done with one center or core set of practices in mind; that is, notions of center and margin in communities are moving targets and are defined from multiple perspectives. Inclusive schools that incorporate these insights are nonexistent. And finally, inclusive education advocates must always be clear about what they ask students and their families. For individuals who inhabit marginal positions due to social class, language, gender, and race, though questions will arise: *Inclusion into what? Do I want to be included in a system that is fraught with systematic barriers for certain groups.*

(p. 357)

Progress is slow where the fundamental assumptions that undergird practice are not examined. Systems persist in their reproduction when leadership for change tackles technical issues without understanding the historical intersectionalities and critical equity concerns that lie at the heart of keeping things the way they are. This is the work of culturally responsive leaders: they must transform systems by being culturally responsive in their own practice.

Conclusion

Moving towards cultural responsivity requires critical examination of all system elements. Changes at one level cannot be presumed to travel intact to the next level because systems change is a cultural activity that is influenced by informal and formal authority at each level of the system, complicated by the intricate social networks of students, families and practitioners, and intersected by race, class, gender, and power.

Examining the equity issues within educational settings based on evidence of the current status of a system offers an initial way in to opening up the dialogue within a system. Leadership for dialogue and action must come from multiple levels of the system with shared intent and mediation strategies. The ensuing discourse must acknowledge the ways in which power and privilege operate within the educational system so that participants can begin to find new ways to practice that open the possibilities for improving access, participation for every student. Lessons from NIUSI emphasize the development of *systems for change* that can travel across activity arenas and create the impetus for locally embedded, systems work that results in improving educational outcomes for marginalized students while simultaneously improving contexts and results for other students as well. Out of this work emerged the following seven principles that help local schools and districts engage difficult questions:

1. The delivery of special education services must be conceptualized as a seamless system of supports and services delivered within the context of an equitable and culturally responsive general education system.
2. Practitioners (including principals, general and special educators, instructional coaches, and related services personnel) must see themselves as members of transdisciplinary teams that share knowledge, skills, and roles in order to design and support comprehensive learning environments for students.
3. Practitioners and families must build a shared vision of education anchored in the concepts of universal design, personalization, formative assessment, and continuous improvement.
4. Equity in terms of opportunities to learn, accountability, and the distribution of resources is essential to culturally responsive systems.
5. Inquiry for improving learning grounded in evidence-based practice is part of a healthy, innovative, and equitable education system.

6. Improvements on behalf of any group of students must be conceptualized as a *systems* change endeavor. Failure to do so creates bureaucratic silos of inefficiency, sluggish communication, and "work arounds" that can mire a system for reasons that are lost in institutional memory but reified in practice.

7. State and local education contexts vary widely because of historical and contemporary political, social, and economic factors that intersect and complicate institutional, group, and individual regulatory and behavioral actions. Notions of transportable, universal research and policy solutions must be tempered by this understanding and emphasis placed on local solutions.

References

Anyon, J. (2005). *Radical possibilities: Public policy, urban education, and a new social movement.* New York: Routledge.

Apple, M. W. (1996). Power, meaning and identity: Critical sociology of education in the United States. *British Journal of Sociology of Education, 17,* 125–144.

Artiles, A. J. (2003). Special education's changing identity: Paradoxes and dilemmas in views of culture and space. *Harvard Educational Review, 73,* 164–202.

Artiles, A. J., & Kozleski, E. B. (2007). Beyond convictions: Interrogating culture, history, and power in inclusive education. *Language Arts, 84,* 35–58.

Artiles, A., Kozleski, E. B., Trent, S. Osher, D., & Ortiz, A. (2010). Justifying and explaining disproportionality, 1968–2008: A critique of underlying views of culture. *Exceptional Children, 79,* 279–299.

Arzubiaga, A., Artiles, A., King, K., & Murri, N. (2008). Beyond culturally responsive research: Challenges and implications of research as situated cultural practice. *Exceptional Children, 74,* 309–327.

Bar-Yam, Y. (2005). *Making things work: Solving complex problems in a complex world.* Brookline, MA: Knowledge Press.

Blackorby, J., & Wagner, M. (1996). Longitudinal postschool outcomes of youth with disabilities: Findings from the National Longitudinal Transition Study (NLTS) of special education students regarding postschool outcomes of American youth with disabilities in their first five years after high school. *Exceptional Children, 62,* 399–413.

Blackorby, J., Wagner, M., Cameto, R., Davies, El., Levine, P., Newman, L., et al. (2005). *Engagement, academics, social adjustment, and independence.* Palo Alto, CA: SRI.

Brayboy, B. (2005). Toward a tribal critical race theory in education. *The Urban Review, 37,* 425–446.

Bronfenbrunner, U. (1979). *The ecology of human development.* Cambridge, MA: Harvard University Press.

Cobb, P., & McClain, K. (2006). The collective mediation of a high-stakes accountability program: Communities and networks of practice. *Mind, Culture, and Activity, 13,* 80–100.

Cole, M. (1996). *Cultural psychology: A once and future discipline.* Cambridge, MA: Harvard University Press.

Cole, M., Engeström, Y., & Vasquez, O. (1997). Introduction. In M. Cole, Y. Engeström, & O. Vasquez (Eds.), *Mind, culture, & activity* (pp. 1–22). Cambridge, UK: Cambridge University Press.

Engeström, Y. (1999). Expansive visibilization of work: An activity-theoretical perspective. *Computer Supported Cooperative Work,* 63–99.

Erickson, F. (1996) Going for the zone: The social and cognitive ecology of teacher-student interaction in classroom conversation. In D. Hicks (Ed.), *Discourse, learning, and schooling (pp. 29–62).* Cambridge, UK: Cambridge University Press.

Erickson, F. (2010). Culture in society and in educational practices. In J. A. Banks & C. A. McGee Banks (Eds.), *Multicultural education: Issues and perspectives* (pp. 33–56). Hoboken, NJ: Wiley.

Ferguson, D. L., Kozleski, E. B., & Smith, A. (2003). Transformed, inclusive schools: A framework to guide fundamental change in urban schools. *Effective Education for Learners with Exceptionalities, 15,* 43–74.

Fullan, M. (2008). *The six secrets of change: What the best leaders do to help their organizations survive and thrive.* San Francisco: Jossey-Bass.

Gallego, M. A., Cole, M., & the Laboratory of Comparative Human Cognition (LCHC) (2001). Classroom cultures and cultures in the classroom. In V. Richardson (Ed.), *Handbook of research on teaching* (pp. 951–997). Washington, DC: American Educational Research Association.

Gay, G. (2000). *Culturally responsive teaching: Theory, research, and practice.* New York: Teachers College Press.

Hartley, D. (2009). Education policy, distributed leadership and socio-cultural theory. *Educational Review, 61,* 139–150.

Hatch, T. (2002). When improvement programs collide. *Phi Delta Kappan, 83,* 626–634.

Heifitz, R. A. (1994). *Leadership without easy answers.* Cambridge, MA: The Belknap Press of Harvard University Press.

Holland, D., & Lachicotte, Jr., W. (2007). Vygotsky, Mead, and the new sociocultural studies of identity. In H. Daniels, M. Cole, & J. V. Wertsch (Eds.), *The Cambridge companion to Vygotsky* (pp. 101–135). Cambridge, MA: Cambridge University Press.

Klingner, J., Artiles, A., Kozleski, E. B., Utley, C., Zion, S., Tate, W., et al. (2005). Conceptual framework for addressing the disproportionate representation of culturally and linguistically diverse students in special education. *Educational Policy Analysis Archives, 13, 38,* Retrieved September 9, 2005, from http://epaa.asu.edu/epaa/v13n38/

Kozleski, E. B. (2004). Technology transfer and the field of education: The research to practice conundrum. *Technology Transfer and Society, 2,* 176–194.

Kozleski, E. B., & Smith, A. (2009). The role of policy and systems change in creating equity for students with disabilities in urban schools. *Urban Education, 44,* 427–451.

Kozleski, E. B., Artiles, A. J., Fletcher, T., & Engelbrecht, P. (2009). Understanding the dialectics of the local and the global in Education for All: A comparative case study. *International Critical Childhood Policy Studies Journal, 2,* 15–29. Retrieved from http://journals.sfu.ca/iccps/index.php/childhoods/index

Kozol, J. (2005). *The shame of the nation: The restoration of Apartheid schooling in America.* New York: Random House.

Lee, C. D. (2007). *Culture, literacy, and learning: Taking bloom in the midst of the whirlwind.* New York: Teachers College Press.

Lichtenstein, B., Uhl-Bien, M., Marion, R., Seers, A., Orton, J. D., & Schreiber, C. (2006). Complexity leadership theory: An interactive perspective on leading in complex adaptive systems. *Emergence: Complexity and Organization, 8,* 2–12.

McKenzie, K. B., & Scheurich, J. J. (2004). Equity traps: A useful construct for preparing principals to lead schools that are successful with racially diverse students. *Educational Administration Quarterly, 40,* 601–632.

National Center for Culturally Responsive Educational Systems (NCCREST) (2008). http://nccrest.eddata.net/maps/index.php?col=RACE_RRW&group=American%2520Indian%252FAlaskan%2520Native&f1=2006-2007&f3=HIGH+INCIDENCE+DISABILITIES+%28ED%2BLD%2BMR%29

No Child Left Behind Act of 2001, 20 U.S.C. §et seq (2010).

Rogoff, B. (2003). *The cultural nature of human development.* New York: Oxford University Press.

Schiller, E., O'Reilly, F., & Fiore, T. (2006). *Marking the progress of IDEA Implementation*: The study of state and local implementation and impact of IDEA. Retrieved October 7, 2008, from *The Study of State and Local Implementation and Impact of the Individuals with Disabilities Education Act* (SLIIDEA): http://www.abt.sliidea.org/reports.htm#Reports.

Shanklin, N., Kozleski, E. B., Meagher, C., Sands, D., Joseph, O., & Wyman, W. (2003). Examining renewal in an urban high school through the lens of systemic change. *International Journal of School Leadership and Management, 231,* 357–378.

Sternberg, R .J. (2007). Who are the bright children: The cultural context of being and acting intelligent. *Educational Researcher, 36,* 148–155.

Van Manen, M. (1990). *Research lived experience: Human science for an action sensitive pedagogy.* Albany, NY: State University of New York Press.

Wagner, M., Newman, L., Cameto, R., Levine, P., & Marder, C. (2003). *Going to school: Instructional contexts, programs, and participation of secondary school students with disabilities. A report from the National Longitudinal Transition Study-2 (NLTS2).* Menlo Park, CA: SRI International. Retrieved 1, 2008, from http: www.nlts2.org/reports/2003_12/nlts2_report_2003_12_complete.pdf

Waitoller, F. R. (2010). *Delving into the seduction of educational reforms: A critical discourse analysis of the justice narratives in the Title I of NCLB.* Manuscript in preparation.

Walker, V. S. (1996). *Their highest potential. An African American school community in the segregated south.* Chapel Hill: The University of North Carolina Press.

10

Inclusive School Reform
Distributed Leadership across the Change Process

Bonnie S. Billingsley

UNIVERSITY OF NORTH CAROLINA AT GREENSBORO

An important question facing educational leaders is how to plan change and build capacity to effectively include and educate students with disabilities in general education settings so that these students can achieve important educational outcomes. School reform is difficult even with knowledgeable and willing participants and leaders often underestimate the complexity involved in the change process (Elmore, 2004; Fullan, 2007). Inclusive reform is viewed as a particularly challenging reform (Mayrowetz & Weinstein, 1999; Sindelar, Shearer, Yendol-Hoppey, & Liebert, 2006) requiring different ways of thinking about the organizational structures of schools (Boscardin & Jacobson, 1997) and how the work of leaders is conceptualized (Mayrowetz & Weinstein). Although the leadership literature on inclusive reform is modest in its scope, there is a specific body of literature that describes the work of leaders as they led change in schools. In this chapter, findings from the research on inclusive school reform in the U.S. are reviewed.

The Context of Inclusive School Reform

Over 35 years ago, the landmark law, The Education for All Handicapped Children's Act, P.L. 94–142 (1975) stated that to the maximum extent appropriate, students with disabilities should be educated in the least restrictive environment (LRE). The LRE principle means that students with disabilities should be educated with their peers without disabilities and should only be removed "when the nature or severity of the disability is such that education in regular classes with the use of supplementary aids and services cannot be achieved satisfactorily" (EHA, 1975, sec. 1412(5)(B)). The vagueness of this language (Crockett & Kauffman, 1999) left a great deal of discretion to school districts as they deliberated placement decisions; and many students with disabilities continued to be served in separate schools and self-contained classrooms (Hasazi, Johnston, Liggett, & Schattman, 1994).

In the years following the passage of P.L. 94–142, some charged that the special education system was flawed, discriminatory, and programmatically ineffective (Davis, 1989). In response to growing criticisms about separate placements for students with disabilities, policymakers and researchers called for the development of a unified general and special education system for all students (Reynolds, Wang, & Walberg, 1987; Stainback & Stainback, 1984; Will, 1986). The call for reform was labeled the Shared Responsibility Initiative, the Regular Education Initiative

(REI) and the Inclusive Schools Movement (Burrello, Lashley, & Beatty, 2001). Despite a prolonged and contentious debate with some voicing cautions or opposition (e.g., Fuchs & Fuchs, 1994; Kauffman, 1989; Zigmond et al., 1995), the movement toward inclusive schools continued to grow.

Since the passage of P.L. 94–142 in 1975, reauthorizations of the law (renamed the Individuals with Disabilities Education Act [IDEA]) have "refined, revised, and renewed the nation's moral and pedagogical commitment to providing well-planned, public, inclusive, and appropriate education to all students with disabilities" (Zigmond, Kloo, & Volonino, 2009, p. 189). Recent evidence suggests that placement trends for almost two decades show not only an increase in placements in general education settings, but an increase in the percentage of students spending most of the day in these settings (34% in 1990 and 58% in 2007) (McLeskey, Landers, Williamson, & Hoppey, in press).

While it is important to acknowledge the progress that has been made in placing students with disabilities in less restrictive settings (e.g., McLeskey et al., in press), defining inclusion as a placement is problematic since it presumes that changing the location where students receive their education makes them members of their classroom communities (Friend & Shamberger, 2011). Over the past decades, scholars have offered various definitions of inclusion. A wide range of components have been described such as defining inclusion as: (a) a philosophy with an inherent social justice perspective; (b) the valuing of diverse learners as part of the human community; (c) an attitude in which all students are welcomed, valued, and experience a sense of belonging in their schools; (d) a belief system used to guide professionals' decisions as they create learning communities and help all students meet valued educational goals; (e) a process, including the removal of barriers to students' participation in schools; and (f) the provision of supports and accommodations in shared environments to help students achieve educational goals; (e.g., Ainscow, 2005; Causton-Theoharis, Theoharis, Bull, Cosier, & Dempf-Aldrich, 2011; Devecchi & Nevin, 2010; Friend & Shamberger, 2011; McLeskey & Waldron, 2011; Peters, 2002; Ryndak, Jackson & Billingsley, 2000).

Given the reality that the "goals of inclusive education are underdeveloped, illusive and difficult to measure" (Peters, Johstone, & Ferguson, 2005, p. 140), leaders face the challenge of working to create clarity about what inclusion means and developing organizational processes to help others work toward an inclusive vision. As Fullan (2007) emphasized, both the what and the how of reform are critical. He stated: "It is possible to be crystal clear about what one wants and totally inept at achieving it. Or to be skilled at managing change but empty-headed about which changes are most needed" (p. 9).

The research literature on inclusive school reform provides some knowledge about leaders' readiness to engage in inclusive change, what leaders did as they moved toward inclusive education, and studies of leadership in existing inclusive schools. Principals are often a focus as scholars have emphasized the importance of their role in how inclusion is accepted and implemented by school staff (DiPaola & Walther-Thomas, 2003; Garrison-Wade, Sobel, & Fulmer, 2007; Guzman, 1997; Hoppey & McLeskey, in press; Ingram, 1997; Keyes, Hanley-Maxwell, & Capper, 1999; Praisner, 2003; Sindelar et al., 2006). Teachers explained the importance of principals' support of inclusive efforts:

> if staff members in a building know that the site administrator supports inclusive education and expects teachers to collaborate with special educators and to teach special education students, then resistance to inclusivity is diminished. The opposite also was felt to be true. Any suggestion or inclination that inclusivity was optional gave permission, of sorts, for marginal support of inclusive education efforts.
>
> *(York-Barr, Sommerness, Duke, & Ghere, 2005, p. 208)*

Unfortunately evidence suggests that many school leaders are not clear about the goals of inclusion and they are not ready to make inclusive education a priority in their schools. For example, barriers to principal leadership include: (a) lack preparation about and experience with students with disabilities; (b) being uncertain or negative about inclusion; (c) viewing inclusive change as others' responsibility; (d) concerns about the impact that students with disabilities will have in general education; (e) concerns about general education teachers' readiness to teach those with disabilities; (f) competing demands on their time; (g) concerns about costs, resources and supports needed for inclusive reform, and; (h) fears about inclusive and high-stakes accountability (e.g., Barnett & Monda-Amaya, 1998; Brotherson, Sheriff, Milburn, & Schetz, 2001; Crockett, Myers, Griffin, & Hollandsworth, 2007; Downing, Eichinger, & Williams, 1997; Praisner, 2003).

Today, the need to educate and support principals as they work to make sure that students with disabilities have opportunities to learn in inclusive settings remains an important priority. This was recently illustrated in a news article that described a professional development effort to "… show principals how to embrace students with special needs, rather than become fearful of how much it might cost to educate the student, or whether the students' scores would lower the school's overall progress" (Padnani, 2010, p. 1).

The emphasis on the principals' role in inclusive reform is understandable given that principals are in a position to shape the organizational conditions necessary for success, such as "shared goals, collaborative work structures and climates, and procedures for monitoring results" (Fullan, 2007, p. 96). While principal leadership is critical to the development of inclusive schools, the work of principals occurs in their interactions with others, often with district leaders, community members, parents, teachers and faculty from IHEs. In this analysis of inclusive school reform, the collective impact of formal and informal leaders is considered as well as the unique contributions of individuals in varied roles.

Two Frameworks for Understanding Inclusive Reform

Two frameworks are used as foundations for this review of inclusive school reform. First, a distributed framework provides a way of considering how varied leaders took responsibility for inclusive school reform through the stages of the change process. In contrast to defining leadership as associated with a specific role (e.g., director of special education, principal, teacher leader), Spillane (2006) conceptualizes leadership as an organizational property. As Spillane elaborated, leadership may be thought of as "activities tied to the core work of the organization that are designed by organizational members to influence the motivation, knowledge, affect, or practices of other organizational members" (pp. 11–12). Distributed leadership provides an "opportunity to stand back and think about exactly how leadership is distributed and the difference made, or not made, by that distribution" (Harris & Spillane, 2008, p. 33).

Analyzing studies using a distributed framework shows the varied roles assumed by formal and informal leaders. Given that expertise is distributed across an organization, it is the organizational unit (e.g., district, school) rather than the formal leader (Spillane, 2006) that is the focus of this analysis. Applying Spillane's ideas, distributed leadership provides a lens for considering how varied individuals within the organization and sometimes across organizations contributed to inclusive change.

Mayrowetz and Weinstein (1999) used a distributive framework in the study of inclusive reform providing evidence that key leadership activities important to inclusive change were shared across individuals in three schools within one district. They used Heller and Firestone's (1995) change leadership function theory, which identified six leadership functions important to change: "(a) providing and selling a vision, (b) providing encouragement and recognition,

(c) obtaining resources, (d) adapting standard operating procedures, (e) monitoring the improvement effort, and (f) handling disturbances" (p. 425). Mayrowetz and Weinstein found that these six functions were implemented by multiple individuals as schools moved toward inclusive change, including those with more and less formal authority. Other scholars have also noted the relevance of a distributed perspective on inclusive reform (Devecchi & Nevin, 2010) and the importance of teacher leadership roles in inclusive education (e.g., Billingsley, 2007; Hoppey & McLeskey, in press; Peters, 2002). Although most studies are not situated in a distributed framework, an analysis of these studies demonstrates that in the majority of studies, both formal and informal leaders provided specific types of leadership, often collaborating together in the creation of inclusive schools.

The second framework used to analyze the research on inclusive school reform is the three phases of the change process described by Fullan (2007) including: (a) initiation and adoption, which involves the activities or processes that lead to change, including decisions to proceed with change; (b) implementation or the initial experiences of trying to put a reform into practice, including initial adoption through years two and three; and, (c) institutionalization, which is the extent to which change is integrated into the system or disappears. Fullan discusses how these three phases may not be clearly distinct and there is not a set amount of time that characterizes each of the three phases of change. He also emphasized that these phases often occur concurrently, e.g., as change is initiated, implementation is also being planned.

To better understand how inclusive change developed or was implemented in schools, three questions were used to guide this analysis:

- How is leadership for inclusive change conceptualized and enacted in districts/schools?
- What were the major activities of inclusive school reform during initiation, implementation, and institutionalization and who assumed responsibility for this work?
- What specific activities and interactions occurred that led to the continuation of inclusive education over time and what interfered with change?

Research on Leadership for Inclusive Reform

A systematic search of the published literature was conducted to identify peer-reviewed research articles that focused on leadership for inclusive school reform in the United States since 1995, a period of time when the leadership for reform literature began to appear with at least some regularity. One literature review addressed what has been learned about maximizing the participation of all students in their school communities in the United Kingdom (Dyson, Howes, & Roberts, 2002), however, no reviews were found of inclusive reform in the United States. While clearly international perspectives and comparative studies about inclusive school reform are important, a focused analysis of U.S. studies provides a better understanding of inclusive reform in this country as well as factors related to more versus less successful efforts.

Terms used for this electronic search included inclusion, inclusive education, inclusive reform, and special education combined with leadership, principals, leaders, administrators and teachers. Eleven studies were found that addressed leadership and how it evolved during the process of change (i.e., Burstein, Sears, Wilcoxen, Cabello, & Spagna, 2004; Downing, Spencer, & Cavallaro, 2004; Fisher, Sax, & Grove, 2000; Fox & Ysseldyke, 1997; Kilgore, Griffin, Sindelar, & Webb, 2001; Mamlin, 1999; Mayrowetz & Weinstein, 1999; Peters, 2002; Rice, 2006; Ryndak, Reardon, Benner, & Ward, 2007; Sindelar et al., 2006). Although less of a focus, selected studies of leadership in existing inclusive schools were also included to provide additional data about leadership in current programs and/or evaluation data on inclusive programs (e.g., Causton-Theoharis et al., 2011; Guzman, 1997; Hoppey & McLeskey, in press; Idol, 1996; Janney, Snell,

Beers, & Raynes, 1995; Keyes et al., 1999; Lieber et al., 2000; Purcell, Horn, & Palmer, 2007; Salisbury & McGregor, 2002). Studies addressing inclusive reform in a particular exceptionality area (e.g., learning disabilities) were not included in this review.

The literature base on leadership for inclusive schools is primarily qualitative and diverse in the student populations, service-delivery models, and school levels studied. Ryndak et al. (2007) studied the inclusion of students with severe disabilities, while others studied the inclusion of students with both lower and higher incidence disabilities (Burstein et al., 2004; Hoppey & McLeskey, in press; Idol, 1996). Some (e.g., Fisher et al., 2000; Kilgore et al., 2001) included all students who received special services in the school (e.g., special education, Title 1, bilingual, magnet resources). School reform also focused on varied service-delivery models. For example, one district's goal was to include all or nearly all students with severe disabilities in general classrooms in their neighborhood schools (Ryndak et al., 2007), whereas others included a mix of service delivery options (Burstein et al., 2004; Idol, 1996). In addition, some focused on specific school levels, including pre-school (Lieber et al., 2000; Purcell et al., 2007), elementary (Causton-Theoharis et al., 2011; Hoppey & McLeskey, in press; Mamlin, 1999), middle (Fox & Ysseldyke, 1997; Kilgore et al., 2001; Sindelar et al., 2006) and high school (Rice, 2006) as well as combined levels (Burstein et al., 2004; Idol; Mayrowetz & Weinstein, 1999; Ryndak et al., 2007; Peters, 2002). While the studies varied significantly in the definitions of inclusion and the timeframes studied, there are some clear themes, particularly related to the activities of change and the activities of formal and informal leaders who led reform efforts.

Phase 1: The Initiation and Adoption of Change

The literature on the initiation and adoption of inclusive reform includes references to where in the organizational hierarchy change originated, the specific activities of planning, and how these activities were distributed and shared across individuals in varied positions. Initiation usually commenced with an emphasis on working to gain the commitment of others, helping individuals make sense of what inclusion means, building capacity through the planning teams and professional development, and garnering resources for inclusive initiatives.

Initiation of Change at Varied Levels. Leadership was initiated at different levels, in some cases from those external to the district (State Education Agencies [SEAs], Institutions of Higher Education [IHEs]), often from district leaders, and sometimes from principals, teachers and parents. Lieber et al. (2000) studied inclusive change in 18 pre-school programs and found district leaders were responsible for the initiation in 13 programs, whereas principals and/ or teachers were responsible for five. In another study of five inclusive preschool programs, Purcell et al. (2007) indicated agents of change were administrative staff from districts, Head Start programs, educational cooperatives and IHEs. Burstein et al. (2004) discussed that while the overall impetus for change initially came from state and district levels, some changes were already occurring at the school level with teachers and parents demonstrating interest in inclusive models. They discussed the nature of teacher leadership in one district: a core group of teachers, dissatisfied with existing service-delivery, initiated inclusive practices and involved others in moving inclusion forward. Although teachers initiated inclusion in some schools, Lieber et al. indicated that these school initiatives rarely spread beyond that particular setting. They cited Fullan (1991) in emphasizing that teacher-initiated change is often limited since teachers usually do not have the contacts to disseminate their views widely. In some cases, parents initiated change (e.g., Burstein et al., 2004; Lieber et al., 2000) and some parents of students with severe disabilities insisted on inclusive classrooms for their children (Ryndak et al., 2007).

Leadership Activities in the Initiation Phase. While inclusive reform was often initiated by key personnel (e.g., Lieber et al., 2000; Mayrowetz & Weinstein, 1999) who "made it happen" (Purcell et al., 2007, p. 91), planning was distributed across individuals in varied positions. The specific roles that external groups, districts, schools, and parents in planning for inclusion are described in this section.

External leadership. SEAs have roles in promoting inclusion through creating incentives for inclusive education through funding and professional development activities, communicating with district personnel, and monitoring progress in educating students in inclusive environments. Some SEA efforts for inclusive reform have been supported with funding from the Office of Special Education Programs (U.S. Department of Education). OSEP created incentives for state leadership of inclusive programs, providing forty million dollars across 26 states over a 13-year period (Fisher et al., 2000).

In several studies SEAs provided intensive professional development for district and school staff about inclusive education (e.g., Burstein et al., 2004; Mayrowetz & Weinstein, 1999; Ryndak et al., 2007). In Florida, the Inclusive Education Technical Assistance Network (IE-TAN), supported by the state, also provided regional representatives who helped districts as they worked for inclusive change (Ryndak et al., 2007). It is likely that at least some reform efforts may have commenced without state assistance since inclusive change was already underway in some districts (Burstein et al., 2004). However, SEAs clearly provided important incentives and supports for inclusive reform.

IHEs were often partners and sometimes leaders in these state-funded initiatives and encouraged districts to apply for state funds for inclusive services (Purcell et al., 2007; Ryndak et al., 2007). Faculty from IHEs also provided guidance and knowledge about inclusion and change processes. To illustrate, Kilgore et al. (2001) guided an inclusive effort in a Florida middle school. They planned retreats, worked to assure that all participants were heard and had opportunities to ask questions. Sindelar et al. (2006), in discussing the same effort, described the use of key principles from the inclusive literature to guide program development including natural proportions, placement in general classrooms with heterogeneous grouping and multidisciplinary interventions. Ryndak and colleagues (2007) also emphasized the importance of critical friends. These friends were described as university and IE-TAN representatives who were well informed about the local initiative and helped those working toward change. As Ryndak and colleagues explained, these critical friends brought in "research-based strategies for developing, implementing, and evaluating services in inclusive general education contexts" and helped with facilitating "sustainable systemic changes across the district" (p. 243). They emphasized that these relationships needed to be based on concern for students, trust, and respect.

District leadership. District leaders advanced an inclusive agenda by initiating and supporting inclusive change and school personnel discussed the importance of this leadership (e.g., Mayrowetz & Weinstein, 1999; Salisbury & McGregor, 2002). While directors of special education were often lead initiators of inclusive reform, other district leaders such as superintendents sometimes initiated change (Lieber et al., 2000; Purcell et al., 2007). District leaders advocated for inclusive change through communicating a clear message that inclusive education was necessary to achieve positive outcomes for students with disabilities (Burstein et al., 2004; Janney et al., 1995). Researchers also described how district leaders worked with others to develop specific plans to promote inclusion through "goals, activities, a timeline, personnel responsible, and a budget" (Burstein et al., 2004, p. 107) and to provide professional development to prepare personnel for new roles (Burstein et al., 2004; Mayrowetz & Weinstein, 1999; Ryndak et al., 2007).

As district leaders initiated change, they sought out help from others. Teams were organized to help solicit support for inclusion, to assess needs, and to plan the inclusive effort (Burstein et al., 2004; Mayrowetz & Weinstein, 1999). Some described how leaders tried to be strategic in finding schools willing to work toward change and also involved those most capable of garnering further support. Mamlin (1999) reported that the district she studied was looking to specific schools as "pathfinders for the rest of the district" (p. 40). One director selected a specific primary school because the school was viewed to be child-centered and he believed the principal's strong relationships with teachers and parents would help facilitate change (Mayrowetz & Weinstein, 1999).

Ryndak and colleagues (2007) provided an in-depth description of how a District Inclusive Education Task Force (DIETF) was charged with the responsibility of systematically planning one district's transition to inclusive education. The team was also responsible for communicating and serving as a link between district personnel, school personnel and families in this transition. The DIETF struggled in their initial year due to the lack of participation of district and school leaders in meetings and the lack of a single individual responsible for inclusion. To address these concerns, the district hired a full-time coordinator to facilitate inclusion, worked with the DIEFT taskforce, and encouraged participation from leadership (improving participation in year 2).

District leaders also supported new inclusive education initiatives through allocating resources. One superintendent stated, "My experience has been that when you mouth the values but you haven't committed money, resources, personnel, or time, then it isn't really going to happen" (Mayrowetz & Weinstein, 1999, p. 436). Mayrowetz and Weinstein reported that the director of special education negotiated a budgetary line item for the inclusion program as students from private schools were brought back into the district. In another school, a district leader worked with an elementary school to create a noncategorical program where teachers worked with students across programs (i.e., special education, bilingual, Title 1, gifted and talented) (Fisher et al., 2000).

A number of researchers discussed the importance of professional development (PD) efforts, describing both formal and informal PD activities designed with the goal of helping others understand a rationale for inclusion and learn about specific inclusive practices. General and special education teachers and administrators participated in these efforts in extended retreats, summer PD workshops, and visits to inclusive schools (Burstein et al., 2004; Mayrowetz & Weinstein, 1999; Ryndak et al., 2007). Teams who attended state sponsored workshops returned to share what they learned with others in their schools (Burstein et al., 2004; Mayrowetz & Weinstein, 1999). Topics for PD included a rationale for inclusion, planning for inclusion, the need to develop a vision of inclusion, and effective practices in inclusive education, including strategies for accommodating and modifying instruction for students with disabilities (e.g., cooperative learning, peer tutoring, circle of friends) and co-teaching (e.g., Burstein et al., 2004; Fox & Ysseldyke, 1997; Mamlin, 1999; Ryndak et al., 2007). In another district, a manual was developed that addressed models for inclusion, development of a vision, curriculum modifications, assessment methods for collaborative classrooms, and ways to facilitate teaming among special and general educators (Burstein et al., 2004).

School leadership. During the initiation phase, districts worked with school personnel to build commitment for inclusion at the building level (e.g., Burstein et al., 2004; Mayrowetz & Weinstein, 1999; Ryndak et al., 2007). Burstein et al. reported that district personnel met with principals and teachers to discuss inclusive goals, consider a rationale for inclusion, as well as discuss research about student outcomes. In another example, Kilgore et al. (2001) described how a committee of teachers and administrators worked during the summer to plan the inclusive model. The committee discussed ways to improve current practices, possible structures for the model, the redistribution of resources, and the roles that both general and support teachers would play in inclusion. Janney et al. (1995) indicated initial discussions with teachers focused on the purposes and benefits of inclusion for students and to consider staff apprehensions and assumptions. By considering teachers' concerns, some reluctant general education teachers became willing to participate, especially when they understood the benefits to students. As part of these collabora-tive efforts, leaders worked to create a democratic process (Kilgore et al., 2001) and empower staff (Janney et al., 1995) as they moved toward inclusive practices.

Researchers pointed out the importance of considering participants' concerns as they planned change. Mayrowetz and Weinstein (1999) indicated that the initial planning team returned from a SEA retreat committed to the idea of including students with disabilities in general classes. However, they spent a great deal of time in the first year helping other school staff work through resistance. In other reform efforts, legal, ethical, pedagogical, safety, and procedural questions were also raised during initial conversations (Janney et al., 1995; Rice, 2006). General educators expressed concerns such as, "What can I actually give, how can they learn from me, they won't be able to keep up, will it hamper my other students' progress" (Janney et al., 1995, p. 433).

Principals took different approaches to addressing teachers' concerns and resistance to inclu-sion. Some continued to work toward developing buy-in by developing shared meanings about inclusion (Mayrowetz & Weinstein, 1999). Some principals encouraged staff to openly disagree, talk with others, and express concerns, sometimes in regularly scheduled meetings (Guzman, 1997; Mayrowetz & Weinstein, 1999; Rice, 2006). Encouraging teachers to voice concerns was viewed as important since taking time to consider their perspectives "demonstrated respect for teachers' professionalism by seeking their recommendations and opinions" (Janney et al., 1995, p. 433). Others dealt with resistance by working with volunteers rather than requiring that they par-ticipate (Fisher et al., 2000). As some researchers explained, once a core group of teachers demon-strated success, others became interested in participating (Burstein et al. 2004; Janney et al, 1995.). However, one principal made it clear that inclusion was not negotiable; however, she tried to create a supportive environment for the critique of possible ways to reach inclusion (Keyes et al., 1999). Janney and colleagues emphasized that resistance should be viewed as a part of the change process, rather than as an indication that it will be impossible to accomplish desired changes.

School staff also worked to develop a shared vision among those who would eventually be responsible for implementing inclusion. The school reform literature emphasizes the importance of a clearly articulated vision (e.g., Fullan, 2007) and those working toward inclusive reform acknowledged the importance of a shared vision in moving forward (e.g., Fox & Ysseldyke, 1997; Lieber et al., 2000; Mayrowetz & Weinstein, 1999; Purcell et al., 2007; Sindelar et al., 2006). Mayrowetz and Weinstein described the formulation of a vision across three schools in a district. They discussed how principals, special and general educators, aides, and parents helped sell the vision of inclusion and the positive results that came out of a year-long planning and "vision-izing" process (p. 432). Similarly, Purcell also emphasized the importance of a shared vision and how the transformation of the concept "occurs over time among those who design, deliver, or use inclusive education, so that it includes the views of all participants" (2007, p. 91).

In a study of six elementary schools identified as having effectively incorporated inclusive practices, Guzman (1997) reported that principals across schools worked with staff to agree col-laboratively on the building philosophy (interpreted as similar to a vision) for inclusion in their schools. The statement was eventually incorporated into a written document emphasizing "a belief in the right of all students to learn, a belief that inclusive classrooms are beneficial for all students, and a commitment to ensuring optimal academic success for all students" (p. 446). In some schools the vision statement was included in the school mission statement, in others it was a separate document.

In contrast to descriptions of how school leaders assisted with planning for reform, Fox and Ysseldyke (1997) described a lack of leadership, which impeded the planning process. They reported that district administrators attempted to sell the inclusion project to the principal and special educators at a middle school, hoping these principals and teachers would then sell the ideas to the general educators. Although the principal provided verbal support, he did not actively support change. Moreover, the special education teachers did not fully commit to the initiative preventing its spread to general education teachers. Fox and Ysseldyke concluded that inadequate staff preparation, lack of resources, and a "top-down" approach led to a failure to secure buy-in for and ownership of inclusion.

In another example of a failed effort, Mamlin (1999) discussed in detail what occurred during initial summer meetings between key stakeholders (i.e., SEAs, IHE, district) and staff from three schools as they developed a restructuring plan for special education. Key school leaders were then encouraged to work with staff to develop the program at the school. However, the plan to involve stakeholders at the school was subverted by one principal, who announced her own plan for inclusion, controlled the "program," and left school staff out of the decision-making process.

Summary. An individual or core group, including state, district and school administrators, teachers and parents, took responsibility for initiating inclusive reform. District leaders typically initiated change, often in partnership with others, such as SEAs and IHEs. Initially, leadership efforts involved communicating a clear message that inclusive education was important, working toward buy-in for inclusion, and providing resources for development. In a number of studies, district and/or school teams were formed to plan and lead the effort. They discussed a rationale for inclusion, considered an inclusive mission or vision, and participated in initial professional development. McLeskey and Waldron (2006) indicated the importance of a carefully constructed team to manage group processes, including "well respected teachers and administrators who are representative of the many perspectives that exist within the school" (p. 273). Scholars also emphasized the importance of listening to concerns and respecting differences as inclusive change is initiated (e.g., Janney et al., 1995; Thousand & Villa, 1995).

Phase 2: The Implementation of Inclusion

The implementation of inclusion differed across schools, which is to be expected given the diverse definitions of inclusive education, the varied contexts of schools, and the different levels of support that were provided for these efforts. Usually, inclusive efforts were focused on including students with disabilities, while a few focused on broader student populations needing assistance (e.g., English for Speakers of Other Languages, Chapter 1, gifted) (Causton-Theoharis et al., 2011; Fisher et al., 2000; Hoppey & McLeskey, in press; Kilgore et al., 2001). The task forces, teams, or informal groups established as part of the initiation of change sometimes continued to guide inclusive change during implementation. School teams also met on a regular basis to continue learning about inclusion and to plan, share ideas, solve problems, share progress, and encourage others (e.g., Burstein et al., 2004; Causton-Theoharis et al., 2011; Mayrowetz & Weinstein, 1999; Ryndak et al., 2007). Mayrowetz and Weinstein showed how there was considerable overlap among leadership tasks among varied school personnel, including teachers, parents and aides. These overlapping functions helped with institutionalizing inclusive reform as discussed in a later section of this chapter.

In contrast to studies that focused on reform specifically for inclusive education, Peters (2002) discussed how inclusive practices grew out of larger school reform efforts, which is consistent with her view of inclusion as a philosophy rather than as an "add-on" reform (p. 289). As Peters explained, school-wide reform in an elementary and middle school allowed for a culture of teacher inquiry, collaboration and leadership. Teachers' collaborative work led to new teaching practices, including "curriculum integration, instructional support and innovation, and systematic assessment strategies for overall school improvement" (p. 295). She went on to state that students with disabilities benefitted from these broader school reform efforts since teachers worked to meet the needs of all students, including those with challenging academic and behavioral issues.

Principal and Teacher Leadership

Although others outside the school (e.g., district leaders), IHEs and parents assisted with the implementation of reform, principals and teachers were responsible for much of the work. The principal was often visible and prominent as they (a) set a positive tone for inclusion (Hoppey & McLeskey, in press; Janney et al., 1995, Mayrowetz & Weinstein, 1999); (b) shared the school vision with varied constituents (Burstein et al., 2004; Guzman, 1997; Mayrowetz & Weinstein); (c) scheduled and attended professional development activities (Burstein et al., 2004; Mayrowetz & Weinstein, 1999; Ryndak et al., 2007); (d) supported staff (Burstein et al., 2004; Guzman, 1997; Hoppey & McLeskey, in press; Idol, 1996; Mayrowetz & Weinstein, 1999; Hoppey & McLeskey, in press); and (e) communicated regularly with parents (Mayrowetz & Weinstein, 1999). Some principals participated in IEP meetings, indicating they wanted to be informed about students and model what they viewed as important (Guzman, 1997). Leaders also provided recognition and encouragement to teachers (Hoppey & McLeskey, in press; Janney et al., 1995; Mayrowetz & Weinstein, 1999) and helped them acquire needed resources (Burstein et al., 2004).

Although principals were key leaders, teachers also took on major roles in inclusive change. In one study of a middle school over a four-year period, teachers served as key players, working closely with administrators to develop the inclusion program. These teachers had responsibility for designing the program, monitoring its operation, and identifying problems (Kilgore et al., 2001; Sindelar et al., 2006). Fox and Ysseldyke (1997) discussed how special education teachers were given the major responsibility for leading implementation of inclusion at the school they studied. In another study, a teacher indicated that the principal gave them the "opportunity to design it and do it any way we wanted to" (Lieber et al., 2000, p. 89). Similarly, teachers "created their service-delivery model and expressed significant ownership of it" (Fisher et al., 2000, p. 225). Teachers appreciated the opportunity to build their own model of inclusion (Kilgore et al., 2001) and the professional autonomy and the freedom to do what was needed (Janney et al., 1995). Hoppey and McLeskey (in press) described how the principal sought to create opportunities for teachers to lead and embed their leadership in collective efforts to address the needs of all students in the school. They also described the nature of the principal's interactions in an established inclusive school, describing how the principal cared for and personally invested in teachers by displaying respect and trust, listening to their concerns and ideas, and treating them fairly.

School Leadership Activities.

The core activities in implementing inclusive education at the school level involved the development of: (a) structures, policies, and resources for inclusion; (b) on-going professional development; (c) teacher collaboration and co-teaching; (d) inclusive classroom environments; and (e) monitoring processes and outcomes. Each of these is described with examples of both formal and informal leaders taking responsibility for each of these key areas.

Structures, policies, and resources. Researchers referred to a number of changes that were necessary to implement inclusion, such as physical and organizational structures, teacher roles, policies for discipline and grading, as well as providing necessary resources. As students were moved from separate facilities to schools, an initial activity was making sure schools were physically accessible (Janney et al., 1995). In some schools special education classes were eliminated (Burstein et al., 2004), requiring new class placements and scheduling. Principals and parents worked together so students with disabilities were placed in classrooms with friends or specific teachers (Fisher et al., 2000; Mayrowetz & Weinstein, 1999).

In some settings, the roles of special educators were retitled, signaling a different relationship between specialists and general educators. For example in one school, all special educators were assigned to grade level teams and were referred to by their grade level rather than their role as special educators (Mayrowetz & Weinstein, 1999). In another school, principals in noncategorical programs began to refer to teachers as resource teachers rather than special educators or Title 1 teachers (Fisher et al., 2000). Similarly, Kilgore et al. (2001) explained that each school team had a co-teacher who was expected to help all students who needed assistance whether or not they were classified with a disability.

Inclusive change also brought about the establishment or modification of policies and procedures. Guzman (1997) discussed the establishment of discipline policies for all students and referenced procedures for accommodating the specific discipline needs of students with disabilities, including procedures for due process. In addition, administrative approval was also needed for grading modifications, allowing teachers to use narratives or other modifications (Mayrowetz & Weinstein, 1999). Lieber et al. (2000) described the development of communication procedures using a notebook for each child so that itinerant teachers, classroom teachers, parents, and related services personnel who were not always on site could document and share important information.

Administrators worked to support inclusive education through providing resources and time. Funds were needed for additional school staff (e.g., to hire substitutes or pay stipends so teachers could attend professional development sessions) as well as to purchase special teaching resources and equipment (Janney et al., 1995; Mayrowetz & Weinstein, 1999; Ryndak et al., 2007). The importance of and need for paraprofessionals was emphasized in several studies (e.g., Fisher et al., 2000; Idol, 1996; Mayrowetz & Weinstein; Peters, 2002). Principals also helped to arrange time for team meetings and discussions about inclusion (Burstein et al., 2004; Mayrowetz & Weinstein).

On-going professional development. Although professional development was often provided during the initiation phase, additional opportunities to continue learning were needed and appreciated by teachers as inclusion was implemented. Fisher et al. (2000) reported that 43% of teachers involved in inclusive change discussed the importance of professional development in biweekly after-school programs and district workshops held throughout the year and during summer months. Janney et al. (1995) reported that over two thirds of teachers interviewed mentioned the value of principals' bringing in new and relevant information through workshops, consultants, visits to other schools and discussions with educators and parents who had experience with inclusion. In one inclusive elementary school, Hoppey and McLeskey (in press) described a principal's commitment to "embedding professional development in the daily work of his teachers" (p. 9) to enhance both their learning and the development of community norms. The principal also supported teachers' growth through their participation in Project INCLUDE, a professional development effort with the goal of addressing the needs of all students in the school, including those with disabilities.

In general, the content of PD efforts was usually not described in detail. However, a range of topics related to inclusive education and teaching students with disabilities were addressed and were similar to those described earlier in the initial stage of reform. Informal learning also occurred through teacher interactions (Causton-Theoharis et al., 2011; Peters, 2002), and special education teachers assumed leadership for helping other teachers with curriculum and instructional needs. Janney and colleagues (1995) indicated special educators provided general educators with information about students with disabilities, their skills, needs, and goals. Rice (2006) discussed how a special educator answered general education teachers' questions, created packets for subject areas with modifications, answered questions about curriculum, and worked with small groups of teachers as needed. In a study of inclusive preschool programs (Purcell et al., 2007), teachers participated in a cooperative that spanned five separate programs that allowed them to work together and problem-solve.

However, not all schools received adequate PD (Fox & Ysseldyke, 1997; Mayrowetz & Weinstein, 1999). Teachers in a new charter school indicated they needed additional PD to implement inclusion in areas such as co-teaching, classroom management and addressing students' social skills (Downing et al., 2004) and others voiced the need for more professional development and desired visits to established inclusive settings (Idol, 1996). As a middle school teacher explained, "There were a couple of videos and that's it. There was no preparation. [The kids] were just there one day in your class" (Mayrowetz & Weinstein, 1999, p. 442). Teachers also indicated that without continued staff development it would be difficult to continue and expand inclusion (Burstein et al., 2004).

Teacher collaboration and co-teaching. Collaboration was viewed as essential to successful inclusion and leaders worked in varied ways to foster collaboration (Burstein et al., 2004), team-teaching (Salisbury & McGregor, 2002), and co-teaching (Causton-Theoharis et al., 2011; Hoppey & McLeskey, in press; Sindelar et al. 2006). Collaboration was described in varied arrangements. In one school, special and general educators developed collaborative teams, shared students and began grouping by need rather than label. In another setting, a special day class was combined with a second grade class. The teachers removed a wall between the classrooms and developed a schedule that included both co-taught whole-class and small-group instruction (Burstein et al., 2004). The roles of co-teachers included developing accommodations and modifications, working with students individually and in small groups, reteaching material, adapting assessments and grading papers (Burstein et al., 2004; Fisher et al., 2000; Sindelar et al., 2006). Idol (1996) describes the importance of the support that teachers received from cooperative teaching, teacher assistance teams, consulting teachers, and departmental level teams. Others describe the benefits of monthly collaboration among pre-school teachers at different locations as they worked together to "collaborate, mentor, and observe each other in practice" (Purcell et al., 2007, p. 92). Teachers also had positive views of their collaborative skills and that of others and valued these interactions (Idol, 1996).

The importance of setting aside time for collaboration (Burstein et al., 2004; Causton-Theoharis et al., 2011) and collaborative work in classrooms (Peters, 2002) was emphasized as schools moved toward greater inclusion. They discussed strategies that were used to create time for teachers to meet and plan together, including regularly scheduled meetings and the hiring of substitutes to cover classes. Burstein et al. also emphasized that the roles of special education teachers in inclusive settings expanded as they began to attend to the "needs of the entire school population" (p. 109).

Teaching and learning in inclusive schools. At the heart of inclusion are the opportunities that students with disabilities have to participate in school and classroom life and achieve valued educational goals. However, in most inclusive reports less attention was given to describing students' instructional programs in these reformed schools. Teachers had primary responsibility for planning and implementing decisions related to curriculum, instruction, and assessment (e.g., Fisher et al., 2000; Fox & Ysseldyke, 1997; Kilgore et al., 2001), which is not surprising, given that administrative involvement in instruction is "among the least frequent activities performed by administrators of any kind at any level" (Elmore, 2004, p. 48).

Many of the descriptions of students' instructional programs in the inclusive setting were general in nature. For example, Sindelar and colleagues (2006) emphasized that teachers used "high quality group instructional practices, which they supplemented with small group" instruction (p. 322). Individualization was also mentioned as well as the need to adapt curriculum (Downing et al., 2004; Sindelar et al., 2006). Sindelar also described more specific strategies used within these settings such as thematic units, varied instructional arrangements, the use of cooperative learning and peer tutoring, as well as the use of mnemonic strategies and split-page note taking. Others gave examples of assigning fewer spelling words, providing instruction in a life skills curriculum and preparing students for transition from school to work (e.g., Downing et al., 2004; Mayrowetz & Weinstein, 1999).

Changes to the instructional program were sometimes superficial and not consistent with inclusion. In a failed attempt at inclusion, Fox and Ysseldyke (1997) described how students with disabilities were sometimes taught outside general education classrooms and attended separate music and art classes to provide special educators with preparation time. When students were in the inclusive classes, they were usually involved with a special education staff member, and observations suggested that general educators made only minor changes in teaching strategies to include students.

Some researchers focused on the importance of helping students with disabilities become part of their school and classroom communities. Janney et al. (1995) discussed that teachers made sure students were in the class picture, in daily roll call, and they displayed students' work. In one school, teachers worked to create a peer-helper program to help with students with severe and multiple disabilities to become part of the school community (Peters, 2002). Fox and Ysseldyke (1997) reported that inclusion did not have positive effects on peer acceptance in the middle school they studied and emphasized the importance of promoting the social acceptance of students with disabilities by incorporating cooperative activities such as peer tutoring and cooperative learning.

Monitoring processes and outcomes. Monitoring is a key leadership function in reform efforts (Mayrowetz & Weinstein, 1999) and may include: (a) learning from the process of change as it develops over time and the effects of reform on staff and students (e.g., through meetings and use of formative student data); and (b) monitoring the outcomes of inclusive reform (e.g., changes in service-delivery, satisfaction with changes, and student achievement and attainment of other goals).

Monitoring the process of reform was not discussed in some reports, but was described in detail in others. Fox and Ysseldyke (1997) described the lack of scheduled meetings to discuss inclusion, which meant that those involved had few opportunities to share what was learned or to monitor student progress. In contrast, Ryndak et al. (2007) discussed multiple methods for monitoring how inclusion was proceeding across the district, including the use of needs assessments across schools to identify issues related to inclusive education and the use of program quality indicators with principals to evaluate inclusive practices at their schools. Mayrowetz and Weinstein (1999) provided a detailed description of how elementary schools monitored progress with regular meetings to discuss school progress, periodic monitoring of student growth, and meetings with parents to discuss student progress. Mayrowetz and Weinstein pointed out that the monitoring process allowed school staff to address and handle problems. In another study, the principal monitored by listening and asking questions such as "So, how's the coteaching going?" (Hoppey & McLeskey, in press, p. 6) and worked with staff to address specific challenges. Guzman (1997) described how five of the six principals in her study scheduled and facilitated an annual retreat with teachers to "evaluate and restructure the special education support model to bring it closer in line with the classroom needs inherent in an inclusive model" (p. 447).

A key outcome of most of the inclusive reform efforts was that students with disabilities were educated in increasingly more inclusive settings, although the extent of participation in general school and settings varied significantly across studies (e.g., Burstein et al., 2004; Causton-Theoharis et al., 2011; Mayrowetz & Weinstein, 1999; Ryndak et al., 2007). Although less of a focus in the literature, some researchers addressed progress monitoring and achievement. In considering student progress over time, one principal collaborated with staff in the use of locally developed measures to inform instructional decisions, leading to more "evidence-based instructional approaches" (Hoppey & McLeskey, p. 7, in press). Some monitored student performance on achievement or mandated tests. For example, Fisher et al. (2000) indicated that student progress was monitored using standardized achievement scores and attendance rates. They did not draw causal connections between the inclusive program and outcomes; rather they indicated, "inclusive education clearly did not negatively affect academic performance, attendance, or parent satisfaction" (p. 218). Ryndak et al. (2007) monitored student performance on mandated tests finding that student outcomes were "maintained or improved" (p. 236). Idol (1996) reported that in three of four elementary settings there was an improvement of overall test scores in the schools which suggested that including students with disabilities did not have a negative effect on overall student performance. Similarly, Causton-Theoharis et al. (2011) reported that "relative stability of achievement … kept the school safe from accountability sanctions" (p. 199).

Several researchers described participant satisfaction with the change toward inclusive change, describing benefits for students and school staff. Researchers described benefits for students with disabilities based on the perspectives of varied groups (e.g., administrators, educators, parents and students). Benefits included feelings of belonging (e.g., Causton-Theoharis et al., 2011) greater academic challenge, great involvement among students with and without disabilities, better role models, less stigma, and improved behavior, social skills, and self-esteem (Burstein et al 2004; Downing et al., 2004; Kilgore et al., 2001). Additional benefits for students without disabilities included students including acceptance of diversity and learning to appreciate differences, pride in helping others, and the development of compassion for others (Burstein et al., 2004; Downing et al.).

When Kilgore et al. (2001) interviewed students, they found that many preferred to be in general education classes, found these settings to be more challenging and interesting, and liked being in contact with non-disabled classmates which made it easier to make friends. The general student population also benefitted from the teaching strategies and extra assistance that were part of inclusive practice (e.g., Burstein et al., 2004; Fisher et al., 2000).

School staff also appeared to benefit from greater inclusion. Some of the benefits were described in general terms, such as the development of an inclusive culture (Fisher et al., 2000; Peters, 2002), teacher learning (Kilgore et al., 2001; Peters, 2002), increased teacher interaction and support (Causton-Theoharis et al., 2011; Peters, 2002) and the development of supportive and caring schools for students and school staff (Burstein et al., 2004; Hoppey & McLeskey, in press). Special educators also became more integrated into the school, developed a better understanding of the general education curriculum, and were renewed by the change in responsibilities (e.g., Burstein et al., 2004; Causton-Theoharis et al., 2011; Peters, 2002).

Other researchers identified concerns or barriers as they studied inclusive change. Causton-Theoharis et al. (2011) identified barriers in moving toward whole-school reform, including the lack of time for teachers and as well as other professionals to collaborate. For example, of paraprofessionals surveyed, 70% indicated they did not have time to receive training or collaborate with their assigned teachers. Increasing caseloads also led to a "thin level of service" (Burstein et al., 2004, p. 111) and special educators struggled to provide appropriate supports. Teachers indicated some students were not ready for inclusion and indicated they missed the sheltered environment of a resource room (Kilgore, et al., 2001). Teachers also questioned the concentration of students with disabilities in a few classes, suggesting that this practice constituted a type of tracking and "was a mistake" (Burstein et al., p. 112). Yet, heterogeneous grouping was more difficult to implement since students were spread across a greater number of classrooms. Another concern was the demands on general educators, especially when they had high caseloads (Burstein et al., 2004) or struggled to manage students who exhibited challenging behaviors (Downing et al., 2004). Causton-Theoharis et al. (2011) also discussed that the negative attitudes of a small minority of staff members influenced school climate and the progress of reform as well as the lack of a shared philosophy on what inclusion means.

Summary. Leadership for inclusive education was shared among a range of formal and informal leaders, although principals and teachers appeared to have primary responsibility. Many of the principals actively supported inclusive reform through providing resources and professional development, supporting collaboration, and encouraging staff. Teachers also provided leadership, as they were primarily responsible for creating instructional programs to meet the needs of individual students. Although we know teachers led changes in instructional programs, these descriptions were general in nature and only a few researchers provided systematic evidence of monitoring student progress. In terms of overall change, some evidence suggests that change became embedded in the school (e.g., Fisher et al., 2000; Mayrowetz & Weinstein, 1999). In others, it was superficial (Fox & Ysseldyke, 1997). Salisbury and McGregor (2002) discussed the concepts of incremental vs. deeper levels of change. The latter require influencing others' "core beliefs and operating principles of schools and hence, deeper levels of change" (p. 268).

Phase 3: The Institutionalization of Reform

Researchers interested in school reform have focused not only on factors that influenced the initiation and implementation of change, but also the extent to which it became institutionalized or embedded in the school and continued over time (Fullan, 2007; Mayrowetz & Weinstein, 1999). Fullan reported that a majority of school reforms do not continue, even those that were well implemented. He identifies specific factors that led to the discontinuation of reform such as insufficient leadership at the district and school levels, insufficient funding and staff support, personnel changes, and lack of opportunities for professional development. Only several studies considered the program continuation beyond the third year of implementation (Mayrowetz & Weinstein, 1999; Purcell et al., 2007; Ryndak et al., 2007; Sindelar et al., 2006).

The distribution of key leadership functions across a range of individuals was a key factor in the institutionalization of reform in two of three schools studied by Mayrowetz and Weinstein (1999). As the researchers pointed out, there were 48 opportunities to provide leadership (6 leadership functions × 8 roles). To clarify, there were six functions outlined earlier (i.e., providing and selling a vision, providing encouragement and recognition, obtaining resources, adapting standard operating procedures, monitoring the improvement effort, and handling disturbances) and eight different leadership roles that could potentially perform each function (e.g., principals, paraprofessionals), equaling 48 possibilities. Across primary and intermediate schools, leaders "performed 38 and 39 functions, respectively, out of a possible 48, whereas those in the middle school executed 27" (p. 443). Mayrowetz and Weinstein concluded that inclusion was institutionalized at the primary school stating that six years after initial training "all teachers now volunteered to be part of the program and that the inclusion team did not meet regularly because it rarely had problems to address" (p. 442). Similar results were found at the intermediate school where inclusion still had strong momentum, despite four teachers who had "persistent misgivings" (p. 442). However, Mayrowetz and Weinstein acknowledged less institutionalization at the middle school and identified possible contributors: fewer individuals performing leadership functions, less involvement from the principal, a less child centered approach and a shorter duration of implementation.

In another study, Ryndak et al. (2007) identified seven variables they considered essential to affect systemic and sustainable changes over time. They reported systemic change in the district over a seven-year period, even in the midst of high stakes assessments and personnel changes. The authors attributed continuation to key variables including: (a) a common vision of desired outcomes and what these outcomes looked like in schools; (b) a shared understanding of the change process; (c) responsibility for the change effort owned by school and district personnel; (d) concurrent and varied efforts at multiple levels; (e) involvement from all types of constituents (e.g., parents, instructional, related services, administrative personnel, and support staff); (f) involvement from all constituents within each type (e.g., related services providers at the school levels and their supervisors at the district level); and (g) involvement of Critical Friends for feedback and strategic planning.

In a study of continuation in five inclusive preschool programs, Purcell et al. (2007) reported that a range of variables supported continuation, although these varied across sites. For example, shared vision, collaborative relationships and formal and informal interagency agreements supported continuation (e.g., school district, Head start, educational cooperatives). In contrast, federal policy changes and ever-changing regulations were challenges to continuation as districts had to constantly alter funding agreements to ensure compliance.

In a study describing the demise of a model middle school inclusion program, Sindelar and colleagues (2006) reported that three primary factors contributed to the loss of the program including: shifting state and district priorities, shifting leadership priorities, and teacher turnover. Reduced support for the program also contributed, but was viewed as a by-product of the three primary factors. After the loss of two principals who provided leadership for the program, a third emphasized recent state and district accountability initiatives and focused school efforts on improving student performance on mandated assessments. Teachers felt pressure as "they were being held to high accountability standards" (Sindelar et al., p. 329) and, as a result, the focus was on low-performing students, not necessarily students with disabilities. This resulted in less support for the program, a reduced number of co-teachers (even while enrollment grew), and less teaming and communication among teachers. High levels of teacher turnover and the loss of key teacher leaders also diluted the initiative. Purcell et al. (2007) also reported that high staff-teacher turnover and less prepared staff challenged continuation and required "starting over" (p. 93) many times. High attrition is a powerful factor known to interfere with the continuation of reform. Unfortunately, most programs do not plan for the orientation and PD needed to support members who arrive after a program begins (Fullan, 2007).

In summary, only several of the studies addressed the institutionalization of reform. However, the research by Mayrowetz and Weinstein (1999) and Ryndak et al., (2007) are important examples of the deliberate work that took place across IHEs, school and districts leaders to maintain the program over time. The factors that these researchers identified as important to continuing change over time are also many of the very factors that are identified as important to initial change and implementation (e.g., vision, support, involvement of key individuals). Therefore, what is done early in the process (i.e., careful and thoughtful initiation, implementation and monitoring) should influence not only the extent to which change is implemented, but also the extent to which it continues over time. Another factor in the Mayrowetz and Weinstein and Ryndak et al. studies is strong support from district and IHE leaders.

Discussion and Implications

In this chapter, published research on inclusive reform in the United States was reviewed to learn about leaders' efforts as they moved from less to more inclusive change and the extent to which these changes were sustained. In addition, studies of leaders in existing inclusive schools were included to provide information about leadership behaviors and contexts that facilitated or interfered with the implementation of inclusion. Studies of inclusive change provide a better understanding of the inner workings of districts and schools as they go about change and provide examples of different types of efforts (e.g., inclusive specific and whole school reform) as well as sustained and less successful efforts.

Across the majority of studies, the initiation of inclusion usually came from outside the school, emphasizing the importance of state and district leadership in developing incentives and supports for inclusive reform. However, it is important not to make too much of this finding given the limited number of studies and the greater likelihood that reform efforts that are funded and supported by IHE faculty will be published. Yet, it is clear that SEAs (and districts) have a role in promoting inclusive schools through approving policy, encouraging inclusive options, building coalitions with key stakeholders, and monitoring progress toward inclusion (Hamre-Nietupski, Nietupski, & Maurer, 1990).

It is not surprising that principals were not usually initiators of reform. Principals have demanding jobs and many do not have experience with inclusion or the preparation to lead inclusive schools (see earlier discussion). However, principals exercised leadership in inclusive reform efforts, usually in response to external expectations. In schools that moved toward greater inclusion, principals supported inclusion in varied ways such as participating in professional development, voicing support for inclusive change, and supporting teachers' efforts (e.g., Burstein et al., 2004; Hoppey & McLeskey, in press; Janney et al., 1995; Mayrowetz & Weinstein, 1999). In schools where inclusive education languished, principal involvement was minimal as they were perhaps not convinced of the value of reform or were focused on other priorities (e.g., Fox & Ysseldyke, 1997; Mamlin, 1999; Mayrowetz & Weinstein, 1999; Sindelar et al., 2006).

A few researchers described broad-based reform efforts, as leaders from multiple settings (e.g., state, district, schools, IHEs) collaborated in the development of some inclusive schools (e.g., Burstein et al., 2004; Causton-Theoharis et al., 2011; Mayrowetz & Weinstein, 1999; Ryndak et al., 2007). Participants collaborated across the boundaries of varied institutions, developed an inclusive vision, structured programs, and worked to address the needs of specific students. As leaders initiated inclusive change, they helped others understand a rationale for change, primarily emphasizing why students with disabilities should receive their education in inclusive environments. Fullan, Cuttress, and Kilcher (2005) referred to the why of change as important for engaging educators in a moral purpose i.e., the need to increase opportunities for those "for whom the school system has been less effective" (p. 54). However, Fullan and colleagues emphasize that commitment to change is not necessarily available at the beginning of the process; rather ownership is "created through a quality change process" (p. 55).

In schools where inclusive practices were developed and sustained over time, an infrastructure of active leadership, supportive policies, adequate resources and on-going professional development helped to move schools toward their inclusive vision (e.g., Burstein et al., 2004; Fisher et al., 2000; Mayrowetz & Weinstein, 1999; Ryndak et al., 2007). In schools where inclusive education took root, advocacy for students with disabilities was shared with many in the school taking initiative in assuring that the needs of these students were met (Mayrowetz & Weinstein). As inclusive practices became embedded, a reculturing, or a transformation of the culture occurred, "changing the way we do things" (Burstein et al., p. 113, citing Fullan, 2001). As Fullan and colleagues (2005) emphasized, "policies take off in learning cultures, but they go nowhere in cultures of isolation" (p. 56). In contrast, when inclusive change was limited to a few in the school or when key leaders left, inclusive efforts languished (e.g., Fox & Ysseldyke, 1997; Mamlin, 1999; Mayrowetz & Weinstein, 1999; Sindelar et al., 2006).

Overall, change processes were emphasized more in the research than actual classroom practices and student outcomes. Researchers documented that students were moved from more to less restrictive settings, yet descriptions about what was provided for students with disabilities in general education classrooms were usually general. Moreover, relatively few studies provided data on student progress or achievement. In addition, while teachers worked out the details of inclusive programs in their schools, there was little description about the nature of the instructional decisions made or what inclusive education looked like in classroom settings. More in-depth investigations are needed of both general and special educators' leadership in inclusive reform—how they viewed their roles, how they made instructional decisions, and how they monitored student learning.

Today, inclusion takes place within the context of standards-based reform, which some view as one of the most challenging requirements in the history of education (O'Donnell & White, 2005). Although little is known about the impact of standards-based reform on inclusion, inclusive education was sustained in one district as standards-based reform was implemented (Ryndak et al., 2007). However, defining success as performance on academic tests was one factor in the demise of an established inclusive middle school program (Sindelar et al., 2006).

Inclusive initiatives must place priority on assuring that students with disabilities receive high quality instruction in general education environments. Although a growing number of students with disabilities are receiving their education in inclusive classrooms, student outcomes are variable because of the "unevenness in the quality of instruction that is provided in these settings" (McLeskey & Waldron, 2011, p. 40). Leaders need to monitor the effects of inclusive education on both the academic progress and the overall well-being of students. As Waldron, McLeskey, and Redd (in press) stated, student data systems helpful to monitoring student progress are needed to assure that the data is relevant to the "content taught, meaningful to teachers, and useful to plan instruction" (p. 17). For students who have IEPs with behavioral, social, vocational, or personal goals, additional measures are needed to assure that instruction meets students' comprehensive needs.

The future of leadership for inclusive reform is likely to be refocused on a broader student population. In a number of studies over the last decade, inclusive change included other student populations, not just those with disabilities (e.g., Causton-Theoharis, 2011; Fisher et al., 2000; Hoppey & McLeskey, in press; Kilgore et al., 2001; Peters, 2002). This is not surprising given that today's leaders must attend to the growing heterogeneity of the student population, including the needs of students who differ in their ability, language, culture, and socioeconomic backgrounds (Salisbury, 2006).

McLeskey and Waldron (2006) proposed Comprehensive School Reform (CSR) as a framework for extending school reform to address the needs of all students. They cited Desimone's (2004) definition of CSR that "focuses on improvement of entire schools rather than on particular populations of students within schools; and it is not limited to particular subjects, programs, or instructional methods" (p. 433). McLeskey and Waldron outline six steps of CSR: (1) broad based support, including central administrators, principals, and teachers; (2) empowering schools to manage change; (3) efforts focused on all students, not just students with disabilities; (4) tailoring change to the needs of students and the specific expertise at the school; (5) incorporating effective practices; and (6) reform designed to make "differences ordinary for students throughout the school" (p. 272).

Comprehensive school reform is consistent with the current interest in professional learning communities, in which teachers have a collective commitment and take responsibility for the implementation of high standards for all students (DuFour, DuFour, & Eaker, 2008; Peters, 2002). Yet, the effects of CSR and PLCs on the education of students with disabilities are not known. If CSR is implemented concurrently with standards-based reform, will the needs of students with disabilities be addressed in a manner that allows these students to meet both the standards designed for all students as well as their individual needs? To what extent are educators prepared to do this work? To what extent will teachers with specific expertise be available and will they have the conditions to assure that the needs of each student are met? In addition, how will special educators participate with others in these communities?

Leaders face a daunting challenge as they continue to move toward inclusive schools in an era of accountability and there is not a precise blueprint that applies across contexts (Fox & Ysseldyke, 1997; Waldron et al., in press). Those interested in inclusive education will benefit from reading key inclusive reform studies in their entirety (e.g., Mayrowetz & Weinstein, 1999; Ryndak et al., 2007; Sindelar et al., 2006). In addition, the specific descriptions of leadership for inclusive schools provides interesting contrasts, including system-wide (e.g., Ryndak et al., 2007) versus school efforts (e.g., Hoppey & McLeskey, in press), whole-school reform (e.g., Causton-Theoharis, 2011; Peters, 2002) vs. reform for students with disabilities (e.g., Mayrowetz

& Weinstein, 1999), more successful (Mayrowetz & Weinstein, 1999; Ryndak et al., 2007) vs. failed (Fox & Ysseldyke, 1997; Mamlin, 1999) or less successful efforts (Rice, 2006).

Leaders also need to develop "understanding and insight about the process of change and the key drivers that make for successful change in practice" (Fullan, 2005, p. 54). As Fullan and colleagues stated, "the presence of change knowledge does not guarantee success, but its absence ensures failure." The following recommendations are based on the inclusive change literature as well as the need to address student outcomes:

1. Incorporate change knowledge in inclusive reform efforts, attending to each phase of the change process;
2. Recognize the collective and specific contributions that policy-makers and leaders in and out of the school can make in the development of inclusive schools and consider partnerships with external groups such as IHEs and other critical friends;
3. Work with stakeholders to understand why inclusion is important and develop not only a shared vision for inclusion, but a specific understanding of what it looks like in practice;
4. Facilitate the development of a culture in which advocacy for students with disabilities (and other student groups) is shared across the school;
5. Provide extended professional development over time for administrators, teachers and others to address not only initial understanding, but to address problems of implementation;
6. Create supportive work contexts that allow for collaborative decision-making and provide necessary supports and resources throughout the phases of change (e.g., personnel, time for teacher collaboration);
7. Encourage questions, expect resistance, listen to concerns and give participants opportunities to own their effort;
8. Emphasize quality instruction as the foundation of inclusive efforts and seek to assure that students' comprehensive needs are met;
9. Monitor the process of moving toward inclusion and assess student outcomes;
10. Build in plans to sustain change as personnel changes occur, providing professional development and support to new hires.

Acknowledgments

I extend my appreciation to my colleagues James McLeskey, Anna-Maria Fall, and Brad Bizzell for their thoughtful comments and suggestions on an earlier version of this manuscript.

References

Ainscow, M. (2005). Understanding the development of inclusive education system. *Electronic Journal of Research in Educational Psychology, 3*(7), 5–20.

Barnett, C., & Monda-Amaya, L. (1998). Principals' knowledge of and attitudes toward inclusion. *Remedial and Special Education, 19,* 181–192.

Billingsley, B. (2007). Recognizing and supporting the critical roles of teachers in special education leadership. *Exceptionality, 15*(3), 163–176.

Boscardin, M. L., & Jacobson, S. (1997). The inclusive school: Integrating diversity and solidarity through community-based management. *Journal of Educational Administration, 35*(3), 466–476.

Brotherson, M. J., Sheriff, G., Milburn, P., & Schetz, M. (2001). Elementary school principals and their needs and issues for inclusive early childhood programs. *Topics in Early Childhood Special Education, 21*(1), 31–45.

Burrello, L. C., Lashley, C., & Beatty, E. E. (2001). *Educating all students together: How school leaders create unified systems.* Thousand Oaks, CA: Corwin Press.

Burstein, N., Sears, S., Wilcoxen, A., Cabello, B., & Spagna, M. (2004). Moving toward inclusive practices. *Remedial & Special Education, 25*(2), 104–116.

Causton-Theoharis, J., Theoharis, G., Bull, T., Cosier, M., & Dempf-Aldrich, K. (2011). Schools of promise: A School district-university partnership centered on inclusive school reform. *Remedial and Special Education, 32*(3), 190–205.

Crockett, J. B., & Kauffman, J. M. (1999). *The least restrictive environment: Its origins and interpretations in special education.* Mahwah, NJ: Erlbaum.

Crockett, J. B., Myers, S. T., Griffin, A., & Hollandsworth, B. (2007). The unintended side effects of inclusion for students with learning disabilities: The perspectives of school administrators. *Learning Disabilities: A Multidisciplinary Journal, 14,* 155–166.

Davis, W. F. (1989). The regular education initiative debate: Its promises and problems. *Exceptional Children, 55*(5), 440–446.

Devecchi, C., & Nevin, A. (2010). Leadership for inclusive schools and inclusive school leadership. In A. H. Normore (Ed.), *Global perspectives on educational leadership reform: The development and preparation of leaders of learning and learners of leadership (Advances in Educational Administration, vol. 11,* pp. 211–241). Bingley, UK: Emerald Group Publishing.

DiPaola, M. F., & Walther-Thomas, C. (2003). *Principals and special education: The critical role of school leaders.* (COPSSE Document No. IB-7). Gainesville: University of Florida, Center on Personnel Studies in Special Education.

Downing, J. E., Eichinger, J., & Williams, L. J. (1997). Inclusive education for students with severe disabilities: Comparative view of principals and educators at different levels of implementation. *Remedial and Special Education, 18*(3), 133–142.

Downing, J., Spencer, S., & Cavallaro, C. (2004). The development of an inclusive charter elementary school: Lessons learned. *Research & Practice for Persons with Severe Disabilities, 29*(1), 11–24.

DuFour, R., DuFour, R., & Eaker, R. (2008). *Revising professional learning communities at work: New insights for improving schools.* Bloomington, IN: Solution Tree.

Dyson A, Howes, A., & Roberts B, (2002). A systematic review of the effectiveness of school-level actions for promoting participation by all students. In *Research evidence in education library.* London: EPPI-Centre, Social Science Research Unit, Institute of Education, University of London.

Education of All Handicapped Children Act of 1975, Public L. No. 94-142.

Elmore, R. F. (2004). *School reform from the inside out: Policy, practice, and performance.* Cambridge, MA: Harvard Education Press.

Fisher, D., Sax, C., & Grove, K. A. (2000). The resilience of changes promoting inclusiveness in an urban elementary school. *The Elementary School Journal, 100*(2), 213–227.

Fox, N., & Ysseldyke, J. (1997). Implementing inclusion at the middle school level: Lessons from a negative example. *Exceptional Children, 64*(1), 81–98.

Friend, M., & Shamberger, C. (2011). Inclusion. In T. L. Good (Ed.), *Twenty-first century education: A reference handbook* (Volume II, Part XI, pp. 124–131). Thousand Oaks, CA: Sage.

Fuchs, D., & Fuchs, L. S. (1994). Inclusive schools movement and the radicalization of special education reform. *Exceptional Children, 60*(4), 294–309.

Fullan, M. (2007). *The new meaning of education change* (3rd ed.). New York: Teachers College.

Fullan, M., Cuttress, C., & Kilcher, A. (2005). 8 forces for leaders of change. *Journal of Staff Development, 26*(4), 54–58.

Garrison-Wade, D., Sobel, D., & Fulmer, C. L. (2007). Inclusive leadership: Preparing principals for the role that awaits them. *Educational Leadership and Administration, 19,* 117–132.

Guzman, N. (1997). Leadership for successful inclusive schools. *Journal of Educational Administration, 35*(5), 439–450.

Harris, A., & Spillane, J. (2008). Distributed leadership through the looking glass, *Management in Education, 22*(1), 31–34.

Hasazi, S. B., Johnston, A. P., Liggett, A. M., & Schattman, R. A. (1994). A qualitative policy study of the least restrictive environment provision of the Individuals with Disabilities Education Act. *Exceptional Children, 60*(6), 491–508.

Hamre-Nietupski, S., Nietupski, J., & Maurer, S. (1990). A comprehensive state education agency plan to promote the integration of students with moderate/severe handicaps. *Journal of the Association for Persons with Severe Handicaps, 15*(2), 106–113.

Harris, A., & Spillane, J. (2008). Distributed leadership through the looking glass. *Management in Education, 22*(1), 31–34.

Hoppey, D., & McLeskey, J. (in press). A case study of principal leadership in an effective inclusive school. *The Journal of Special Education.*

Individuals with Disabilities Education Improvement Act, 20 U.S.C. §1401 et seq. (2004).

Idol, L. (1996). Toward inclusion of special education students in general education: A program evaluation of eight schools. Remedial and Special Education, 27(2), 77–94.

Ingram, P. D. (1997). *Leadership behaviors of principals in inclusive educational settings. Journal of Educational Administration, 35*(5), 411–427.

Janney, R., Snell, M. E., Beers, M. K., & Raynes, M. (1995). Integrating students with moderate and severe disabilities into general education classes. *Exceptional Children, 61*(5), 425–439.

Kauffman, J. M. (1989). The regular education initiative as Reagan-Bush education policy: A trickle-down theory of education of the hard-to-teach. *Journal of Special Education, 23,* 256–278.

Keyes, M., Hanley-Maxwell, C., & Capper, C. (1999). `Spirituality? It's the core of my leadership': Empowering leadership in an inclusive elementary school. *Educational Administration Quarterly, 35*(2), 203–237.

Kilgore, K., Griffin, C., Sindelar, P., & Webb, R. (2001). Restructuring for inclusion: A story of middle school renewal (Part I). *Middle School Journal, 33*(2), 44–51.

Lieber, J., Hanson, M. J., Beckman, P. J., Odom, S. L., Sandall, S. R., Schwartz, I. S., et al. (2000). Key influences on the initiation and implementation of inclusive preschool programs. *Exceptional Children, 67*(1), 83–98.

Mamlin, N. (1999). Despite best intentions: When inclusion fails. *Journal of Special Education, 33*(1), 36–49.

Mayrowetz, D., & Weinstein, C. (1999). Sources of leadership for inclusive education: Creating schools for all children. *Educational Administration Quarterly, 35*(3), 423–449.

McLeskey, J., Landers, E., Williamson, P., & Hoppey, D. (in press). Are we moving toward educating students with disabilities in less restrictive settings? *Journal of Special Education.*

McLeskey, J., & Waldron, N. L. (2006). Comprehensive school reform and inclusive schools. Comprehensive school reform and inclusive schools. *Theory into Practice, 45*(3), 269–278.

McLeskey, J., & Waldron, N. L. (2011). Educational programs for elementary students with learning disabilities. Can they be both effective and inclusive? *Learning Disabilities Practice, 26*(1), 48–57.

O'Donnell, R. J., & White, G. P. (2005). Within the accountability era: Principals' instructional leadership behaviors and student achievement. *NASSP Bulletin, 89*(645), 56–71.

Padnani, A. (2010 February 2). Principals are urged to stress special education. Staten Island Real-Time News. Retrieved from http://www.silive.com/news/index.ssf/2010/02/principals_are_urged_to_stress.html

Peters, S. (2002). Inclusive education in accelerated and professional development schools: A case-based study of two school reform efforts in the USA. *International Journal of Inclusive Education, 6*(4), 287–308.

Peters, S., Johstone, C., & Ferguson, P. (2005). A disability rights in education model for evaluating inclusive education. *International Journal of Inclusive Education, 9*(2), 139–160.

Purcell, M. L., Horn, E., & Palmer, S. (2007). A qualitative study of the initiation and continuation of preschool inclusion programs. *Exceptional Children, 74*(1), 85–99.

Praisner, C. L. (2003). Attitudes of elementary school principals toward the inclusion of students with disabilities. *Exceptional Children, 69*(2), 135–145.

Reynolds, M. C., Wang, M. C., & Walberg, H. J. (1987). The necessary restructuring of special and regular education. *Exceptional Children, 53*(5), 391–398.

Rice, N. (2006). Opportunities lost, possibilities found: Shared leadership and inclusion in an urban high school. *Journal of Disability Policy Studies, 17*(2), 88–100.

Ryndak, D. L., Jackson, L., & Billingsley, F. (2000). Defining school inclusion for students with moderate to severe disabilities: What do experts say? *Exceptionality, 8*(2), 101–116.

Ryndak, D., Reardon, R., Benner, S. R., & Ward, T. (2007). Transitioning to and sustaining district-wide inclusive services: A 7-year study of a district's ongoing journey and its accompanying complexities. *Research & Practice for Persons with Severe Disabilities, 32*(4), 228–246.

Salisbury, C. L. (2006). Principals' perspectives on inclusive elementary schools. *Research & Practice for Persons with Severe Disabilities, 31*(1), 70–82.

Salisbury, C. L., & McGregor, G. (2002). The administrative climate and context of inclusive elementary schools. *Exceptional Children, 68*(2), 259–281.

Sindelar, P., Shearer, D., Yendol-Hoppey, D., & Liebert, T. (2006). The sustainability of inclusive school reform. *Exceptional Children, 72*(3), 317–331.

Spillane, J. P. (2006). *Distributed leadership* , San Francisco: Jossey-Bass.

Stainback, S., & Stainback, W. (1984). A rationale for the merger of special and regular education. *Exceptional Children, 51*(2), 102–111.

Thousand, J. S., & Villa, A. (1995). Managing complex change toward inclusive schooling. In Thousand, J. S. & Villa, R. A. (Eds.), *Creating an inclusive school.* Alexandria, VA: Association for Supervision and Curriculum Development.

Waldron, N., McLeskey, J., & Redd, L. (in press). Setting the direction: The role of the principal in developing an effective, inclusive school. *The Journal of Special Education Leadership.*

Will, M. C. (1986). Educating children with learning problems: A shared responsibility. *Exceptional Children, 52,* 411–415.

York-Barr, J., Sommerness, J., Duke, K., & Ghere, G. (2005). Special educators in inclusive education programmes: Reframing their work as teacher leadership. *International Journal of Inclusive Education* (2), 193–215.

Zigmond, N., Jenkins, J., Fuchs, L., Deno, S., Fuchs, D., Baker, J. N., et al. (1995). Special education in restructured schools: Findings from three multi-year studies. *Phi Delta Kappan, 76,* 531–540.

Zigmond, N., Kloo, A., & Volonino, V. (2009). What, where, and how? Special education in the climate of full inclusion, *Exceptionality, 17*(4), 189–204.

11

Collaborative Decision-Making in Multicultural Contexts

John J. Hoover, Amy Eppolito, Janette K. Klingner, and Leonard Baca

UNIVERSITY OF COLORADO AT BOULDER

Research on the value and effectiveness of collaboration when making educational decisions is extensive and comprehensive (Friend & Cook, 2010; Heron & Harris 2000; McLeskey, Rosenberg & Westling, 2010; Walter-Thomas, Korinek, McLaughlin, & Williams, 2000). According to Friend and Cook, collaboration includes several characteristics that collectively facilitate meaningful decision-making. These qualities include shared contributions that are equally valued, clear purpose and mutual goal(s), team member participation and accountability, and shared expertise and resources. Effective school and team leadership is facilitated through collaboration as team members support each other and their students. Discussing collaboration, McLeskey and colleagues wrote that administrators and teachers must work cooperatively to "change their practices, the roles they play, and the very structure of their schools" (2010, p. 212). This statement is particularly appropriate in today's educational climate as more and more schools transition to response to intervention (RTI) models (Hoover, Baca, Love, & Saenz, 2008; Spectrum K12, 2010; Zierkel & Thomas, 2010), and as diversity in our classrooms continues to increase (Klingner & Edwards, 2006; Klingner, Hoover, & Baca, 2008). Both RTI and increased diversity highlight the reality that no one or two educators in a school possess sufficient expertise and the resources to adequately meet the needs of all learners. In support, Thousand, Villa and Nevin (2007) wrote that

> Collaboration has become more and more of a norm in North American schools due to a number of legal, practical, and ethical reasons all related to providing all students both access to quality instruction and equity in educational experience.
>
> *(p. 110)*

Villa and Thousand (2005) also suggested that collaboration is an essential aspect within teaching and learning. As a result, the need for collaboration to address contemporary educational challenges is highly evident as supported by recent research results.

For example, Jackson and Bruegmann (2009) evaluated over a decade of student achievement data and concluded that teacher collaboration leads to greater student achievement. They attributed these gains, in part, to the process of teacher peer learning resulting from constructive collaboration. Idol, Nevin, and Paolucci-Whitcomb (2000) reviewed over two dozen research-based studies on the effectiveness of collaboration and concluded that most yielded positive results. In addition, Kampwirth (2006) summarized results of several studies on collaborative consultation that indicated effectiveness in reducing referrals and placements (see Busse, Kratochwill, & Elliot, 1995; Gutkin, Henning-Stout, & Piersel, 1988; Idol, 2000). Based on results, Kampwirth wrote that "students served by consultees involved in experimental (i.e., structured, data-oriented) studies improved considerably more than did control students" (p. 19).

In their study, Gravois and Rosenfield (2006) found that over a two-year period collaborative consultative support provided to teachers increased student achievement for those who were struggling, and reduced the need for formal referral especially for minority students. Gravois and Rosenfield studied the effects of support provided to general classroom teachers by instructional consultation teams on overidentification of minority students for special education. The teams provided data-driven support in systematic ways to assist classroom teachers to meet the needs of learners. A key feature of their method is the one-on-one interactions between a team member and the classroom teacher rather than group meetings with the teacher. This individual effort by a team member included support in designing and implementing instructional or management practices to meet specified, measurable goals by providing collaborative support through ongoing communication and systematic problem-solving. Annual referral data were collected and compared across time with a decrease in referrals observed. These authors found that the "odds of minority students' being referred and placed in special education decreased by almost half" (p. 42) for students supported by the instructional consultation teams.

In regards to leadership, McLeskey et al. (2010) wrote that research has shown that support for collaborative problem-solving teams from the school principal along with school staff members creates a positive environment for student learning. These authors also discussed the notion that collaboration has positive effects on school-home interactions, writing that "extensive evidence reveals that home-school collaboration can result in significant improvement in student achievement and behavior" (p. 239). Collaboration may also assist in alleviating parental concerns about becoming involved due to cultural issues that interfere with effective communication (Martuszny, Banda, & Coleman, 2007).

As shown, research results over time suggest that the process of collaboration to provide effective education for students who struggle, those who are being considered for a special education referral and for culturally and linguistically diverse learners may have positive effects on reducing unnecessary referrals and placements. In this chapter, we discuss different issues related to collaborative decision-making in special education. First, we provide an overview of historical perspectives on special education decision making. We compare and contrast decision-making by pre-referral intervention teams with decision-making in Response to Intervention (RTI) models. Next, we discuss issues specific to RTI decision-making in diverse schools. Then, we describe the role of administrative leadership in collaborative decision-making. We finish by discussing implications for practice and for future research.

A Comparison of Historical and Contemporary Perspectives on Special Education Decision-Making

For over a century, educators in public and private schools and institutions have engaged in processes to best understand the needs of individuals with disabilities. Historically, the education of students with disabilities has moved through several periods, each of which provided for less restrictive and more inclusive forms of instruction (i.e., institutionalization, self-contained classrooms, mainstreaming, full inclusion). A common element with each type of instruction and educational placement is the use of some process for identifying learning needs and making decisions about the education of the student. Although there was and continues to be much controversy and debate over the most appropriate educational settings for students with varying degrees of disabilities, in most situations a team of professionals uses various forms of assessment information to make decisions about students' needs. Additionally, there are added complexities associated with meeting needs and providing appropriate placements for students with disabilities who bring cultural and linguistic diversity to the teaching and learning situation.

To best understand the special education decision-making process, a review of how decision-making teams approached their tasks of collecting, organizing and interpreting academic and social-emotional information is necessary. Specifically, in K–12 schools, for nearly five decades, decisions about struggling students centered on identifying intrinsic disorders within the learner; today, these decisions have a central focus on quality of instruction. The contemporary model for making special education decisions is framed within RTI models, while previous efforts took place within prereferral intervention models. RTI represents a preventative and early intervening approach, deviating from the prereferral model that required a student to demonstrate significant problems for an extended period of time (e.g., two years) prior to receiving targeted or more intensive instructional support (Hoover, 2009; Mellard & Johnson, 2008).

Although there are similarities between the previous (i.e., prereferral) and contemporary (i.e., RTI) models, the types of information and how that information is interpreted represent significant historical differences. Table 11.1, developed from Hoover and Love (2011) and Hoover (2010) illustrates some key differences between RTI and prereferral models.

As shown, differences between these frameworks are seen in how struggling learners are taught and progress monitored reflecting quality of instruction decision-making. This section provides a review of the decision-making process from both historical and contemporary perspectives highlighting key aspects along with comparison of similarities and differences as reflected prior and subsequent to the rise of response to intervention, a period that began more formally in the mid-1990s. These discussions pertain to any struggling student in grades K–12, with specific emphasis on decision-making to meet the needs of struggling learners representing cultural and linguistic diversity. Diverse learners bring unique challenges to school problem-solving teams that have and continue to lead to unnecessary referrals and inappropriate placements into special education. Clarification of the role of diversity within contemporary decision-making structures assists team members to make more informed instructional and eligibility decisions for all students. Historically, this process has occurred with a prereferral intervention model; however, a shift from this model is currently underway as more and more school systems implement response to intervention models.

Decision-Making Elements of the Prereferral Intervention Model

The contemporary model for addressing the needs of struggling learners, currently framed within RTI, builds upon previous successes and challenges associated with the prereferral model implemented for the past several decades. Specifically, an RTI model requires educators to transition

Table 11.1 Comparison of RTI and Preferral Models of Instructional Decision Making

RTI Model	Prereferral Model
Screening of all learners	Screening may not be completed for all learners
Evidence-based practice required	Use of evidence-based interventions not required
Actual-Expected Achievement discrepancy	Potential-Achievement discrepancy
Frequent progress monitoring	Infrequent required monitoring of learner progress
CBM assessment emphasis	Extensive use of norm reference devices
Early Intervening/Prevention	Wait to Fail
Quality of instruction focus	Intrinsic disorder focus

away from a diagnostic mode of thinking to a preventative way of viewing the instructional needs of students who struggle in school. This transition reflects the movement away from a wait to fail process that focused primarily on eligibility decisions, to one of instructional quality that focuses primarily on effective instruction and associated instructional adjustments when considering struggling learners (Hoover, 2011). Although some similar elements exist between these two decision-making frameworks, as discussed below, the purpose for which the needs of struggling students is considered represents a significant shift in the decision-making outcome within RTI models (i.e., instructional quality rather than eligibility resulting from wait to fail).

Over the past several decades we have seen the implementation of school-based collaborative and consultative teams that were developed with the purpose of assisting teachers to work with struggling students as well as to identify learning and behavioral disabilities. These teams have acquired various labels over the years including: Teacher Assistance Teams (TATs) (Chalfant, Psych, & Moultrie, 1979), School Consultation Committees (McGothlin, 1981), the Prereferral Intervention Model (Graden, Casey, & Bonstrom, 1983), Collaborative Peer Problem Solving (Pugach & Johnson, 1988), Intervention Assistance Teams (Graden, 1989), Child Study Teams (Moore, Fifield, Spira, & Scarlato, 1989), Mainstream Assistance Teams (Fuchs, Fuchs, & Bahr, 1990), Instructional Support Teams (Kovaleski, Tucker, Duffy, Lowery, & Gickling, 1995), and Instructional Consultation Teams (Rosenfield & Gravois, 1996). Although these models varied slightly in their title and implementation, they had similar goals in having a multidisciplinary team or a team of general education teachers that would assist mainstream teachers in developing interventions or strategies to help meet the needs of students in the regular classroom. The teams mostly followed similar procedures: (a) request for a consultation, (b) consultation, (c) observation, (d) conference, and (e) formal referral for special education eligibility (Graden et al., 1985). The most commonly implemented process of decision-making was through the Pre-referral Intervention Model (PIT), which as previously discussed, was originally designed as a collaborative problem-solving model that utilized a systematic problem-solving format (Burns, Appleton, & Stehouwer, 2005; Nelson, Smith, Taylor, Dodd, & Reavis, 1991). However, these teams have been criticized as functioning more as a decision-making process for referral to special education rather than as the problem-solving process as they were intended (Burns et al., 2005). An understanding of the practices associated with prereferral over the past several decades assists to frame how this initially well-intended process inadvertently led to misplacements into special education and associated misdiagnosis of disabilities, especially for culturally and linguistically diverse learners.

The literature shows us that decision-making teams have faced many challenges in collecting information and interpreting that information to make valid decisions. In the 1980s there were several studies of team meetings and their decision-making processes that highlighted these challenges (Abelson & Woodman, 1983; Bray, Coleman, & Gotts, 1981; Mehan, Hartwick, & Meihls, 1986; Moore et al., 1989; Ysseldyke, Algozzine, Richey, & Graden, 1982). Several of these studies, as well as more recent ones, provide a great deal of insight on how the roles of the team members and interactions among team members can affect the decision-making process. Working with culturally and linguistically diverse student populations adds another level of complexity to the decision-making process (Carrasquillo & Rodriguez, 1997; Figueroa & Newsome, 2006; Klingner & Harry, 2006; Wilkinson, Ortiz, Robertson, & Kushner, 2006). Historically, there has been an underlying presumption that the learning problems lie within the child, and there is little consideration as to other factors that may be influencing the child's academic struggles such as teacher quality, quality of the instruction, or the child's cultural and linguistic background. One of the critical issues we have seen with pre-referral decision-making teams is that they collect extensive amounts of data but tend to make decisions independent of the data (Mehan et al., 1986; Ysseldyke et al., 1982).

How have pre-referral teams been collecting and interpreting information? The information collected by pre-referral teams has mainly fallen into three categories: (a) student's response to pre-referral interventions, (b) informal teacher reports or anecdotal information, and (c) formal evaluations/IQ scores. Although utilizing all of these data points could provide sufficient evidence for valid decisions, teams have struggled to either collect this information accurately or to make their decisions based on the evidence provided. For example, many teams have faced challenges in designing quality interventions, implementing them with fidelity, monitoring their effectiveness, and connecting the results to the decisions.

Flugum and Reschly (1994) measured the quality of interventions provided to 312 students who had been referred for interventions and the extent to which they were provided. They found that many students were not receiving the necessary interventions or were receiving them sporadically, and the majority of interventions were lacking in quality. Truscott, Cohen, Sams, Sanborn, and Frank (2005) conducted a survey across the states and found that interventions seldom required any significant change in instruction or behavior, and only a few schools mentioned monitoring the interventions. In a study by Wilkinson et al. (2006) focusing on bilingual students, the authors found that an expert panel disagreed with decisions made by the teams in referring bilingual students to special education due to concerns with intervention efforts. The interventions were not well documented and some students were referred even though they demonstrated success with the interventions or were making similar progress to their peers. So although teams have been functioning with the intent of providing and monitoring interventions to aid in decision making, implementation has fallen short of the goal.

Another piece of data that teams have relied on has been the informal judgment of the classroom teacher. A survey of pre-referral teams in three states reported that 94% of team members indicated that teacher judgment of intervention effectiveness was the most frequently used index for decisions without using objective, data-based evaluation methods (Bahr, Whitten, Dieker, Kocarek, & Manso 1999). Although teachers' input is valuable and necessary, teachers' reports of student progress are variable and depend on the views of the individual teacher, which are subjective and inherently biased. A number of studies show that psychologists place a heavy emphasis on teachers' informal diagnoses of students in team meetings (Harry & Klingner, 2005; Mehan et al., 1986). This becomes especially problematic when working with culturally and linguistically diverse students because many teachers do not understand the influences of language and culture on learning.

According to Klingner and Harry (2006), school personnel are frequently confused as to when to refer an ELL for interventions or special education. In some cases, teachers have misinterpreted a student's lack of English proficiency as low IQ or a learning disability. Carrasquillo and Rodriguez (1997) reviewed the records of bilingual students either referred to or placed in special education classes and found that most bilingual students referred to special education had been in the country for less than three years. This indicates that language proficiency may not have been fully addressed or considered.

Formal evaluations can be useful tools in making decisions, but they have their limitations in providing teams with accurate results that are culturally and linguistically valid. Teams have gradually moved away from relying solely on formal assessments; however we found some interesting trends in the literature relating to assessment issues. With regards to the use of IQ tests in decision-making meetings, some researchers found that the more test information that was presented on a struggling student, the more likely the student was to be referred and classified as learning disabled (LD) (Ysseldyke et al., 1982).

A number of studies have analyzed the ability of psychologists in conducting nondiscriminatory assessments. Ochoa and colleagues (Ochoa, González, Galarza, & Guillemard, 1996; Ochoa, Powell, & Robles-Piña, 1996; Ochoa, Rivera, & Powell, 1997) conducted a survey of

859 National Association of School Psychologist (NASP) members to investigate their practices. In one study they explored which factors these professionals used to comply with IDEA's exclusionary clause for bilingual students and ELLs. They identified important factors that were overlooked, including how many years the student had received instruction in English and whether a test score discrepancy existed in both English and the student's native language. They also found that a little over half of the psychologists used bilingual interpreters but that only a small percentage of them were trained.

Figueroa and Newsome (2006) conducted a smaller study analyzing 19 psychological reports in terms of their use of legal and professional directives on how to test English Language Learners to determine if the directives were present and appropriate. They found that the reports seldom adhered to professional and legal guidelines, indicating that the psychologists were not considering or assessing the effects of bilingualism on learning. The reports never included discussion of the possibility of other factors affecting the students' learning, such as subtractive bilingualism or flaws in the schooling process. Klingner and Harry (2006) found that although bilingual assessors evaluated students' language proficiency, they rarely attended referral meetings. Carrasquillo and Rodriguez (1997) suggested that accessible assessments may not accurately measure ELLs' academic and linguistic needs. So we see from the research that in some cases the professionals evaluating students did not strongly consider the native language of the student being tested. They relied solely on English language tests and disregard whether underachievement is due to limited English proficiency (Klingner, Artiles, & Barletta, 2006).

Although there has been a great deal of effort among decision-making teams to work collaboratively to serve struggling learners, we see reoccurring themes in the literature suggesting that collaborative problem solving remains an ongoing challenge. For example, team members often have limited training in the decision-making process or in working with culturally and linguistically diverse students. The roles of team members are rather undefined, and team members are often unsure of how their expertise can contribute to the discussion. Often, it is unclear who actually makes the final decisions.

A number of researchers have noted that a hierarchy of team members seems to be pervasive among decision-making teams (Mehan et al., 1986; Klingner & Harry, 2006) and that information provided at meetings varies according to the expertise and perceived status of the member presenting the information, with certain members' voices "heard" more than others. School psychologists, followed by special education teachers, tend to have the most influence on decisions, with classroom teachers and parents having the least amount of influence (Frankenberger & Harper, 1988; Knoff, 1983). Historically, the school psychologist has significant influence on the nature of the conversation, the team norms, how information is interpreted, and overall how decisions are finalized (Frankenberger & Harper, 1988; Gutkin & Nemeth, 1997; Klingner & Harry, 2006; Knoff, 1983; Mehan et al., 1986). On the other hand, Klingner and Harry (2006) found that the parents of bilingual students and their advocates were rarely listened to in team meetings, and there often were misunderstandings among parents as to how the special education referral process works and their role, which may have led to reluctance on the parents' part to participate fully.

The above discussions highlight some of the issues that have dominated problem-solving team decision-making within prereferral intervention models. The next section provides a discussion about RTI and its decision-making process for struggling learners, including culturally and linguistically diverse students.

RTI Team Decision-Making

RTI provides a promising new framework for viewing teaching and learning for students who struggle, have disabilities, or otherwise demonstrate at-risk factors in education. In most school systems nationwide, response to intervention models include collaborative problem solving (Hoover, Baca, Wexler, Love, & Saenz, 2008). Most models of RTI include three tiers or layers of instruction each increasing in duration and intensity should learners exhibit continued lack of adequate progress (Mellard & Johnson, 2008):

Tier 1—Core, general class instruction using only research-based curriculum implemented to all learners in which progress is periodically screened (e.g., 3–4 times per year). A minimum of 80% of students is expected to make adequate progress toward curricular benchmarks in Tier 1 (Yell, 2004).

Tier 2—Supplemental instructional supports delivered through push-in or pull-out arrangements in which evidence-based interventions (e.g., reciprocal teaching, direct instruction, etc.) are employed to complement, not replace, Tier 1 core instruction; progress is more frequently monitored (e.g., bi-weekly, monthly). Expectations are that 15%–20% of learners will require some form of Tier 2 supports during their schooling (Yell, 2004).

Tier 3—Intensive instruction is reserved for meeting the most significant needs, including special education disability needs, in which highly focused and targeted instruction is provided in one-to-one or small groups (i.e., 2–3 students); student progress is more aggressively monitored (e.g., weekly, daily). Tier 3 intensive interventions may include alternate curriculum differing from that used in Tiers 1 and 2 and is reserved for 1%–5% of the student population (Yell, 2004).

Below is an overview of selected problem-solving models followed by how these may be applied in an RTI multi-tiered instructional framework.

Collaborative Problem-Solving Models. Although a variety of collaborative problem-solving models exist, most contain similar steps or procedures that guide decision making to meet the learning needs of all students. For example, Marston, Muyskens, Lau, and Canter (2003) described key aspects of the problem-solving model used in Minneapolis schools. Their model is termed the Problem Solving Model (PSM) and includes three primary stages:

Classroom interventions. In this initial stage screening data are gathered and teachers differentiate instruction to meet individual needs that arise. Information is also gathered on a variety of variables that may influence screening data including cultural factors for diverse learners. This is an essential aspect of the problem-solving model since consideration of cultural and linguistic diversity assists to provide sufficient opportunities to learn for diverse students.

Problem-solving team interventions. If the stage or Tier 1 differentiations are unsuccessful at helping students progress toward grade or age level benchmarks a more targeted instructional program (e.g., Tier 2 supplemental instruction) is developed for implementation in the general classroom curriculum. This may include use of interventions designed to meet specific levels of performance and closely monitoring students' progress (i.e., ongoing progress monitoring). Given the emphasis in the PSM on identifying cultural factors that may be influencing learning, this stage includes consideration of cultural and linguistic variables.

Special education referral and due process procedures. In the PSM, should the learner fail to respond satisfactorily to implementation of instructional efforts in the second stage then consideration for special education may begin. At this time parent/guardian consent is obtained and the comprehensive evaluation for special education ensues building on the body of evidence previously collected in stages one and two (Marston et al., 2003).

As seen, this process contains three clearly defined stages in which instructional efforts are implemented in preventative ways prior to considering students for special education. In addition, attention directed toward cultural and linguistic variables helps to ensure that sufficient opportunities to learn exist for diverse learners, thereby closing the opportunity gap. It should be noted that the model summarized above is only one type of problem-solving model. The reader is referred to Brown-Chidsey and Steege (2005), Burns and Gibbons (2008) and Deno (2005) for additional models and further discussion. However, whichever collaborative problem-solving model is used within an RTI model, its effects on student progress are highly promising for all students and especially culturally and linguistically diverse learners, as discussed in subsequent sections of the this chapter.

Collaborating to Facilitate Learning for Culturally and Linguistically Diverse Students. Harris (1996) has emphasized that collaborators should have a unique set of multicultural skills when working with culturally diverse students. Some of the skills she recommends are:

1. Making sincere attempts to understand the world from others points of view.
2. Respecting individuals from other cultures.
3. Identifying needed multicultural knowledge base.
4. Working effectively with an interpreter or translator.
5. Acknowledging cultural differences in communication and relationship building.
6. Ensuring that problem identification does not conflict with cultural beliefs.
7. Using information regarding socially hidden aspects of power that privilege or silence culturally diverse groups in problem solving.

Advantages to RTI. Schwanz and Barbour (2005) suggested that problem-solving team efforts within an RTI model reduce special education referrals by improving achievement and behavior. The structure and process in the decision-making models within RTI are similar in design and scope to those found previously in the prereferral models. However, as previously illustrated in Table 11.1, the RTI model represents a shift in use of instructional data and information away from identifying a disability to ensuring quality of instruction. Schwanz and Barbour (2005) also summarized differences between the models:

> Problem-Solving Outcomes within RTI—Primary outcomes are to select and ensure proper implementation of evidence-based practices to meet learner needs in the general education curriculum.
> Problem-Solving Outcomes within Prereferral Intervention—Primary outcome is typically seen as a process for gathering necessary materials and evidence in order to make a formal referral for special education eligibility and/or placement.

In addition, Gresham (2005) identified four advantages that RTI holds over the prereferral model: (a) early identification of learning problems, (b) use of a risk model rather than a deficit model, (c) reduction of identification biases, and (d) focus on student outcomes. Therefore, although RTI decision-making structures may remain similar to previous structures, several key differences exist that attempt to address the major short comings of the prereferral model, four of which are discussed below:

1. *Emphasis placed on prevention rather than wait to fail.* RTI decision-making is designed to focus on preventative measures to minimize problems from becoming more significant prior to receiving necessary instructional supports. An emphasis on prevention reduces unnecessary

referrals to and placements in special education as evidenced by success in several state and school initiatives (see Table 11.2).

2. *Dual Discrepancy.* Problem-solving teams in prereferral models relied extensively on the discrepancy between intellectual ability and actual achievement and research shows that many states and school systems are de-emphasizing use of this practice (Hoover et al., 2008, Spectrum K12, 2010; Zierkel & Thomas, 2010). Rather, consideration of two interrelated alternate discrepancies is suggested: (a) discrepancy between actual and expected achievement, and, (b) discrepancy between actual and expected rate of progress toward achievement, both relative to grade and age level peers (Burns & Gibbons, 2008; Mellard & Johnson, 2008).

3. *Use of quantified data to base instructional decision-making.* Problem-solving teams within RTI models use objective and quantified achievement and behavioral data to make instructional adjustments. Research suggests that the use of quantifiable and verifiable student data provides a more solid foundation for making curricular decisions over teacher referral information (VanDerHeyden & Witt, 2005).

4. *Implementation of evidence-based practice.* Unlike prereferral intervention models, all instruction within RTI models provided to students must be evidence-based to ensure that learners receive sufficient opportunities to learn.

Although not all-inclusive, these four components within response to intervention models clearly differentiate the RTI problem-solving outcomes from problem-solving results previously obtained through prereferral intervention models. The nation-wide transition from the prereferral model to the contemporary response to intervention model has only recently been undertaken in most of today's districts and schools (Hoover, 2011). However, a few states and school systems have been implementing a problem-solving model within an RTI framework for a decade or more. Several of these efforts are summarized in Table 11.2. The purpose of the table is to summarize recent educational efforts underway across the country where the focus is placed on the use of problem-solving teams to address student needs in a preventative manner, deviating significantly from the previous prereferral diagnostic approach. Additionally, Table 11.2 highlights salient points specific to our discussion of problem-solving team leadership and collaboration in the contemporary era in today's schools. The reader is referred to the sources cited in the development of the table for a more detailed description and discussion of these state and district problem-solving efforts within RTI frameworks.

Table 11.2 State/District Problem-Solving Team Initiatives

State	Site Description	Key Specifics	Relevant Research Findings
Wisconsin	Public Charter HS	900 students	Increased student participation in state-wide testing from 10–99%
Iowa	Heartland Area Education Agency	84 Schools	Increased data-driven instructional decisions Relied upon direct measures for decisions Effects on achievement are being monitored through 2014; Initial results are promising Special education decisions have been made without consideration of IQ-achievement published tests for over 10 years
Minnesota	Minneapolis PS	Alternate Assessment system and use of data	Disability terms were replaced with non-categorical classifications Placement for high incidence disabilities remained low at 7% of student population Progress monitoring and formative assessment continues to guide decision-making

(continued)

Table 11.2 Continued

State	Site Description	Key Specifics	Relevant Research Findings
Ohio	State-wide initiative	300+ schools	Data used to make instructional decisions Model emphasizes collaborative problem-solving Requires a school-wide effort
Illinois	State-wide initiative	State and Regional Problem-Solving Model	Survey/achievement data results indicated academic and behavioral improvements within a 2-4 year period Amount of time required to provide needed assistance was reduced by nearly 60% Initial evaluations for special education were reduced Building principal support is critical to success of problem-solving team efforts Continuous communication and collaboration are essential
Minnesota	St. Croix River Education District	Five school districts with 9000 students	Percentage of students achieving at benchmark increased significantly in the area of reading (< 40% to near 70%) Students placed in special education for learning disabilities dropped by over 40% Structured problem-solving procedures must be in place to best meet all learner needs Results suggest that this problem-solving model reduces LDs and academic failure
Idaho	State-wide initiative	Results-based problem-solving model in over 150 schools	Standard-treatment practices should be included in problem-solving model Sharing responsibility/collaboration is essential Problem-solving team is able to replace the prereferral team Up to 3% decrease in special education occurred across districts Building administrative leadership is essential to success of problem-solving teams
Michigan	State-wide Initiative	School-wide Effort in four Schools with 1300 students	Building principal support and active participation essential to successful school-wide implementation of problem-solving team Preliminary achievement suggest positive growth for students Building teams serve as the foundation for school level efforts

Note: Table developed from information found in Canter (2004); Staum, & Ocampo, 2004; Jimerson, Burns & VanDerHeyden, 2007); Ikeda, Rahn-Blakeslee, Niebling, Gustafson, Allison, & Stumme, 2007; Marston, Lau, & Muyskens, 2007; Graden, Stollar, & Poth, 2007; Bollman, Silberglitt, & Gibbons, 2007; Callender, 2007; Ervin, Schaughency, Goodman, McGlinchey, & Matthews, 2007; Peterson, Prasse, Shinn, & Swerdlik, 2007

As shown, results from the problem-solving efforts within various states and school systems suggest that the effects from a decision-making model that is preventative rather than reactive (i.e., wait to fail) are positive. Selected implications of these results are highlighted below.

Principal Leadership. Research results confirm the significance and need for ongoing principal support and leadership to bring the best out of school problem-solving teams. Hall (2008) discussed several ways principals demonstrate needed leadership to support RTI implementation including motivating staff to see its positive aspects, managing those who may resist RTI change, facilitate the process and procedures for effective RTI decision-making, actively participate in data analysis meetings and discussions (i.e., universal screening/progress monitoring data), and support efforts to evaluate the effectiveness of each tier of instruction.

Impact on Achievement. In many of the sites, the problem-solving teams facilitated school-wide efforts that led to increased student progress towards benchmarks.

Referral/Placements. In several sites the percentage of students being referred for special education and/or placed into special education was reduced through the efforts of problem-solving teams.

Prevention Efforts. The time required to receive necessary interventions decreased along with improved quality of interventions for struggling learners, due to preventative and early intervening instruction facilitated by problem-solving teams.

Use of Data. Instructional decisions relied more extensively on objective achievement and behavioral data than previous efforts through prereferral intervention models.

RTI Problem-Solving Team Efforts for Diverse Learners

Much research has been conducted over the past decade on the potential effectiveness of collaborative problem-solving teams' abilities to address general student needs in the teaching and learning environment. Conversely, fewer studies have been undertaken to specifically examine the effects of problem-solving models on the education of culturally and linguistically diverse learners. While not as extensive, some recent research projects have been undertaken that illustrate that collaborative problem solving has the potential to reduce the disproportionate referral to and placement of culturally and linguistically diverse students in special education, as illustrated in Table 11.3.

As shown, Table 11.3 illustrates selected research studies specific to RTI collaborative problem-solving efforts for diverse learners, thereby reflecting a multicultural perspective in the decision-making process. Below is a summary of conclusions that may be drawn from these research projects for meeting core, supplemental and intensive instructional needs of diverse learners, as summarized in the table:

- Structured program interventions such as Tier 2 small group instruction assist diverse learners in the area of reading;
- More informed instructional decisions are made when diverse students' rates of progress and proficiency levels are addressed by the problem-solving team, rather than simply considering proficiency level alone;
- Team collaboration leads to greater understanding of diverse learners' needs, which in turn facilitates more effective instructional decision-making;
- Screening and progress monitoring of diverse learners that rely on multiple forms of data rather than extensively on teacher perceptions provide for better informed teams who use objective data for making more accurate instructional decisions;
- Systematic analysis of student data leads to less unnecessary and misinformed referrals to special education for diverse learners;
- Problem-solving teams who use progress data to make instructional decisions provide diverse students greater opportunities to learn by reducing unnecessary placements into special education.

Although less research has been conducted on the problem-solving process when considering the needs of diverse learners, that which has been conducted demonstrates encouraging results for collaboration within multicultural contexts. Additional research is needed to help further clarify best collaborative decision-making team practices in culturally and linguistically diverse contexts.

Table 11.3   RTI Problem-Solving Decision Making for Diverse Learners

Research Project Overview	Key Relevant Finding(s)
First graders in a CA school with over 90% ELLs were screened and the lowest performing students were provided small group intervention. Data collection included achievement scores and classroom observations (Healy, Vanderwood, & Edelston, 2005)	Problem-solving team compared actual scores with expected trend line scores along with classroom observation data to confirm fidelity of instruction. Research results suggest that a structured intervention program (i.e., Tier 2 instruction in a small group) is effective for meeting the needs of struggling ELLs in reading.
A pilot project examining school-based problem solving teams in three elementary schools with significant ELL populations was conducted to identify key issues encountered by the school teams in implementing RTI in their schools. Project documented interactions with the school team members, issues discussed and suggestions for addressing the issues (Hoover & Love, 2011)	Problem-solving teams indicated that while proficiency levels were obtained for ELLs their rate of progress was often not considered. Results suggest that when both proficiency and rate of progress are considered problem-solving teams are more informed, thereby leading to more accurate instructional decisions for ELLs.
A study was conducted designed to investigate the use of an RTI model to address reading skills in three highly ELL populated urban schools. A key component is the inclusion of a problem-solving school team which met weekly to discuss student progress (Rinaldi, Averill, & Estabrook, 2010)	Student success was attributed in part to team collaboration and problem solving along with greater awareness of ELL needs. Researchers conclude the RTI problem solving process is effective in monitoring reading needs of ELLs. RTI team collaboration and training helped both teachers and administrators to better understand and meet the needs of ELLs.
Study investigated effects of the 'problem validation screening (PVS) model' which is a universal screening model designed to provide problem-solving teams with information for making screening decisions for low-performing, minority and male students. Study compared this RTI process with the teacher referral method. Data from four screening measures were compared with teacher referral documentation by the problem-solving team (VanderHeyden & Witt, 2005).	Overall, results support the use of an RTI process for screening students. Teacher referrals were found to be less accurate than the PVS model. Researchers found that when combined with use of interventions universal screening reduced disproportionality. Additionally, RTI process for screening was found to reduce disproportionality by more accurately screening learners by race than the teacher prereferral process.
The process of using Instructional Consultation Teams to affect disproportional referral and placement of minority students into special education was studied. Experimental and control schools were included and most students were categorized as African American or Caucasian (Gravois & Rosenfield, 2006).	Problem-solving team members emphasized collaboration and systematic analysis of charted classroom data. After two years the use of an Instructional Consultation Team model reduced the chances of minority students being referred and placed in special education by half as compared to the control schools. Also, results showed that the ratio of minority students referred and placed into special education was reduced by more than 50%.
Tucker and Sornson (2007) conducted a review of research on the effects of Instructional Support Teams (IST) on special education referrals as implemented in several states. One component of this research studied the effects of an IST or similar type problem-solving model on referrals and placement of minority students in special education.	Summary reporting of this research review indicated that in one of the states studied a significant reduction in referrals for minority students occurred. Specifically, over a three-year span once the instruction support model was introduced as the problem-solving approach referrals for Hispanic and African American students were reduced from 95% to 7% and 36% to 3%, respectively. The IST decision-making process led to more support in the general Tier 1 instruction, thus reducing the need for referrals. Other states showed similar reductions in referrals for minority students.

Administrative Leadership in Collaborative Decision-Making

Contemporary decision-making resulting from collaborative problem solving for struggling learners requires commitment and involvement from school and district administrators as well as teachers and support personnel. Much research documents the importance of administrative support and participation in order for problem-solving to lead to successful implementation of team decisions (e.g., Bottoms, 2003; Ervin, Schaughency, Goodman, McGlinchey, & Mathews, 2007; Hall, 2008; Howell, Patton & Deiotte, 2008). While this leadership is necessary for guiding decision-making for all learners, it is especially important for diverse students who require culturally and linguistically responsive supports to be successful within the initial instructional tiers (i.e., Tiers 1, 2) in RTI models.

As previously discussed, the framework of RTI shows promise for all struggling learners, especially diverse students; however, school-based problem-solving models within RTI require structure, leadership and ongoing support to be successful. When implementing RTI, administrators may demonstrate needed leadership and support as they: (a) coordinate curriculum and assessment considerations, (b) address teachers' professional developmental needs, (c) attend to school climate issues, and (d) orchestrate and respond to multiple (often contradictory) reforms (Adelman & Taylor, 2002). Hall (2008) discussed the foundation of administrative support, stating that a "principal's commitment is essential" (p. 37). Specifically, administrative leadership must provide a clear direction for instructional success to occur. This includes establishing clearly defined goals that collaborative problem-solving teams strive to achieve. Goals such as reducing the percentage of students achieving below grade level in reading comprehension, increasing positive behaviors in every classroom, or reducing unnecessary referrals to special education are examples of the types of goals collaborative efforts might address in school-wide efforts to meet the needs of all learners. Within multicultural contexts, a critical administrative leadership goal is the reduction of disproportionate referrals and placements of culturally and linguistically diverse learners into special education, resulting from misinterpreting learning differences from disabilities.

When considering administrative leadership, Howell, Patton, and Diottee (2008) wrote that "there is overwhelming evidence that strong leadership is provided by setting direction, developing staff, and developing the organization" (p. 18). In support of these elements, a building principal should maintain leadership in all aspects of RTI (Hall, 2008), which includes communication, collaboration, and implementation driven by a school's problem-solving team structured in a manner previously discussed. Before beginning RTI in a school, administrative leaders can lay the groundwork for successful implementation in multiple ways (Crockett & Gillespie, 2007). Crockett and Gillespie recommend establishing a leadership team. One of this team's first tasks should be to determine the quality of core, or Tier 1, instruction and then to develop a plan for improving the core. As Crockett and Gillespie stated, "The critical role that principals play by enhancing instructional quality ... cannot be overstated" (p. 7). Plans are also needed for (a) how to select and evaluate the quality and effectiveness of Tier 2 and Tier 3 interventions such as ensuring that outcomes for successful progress are clearly defined, (b) how to monitor students' progress, and by whom including progress monitoring schedules and measures, (c) how parents will be involved such as detailing the process for including parents in multi-tiered instructional decision-making for students who struggle, and (d) how special education eligibility will be determined, which includes delineating the types of achievement data required and decision points adhered to within an RTI model in order to clarify eligibility due to a disability.

Providing professional development in appropriate evidence-based interventions is one of an administrator's essential tasks (Boscardin, 2004). The need for this is particularly acute in culturally and linguistically diverse settings with students who typically underachieve. Describing the critical role of administrators, Movit, Petrykowska, and Woodruff (2010) wrote, "To support teachers in their efforts to utilize culturally and linguistically responsive practices, administrators should provide and encourage teachers to take advantage of professional development opportunities that will help them to develop strategies to meet the needs of all students" (p. 5). Webb-Johnson (2008) stressed the importance of culturally responsive staff development to address disproportionate patterns of ineffective instruction for learners in our schools. Professional development should help educators involved in making decisions about culturally and linguistically diverse students understand the second language acquisition process and how to distinguish between learning disabilities and language acquisition or learning differences (Klingner, Hoover, & Baca, 2008).

As discussed, evidence shows that administrative support is a cornerstone to efforts undertaken by collaborative problem-solving teams in meeting the needs of diverse learners. However, some research in the area of diversity and administrative leadership suggests that further progress is required to adequately meet the instructional needs of all learners. For example, Liu, Thurlow, Koo, and Barrera (2008) conducted an online principal survey of middle and junior high schools examining, in part, the principals' roles in supporting teachers in the education of English language learners, including those with disabilities. They noted from their review of research that administrative support for the successful education of ELLs should include several elements:

- Communicating the attitude that all students can learn and achieve at high levels;
- Being personally knowledgeable of ELLs' characteristics and needs and expect the same for all staff;
- Facilitating the development to increase capacity to meet the learning and behavioral needs of ELLs;
- Reducing academic barriers to increase ELL achievement, development and sufficient opportunities to learn; and,
- Creating an environment that promotes positive staff attitudes toward the education of ELLs.

These are not all-inclusive; however, they represent several strengths that support administrative efforts to further advance the success of the work undertaken by collaborative problem solving for culturally and linguistically diverse learners. As can be seen, the importance of administrative support so that school staff have the needed skills and resources to best implement instruction for diverse students is a common theme. Although these and similar administrative supports are deemed necessary, the research of Liu et al. (2008) suggested that principals: (a) may be less familiar with needs and instructional interventions to educate ELLs with disabilities than with the general population of learners; and (b) may defer some of the instructional leadership concerning the education of ELLs with disabilities to the district level, which the researchers noted may be an effective strategy. However, they also concluded that if building administration possessed greater knowledge and skills in the education of ELLs, including those with disabilities, more direct instructional leadership could occur. Liu et al. further suggested that additional research is needed to more clearly understand how principal (and other administrative) leadership can be provided and its effects on ELL school achievement.

Conclusion

In conclusion, we recommend using a flexible, proactive approach to collaborative decision-making in RTI that (a) builds on the strengths, interests, and expertise of school personnel; (b) provides ongoing professional development that enhances educators' capacity to provide appropriate instruction and to make well-informed decisions; (c) involves families in the decision-making process; and (d) focuses on students' strengths as well as needs.

We offer a set of questions for school leaders to ask themselves as they guide collaborative decision-making in multi-lingual, multicultural schools. This list is not meant to be all-inclusive, but rather, to reflect a starting point (adapted from Klingner, Méndez Barletta, & Hoover, 2008):

1. Who benefits from decisions? Who doesn't? Can I detect patterns in which some groups in the school benefit more than others from certain decisions?

2. Does the representation of students who have difficulties or are succeeding in my school match the general representation of students in the school, or are some student groups over- or under-represented?

3. Do I adequately capitalize on cultural and linguistic diversity and build on students' and families' strengths?

4. Do I continue to develop my own knowledge and expertise regarding optimal educational practices for culturally and linguistically diverse students?

5. Do I exemplify a positive, supportive, respectful attitude towards teachers, students, and families?

6. Do I actively seek out and employ faculty, support personnel, and office staff who demonstrate the ability to meaningfully and respectfully interact with individuals from diverse cultural backgrounds?

7. Do I demonstrate my commitment to collaborative problem-solving by making sure that teachers and support staff have adequate time in their schedules to meet (e.g., common planning time; early release days) and the resources they need?

8. Does my school have a school leadership team made up of diverse individuals with expertise in the languages and cultures of the students, including parents?

9. Does my school have a system for problem-solving and decision-making that includes diverse individuals with expertise in the languages and cultures of students?

10. Do I make sure that teachers and support personnel are provided with professional development in how to meet the needs of culturally and linguistically diverse students?

References

Abelson, M. A., & Woodman, R. W. (1983). Review of research on team effectiveness: Implications for teams in schools. *School Psychology Review, 12*, 125–136.

Adelman, H. S., & Taylor, L. (2002). Building comprehensive, multifaceted, and integrate approaches to address barriers to student learning. *Childhood Education, 78*, 261–268.

Bahr, M., Whitten, E., Dieker, L., Kocarek, C., & Manso, D. (1999) A comparison of school-based intervention teams: Implications for educational and legal reform. *Exceptional Children, 66*(1), 67–83.

Bollman, K. A., Silberglitt, B., & Gibbons, K. A. (2007). The St. Croix River education district model: Incorporating systems-level organization and a multi-level problem-solving process for intervention delivery. In S. R. Jimerson, M. K. Burns, & A. M. VanDerHeyden (Eds.), *Handbook of response to intervention: The science and practice of assessment and intervention* (pp. 319–110). New York: Springer.

Boscardin, M. L. (2004). Transforming administration to support science in the schoolhouse for students with disabilities. *Journal of Learning Disabilities,37*, 262–269.

Bottoms, G. (2003). What school principals need to know about curriculum and instruction. *ERS Spectrum, 21*(1), 29.

Bray, N., Coleman, M., & Gotts, E. (1981). The Interdisciplinary team: challenges to effective functioning. *Teacher Education and Special Education, 4*(1), 44–49.

Brown-Chidsey, R., & Steege, M. W. (2005). *Response to intervention: Principles and strategies for effective practice.* New York: Guildford Press.

Burns, M., Appleton, J., & Stehouwer, J. (2005). Meta-analytic review of Response-to-Intervention Research: Examining field-based and research-implemented models. *Journal of Psychoeducational Assessment, 23*, 381–394.

Burns, M. K., & Gibbons, K. A. (2008). *Implementing response-to-intervention in elementary and secondary schools: Procedures to assure scientific-based practices.* New York: Taylor & Francis.

Busse, R., Kratochwill, T., & Elliott, S. (1995). Meta-analysis for single case outcomes: Applications to research and practice. *Journal of School Psychology, 33*, 269–285.

Callender, W. A. (2007). The Idaho results-based model: Implementing response to intervention statewide. In S. R. Jimerson, M. K. Burns, & A. M. VanDerHeyden (Eds.), *Handbook of response to intervention: The science and practice of assessment and intervention* (pp. 331–342). New York: Springer.

Canter, A. (2004, December). A problem-solving model for improving student achievement. *Principal Leadership Magazine 5*(4). Retrieved June 3, 2010, from http://www.nasponline.org/resources/principals/nassp_probsolve.aspx

Carrasquillo, A. L., & Rodriguez, J. (1997). Hispanic limited English-proficient students with disabilities. *Learning Disabilities: A Multidisciplinary Journal, 8*(3), 167–174.

Chalfant, J. C., Psych, V., & Moultrie, R. (1979). Teacher assistance teams: A model for within-building problem solving. *Learning Disabilities Quarterly, 2*, 85–96.

Crockett, J. B., & Gillespie, D. N. (2007). Getting reading for RTI: A principal's guide to response to intervention. *ERS Spectrum, 25*(4), 1–9.

Deno, S. L. (2005). Problem-solving assessment. In R. Brown-Chidsey (Ed.), *Assessment for intervention: A problem-solving approach* (pp. 10–40). New York: Guilford Press.

Ervin, R. A., Schaughency, E., Goodman, S. D., McGlinchey, M. T., & Mathews, A. (2007). Moving from a model demonstration project to a statewide initiative in Michigan: Lessons learned from merging research–practice agendas to address reading and behavior. In S. R. Jimerson, M. K. Burns, & A. M. VanDerHeyden (Eds.), *Handbook of response to intervention: The science and practice of assessment and intervention* (pp. 354–377). New York: Springer.

Figueroa, R., & Newsome, P. (2006). The diagnoses of LD in English Language Learners: Is it nondiscriminatory? *Journal of Learning Disabilities, 39*, 206–214.

Flugum, K. R., & Reschly, D. J. (1994). Prereferral interventions: Quality indices and outcomes. *Journal of School Psychology, 32*(1), 1–14.

Frankenberger, W., & Harper, J. (1988). Perceived importance of contributions made by professionals participating on multidisciplinary evaluation teams. *Mental Retardation and Learning Disability Bulletin, 16*(2), 29–35.

Friend, M., & Cook, L. (2010). *Interactions: Collaboration skills for school professionals*. Columbus, OH: Pearson Merrill.

Fuchs, D., Fuchs, L. S., & Bahr, M. W. (1990) Mainstream assistance teams: A scientific basis for the art of consultation. *Exceptional Children, 57*, 128–139.

Graden, J. L., Stollar, S. A., & Poth, R. L. (2007). The Ohio Integrated Systems Model: Overview and lessons learned. In S. R. Jimerson, M. K. Burns, & A. M. VanDerHeyden (Eds.), *Handbook of response to intervention: The science and practice of assessment and intervention* (pp. 288–299). New York: Springer.

Graden, J. L. (1989) Redefining "prereferral" intervention as intervention assistance: Collaboration between general and special education. *Exceptional Children, 56*, 227–231.

Graden, J. L., Casey, A., & Bonstrom, O. (1983). Pre-referral interventions: Effects on referral rates and teacher attitudes (Report No. IRLD-RR-140). Minneapolis: Minnesota University Institute for Research on Learning Disabilities. (ERIC Document Reproduction Service No. ED 162451)

Gravois, T. A., & Rosenfield, S. A. (2006). Impact of instructional consultation teams on the disproportionate referral and placement of minority students in special education. *Remedial and Special Education, 27*(1), 42–52.

Gresham, F. M. (2005). Response to intervention: an alternative means of identifying students with emotional disturbance. *Education and Treatment of Children, 28*, 328–344.

Gutkin, T. B., & Nemeth, C. (1997). Selected factors impacting decision making in prereferral intervention and other school-based teams: Exploring the intersection between school and social psychology. *Journal of School Psychology, 35*, 195–216.

Gutkin, T. B., Henning-Stout, M., & Piersel, W. C. (1988). Impact of a district-wide behavioral consultation prereferral intervention service on patterns of school psychological service delivery. *Professional School Psychology, 3*, 301–308.

Hall, S. L. (2008). *A principal's guide: Implementing response to intervention*. Thousand Oaks, CA: Corwin Press.

Harris, K. C. (1996). Collaboration within a multicultural society: Issues for consideration. *Remedial and Special Education, 17*(6), 335–362.

Harry, B., & Klingner, J. K. (2005). *Why are so many minority students in special education? Understanding race and disability in schools*. New York: Teachers College Press.

Healy, K., Vanderwood, M. L., & Edelston, D. (2005). Early Literacy Interventions for English Language Learners: Support for an RTI Model. *California School Psychologist. 10*, 55–63.

Heron, T. E., & Harris, K. C. (2000). *The educational consultant*. Austin, TX: Pro-Ed.

Hoover, J. J. (2011). *Response to intervention models: Curricular implications and interventions*. Boston, MA: Pearson Allyn & Bacon.

Hoover, J. J. (2010). Special education eligibility decision making in response to intervention models. *Theory Into Practice, 49*(4), 289–296.

Hoover, J. J. (2009). *RTI assessment for struggling learners*. Thousand Oaks, CA: Corwin Press.

Hoover, J. J., & Love, E. (2011) Supporting school-based response to intervention: A practitioner's model. *Teaching Exceptional Children, 43*(3), 4-48

Hoover, J. J., Baca, L. M., Wexler Love, E., & Saenz, L. (2008). *National implementation of Response to Intervention (RTI): Research summary*. University of Colorado, Boulder-BUENO Center. Retrieved February 15, 2009, from National Association of State Directors of Special Education (NASDSE) Website: http://www.nasdse.org

Howell, R., Patton, S., & Deiotte, M. (2008). *Understanding response to intervention: A practical guide to systemic implementation*. Bloomington, IN: Solution Tree.

Idol, L. (2000). The scientific art of classroom consultation. *Journal of Educational and Psychological Consultation 1*(1), 3–22.

Idol, L., Nevin, A., & Paolucci-Whitcomb, P. (2000). *Collaborative consultation* (3rd ed.). Autsin, TX: Pro-Ed.

Ikeda, M. J., Rahn-Blakeslee, A., Niebling, B. C., Gustafson, J. K., Allison, R., & Stumme, J. (2007). The Heartland Area Education Agency 11 problem-solving approach: An overview and lessons learned. In S. R. Jimerson, M. K. Burns, & A. M. VanDerHeyden (Eds.), *Handbook of response to intervention: The science and practice of assessment and intervention* (pp. 255–268). New York: Springer.

Jackson, C. K., & Bruegmann, E. (2009). *Teaching students and teaching each other: The importance of peer learning for teachers*. Retrieved June 1, 2010, from Cornell University, School of Industrial and Labor Relations Website: http://digitalcommons.ilr.cornell.edu/workingpapers/77/

Jimerson, S. R., Burns, M. K., & VanDerHeyden, A. M. (Eds.). (2007). *Handbook of response to intervention: The science and practice of assessment an intervention*. New York: Springer.

Kampwirth, T. J. (2006). *Collaborative consultation in the schools: Effective practice for students with learning and behavior problems*. Columbus, OH: Pearson.

Klingner, J. K., Artiles, A., & Barletta, L. M. (2006). English Language Learners who struggle with reading: Language acquisition or LD? *Journal of Learning Disabilities, 39*, 108–128.

Klingner, J. K., & Edwards, P. E. (2006). Cultural considerations with response to intervention models. *Reading Research Quarterly, 41*, 108–115.

Klingner, J. K., & Harry, B. (2006). The special education referral and decision-making process for English Language Learners: Child study team meetings and placement conferences. *Teachers College Record, 108*, 2247–2281.

Klingner, J., Hoover, J. J., & Baca, L. (Eds.). (2008*). Why do English language learners struggle with reading? Distinguishing language acquisition from learning disabilities*. Thousand Oaks, CA: Corwin Press.

Klingner, J., Méndez Barletta, L., & Hoover, J. (2008). Response to intervention models and English language learners. In J. K. Klingner, J. Hoover, & L. Baca (Eds.), *Why do English language learners struggle with reading? Distinguishing language acquisition from learning disabilities?* (pp. 37–56). Thousand Oaks, CA: Corwin Press.

Knoff, H. M. (1983). Investigating the disproportionate influence and status of multidisciplinary child study teams. *Exceptional Children, 49*, 367–370.

Kovaleski, J. F., Tucker, J. A., Duffy, D. J., Jr., Lowery, P. E., & Gickling, E. E. (1995). School reform through instructional support: The Pennsylvania initiative. Part I: The instructional support team (IST) — Part II: Instructional evaluation. *Communique, IST-400; IST 1* (2).

Liu, K., Thurlow, M., Koo, H., & Barrera, M. (2008). *Middle school principals' perspectives on academic standards-based instruction and programming for English language learners with disabilities* (ELLs with Disabilities Report 22). Minneapolis: University of Minnesota, National Center on Educational Outcomes.

Marston, D., Lau, M., & Muyskens, P. (2007). Implementation of the problem-solving model in the Minneapolis public schools. In S. R. Jimerson, M. K. Burns, & A. M. VanDerHeyden (Eds.), *Handbook of response to intervention: The science and practice of assessment and intervention* (pp. 279–287). New York: Springer.

Marston, D., Muyskens, P., Lau, M., & Canter, A. (2003). Problem-solving for decision-making with high incidence disabilities: The Minneapolis experience. *Learning Disabilities Research and Practice, 18*, 187–200.

Martuszny, R., Banda, D., & Coleman, T. (2007). A progressive plan for building collaborative relationships with parents from diverse backgrounds. *Teaching Exceptional Children, 39*(4), 24–31.

McLeskey, J., Rosenberg, M. S., & Westling, D. L. (2010). *Inclusion: effective practices for all students*. Upper Saddle River, NJ: Pearson.

McGlothin, J. E. (1981). The school consultation committee: An approach to implementing a teacher consultation model. *Behavioral Disorders, 6*, 101-107.

Mehan, H., Hartwick, A., & Meihls, J. L. (1986). *Handicapping the handicapped: Decision-making in students' educational careers*. Stanford, CA: Stanford University Press.

Mellard, D. F., & Johnson, E. (2008). *RTI: A practitioner's guide to implementing response to intervention*. Thousand Oaks, CA: Corwin Press.

Moore, K. J., Fifield, M. B., Spira, D. A., & Scarlato, M. (1989). Child study team decision making in special education: Improving the process. *Remedial and Special Education, 10*, 50–58.

Movit, M., Petrykowska, I., & Woodruff, D. (2010, May). *Information brief: Using school leadership teams to meet the needs of English Language Learners*. Washington, DC: National Center on Response to Intervention.

Nelson, J. R., Smith, D. J., Taylor, L., Dodd, J. M., & Reavis, K. (1991). Prereferral intervention: A review of the research. *Education and Treatment of Children, 1*(4), 243-253.

Ochoa, S. H., González, D., Galarza, A., & Guillemard, L. (1996). The training and use of interpreters in bilingual psychoeducational assessment: An alternative in need of study. *Diagnostique, 21*(3), 19–22.

Ochoa, S. H., Powell, M. P., & Robles-Piña, R. (1996). School psychologists' assessment practices with bilingual and limited-English-proficient students. *Journal of Psychoeducational Assessment, 14,* 250–275.

Ochoa, S. H., Rivera, B. D., & Powell, M. P.(1997). Factors used to comply with the exclusionary clause with bilingual and limited-English-proficient pupils: Initial guidelines. *Learning Disabilities Research & Practice, 12,* 161–167.

Peterson, D. W., Prasse, D. P., Shinn, M. R., & Swerdlik, M. E. (2007). The Illinois flexible service delivery model: A problem-solving initiative. In S. R. Jimerson, M. K. Burns, & A. M. VanDerHeyden (Eds.), *Handbook of response to intervention: The science and practice of assessment and intervention* (pp. 300–318). New York: Springer.

Pugach, M., Johnson, L. J. (1988). *Peer collaboration: Enhancing teacher problem solving capabilities for students at risk.* Paper presented at the annual meeting of the American Research Associations. New Orleans. (ERIC Document reproduction service no. SP 030 114).

Rinaldi, C., Averill, O., & Estabrook, S. (2010, March). *Implementing a Response to Intervention Model with ELLS: An urban case study.* Research presented at TESOL's 44th Annual Convention, Boston, MA.

Rosenfield, S. A., & Gravois, T. A. (1996). *Instructional consultation teams: Collaborating for change.* New York: Guilford Press.

Spectrum K12. (2010). *RTI adoption report.* Retrieved June 4, 2010, from http://www.spectrumk12.com/rti/the_rti_corner/rti_adoption_report

Schwanz, K. A., & Barbour, C. B. (2005, June). Problem-solving teams: Information for educators and parents. *National Association of School Psychologists Communiqué, 33*(8).

Staum, M., & Ocampo, L. (2004). Case study: Optimizing success through problem solving. *Principal Leadership Magazine* (4). Retrieved June 3, 2010, from http://www.nasponline.org/resources/principals/nassp_probsolve.aspx

Thousand, J. S., Villa, R. A., & Nevin, A. I. (2007). *Differentiating instruction: Collaboratively planning and teaching for universally designed learning.* Thousand Oaks, CA: Corwin Press.

Truscott, S. D., Cohen, C. E., Sams, D. P., Sanborn, K. J., & Frank, A. J. (2005). The current state(s) of prereferral intervention teams: A report from two national surveys. *Remedial and Special Education, 26,* 130–140.

Tucker, J. A., & Sornson, R. O. (2007). One student at a time; one teacher at a time: Reflections on the use of instructional support. In S. R. Jimerson, M. K. Burns, & A. M. VanDerHeyden (Eds.), *Handbook of response to intervention: The science and practice of assessment and intervention* (pp. 269–278). New York: Springer.

VanDerHeyden, A. M., & Witt, J. C. (2005). Quantifying context in assessment: Capturing the effect of base rates on teacher referral and problem-solving model of identification. *School Psychology Review, 34,* 161–183.

Villa, R. A., & Thousand, J. S. (2005). *Creating an inclusive school* (2nd ed.). Alexandria, VA: Association for Supervision and Curriculum Development.

Walter-Thomas, C., Korinek, L., McLaughlin, V., & Williams, B. (2000). *Collaboration for inclusive education.* Boston: Allyn & Bacon.

Webb-Johnson, G. (2008, December). *Culturally responsive leadership: An ethnic imperative for staff development leaders and providers.* Presentation at the 40th Annual National Staff Development Council, Washington, DC.

Wilkinson, C., Ortiz, A., Robertson, P., & Kushner, M. (2006). English language learners with reading-related LD: Linking data from multiple sources to make eligibility decisions. *Journal of Learning Disabilities. 39,* 129–141.

Ysseldyke, J. E., Algozzine, B., Richey, L., & Graden, J. (1982). Declaring students eligible for learning disability services: Why bother with the data? *Learning Disability Quarterly, 5,* 37–44.

Zierkel, P. A., & Thomas, L. B. (2010). State laws for RTI: An updated snapshot. *Teaching Exceptional Children, 24*(3), 56–63.

12

Leadership and Collaboration in Home-School Partnerships

Beth Harry

UNIVERSITY OF MIAMI

Special education leaders must take their cue from the law. The Individuals with Disabilities Education Act (IDEA), in its 1997 and 2004 revisions, has intensified its requirements for the role of parents in the provision of special education services. School districts must ensure not only that caregivers receive all appropriate notices of meetings and reports but also that they understand the proceedings of individualized education program (IEP) conferences, have been provided with interpreters wherever necessary, have been consulted regarding the scheduling of such meetings, and have documented all efforts at these communications with parents.

These requirements reflect the high ideals of special education law; but can the law legislate truly collaborative practice? Clearly, the law can only provide for a basic floor of collaboration, leaving it to policy makers, professional organizations, and administrators themselves to infuse the spirit of the law into daily practice. Special education policy makers have not been tardy in working toward this goal. The Council for Exceptional Children (CEC), in conjunction with the Council of Administrators of Special Education (CASE), has developed and continued to revise The Professional Standards for Administrators of Special Education, which, as noted by Boscardin, Mainzer, and Kealey (2011), were first presented in 1998, then revised in 2003, and again in 2009. The 2003 and 2009 versions were published in *What Every Special Educator Must Know: Ethics, Standards, and Guidelines for Special Educators* (CEC, 2003, 2009). Boscardin et al., explained that the historical development of the field of special education administration—a composite of special education, general education, and educational administration—was "dominated by the assumptions, practices, and knowledge traditions of the discipline of special education" (p. 3). Thus, the need for a more inclusive vision led to the most recent revisions of the standards, resulting in a broader view of administrators' roles, which goes beyond the required basic skills related to instruction and emphasizes an additional level of skills at the school and district levels.

Based on a well-triangulated research methodology described by Boscardin, McCarthy, and Delgado (2009), the six CEC standards were revised to include: Leadership and Policy, Program Development and Organization, Research and Inquiry, Evaluation, Professional Development and Ethical Practice, and Collaboration. The latter standard, which is the focus of this chapter, specifies a set of knowledge and skill competencies whose language repeatedly emphasizes the idea of leadership for collaboration. As seen below, despite repeated use of the terms "families" and "all stakeholders," it is clear that the onus is on the leader to create these partnerships.

Knowledge:
1. Collaborative theories and practices that support the administration of programs and services for individuals with exceptional learning needs and their families.
2. Administrative theories and models that facilitate communication among all stakeholders.
3. Importance and relevance of advocacy at the local, state, and national level for individuals with exceptional learning needs and their families.

Skills:
1. Utilizes collaborative approaches for involving all stakeholders in educational planning, implementation, and evaluation.
2. Strengthens the role of parent and advocacy organizations as they support individuals with exceptional learning needs and their families.
3. Develops and implements intra- and interagency agreements that create programs with shared responsibility for individuals with exceptional learning needs and their families.
4. Facilitates transition plans for individuals with exceptional learning needs across the educational continuum and other programs from birth through adulthood.
5. Implements collaborative administrative procedures and strategies to facilitate communication among all stakeholders.
6. Engages in leadership practices that support shared decision making.
7. Demonstrates the skills necessary to provide ongoing communication, education, and support for families of individuals with exceptional learning needs.
8. Consults and collaborates in administrative and instructional decisions at the school and district levels.

This wide range of knowledge and skills seems to be a tall order. Indeed, in a survey of 240 special education administrators' self-ratings on the CEC standards, Wigle and Wilcox (2002) found that the administrators felt that they were not highly skilled in more than half of the (then current) CEC standards, assessment and collaboration being rated in the lowest quartile. As will be demonstrated below, however, no one practice stands on its own, and research on administrators' effectiveness in collaboration points to the interrelatedness of the six areas specified. In fact, Boscardin (2005) has argued that to be an effective special education leader, administrators really need to be well grounded in many aspects of special education and are envisioned as instructional leaders rather than mainly as managers.

This review is organized around two main questions: First, what is the meaning of collaboration and why is it so difficult to achieve? Second, what constitutes leadership for collaboration in this field and what are the challenges it faces in different service delivery contexts?

The Meaning of Collaboration

What constitutes collaboration? The history of the development of parent–professional collaboration in special education is interesting, and even the most critical view of its implementation must acknowledge the huge distance that the field has travelled since the beginnings of the parent advocacy movement after the Second World War. An article in the *American Journal on Mental Deficiency* in 1949 (Aldrich, 1947) prompts an appreciation of this journey. An obstetrician named Dr. Aldrich published an article entitled "Preventive medicine and the birth of a Mongolian idiot" in which he described a method of placing newborns with Down Syndrome into institutions. Not allowing the mother to see the infant, the doctor would inform the father and other key members of the family of the child's condition and would persuade them of the dire impact the presence of this child would have on the family. The mother would then be informed of the family's decision and the child whisked away to an institution. Dr. Aldrich claimed that his approach had failed in only 3 cases over the 14 years of his practice. The heartbreaking situation that grew out of this approach is well known and needs no elaboration here.

As the parent movement gradually made progress, culminating in the passage of the Education for All Handicapped Children's Act (EHA) in 1975, relationships between parents and professionals improved but went through many transformations. As described by Ferguson (2002), the range of professional views of parents included casting parents as neurotic, as victims, as dysfunctional, and as powerless. Finally, Ferguson argued, professionals have come to understand that what might appear as resistance by families is in reality a means of coping and adapting to the changing needs of their children.

The re-framing of requirements for parental participation in IDEA 1997 and 2004 has made the shift official. While both parts of the law call for collaborative processes, the requirements of Part C of IDEA have resulted in an explicit mandate for family centered practice. Perhaps most challenging is the recommendation in Part C that, "to the maximum extent appropriate to the needs of the child, early intervention services must be provided in natural environments, including the home and community settings in which children without disabilities participate" 34 CFR §303.12b (1999). The law further describes "natural environments" as "settings that are natural or normal for the child's age peers who have no disabilities" 34 CFR §303.18 (1999). However, the literature emerging on this requirement reflects a steady trend of concerns about resistance of therapists to accept the demands of this model, along with a list of logistical issues related to cost of these services, travel time, and doubts about whether providing services in the natural environment necessarily means that the services will be delivered in a family centered manner (Campbell & Sawyer, 2007).

Responding to the law's call for collaboration, early intervention scholars have spelled out key components of this concept, resulting in what Harry (2008) referred to an ideal yet elusive vision. Officially enshrined in the law, the notion of a family centered model has been supported fully by the field, and it has been almost two decades since Dunst, Johanson, Trivette, and Hamby (1991) offered a definition of family centered practice as "a combination of beliefs and practices that define particular ways of working with families that are consumer driven and competency enhancing" (p. 115). Detailed recommendations for what this should look like in practice have been offered by numerous leaders in the field (e.g., Dunst, Trivette, & Hamby, 2006; Turnbull, Turnbull, Erwin, Soodak, & Shogren, 2000).

The development of this vision has been supported by research efforts that have sought families' own definitions of effective collaboration (Blue-Banning, Summers, Frankland, Nelson, & Beegle, 2004; Dunst, 2002; Dinnebeil, Hale, & Rule, 1996; Summers, Hoffman, Marquis, Turnbull, and Poston, 2005). The latter research team, using a survey that included 137 families of widely ranging age, socioeconomic status and ethnicity, produced six main characteristics that parents identified as constituting effective collaboration: (a) positive, understandable, and respectful communication; (b) commitment to the child and family; (c) equal professional and parent power in decision-making and service implementation; (d) professional competence; (e) mutual trust; and (f) mutual respect. Based on these results, Summers et al. (2005) developed the Family-Professional Partnership Scale for assessing "parents' perceptions of the importance of, and their satisfaction with" (p. 65), their professional partnerships. Follow-up work by Summers et al. (2005) revealed that parental satisfaction varied significantly by age of child, with parents of younger children expressing greater satisfaction. The authors noted that one limitation to these findings continues to be the relatively low numbers of responses from families of diverse ethnicities and low income status.

An Elusive Vision

The vision of participation and collaboration with parents is elusive for several reasons, all of which are intensified in the case of families from culturally and linguistically diverse (CLD) backgrounds. Indeed, the low level of CLD parents' involvement is well known both in early intervention and in school age studies. For example, a survey by Griffith (1998) of parent and students perceptions regarding the effectiveness of school structures in 122 public elementary schools found that lower parent participation was associated with being of minority ethnicity, low socioeconomic status (SES), and having a child in special education or English as a Second Language programs. In early intervention, even allowing for five levels of engagement in a home visiting program, Wagner, Spiker, Linn, Gerlach-Downie, and Hernandez (2003) noted low engagement of Black and Latina mothers.

With regard to parental satisfaction, three reasons for difficulty in assessing this aspect are evident in the literature. First, it can be difficult to assess how satisfied parents really are because satisfaction is inherently subjective and depends totally on a comparison to one's expectations. Singer (2002) observed that while caregiver satisfaction should tell us much about the effectiveness of home-school collaboration, he also noted that parental satisfaction was often higher than researchers' expectations. This not uncommon observation has long been explained by several studies in terms of differing cultural norms for parent participation (Harry, 1992; Lai & Ishiyama, 2004; McNaughton, 1994; Meyers & Blacher, 1987). In discussing cultural differences, scholars such as Kalyanpur and Harry (1999) and Lynch and Hanson (2004) have emphasized that immigrant groups whose children would not have received services in their homelands may hold expectations much lower than what the field considers good practice. Another explanation is that parents who do not feel entitled or empowered may refrain from expressing dissatisfaction because of habits of deference to professionals. For example, in a study of the experiences of eight culturally diverse families Harry, Kalyanpur, and Day (1999) quoted a Dominican father of a boy with Down Syndrome who explained that when the school district informed the family that their son's placement would be changed to a school some 10 miles away, the family would not think of questioning the decision, since "they are the ones who know … If kids have to be moved to another school, one can't be opposed" (p. 195).

Second, as Kalyanpur and Harry (1999) have argued at length, special education services continue to be premised on a model of delivery of services by expert professionals. Teachers and all other service providers undergo extensive training that teaches them skills that are presumably beyond the reach of the average parent. Moving from this model to one of collaboration is difficult because most professionals have been taught that *they* have the answers. Programs that effectively teach practitioners to develop a critical view of their own practice and as well as collaborative skills based on genuine mutual respect are either rare or not well documented (Fults & Harry, 2011).

A third reason that the vision of collaboration is elusive is that professionals may have difficulty distinguishing between being friendly with parents and sharing power with parents. This relates to the foregoing point about professional enculturation. Dunst and colleagues (2006) made this point powerfully as they distinguished between relational and participatory practices, pointing out that service providers may create respectful and friendly relationships with caregivers yet fail to include them in making decisions about services.

Of course, it is not only early interventionists that have called for high quality parent-professional collaboration, and several scholars have specified particular areas for attention. For example, Harry (1992) spelled out specific steps needed to restructure the balance of power in IEP meetings between professionals and African American parents; Argus-Calvo, Tafoya, and Grupp (2005) emphasized the need for parental collaboration in the implementation of prereferral practices; and Osher and Osher (2002) advocated a "paradigm shift" to "family driven" approaches that place the real power in the hands of parents. Turnbull et al.'s (2010) classic text, now in its sixth edition has consistently presented an ideal model of collaboration both for IEP and IFSP development.

Leadership and Collaboration in Differing Service-Delivery Contexts

Is it the absence of leadership that supports the continuing discrepancy between a vision of collaboration and its effective implementation? How do varying contexts of service-delivery affect the development of home-school partnerships?

First, we must ask who the leaders are that would be responsible for promoting, supporting, and ensuring collaborative practices with parents. The answer to this varies with the type and level of the program. In Early Intervention, services may include center-based programs, home visiting programs, parent-as-teacher (PAT) programs, and interagency collaboration with other agencies that include but do not necessarily focus on serving children with disabilities, such as Head Start or Early Head Start. However, the answer to who administers these programs varies widely, ranging from Early Childhood program directors to elementary school principals. Early childhood programs falling under Part B of the law may be housed in varying locations and be directed by a range of administrative leaders. This is an important distinction since, in elementary education, special education leadership generally falls to the building administrators, who may or may not be special educators by training.

A search of literature based on the key words—administration, parents, collaboration, and special education, produced literature mainly from Early Intervention (EI) and Early Childhood Special Education (ECSE) programs. This is not surprising since the greatest concern regarding collaboration is generated by Part C of IDEA and research has shown that parental participation in special education program planning decreases with the age of the child and severity of the child's disability (Hernandez, Harry, Newman, & Cameto, 2008) as does satisfaction with services (McWilliam et al., 1995; Summers et al., 2005). I will discuss the findings of this literature first and will then turn to literature on school-age programs.

Leadership for Collaboration in Early Intervention Programs

Studies of collaboration in early intervention have been careful to specify the components of collaborative partnerships between professionals and family members. Analyses of these components have resulted in a helpful distinction between interpersonal relationships in collaboration and organizational factors that help or hinder collaborative efforts (Dinnebeil, Hale, & Rule, 1999; Park & Turnbull, 2003). Building on this base, Dinnebeil et al., conducted a survey that resulted in responses from 397 parents and 226 service coordinators from across the nation. Once more, the caveat must be made that the 76% of the respondents were White and 94% were high school graduates. Further, the authors pointed out other limitations, including possible coding biases and the fact that respondents tended to focus on personal qualities of service providers rather than administrative components per se. Nevertheless, the study revealed five categories of organizational influences on collaboration: (a) program climate and philosophy—whether or not there was a true commitment to collaboration; (b) available service delivery options, such as home visits, provision of resources and transportation, one-to-one versus group therapy, as well as whether families were fully informed of the range of options; (c) effective structures for teaming, such as appropriate scheduling and sharing of resources and information; (d) administrative policies and practices, such as flexibility, training opportunities, supervision of service providers, monetary support, and good hiring decisions, and (e), community context, such as funding, relationships with other agencies, external bureaucratic demands, and the scheduling of contracted service providers.

Further study by Epley et al. (2010) focused on three "administrative structures ... an agency's leadership and vision, organizational climate, and resources ... the general operating processes that enable the staff to deliver services in a way that embodies recommended practices" (p. 20). Furthering the work of Dinnebeil et al (1999), these researchers asked what factors influence administrative structures, and how these structures affect services to families. Using a case-study methodology, Epley et al., compared the practices of two EI (birth to 3) sites that utilized a home visiting model and provided services to diverse children and their families. While both were in the same Midwest state and had the state department of health as the lead agency, the local contexts for the programs were very different, one being located within a larger metropolitan area and the other serving multiple rural communities across 12 counties. The former program fell within the purview of the local school district while the latter was a community-based, not-for-profit child development center. Using focus groups, individual interviews, and home observations, the study sought to identify the factors influencing the three administrative structures.

The study by Epley et al. (2010) was particularly instructive because of the nuanced interpretations of the data, showing how complex are the needs of programs seeking to be truly family centered and collaborative. For example, in the two very different programs studied, contrasting strengths and limitations of leaders' visions emerged: In the program with a PAT orientation, a pervasive vision of inclusive home-based services was inspiring to service providers, but the lack of special education training on the part of the director impeded the implementation of evidence-based practices such as routine-based interventions. In the community-based program, a director who was committed to evidence-based EI practices had difficulty monitoring the fidelity of implementation of these field-based practices. Aspects of organizational climate that affected these programs included opportunities for collaboration among the service providers and gaining a balance between service providers' autonomy and accountability. Resources also proved very important, with the not-for-profit agency having more flexibility to access funds and make administrative decisions than did the program that was based in the school district. A problem of equity and transparency arose here as providers would make under the table provisions that they felt were needed but were not officially sanctioned by the budget, such as hiring a parent to work as a family support specialist. In both programs documentation of services seemed to be a challenge but for very different reasons: In the school district program there was a fear of documenting the ad hoc decisions and in the agency program there seemed to be an aversion to excessive paperwork. Overall, the study revealed the complexity of balancing vision and specialized knowledge, accountability and autonomy, and adequate and flexible resources.

Leadership for Collaboration in Pre-School Programs

Issues of leadership may be somewhat different in inclusive pre-school programs as compared to community based, early intervention services. Several studies have highlighted the importance of administrative influences, especially principals, on such programs (Buysse, Wesley, & Keyes, 1998; Lieber et al., 1997, 2000).

Furthering this line of work, a study by Brotherson, Sheriff, Milburn, and Schertz (2001) focused on the role of elementary school principals in effecting inclusion programs in their schools. These researchers emphasized the role of the principal because he/she is often the designated district representative at IEP meetings. In this study, the views of 694 principals in the state of Iowa pointed to the considerable frustration they felt in being expected to direct Early Childhood programs. While the principals expressed support for the principles of inclusion, they tended to see the challenges as being beyond their purview. Six main themes emerged, indicating that principals were concerned about: (a) the large numbers of children needing services; (b) the lack of adequate personnel; (c) the lack of adequate funding, space, logistical problems, and incompatibility of regulations among EC programs; (d) the need for more preventive and earlier support to families; (e) the need for greater inter-agency collaboration, and (f) the principals' own need for training. The researchers concluded that the principals did not see the need for greater agency on their own parts and tended to see the increasing demand for services as a trend that could be prevented by earlier intervention and family support, but did not hold a family-centered approach as appropriate to their roles. Overall, the main point that emerged was that the principals did not see EC programs as a natural part of their range of responsibility. Rather, they felt that this was an unreasonable stretch for them as a result of which they tended to rely on their EC teachers for knowledge of appropriate practices. Pianta, Cox, Taylor, and Early (1999) found similar concerns expressed by kindergarten teachers, for example, that there was a lack of transition planning and that principals paid inadequate attention to scheduling issues that included summer programming.

The dilemma faced by elementary school principals supervising these programs is understandable. As Marvin, LaCost, Grady, and Mooney (2003) observed in their study of state mandated programs in Nebraska, state mandates for early childhood programs have "forced school districts to redefine their mission" (p. 218). Citing Brotherson et al. (2001), these authors pointed out that principals have not historically been accustomed to having responsibility for such programs and may not be prepared either for the content of the programs or for the kind of supervision needed by programs that involve families and also other agencies.

The study by Marvin et al. (2003) revealed that in these programs elementary principals may be responsible but other administrators may be too. In a small state such as Nebraska, projects are often cooperative ventures across districts, which requires EC administrators to "take on the role of program coordinator, special education director, or project supervisor, working out of regional educational service unites or in cooperation with local elementary principals of schools where programs may be housed" (p. 219). The state department's awareness of the challenges facing project directors was evidenced by the fact that this research grew out of a state-funded project to enhance public school administrators' knowledge of EC programs for zero to five. The purpose of the study was to ascertain EC teachers' perceptions of administrative support: 176 surveys returned (56%) by ECSE and other EC teachers: half were administered by school principals, roughly other half were directors of the EC programs either on or off-site. Nearly two thirds reported that administrators relied on teachers' expertise for decisions but the majority did state that administrators were supportive of their work. Overall, there was considerable satisfaction with immediate supervisors but there was also an expressed need for more professional development for administrators, such as ensuring space, hiring qualified EC personnel, supporting inclusionary practices, providing assessment tools that are appropriate for EC practices; supporting collaboration between kindergarten and pre-k teachers especially regarding children's transitions; and figuring out how to supervise staff who are providing community based services. Finding that administrators who were not principals were more likely to be flexible in scheduling, the researchers interpreted this as indicating that principals may see EC program needs as conflicting with other building needs.

Kaczmarek, Goldstein, Florey, Carter, and Cannon (2004) conducted a study that shed an interesting light on the question of the stressors experienced by principals. These researchers evaluated a preschool model that used parents of children with disabilities as family consultants (FCs) whose responsibility was to "augment the support provided by classroom professionals" (p. 214). As paraprofessionals, the FCs acted as a "liaison between families and professional staff, the agency, and the broader community" (214). The building administrators were very supportive of the program, to the extent that midway through the project they requested expansion of the program to other sites and agreed to provide for more such support. Their willing support of the project echoes concerns in the study by Marvin et al. (2003) about supervision and accountability of community based services since it highlights the principals' need for personnel who could attend to the community or home-based needs of families of young children with disabilities—a range of needs that cannot simply be met in a center-based program and which principals are ill equipped to supervise and sustain.

Marvin et al. (2003) emphasized the need for the provision of professional development for administrators, certification programs for EC administrators, opportunities for networking with community agencies, coordination of staff development, space, supplies, and curricula between EC and K teachers. This very detailed and informative study concluded that, "Quality EC programs need personnel who can provide program management and leadership, inspiration, and knowledge of recommended practices, laws, and child development" (p. 228).

As noted at the beginning of this chapter, the wide range of knowledge and skills needed by special education administrators points to the challenge inherent in the trans-disciplinary model espoused by early intervention. This becomes even more notable in studies that directly address inter-agency collaboration in Early Intervention. For example, in studying the components that make for effective service integration between Part C programs and Early Head Start programs, Summers et al. (2001) surveyed the perceptions of staff and families served by six local EHS programs and Part C agencies in five states. While this study focused more on interagency collaboration than on collaboration with parents per se, certain management issues were seen to affect parents, such as the effects of staff turnover on the continuity of relationships with providers, parents having to serve as the communication bridge or middle-man" between service providers, and communication regarding children's transitions.

In sum, the EI literature suggests that leadership in programs for children from birth through kindergarten is most effective when program administrators have the special education program as their focal responsibility. Elementary school principals, regardless of their individual philosophical persuasions, are often either not prepared for, or sensitized to the needs of pre-school programs and the types of administrative structures that such programs demand. Further, expecting them to meet the widely varying needs of pre-school and school-age populations may be demanding just too much.

Leadership for Collaboration in School-Age Programs

Turning to how the foregoing issues might apply to special education programs within age 6 to 21 schooling, it is instructive to note the language of Epstein (2001), a leading voice in school-family partnerships, who has argued that schools must create intentional structures for collaboration. In special education, one would think that these intentional structures should be in place, given the requirement for parent conferences around IEP development and implementation and given the legal requirement for the presence of a representative of the school district (usually interpreted as a building administrator) at IEP meetings. There is no dearth of literature on models for accomplishing such collaboration, yet studies do not show that these intentional structures result in true collaboration.

Overall, the literature on public schooling is not as abundant or as clear cut as is the EI literature, since studies focusing on parent-professional collaboration in school age programs have not paid much direct attention to the effects of leadership. Apart from a few studies that have included such a focus, information on this topic tends to be more embedded in study of broader issues. Looking for administrator roles in home-school special education collaboration means seeking information on the roles of building principals in general education as well, since the placement process is really a continuum along which key decisions and practices can make a difference to whether a child will be determined eligible for special education services. This means examining pre-referral and placement processes such as Child Study Teams or IEP meetings, as well as administrators' roles in supporting or requiring effective school to home communication around the progress of children already served by special education. For the most part, studies focusing on decision-making processes regarding special education reveal that the most influential role is played by the assessor—usually a psychologist—and that the manner of conducting assessments for placement is far from collaborative with parents or with teachers and other school personnel (Harry, Klingner, Sturges, & Moore, 2002; Knotek, 2003; Mehan, Hartwick, & Meihls, 1986).

Reports from an ethnographic study by Harry and Klingner (2006) and Klingner, Harry, and Felton (2003) of the processes by which Black and Hispanic students were placed in special education programs revealed a host of problems that contributed to inappropriate placement, including weak school leadership. First, district-based special education superintendents and senior administrators had little to do with the assignment of principals to elementary schools and there seemed to be no particular attention paid to considering the special education preparation of building administrators. Indeed, assignment of principals to schools seemed almost whimsical, as indicated by a practice that allowed the district superintendent to recommend candidates for the principal positions, and a pattern of dramatic turnover—up to as many as four principals in 12 years—especially in the lowest performing schools.

Further, it was clear that children of color in the highest poverty neighborhoods were placed at increased risk of special education placement by administrative decisions such as assignment of the weakest teachers to the weakest students and overloaded scheduling by which a host of overlapping or competing programs were adopted within a school. The latter situation caused one teacher to exclaim: "We're the ones who make them [the children] hyper!" (Harry & Klingner, p. 36). With regard to collaboration with parents, the data revealed a clear cut pattern of pervasive negativity toward those parents living in poverty and an explicit assumption that the children's difficulties or disabilities "came from the home" (p. 71).

Another aspect of administration policy that impacted collaboration in this study was the question of parental presence in the school. School policies on this varied widely, depending totally on the principal. In one school serving a low income, African American population, parents expressed great dissatisfaction at the decision of a new principal, herself African American, to require parents to go to the front office and make an appointment to visit their child's classroom. This was the opposite of the previous principal's open-door policy. The most exemplary teacher in this small school, an African American woman who had been there for 13 years, was as incensed by this as were the parents and she simply ignored the policy telling the parents they could come in whenever they wanted. This teacher was committed to anticipating and addressing children's learning and behavioral difficulties in proactive ways to prevent their referral to special education and considered her relationships with parents a central part of this process.

Like the kindergarten teacher above, there were other personnel in this study whose personal relationships with family members contrasted with administrative policies that undermined collaboration. Indeed, perhaps the most effective collaboration noted was effected by community liaison workers in two schools, who were hired with Title One funds for the purpose of encouraging parent participation in school-based meetings such as Child Study teams or IEP meetings. Because these personnel had the trust of the community and respected the parents, they were able to achieve close to 100% attendance at IEP and Child Study Team meetings. This pattern is reminiscent of a study of an urban school district that developed a structured home liaison program that featured conflict resolution, cultural brokering and direct support to parents (Howland, Anderson, Smiley, & Abbott, 2006).

In Harry and Klingner's (2006) study, occasional effective leadership was noted in the case of a few individual school leaders. Against a backdrop of generally negative attitudes and behaviors displayed at IEP or Child Study Team meetings, a powerful contrast was presented by these few administrators who did participate or intervene to affect decisions regarding pre-referral interventions or placement outcomes. For example, an assistant principal in a school serving a very poor, predominantly Black neighborhood, stood out in her support of parent perspectives at these meetings, and in one case, actually went against the grading and communication practices of a second grade classroom teacher who argued that she would not send children's weekly work folders home because she didn't think the parents would send them back. In two other schools, it was the school counselor who stood out as advocates for parent perspectives, while the building administrators were seldom present or would stop by mainly to sign their line on the required paperwork. In no school did the researchers observe collaboration between psychologists and parents.

A strong body of research on attitudes toward families of culturally and linguistically diverse students in special education underscores the findings of Harry and Klingner (2006), but these studies do not give much information on the role of administrators in the ineffective collaboration. For example, a line of research on 250 Mexican and Puerto Rican mothers' perspectives highlighted issues of cultural discrimination and alienation (Bailey, Skinner, Correa, et al., 1999; Bailey, Skinner, Rodriguez, Gut, & Correa, 1999; McHatton & Correa, 2005). Similarly, Knotek's (2003) powerful ethnographic study of the placement process reported non-collaborative and prejudicial processes in placing Black children referred for special education, but none of these studies specified the roles of administrators.

Collaboration within Increasingly Inclusive Models of Education

Over the past decade, the emerging requirements for more inclusive models and greater accountability in public schools has meant a re-visioning of the role of special education leaders.

In 2003, Lashley and Boscardin (2003) described special education administration as being at a "crossroads" at which the traditional emphasis on special education knowledge needed to be complemented by extensive knowledge of general education. Since that time, the law's call for students to be served in general education settings at least 80% of the time has made this challenge even greater. Inclusive placements require not only increased skill in assessment, data monitoring, and differentiated instruction, but also in collaboration with families, since the entire assessment and placement process should be based on collaborative efforts.

One specific aspect of these shifting roles arises with regard to the increasing implementation of tiered models of instruction and assessment, generally subsumed under the rubric of Response to Intervention (RTI), which should provide strong support for collaboration with parents. RTI models so far, however, do not specifically state what the role of administrators would be. For example, a joint paper by the National Association of State Directors of Special Education and the Council of Administrators in Special Education (2006) refers to the need for integrated, coordinated assessments and services but does not specifically mention parents or collaboration outside of RTI team processes.

Regardless of which model is used, a key caveat regarding inclusion is the fact that inclusive practice continues to lie in the shadow of the disproportionately high placement of students of color in high incidence disability categories, and in unduly restrictive placements of such students (Donovan & Cross, 2002; Fierros & Conroy, 2002). This decades-old pattern, along with the steady line of research (cited above) showing the impact of negative stereotyping on parent-professional collaboration, points to the need for explicit policy language related to diversity.

This aspect of inclusive practice has intense implications for administrators, yet appears to be weakly represented in the new Administrator of Special Education standards cited at the beginning of this chapter (CEC, 2009). The term "diversity" is mentioned twice in the standards, both times in relation to the need for a knowledge base regarding the impact of diversity on educational expectations and programming (see Boscardin et al., 2009). While this is important, no direct reference to diversity appears in the collaboration standard and there is no explicit call for skills related to the challenge of crossing borders of racial, cultural, language, or social class diversity. Of course, such values are implicit in the use of inclusive terms such as "all stakeholders" and in the general tenor of the competencies listed. However, scholars who have investigated the skills needed by educators (for example, Kalyanpur & Harry, 1999; Trent, Kea, & Oh, 2008) typically emphasize the need for explicit attention to diversity, if only because professionals are often unaware of the depth of their prejudices and the ways in which negative stereotyping affects their decisions about children and families. With specific regard to administrators, the need for well practiced skills in this area has been noted by Voltz and Collins (2010), who argued that current needs include specific attention to issues such as administrators using effective teacher recruitment and retention strategies for high need schools, as well as induction strategies that will strengthen the skills and attitudes of new teachers in working with a diverse range of families. Certainly, leaders who are effective "border-crossers" are needed as models for other professionals.

Conclusion

This review might leave the reader feeling as if special education leaders might need a magic wand in order to bring about effective home-school collaboration in their programs. There is no doubt that a tremendous range of skills is needed. Marvin et al. (2003) summarized key administrative characteristics as "listening to staff member concerns, establishing a shared vision among staff and families, acknowledging the abilities of staff members; providing appropriate resources for staff planning and training and for networking with community agencies" (p. 218). This list reflects interpersonal process and organizational knowledge and skills but does not mention the special education expertise of the leader. The summary by Epley et al. (2010) offers a more comprehensive view, specifying leadership and vision, organizational climate, and resources, and seems to subsume disciplinary knowledge within the concept of leadership. This study concluded that size, location and "administrative home" of the program influenced the effects of the leaders' vision, organizational climate and resources. Clearly, if resources are a key part of effective leadership, then special education leaders must be skilled not only in interpersonal and organizational matters but in creative and persistent methods of securing and extending economic, human, and logistical resources.

Beyond these abilities, special education leaders' values, knowledge, and interpersonal skills must rise to the multicultural climate of our times. Voltz and Collins (2010) and Boscardin, Brown-Chidsey, and Gonzalez-Martinez (2001), have emphasized the need for these leaders to have a keen understanding of culturally responsive practices. It is here that I believe the greatest challenge lies. The chasm that has come to be seen as marking two Americas is nowhere so evident as in education. Although special education represents one of the nation's most powerful civil rights movements, the separate structuring of special and general education has extended rather than diminished the stigmatizing of students with learning or developmental difficulties, and the overrepresentation of poor and minority students in these programs has continued to undermine the field's goal of equity. Families of such children have continued to be marginalized by the pervasive negativity that sustains racial and class-based prejudices. While it is clear that individual service providers, whether in birth to three, pre-school, or school age programs, can make tremendous positive contributions to families' empowerment, individual provisions are inherently limited if they are not supported by a clear vision of and commitment to equity, deep-seated knowledge of evidence based special education practices, effective organizational structures, and an ability to garner and sustain adequate resources.

References

Aldrich, C. A. (1947). Preventive medicine and mongolism. *American Journal of Mental Deficiency, 69*, 391–401.

Argus-Calvo, B., Tafoya, N., & Grupp, L. (2005). Pre-referral: A time to empower culturally and linguistically diverse families through a culturally sensitive approach. *Multiple Voices for Ethnically Diverse Exceptional Learners, 8*(1), 71–83.

Bailey, D., Skinner, D., Rodriguez, P., Gut, D., & Correa, V. (1999). Awareness, use, and satisfaction with services for Latino parents of young children with disabilities. *Exceptional Children, 65*, 376–381.

Bailey, D. B., Skinner, D., Correa, V., Arcia, E., Reyes-Blanes, M., Rodriguez, P., et al. (1999). Needs and supports reported by Latino families of young children with developmental disabilities. *American Journal on Mental Retardation, 104*(5), 437–451.

Blue-Banning, M., Summers, J. A., Frankland, H. C., Nelson, L. L., & Beegle, G. (2004). Dimensions of family and professional partnerships: Constructive guidelines for collaboration. *Council for Exceptional Children, 70*(2), 167–184.

Boscardin, M. L. (2005). The administrative role in transforming secondary schools to support inclusive evidence-based practices. *American Secondary Education, 33*(3), 21–32.

Boscardin, M. L., Brown-Chidsey, R., & Gonzalez-Martinez, J. C. (2001). The essential link for students with disabilities from diverse backgrounds: Forging partnerships with families. *Journal of Special Education Leadership, 14*, 89–95.

Boscardin, M. L., Mainzer, R., & Kealy, M. V. (2011). Commentary: A response to preparing special education administrators for inclusion in diverse, standards-based contexts. *Teacher Education and Special Education, 34*(1), 71–78.

Boscardin, M. L., McCarthy, E., & Delgado, R. (2009). An integrated research-based approach to creating standards for special education leadership. *Journal of Special Education Leadership, 22*(2), 68–84.

Brotherson, M. J., Sheriff, G., Milburn, P., & Schertz, M. (2001). Elementary school principals and their needs and issues for inclusive early childhood programs. *Topics in Early Childhood Special Education, 21*(1), 31–45.

Buysse, V., Wesley, P., & Keyes, L. (1998). Implementing early childhood inclusion: Barrier and support factors. *Early Childhood Research Quarterly, 13*(1), 169-184.

Campbell, P., & Sawyer, L. B. (2007). Supporting learning opportunities in natural settings through participation-based services. *Journal of Early Intervention, 29*(4), 287–305.

Council for Exceptional Children. (2003). *What every special educator must know: Ethics, standards, and guidelines for special educators.* Arlington, VA: Author.

Council for Exceptional Children. (2009). *What every special educator must know: Ethics, standards, and guidelines for special educators.* Arlington, VA: Author.

Dinnebeil, L. A., & Hale, L. M., & Rule, S. (1996). A qualitative analysis of parents' and service coordinators' descriptions of variables that influence collaborative relationships. *Topics in Early Childhood Special Education, 16*(3), 322–347.

Donovan, M. S., & Cross, C. T. (2002). *Minority students in special and gifted education.* Washington, DC: National Research Council.

Dunst, C. J. (2002). Family-centered practices: Birth through high school. *The Journal of Special Education, 36*(3), 139–147.

Dunst, C. J., Johanson, C., Trivette, C. M., & Hamby, D. (1991). Family oriented early intervention policies and practices: Family-centered ornot? *Exceptional Children, 58*, 115–126.

Dunst C. J., Trivette C. M., & Hamby D. W. (2006). *Family support program quality and parent, family and child benefits.* Asheville, NC: Winterberry Press.

Education for All Handicapped Children Act, 20 U.S.C. §1400 et seq. (1975).

Epley, P., Gotto, G., Summers, J., Brotherson, M., Turnbull, A., & Friend A. (2010).Supporting families of young children with disabilities: Examining the role of administrative structures. *Topics in Early Childhood Special Education* [serial online], *30*(1), 20–31.

Epstein, J. L. (2001). *School, family, and community partnerships: Preparing educators and improving schools.* Boulder, CO: Westview Press.

Ferguson, P. M. (2002). A place in the family: An historical interpretation of research on parental reactions to having a child with a disability. *The Journal of Special Education, 36*(3), 124–130.

Fierros, G. E., & Conroy, J. W. (2002). Double jeopardy: An exploration of restrictiveness and race in special education. In D. J. Losen & G. Orfield (Eds.), *Racial inequity in special education* (pp. 39-70). Boston, MA: Harvard Education Press.

Fults, R., & Harry, B. (2011, June). Combining family centeredness and diversity in early childhood teacher training programs. *Teacher Education and Special Education: The Journal of the Council for Exceptional Children.* Retrieved from http://tes.sagepub.com/content/early/2011/06/04/0888406411399784

Griffith, J. (1998). The relation of school structure and social environment to parent involvement in elementary schools. *The Elementary School Journal, 99*(1), 53–80.

Harry, B. (2008). Family-professional collaboration with culturally and linguistically diverse families: Ideal vs. reality. *Exceptional Children, 72*(3), 372-388.

Howland, A., Anderson, J., Smiley, A., & Abbott, D. (2006). School liaisons: Bridging the gap between home and school. *The Journal of Special Education, 37*(1), 2–14.

Harry, B., Kalyanpur, M., & Day, M. (1999). *Building cultural reciprocity with families: Case studies in special education.* Baltimore, MD: Brookes.

Harry, B., & Klingner, J. (2006). *Why are so many minority students in special education? Understanding race and disability in schools.* New York: Teachers College Press.

Harry, B., Klingner, J., Sturges, K., & Moore, B. (2002). Of rocks and soft places: Using qualitative methods to investigate the processes that result in disproportionality. In D. Losen & G. Orfield (Eds.). *Issues in the disproportionate placement of minorities in special education* (pp. 71-92). Boston, MA: Harvard Publishing Group.

Hernandez, J. E., Harry, B., Newman, L., & Cameto, R. (2008). Survey of family involvement in and satisfaction with the Los Angeles Unified School District special education processes. *Journal of Special Education Leadership, 21*(2), 84–93.

Howland, A., Anderson, J., Smiley, A., & Abbott, D. (2006). School liaisons: Bridging the gap between home and shcool. *The School Community Journal, 16*(2), 47–68.

Individuals with Disabilities Education Act, 20 U.S.C. §1400 et seq. (1997).

Individuals with Disabilities Education Improvement Act , 20 U.S.C. §1400 et seq. (2004).

Kaczmarek, L. A., Goldstein, H., Florey, J. D., Carter, A., & Cannon, S. (2004). Supporting families: A preschool model. *Topics in Early Childhood Special Education, 24*(4), 213–226.

Kalyanpur, M., & Harry, B. (1999). *Culture in special education: Building reciprocal family-professional relationships.* Baltimore, MD: Brookes.

Klingner, J. K., Harry, B., & Felton, R. (2003). Understanding factors that contribute to disproportionality: Administrative hiring decisions. *Journal of Special Education Leadership, 16*(1), 23–33.

Knotek, S. (2003). Bias in problem-solving and the social process of student study teams: A qualitative investigation. *The Journal of Special Education 37*(1), 2–14.

Lai, Y., & Ishiyama, F. I. (2004). Involvement of immigrant Chinese Canadian mothers of children with disabilities. *Exceptional Children, 71*(1), 97–108.

Lashley, C., & Boscardin, M. L. (2003). Special education administration at a crossroads. *Journal of Special Education Leadership, 16*, 63–75.

Lieber, J. A., Beckman, P. J., Hanson, M. J., Janko, S., Marquart, J. M., Horn, E. M., et al. (1997). The impact of changing roles on relationships between adults in inclusive programs for young children. *Early Education and Development, 8,* 67-72.

Lieber, J. A., Hanson, M. J., Beckman, P. J., Odom, S. L., Sandall, S., Schwartz, I., et al. (2000). Key influences on the initiation and implementation of inclusive preschool programs. *Exceptional Children, 67*(1), 83–98.

Lynch, E. W., & Hanson, M. J. (2004). *Developing cross-cultural competence: A guide for working with children and their families (3rd ed.).* Baltimore, MD: Brookes.

Marvin, C., LaCost, B., Grady, M., & Mooney, P. (2003). Administrative support and challenges in Nebraska Public School Early Childhood Programs. Preliminary study. *Topics in Early Childhood Special Education, 23*(4), 217–228.

McWilliam, R. A. Lange, L., Vandivere, P., Angell, R., Collins, L., & Underdown, G. (1995). Satisfaction and struggles: Family perceptions and early intervention services. *Journal of Early Intervention, 19*(1), 43–60.

McHatton, P. A., & Correa, V. (2005). Stigma and discrimination: Perspectives from Mexican and Puerto Rican mothers of children with special needs. *Topics in Early Childhood Special Education, 25*(3), 131–142.

McNaughton, D. (1994). Measuring parent satisfaction with early childhood interventions programs: Current practice, problems, and future perspectives. *Topics in Early Childhood Special Education, 14*(1), 26–48.

Mehan, H., Hartwick, A., & Meihls, J. L. (1986). *Handicapping the handicapped: Decision-making in students' educational careers.* Stanford, CA: Stanford University Press.

Meyers. C. E., & Blacher, J. (1987). Parents' perceptions of schooling for severely handicapped children: Home and family variables. *Exceptional Children, 53*, 441–449.

National Association of State Directors of Special Education and the Council of Administrators of Special Education. (2006). *A joint paper on Response to Intervention.* Retrieved February 17, 2012. http://www.opi.mt.gov/pdf/SpecED/Training/RTl/RtI_AdminPersp.pdf

Osher, T. W., & Osher, D. M. (2002). The paradigm shift to true collaboration with families. *Journal of Child and Family Studies, 11*(1), 47–60.

Park, J., & Turnbull, A. P. (2003). Service integration in early intervention: Determining interpersonal and structural factors for its success. *Infants and Young Children, 16*(1), 48–58.

Pianta, R., Cox, M., Taylor, L., & Early, D. (1999). Kindergarten teachers' practices related to the transition to school. Results of a national survey. *Elementary School Journal, 100*(1), 71–86.

Singer, G. H. S. (2002). Suggestions for a pragmatic program of research on families and disability. *The Journal of Special Education, 36*(3), 148–154.

Summers, J. A., Hoffman, L., Marquis, J., Turnbull, A., & Poston, D. (2005). Relationship between parent satisfaction regarding partnerships with professionals and age of child. *Topics in Early Childhood Special Education, 25*(1), 48–58.

Summers, J. A., Hoffman, L., Marquis, J., Turnbull, A., Poston, D., & Nelson, L. L. (2005). Measuring the quality of family-professional partnerships in special education services. *Exceptional Children, 72*(1), 65–81.

Summers, J. A., Steeples, T., Peterson, C. Naig, L., McBride, S., Wall, S., Liebow, H., et al. (2001). Policy and management supports for effective service integration in Early Head Start and Part C programs. *Topics in Early Childhood Special Education, 21*(1), 16–30.

Trent, S. C., Kea, C. D., & Oh, K. (2008). Preparing pre-service educators for cultural diversity: How far have we come? *Exceptional Children, 74*, 328–350.

Turnbull, A., Turnbull, H. R., Erwin, E. J., Soodak, l. C., & Shogren, K. A. (2010). *Families, professionals, and exceptionality: Positive outcomes through partnerships and trust.* Upper Saddle River, NJ: Prentice Hall.

Voltz, D. L., & Collins, L. (2010). Preparing special education administrators for inclusion in diverse, standards-based contexts: Beyond the Council for Exceptional Children and the Interstate School Leaders Licensure Consortium. *Teacher Education and Special Education 33*(1), 70–82.

Wagner, M., Spiker, D., Linn, M., Gerlach-Downie, S., & Hernandez, F. (2003). Dimensions of parental engagement in home visiting programs: Exploratory study. *Topics in Early Childhood Special Education, 23*(4), 171–183.

Wigle, S. B., & Wilcox, D. J. (2002). Special education directors and their competencies on CEC-identified skills. *Education, 123*, 276–288.

13

Building Trust and Responding to Conflict in Special Education

Barbara J. Lake

VIRGINIA TECH

Art Stewart

VIRGINIA DEPARTMENT OF EDUCATION

An under-researched but critical area of study for special education leaders is conflict and conflict resolution. Collectively, school districts across the United States are spending more than $90 million per year in conflict resolution (Mueller, 2009). Due to its costly nature (both in terms of financial costs as well as emotional costs), it is important to understand the specific complexities that accompany special education conflicts. Stakeholders have vested interests in resolving conflicts as economically and as expeditiously as possible; however, data indicate that few of the stakeholders (parents, special educators, and school administrators) have had formal or sufficient training in understanding and responding to conflict (Schrag & Schrag, 2004). While research in special education conflict resolution is limited (Lake & Billingsley, 2002; Mueller, 2009; Nowell & Salem, 2007; Reiman et al., 2007; Schrag & Schrag, 2004), there is robust dialogue conducted in on-line environments, at conferences, and in trainings focused on enhancing practice and effectiveness in resolving special education disputes. There is mounting concern for the prevention of relationship-damaging conflict as well as careful handling of conflicts to preserve present and future parent-school relationships. Developing and protecting collaborative working relationships between parents and school personnel have been identified as key elements in the success of special education programs, leading to improvement in educational outcomes (Nowell & Salem, 2007).

Five major areas appear to constitute about 70% of the dispute resolution cases in the special education dispute resolution databases (Schrag & Schrag, 2004). The five categories are: (a) Individualized Educational Plans (IEP's), (b) Placement, (c) Free and Appropriate Public Education (FAPE), (d) Identification and Evaluation, and (e) Multiple Issues. Disputes are not evenly distributed across disability areas. Schrag and Schrag (2004) reported that while students with autism represented about 1% of the population of students with disabilities, they represented over 11% of the dispute resolution population. Students with other disabilities such as deaf-blindness, emotional disturbance, hard of hearing, multiple disabilities and traumatic brain injury tend to utilize the system beyond their representation as well.

Another pattern in dispute resolution cases is the predominance of cases involving male students with the maximum number of cases occurring with students in their early teens (Schrag & Schrag, 2004). This is not surprising given that there are far more males than females in special education. Rural districts may be particularly vulnerable to parent-initiated due process hearings (Scheffel, Rude, & Bole, 2005). Opuda (1999) found that families who reported higher annual income were more often inclined to withdraw their due process request rather than receive a decision, while parents with lower household income levels tended more often to receive a decision rather than withdraw their request for a hearing.

The importance of studying special education conflict in the context of school leadership is that knowledge can provide guidance for resolving conflicts in a mutually satisfying manner. Given the sometimes highly emotionally charged special education environment and the potential longevity of relationships with parents, the need to decrease the effects of adversity between parents and school personnel is critical. Mutually agreed-upon solutions provide the potential for strengthening trust and increasing the likelihood of maintaining "healthy" parent-school relationships.

The purpose of this chapter is to: (a) briefly review the historical progression and the development of special education conflict resolution practice; (b) provide an understanding about factors that contribute to conflict, with a focus on interactions that are specific to relationships in special education; and (c) outline recommendations for resolving special education conflict with a discussion that encourages prevention and early response to conflict.

Historical Progression of Conflict Resolution in Special Education

Though research into special education conflict is limited, we can trace a historical path that began in 1975 with the passage of the Education for All Handicapped Children Act (PL. 94-142). Early special education legislation focused on assuring access to education for students with disabilities who previously had been denied an education in public schools. This early legislation that granted and defined educational rights for students and their families came about as civil rights legislation granting access to public school education for students with disabilities (Crockett & Kaufman, 1999).

Congress recognized that along with granting educational rights would come disagreements, and lawmakers anticipated that disputes between parents and school officials would inevitably occur. Strengthening of procedures and mechanisms for dispute resolution continued in 1990 with the Individuals with Disabilities Education Act (IDEA; P.L. 101-476), again in the 1997 IDEA Reauthorization (P.L. 105-17), and most recently with the 2004 Reauthorization of IDEA.

Four types of dispute resolution procedures are afforded to parents and schools under IDEA: negotiation and consultation, complaint procedures, due process hearings, and mediation. Negotiation and consultation are evident when parents and school sit down to craft each Individualized Education Plan and when they amend or discuss provisions of IEPs. Formal complaint procedures involve a written request to one's State Education Agency (SEA). Within the formal complaint resolution process, parents or school personnel may submit a written complaint regarding the identification, evaluation, placement or provision of FAPE for a particular special education student. The SEA then responds to the complaint in writing.

Due process proceedings are modeled after court hearings in which the school district and child's family participate in a legal procedure focused on evaluating and resolving the issue in conflict. A hearing officer is required to objectively listen to both sides of the issue and make a decision following special education law and regulations.

Finally, mediation is a process that attempts to resolve disagreements through a trained and impartial mediator, in a forum less formal and contentious than due process hearings. A trained mediator assists in negotiations between home and school representatives and attempts to facilitate mutually agreeable resolution steps.

IDEA established these four formal procedures for resolving disputes described above and each procedure has limitations. While due process proceedings and legal actions proved necessary (to grant access, make interpretations, set precedents, etc.), both scholars and practitioners have discussed the "ills" of due process proceedings (Budoff & Orenstein, 1982; Fielding, 1990; Goldberg, 1989; Hehir, 1992; Mueller, 2004; Nowell & Salem, 2007). Major problems arising out of due process hearings are: (a) further strained relations between parents and school, (b) high financial costs, and (c) emotional strains (Mueller, 2009).

When parents and school personnel reach an impasse that results in a due process hearing request, the gathering tension and animosity can be overwhelming. Parents and school personnel often judge each other negatively leading to a more contentious atmosphere (Opuda, 1999; Shortt, Douglas, & McLain, 2000), which may limit future collaboration. Although due process hearings are a necessary part of dispute resolution in special education, other methods of resolving conflicts are less costly and less adversarial.

Special Education Mediation

Congress turned toward mediation largely because of the possibility that mediation would resolve conflicts less expensively without exacerbating negative relationships. Interest in special education mediation was strengthened again in the 1997 IDEA Amendments, which required states previously not utilizing mediation to offer it as an option for parents and schools to settle disputes.

Mediators are trained as non-evaluative facilitators of the process of resolving disputes. They are trained not to offer opinions or solutions to the issues in dispute but rather to focus on assisting parties to hear one another's concerns, identify common interests, and seek creative, mutually agreeable resolutions (Nowell & Salem, 2007).

Research studies on mediation consider participant satisfaction, fairness, and implementation of mediation agreements. The results of these studies are mixed (D'Alo, 2003; Mueller, 2004; Nowell & Salem, 2007; Reiman et al., 2007; Schrag & Schrag, 2004). In an investigation of the use and effectiveness of special education mediation across seven states, Schrag and Schrag (2004) stated that one third of parents indicated that they would not use mediation again. Parents indicated agreements were ineffective, did not enhance their child's education, or that the mediation agreements were not implemented by the school. Mueller (2009) also reported negative relational aspects of mediation such as increased adversarial relationship between parents and school personnel, dashed parents' expectations concerning hopes for positive change, reinforced parents' perceptions of powerlessness, and decreased parents' hope for the future. However, Mueller (2009) also reported positive relational aspects of mediation including (a) increased school responsiveness to parents' concerns, (b) decreased negative interactions with school personnel, (c) increased parent involvement in special education advocacy, and (d) increased school respect for parents' knowledge, rights, and decision-making roles.

Resolution Meeting Requirement Added

In a subsequent IDEA Reauthorization (2004), a new formal dispute resolution procedure labeled a "resolution meeting" was added. The intent of a resolution meeting is for "the parents of the child to discuss their due process complaint, so that the local education agency (LEA) has an opportunity to resolve the dispute that is the basis for the due process complaint" (IDEA [2004] 34C.F.R &300.510(2). A resolution meeting must be held within 15 days of receiving notice of a parent's due process complaint and must include parents, LEA representative, and relevant individualized education plan (IEP) team members. Attorneys cannot be included in the resolution meeting unless both parties have an attorney present. There is no stipulation regarding confidentiality, meaning that discussions during the resolution meeting can be used as evidence should the disagreement go forward to a due process hearing (Mueller, 2009).

Expanded Options for Resolving Conflicts

In addition to mandated conflict resolution procedures, LEAs and states have attempted to use conflict resolution processes and mechanisms not required under IDEA. Specifically, ten processes were identified in results from a national survey of eight states' use of non-IDEA required alternative dispute resolution processes (Henderson, 2008). The 10 specific non-mandated Alternative Dispute Resolution (ADR) processes are: conflict resolution skills training, stakeholder management or oversight council, parent–parent assistance, dispute resolution case managers, telephone intermediary, IEP facilitation, non-IDEA mediation, third party opinion or consultation processes, early complaint resolution and resolution meeting facilitation. Use of these procedures offers expanded options for resolving conflict.

Understanding Conflict in Special Education

A discussion of conflict in special education is incomplete without recognizing the powerful dynamics that are often an inherent part of special education disagreements. Identity-driven conflicts are rooted in the articulation of, and the threats or frustrations to, people's need for dignity, recognition, safety, control, purpose, and efficacy. Unfortunately, issues are too rarely framed that way (Rothman, 1997). Rather, issues in conflict are more likely to be framed as a lament about past events and perceived wrongdoings. Those attempting to solve special education conflicts need to understand the necessity of probing for the values, fears, and beliefs which often are motivating factors in conflict, but are factors that may not be identified as presenting issues in conversation. School personnel are generally inexperienced and untrained negotiators; therefore, issues may sometimes be unclear, ambiguous, or not easily recognizable in the course of discussions about problem issues (Stewart, 2003).

Because events in a school day occur under compressed timelines, this may compel people to proceed with their first, intuitive framing of an issue rather than spending time to make sure that issues are framed in a way that will allow the most engaging and motivating discussion. Imposed timelines also encourage a rush to the bottom line, which ignores the time people need to consider new information and to adjust their thinking and commitment. A rush to seeking consensus will short-circuit this important middle step. If (in parent-school relationships) we are to influence and inform each other about essential concerns that are relevant to a child's future, recognizing and allowing sufficient time for problem solving is critical (Stewart, 2004).

An additional factor that may complicate special education conflict discussions is a feeling of vulnerability. Parents' relationships to their children make them emotionally and psychologically vulnerable. Parents may also be coping with the feelings of responsibility, sometimes guilt, or shame. These feelings may be unrelated to the matter in dispute, but may be highly relevant to what they can accept in terms of an agreement (D'Alo, 2003). Feelings of vulnerability are also experienced and reported by school personnel. Administrators have reported that they feel the ominous threat of a potential costly lawsuit and the negative consequences that accompany litigation (Lake & Billingsley, 2000; Mueller, 2009; Opuda, 1999). As Bartlett, Weisenstein, and Eitschedit (2001) noted, "The possibility of due process hangs over most inclusive school environments like a mysterious and ever-present threat" (p. 48).

The need for a continued relationship that survives the rigors of time, changing circumstances and divergent viewpoints (Brock & Shanberg, 1990) makes the stakes high when conflicts arise. The potential for conflict is heightened due to the need for on-going interactive communication between parents and schools regarding students' individualized educational plans. For example:

> Parents and various professionals associated with a child with disabilities are constantly relating to one another as educational decisions are made about that child; however this

may result in relationship conflict. We often hear professionals say, "Parents are never realistic, they only think of their child, they're too emotional and they don't communicate unless they are angry or want something." On the other hand, we hear parents say, "Professionals assume they know best and that we as parents know nothing, they don't value our input, they usurp our right to know and decide, and they blame or judge us if we don't do what they say."

(Amon & Karstaedt, n.d.)

Voices of those who have experienced special education conflict have been reported in several qualitative studies (e.g., Blue-Banning, Summers, Frankland, Nelson, & Beegle, 2004; Lake & Billingsley, 2000; Mueller, 2009; Neely, 2005; Nowell & Salem, 2007; Opuda, 1999). An examination and review of actual participants' comments from parents, teachers, school administrators, hearing officers, and mediators who were involved in a special education conflict reveal the following themes that serve either to escalate or deescalate conflict in special education:

- Sensitivity to the needs and perspectives of others
- Trust
- Communication and the importance of listening
- Recognizing and understanding power
- Feeling de-valued in the parent-school partnership

These themes provide a framework for understanding how conflicts may play out in the unique day–to-day operations of special education programming and decision-making.

Sensitivity to the Needs and Perspectives of Others

Differences between parents' views of their children and school personnel's views can escalate conflict (Fish, 1990; Lake & Billingsley, 2000; Turnbull, Turnbull, Erwin, & Soodak, 2006). Parents have repeatedly stated in studies of special education conflict that it is important for school personnel to view their children as individuals with unique strengths and abilities and that school personnel *not* discuss their child from a "deficit perspective" (Turnbull et al., 2006; Zaretsky, 2004). Viewing a student in his/her entirety is a perspective that parents have reported as critical during educational planning (Blue-Banning et al., 2004; Turnbull, 2010).

School officials have reported that, justifiably, schools and parents view their children differently. Though the differences are understandable, not being able to acknowledge the perspective of another may increase the likelihood of conflict. Parents have reported that schools focused too often on a child's weaknesses and did not seem to take into account what the whole child was like. School personnel have reported that parents became single-minded and sometimes selected one right thing and excluded acceptable choices for particular students. A mediator shared this insight:

A parent's report of his/her child's abilities are often one-on-one, with the parent's full attention at all times. That's not the classroom circumstance. So the teacher's observation, which may differ from the parents' is equally correct. The teacher reports on circumstances under which they observe and know the child. We have to get past thinking that those are mutually exclusive observations. And come to realize that, like us, kids are different in different circumstances. And people's observations are what they know. And they can and should inform each other.

(Lake & Billingsley, 2000, p. 245)

"What surfaces most frequently (in post mediation interviews) is that parents wished that the school district *understood* them and realized that it (the school district) needed to *hear* and *understand* them" (D'Alo, p. 225). In a study by Blue-Banning et al. (2004), parents of children with and without disabilities, service providers, and school administrators have emphasized the need for communication to be two-way, that is for professionals and parents to listen carefully and non-judgmentally to what the other has to say. As one father put it:

> The first thing is to listen to us … I think some of these people have preconceived notions about everything … So if I tried to tell them (professionals) something it'd be LISTEN TO ME!
>
> *(p. 175)*

Another parent reported:

> I felt like I was constantly being just patted on the head and told to go home and everything would be fine, And they hardly ever listened to the concerns with an open ear at all. It was just go away, you're bothering me. I think they were trying to humor me, not really listen to me …
>
> *(Lake & Billingsley, 2000, p. 247)*

School professionals have emphasized the importance of frequent and honest communication with families, and have spoken of the need to listen carefully and respectfully. Many professionals and parents alike have said that school officials need to avoid jargon and check tactfully to make sure that all parents understood reports, description of rights, and other documents they were receiving (Blue-Banning et al., 2004; Nowell & Salem, 2007; Turnbull et al., 2006; Zaretsky, 2004). Investigating the perspective of culturally and linguistically diverse families participating in IEP meetings, Cho and Gannotti (2005) reported that limited English ability was *not* a barrier in negotiations, as long as professionals were willing to take the time to communicate with them by listening carefully and rephrasing the parent's words in correct English to clarify and avoid misunderstandings.

Trust

Much has been written about the relevancy of trust in establishing parent-school relationships. In a study by Blue-Banning et al. (2004), parents used the term "trust" in the context of three distinct meanings. First trust meant *reliability* in the sense that people who are trustworthy can be depended on to follow through with an action, to do what they say they are going to do, or otherwise fulfill promises. Second, trust meant *safety*. This not only meant that the child was clean, warm, fed and protected, but also making sure the child was treated with dignity and protected from such "hurts" as teasing from peers. Third, trust included *discretion*. Participants in this study gave both positive and negative examples of partnerships in which professionals could be trusted with confidential or personal information about a family, or in which professionals violated their confidence.

The theme of trust and reliability has also been viewed as an important factor for professionals:

> I think it really comes back to trust. And to the kind of trust that you can establish with that family so that they KNOW that this is a person they can depend on to give them if not the answer, then to help them find it wherever it exists. Or to be that listening ear. Maybe

there isn't an answer to what the problem is, but at least here's somebody there who isn't going to judge them.

(Banning et al., 2004, p.179)

Trust is one of the "hostages" that conflict takes (Stewart, 2007). The importance of preserving trust is perhaps the one most important research finding from special education conflict resolution research. During meetings of the President's Commission on Excellence in Special Education (2002), Jim Rosenfield (attorney) commented:

> The fact that law suits do not reconcile the parties suggests that there is a need for alternative, additional dispute resolution mechanisms ... Until there is a non-adversarial dispute resolution alternative available designed to rebuild parent/school trust that is inherent in the complex task of educating a child with disabilities, the adversarial nature of parent/ school relations will never be reduced for very long.

(pp. 135, 142)

In a trusting relationship, members of the partnership share a sense of assurance about the reliability or dependability of the character, ability, strength or truth of the other (Blue-Banning et. al., 2004). An important advantage of preserving trust in the midst of adversity is that with trust intact, the avenues of communication between parents and schools and processes for decision-making are better supported. This allows both parties in conflict to exercise receptivity to alternative ways of viewing the situation and alternative ways of considering solutions.

The Beach Center on Disability (2010) suggests these actions to encourage parental involvement in a trusting relationship between parents and their child's service providers:

- Learn and share new information with parents. Frequently update parents on students' progress.
- Demonstrate honesty by admitting when you do not know, but be willing to seek more information and share what you discover.
- Demonstrate dependability by consistent actions.
- Show parents what steps have been taken to ensure the "safety" of their children.
- Preserve privacy and confidentiality.

The importance of preserving trust is highlighted by reports from parents in both "intact-trust" relationships and from those in "broken-trust" relationships. Parents in "broken trust" relationships reported that they had difficulty accepting suggestions from school personnel. Parents in this group reported that they were less satisfied and less inclined to see their parent-school relationship as one of mutual benefit. They expected fewer positive outcomes from their schools and viewed their school personnel as being uncaring, unresponsive, or detrimental to their child's well being. Parents in broken-trust relationships lacked the confidence to fully accept school personnel's demonstration of good faith efforts (Lake & Billingsley, 2000).

However, if trust was intact between parents and school personnel, parents in a dispute reported that they felt a certain amount of predictability and security about the actions of school personnel. They expressed that they were able to tolerate negative events periodically, without attaching too much importance to one single event. They generally could verbalize that school personnel were professionally capable and were considerate of their children's needs. If trust was not broken, parents appeared willing to give the school personnel the benefit of the doubt when minor events became problematic in the course of a school week (Lake & Billingsley, 2000).

229

Communication and the Importance of Listening

The lack of communication, lack of follow up, misunderstood communication, and timing of communication have been identified as factors that escalate conflicts. Deciding not to communicate with a party in conflict has been viewed as a tactic that distances one from having to "face" the conflict. The perception of withholding information or communication that was perceived as untrue or deceitful has also been identified as a factor that escalated conflicts (Lake & Billingsley, 2000; Mueller, 2009). The importance of communication is critical, for it is the basis for establishing trust, expressing respect, and conferring equality for families (Blue-Banning et al., 2004; Turnbull, 2010). School officials have stressed the importance of communication:

> Many, many times if I had known what the parent had been up against, I might have been able to intervene, before they got to the point of breaking ... I think one of the most important things parents can do is somehow contact the (special education) director and say, "This is my problem, this is what I am looking for as a resolution, and what do you see?"
>
> *(Lake & Billingsley, 2000, p. 247)*

Another special education director spoke of feelings of injustice when parents hit him with issues, suddenly without warning:

> Parents may not be happy with something, but they don't tell us. And then ... they show up with their lawyer or their advocate.... And so I guess it's important to get parents to talk to the school system and explain what they're unhappy with, and see if we can work it out before the lawyers and advocates come along, because that causes a lot of stress.
>
> *(Lake & Billingsley, 2000, p. 247)*

A history of past unsuccessful meetings and unresolved issues may intensify difficulty in communicating. Approaching conversations with an unguarded and open stance helps to elicit the same in return. If one regards one's first task as trying to understand people, what their experience is, and has been, one is more likely to become engaged in listening to them productively. In order to proceed away from an adversarial framing of issues in conflict, adjustments can be made through listening to develop a better understanding of each party's best thinking, their commitment and their rationale (Stewart, 2007). Discussing the observations and concerns behind conclusions opens the discourse to include interests and to reveal common objectives. Once the discussion brings the larger focus of underlying interests into play, the range of possible acceptable outcomes to a presenting challenge is enlarged, and the likelihood of agreement is improved. Seeking to discover one's aspirations, values, and long-term goals can ease the strain on communicating in the face of adversity. Exploring fears either party may have (that may not have been explicitly revealed) can inform negotiation. Summarizing what one has heard may provide needed assurance as well as provide shape and focus to discussions (Stewart, 2007).

Recognizing and Understanding Power

Parents and school employees have revealed bases of power and tactical maneuvers that were employed in an attempt to get what they wanted or put an end to a conflict. For example, a parent described this interactive power play between herself and the school system in this manner:

No matter now angry I got, the angrier they got back. The angrier I got, the worse the response was. It was fighting, all the time. It was like pushing back the water. No matter where you pushed, you were met with resistance everywhere.

(Lake & Billingsley, 2000, p. 247)

Power is a factor in every negotiation. Power is transactional, shifts during negotiation and is not always knowable (Stewart, 2007). Lake and Billingsley (2000) recognized the reciprocity factor in the imbalance of power. Power is reciprocal—parents have it, school systems have it—both parties have it. It is spread across the dimensions of control of resources, information, legal and regulatory requirements, aspirational level of participants, values, grasp of issues, persuasive ability, and other factors (Stewart, 2007). Since it is always present in negotiations and shifts with each issue discussed, concern is not that it is present, but that power not be used to intimidate, silence participants, or force a consent, not freely chosen (Stewart, 2007).

Regardless of how the dynamics of power played out in individual conflict cases, parents, school officials, and mediators have recognized the human costs of the consequences of misuse of power. The threat of a lawsuit puts parents in a very powerful position. A mediator reported "A parent who will take you to the cleaners at any cost is in a very powerful position" (Lake, 1998, p. 165).

Feeling De-valued in the Parent-School Partnership

When parents reported feeling de-valued in the parent-school relationship or when they gave examples of the perceived devaluation of their children's strengths and abilities, conflicts escalated (Lake & Billingsley, 2002; Mueller, 2009; Zaretsky, 2004). For example, a parent shared:

He (special education director) was very belligerent and insulting … he would say things like, "Well your son is retarded. There is nothing else we can do for him. You'd better accept the fact." And he said all kinds of insults like that (when there were no other witnesses), which puts parents, such as myself, on the defensive.

(Lake & Billingsley, 2000, p. 247)

Zaretsky (2004) reported that one principal described an experience in which he felt devalued:

How do you always get a parent to listen? I was so frustrated by her (parent) refusal to listen to anything we had to say. She wanted to remove him from special education, but I knew he would die without support. It's tough going sometimes. Emotions complicate things. That's why you have to try to separate the personal and the emotional from the professional dialogue.

(p. 275)

Recommendations for Resolving Special Education Conflict

To date, our examination of the literature specific to dispute resolution in special education offers a snapshot of a discipline whose research base is in its infancy. Most conspicuously absent is research addressing the efficacy of actual practices (tactics, strategies, interventions) employed in mediation, resolution sessions, facilitated IEP meetings and other early/innovative dispute resolution strategies (Reiman et al., 2007). What research has provided is a framework in which one can examine the most critical elements of conflict that directly affect relationships with parents, and which directly affect substantive educational outcomes for students.

Researchers have identified conditions that are "favorable and necessary" for conflict to be handled so that relationships stay healthy and intact. Participants themselves have offered what they perceive is "needed" in order for a conflict to be handled in such a way that they can respect. D'Alo (2003) identifies three benefits that disputants are generally looking for in a dispute resolution:

1. A substantively fair and just result;
2. An opportunity for voice, acknowledgement of their voice, and dignified and respectful treatment;
3. Achievement of other personal and emotional goals, such as reconciliation, or at least not feeling worse, emotionally and psychologically (Sternlight, 2003).

In essence, skills in meeting the procedural justice, personal, and emotional goals are needed in any resolution of a conflict, especially one that requires an on-going working relationship. In addition to fairness, opportunity to be heard and reconciliation, participants in a dispute need freedom of choice, acceptance of one's child, a sense of belonging, and a sense of comfort (Stewart, 2007).

Implications for practice in this section are focused on two primary areas: responding positively to conflict and resolving conflicts with relationships intact. If these two foundational principles are achieved, financial and human costs of conflict will likely decrease and adversarial actions will likely be minimized.

Proactive Policies and Early Response to Conflict

A starting point for developing a proactive stance is acknowledging the complexity of special education decision making, acknowledging that decisions are emotionally laden for all parties, and understanding the needs of all parties involved. Conflict can be viewed as a positive opportunity to improve communication, to deepen understanding of complex special education issues, and to realize the chance to be heard. Viewing conflict as an indicator where change may be needed is a first step in responding positively when inevitable conflict occurs. One of the strongest motivators for responding early to conflict is that by doing so, school personnel may protect the trusting relationship that may have taken months or years to develop with parents (Lake, 1998).

As students with challenging academic and behavioral needs participate in a wider array of settings, programs, and opportunities, the need for school leaders who understand the complexities of varied systems becomes essential to student success (Garrison-Wade, Sobel, & Fulmer, 2007). School districts should analyze their own systems and explore policy that promotes early response to conflict at the building level. Strategic focus on early response to conflict is essential in preserving working parent-school relationships.

Need for Professional Development

School administrators report that they are deficient in understanding special education laws and regulations and that they refer to their special education director for guidance and clarification (Garrison-Wade et al., 2007). Parents have expressed through various questionnaires that they desire more information about how to handle conflict. Training programs for teachers and administrators that include a course in Conflict Resolution in Special Education are needed and helpful. For instance, principals described how their conflict-resolution training helped them remain calm and emotionally detached during heated debates with school advocates (Zaretsky, 2004).

Responding to Conflict with Culturally Responsive Actions

With schools becoming increasingly more diverse, it is necessary that our attitudes and actions in handling conflict become culturally responsive as well. For example, while most parents report feeling overwhelmed by school conflict, the stress may be exacerbated in situations such as single-parent families, foster or adoptive families, families with large number of children and homeless families (Fish, 1990). There may be additional strains on negotiating with families whose native language is something other than English. Those involved in handling conflict at every level must be sensitive to cultural, linguistic and class differences (Engiles, Fromme, LeResche, & Moses, 1999).

Operationally Defining Terms Such As Trust and Respect

Professionals and parents may have difficulty implementing collaborative partnerships, especially in the face of adversity because they may not fully understand what is expected of them (Blue-Banning et al., 2004; Turnbull, 2010). It is possible that a deeper understanding of the meaning of factors such as mutual respect and trust could lead to better guidelines for practice. What, for example, are the specific actions that parents interpret as "respect"? What are the specific indicators of professional behavior that allow educators to be viewed as "trustworthy" in the eyes of parents involved in conflict?

Sharing Data and Success Stories

Professional collaboration across disciplines is critically lacking in the area of special education conflict resolution. There are not sufficient opportunities for mediators and school personnel to share information and strategies that are known to be helpful in resolving disputes. Though both educators and mediators are attempting to craft the best outcome for students in a school conflict, they may not share information that informs each other.

Organizations such as National Association of State Directors of Special Education (NASDSE) and Consortium for Appropriate Dispute Resolution in Special Education (CADRE) and others have been involved in numerous data base analyses and longitudinal effectiveness studies and about special education conflict resolution (i.e., Initial Review of Research on Appropriate Dispute Resolution in Special Education, 2007 [Reiman, Beck, Peter, Zeller, Moses, & Engiles, 2007]; National Dispute Resolution Use and Effectiveness Study, 2004; State Mediation Systems-A NASDSE Report, 2003 [Markowitz, Ahearn, & Schrag, 2003]). Results of these studies are not readily made accessible or included in the body of literature that comprises scholarly research. There needs to be a mechanism to bridge the gap and share data, in and among pre-service training programs, in-service training, and specifically personnel preparation programs with educational leadership as their focus.

Learning from Mediators

Mediators are trained to let parties know that their issues will be addressed and that resolving them is part of their goal. Untrained problem solvers and negotiators, such as most school administrators, often approach negotiations instinctively. Well-intentioned people may not have identified the names for the techniques that they are using to problem-solve or they may not know the choices they have to employ different problem-solving strategies. They may not recognize strategies that are available for maximizing outcomes at each stage of a conflict. However, from conflict theorists (Deutsch, 1973; Fisher & Ury, 1981) we know that conflicts follow a similar pattern and identified strategies *can* diminish the negative effects of conflict. Understanding and incorporating pragmatic and established problem-solving strategies into school negotiations can result in moving school leaders from reflexive/reactive negotiators to reflective negotiators (Stewart, 2003).

An attitude that diminishes the possibility of agreement is that there is just *one right way*, just one supportable outcome. Maintaining a flexibility of mind in order to adjust to what a situation presents heightens the likelihood of a consensual outcome. Having the confidence to admit that what you are doing is not working can earn respect. Acknowledging that missteps have occurred helps clear the air, reinforce credibility and trust, and helps to create a foundation for a new possibility. A lot has been written about the value of an apology in negotiations (Stewart, 2003). It has the power and possibility to bring closure to lamented events, implies that there is a shared viewpoint and a shared regret, and evokes a stance toward each other that can be enlisted for productive discussion of next steps.

The interactive nature of conflict makes it a complex subject. When special education conflict is also viewed through the defining parameters imposed by civil rights and disability legislation, parent school conflict is elevated to a position of significance to school administrators, both from a financial and a programmatic perspective. Complexities demand that both scholars and practitioners examine problematic issues and foster discourse between educators and those who are experts in dispute resolution. Shaping discussions for students' educational benefit when conflict occurs requires a multi-focused approach given the many variables that contribute to any given conflict.

Conclusions

Tina Diamond, OSEP Project Officer, states in a CADRE webinar "knowledge about dispute resolution cannot be generated by typical research methods alone" (Diamond, 2011). With a 35-year-old history of resolving conflicts in special education, why has so little of what is known to be effective practice from the field of dispute resolution not been more readily available to teachers and educational leaders? What literature and which practices have been deemed worthy of being included in our preparation of educational leaders? Have we incorporated what has been researched and considered best practice in the field of negotiation and conflict resolution into our mind set as educators or into our daily decision-making practices?

Perhaps a closer examination and integration of proven dispute handling techniques from other fields such as labor relations, domestic and environmental dispute resolution would assist educators in understanding the specifics of negotiating and resolving conflicts (Lake, 1998; Reiman et al., 2007; Schrag & Schrag, 2004; Stewart, 2007). Studies from these areas employ more rigorous research methodology than the alternative dispute resolution literature in special education (Reiman et al., 2007) and potentially offer a much larger body of research to examine.

Regardless of what dispute resolution literature is examined, a more concentrated and focused effort needs to be spent analyzing what has been learned. Reiman et al. (2007) suggest that as the body of research literature in special education conflict resolution develops, it may be helpful to categorize levels of practice as (a) emerging, in which a body of anecdotal evidence exists for a practice, but no scientifically based research exists; (b) promising, in which some data exist to support a practice but it is not of sufficient rigor or magnitude to determine effectiveness; and (c) evidence-based, in which a practice is supported by rigorous scientifically based research designs (Odom et al., 2005). More systematic organization of data about conflict resolution combined with more systematic sharing of data can support educators' use of processes and conflict resolution strategies that have some basis in theory and research.

Although research is limited (and needs to be continued), there is a historic and evolving body of hard-earned craft knowledge that has resulted from parents, teachers, school administrators, advocates, hearing officers, and mediators who have participated in resolving conflicts at the grass roots level (Reiman et al., 2007). This craft- knowledge has much to offer in understanding what results in stalled or successful negotiations. Research based practice in special education conflict resolution is being examined and reviewed with the intent of informing stakeholders of the most promising attitudes and actions that can resolve conflict with relationships intact. It is imperative that what has been learned from the reports of those in the midst of parent-school conflict be heard and acknowledged.

References

Amon, C., & Karstaedt, C. (n.d.). *Mediation: Putting theory into practice* (Seminar No.10). Denver, CO: Department of Education.

Bartlett, L. D., Weisenstein, G. R., & Etscheidt, S. (2001). *Successful inclusion for educational leaders.* Upper Saddle River, NJ: Prentice Hall.

Beach Center on Disability. (2010). How can service providers develop trust with parents of children with disabilities. Retrieved on January 8, 2010, from http://www.beachcenter.org/resource_library/beach_resource_detail_page.aspx?intResource

Blue-Banning, M., Summers, J., Frankland, H. C., Nelson, L., & Beegle, G. (2004). Dimensions of family and professional partnerships: Constructive guidelines for collaboration. *Exceptional Children, 70*(2), 167–184.

Brock, K. A., & Shanberg, R. (1990). Avoiding unnecessary due process hearings. *Journal of Reading, Writing, and Learning Disabilities, 6*(1), 33–39.

Budoff, M., & Orenstein, A. (1982). *Due process in special education: on going to a hearing.* Cambridge, MA: The Ware Press.

Cho, S. J., & Gannotti, M. E. (2005). Korean-American mother's perception of professional support in early intervention and special education programs. *Journal of Policy and Practice in Intellectual Disabilities, 2*(1), 1–9.

Crockett, J. B., & Kaufman, J. M. (1999). *The least restrictive environment: Its origins and interpretation in special education.* Mahwah, N J: Erlbaum.

D'Alo, G. E. (2003). Justice, understanding, and mediation: When talk works, should we ask for more? *Negotiation Journal, 19*(3), 215–227.

Deutsch, M. (1973). *The resolution of conflict: Constructive and destructive processes.* New Haven, CT: Yale University Press.

Diamond, T. (2011, February 3). CADRE's exemplar initiative [Webinar]. Retrieved August 5, 2011, from http:www.directionservice.org/cadre/raisesearch.cfm

Engiles, A., Fromme, C., LeResche, D., & Moses, P. (1999). *Keys to access: Encouraging the use of mediation by families from diverse backgrounds.* Eugene, Oregon: Consortium for Appropriate Dispute Resolution in Special Education (CADRE).

Fielding, P. (1990). Mediation in special education. *Journal of Reading, Writing, and Learning Disabilities, 6*(1), 41–42.

Fish, M. C. (1990). Family-school conflict: Implications for the family. *Journal of Reading, Writing, and Learning Disabilities, 6*(1), 71–79.

Fisher, R., & Ury, W. (1981). *Getting to yes: Negotiating agreement without giving in.* Boston, MA: Houghton-Mifflin.

Garrison-Wade, D., Sobel, D., & Fulmer, C. L. (2007). Inclusive leadership: Preparing principals for the role that awaits them. *Educational Leadership and Administration, 19*, 117–132.

Goldberg, S. S. (1989). The failure of legalization in education: Alternative dispute resolution and the Education for All Handicapped Children Act of 1975. *Journal of Law and Education, 18*(3), 441–454.

Hehir, T. F. (1992, Spring). The impact of due process on the programmatic decisions of special education directors. *The Special Education Leadership Review, 1*(1), 63–76.

Henderson, K. (2008, May). Optional IDEA alternative dispute resolution. Project Forum. National Association of State Directors of Special Education. Alexandria, VA.

Lake, B. J. (1998). *Factors that escalate parent-school conflict and the value of mediation in special education.* Unpublished doctoral dissertation, Virginia Tech, Blacksburg, VA.

Lake, B. J., & Billingsley, B. S. (2000). An analysis of factors that contribute to parent-school conflict in special education. *Remedial and Special Education, 21*(4), 240–256.

Markowitz, J., Ahearn, E., & Schrag, J. (June 2003). *Dispute resolution: A review of systems in selected states.* Alexandria, VA: Project FORUM, National Association of State Directors of Special Education.

Mueller, T. G. (2004). A tale of two districts fostering the home-school partnership: Conflict prevention and alternative dispute resolution practices in special education (Doctoral dissertation, University of California at Santa Barbara, 2004). *Dissertation Abstracts International, 65*(06). (UMI No. 3136884)

Mueller, T. G. (2009). Alternative dispute resolution: A new agenda for special education policy. *Journal of Disability Policy Studies, 20*(1), 4–13.

Neely, H. (2005). *Special education conflict management at the school building level: A multi-vocal synthesis.* Unpublished doctoral dissertation, Virginia Tech, Blacksburg, VA.

Nowell, B. L., & Salem, D. A. (2007). The impact of special education mediation on parent-school relationships: Parents' perspective. *Remedial and Special Education, 28*(5), 304–315.

Odom, S. L., Brantlinger, E., Gersten, R., Horner, R. H., Thompson, B., & Harris, K. R. (2005). Research in special education: Scientific methods and evidence-based practices. *Exceptional Children, 71*(2), 137–148.

Opuda, M. A. (1999). *Comparison of parents who initiated due process hearings and complaints in Maine.* Unpublished doctoral dissertation, Virginia Tech, Blacksburg, VA.

President's Commission on Excellence in Special Education. (2002, April 23). *Task force on system administration,* Washington, DC: Office of Special Education and Rehabilitative Services, U.S. Department of Education.

Reiman, J., Beck, L., Peter, M., Zeller, D., Moses, P., & Engiles, A. (2007). *Initial review of research literature on appropriate dispute resolution (ADR) in special education.* Eugene, Oregon: Consortium for Appropriate Dispute Resolution in Special Education (CADRE).

Rothman, J. (1997). *Resolving identity-based conflict.* San Francisco: Jossey-Bass.

Scheffel, D .L., Rude, H. A., & Bole, P. T. (2005). Avoiding special education litigation in rural school districts. *Rural Special Education Quarterly, 24*(4), 3–8.

Schrag, J. A., & Schrag, H. L. (2004, Summer). National dispute resolution use and effectiveness study. Alexandria, VA: NASDSE. Retrieved from http://www.directionservice.org/cadre

Shortt, T., Douglas, J., & McLain, J. (2000). Building the foundation for special education mediation in Virginia's high schools. *NASSP Bulletin, 84*(613), 35–40.

Sternlight, J. (2003). ADR is here: Preliminary reflections on where it fits in a system of justice. *Nevada Law Journal, 3,* 289–304.

Stewart, A. (2003). *What can you expect when you mediate?* Virginia Department of Education, Office of Dispute Resolution and Administrative Services. Retrieved from http.://www.doe.virginia.gov/special_ed/resolving.../expect_mediate.pdf

Stewart, A. (2004, Spring). *Mediators negotiate and negotiators mediate.* Virginia Council of Administrators of Special Education. Retrieved from http://www.directionservice.org/cadre/pdf/stewart1.pdf

Stewart, A. (2007). *Training manual and materials.* Cambridge, MA: Community Dispute Resolution Center.

Turnbull, A. (2010). *How can service providers develop trust with parents of children with disabilities.* Lawrence, KS: Beach Center on Disability, University of Kansas.

Turnbull, A. P., Turnbull, H. R., Erwin, E., & Soodak, L. (2006). *Families, professionals, and exceptionality: positive outcomes through partnerships and trust.* Upper Saddle River, NJ: Pearson/Merrill-Prentice Hall.

Zaretsky, L. (2004). Advocacy and administration: From conflict to collaboration, *Journal of Educational Administration 42*(2), 270–286.

Section IV

Instructional Leadership and the Evaluation of Educational Outcomes
Introduction

Educating students with disabilities is an important dimension of school improvement, and special education is now a major concern for educational leaders responsible for ensuring that students have equitable opportunities to learn in the context of challenging standards and high stakes accountability. There is growing evidence that gains in academic achievement and social growth are closely tied to school leaders who make instruction and learning the driving force behind their leadership. Although educational leadership is only indirectly linked to student learning, it is "second only to classroom instruction among all school related factors that contribute toward what students learn at school" (Leithwood, Louis, Anderson, & Wahlstrom, 2004, p. 5). The chapters in this section address content essential to providing instructional leadership that improves the quality of teaching and learning from early intervention services starting at birth through post-secondary transition to adulthood.

If the goal of reform is to improve the quality of education that students receive, then school leaders would do well to target teachers for support because education cannot improve if instruction remains the same. Deshler and Cornett (Chapter 14) address leadership to improve teacher effectiveness in the context of the school-wide instructional framework known as Response to Intervention (RTI), and they also address the meaning of high quality instruction for every child. Supporting teachers as they improve the quality of instruction requires that educational leaders scaffold the organizational reforms and the pedagogical changes made in each classroom, school, and district office. Much has been written about instructional practices that positively impact student achievement, and volumes of research justify these claims; however, little is known about how teachers in classrooms instruct their students once the classroom door has been closed. In that spirit, Deshler and Cornett share results from one small-scale descriptive study as a model for additional research to help leaders for special education understand the state of instruction in other schools and districts.

Ensuring that students with disabilities have access to quality teachers is a leadership priority because quality instruction is essential to students' success in school. Brownell, Billingsley, McLeskey, and Sindelar (Chapter 15) describe the ways in which the supply of special and general education teachers prepared to instruct students with disabilities is likely to contribute to the successful education of these students. These authors also summarize research that supports four major strategies for ensuring that students with disabilities have access to quality teachers. These strategies include designing effective beginning teacher induction programs, implementing effective professional development efforts, providing supportive work contexts, and designing and implementing teacher evaluation systems that identify quality teachers and inform efforts to support teacher development.

Cook and Smith (Chapter 16) address instructional leadership by examining the use of evidence-based practices in special education. Using the most effective instructional technique lies at the heart of special education. Traditionally, special educators have used approaches such as personal experience, anecdotal information, and tradition to determine what works and to decide how and what to teach students with disabilities. These approaches, however, are vulnerable to both Type I (i.e., false positives) and Type II (i.e., false negatives) errors. Evidence-based practices (EBPs)—instructional approaches supported by a number of research studies that meet rigorous standards regarding research design, methodological quality, and magnitude of effect—represent a reliable approach for identifying effective practices. Cook and Smith present a rationale for using EBPs to determine what works for teaching students with disabilities; criteria for identifying EBPs in special education; and considerations for educational leaders seeking to facilitate the adoption and maintenance of EBPs.

Ensuring safe and productive learning environments is also a high priority for educational leaders, and Sugai, O'Keeffe, Horner, and Lewis (Chapter 17) focus on the topic of leadership and school-wide positive behavior support. Student engagement and academic achievement, in part, are linked to the use of effective instructional materials and strategies. However, if student engagement is to be maximized, effective classroom and school-wide behavioral practices also must be in place. School leaders are important to ensuring that the academic-behavior association is clearly understood, formally addressed, and effectively managed. These authors provide an overview of the role of school leadership in the adoption and implementation of the systems and practices of school-wide positive behavior support at the classroom, school, district, and state levels.

Snyder, Crowe, and Crow (Chapter 18) focus on the education of very young children by extending the discussion of effective leadership practices and the evaluation of educational outcomes to early intervention and early childhood special education. They situate this discussion in the context of responsive instructional leadership. By responsive, they mean actions taken relative to internal or external situations or changes so the circumstances of an intervention program are maintained or improved. Responsive instructional leadership focuses on actions taken to improve or maintain instructional quality, instructional effectiveness, and to evaluate whether desired outcomes in early intervention and early childhood special education are being achieved.

Test, Mazzotti, and Mustian (Chapter 19) shift the emphasis from early learning to post-school outcomes for older students with disabilities by discussing leadership for transition-focused education. Test and his colleagues provide information about transition-related educational policy, evidence-based practices and predictors for secondary transition, and strategies for their use in schools and classrooms. They conclude their discussion with implications for practice and recommendations for educational leaders about secondary transition in school reform and improving school completion rates.

The chapters in this section inform the practice of effective instructional leadership that fosters the academic learning and social growth of children and youth with disabilities in the context of schools and other instructional settings. How instructional leaders carry out these practices, and interact with others in the process, may be what is most important in influencing what teachers do to deliver equitable and beneficial special education.

References

Leithwood, K., Louis, K. S., Anderson, S., & Wahlstrom, K. (2004). *How leadership influences student learning.* Minneapolis, MN: Center for Applied Research and Educational Improvement, University of Minnesota, and Ontario Institute for Studies in Education at the University of Toronto.

14

Leading to Improve Teacher Effectiveness
Implications for Practice, Reform, Research, and Policy

Donald D. Deshler

UNIVERSITY OF KANSAS

Jake Cornett

SRI INTERNATIONAL

During the past 20 years there has been a marked decrease in the amount of time students with disabilities spend outside of general education classrooms (Snyder & Dillow, 2010). Whereas in 1989, 31.7% of students with disabilities spent 80% or more of the school day in general education classrooms, by 2007 the number of students doing so had grown to 56.8% (Snyder & Dillow, 2010). Because students with disabilities spend larger portions of the school day inside general education, these classroom are more academically diverse today than at any time in the preceding 20 years. Given these facts, access to the general curriculum requires that general and special educators use instructional activities and practices that support a broad range of student abilities. For many teachers, their pre-service training was not designed for nor prepares them for the realities of instructing diverse learners[1] within the same classroom.

As research has shown, student academic outcomes are highly dependent on the quality of instruction (Darling-Hammond, 2000; Sanders & Horn, 1998; Sanders & Rivers, 1996; Wenglinsky, 2000; Westbury, 1993). Fundamental changes in how classroom teachers think about and conduct the business of teaching and learning are extremely difficult to generate, and harder to sustain (Elmore, 1996; Desimone, Porter, Garet, Yoon, & Birman, 2002; Knapp, 1997; Supovitz, 2006). Schools and teachers regularly make surface changes—adopting new textbooks, curricula, or information reporting system —but such changes rarely impact teaching and learning once the classroom door has been closed (Elmore, 1996). In part this is due to the egalitarian (City, Elmore, Fiarman, & Teitel, 2009), autonomous, and discretionary (Mehta, 2006) character of education in the United States and the organizational structures that conserve the status quo and thereby circumvent reform efforts (Skrtic, 1995, 2005). Nevertheless, meaningful access to the general education curriculum requires deep changes in how teachers conduct themselves and relate to their students in the classroom (Mellard & Deshler, 2004), and how they interact with one another, other professionals, and the community. One such educational reform framework that has shown promise is response to intervention (RTI).

Response to Intervention as School-wide Reform

Response to Intervention is a school-wide reform logic model used to tailor instruction to better match each student's need. It is also referred to as Response to Instruction or multi-tiered systems of support, which generally signify the same logic model. There are numerous approaches to RTI being written about in academic and professional literature. All of these seem to have five practices in common: universal screening, intervention, progress monitoring, use of data to make decisions, and at least three increasingly intense tiers of support. These five practices are the defining features of response to intervention. Although these five elements are common to the various approaches to RTI, some approaches have additional elements in their implementation design (e.g., fidelity estimation of individual interventions, etc.). How these practices are implemented in schools are what we refer to as the technical aspects of RTI, these will not be discussed here.[2] By virtue of the tiered support structure and prevention logic, RTI is a school-wide framework. As such, the effects of RTI should be realized at the school level.

School-wide RTI operates on three basic assumptions: (a) teacher instruction is the most powerful predictor of student success; (b) all students can learn; and (c) schools must provide *all* students a beneficial education, which begins with preventing failure. Therefore, decisions made by teachers about student instruction should be data driven and responsive to student need. RTI in this manner can also reduce the number of children who are identified as having a learning disability when their academic difficulty is actually due to cultural differences or lack of adequate instruction (Cortiella, 2005). When implementing the RTI framework, high quality instruction is the primary focus at each tier. This is because instruction is the basic foundation of the logic model.

Multitier system of support. Most RTI conceptual models have three to five tiers of support for students. Key to the RTI model is the concept that different students require differing levels of support according to their needs; and, that schools should use a multi-tiered approach to providing these differing levels of support. The first tier of instruction is referred to as core or universal, which indicates that all students within the school are supported by this tier. The goal of universal supports is to provide the highest quality instruction and curriculum while screening all students to identify those at risk of failure. As the tiers increase—from one to two, and two to three—the level of specialized support and instructional attention increase also. These tiers exist to provide a framework for preventing student failure and for appropriately supporting students so all can benefit maximally from the instruction they receive. RTI is distinct from the three-tiered model previously applied to education in which general education, Title I supports, and special education were stacked on each other; school-wide RTI supports are fluid and integrated across funding streams, support providers, and instructional settings.

A Systems-Focused View of RTI

This chapter considers three topics relevant to the implementation and enculturation of school-wide RTI. The first section will focus on professional learning and systems of support that scaffold the learning of new practices by teachers. If the goal of reform is to improve the quality of education that students receive, then teachers ought to be targeted first for support because education cannot improve if instruction remains the same. To accomplish this, copious support from other skilled professionals is needed (Elmore & Burney, 1997; Fuchs & Deshler, 2007). Also presented in this section is a conceptual framework for job-embedded coaching supports.

The second section will focus on organizational supports provided by school district administrators and school leaders. Supporting teachers as they improve the quality of instruction requires that leaders scaffold the organizational reforms and the pedagogical changes made in each classroom, school, and district office (Sailor, 2009). The focus of changes within the organization must be carefully planned, executed, and adapted to meet the unique needs of each school while maintaining sharp focus on improving the educational experience of all children.

The third section will focus on the meaning of high quality instruction for every child. This is the linchpin that determines success or failure of RTI. Much has been written about instructional practices positively impacting student achievement, and volumes of research justify these claims, however little is known about how teachers in classrooms instruct their students once the classroom door has been closed. There is a need for large-scale instructional-epidemiological studies of methods and practices used by teachers. Findings from these studies would inform policy decisions and allow school and school district leaders to wisely target their resources to move their staff from where they are today to where they need to be tomorrow. In that spirit, results from one small-scale descriptive study will be presented. Methods used in this study may serve as a model for additional research to understand the *state of instruction* in other schools and districts.

Ongoing, Job-Embedded Professional Learning and Support

Prior to 2000, the dominant approach to professional development, or in-service training, consisted of a series of workshops spread throughout the school year that lasted several hours to several days (Little, 1989). These one-shot workshops were intended to help teachers learn new pedagogy from emerging educational research. Often, professional consultants traveled from district to district facilitating these in-service trainings for teachers and other service providers. However, as research indicated that the workshop model was ineffective at achieving transfer of new pedagogy into classroom practice (Bush, 1984; Knight & Cornett, 2009; Little, 1993; Showers, 1982, 1984) job-embedded professional development supplanted the consultant-workshop model.

Job-embedded professional development occurs in the context where one practices their profession. For nurses this learning occurs in hospitals and clinics whereas for teachers job-embedded learning occurs in schools and classrooms. This type of learning is most effective when it focuses on problems of practice that have been identified by teachers (Darling-Hammond, Wei, Andree, Richardson, & Orphanos, 2009; Elmore, 2004; Fullan, 2007). There are several prominent types of job-embedded professional development that have emerged in the literature, they include lesson study, professional learning communities, critical friends groups, and coaching (City et al., 2009; Cornett & Knight, 2008; DuFour & Eaker, 1998; Dunne, Nave, & Lewis, 2000; Joyce & Showers, 2002; Knight, 2007; Watanabe, 2002). Moreover, leading systems change experts in both general education and special education have suggested that ongoing, job-embedded support is a critical element of any school reform (Darling-Hammond et al., 2009; Elmore, 2004; Fullan, 2007), including implementation of Response to Intervention (Lenz, Ehren, & Deshler, 2005; Sailor, 2008/2009, 2009), Positive Behavioral Interventions and Supports (Sugai et al., 2010), and other reforms (e.g., Bean Draper, Hall, Vandermolen, & Zigmond, 2010; Biancarosa, Bryk, & Dexter, 2010).

School districts around the United States and local education agenciess abroad are investing heavily in school-based coaching programs as their primary means of professional development. Since 2000, coaching has increasingly been at the forefront of the implementation strategy for major reform policies in the United States including Reading First, Striving Readers, and the professional development provisions of the No Child Left Behind Act. As Darling-Hammond and colleagues aptly stated, coaching is "one of the fastest growing forms of professional development today" (Darling-Hammond et al., 2009, p. 11). Until recently, policy and systems change experts have advocated for coaching on the basis of prescriptive literature and practice alone, not from rigorous research of the effects of coaching on teachers or student learning.

To date, there is no undergirding unified theory to explain the learning principles and mechanisms of coaching. Although several approaches to coaching have described a "theory of action" (e.g., Costa & Garmston, 2002; Knight, 2007; West & Staub, 2003), it appears somewhat disconnected from other theory, or cannot be applied to other approaches to school-based coaching. Presented here is a unified theory, a theory that relies on established social and cognitive psychology by incorporating existing learning theories into the teaching and learning process of schools. This unified theory can be applied to multiple approaches of school-based coaching and can therefore be used as the basis for comparative research between various approaches. At least in part, the lack of theoretical grounding for coaching has impeded research on the effects. With the following description of a conceptual framework, we intend to diminish this impediment.

Conceptual Framework for Coaching

The conceptual framework for coaching is depicted graphically in Figure 14.1. Our four-part framework has three active processes. The four parts of the framework are (a) coaches, (b) teachers, (c) students, and (d) context with each playing an important and unique role in the moderation of new skill acquisition by teachers. The three active processes that occur between the coach and teacher are (a) job-embedded learning, (b) modeling and observing of skilled practice, and (c) collaborative feedback. Within each of these three processes is an empirically supported theory of learning that guides this model of professional support. When taken as one unified theory, coaches work collaboratively with teachers to develop high level instructional skills that can in turn support high quality curriculum. As such, the effect of the coach on student level outcomes is moderated by multiple teacher variables, including the teacher's content knowledge, curricular knowledge, professional training, and mastery of diverse instructional methods and activities.

Job-Embedded Learning. The first process of the conceptual framework recognizes the inherent differences in instruction from classroom to classroom. In recognizing the importance of these differences, situational learning theory (Lave, 1988; Lave & Wenger; 1990) roots the process of job-embedded learning. According to this learning theory, social interaction is a critical element of situated learning. Learners must become involved in a community of practice embodying belief, behavior, and implicit skill. With exposure over time to these complex social interactions, there is a gradual acquisition of knowledge and skill as the more novice learner adopts the practices of the more skilled expert within the context of everyday activities. When applied to coaching, this means coaches and teachers work within the school and classroom. This theory places great emphasis on the micro-cultures that develop in schools and classrooms and the importance of learning new practice in the midst of these environments and micro-cultures.

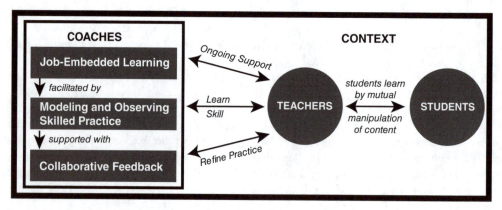

Figure 14.1 Conceptual framework for coaching as a model of job-embedded support

Modeling and Observing Skilled Practice.   The second process of the conceptual framework recognizes that knowledge workers learn new skills through observational learning of other skilled and knowledgeable peers. According to Davenport (2005), knowledge workers are individuals who are highly skilled, educated, and experienced; their work involves the creation, distribution, analysis, or application of knowledge. These valuable workers engage is regular and spontaneous problem solving, decision-making, and collaboration in the course of their work. In short, knowledge workers are thinking for a living; and, they are found in multiple sectors of industry. Teachers are knowledge workers because they work to create knowledge within their classroom.

Often, the skills that knowledge workers possess are difficult to learn due to the complicated and sometimes innate character of the processes used to create, analyze, and apply knowledge for effective problem solving and decision-making. Therefore, knowledge workers often rely on observational learning to improve their practice. To ground this type of observational learning we rely on social learning theory (Bandura, 1977). Social learning theory states that people learn new behavior through observational learning of social factors in their environment. If new skill is observed or demonstrated, and positive outcomes result, the behavior is more likely to be modeled, imitated, and adopted into the practice of others.

Collaborative Feedback.   The third process of the conceptual framework recognizes job-embedded professional learning for teachers is inherently an informal educational process. When learning is informal, traditional methods of curricular learning are less effective. To address this, we turn to dialogue as the means to informal learning (Freire, 1972). Dialogue is "a kind of social relation that engages its participants" (Burbules, 1993, p. 19) for the purpose of creating new understanding. This is an exploratory process whereby the direction of conversation is shaped equally and mutually by those involved, by the coach and the teacher. This mutual shaping allows each person involved in the dialogue to form new insights by reflecting on their experience of an event important to them. When applying this to the coach-teacher interaction, feedback is gleaned during the dialogical exchange between two professionals. Dialogue requires mutual trust, respect, willingness to listen, and readiness to risk one's opinions as an "ideal that can orient our practical and political lives" (Bernstein, 1983, p. 163). Bohm and his colleagues suggested there are three basic conditions for dialogue: (a) suspended assumptions, (b) viewing each other as peers or colleagues, and (c) initial facilitation to guide the dialogue (Bohm, Factor, & Garrett, 1991a,b; Bohm & Peat, 1987).

Effects of Coaching on Teaching Practice and Student Learning

Currently, coaching programs primarily focus on either content coaching or instructional coaching (Lockwood, McCombs, & Marsh, 2010). Both of these approaches to coaching use on-site specialists to support classroom teachers who are learning new pedagogy or implementing new instructional models or curriculum. Content coaches tend to focus on content specific elements of teaching-and-learning (West & Staub, 2003) whereas instructional coaches focus on general instructional practice, classroom management, teaming, and the use of data to inform instruction (Knight, 2007). Regardless of the specific approach to coaching or the content area to which it is applied, several key differences exist between this form of professional development and previously used models. Namely, the coach is school-based, works collaboratively, and primarily works with teachers one-on-one or in small groups for prolonged periods of time. It is this job-embedded feature that allows for substantial and ongoing changes to occur in the professional practice of teachers. This is a key element of RTI adoption and implementation.

Organizing Schools for Instructional Effectiveness

As special education leaders contemplate ways to improve services for students with disabilities in their LEAs, they should consider three factors that are generally involved in the change process. Two of these elements (technical problems and adaptive problems) have been described by Ronald Heifetz and his colleagues from the Center for Public Leadership at Harvard University (Heifetz, 1994; Heifetz & Linsky, 2002). Technical problems are generally ones that can be addressed by applying a specific procedure or going through a set of steps to solve the problem. For example, within an RTI model, one of the technical problems/challenges is determining when to move a student from one tier of instruction to another. This challenge can be addressed by spelling out and applying a specific progress monitoring and decision-making routine.

An adaptive problem, on the other hand, requires people to change their attitudes/opinions or their values. In short, for these kinds of problems to be solved, people must change how they think about and do their jobs—a much more difficult challenge to address. Again, within a RTI framework, special educators may be asked to perform their roles in markedly different ways—ways that may conflict with how they were trained or how they initially perceived their professional identity. It is critical for school leaders to differentiate the types of problems that they are facing (i.e., technical or adaptive) because the nature and the relative ease or difficulty of the solution(s) may be dramatically different.

The third factor that plays a central role in influencing the change process is strong sense of the overall moral purpose of schooling. Fullan (2003) writes about the "moral imperative" for school leaders. That is, seeing that a foundational part of their role is to ensure that the systems they lead are deeply focused on practices enabling all students to learn, reducing the gap between high and low performers, and ensuring students are prepared to be successful citizens and workers.

Using the above three factors as a backdrop against which school leaders should approach school improvement, and in light of the information presented in the previous section on job-embedded supports, a logical question to ask is what specific strategies can school leaders use to bring about significant change in the quality of instruction on a sustained basis? The following section provides a bulleted summary of the relevant professional literature on leadership strategies that support improvements in the quality of instruction. The final two bullet points (principles of change and the central role of the district) are discussed in greater detail in the last part of this section.

Leadership Strategies that Support School Improvement

The most heavily weighted strategies that have emerged from the professional literatures that leaders can leverage to improve student achievement are the following:

- jealously guard the learning time in core academic areas of reading, writing, math, and science (Odden, 2009);
- recognize the importance of and plan for additional learning time and increased individualized instructional time for struggling students using experimental and/or clinical teaching methods (Ehren, Deshler, & Graner, 2010);
- base teacher evaluations on effective use of instructional activities and learning arrangements shown to positively impact student success (Hulleman & Cordray, 2008);
- foster collaborative teaming, planning, and problem-solving that examines data in reference to individual student progress and instructional practice (Lenz & Adams, 2006; Odden, 2009);

- promote learning across professionals within the organization to build capacity through continuous growth (Bain, 2007; Fullan, 2007; Supovitz, 2006);
- ensure that every human and financial resource is aligned between district and schools, is benefiting students, and is being used fully (Marzano & Waters, 2009; Sailor, 2009);
- make staffing decisions (both course assignments and retention decisions) and master schedule decisions (what classes are offered at what time and how many periods) based on student academic and social needs and not teacher preferences or seniority (Weisberg, Sexton, Mulhern, & Keeling, 2009);
- recruit skilled professionals who are willing to collaborate with others, and encourage those who are unwilling to learn, to improve their practice, or to collaborate with others to leave the profession (Odden, 2009; SMHC, 2009);
- adhere to known principles of organizational and individual change when articulating strategic plans and when working on school improvement agendas (Deshler, Deshler, & Biancarosa, 2007; Fullan, 2010); and
- recognize and leverage the central role that should be played by the district in bringing about improvements at the school level (Marzano & Waters, 2009; Zavadsky, 2009).

Because less attention has traditionally been given to the last two factors in the above listing, they will be elaborated in the sections below.

Adhere to Known Principles of Change

While most efforts to change schools are well-intentioned, often they are hastily adopted and initiated through a top-down approach thus ignoring many principles of organizational change (Fullan, 2010). When educators are subjected to one reform after the other, they acquire what Morgan (2001) refers to as "change fatigue." Deshler and colleagues (2007) propose three principles of organizational change that can be used at the school and district level to build a foundation for successful changes. A brief synopsis of each follows.

Organizations and People Must Be Ready to Make Change.
Determining readiness to undertake a change effort is an essential first step. Among the things that will signal a readiness to change are: (a) a compelling need to change; (b) key stakeholders acknowledge an understanding of the need to change; (c) there is strong leadership commitment as evidenced by words and actions; (d) those involved in the change effort possess the necessary skills, attitudes, and dispositions to make it successful; (e) the existing organization has the systems and processes in place to support the change; (f) the capability exist to deal with the responses of various stakeholders to the proposed change (some of which may be ones of resistance); and (g) there are not competing events or initiatives that will detract from or hamper the implementation of the proposed change.

The work of Spillane and his colleagues (e.g., Spillane, Reiser, & Reimer, 2002) have underscored the importance of readiness from a slightly different perspective. Specifically, their research has described the importance of "human sense-making" in understanding and implementing proposed changes.

> Successful implementation of complex policies usually necessitates substantial changes in the implementing agents' schemas. Most conventional theories of change fail to take into account the complexity of human sense making.... Sense making is not a simple decoding of the policy message... (but) an active process of interpretation that draws on the individual's rich knowledge base of understandings, beliefs, and attitudes

(p. 392)

Hence, those who are the targets of change initiatives must be given the opportunity to "make sense of" the proposed change by being able to ask questions, provide input, become proficient with required new skills, and figure out the adjustments in their newly assigned role.

Key Stakeholders Must Be Engaged in Decision Making.   An effective strategy for engaging people in the change process is to form teams that have a clear charter and a set of objectives to accomplish. Well-run teams involve people in creating solutions. When stakeholders are involved in making certain types of decisions, they gain some ownership in the initiative and hopefully find a stake that will help them through the transition they must personally or professionally make. Among the kinds of decisions that teams or committees can participate in making include, deciding interventions to implement and in what sequence; what should be piloted and how; how success will be measured; and what professional development and/or coaching will be needed.

Central to most RTI models are decision-making teams. While there are a variety of ways that leadership within schools can be structured, having key teachers and administrators centrally involved in a decision making body that is responsible for improving the literacy performance of all students in the school is foundational to improving student outcomes on essential metrics. This team should be responsible for reviewing performance data on the student body, making decisions about professional development offerings that would support staff in addressing student needs, determining ways to implement and monitor the effectiveness of targeted interventions, etc. When responsibility for addressing the literacy needs of the school is given to a team with this specific charge, ownership of the problem is shared and the probability for progress is enhanced.

Self-Assessments That Measure Progress Toward Key Goals Must Be Used to Define Success.   The literature on change and improvement, whether at the organizational or individual level has multiple references to the important role feedback plays in accelerating improvement when it is provided in a timely fashion. Several school improvement initiatives have described the powerful role that feedback plays in improving student outcomes either academically or behaviorally (e.g., Goldenberg, Saunders, & Gallimore 2004; Horner, Sugai, & Horner, 2000). Alan Bain's (2007) research on the self-organizing school also has feedback as one of the central design characteristics of schools that are successful in improving student outcomes. Specifically, these schools see their feedback systems as a way that a complex system "talks to itself." In Bain's framework, the whole system learns to interact through the constant exchange of feedback among individuals with the overall benefit accruing to the system as a result. Feedback is seen as the mechanism that makes it possible for teachers, administrators, and staff to grow in their capacities and for the system to produce emergent solutions. For individuals within a system to embrace feedback as a central function for growth and improvement, it is foundational that three features are present: (a) transparency (i.e., instructional decision making and implementation is openly observed and discussed); (b) non-judgmentalism (i.e., candid discussion focuses on specific teaching practices without judging the person), and (c) supportive coaching (i.e., a means must be provided whereby individuals can improve their practice) (Fullan, 2009).

Recognize The Central Role Played by the District

School improvement efforts are generally conceptualized as taking place at the classroom or school level. This is understandable and consistent with Elmore's call for focusing on the instructional core. However, there is growing evidence that well-functioning school districts that do things to support and facilitate the implementation of evidence-based instructional practices can have a significant impact on student outcomes. This fact has been strongly underscored by examining the increasing number of school districts that are dramatically changing the performance of multiple schools in their district and not merely having a handful of schools achieve. Specific examples of school districts accomplishing this are those awarded the Broad Prize from the Eli and Edythe Broad Foundation. Since 2002, these prizes are given to urban school districts that demonstrate the greatest overall performance and improvement in student achievement while reducing gaps among low-income and minority students.

In an analysis of the most recent award winning districts, Zavadsky (2009) identified a set of common characteristics that defined how they beat the odds in raising the performance of their students. The shared characteristics were: (a) an adoption of a long-term view and resisting temptation to veer off course or get pulled in too many directions; (b) a clear definition of what students are to know and be able to do; (c) steps to ensure that teachers felt supported and respected; (d) adoption and execution of a few strategies very well with a laser-like focus on teaching and learning; and (d) alignment of all appropriate elements that support instruction across all organizational levels of the district to produce a seamless educational program for students.

Zavadsky draws the following conclusion about the central role of the district in promoting school success:

> The district serves as a key force or driver for pulling the pieces together. This concept is a departure from research in the 1990s that characterized districts as overbureaucratized organizations that impeded more than helped schools and teachers ... districts [are] making a shift from a fragmented operational focus to building a common base or vision and then building the infrastructure to support the vision ... the central office is a logical centralized catalyst for building commitment and alignment across district levels ... [as it] focuses on student improvement and raising standards (by setting the vision), continually reviewing and redefining instruction, emphasizing the use of data, and aligning operations and supports around common goals.
>
> *(pp. 5–6)*

Marzano and Waters (2009) conducted a meta-analysis of the empirical literature to determine the effects of district behavior on student achievement. As they worked to answer two basic questions, they came to very similar conclusions as did Zavadsky (2009). The two questions they sought to answer were: (a) What is the strength of the relationship between district-level administrative actions and average student achievement? (b) What are the specific district leadership behaviors that are associated with student achievement? They identified 27 studies that met their review criteria. These studies included data from 2,714 districts, approximately 4,500 ratings of superintendent leadership, and 3.4 million student achievement scores.

Their answer to the first question was a computed correlation between district leadership and student achievement of .24; this was statistically significant. In explaining this correlation Marzano and Waters said:

> consider an average superintendent (i.e., he is at the 50th percentile in terms of his leadership skills). Also assume that this superintendent is leading a district where the average student achievement is also at the 50th percentile. Now assume that the superintendent improves his or her leadership abilities by one standard deviation). Given the correlation of .24, we would predict that the average student achievement in the district would increase by 9.5 percentile points or to the 59.5th percentile.
>
> *(2009, pp. 4–5)*

Thus, these findings suggest that when district leaders are carrying out their leadership responsibilities effectively, student achievement across the district is positively affected.

The answer to Marzano and Waters (2009) second question also overlaps with some of Zavadsky's (2009) conclusions. Specifically, they found there to be five district-level leadership "responsibilities" or "initiatives" with a statistically significant correlation with student achievement. These five factors were: (a) ensuring collaborative goal setting; (b) establishing non-negotiable goals for achievement and instruction; (c) creating board alignment with and support of district goals; (d) monitoring achievement and instructional goals; and (e) allocating resources to support the goals for achievement and instruction.

In light of the findings from both the Zavadsky (2009) and Marzano and Waters (2009) studies, as school leaders ponder ways to improve student outcomes, it is essential for them to consider the role of the district in their strategic planning. This is especially true in places where an RTI framework is being implemented. Because of the primary emphasis that RTI leaders have given to classroom and school-level implementation factors, we can now see that it is important to give consideration to the roles that districts can play to ensure optimal implementation of this model.

High Quality Instruction for Every Child

School and district leaders play a central role in ensuring every child, including those with disabilities, are in a school environment that embodies the very best that is known about high quality instruction. Foremost among the tasks facing school leaders are the following, ensure: (a) teaching behaviors manifested by classroom teachers align with the professional literature on instructional effectiveness; (b) teachers have time to engage in collaborative planning with other teachers to optimize learning for students across teachers, settings, and curriculum content; (c) professional development and coaching supports prepare teachers to use effective teaching behaviors at high levels of proficiency; and (d) there is an internal alignment of responsibility, expectations, and accountability for the implementation of teaching behaviors that lead to a better education for a greater number.

Rosenshine and Stevens (1986) synthesized the work of several leading scholars (Gagné, 1970; Good & Grouws, 1979; Hunter & Russell, 1981) on effective teaching practice that described a general model of effective instruction 35 years ago, which was rooted in information processing research, and the emerging research on explicit and direct instruction. The six teaching functions they described were, "1. review, check previous day's work (and reteach, if necessary); 2. present new content/skill; 3. guided student practice (and check for understanding); 4. feedback and correctives (and reteach, if necessary); 5. independent student practice; and 6. weekly and monthly reviews" (Rosenshine & Stevens, 1986, p. 379). In the intervening years since Rosenshine and Stevens described these functions, educational researchers have established a clear link between skilled instructors and increased student academic outcomes (Hattie, 1999; Sanders & Rivers, 1996). This type of "process-product" research indicates that explicit, direct, and scaffolded instruction has a positive effect on academic outcomes (Brophy & Good, 1986; Swanson & Deshler, 2003). Moreover, in 2003 Hattie used a complex statistical modeling strategy to estimate sources of variance within student achievement outcomes. Hattie found that teacher knowledge and practice account for approximately 30% of the total variance found in student achievement, while student factors account for approximately 50%. The student's home life, school, and peers account for the remaining 15% to 30% of variance. Beyond what students arrive prepared to do, teacher effects are the largest single contributor to student achievement.

Teachers impact student academic success by virtue of the control they exercise over a set of coordinated instructional and management activities. To meet the needs of all learners, teachers must effectively plan and manage the instructional period, keep students engaged in the learning, create opportunity for individualized instruction, and match instructional activity to the skill being learned and the knowledge level of the students. Although much is known about the efficacy of various teaching approaches, curricula, school-wide initiatives, and the influence of parenting on student achievement (Hattie, 2009), there remains a paucity of descriptive literature that characterizes adoption of best practice. The remainder of this section will summarize the findings of a recently conducted review of the empirical literature on effective teaching variables and the findings of a small-scale descriptive study designed to measure the degree to which instructional variables are found in settings where students with disabilities are taught.

Findings from a Small-Scale Descriptive Study of Classroom Instruction

There is relatively little known about how high school teachers manage their classroom or engage students in the content. As a preliminary analysis of how this information could be gathered, an observational time study of typical high school instruction was designed and conducted in the spring of 2010 (Cornett, 2010). Three types of instructional settings were observed. The first setting observed, adapted classrooms, use the same curriculum as regular education classes; however, the instructor is a certified special educator and all students enrolled in the class are qualified for special education services. McCall and Skrtic (2009) have referred to these classes as "*special* regular classrooms." Students in these adapted classrooms receive credit that applies toward earning a regular diploma. The second setting observed, co-taught classrooms, are taught by a general education teacher and a certified special educator (Hudson, 1990; Schulte, Osborne, & McKinney, 1990). In these classes, the general educator was primarily responsible for teaching the content with the special educator acting in a support capacity. The third setting observed, resource classrooms, are taught by a certified special education teacher; all students enrolled in the class are qualified for special education services (Wiederholdt, 1974). The defining features of resource rooms vary considerably. Some are designed to somewhat mirror the general education curriculum with added supports. Others are designed primarily to support the acquisition of critical skills to meet individual student needs or to provide instruction to small homogeneous groups of students (Kozleski, Mainzer, & Deshler, 2001).

Across the content areas, teachers were observed using momentary time sampling (MTS) relative to focus area: student engagement, transition time, learning arrangement, and instructional activity. Two independent observers conducted the observations over a three-day time period; one served as the primary data collector and the second as the inter-observer agreement data collector. Data collection was conducted in real-time using MTS, beginning when the teacher started instruction and ending when the teacher stopped instruction. Data was collected during each interval in each of the four focus area such that four observations were recorded during every 30-second observation interval. In total, approximately 8,000 individual observations were recorded. Inter-observer reliability was 95.6%.

Hattie's (2009) synthesis of 815 meta-analyses summarized the efficacy evidence of several teaching approaches. When examining effect sizes reported in educational research, Hattie found that 90% were reported to be positive. Of the remaining 10% of effects, half were expected to be negative (e.g., high student mobility). In brief, this suggests that almost everything positively impacts student achievement. Given this, how do educational leaders differentiate between what works and what works best? Hattie reported that the average effect size of all measured influences in education was $d = .40$. He suggested that effect size of $d = .40$ should therefore be used as the hinge point, or benchmark, for indicating whether or not an educational innovation exceeds the typical average effect of teachers. Effect sizes that exceed the hinge-point of $d = .40$ fall within the "zone of desired effects" (p. 19). However it is important to note that this benchmark value "is not a magic number...but a guideline to begin discussions about what we can aim for if we want to see students change" (p. 17). In effort to make the results of this observational descriptive study meaningful and interpretable, the findings will be presented alongside mean effect size calculations performed previously by Hattie, when available.

Student Time-on-Task. Research on classroom management indicates a variety of instructional activities and classroom management techniques can reduce the likelihood of student problem behavior and enhance student achievement (Doyle, 1986). McNamara and Jolly (1990a,b) investigated ways to increase on-task behavior while reducing off-task and disruptive behaviors of 12- and 13-year-old students, they concluded that, "when disruptive behavior is dealt with by the promotion of on-task behaviors then all types of off-task behavior, from innocuous to grossly disruptive, are reduced" (1990b, p. 248). When off-task and disruptive behavior are reduced, the opportunity for student learning increases. Results from the descriptive study indicated that on average students were on-task 83.9% of all intervals, with no significant difference between the three instructional settings (Cornett, 2010). According to Hattie's (2009) synthesis, the average effect size of time on task is moderate (d = .38) but does not fall within the zone of desired effects (i.e., according to his operational definition an effect size of d = .40 or greater). Karweit's (1984, 1985) syntheses indicated time on task is not analogous to engagement; engagement results from several co-varying factors that include classroom management, lesson design, instructional pedagogy, student enthusiasm for the content, student respect for their teacher, and others. In secondary schools, some students choose to stay overtly on task during instructional time in order to avoid reprisal from the instructor, but level of engagement and the degree that the student is attending to the academic task remain low. In conclusion, not only must students be on-task but the preconditioning factors leading to engagement must also be present; teachers must use the best of classroom management and instructional practices if we expect to impact student achievement.

Transitioning Between Activities. While students transition between places, activities, phases of a lesson, or lessons there is great opportunity for wasted time and off-task behavior; moreover, there is little opportunity for student learning. Transition periods are lost instructional time that teachers should endeavor to reduce. Researchers working in elementary classrooms found that approximately 31 transitions occur daily accounting for about 15% of classroom time (Burns, 1984; Gump, 1967). However, much less is known about the frequency or duration of transitions in high school classrooms. It is commonly assumed that because the seating structure or "room arrangements in secondary classes typically remain the same across activities, major transitions take less time" (Doyle, 1986, p. 406). Therefore, transitions in high school classrooms should take less time than in elementary school (Doyle, 1986) and be fewer in number. Results from the descriptive study indicate that very little time was lost in major transitions during the class period. Transition time accounted for 4.4% of all intervals (Cornett, 2010), which is markedly less time than the 15% of classroom time suggested by Burns (1984) and Gump (1967). Further, results indicated no significant difference in major transition time between the three instructional settings (Cornett, 2010). In conclusion, little time was lost between transitions that occurred in these high school classrooms.

Learning Arrangement. Although whole or large group instruction is commonly viewed as most prevalent in high schools, it is not regarded as an appropriate learning arrangement for extended periods of time in academically diverse classrooms (Archer & Hughes, 2011). During whole group instruction, the teacher gears the lesson to the average ability of the students in the classroom. The hope is that it will meet the educational need of the greatest number of students (Ornstein, 1995). High school students within the same classrooms have diverse academic needs, and whole group instruction only meets the needs of the few students whose ability is near the group average. Results from the descriptive study indicate that in each of the three settings, whole group instruction consumed the largest portion of observation intervals (Cornett, 2010). The percentage of intervals teachers used whole group instruction in adapted, co-taught, and resource rooms is 37.5, 51.0, and 55.5, respectively.

Small group instruction allows students to excise different skills not used in whole or large group instruction. Cohen (1994) found that students who worked well together in small groups were better able to manage competition and conflict among team members, listen to and combine different points of view, construct meaning, and provide support to one another; moreover, these 21st century social skills carryover to college readiness and academic achievement (Springer, Stanne, & Donovan, 1999). Hattie (2009) reported a moderate effect size for small group learning ($d = .49$), which is within the zone of desired effects. However, the average effect size of individualized instruction is small ($d = .23$) and does not reach the threshold of desired effects. This suggests the instructional method used during one-on-one instruction has a larger effect than the learning arrangement. During the descriptive study, small group instruction occurred only in adapted classrooms, and infrequently in that setting (Cornett, 2010). Teacher led one-on-one instruction occurred during 28.8% of the intervals in the resource room setting whereas 4.7% in the co-taught classrooms and not at all in adapted classrooms. In summary, the learning arrangement of the class was primarily independent work or large group instruction with little opportunity for small group learning.

Instructional Activity.   Skilled teachers use a variety of instructional activities to mediate content learning for diverse learners. In our review of the literature on instruction, we identified 30 activities to include in this focus area. The activities ranged from providing explicit feedback, to showing video, and use of formative progress measures. The 30 instructional activities included in the descriptive study have been grouped according to 11 categories described by Hattie (2009). Three observed instructional activities (i.e., academic directions, procedural directions, and lecture) are not included in Hattie's synthesis, but are reported below. Finally, time that teachers were not engaged in instruction is included below and will be reported first. Figure 14.2 shows the mean percentage of intervals in which teachers in all settings engaged in the instructional activities or did not engage in any instructional activity.

The data in Figure 14.2 are arranged from most to least frequently observed instructional activity. Instructional activities that exceed effect size of .40 fall within Hattie's (2009) zone of desired effects and are shown as solid black circles. Activities associated with effect sizes below .40 are shown as gray circles. Activities not associated with an effect size are shown as gray crosses. The diameter of the circles illustrates the effect size of the instructional activity; the larger the circle, the larger the effect of the activity on student achievement. For example, the diameter of formative progress monitoring ($d = .90$) is approximately twice as large as questioning ($d = .46$).

The mean percentage of intervals in which teachers in all settings engaged in any type of instruction was 76.8 whereas the mean percentage not engaged in instruction was 23.2. During a 45-minute class period, teacher disengaged time represents approximately 10.5 minutes per class per day, or about 50 minutes per week per class of instructional time that is not utilized. Teacher disengaged from instruction was the most frequently observed behavior. As seen in Figure 14.2, instructional activities within the zone of desired effects only consumed 28.2% of instructional time. This is significantly less than we expected and hoped to see. Table 14.1 shows the mean percent intervals within each of the instructional activities included in Figure 14.2.

Among instructional activities that have large positive impact on student achievement are various forms of feedback. Formative evaluations are a powerful type of feedback allowing students to understand where mistakes are made in the sequence of learning new concepts,

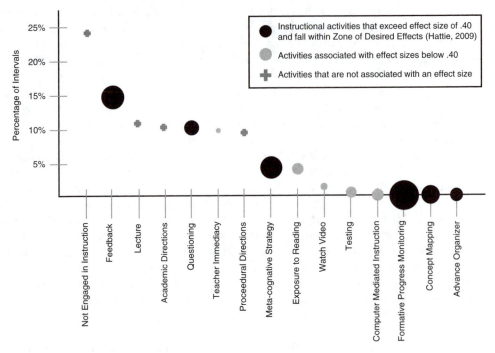

Figure 14.2 Instructional activity by percentage of interval observed by effect size

procedures, or strategies. In their meta-analysis, Fuchs and Fuchs (1986) found that formative evaluations increased achievement for students with a learning disability. Likewise, Hattie (2009) reports an average effect size of *d* = .90, which ranks third among all effects reported in his synthesis. Results from the descriptive study suggest that this type of feedback rarely occurs; with no instance of formative evaluation observed in any setting. However, other types of feedback were observed during 15.5% of observation intervals. Table 14.1 indicates that among the sub-types of feedback, elaborated feedback was most common. Hattie reports that feedback is "among the most powerful influences on achievement" (2009, p. 173), with the average effect size well into the zone of desired effects, *d* = .73.

Small-Scale Descriptive Study Conclusions.   Results from the descriptive study show little time was spent using instructional activities that research indicates are appropriate for diverse academic learners (e.g., concept mapping, strategy instruction, formative assessment). Instructional activities that occurred frequently (e.g., giving academic or procedural direction, and lecturing) are not associated with student academic outcomes in the empirical or prescriptive literature. Moreover, a tremendous amount of instructional time was lost due to teacher disengagement. Typical behavior during disengaged time was checking, writing, or reading e-mail at a computer in the classroom or preparing to teach the lesson in the next class period. In part, this suggests a systemic problem may exist in schools and raises a number of questions about what barriers prevent teachers from engaging with students during the whole instructional period: (a) Why do teachers receive such a large volume of e-mail that they cannot be responded to before and after school? (b) Do teachers have adequate time to co-plan within co-taught classrooms? (c) Is adequate preparation time provided to teachers?

Students spent the observed class period engaged primarily in whole group or independent learning arrangements. When taken together, findings from this study raise serious questions

Table 14.1 Instructional Activity by Subcategory and Mean Percentage of Intervals

d (Hattie, 2009)	Instructional Activity and Subcategory	Mean Percent
0.90	Formative Progress Monitoring	0.0
0.73	Feedback	15.5
	Review Fact, Concept, Procedure	0.7
	Review by Generalization	0.1
	Elaborated Feedback	8.3
	Simple Feedback	6.4
0.69	Meta-cognitive Strategy	3.9
	Reading Strategy	0.3
	Review Skill or Strategy	0.1
	Implicit Model	0.9
	Explicit Model	0.7
	Describe	1.8
0.57	Concept Mapping	0.0
	Post Organizer	0.0
	Other Graphic Device	0.0
0.46	Questioning	8.9
	Questioning for Self Answer	0.2
	Questioning for Verbal Response	7.8
	Questioning for Written Response	0.8
	Questioning for Action Response	0.1
0.41	Advance Organizer	0.0
0.37	Computer Mediated Instruction	0.0
0.36	Exposure to Reading	4.0
	Read to Students	2.3
	Shared Reading	1.6
	Simple Silent Reading	0.0
	Augmented Silent Reading	0.0
0.34	Testing	0.4
	Test	0.0
	Quiz	0.4
0.22	Watch Video	0.7
0.16	Teacher Immediacy	9.7
	Physical Observation	7.9
	Listen	1.7
None Reported	Academic Directions	10.8
None Reported	Procedural Direction	10.2
None Reported	Lecture	12.8
None Reported	Not Engaged in Instruction	23.2

about meaningful access to the general education curriculum for students with disabilities. The results from the co-taught classrooms indicate that physical inclusion in the general education classroom does not guarantee access to the general curriculum as indicated by effective and differentiated instructional activities. Moreover, it is questionable whether co-taught classrooms are the least restrictive environment given the learning arrangements students are placed into and the instructional activities teachers use. However, the same conclusion can be drawn regarding adapted and resource classroom instruction. In summary, the quality of education, as assessed by the instructional and management activities observed in this study, is of questionable quality in each of the three instructional settings and raise questions about the quality of education not only for students with disabilities but for all students.

We undertook this small-scale descriptive study for two primary reasons. First, to demonstrate that high quality instructional-epidemiological research is possible and, second, to gather information about the educational experience of students with disabilities who spend most of their school-day within general education classrooms. However, the results reported here raise more questions than are answered. For those of us committed to bettering the educational experience and outcomes of students with disabilities, these findings should serve as a call to action. We need to critically examine our practice, teacher training programs, and supervision systems. Then, shift policy to ensure that (a) student teachers are taught the best instructional practice; (b) general educational teachers are supported by coaches and special educators in learning differentiated instruction; and (c) school and district leaders develop staff evaluation systems that specifically look for best instructional practice shown to benefit diverse learners.

Recommendations for Special Education Leaders Practice and Future Research

Thirty-five years ago more than half of all of American children with disabilities were not receiving appropriate educational services. Remarkable changes have occurred since the initial passage of P. L. 94-142 in 1975. Today, schools are much more sophisticated in offering systems of differentiated instruction for all students regardless of cognitive, emotional, or physical limitations. However, while the vast majority of students with disabilities are welcomed into classrooms, their successful access to the general education curriculum still remains a challenge on many fronts. Among the challenges still to be overcome are disproportionate placement of minority students, high teacher turn-over, burdensome paperwork, and less than stellar evidence of student achievement.

The overriding message of this chapter is that any turn around or school improvement initiative for students with disabilities must place high quality instruction at the very center of its change strategy. This message parallels what David and Cuban (2010) found in a recent analysis of twenty-three school reform models (one of which was RTI). Namely, while changes in school structures and organizational factors (e.g., altering school schedules, infusing technology, etc.) may play an important role, their influence on student achievement pales in comparison to the relative power of high quality instruction as the centerpiece of school reform. Therefore, a core question for all school leaders to ask is what kinds of strategies can school leaders use to bring about significant change in the quality of instruction on a sustained basis?

In this chapter we have tried to make the case that there is a growing evidence base on high leverage teaching variables that teachers and administrators can draw upon in planning, implementing, and evaluating the instruction that is provided to students. Practitioners now have a growing amount of information on a broad array of teaching variables that will produce the largest effect sizes if they are used with fidelity and with sufficient intensity. There are two recently published books containing thorough reviews of the literature on instructional variables and teaching routines shown to produce the greatest amount of student achievement. The information covered in these books should be understood and applied by special education leaders in planning professional development programs and in guiding their decisions to hire new staff and evaluate the instructional practices of current staff. The first book is *Explicit Instruction: Effective and Efficient Teaching* by Anita Archer and Charles Hughes (2011); the second is *Visible Learning: A Synthesis of over 800 Meta-analyses Relating to Achievement* by John Hattie (2009).

To help ensure satisfactory rates of implementation of these high-leverage teaching practices, we have argued that school leaders should carefully examine the professional learning practices they employ to determine the degree to which they reflect what multiple studies have now told us. Namely, one-shot workshops with no opportunity to practice newly taught instructional procedures in their classroom settings without ample, high quality coaching and feedback simply *do not work*. Continued investments by administrators in one-shot workshops is a waste of resources. However, to the degree that school leaders use coaches to provide job-embedded learning, teacher capacity will grow and the chances of their proficient application of evidence-based practices to improve student outcomes will increase.

Finally, informed leadership strategies and values that make high quality instruction their top priority leads to an unrelenting focus on the goal of enabling all of their teachers to proficiently implement evidence-based practices. Such strategies and values include the following: very carefully protecting instructional time, making teacher collaboration and co-planning a high priority, providing differentiated instruction through instructional tiers of varying intensity, aligning financial and human resources between the district and schools, basing teaching assignments on student and not teacher/administrator needs, adhering to known principles of organizational and individual change, and leveraging district resources and capacities to support the instructional mission of schools.

To better equip special education leaders to be even more influential in impacting teacher effectiveness, answers to the following research questions should be sought:

- *What are the cost implications of implementing ongoing, job-embedded professional learning and support?* While models of professional development other than one-shot workshops have strong face validity and growing evidence of their effectiveness on student achievement, there is a paucity of evidence regarding the costs of such models. To gain traction over the long haul and to have viability in times of limited economic resources, studies that demonstrate the cost-effectiveness of models characterized by such things as job-embedded professional learning and ongoing coaching must be determined. Some preliminary investigations have yielded favorable results (e.g., Knight, 2010; Levin, Catlin, & Elson, 2010); however, more thorough investigations remain to be done.
- *What leadership approaches best support ongoing, job-embedded professional learning and support?* There is more knowledge and conceptual understanding about the types of professional learning and support detailed in this chapter than there is knowledge of how to best prepare educational leaders to successfully vision, implement, and sustain ongoing, job-embedded professional learning and support on the front lines. Determining the skills, dispositions, and values essential for school leaders to most effectively implement this approach to professional development and identifying how to equip school leaders with these necessary skill is vital. Guidance for addressing these issues may be found, in part, in the report prepared by the Southern Regional Education Board entitled *Schools Need Good Leaders Now: State Progress in Creating a Learner-Centered School Leadership System* (Fry, Bottoms, O'Neill, & Walker 2007). The strategies described in this report are relevant because it places high quality instruction at the heart of all school leader training—this is the same posture described in this chapter.
- *To what degree do current special education leadership preparation programs prepare leaders to understand instructional effectiveness?* If special education leaders are to provide the necessary leadership

that will result in a significant changes in the quality of instruction provided to students with disabilities, they must have a deep understanding of what constitutes high quality instruction, how to measure and observe it in practice, how to provide meaningful and actionable feedback to teachers, and how to conceptualize and implement professional learning experiences on instructional effectiveness. A careful analysis of the curriculum and practicum offerings in existing leadership preparation programs will provide a baseline for determining the kinds of changes that should be made in these programs to better prepare special education leaders with the proper skill sets and dispositions around high quality instruction.

* *How can technological advancements be leveraged to increase the effectiveness of special education leaders in raising the quality of instruction of all teachers?* One of the most powerful factors in altering adult behavior is timely, specific, frequent, and elaborated feedback. Providing that kind of feedback to large numbers of teachers can be complex and time consuming at best and overwhelmingly daunting at worst. With the burgeoning number of technological advances available, it is important to accelerate the number of studies being done on ways these innovations can be used to capture, categorize, and analyze instructional behaviors that can be examined and acted upon by practitioners and their coaches.

* *What kinds of large-scale epidemiological studies of instructional practices can best inform leadership practices, policy, and future research?* The findings of the Cornett (2010) study discussed in this chapter underscores the valuable array of data that can emerge through observational studies focusing on instructional practice. This study, however, was very limited in scope. Much larger studies in a broad array of settings (e.g., various instructional tiers in an RTI framework) are needed. A detailed picture of where classroom practice stands currently will be informative to educational leaders and teachers as well as policy makers. This baseline information will be invaluable in providing direction for future research, practice, and policy around issues of instructional effectiveness.

Notes

1 We use the term "diverse learners" broadly. The term encompasses racial diversity, gender diversity, ethnic diversity, socioeconomic diversity, and disability.

2 For information about these technical aspects of RTI, see the following: Sailor (2009); Shores and Chester (2009).

References

Archer, A. L., & Hughes, C. A. (2011). *Explicit instruction: Effective and efficient teaching.* New York: Guilford.

Bain, A. (2007). *The self-organizing school: Next-generation comprehensive school reforms.* Lanham, MD: Rowman & Littlefield Education.

Bandura, A. (1977). *Social learning theory.* New York: General Learning Press.

Bean, R. M., Draper, J. A., Hall, V., Vandermolen, J., & Zigmond, N. (2010). Coaches and coaching in reading first schools. *The Elementary School Journal, 111,* 87–114.

Bernstein, R. J. (1983). *Beyond objectivism and relativism: Science, hermeneutics and praxis.* Oxford, UK: Blackwell.

Biancarosa, G., Bryk, A. S., & Dexter, E. R. (2010). Assessing the value-added effects of literacy collaborative professional development on student learning. *The Elementary School Journal, 111,* 8–34.

Bohm, D., Factor, D., & Garrett, P. (1991a). *Dialogue: A proposal 1/2.* Retrieved from: http://www.world.std.com/~lo/bohm/0000.html

Bohm, D., Factor, D., & Garrett, P. (1991b). *Dialogue: A proposal 2/2.* Retrieved from: http://www.world.std.com/~lo/bohm/0001.html

Bohm, D., & Peat, D. (1987). *Science, order, and creativity.* New York: Bantam.

Burns, R. B. (1984). How time is used in elementary schools: The activity structure of classrooms. In L. W. Anderson (Ed.), *Time and school learning: Theory, research and practice* (pp. 91–127). London: Croom Helm.

Brophy, J. E., & Good, T. L. (1986). Teacher behavior and student achievement. In M. C. Wittrock (Ed.), *Handbook of Research on Teaching* (3rd ed.; pp. 328–375). New York: MacMillan.

Burbules, N. (1993) *Dialogue in teaching: Theory and practice.* New York: Teachers College Press.

Bush, R. N. (1984). *Effective staff development. In making our schools more effective: Proceedings of three state conferences.* San Francisco: Far West Laboratories.

City, E. A., Elmore, R. F., Fiarman, S. E., & Teitel, L. (2009). *Instructional rounds in education: A network approach to improving teaching and learning.* Cambridge, MA: Harvard Education Press.

Cohen, E. G. (1994). Restructuring the classroom: Conditions for productive small groups. *Review of Educational Research, 64,* 1–35.

Cornett, J. (2010). What's evidence got to do with it? An observational study of research-based instructional behavior in high school classes .Masters Thesis, University of Kansas. *Masters Abstracts International, 48,* 5. (UMI No. 1476574)

Cornett, J., & Knight, J. (2008). Research on coaching. In J. Knight (Ed.), *Coaching: Approaches and perspectives* (pp. 192–216). Thousand Oaks, CA: Corwin.

Cortiella, C. (2005). *A parent's guide to response-to-intervention* [Parent advocacy brief]. New York: National Center for Learning Disabilities.

Costa, A. L., & Garmston, R. J. (2002). *Cognitive coaching: A foundation for renaissance schools* (2nd ed.). Norwood, MA: Christopher-Gordon.

Darling-Hammond, L. (2000). Teacher quality and student achievement: A review of state policy evidence. *Education Policy Analysis Archives, 8,* 1–44.

Darling-Hammond, L., Wei, R. C., Andree, A., Richardson, N., & Orphanos, S. (2009). *Professional learning in the learning profession: A status report on teacher development in the United States and abroad.* Dallas, TX. National Staff Development Council.

Davenport, T. H. (2005). *Thinking for a living: How to get better performances and results from knowledge workers.* Cambridge, MA: Harvard Business Press.

David, J. L., & Cuban, L. (2010). *Cutting through the hype: The essential guide to school reform.* Cambridge, MA: Harvard Education Press.

Deshler, R. T., Deshler, D. D., & Biancarosa, G. (2007). School and district change to improve adolescent literacy. In D. D. Deshler, A. S. Palincsar, G. Biancarosa, & M. Nair (Eds.), *Informed choices for struggling adolescent readers: A research-based guide to instructional programs and practices* (pp. 92–110). Newark, DE: International Reading Association.

Desimone, L. M., Porter, A. C., Garet, M. S., Yoon, K. S., & Birman, B. F. (2002). Effects of professional development on teachers' instruction: Results from a three-year longitudinal study. *Educational Evaluation and Policy Analysis, 24,* 81–112.

Doyle, W. (1986). Classroom organization and management. In M. C. Wittrock (Ed.), *Handbook of Research on Teaching* (3rd ed.; pp. 392–431). New York: MacMillan.

DuFour, R., & Eaker, R. (1998). *Professional learning communities at work.* Bloomington, IN: National Educational Service.

Dunne, F., Nave, B., & Lewis, A. (2000). Critical friends groups: Teachers helping teachers to improve student learning. *The Research Bulletin, 28.* Bloomington, IN: Center for Evaluation, Development and Research.

Ehren, B. J., Deshler, D. D., & Graner, P. S. (2010). Using the content literacy continuum as a framework for implementing RTI in secondary schools. *Theory Into Practice, 49,* 315–322.

Elmore, R. F. (1996). Getting to scale with good educational practice. *Harvard Educational Review, 66,* 1–26.

Elmore, R. F. (2004). *School reform from the inside out: Policy, practice, and performance.* Cambridge, MA: Harvard Education Press.

Elmore, R. F., & Burney, D. (1997). *Investing in teacher learning: Staff development and instructional improvement in Community School District #2, New York City.* Washington, DC: National Commission on Teaching and America's Future.

Freire, P. (1972) *Pedagogy of the oppressed.* New York: Continuum.

Fry, B., Bottoms, G., O'Neill, K., & Walker, S. (2007). *Schools need good leaders now: State progress in creating a learning-centered school leadership system.* Atlanta, GA: Southern Regional Education Board.

Fuchs, D., & Deshler, D. D. (2007). What we need to know about responsiveness to intervention (and shouldn't be afraid to ask). *Learning Disabilities Research & Practice, 22,* 129–136.

Fuchs, L. S., & Fuchs, D. (1986). Effects of systematic formative evaluation: A meta-analysis. *Exceptional Children, 53,* 199–208.

Fullan, M. (2003). *The moral imperative of school leadership.* Thousand Oaks, CA: Corwin Press.

Fullan, M. (2007). *The new meaning of educational change* (4th ed.). New York: Teachers College Press.

Fullan, M. F. (2009). *The challenge of change.* New York: Corwin.

Fullan, M. (2010). *Motion leadership: The skinny on becoming change savvy.* Thousand Oak, CA: Corwin Press.

Gagné, R. (1970). *The conditions of learning.* New York: Holt, Rinehart & Winston.

Goldenberg, C., Saunders, W., & Gallimore, R. (2004). *Settings for change: A practical model for linking rhetoric and action to improve achievement for diverse students.* Final Report to the Spencer Foundation (Grant #19800042).

Good, T. L., & Grouws, D. A. (1979). The Missouri mathematics effectiveness project. *Journal of Educational Psychology, 71*, 355–362.

Gump, P. V. (1967). *The classroom behavior setting: Its nature and relation to student behavior (Final report).* Washington, DC: U. S. Office of Education, Bureau of Research. (ERIC Document Reproduction Service No. ED 015 515)

Hattie, J. A. (1999, June). *Influences on student learning* [Inaugural professorial address, University of Auckland, New Zealand]. Retrieved April 11, 2010, http://www.education.auckland.ac.nz/uoa/home/about/staff/j.hattie/hattie-papers-download/influences

Hattie, J. A. C. (2009). *Visible learning: A synthesis of over 800 meta-analyses relating to achievement.* New York: Routledge.

Heifetz, R. A. (1994). *Leadership without easy answers.* Cambridge, MA: Harvard University Press.

Heifetz, R. A., & Linsky, M. (2002). *Leadership on the line: Staying alive through the dangers of leading.* Cambridge, MA: Harvard Business School Press.

Horner, R. H., Sugai, G., & Horner, H. F. (2000, February). A schoolwide approach to student discipline. *The School Administrator, 2*, 20–23.

Hudson, F. (1990). *Research reports for Kansas City, Kansas public schools division of special education on CTM-collaborative teaching model at Stony Point Sough Elementary School, 1989–90.* Kansas City: University of Kansas Medical Center, Department of Special Education.

Hulleman, C. S., & Cordray, D. S. (2008). Moving from the lab to the field: The role of fidelity and achieved relative intervention strength. *Journal of Research on Educational Effectiveness, 2*, 88–110.

Hunter, M., & Russell, D. (1981). Planning for effective instruction: Lesson design. In *Increasing your teaching effectiveness.* Palo Alto, CA: The Learning Institute.

Joyce, B., & Showers, B. (2002). *Student achievement: Through staff development* (3rd ed.). Alexandria, VA: Association for Supervision and Curriculum Development.

Karweit, N. (1984). Time-on-task reconsidered: Synthesis of research on time and learning. *Educational Leadership, 41*, 32–35.

Karweit, N. (1985). Should we lengthen the school term? *Educational Researcher, 14*, 9–15.

Knapp, M. S. (1997). Between systemic reforms and the mathematics and sciences classroom: The dynamics of innovation, implementation, and professional learning. *Review of Educational Research, 2*, 227–266.

Knight, J. (2007). *Instructional coaching: A partnership approach to improving instruction.* Thousand Oaks, CA: Corwin Press.

Knight, D. S. (2010). *The economic cost of instructional coaching* (master's thesis). Available at http://disexpress.umi.com/dxweb#results. (Order No. AAT 1484285.)

Knight, J., & Cornett, J. (2009, April). *Studying the impact of instructional coaching.* Paper presented at the annual meeting of the American Educational Research Association, San Diego, CA.

Kozleski, E., Mainzer, R., & Deshler, D. D. (2001). *Bright futures: An agenda for action for changing the conditions of teaching in special education.* Reston, VA: Council of Exceptional Children.

Lave, J. (1988). *Cognition in practice: Mind, mathematics, and culture in everyday life.* Cambridge, UK: Cambridge University Press.

Lave, J., & Wenger, E. (1990). *Situated learning: Legitimate peripheral participation.* Cambridge, UK: Cambridge University Press.

Lenz, B. K., & Adams, G. (2006). Planning practices that optimize curriculum access. In D. D. Deshler & J. B. Schumaker (Eds.), *Teaching adolescents with disabilities: Accessing the general education curriculum* (pp. 35–78). New York: Corwin.

Lenz, B. K., Ehren, B. J., & Deshler, D. D. (2005). The content literacy continuum: A school reform framework for improving adolescent literacy for all students. *Teaching Exceptional Children. 37*, 60–63.

Levin, H. M., Catlin, D., & Elson, A. (2010). Adolescent literacy programs: Costs of implementation. New York: Carnegie Corporation of New York.

Little, J. W. (1989). District policy choices and teachers' professional development opportunities. *Educational Evaluation and Policy Analysis, 11*, 165–179.

Little, J. W. (1993). Teachers' professional development in a climate of educational reform. *Educational Evaluation and Policy Analysis, 15*, 129–151.

Lockwood, J. R., McCombs, J. S., & Marsh, J. (2010). Linking reading coaches and student achievement: Evidence from Florida middle schools. *Educational Evaluation and Policy Analysis, 32*, 372–388.

Marzano, R. J., & Waters, T. (2009). *District leadership that works: Striking the right balance.* Bloomington, IN: Solution Tree Press.

McCall, Z., & Skrtic, T. M. (2009). Intersectional needs politics: A policy frame for the wicked problem of disproportionality. *Multiple Voices, 11*, 3–23.

McNamara, E., & Jolly, M. (1990a). The reduction of disruptive behavior using feedback of on-task behavior: An across setting study of a class of 12- and 13-year-olds. *Behavioural Psychotherapy, 18*, 103–119.

McNamara, E., & Jolly, M. (1990b). Are disruptive behaviours reduced when levels of on-task behaviours increase? An across settings study of a class of 12- and 13-year-old pupils—II. *Behavioural Psychotherapy, 18*, 239–249.

Mehta, J. D. (2006). The transformation of American educational policy, 1980–2001: Ideas and the rise of accountability politics. Doctoral dissertation, Harvard University, Cambridge, MA. Retrieved May 25, 2009, from Dissertations & Theses: Full Text. (University Microfilms No. AAT 3245170)

Mellard, D. F., & Deshler, D. D. (2004). LD identification: It's not simply a matter of building a better mousetrap. *Learning Disability Quarterly, 27*, 229–242.

Morgan, N. (2001). How to overcome "change fatigue." *Harvard Management Update, 6*, 1–3.

Odden, A. (2009). *Ten strategies for doubling student performance.* Thousand Oaks, CA: Corwin.

Ornstein, A. C. (1995). Synthesis of research: Teaching whole-group classrooms. *Peabody Journal of Education, 70*, 104–116.

Rosenshine, B., & Stevens, R. (1986). Teaching functions. In M. C. Wittrock (Ed.), *Handbook of Research on Teaching* (3rd ed.; pp. 376–391). New York: MacMillan.

Sailor, W. (2008/2009). Access to the general curriculum: Systems change or tinker some more? *Research & Practice for Persons with Severe Disabilities, 33*, 249–257.

Sailor, W. (2009). *Making RTI work: How smart schools are reforming education through schoolwide response-to-intervention.* New York: Jossey-Bass.

Sanders, W. L., & Horn, P. (1998). Research findings from the Tennessee Value-Added Assessment System (TVAAS) database: Implications for educational evaluation and research. *Journal of Personnel Evaluation in Education, 12*, 247–256.

Sanders, W. L., & Rivers, J. C. (1996). *Cumulative and residual effects of teachers on future student academic achievement.* Knoxville, TN: University of Tennessee.

Schulte, A., Osborne, S., & McKinney, J. (1990) Academic outcomes for students with learning disabilities in consultation and resource programs. *Exceptional Children, 57*, 162–172.

Shores, C., & Chester, K. (2009). *Using RtI for school improvement: Raising every student's achievement score.* Thousand Oaks, CA: Corwin.

Showers, B. (1982). *Transfer of training: The contribution of coaching.* Eugene, OR: Centre for Educational Policy and Management.

Showers, B. (1984). *Peer coaching: A strategy for facilitating transfer of training.* Eugene, OR: Centre for Educational Policy and Management.

Skrtic, T. M. (Ed.). (1995). *Disability and democracy: Reconstructing (special) education for postmodernity.* New York: Teachers College Press.

Skrtic, T. M. (2005). A political economy of learning disabilities. *Learning Disability Quarterly, 28*, 149–155.

SMHC. (2009). *Taking human capital seriously: Talented teachers in every classroom, talented principals in every school.* Madison, WI: Consortium for Policy Research in Education.

Snyder, T. D., & Dillow, S. A. (2010). *Digest of Education Statistics 2009* (NCES 2010-013). National Center for Education Statistics, Institute of Education Sciences, U.S. Department of Education. Washington, DC.

Spillane, J. P., Reiser, B. J., & Reimer, T. (2002). Policy implementation and cognition: Reframing and refocusing implementation research. *Review of Educational Research, 72*, 387–431.

Springer, L., Stanne, M. E., & Donovan, S. S. (1999). Effects of small-group learning on undergraduates in science, mathematics, engineering, and technology: A meta-analysis. *Review of Educational Research, 69*, 21–51.

Sugai, G., Horner, R. H., Algozzine, R., Barrett, S., Lewis, T., Anderson, C., Bradley, R., et al. (2010). *School-wide positive behavior support: Implementers' blueprint and self-assessment.* Eugene, OR: University of Oregon.

Supovitz, J. A. (2006). *The case for district-based reform: Leading, building, and sustaining school improvement.* Cambridge, MA: Harvard Education Press.

Swanson, H. L., & Deshler, D. D. (2003). Instructing adolescents with learning disabilities: Concerting a meta-analysis to practice. *Journal of Learning Disabilities, 36*, 124–135.

Watanabe, T. (2002). Learning from Japanese lesson study. *Educational Leadership, 59*, 36–39.

Weisberg, D., Sexton, S., Mulhern, J., & Keeling, D. (2009). *The widget effect: Our national failure to acknowledge and act on teacher differences.* Boulder, CO and Tempe, AZ: Education and the Public Interest Center & Education Policy Research Unit.

Wenglinsky, H. (2000). *How teaching matters: Bringing the classroom back into discussions of teacher quality.* Princeton, NJ: Policy Information Center.

West, L., & Staub, F. C. (2003). *Content-focused coaching: Transforming mathematics lessons.* Portsmouth, NH: Heinemann.

Westbury, I. (1993). American and Japanese achievement again: A response to Baker. *Educational Researcher, 22*, 21–25.

Wiederholdt, J. L. (1974). Planning resource rooms for the mildly handicapped. *Focus on Exceptional Children, 8*, 1–10.

Zavadsky, H. (2009). *Bringing school reform to scale: Five award-winning urban districts.* Cambridge, MA: Harvard Education Press.

15

Teacher Quality and Effectiveness in an Era of Accountability
Challenges and Solutions in Special Education?

Mary T. Brownell

UNIVERSITY OF FLORIDA

Bonnie S. Billingsley

UNIVERSITY OF NORTH CAROLINA AT GREENSBORO

James McLeskey and Paul T. Sindelar

UNIVERSITY OF FLORIDA

Quality teachers are considered one of the most important resources for improving student achievement in schools. Over the past decade or so, researchers have demonstrated repeatedly, using value-added growth modeling, the contribution that teachers make to the achievement of students (Hanushek, Rivkin, & Kain, 2005; Kane, Rockoff, & Staiger, 2008). Next to students themselves, teachers produce the largest effect on student achievement in the educational system. As a result, many federal and state initiatives have emerged over the last decade whose main intention is to support strategies for securing and developing quality teachers (e.g., The Reading First Initiative, Teacher Quality Enhancement Grants). These initiatives have had a profound impact on both the initial preparation and on going professional development of teachers in general and special education. The Individuals with Disabilities Education Act and the No Child Left Behind Act (NCLB) acknowledged research demonstrating the role that content knowledge played in effective instruction by insisting that all teachers have the necessary subject matter knowledge they need to teach to be designated as highly qualified. Additionally, both pieces of legislation recognize the important role that professional development and induction of beginning teachers play in helping teachers to provide evidence-based instruction. The Reading First Program, President George W. Bush's signature program funded under NCLB, is the best example of a comprehensive professional development effort to improve the quality of teachers' reading instruction that has ever been undertaken by the federal government.

Students with disabilities, unfortunately, are at risk for having teachers that are not qualified to assist them with their learning and behavior needs. The majority of these students spend much of their day in general education classrooms (McLeskey, Landers, Williamson, & Hoppey, 2010) where their teachers struggle to address the diversity of students' achievement needs, even when provided considerable support via professional development (Garet et al., 2008; Roehrig, Brownell, Schatschneider, & Petscher, 2010). Moreover, there is the possibility that they will not have access to a quality special education teacher either. Historically, there has been a chronic shortage of special education teachers (Boe & Cook, 2006; McLeskey, Tyler, & Flippin, 2004; U.S. Department of Education, 2010); thus, schools have often been in the position of hiring teachers that are not certified in special education (Boe & Cook, 2006). Additionally, to address shortages of certified teachers, policies and strategies have been put into place that may exacerbate them. Under pressure to staff schools with qualified special education teachers, many policy makers and school district leaders have advocated for routes to the classroom that require minimal upfront preparation. Perhaps the best illustration of this point is federal legislation that allows special education teachers to be identified as highly qualified with minimal preparation. According to the Individuals with Disabilities Education Act (IDEA), teachers are highly qualified to teach if they have a bachelor's degree and have passed a certification exam in special education and any content area they are assigned to teach. Fast routes to the classroom, however, are likely to exacerbate both supply and quality problems. For one, such teachers are more likely to leave the schools that need them most (Sindelar et al., 2010); and secondly, these teachers are unlikely to be qualified to meet the needs of students with disabilities (Feng & Sass, 2010).

In the following sections of this chapter, we discuss the shortages of qualified teachers for students with disabilities and the contributing factors. We also describe how attempts to ameliorate shortages have created additional problems for securing adequate numbers of quality teachers. We go on to analyze the research behind strategies that have been promulgated for improving the quality of teachers for students with disabilities and their retention in the work place, and provide some thoughts about what research is needed to improve practice in these areas.

Shortages of Qualified Teachers for Students with Disabilities

For at least the last two decades, there has been a severe, chronic shortage of qualified special education teachers (SETs) (Boe & Cook, 2006; McLeskey et al., 2004; U.S. Department of Education, 2010). During this time, from 7.4% to 12.4% of the special education teaching force has lacked credentials as fully certified or highly qualified (McLeskey & Billingsley, 2008; U.S. Department of Education, 2010). School districts in all geographic areas of the U.S. reported difficulty finding sufficient numbers of qualified SETs (AAEE, 2008), resulting in a shortage of approximately 35,000 teachers during the 2007–08 school year (U.S. Department of Education, 2010).

A major contributing factor to the SET shortage is the lack of a sufficient supply of first time, fully certified teachers who are produced by teacher preparation programs (Cook & Boe, 2007). The inadequate supply of SETs has been worsened by the decline in production of special education degree programs, as well as the growth in special education teaching positions that has occurred over the last 20 years (Boe & Cook, 2006; Cook & Boe, 2007). This has resulted in school districts hiring many of their first-time teachers from out of field or without extensive teacher preparation, and a shortage in special education that is somewhat greater than in general education (Boe & Cook, 2006).

The difficulty in finding qualified SETs is most extreme at the secondary level (Billingsley, Fall, & Williams, 2006; McLeskey & Billingsley, 2008). Research has shown that one contributor to effective teaching at the secondary level is subject matter knowledge (Wilson, Floden, & Ferrini-Mundy, 2002). SETs who teach English, math, social studies, and science at the secondary level often lack this content knowledge. For example, Boe and Borush (cited in McLeskey & Billingsley, 2008) speculated that 82% to 99% of SETs would not meet the highly qualified criterion of NCLB and lacked sufficient knowledge in the content area they were teaching. Similarly, Billingsley and colleagues (2006) found that only a small percentage of secondary SETs were certified in core academic areas.

It is noteworthy that trends in the shortage of highly qualified SETs have changed significantly in the last 5 years. For example, the total number of SETs in the U.S. for students ages 6–21 peaked in 2005–06 at 426,493, and has since declined by over 8% to 390,421 in 2007–08. A decline has also occurred in the number of SETs who lack certification or are not highly qualified. This number peaked in 2002–03 at over 49,000 (over 12% of the teaching force), and has since declined to approximately 35,000 (about 9% of the teaching force).

Although it is not clear why shortages have decreased, it is likely that the highly qualified requirement of the NCLB Act had some influence, as well as the economic crisis in the United States, which has significantly reduced funding for public schools in many states. An additional factor that very likely contributed to these changes was a reduction of approximately 3% in the proportion of school age students identified with disabilities (McLeskey et al., 2010). We would speculate that these factors likely contributed to both the decline in the special education teaching force, as well as the decrease in the number of teachers who are not highly qualified. These numbers suggest a positive trend toward higher percentages of highly qualified SETs, but it is too soon to conclude that real and substantial change is occurring. We can thus only conclude that in spite of these changes, the shortage of highly qualified SETs remains a significant problem.

A final important consideration regarding the SET shortage is the distinct possibility that in the future shortages may be less pervasive and general than has been true in the past. For example, in spite of the overall decline in the SET shortage, we anticipate that shortages of culturally diverse teachers (Tyler, Yzquierdo, Lopez-Reyna, & Flippin, 2002) are likely to persist. We also anticipate that high poverty urban and rural schools are likely to continue to experience SET shortages (Fall & Billingsley, 2008), in spite of adequate supplies elsewhere in the same states (Lauritzen & Freeman, 1993). Shortages at high poverty schools are likely to persist because, with reduced funding, school districts will not have adequate funds to cover the salary differentials necessary for hard-to-staff schools to recruit and retain fully qualified teachers (Hanushek, Kain, & Rivkin, 2004; Imazeki, 2003). Furthermore, certain areas of certification—EBD, deaf and hard of hearing, visual impairments—are also likely to continue to experience shortages, the latter two because of limited training capacity (Corn & Spungin, 2003; Johnson, 2003). EBD will remain an area of significant demand because of the high turnover in such positions.

To address the teacher shortage in special education, policy makers have touted alternatives to traditional programs that are designed to streamline preparation and attract to the field capable individuals who eschewed lengthy formal preparation. Indeed, increasing numbers of teachers including SETs (Boe, Sunderland, & Cook, 2006; Feistritzer, 2008) are entering the profession via alternative preparation routes. However, in special education, most of these routes are comparable to traditional, on-campus programs in length and rigor, and most are offered by colleges and universities that also conduct on-campus training (Rosenberg, Boyer, Sindelar, & Misra, 2007; Sindelar et al., 2010).

In contrast to these intensive programs, Rosenberg et al. (2007) reported that approximately 10% of alternate route programs from their sample were *fast track*, in that they were short in duration and immediately placed candidates in classrooms as teachers of record. Although there is no evidence linking length of preparation and student achievement, length of preparation has been linked to other important outcomes. For example, Boe, Shin, and Cook (2007) reported that SETs with extensive preparation were (a) more likely to be fully certified in their main teaching assignment, (b) less likely to be teaching out of field, and (c) more likely to report feeling well-prepared for their work.

These findings are based on analyses of the 1999–2000 administration of the Schools and Staffing Survey (SASS). To define *extensive teacher preparation* (as well as *some teacher preparation* and *little or no teacher preparation*), Boe et al. (2007) were limited to information available from SASS.

Thus, extensive preparation comprised at least 5 to 9 weeks of practice teaching and at least three of four training components (courses in selecting and adapting instructional materials; courses in educational psychology; classroom observations; and feedback on teaching). At best, SASS respondents with extensive preparation were known to have completed 10 or more weeks of practice teaching and all four training components.

Although this definition sets a low bar for defining extensive training, Sindelar et al. (2010) reported corroborating findings from a study of 31 alternative route SET preparation programs. These authors found that attrition was greater among teachers who completed brief, district-sponsored alternative route programs than among teachers who completed more extensive (but alternative) preparation. In particular, many fast-track graduates planned to leave special education teaching for jobs in general education. Graduates of these fast-track programs completed, on average, 146 clock hours of training, much of it in general education courses. Graduates of more extensive alternative preparation models averaged from 500 to 900 clock hours.

Still another challenge related to providing high quality instruction for students with disabilities is ensuring that general education teachers are prepared to meet their needs (Conderman & Johnston-Rodriguez, 2009; Harvey, Yssel, Bauserman, & Merbler, 2010). Currently 80% of students with disabilities are included in general education classrooms for a substantial portion of the school day (McLeskey et al.,2010). The need to provide high quality, effective instruction in these settings has been highlighted recently by the increasingly wide spread use of Response to Intervention (RTI) instructional models and multi-level frameworks to deliver instruction (Spectrum K12, 2009; Sugai & Horner, 2009; Torgesen, 2009). Inclusive programs and multi-level frameworks require that general education teachers have skills to differentiate instruction, collaborate, and provide effective, evidence based practices to meet student needs (Conderman & Johnston-Rodriguez, 2009; Gersten et al., 2009; Harvey et al., 2010).

Available evidence indicates that general education teachers are often not well prepared to meet the needs of students with disabilities (DeSimone & Parmer, 2006; McHatton & McCray, 2007). Furthermore, most general education teacher education programs provide little preparation for beginning teachers in special education (Harvey et al., 2010; McHatton & McCray, 2007). The demands placed on both special and general education teachers are likely to increase in the coming years, as inclusive programs become more prevalent (Zigmond, Kloo, & Volonino, 2009). School districts increasingly use RTI or multi-tiered frameworks for instructing students with disabilities that draw on the careful integration of research in general education, special education, and related fields, such as cognitive psychology, to provide well-crafted, differentiated instruction within the content areas that also supports the literacy and numeracy needs of students with disabilities (Brownell, Sindelar, Kiely, & Danielson, 2010; Bryant & Barrera, 2009; Spectrum K-12, 2009).

Strategies for Improving the Quality of Teachers for Students with Disabilities

In order to develop the quality general and special education teachers we need, a comprehensive, seamless approach to teacher learning must be embraced (Feiman-Nemser, 2001). This approach should consider what underlies expert teaching, teachers' developmental needs as they progress from novice to more expert status, and the learning supports that address such a progression. Increased emphasis on teacher quality has resulted in a flurry of studies designed to understand better the knowledge and classroom practices of our nation's most effective teachers. Findings from these studies suggest that expert teachers, in both general and special education, are those who have knowledge of their content and how to enact it (Brownell et al., 2007; Hill et al., 2008; Piasta, Connor, Fishman, & Morris, 2009). These teachers not only know their subject, but they understand how to represent it for students; they have pedagogical content knowledge. Such pedagogical content knowledge (PCK) is evident in two types of studies: (a) observation studies of classroom performance in reading and mathematics (Baker, Gersten, Haager, & Dingle, 2006; Griffin, Jitendra, & League, 2009; Hill et al., 2008), and (b) studies of PCK that demonstrate relationships between surveys of knowledge and student achievement in math (Hill, Rowan, & Ball, 2005) or observed classroom practice in reading (Brownell et al., 2007; Carlisle, Kelcey, Berebitsky, Phelps, & Johnson, 2009). Additionally, expert teachers are able to use their knowledge to craft instruction that is responsive to students' needs.

In addition to the knowledge needed for instruction, general and special education teachers will need a strong understanding of how to work together productively. Unfortunately, many special and general education teachers are not sufficiently prepared to work together or work productively with families (McKenzie, 2009). Beginning teachers find the demands of providing services to students with disabilities even more complex, whether they are prepared in special or general education. Even when teaching typically developing students, beginning general education teachers struggle with classroom management, teaching content, and being responsive to the needs of individual students (Reynolds, 1995). Special education teachers perceive themselves as having similar struggles, but they also have the added struggles of forging collaborative relationships with parents and general education colleagues that are not always supportive and coping with the procedural demands of serving students with disabilities (Billingsley, 2004; Billingsley, Griffin, Smith, Kamman, & Israel, 2009). Further, many SETs are likely to have entered the classroom without any preparation or very little preparation (Boe & Cook, 2006) and these teachers may require considerable support.

Developing such complex knowledge and skills sets will necessitate effective professional learning strategies that recognize the developmental differences of more novice versus expert teachers. Yet, what do we know about effective strategies for improving the quality of beginning and more experienced teachers working with students with disabilities?

Induction Supports for Early Career Teachers

In special education, the research on effective induction and mentoring programs could be described as superficial and thin. A systematic review of the literature revealed a limited number of studies related to beginning teacher induction in special education and these studies were based largely on teachers' perceptions (Billingsley et al., 2009). Further, findings from this literature review support only the most global recommendations for improving beginning SETs' quality. Billingsley and her colleagues found that the personal and professional characteristics of mentors were important to beginning SETs. Mentoring relationships were perceived as satisfying when beginning SETs had access to mentors that were emotionally supportive and good communicators. Moreover, beginning SETs preferred and were more likely to access mentors with backgrounds in special education, those with similar teaching styles, and those who taught similar students, both in terms of disability category and grade level.

Both formal and informal sources of induction support are also perceived by beginning SETs as helpful (Billingsley et al., 2009). When beginning SETs participated in a formal induction program that included certain components, they tended to perceive themselves as competent and indicated that they were likely to remain in special education (Gehrke & McCoy, 2007; Griffin, 2005; Irinaga-Bistolas, Schalock, Marvin, & Beck, 2007; Martinez & Mulhall, 2007; Nielsen, Barry, & Addison, 2006; Tucker, 2000). These programs included some or most of the following components: (a) a beginning teacher orientation, (b) formal observations of beginning SETs as well as unscheduled visits designed to provide formative feedback and emotional support, (c) evaluation and feedback on teaching standards, (d) monthly seminars, (e) support groups, and (f) the delivery of content germane to special education. Beginning SETs perceived regularly scheduled meetings as a way of promoting collaboration and facilitating communication between mentors and mentees. Beginning SETs also rated informal support (i.e., unscheduled meetings with mentors and colleagues, unscheduled visits to check in on a beginner who is struggling) as more helpful than formal supports. Additionally, beginning SETS thought that the frequency with which they received support and the proximity of that support was important.

The content of mentoring support has also been examined in the literature (Billingsley et al., 2009). Beginning SETs value support that helps them cope with their job emotionally. They also see supports that allow them to understand and carry out the procedural requirements associated with special education placement and evaluation as important. Further, they appreciate instructional assistance with both curricular materials and learning new approaches for teaching their students, particularly when it fits with the needs of their students (Gehrke & Murri, 2006). However, little is known about the extent to which new special educators receive these instructional and curricular supports. In a recent study of general education teachers, Kardos and Johnson (2010) reported that across three states less than 60% of new teachers had three or more conversations with their mentor about substantive aspects of teaching and only 41% were observed teaching even one time. Perhaps one reason that emotional support is viewed as so helpful to special educators is that many new teachers receive very little instructional assistance from their mentors. Additional study is needed to learn more about the substantive content of mentoring in special education.

Although teachers seem to value mentors with certain personal and professional qualities and specific types of professional support, we have little knowledge of how these qualities and supports affect beginning SETs instructional and collaborative practice. For example, we need to know more about the substantive nature of mentor assistance, the extent to which specific types of instructional assistance are helpful and aspects of instructional coaching that have a positive influence on mentees' practices. Moreover, studies have not revealed how induction and mentoring programs can help SETs who have received little formal preparation or how these programs help beginning general education teachers work more effectively with both students with disabilities. We only know that beginning SETs seem to value mentor characteristics and supports described in this section.

The Role Curriculum Plays in Supporting Teacher Learning

Curriculum materials, when well designed, can be educative tools for teachers. Schneider and Krajcik (2002) showed how curriculum materials could be designed to support reform-based practices in science education. Teachers that used the educative features of the curriculum materials were more successful in translating reform-based science practices into their instruction. Interviews with teachers suggested that the curriculum's educative features seemed to help them understand specific ideas in lessons by helping them acquire the underlying PCK necessary for teaching those ideas.

Although curriculum can be helpful for all teachers, well-designed materials can be particularly helpful for beginning teachers in both general and special education, as it can provide the practical tools necessary for enacting effective instruction. Seven studies in general education and three studies in special education showed that access to structured curriculum supported the instructional practices of both general and special education teachers. Specifically, structured curriculum (a) helped beginning general education teachers feel less overwhelmed by the daily demands of course preparation than their counterparts who lacked such curriculum (Chubbuck, Clift, Allard, & Quinlan, 2001; Kauffman, Johnson, Kardos, Liu, & Peske, 2002), (b) supported the classroom practice of general and special education teachers, sometimes improving the instruction of weaker teachers (Bishop, Brownell, Klingner, Menon, Galman,

& Leko, 2010; Grossman et al., 2000; Grossman & Thompson, 2004), (c) helped beginning special education teachers apply research-based principles acquired during their professional preparation in the classroom (Leko & Brownell, in press), and (d) helped teachers without any formal preparation in special education learn how to teach reading to students with disabilities (Kamman, 2009).

Curriculum combined with professional development or mentoring was more helpful to beginning general education teachers than simply having access to curriculum (Valencia, Place, Martin, & Grossman, 2006). Leko and Brownell (2011) found that special education preservice teachers were better able to utilize what they had learned about reading instruction in their preservice program when they had access to structured curriculum and cooperating teachers experienced in teaching reading to students with disabilities that mentored them. Specifically, the curriculum provided a structure for their instruction and the cooperating teacher provided concrete ideas for improving their instruction and allowed them some flexibility in applying new ideas. Further, Kamman (2009), in her study of beginning special education teachers who were not prepared formally to teach, found that mentoring focused on the curriculum allowed these teachers to acquire more knowledge about teaching reading and improve their instructional practice in this area.

Overly scripted materials, however, can become a liability when beginning teachers have well-developed understandings of classroom instruction and thereby feel constrained by the scripted curriculum. In two separate studies, researchers demonstrated that beginners with a strong understanding of their content and pedagogy were frustrated by district mandates to use overly structured curriculum (Crocco & Costigan, 2007; Smagorinsky, Lakly, & Johnson, 2002). From their perspective, overly structured curriculum interfered with their ability to use what they had learned in their professional preparation or organize instruction in ways that they thought were most beneficial to students. Findings from two separate qualitative studies showed that overly scripted curriculum challenged both beginning and experienced special education teachers to incorporate research-based strategies learned in a professional development effort into their instruction (Brownell, Lauterbach, et al., 2010; Dingle, Brownell, Leko, Boardman, & Haager, 2010).

Providing Quality Professional Development

Few researchers have studied professional development efforts for special education teachers. Instead, researchers have focused mostly on defining the features of effective professional development for general education teachers working in inclusive classrooms that include students with disabilities. The majority of these studies have focused on teaching general education teachers to use selected evidence-based strategies, mostly in reading. Two reviews of these studies have shown that teachers can learn to implement research-based strategies when (Klingner, 2004; Pugach, Blanton, Correa, McLeskey, & Langley, 2009):

- Strategies fit the reality principle (i.e., they align well with the demands of their class);
- Conceptual underpinnings of a strategy's components are taught in depth;
- Active learning opportunities that support teachers' implementation are available, including expert coaches and peer mentors that model targeted strategies in the classroom as well as observe strategy implementation and provide feedback;
- Collaborative opportunities (with peers and experts) to discuss strategy implementation and analyze its effectiveness are available;
- Opportunities to observe the positive impact of strategy implementation on student achievement exist; and

- Contextual supports for learning are present, such as availability of instructional materials needed to implement new strategies and administrators that support and monitor strategy implementation.

Although the majority of professional development studies have focused on helping general education teachers implement reading strategies in inclusive classrooms, two different groups of researchers (Brownell, Boardman et al., 2010; McCutchen, Green, Abbott, & Sanders, 2009) have focused simultaneously on developing teachers' reading content knowledge (e.g., information about phonology and orthography) and knowledge of research-based reading strategies, the PCK of reading. These researchers have shown that both general and special education teachers benefit from professional development efforts that embrace many of the supports described above as well as extended opportunities to learn content. In both studies, teachers participated in up front professional development institutes that taught both the content knowledge needed for teaching reading and strategies for teaching that content. Additionally, in a study conducted by Brownell and her colleagues (2010), teachers seemed to benefit from curricular materials that assisted them in selecting appropriate word patterns for decoding instruction. Findings from these studies show that when teachers acquire PCK, they are likely to implement research-based reading strategies accurately and effectively, and in turn, affect student achievement.

Findings from the special education research on PD support those in general education, at least in a broad sense. Laura Desimone (2009) proposed a framework for designing and studying professional development, based on the professional development research in general education. Her framework is comprised of the following components: (a) content focus that helps teachers understand the subject matter and how students learn it; (b) duration or extended opportunities to learn; (c) active learning opportunities (e.g., modeling new practices for teachers, discussing implementation efforts); (d) collective participation through various structures such as teacher study groups and grade level teams; and (e) coherent learning opportunities (i.e., professional development opportunities are consistent with school, district, and state standards and curricular expectations). Of these five components, Desimone argued that content focus was likely to be the most powerful, as it received some of the strongest support from longitudinal, correlational and quasi-experimental research (Banilower, Heck, & Weiss, 2005; Carpenter, Fennema, Peterson, Chiang, & Loef, 1989; Cohen & Hill, 2000; Desimone, Porter, et al., 2002).

Determining the content knowledge of professional development efforts will not be a simple matter, especially if those efforts involve general and special education teachers. First, the content and methods for teaching advocated in general education are not always the same as those advocated in special education and these differences are apparent in many academic areas, including reading, mathematics, and writing (Troia & Graham, 2002; Woodward & Montague, 2002). Second, there is some research suggesting that teachers might need to apply the content they are learning differently depending on the needs and abilities of their students. As an example, Connor, Morrison, and Underwood (2007) showed that students with poor decoding and vocabulary knowledge benefitted most from teacher-managed code instruction; whereas, students with average or above average knowledge in these areas benefitted most from child-managed comprehension instruction. Additionally, Woodward and Baxter (1997) found that Everyday Mathematics, a curriculum that embraced the standards of the National Council of Mathematics for Teachers, was most beneficial to average and high ability students, but the impact on low achieving students was more questionable. Findings from the Connor et al study and Woodward et al study make it clear that the content addressed in professional development efforts must be differentiated according to the types of students teachers are addressing. The potential need to differentiate content while at the same time promoting collaborative conversations about the PD content will challenge most faculty crafting professional development efforts.

Considering Individual Teacher Learning and the Potential Learning Opportunities in the Collaborative Group

Even when conditions for teacher learning are sufficient and contextual supports are present, not all teachers learn similarly nor are all collaborative learning opportunities equally powerful. Differences in individual qualities and contextual conditions influence teachers' abilities to profit from various learning opportunities. Three studies in the special education literature (Brownell, Adams, Sindelar, Waldron, & vanHover, 2006; Brownell, Lauterbach, et al., 2010; Dingle et al., 2010) have shown that general and special education teachers seem to implement strategies acquired during professional development efforts effectively when they have (a) a fair amount of knowledge for teaching content and/or knowledge for providing direct, explicit instruction to students with disabilities is strong; (b) beliefs about instruction that align with strategies they are learning; (c) motivation to learn new strategies; and (d) ability to analyze the quality of their instruction and its impact on groups of students as well as individual students. In fact, special and general education teachers that exhibit all these individual qualities seem to take up strategies learned in professional development efforts quickly and effectively. Teachers that exhibit fewer of these qualities seem to need extra support in the learning process, including coaching, more feedback, and assistance developing lessons. The role that individual teacher qualities plays in what general and special education teachers learn is important to consider in any professional development or induction effort. Many general and special education teachers enter the classroom through a variety of preparation routes and have different prior experiences; as such they are likely to vary on many of these individual qualities and may need differentiated supports to learn. Levin and Marcus (2010) also studied various collaborative teacher meetings in one high school. These researchers found that teachers took the most turns during collaborative discussions when the intended purpose was to discuss instruction and when protocols for discussion, such as an agenda and set of lesson planning tasks to be completed, where present. Despite the high level of teacher talk about instruction, teachers felt that it was too general and not sufficiently specific to help them deepen either their content knowledge or pedagogical content knowledge.

The collective expertise available in a collaborative group and teachers' ability to engage in more productive discourse should also influence the type of learning opportunities availed to teachers though these concepts are rarely studied in general or special education. Little (2003) studied the discourse of high school level teams, examining the learning opportunities teachers presented through their discussions of classroom practice. Little found that when teachers tried to problem solve, they often focused on their classroom practice. However, their discussions of classroom practice were often too condensed and brief to be useful, as teachers found themselves struggling to balance the need to reflect on practice versus the need to complete curriculum development tasks.

In a dissertation study of grade level inclusion teams, Williamson (2006) found that teachers tended to spend the most time discussing students academic and behavior problems. Additionally, teachers engaged in the most productive discussions when they used tentative language, such as "You might think about" or "Could you approach the problem this way?"

We only identified one study that examined the discourse of special education teachers participating in a content focused professional development effort (Leko, Brownell, Kiely, Osipova, Dingle, & Mundy, 2010). In this study, teachers that demonstrated high knowledge and a strong proclivity for inquiry presented more potential opportunities for their colleagues to learn than those whose discourse could not be characterized in these ways. These high knowledge, strong inquiry teachers used language that was grounded in both the content and pedagogical knowledge of reading and described their practices in specific ways. They also asked more questions about their practice and were more open to feedback than their counterparts that would not be characterized similarly. These teachers provided more concrete representations of teaching practice and modeled a critical stance on their teaching. Even low knowledge, strong inquiry teachers were able to provide learning opportunities when they asked questions to gain better understanding or more knowledge. Leko and her colleagues could not discern, however, the degree to which other teachers profited from learning opportunities presented.

These few studies of collaborative discourse suggest that far more attention must be paid to collaborative learning structures than currently is the case. We need a better understanding of how teachers' knowledge and ability to articulate that knowledge, as well as ways of reflecting on their practice and discussing the practices of other teachers help those involved in collaboration learn.

Crafting Work Environments That Support Teaching Effectiveness and Retention

Teacher learning does not exist in a vacuum but in an environment that enables teachers to apply and continue to refine their knowledge and skills. Additionally, even when teachers have considerable knowledge and skills, they will not be effective unless the environment is designed in a way that they can demonstrate their abilities. Thus, leaders interested in supporting effective teaching for students with disabilities must consider: (a) the opportunities their teachers have to apply their skills and knowledge towards improving student achievement, (b) how to develop cultures that support both teacher learning and professional collaboration, and (c) strategies for retaining quality teachers.

Assuring Sufficient Opportunities to Teach.
Teachers' knowledge and skills are foundational to helping students with disabilities achieve maximum outcomes; however, they are not sufficient to provide students with disabilities the types of learning opportunities they need. For general and special education teachers to be effective, they require opportunities to teach. Ladson-Billings (2008) refers to opportunities to teach as the use of one's "knowledge, skills, and abilities ... in an environment conducive to teaching and learning" (p. 207). Working conditions mediate teachers' effectiveness and consequently their ability to have an impact on student learning (Hirsch, Emerick, Church, & Fuller, 2007; Johnson & the Project on the Next Generation of Teachers, 2004). Both general and special education teachers have expressed concern about workloads, lack of time to do their jobs well, and inadequate opportunities to collaborate with their peers (Billingsley, 2004; Billingsley et al., 2009; Loeb, Elfers, Knapp, Plecki, & Boatright, 2004). Working conditions tend to be less favorable in high poverty settings with teachers having fewer resources, higher and more diverse caseloads, and less support from principals and colleagues (Fall & Billingsley, 2011; Oakes & Saunders, 2004).

SETs in particular experience role ambiguity as they strive to make sense of uncertain roles and as they deal with the varied demands (Billingsley, 2004; Gersten et al., 2001). Numerous non-instructional tasks (Vannest & Hagan-Burke, 2010), working across a range of grades and subjects (Billingsley et al., 2009), handling rising caseloads (McLeskey et al., 2004), and challenging accountability requirements make special education teaching a challenging job.

More than half of SETs in a national sample reported that routine duties and paperwork interfered with their teaching to a great extent (with fewer general educators perceiving such interference) (Paperwork in Special Education, 2002). While past research on teachers' work activities has relied primarily on SETs' self-reports, a recent study by Vannest and Hagan-Burke (2010) provides observational evidence of the challenges SETs' encounter in managing varied activities as they try to provide instruction to students with disabilities. They observed 36 special educators in four different instructional arrangements for 2,200 hours. On average, they found SETs' spent their time: teaching academics (15.6%), instructional support (14.6%), paperwork (12.1%), personal time (9.4%), consulting/collaboration (8.6%), "other responsibilities (7.9%), supervision (7.2%), discipline (7.0%), and planning (5.4%)" (p. 138). They spent less time in assessment and nonacademic instruction (4.4%), with the least amount of time spent in IEP meetings (2.9). Also of interest is the variation that occurred across some categories. For example, although paperwork required an average of 12.1% of SETs' time, some teachers spent as much as 50% of their time on the activity. As the authors point out, it is the number of activities that SETs are responsible for, rather than any single activity, that erodes the time they have for instruction.

Moreover, the amount of time special education teachers have to spend with their students and the numbers of students they teach at any particular time matters. In a study of special education teachers, Brownell and her colleagues (2007) found that the relationship between the quality of special education teachers reading instruction and student achievement gains in reading were moderated by the time they had to teach the students and the instructional group size. Special education teachers with strong instructional practices that also had more time to teach and smaller groups of students to teach were more effective than their equally competent counterparts in producing student achievement gains. Clearly, if special education teachers are to be effective in their instruction, serious thought will need to be given to identifying how district, school, classroom, and teacher variables interact to influence SETs' work and time use.

SETs also have formidable content and pedagogical demands. They often teach across several grade levels and content areas. New teachers struggle with these demands, sometimes reporting that they learn the curriculum along with their students (Billingsley et al., 2009). The expectation that SETs should be prepared to teach any content area across K-12 is unrealistic and might explain why curriculum materials are such a helpful form of support. To better prepare SETs for the demands of their work, Brownell, Sindelar, Kiely, and Danielson (2010) emphasized that teacher preparation should focus on elementary or secondary levels given that instructional demands vary based on the grade levels taught.

To complicate matters, the RTI movement provides additional challenges for SETs and GETs. RTI has no well-defined roles for school professionals—at least not yet. With leadership, however, RTI offers a unique opportunity for educators to re-define and clarify the roles of both general and special education teachers (Brownell, Sindelar, et al., 2010). These multilevel frameworks also provide an opportunity to improve upon the quality of teacher collaboration, in which many SETs have been relegated to quasi-paraprofessional status. As programs are developed and implemented, roles are being defined. Brownell and her colleagues have called for special education teacher educators to modify their programs so as to prepare specialists to deliver tier three interventions and to support and participate in tier two collaboration. Preparing for such complex roles would require extensive training, but specialists of this sort would play a distinct and critical role in a multi-level system.

Developing School Cultures That Support Special Educators' Work. At a broader level, the commitments that leaders and general educators have toward the education of students with disabilities influences what SETs are able to achieve in schools. Special educators enter their work in schools expecting to collaborate with general educators in meaningful ways to assure that their students have opportunities to achieve the standards set for all students. Yet, studies of SETs suggest many of them struggle in these collaborations, meeting indifference or even hostility (Billingsley et al., 2009; Gehrke & Murri, 2006). Special educators also face other barriers to collaboration including heavy caseloads or a lack of time or schedules for collaborative work (Griffin et al., 2009; Kilgore, Griffin, Otis-Wilborn, & Winn, 2003). Even when SETs co-teach in general education classrooms, they may function as teacher assistants rather than skilled teachers (Weiss & Lloyd, 2002).

At the foundation of these barriers is a lack of a "school-wide philosophy, strategies, or structures to support the inclusion of students with disabilities into general education programs" (Kilgore et al., p. 41). Principals are in an important position to help shape the school culture and how others respond to the work of special educators. To elaborate, leaders can have an important impact on the school communities' understanding of special education, the structures that support special educators' work as well as helping teachers address the challenges they encounter. More specifically, principals show their commitment to inclusive education through mission or vision statements, verbally as they interact with various stakeholder groups and by supporting the education of students with disabilities. York-Barr, Sommerness, Duke, and Ghere (2005), in a study of special education teachers' perspectives about their work, emphasized the importance of explicit administrator support for inclusive education, indicating that when administrators clearly value having students with disabilities in the school and communicate clear expectations to school staff about inclusion, they remove "an invisible barrier" (p. 208). York-Barr and colleagues (2005) stated:

> if staff members in a building know that the site administrator supports inclusive education and expects teachers to collaborate with special educators and to teach special education students, then resistance to inclusivity is diminished. The opposite also was felt to be true. Any suggestion or inclination that inclusivity was optional gave permission, of sorts, for marginal support of inclusive education efforts.
>
> *(p. 208)*

Principals can also foster productive collaborative relationships by providing necessary professional development on collaboration, ensuring that there is scheduled time for collaboration and encouraging mentor teachers to include new special educators in their collaborative work. Inclusive and collaborative practices may not be understood by principals which is not surprising because these leaders may have had little if any preparation in special education (Garrison-Wade, Sobel, & Fulmer, 2007).

Teacher Evaluation in Special Education

Any attempt to improve the quality of special education teachers would be incomplete without effective measures for evaluating them. Valid evaluation systems are necessary for determining (a) those areas of special education teacher quality that need strengthening, (b) the effectiveness of strategies employed to improve quality, and (c) to make retention, tenure and promotion decisions. Presently, the national policy conversation focuses almost exclusively on evaluating teachers using student achievement to make tenure and promotion decisions, with little rhetoric focused on using evaluation as a tool for determining if teachers' opportunities to learn are adequate.

Those in favor of using teacher evaluation, as a way of recognizing the best and weeding out the less desirable, propose that replacing outdated, perfunctory teacher evaluation systems with rigorous teacher performance measures, ones that rely heavily on growth models of student achievement, is an important policy lever for improving both teacher and student performance (Goldhaber, 2010). Such views of teacher evaluation have received considerable support at the federal level. The Obama administration has made teacher effectiveness and evaluation a prominent part of the national education reform agenda (U.S. Department of Education, 2010). Race to the Top grant applicants must include student performance data in their proposed systems of teacher evaluation. In response, states are making radical revisions to their teacher evaluation systems, incorporating value-added approaches for evaluating the effects of teachers on student performance (Steele, Hamilton, & Stecher, 2010) and valid observation systems for evaluating teaching processes (e.g., Danielson, 2007; Pianta & Hamre, 2009).

Unfortunately, there is little to guide states and districts as they consider evaluating special educators and teachers of English Language Learners (Holdheide, Goe, Croft, & Reschly, 2010). As a field, we have limited research identifying the dimensions of teacher quality in special education (Brownell et al., 2009) and we have been unable to articulate how special education teaching might be similar to or different from teaching in general education. Thus, it will come as no surprise that special education teachers are often evaluated using the same criteria as general education teachers with little recognition about the ways in which their instructional assignments might be different. A recent examination of Successful Race to the Top applications revealed little to no differentiation between special education teachers and general education teachers in the evaluation process (Brownell, Lignugaris-Kraft, & Salzberg, 2010). Further, in a survey of district and state administrators, Holdheide and colleagues reported that only 26% of district and state teacher administrators indicated that their evaluation systems allowed for a different or slightly modified evaluation process for special educators, raising questions about how SET evaluations will recognize the ways in which special education teaching might differ from general education teaching.

How Should Districts and States Proceed?

Given the state of research in this area and the complexity of special education teaching, state and district administrators would be advised to consider employing multiple measures for evaluating special education teachers. Even in general education, scholars agree the multiple measures are the only way to capture the complex dimensions of teaching (Rockoff, Jacob, Kane, & Staiger, 2009). The Bill and Melinda Gates Foundation incorporates multiple measures "anchored in students achievement" (p. 2) including rigorous classroom observations, student feedback, pedagogical content knowledge and school working conditions (Working with Teachers to Develop Fair and Reliable Measures of Effective Teaching, 2010).

As in general education, multiple measures are essential for assessing teacher effectiveness in special education. Multiple measures of teacher quality are the only strategy for assessing the degree to which special educators are successful in fulfilling their various roles, including: (a) providing direct instruction, (b) collaboration with general education teachers and parents, (c) developing individualized education programs, and (d) supervising paraprofessionals. Each of these roles demands a particular knowledge and skill set that must be evaluated validly.

Yet, how should such a complex set of abilities be evaluated in a way that balances rigor with practicality? In general education, scholars are using a variety of measures to determine teachers' effectiveness and some of these may be applicable to special education teachers. As special education researchers and practitioners consider these evaluation systems and craft new ones, they must be able to balance rigor, practicality, and face validity or credibility. Evaluations that are useful for a wide range of teaching situations obviously are more useful than those that can be applied only to a particular content area, and evaluations that can be implemented with a modest use of resources will also be more realistic. Finally, teachers must find the evaluation systems be fair or valid. They must be able to distinguish among colleagues who are effective and those deemed as less effective.

Teacher Observations. Observations systems are the most frequently used data source in teacher evaluations (Holdheide et al., 2010), and these have traditionally been used for formative evaluation purposes. Recently, traditional teacher evaluations have come under sharp criticism, as some researchers have shown that as many as 98% of teachers are deemed satisfactory according to their observed performance. These observations systems fall into two types. The first type assesses teacher effectiveness across content domains: the Classroom Assessment Scoring System (CLASS); Pianta & Hambre (2009) and Danielson's Framework for Teaching (Danielson, 2007). Teacher performance on the CLASS and Danielson's framework have been linked to student achievement data in general education and are the object of further analysis in the MET study of teacher quality in general education. The second type of assessment is focused on specific content areas, such as language arts, mathematics and science, English Language Learners, and special education. These include (a) Mathematical Quality of Instruction (MQI), Protocol for Language Arts Teaching Observations (PLATO; Grossman, Loeb, Cohen, et al., 2010), Quality Science Teaching (QST; Pecheone as cited in the Gates Foundation, 2010), and Reading in Special Education (RISE; Brownell et al., 2009). The MQI and the RISE have validity and reliability data; whereas the other two observation systems are undergoing validity studies. The advantage of content specific observations is that they are likely to be more useful in helping teachers improve specific instructional practices in their subject area; however, they are more challenging to implement because evaluator training will be required for multiple instruments.

The concern about most evaluation systems is that they have only been used to assess general education teachers, with the exception of the RISE, and therefore, researchers do not understand if these systems can effectively assess the nuances of special education teachers. As an example, Danielson's framework (2007) is a widely used teacher observation system (Heneman, Milanowski, Kimball, and Odden, 2010; Kane, Taylor, Tyler, & Wooten, 2010; Milanowski 2004); yet, researchers have only minimal validity date about its use with special educators. Only two studies have used Danielson's framework to compare the effectiveness of special education teachers graduating from traditional and emergency teacher preparation routes (Nougaret, Scruggs, & Mastropieri, 2005) and from traditional and alternative route programs (Sindelar, Daunic, Rennells, 2004). In both cases the instrument has been productive in differentiating teachers entering special education teaching through different routes. Other validity concerns center on the rater's qualifications. In many cases principals evaluate special education teachers, but are they capable of validly assessing them? To use evaluation systems effectively, particularly comprehensive ones, we need to what types of special training observers need to evaluate the nuances of special education teaching (Holdheidi et al., 2010).

Clearly, to create a credible and useful evaluation system, practitioners need research demonstrating that the observation tools they select can validly and reliably assess the classroom practice of special education teachers and can provide information that will enable special education teachers to improve their instruction. Additionally, district administrators will need to understand what training evaluators will need to successfully assess the classroom practice of special education teachers.

Value-Added/Student Growth Measures. Value-added models are currently being hailed as necessary mechanism for identifying effective teachers and ridding the system of ineffective ones. Further, their use is required in Race to the Top applications, as states must use teachers' impact on student achievement as a substantial portion of their evaluation system. Value-added measures use statistical procedures to estimate the effects of teachers and/or schools on student achievement, and research demonstrates that they can be effective in identifying those general education teachers who should receive tenure or be retained in schools; yet, these measures are not without their problems, particularly in special education (Reshley, Holdheidi, Billingsley, & Bagshaw, 2010). Reliability estimates for value added measures are between .30 and .60 (Goldhaber, 2009); thus, a teacher has a relatively good chance of being identified as effective one year, but not the next (Glazerman et al., 2010). Additionally, value-added measures are far more reliable when you have 3 years of data versus 1 and they are more reliable estimates of teacher effectiveness in math than reading. Thus, there are questions about using value-added scores on a yearly basis to evaluate teachers.

Furthermore, there are specific concerns about using value-added techniques in special education. Buzick and Laitusis (2010) identified five major problems associated with using growth scores for students with disabilities:(a) the impact of test modifications on test performance and how these modifications are used differently over time; (b) large scale assessments designed for typically developing students may lack the precision to measure growth reliably in the disability population; (c) comparability of standard and modified assessments in large scale, longitudinal data bases; (d) small numbers of students in different disability subgroups and comparability of performance across those subgroups; and (e) number of students that change disability classification over time. In addition to these concerns, most scholars and practitioners are concerned about how one might attribute gains in student performance to the special education teacher. Although Feng and Sass (2010) successfully used value-added measures to determine the effects of special education teachers on the achievement gains of students with disabilities, they omitted special education teachers who were not the primary teacher of record for mathematics or reading.

To this point, no one has been able to validly determine how variance in student performance can be attributed to the special or general education teacher when they share instructional responsibility for students with disabilities. Since special education teachers are likely to be providing tier two and tier three instruction in a RTI framework or be co-teaching in a general education classroom, it seems nearly impossible to validly and reliably determine what these individual teachers' contributions to student growth might be. In some Race to the Top states, administrators are treating them as a team; yet, doing so raises a different set of issues. What happens when the special or general education teacher differ in skills and knowledge, with one teacher demonstrating substantial competence and the other one demonstrating significant needs? Also, what happens in situations where special education teachers have little power in the instructional arrangement and have little opportunity to demonstrate their effectiveness? These questions must be answered if teacher evaluations based on value-added measures student performance are to be credible in the minds of general and special education teachers.

Other Measures.   Observations of teachers and value-added measures, however, only capture specific aspects of teacher effectiveness, providing academic instruction. Both special and general education teachers also have knowledge that influences the classroom practices they exhibit. Surveys of the content knowledge needed for instruction in reading and mathematics have demonstrated relationships between the amount of knowledge teachers have, the classroom practices they use, and in some cases, student achievement gains. Though these measures have not been developed specifically for special education teachers, they have been used successfully to predict classroom reading practices (Brownell et al., 2007). Less clear in the areas of reading and literacy are the roles that special versus general education teachers play in instruction and what knowledge they will need to execute those instructional roles (Brownell, Sindelar, Kiely, & Danielson, 2010).

Special education teachers also play roles in helping students learn to manage their behavior, develop social skills, and learn adaptive skills, and thus far, we have few assessments that assess knowledge and practices and their relationship to student outcomes in these areas. Further, special education teachers spend their time in a range of other activities, many of which do not involve direct instruction, such as collaborative planning and running Individualized Education Program meetings (Vannest & Hagan-Burke, 2010). How these activities can be evaluated effectively remains a question. Some scholars have developed ways of assessing co-teaching, but we were unable to determine the validity and reliability of these assessments (Adams, Cessna, & Friend, 1993; Wilson, 2005). Other aspects of special education teachers' roles, such as supervising paraprofessionals, have been unaddressed from an evaluative perspective. Further, studies examining how special education teachers spend their time, how these teachers are treated in co-teaching situations, and how time allotted for instruction and instructional group size moderates teacher effectiveness raises real questions about how fair evaluation procedures can be crafted when working conditions do not support special education teacher effectiveness. Alternatively, evaluation systems could be put in place that incorporate schools' capacity for creating conditions that support special education teachers in their roles. Adding school support for teacher effectiveness into any evaluation system just might create the working conditions special education teachers need to be successful.

As new systems of teacher evaluation are put into place, we wonder how the complexity of special education teaching will be captured accurately and validly and will the voices of those knowledgeable about special education be included in conversations about how to best evaluate these teachers. Or, will the unique needs of special education teachers be overlooked in evaluation systems because the issues are too complex and administrators are too overwhelmed just dealing with the formidable demands of current accountability requirements, building data infrastructures, and addressing the concerns of various groups (e.g., teachers, unions). Administrators and teachers knowledgeable about special education are important stakeholders and need to have input into evaluation policies. Ideally, evaluations will be piloted and gradually phased in so adjustments can be made to assure that evaluations meet criteria we described earlier: credible, practical, rigorous, and valid.

An optimistic perspective is that the evaluation of special education may allow the creation of solutions to problems that have plagued SETs' work in schools (e.g., Billingsley et al., 2009; Billingsley, 2004). If school leaders begin to understand what SETs do, and begin to respond with structures and schedules conducive to collaboration and using instructional time well, improvements may result that have an impact on special educators' and general educators' teaching and in turn students with disabilities achievement.

Conclusions

Improving the quality of the teachers instructing students with disabilities will require our field to shift away from its historical attention to securing adequate numbers of teachers to a laser-like focus on strategies for improving teacher quality. Fast-track alternatives to the classroom must be discouraged and strategies for ensuring increased numbers of fully prepared special education teachers encouraged and supported politically. Teacher learning, however, cannot stop after initial preparation. Administrators and teacher educators must create strategies that ensure the implementation of well-integrated systems of teacher education that begin with teachers' initial preparation to work with students with disabilities and continue through carefully planned induction and throughout the career span. Such systems must ensure that general education teachers can integrate content knowledge into strategies that support universal design for learning and provide special education teachers with both the content and intervention knowledge that enables them to support and extend instruction provided in general education. High quality, coherent teacher education, however, will not be enough. Administrators and teacher educators must be accountable for providing the work contexts that support general and special teachers in providing effective instruction. Caseloads, time to plan, and time to teach will be essential to supporting effective teaching. Additionally, evaluation systems that identify teachers' learning needs, provide a basis for teacher education efforts, and promote accountability will help to ensure that special and general educators develop into effective teachers.

Implementing the practices recommended here will not be easy, such a comprehensive approach to improving teacher quality for students with disabilities will challenge colleges of education, schools, state departments of education, and policy makers to act and work in ways that have eluded them previously. They will need courage to resist simple solutions to teacher shortages, such as increasing the number of available fast tracks to the classroom, and instead, engage in coordinated, sustained efforts to design and implement long term, and sometimes costly, strategies for improving teacher quality.

References

Adams, L., Cessna, K., & Friend, M. (1993). *The Colorado assessment of co-teaching* (COACT). Ft. Collins: Colorado State University.

American Association for Employment in Education (AAEE). (2008). *Educator supply and demand in the United States: Executive Summary.* Retrieved April 12, 2010, from http://www.aaee.org

Baker, S., Gersten, R., Haager, D., & Dingle, M. (2006). Teaching practice and the reading growth of first-grade English learners: Validation of an observation instrument. *Elementary School Journal, 107,* 199–219.

Banilower, E., Heck, D., & Weiss, I. (2005). Can professional development make the vision of the standards a reality? The impact of the National Science Foundations Local Systemic Change Through Teacher Enhancement Initiative. *Journal of Research in Science Teaching, 44*(3), 375–395.

Billingsley, B. S. (2004). Special education teacher retention and attrition: A critical   analysis of the research literature. *Journal of Special Education, 38*(1), 39–55.

Billingsley, B., Fall, A., & Williams, T. O. (2006). Who is teaching students with emotional disorders? A profile and comparison to other special educators. *Behavioral Disorders, 31*(1), 252–264.

Billingsley, B. S., Griffin, C. C., Smith, S. J., Kamman, M., & Israel, M. (2009). *A review of teacher induction in special education: Research, practice, and technology solutions.* (NCIPP Doc. No. RS-1). Retrieved February 8, 2010, from University of Florida, National Center to Inform Policy and Practice in Special Education Professional Development Web site: http://ncipp.org/reports/rs_1.pdf

Bishop, A. G., Brownell, M. T., Klingner, J. K., Leko, M. M., & Galman, S. (2010). Differences in beginning special education teachers: The influence of personal attributes, preparation, and school environment on classroom reading practices. *Learning Disability Quarterly, 33,* 75–92.

Boe, E., & Cook, L. (2006). The chronic and increasing shortage of fully certified teachers in special and general education. *Exceptional Children, 72*(4), 443–460.

Boe, E. E., Shin, S., & Cook, L. H. (2007). *Does teacher preparation matter for beginning teachers in either special or general education? Journal of Special Education, 41,* 148-170.

Boe, E., Sunderland, B., & Cook, L. (2006, November). *The supply of teachers from traditional and alternative routes of preparation.* Paper presented at the annual meeting of the Teacher Education Division of the Council for Exceptional Children, San Diego.

Brownell, M. T., Adams, A., Sindelar, P. T., Waldron, N., & vanHover, S. (2006). Learning from collaboration: The role of teacher qualities. *Exceptional Children, 72,* 169–185.

Brownell, M. T., Bishop, A. G., Gersten, R., Klingner, J. K., Penfield, R., Dimino, J., et al. (2009). The role of domain expertise in beginning special education teacher quality. *Exceptional Children, 75, 4,* 391–411.

Brownell, M. T., Boardman, A., Haager, D., & Klingner, J. (2010, June). *The influence of collaborative professional development groups and coaching on the literacy instruction of upper elementary special education teachers.* Presented at the Fifth Annual Institute for Education Research Conference. National Harbor, MD.

Brownell, M. T., Haager, D., Bishop, A. G., Klingner, J. K., Menon, S., Penfield, R., & Dingle, M. (2007, April). *Teacher quality in special education: The role of knowledge, classroom practice, and school environment.* Paper presented at the annual meeting for American Education Research Association, Chicago, Illinois.

Brownell, M. T., Lauterbach, A., Dingle, M. T., Boardman, A., Urbach, J., & Leko, M. (2010, April). *Individual and contextual factors influencing special education teacher learning in literacy learning cohorts.* Paper presented at the Annual Meeting for American Education Research Association, Denver, CO.

Brownell, M. T., Lignugaris-Kraft, B., & Salzberg, C. (2010, November). *Evaluating special education teachers: Challenges and reasonable possibilities.* Paper presented at the Annual Meeting of the Teacher Education Division, Council for Exceptional Children. St. Louis, MO.

Brownell, M. T., Sindelar, P. T., Kiely, M. T., & Danielson, L. C. (2010). Special education teacher quality and preparation: Exposing foundations, constructing a new model. *Exceptional Children, 76*(3), 357–377.

Bryant, D., & Barrera, M. (2009). Changing roles for educators within the framework of Response-to-Intervention. *Intervention in School and Clinic, 45*(1), 72–29.

Buzick, H. M., & Laitusis, C. C. (2010). Using growth for accountability: Measurement challenges for students with disabilities and recommendations for research. *Educational Researcher, 39,* 537–544. Retrieved from http://edr.sagepub.com/content/39/7/537. doi: 10.3102/0013189X10383560

Carlisle, J., Kelcey, B., Berebitsky, D., Phelps, G., & Johnson, D. (2009, April). *Dimensions of teachers' early elementary reading instruction.* Paper presented at the annual meeting of the American Education Research Association, San Diego, CA.

Carpenter, T. P., Fennema, E., Peterson, P. L., Chiang, C., & Loef, M. (1989). Using knowledge of children's mathematics thinking in classroom teaching: An experimental study. *American Educational Research Journal, 26*(4), 499–531.

Chubbuck, S. M., Clift, R. T., Allard, J., & Quinlan, J. (2001). Playing it safe as a novice teacher: Implications for programs for new teachers. *Journal of Teacher Education, 52*, 365–376.

Cohen, D. K., & Hill, H. (2000). Instructional policy and classroom performance: The mathematics reform in California. *Teachers College Record, 102*(2), 294–343.

Cook, L., & Boe, E. (2007) National trends in the sources of supply of teachers in general and special education. *Teacher Education and Special Education, 30*(4), 217–232.

Conderman, G., & Johnston-Rodriguez, S. (2009) Beginning teachers' views of their collaborative roles. *Preventing School Failure, 53*(4), 235–244.

Connor, C. M., Morrison, F. J., & Underwood, P. S. (2007). A second chance in second grade: The independent and cumulative impact for first- and second-grade reading instruction and students' letter-word reading skill growth. *Scientific Studies of Reading, 11,* 199–233.

Corn, A. L., & Spungin, S. J. (2003). *Free and appropriate public education and the personnel crisis for students with visual impairments and blindness* (COPSSE Document No. IB-10). Gainesville: University of Florida, Center on Personnel Studies in Special Education. Retrieved from http://www.coe.ufl.edu/copsse/docs/IB-10/1/IB-10.pdf

Crocco, M., & Costigan, A. (2007). The narrowing of curriculum and pedagogy in the age of accountability: Urban educators speak out. *Urban Education, 42*(6), 512–535.

Danielson, C. (1996). *Enhancing professional practice: A framework for teaching.* Alexandria, VA: Association of Supervision and Curriculum Development.

Danielson, C. (2007). *Enhancing professional practice: A framework for teaching* (2nd ed.). Alexandria, VA: Association for Supervision and Curriculum Development.

DeSimone, J., & Parmar, R. (2006). Issues and challenges for middle school mathematics teachers in middle school inclusion classrooms. *School Science and Mathematics, 106*(8), 338–348.

Desimone, L. M., Porter, A. C., Garet, M., Yoon, K. S., & Birman, B. (2002). Does professional development change teachers' instruction? Results from a three-year study. *Educational Evaluation and Policy Analysis, 24*(2), 81–112.

Desimone, L. (2009). Improving impact studies of teachers' professional development: Toward better conceptualizations and measures. *Educational Researcher, 38,* 181–199. doi: 10.3102/0013189X08331140.

Dingle, M., Brownell, M. T., Leko, M., Boardman, A., & Haager, D. (2010). *Developing Effective Special Education Reading Teachers: The Influence of Professional Development, Context and Individual Qualities.* Manuscript under review.

Fall, A. M., & Billingsley, B. (2008). Disparities in teacher quality among early career special educators in high and low poverty districts. In Scruggs, T. E., Mastropieri & M.A. (Eds.), *Advances in learning and behavioral disabilities: Personnel preparation* (Vol. 21, pp. 181–206). Stanford, CT: JAI.

Fall, A. M., & Billingsley, B. (2011). Disparities in work conditions among early career special educators in high- and low-poverty districts, *Remedial and Special Education. 32*(3), 64–78.

Feiman-Nemser, S. (2001). From preparation to practice: Designing a continuum to strengthen and sustain teaching. *Teachers College Record, 103,* 1013-1055.

Feistritzer, C. E. (2008). *Alternative teacher certification: A state-by-state analysis 2008.* Washington, DC: National Center for Education Information.

Feng, L., & Sass, T. (2010). *What makes special education teachers special? Teacher training and achievement of students with disabilities.* Calder Urban Institute (Working Paper 49). Retrieved from http://www.caldercenter.org/publications.cfm

Garet, M., Cronen, S., Eaton, M., Kurki, A., Ludwig, M., Jones, W., et al. (2008). *The impact of two professional development interventions on early reading instruction and achievement.* Report for the National Center for Educational Evaluation and Regional Assistance, Institute for Education Sciences, U.S. Department of Education (NCEE 2008–4030). Washington, DC: U.S. Department of Education.

Garrison-Wade, D., Sobel, D., & Fulmer, C. L. (2007). Inclusive leadership: Preparing principals for the role that awaits them. *Educational Leadership and Administration, 19*, 117-132.

The Gates Foundation (2010). *Working with teachers to develop fair and reliable assessments of effective teaching.* Retrieved on February 9, 2011, from http://www.metproject.org/

Gehrke, R. S., & McCoy, K. (2007). Sustaining and retaining beginning special educators: It takes a village. *Teaching and Teacher Education, 23,* 490–500.

Gehrke, R. S., & Murri, N. (2006). Beginning special educators' intent to stay in special education: Why they like it here. *Teacher Education and Special Education, 29*(3), 179–190.

Gersten, R., Compton, D., Dimino, J., Santoro, L., Linan-Thompson, S., & Tilly, D. (2009). *Assisting students struggling with reading: Response to intervention and multi-tier intervention in primary grades* (NCEE 2009-4045). Washington, DC: Institute for Education Sciences.

Glazerman, S., Goldhaber, D., Loeb, S., Staiger, Raudenbush, S., & Whitehurst, G. (2010). *Value-added: It's not perfect, but it makes sense.* Retrieved December 15, 2010, from http://cepa.stanford.edu/news/value-added-its-not-perfect-it-makes-sense

Goldhaber, D. (2009, April). *Teacher quality and value-added measurement.* Presented at the TQ Center Workshop. Retrieved on February 9, 2011, from http://www.tqsource.org/webcasts/teacherEffectivenessWorkshp/index.php

Goldhaber, D. (2010). *When the stakes are high, can we rely on value-added? Exploring the use of value-added to inform teacher workforce decisions.* Center for American Progress. Retrieved from http://www.americanprogress.org

Griffin, M. L. (2005). *Perspectives of mentors and mentees involved in a special education resident teacher program.* Unpublished doctoral dissertation, University of North Dakota, Grand Forks.

Griffin, C. C., Jitendra, A. K., & League, M. B. (2009). Novice Special Educators' Instructional Practices, Communication Patterns, and Content Knowledge for Teaching Mathematics. *Teacher Education and Special Education, 32*(4) 319–336. doi: 10. 117710888406409343540

Grossman, P. L., Loeb, S. Cohen, J., Hammerness, K., Wyckoff, J., Boyd, D., et al. (2010). *Measures of instructional practice in middle school English Language Arts and teachers' value-added scores.* Calder Urban Institute (Working Paper 45). Retrieved from http://www.caldercenter.org/publications.cfm

Grossman, P. L., & Thompson, C. (2004). *Curriculum materials: Scaffolds for new teacher learning?* Seattle: University of Washington, Center for the Study of Teaching and Policy.

Grossman, P. L., Valencia, S. W., Evans, K., Thompson, C., Martin, S., & Place, N. (2000). Transitions into teaching: Learning to teach writing in teacher education and beyond. *Journal of Literacy Research, 32*(4), 631–662.

Hanushek, E. A., Kain, J. F., & Rivkin, S. G. (2004). The revolving door: Factors affecting teacher turnover. In W. J. Fowler, Jr. (Ed.), *Developments in school finance: 2003* (pp. 7–15). Washington, DC: U. S. Department of Education, National Center on Educational Statistics.

Hanushek, E. A., Rivkin, S. G., & Kain, J. F. (2005). Teachers, schools, and academic achievement. *Econometrica, 73,* 417–458.

Harvey, M., Yssel, N., Bauserman, A., & Merbler, J. (2010). Preparation for inclusion: An exploration of higher education teacher-training institutions. *Remedial and Special Education, 31*(1), 24–33.

Heneman, H. G., Milanowski, A., Kimball, S., & Odden, A., (2010). Standards-based teacher evaluation as a foundation for knowledge- and skill-based pay. CPRE Policy Briefs. RB-45. (Eric document: ED 493116).

Hill, H. C., Blunk, M. L., Charalambos, C. Y., Lewis, J. M., Phelps, G. C., Sleep, L., & Ball, D. L. (2008). Mathematical knowledge for teaching and the mathematical quality of instruction: An exploratory study. *Cognition and Instruction, 26,* 1–81.

Hill, H. C., Rowan, B., & Ball, D. L. (2005). Effects of teachers' mathematical knowledge for teaching on student achievement. *American Educational Research Journal, 42,* 371–406.

Hirsch, E., Emerick, S., Church, K., & Fuller, E. (2007). *Teacher working conditions are student learning conditions: A report on the 2006 North Carolina Teacher Working Conditions Survey.* Hillsborough, NC: Center for Teaching Quality. Retrieved December 12, 2008, from http://www.teachingquality.org/pdfs/twcnc2006.pdf

Holdheide, L. R., Goe, L., Croft, A., & Reschly, D. J. (2010). *Challenges in evaluating special education teachers and English language learner specialists.* Washington, DC: National Comprehensive Center for Teacher Quality.

Imazeki, J. (2003). Teacher attrition and mobility in urban districts: Evidence from Wisconsin. In C. F. Roellke & J. K. Rice (Eds.), *Fiscal issues in urban schools* (pp. 119–136). Greenwich, CT: Information Age.

Irinaga-Bistolas, C., Schalock, M., Marvin, R., & Beck, L. (2007). Bridges to success: A developmental induction model for rural early career special educators. *Rural Special Education Quarterly, 26*(1), 13–22.

Johnson, H. A. (2003). *U. S. deaf education teacher preparation programs: A look at the present and a vision for the future* (COPSSE Document No. IB-9). Gainesville, FL: University of Florida, Center on Personnel Studies in Special Education. Retrieved from http://www.coe.ufl.edu/copsse/docs/IB-9/1/IB-9.pdf

Johnson, S. M., & The Project on the Next Generation of Teachers (2004). *Finders and keepers: Helping teachers survive and thrive in our schools.* San Francisco: Jossey-Bass.

Kamman, M. L. (2009). *Understanding the role curriculum and supports for its implementation play in how test-only beginning special education teachers learn about and enact reading instruction.* Unpublished doctoral dissertation, University of Florida, Gainesville.

Kane, T. J., Taylor, E. S., Tyler, J. H., & Wooten, A. L. (2010). *Identifying effective classroom practices using student achievement data.* Working Paper 15803. Retrieved February 9, 2011, from http://www.nber.org/papers/w15803

Kane, T., Rockoff, J., & Staiger, D. O. (2008). What does certification tell us about teacher effectiveness? Evidence from New York City. *Economics of Education Review, 27,* 615–631.

Kardos, S. M., & Johnson, S. M. (2010). New teachers' experiences of mentoring: The good, the bad, and the inequity. *Journal of Educational Change* (11), 23–44.

Kauffman, D., Johnson, S. M., Kardos, E. L., Liu, E., & Peske, H. G. (2002). Lost at sea: New teachers' experiences with curriculum and assessment, *Teachers College Record, 104*(2), 272–300.

Kilgore, K. L., Griffin, C. C., Otis-Wilborn, A., & Winn, J. (2003). The problems of beginning special education teachers: Exploring the contextual factors influencing their work. *Action in Teacher Education, 25*(1), 38–47.

Klingner, J. K. (2004). The science of professional development. *Journal of Learning Disabilities, 37*, 248–255.

Leko, M., & Brownell, M. T. (2011). Understanding the various influences on special education preservice teachers' appropriation of conceptual and practical tools for teaching reading. *Exceptional Children, 97*, 229–251.

Leko, M. M., Brownell, M. T., Kiely, M. T., Osipova, A., Dingle, M., & Mundy, C. (2010, April). *Maximizing Learning Opportunities in a Special Education Professional Development Project.* Paper presented at the Annual American Educational Research Association Conference. Denver, CO.

Little, J. W. (2003). Inside teacher community: Representations of classroom practice. *Teachers College Record, 105*(6), 913–945.

Loeb, H., Elfers, A. M., Knapp, M. S., Plecki, M. L., & Boatright, B. (2004). Preparation and Support for Teaching: A Survey of Working Conditions of Teachers. Retrieved January, 2011, from http://depts.washington.edu/ctpmail/PDFs/Survey2WorkingPaper.pdf

Martinez, E., & Mulhall, L. (2007). Transition mentoring: Supporting teachers through the induction phase of the teaching profession. Doctoral dissertation, Teachers College, Columbia University, New York. *Dissertation Abstracts International, 67,* 2537.

McCutchen, D., Green, L., Abbott, R., & Sanders, E. A. (2009). Further evidence for teacher knowledge: Supporting struggling readers in grades three through five. *Reading and Writing, 22,* 401–423. doi:10.1007/s11145-009-9163-0

McHatton, P., & McCray, E. (2007). Inclination toward inclusion: Perceptions of elementary and secondary education teacher candidates. *Action in Teacher Education, 29*(3), 25–32.

McKenzie, R. G. (2009). A national survey of pre-service preparation for collaboration. *Teacher Education and Special Education 32,* (4) 379-393. doi: 10.1177/10888406409346241

McLeskey, J., & Billingsley, B. (2008). How does the quality and stability of the teaching force influence the research-to-practice gap? A perspective on the teacher shortage in special education. *Remedial and Special Education, 29*(5), 293–305.

McLeskey, J., Landers, E., Williamson, P., & Hoppey, D. (2010). Are we moving toward educating students with disabilities in less restrictive settings? *Journal of Special Education.*doi: 10.1177/0022466910376670.

McLeskey, J., Tyler, N., & Flippin, S. (2004). The supply of and demand for special education teachers: A review of research regarding the nature of the chronic shortage of special education teachers. *Journal of Special Education, 38*(1), 5–21.

Milanowski, A. (2004). The criterion-related validity of the performance assessment system in Cincinnati. *Peabody Journal of Education, 79*(4), 33–53.

Nielsen, D. C. Barry, A. L., & Addison, A. B. (2006). A model of a new-teacher induction program and teacher perceptions. *Action in Teacher Education, 28*(4), 14–24.

Nougaret, A., Scruggs, T., & Mastropieri, M. (2005). Does teacher education produce better special education teachers? *Exceptional Children, 71,* 217–229.

Oakes, J., & Saunders, M. (2004). Education's most basic tools: Access to textbooks and instructional materials in California's public schools. *Teachers College Record, 106*(10), 1967–1988.

Pianta, R. C., & Hamre, B. K. (2009). Conceptualization, measurement, and improvement of classroom processes: Standardized observation can leverage capacity. *Educational Researcher, 38*(2), 109–119.

Piasta, S. P., Connor, C. M., Fishman, B. J., & Morris, F., J. (2009). Teachers' Knowledge of Literacy Concepts, Classroom Practices, and Student Reading Growth. *Scientific Studies of Reading, 13,* 224–248.

Pugach, M. C., Blanton, L., Correa, V. I., McLeskey, J., & Langley, L. (2009). *The role of collaboration in supporting the induction of new special education teachers.* Report for the National Center to Inform Policy and Practice in Special Education Professional Development (NCIPP Document Number RS-2). Retrieved from http://www.ncipp.org

Reshley, D., Holdheidi, L. Billingsley, B., & Bagshaw, T. (2010, July). *Challenges in evaluating special education teachers.* Washington, DC: U.S. Department of Education, Office of Special Education Programs.

Reynolds, A. (1995). The knowledge base for beginning teachers: Education professionals' expectations versus research findings on learning to teach. *Elementary School Journal, 95,* 199–221.

Rockoff, J. E., Jacob, B. A., Kane, T. J., & Staiger, D. O. (2009). Can you recognize an effective teacher when you recruit one? *Education Finance and Policy, 6,* 43–74.

Roehrig, A., Brownell, M. T., Schatschneider, C., & Petscher, Y. (2010). *Predicting reading first student outcomes: How professional development, context, and individual teacher variables interact.* Manuscript under review.

Rosenberg, M. S., Boyer, K. L., Sindelar, P. T., & Misra, S. (2007). Alternative route programs to certification in special education: What we know about program design, instructional delivery, and participant characteristics. *Exceptional Children, 73,* 224–241.

Schneider, R. M., & Krajcik, J. (2002). Supporting science teacher learning: The role of educative curricular materials. *Journal of Science Teacher Education, 13,* 221–245.

Sindelar, P. T., Daunic, A., & Rennells, M. (2004). Comparisons of traditionally and alternatively trained teachers. *Exceptionality, 12,* 209–223.

Sindelar, P. T., Rosenberg, M. S., Corbett, N. L., Dewey, J., Denslow, D., & Lotfinia, B. (2010). *Cost effectiveness of alternative route special education teacher preparation.* Manuscript submitted for publication.

Smagorinsky, P., Lakly, A., & Johnson, T. S. (2002). Acquiescence, accommodation, and resistance in learning to teach within a prescribed curriculum. *English Education, 34,* 187–213.

Spectrum K-12. (2009). *Response to intervention (RTI) adoption survey.* Retrieved April 8, 2009, from http://www.spectrumk12.com/

Steele, J. L., Hamilton, L.S., & Stecher, B. M. (2010). *Incorporating student performance measures into teacher evaluation systems.* Santa Monica, CA: Rand Corporation. Retrieved from http://www.rand.org/

Sugai, G., & Horner, R., (2009). Responsiveness-to-intervention and school-wide positive behavior supports: Integration of multi-tiered system approaches. *Exceptionality, 17*(4), 223–237.

Torgesen, J. (2009). The response to intervention instructional model: Some outcomes from a large-scale implementation in reading first schools. *Child Development Perspectives, 3*(1), 38–40.

Troia, G., & Graham, S. (2002). The effectiveness of a highly explicit, teacher-directed strategy instruction routine: Changing the writing performance of students with learning disabilities. *Journal of Learning Disabilities, 35,* 290–305.

Tucker, T. N. (2000). Impacts of an induction program for beginning special education teachers.Doctoral dissertation, University of Sarasota, FL. *Dissertation Abstracts International, 60*(10), 3600.

Tyler, N., Yzquierdo, Z., Lopez-Reyna, N., & Flippin, S. (2002). *Diversifying the special education workforce* (COPSSE Document No. RS-3). Gainesville: University of Florida, Center on Personnel Studies in Special Education. Retrieved from http://www.coe.ufl.edu/copsse/docs/RS-3/1/RS-3.pdf

U.S. Department of Education. (2010). Individuals with Disabilities Education Act (IDEA). Retrieved March 1, 2010, from http://www.ideadata.org/

Valencia, S. W., Place, N. A., Martin, S. D., & Grossman, P. L. (2006). Curriculum materials for elementary reading: Shackles and scaffolds for four beginning teachers. *Elementary School Journal, 107*(1), 93–121. Retrieved fromhttp://sed.sagepub.com/content/36/2/89. doi: 10.1177/00224669020360020401

Vannest, K. J., & Hagan Burke, S. (2010). Teacher time use in special education. *Remedial and Special Education, 31*(2), 126–142.

Weiss, M. P., & Lloyd, J. W. (2002). Congruence between roles and actions of secondary special educators in co-taught and special education settings. *The Journal of Special Education, 36,* 58–68.

Williamson, P. (2006). *Grade level team meetings: How dialogue shapes teacher problem and response construction.* Doctoral dissertation. University of Florida, Gainesville. Retrieved from http://gradworks.umi.com/32/28/3228865.html

Wilson, G. L. (2005). A supervisor's guide for observing co-teachers. *Intervention in School and Clinic, 40,* 271–275.

Wilson, Floden & Ferrini-Mundy. (2002). Teacher preparation research: An insider's view from the outside. *Journal of Teacher Education, 53*(3), 190–204

Woodward, J., & Baxter, J. (1997). The effects of an innovative approach to mathematics on academically low-achieving students in inclusive settings. *Exceptional Children, 63,* 377–388.

Woodward, J., & Montague, M. (2002). Meeting the challenge of mathematics reform for students with learning disabilities. *The Journal of Special Education, 36,* 89–101.

Working with Teachers to Develop Fair and Reliable Measures of Effective Teaching. (2010) MET Project White Paper. Seattle, Washington: Bill & Melinda Gates Foundation, 1. Retrieved from http://www.metproject.org/downloads/met-framing-paper.pdf.

York-Barr, J., Sommerness, J., Duke, K., & Ghere, G. (2005). Special educators in inclusive education programmes: Reframing their work as teacher leadership. *International Journal of Inclusive Education, 9,* 193–215.

Zigmond, N., Kloo, A., & Volonino, V. (2009). What, where, how? Special education in the climate of full inclusion. *Exceptionality, 17,* 189–204.

16

Leadership and Instruction
Evidence-Based Practices in Special Education

Bryan G. Cook and Garnett J. Smith

UNIVERSITY OF HAWAII AT MANOA

For teachers to use evidence to improve teaching and learning in their classrooms they need ... evidence about their own practice and its impact on students, and knowledge or research evidence ... to give direction for improvement to practice. Teachers, however, cannot be expected to know and do all this on their own, but need the support of well informed leaders who have sufficient knowledge both to lead teachers' evidence-informed inquiry and to engage in their own inquiry into the effectiveness of their leadership practice in promoting teacher and student learning.

(Timperley, 2010, p. 1)

At the heart of schooling is the desire to improve those student outcomes deemed important for the development and success of individual students as well as the broader community. The focus on improving student outcomes appears to be particularly important for special education, because of the unique and typically problematic learning characteristics and outcomes of students with disabilities (Snell, 2003). However straightforward and amenable the goal of improved student outcomes appears to be, it begs an important question: What instructional practices can educators use to optimally improve targeted student outcomes? Or, more colloquially, how can educators know what works? In this chapter, we discuss evidence-based practices (EBPs), a contemporary reform that has the potential to transform education by meaningfully enhancing student outcomes (e.g., Cook, Smith, & Tankersley, 2011; Slavin, 2002). Specifically, we begin by discussing why using personal experience to determine what works may lead to false positives and false negatives, then describe the contributions and limitations of educational research and evidence-based reviews for identifying effective practices, provide an overview of EBPs in special education, and conclude with a discussion of how special education leaders (e.g., school, district, and state administrators; teacher educators) can facilitate the implementation of EBPs.

False Positives, False Negatives, and Instruction for Students with Disabilities

Most special educators have relied primarily on sources such as personal experience, anecdotal information (e.g., stories about the experiences of others), and tradition (e.g., customary practice based on the collective experiences of a community) to determine what works and to make instructional decisions. In many instances, one's own previous experiences, others' experiences, and traditional practice have provided reliable guidance and resulted in effective instruction for students with disabilities. In fact, at the heart of these approaches lies empirical exploration, the same foundation as scientific research (Hemsley-Brown & Sharp, 2003). That is, personal experience, anecdotal information, and tradition all involve individuals observing teaching and student learning, forming hypotheses as to the effects of specific practices, and confirming or denying those hypotheses through subsequent experiences and observations. Although these approaches typically rely on a limited number of informal perceptions, they have resulted in a large corpus of craft knowledge that is often both practical and effective (Nelson, Leffler, & Hansen, 2009).

Inattentional Blindness, Illusory Causation, and Type I Errors

Individual perception and experience, however, are fallible (see Chabris & Simons, 2010) and can lead to erroneous conclusions about what works in teaching students with disabilities. For example, psychologists have documented the existence of *inattentional blindness*, in which individuals do not perceive unexpected stimuli when they are focused on another task. For example, Simons and Chabris (1999) instructed undergraduate students to view a short video clip and keep count of how many times team members passed a basketball to each other. In the midst of the video, someone in a gorilla outfit walks into the middle of the picture, beats their chest, and walks away (on screen for seven seconds). Remarkably, when asked, half of the participants reported not seeing the gorilla in the video. Because they were focused on a task and clearly did not expect to see a gorilla, they did not perceive this seemingly obvious stimulus. As Most, Scholl, Clifford, and Simons (2005) noted in summarizing a series of related experiments, "Quite literally, the probability that people will notice an unexpected object depends largely on what they have set their minds to see" (p. 237). Preconceptions may so markedly influence one's interpretations and memories of experiences (e.g., Halberstadt, Winkielman, Niedenthal, & Dalle, 2009) that "believing is seeing" may be more accurate version of the old axiom "seeing is believing."

Humans' perceptual weaknesses may be especially acute in relation to determining whether one phenomenon (e.g., an instructional practice) causes another (e.g., improved student outcomes). Psychologists refer to the tendency of humans to ascribe causality when it actually does not exist as *illusory causation*. "Considerable evidence indicates that people overattribute causality to a given stimulus when it is salient or the focus of their attention—the so-called illusory-causation phenomenon" (Lassiter, Geers, Munhall, Ploutz-Snyder, & Breitenbecher, 2002, p. 299). Lassiter et al. found that individuals selectively register or extract information from their observations based on their initial points of view. Thus, individuals appear prone to pay attention to what they already believe to be true, thereby establishing the perception of causal relationships consistent with their a priori beliefs regardless of whether such a relationship exists in reality.

Shermer (2002) has suggested that humans are hard-wired with a proclivity for seeing patterns and making causal connections. Humans' tendencies to draw causal connections may be evolutionarily adaptive, in that the harm caused by mistakenly identifying causal connections (i.e., Type I errors, false positives) in our species' formative years (e.g., believing that a predator caused a noise in the bushes when it was really just the wind) was typically minimal compared to the dangers associated with making Type II errors (i.e., false negatives; e.g., believing that the wind caused a rustling in the bushes when it was really a predator) (Shermer, 2010). Moreover, it appears that the more unpredictable and out-of-control the environment, the more humans strive to make sense of their surroundings by identifying patterns and making causal connections; and are thus more likely to make Type I errors and identify illusory causal relationships (Whitson & Galinsky, 2008).

One can easily envision how these phenomena might play out in classroom settings, which often are unpredictable and chaotic environments in which teachers are actively engaged in specific tasks. Imagine, for example, that a new teacher is struggling to impact positively the behavior and performance of her students. She recently received professional development on a practice, read about how experts support it, and talked to other teachers who reported the technique to be successful. The teacher is enthusiastic about the practice, has invested considerable time, energy, and even money into preparing to implement it, and fully expects it to be effective. Because of the chaotic nature of the instructional environment and her positive expectations, upon implementation the teacher is likely to (a) search hard for links between her instructional behavior and improved student behavior, and (b) overattend to indications of the practice's success (e.g., a small group of students performing well) while misperceiving or ignoring other stimuli indicating that the practice is less than effective (e.g., a group of students whose performance gains are minimal). Accordingly, the teacher comes to believe that the practice truly works, continues to use the practice, and spreads the word regarding its positive impact to colleagues.

This propensity for teachers to perceive illusory causal relationships between instruction and student performance may be a cause of educators' continued beliefs in and application of practices shown to be ineffective (i.e., Type I errors). Based on their own or others' experiences and perceptions, well-intentioned special educators have embraced a litany of practices as effective that actually do not have a meaningful, and may even have a negative, impact on student outcomes (e.g., colored lenses, facilitated communication, dietary interventions, learning styles, patterning; see Mostert, 2010).

Inattentional Blindness and Type II Errors

It may seem that one of the benefits of practitioners' apparent inclination to overidentify causal relationships is that they seldom commit Type II errors, or fail to recognize when a practice actually does cause improved student outcomes. However, relying on personal experience and subjective observations to determine what works may also contribute to incorrectly perceiving that an effective practice does not work—inattentional blindness can work both ways. That is, if practitioners expect that a practice will not work, they may not attend to unexpected indications that the practice is working. For example, Direct Instruction, an instructional practice with strong empirical support, is often rejected and viewed as ineffective by teachers (e.g., Ziffer, 2006)—perhaps because some teachers perceive its scripted, teacher-directed lessons as overly constraining, not sufficiently student-centered, and therefore unlikely to work. Similarly, positive reinforcement, a mainstay of effective classroom management, may often be perceived as ineffective not because of actual student outcomes, but because it clashes with many individuals' traditional beliefs regarding how problem behaviors should be handled (e.g., Maag, 2001).

Due at least in part to over-reliance on personal experience, anecdotal information, and tradition for determining what works, a research-to-practice gap has evolved in which special educators commonly implement practices that are ineffective and sometimes fail to use those practices that are the most effective (Carnine, 1997; Cook & Schirmer, 2006). Although the gap between research and practice impacts the learning of all students, it is especially harmful to students with disabilities, who typically require the most effective instruction to reach their goals (Dammann & Vaughn, 2001). Because of the shortcomings of traditional approaches for determining what works, special educators need a more trustworthy mechanism for evaluating instructional practices, such as research.

Using Research to Identify Effective Practices

Scientific research represents one way to improve the reliability with which the effectiveness of education practices is determined. It is important to realize that research findings (a) are far from infallible and (b) can be difficult for teachers to interpret and apply (e.g., Gallagher, 2004). Yet educational research is essentially a refined and systematic application of the observational, trial-and-error process that teachers go through every day to form their personal perspectives on what works, conducted in ways that systematically guard against Type I and Type II errors (see Cook et al., 2011). Without the safeguards that characterize high quality group experimental or single-subject research designs—two research approaches that are uniquely suited for determining whether a practice *causes* changes in student outcomes (Cook, Tankersley, Cook, & Landrum, 2008)—it is easy for educators to make Type I and Type II errors. For instance, if a teacher implements a new practice and observes that students do well on subsequent quizzes, it seems reasonable to conclude that the practice works. However, it is possible that students would have done just as well, if not better, without the intervention. Group experimental and single-subject research incorporate systematic design features that guard against these types of spurious conclusions.

Group Experimental Studies and Control Groups

True group experimental research involves random assignment of participants (e.g., students) to two or more groups (experimental studies can involve more than two groups, but we limit our discussion here to two-group experiments): an experimental group, which receives the intervention, and a control group, which does not. The educational experiences of the two groups should be as similar as possible (e.g., the same or equivalent instructors, physical conditions, time devoted to instruction) except for the implementation of the practice being examined. The control group often receives typical instruction and, therefore, represents the outcomes that would be expected in the absence of the intervention; to which the performance of the experimental group is compared. To the degree that (a) the two groups are functionally equivalent on relevant characteristics (e.g., age, ability) and (b) everything about the two groups' educational experiences are functionally equivalent except for the presence of the intervention, any robust differences between the two groups on outcome changes can be ascribed logically to the intervention (Cook, Cook, Landrum, & Tankersley, 2008). Thus, the presence of a control group provides a meaningful comparison and guards against the possibility an intervention is perceived as effective when it actually produced no better (or worse) outcome gains than would have occurred in its absence.

Quasi-experimental group studies follow the same logic, but do not randomly assign study participants to control and intervention groups. Rather, intact groups (e.g., students in particular classes) are assigned to the comparison or intervention group based on convenience. Every effort is made to ensure that participants and conditions in the two groups are as similar as possible, statistically adjust for any meaningful differences between the groups, or both. Yet, even when groups are demonstrably similar in terms of membership and conditions, differences are adjusted for statistically, or both, it is possible that unmeasured disparities between the groups (e.g., one group has a more experienced teacher than the other) may influence the relative impact of the intervention—resulting in either Type I or Type II errors. Therefore, although quasi-experimental studies are used to determine whether practices work in special education, it should be recognized that they are more prone to false positive and false negatives than true group experiments (Cook, Cook, Landrum, & Tankersley, 2008).

Single-subject Research and Intra-individual Comparisons

Single-subject research designs employ a different logic to rule out the possibility that outcome changes might have occurred in the absence of the intervention. In single-subject research, student performance data collected while the intervention is in place are compared to performance data from the same individual when the intervention is not being implemented (i.e., intra-individual comparison) to determine if the intervention is functionally related to improved student outcomes (Kazdin, 2010).

Student performance is measured initially during a baseline phase of typical instructional conditions. To guard against Type I errors, single-subject researchers do not introduce the intervention until baseline data indicate that performance is not improving on its own. If baseline data show that student performance is improving without the intervention, it is reasonable to conclude that any improvements observed during a subsequent intervention phase may have occurred anyway (i.e., without implementing the intervention). Comparing baseline data and intervention outcomes for the same student also guards against Type II errors. For example, imagine that self-monitoring is implemented to improve the amount of time a student spends reading. Even after the intervention has been implemented, the student still does not read as much as the other children in class. In the absence of baseline data, the teacher may perceive that the intervention was ineffective. However, baseline data indicate that without the intervention, the child engaged in reading much less and was not improving at all before the intervention, indicating that the self-monitoring is associated with increased reading time for that child.

Other design components in single-subject research further guard against Type I and Type II error. For example, in an ABAB (reversal) design, a baseline phase is followed by an intervention phase, which is followed by a second baseline phase, which is in turn followed by a return to the intervention. Single-subject studies also typically involve multiple individuals. Thus, only when outcomes are (a) relatively low and not improving during both baseline phases, (b) relatively high during both intervention phases, and (c) these patterns hold across multiple participants can research consumers confidently conclude that it was the intervention that caused the improved student outcomes (Alberto & Troutman, 2008).

Other Safeguards Against Type I and Type II Errors in High Quality Research

Haphazard observations and poorly constructed assessments (e.g., tests that are biased, have little to do with targeted outcomes, are overly aligned with the intervention) can make it appear that an ineffective practice worked (Type I error) or that an effective practice did not work (Type II error). So high quality research studies use measures of student performance and behavior shown to be reliable (i.e., consistent) and valid (i.e., meaningful) (e.g., direct observations of behaviors, standardized assessments, curriculum-based measurement). By using reliable and valid measures, researchers reduce the possibility that student performance appears to improve more or less than it actually did due to measurement error.

High quality research also guards against Type I and Type II errors by examining and providing evidence of adequate treatment fidelity. Treatment fidelity, also known as treatment integrity and implementation fidelity, refers to the degree to which an intervention or practice is used as designed (e.g., Lane, Bocian, MacMillan, & Gresham, 2004). If all of the elements of a practice are not implemented or the practice was not applied as frequently as it was designed to be, it might appear that it is ineffective when in reality the disappointing student outcomes may be due to the practice being used inappropriately (i.e., a Type II error). In contrast, implementing a practice more frequently than designed or including additional resources that are not part of the intervention (e.g., additional classroom personnel) may make a practice appear more effective than it actually is (i.e., a Type I error). See Gersten et al. (2005) and Horner et al. (2005) for more detailed discussions of these and additional quality indicators that are present in high quality group experimental and single-subject research, respectively, in special education that limit the likelihood of Type I and Type II errors.

Issues with Using Research to Determine What Works in Special Education

The safeguards incorporated into high quality group experimental and single-subject research greatly reduce the likelihood of making Type I and Type II errors when determining what works in special education in comparison to relying on personal experience, anecdotal information, or tradition. However, determining what works based on a research study does not eliminate the possibility of false positives or false negatives. Indeed, accessing research may raise some additional, potentially problematic issues for special educators seeking to determine what works. For example, the abundance of research available to educators can be overwhelming (Landrum & Tankersley, 2004; Nelson et al., 2009). Since the advent of the Internet, teachers can access a wealth of research on a vast array of interventions within seconds. Although this abundance of resources and the ease with which they are accessed can be valuable tools, they also provide new means for making Type I and Type II errors.

Unfortunately, much of the research available, especially on the Internet, is not of high quality or peer-reviewed. The authors of these research reports may, then, reach spurious findings, draw misleading conclusions that are not supported fully by their results, or both. If special educators rely on a single study to make decisions, especially if the study is not of high quality or utilizes a design from which causality cannot be inferred (e.g., correlational studies, qualitative studies), they can easily be led to believe that an effective practice does not work, or that an ineffective practice should be implemented. Science is a gradual, imperfect process. No research study can result in 100% certainty. Rather, one places incrementally greater confidence in a hypothesis (e.g., practice A causes improved student outcomes) as the findings of multiple, high quality research studies utilizing appropriate research designs accrue and converge to show repeatedly that a practice has robust effects on student outcomes (e.g., Cook et al., 2011; Sagan, 1996; Shermer, 2002).

One might hope, then, that special educators use the wealth of resources available to them to make instructional decisions based on critical readings of entire research bases. However, most practitioners have neither the time nor the training to critically analyze an entire corpus of research literature for every instructional decision they have to make. Given the infeasibility of practitioners conducting in-depth and critical analyses of multiple literature bases, many special educators interact with research haphazardly and indirectly. That is, practitioners' exposure to research on a topic often consists of a cursory reading of the first one or two studies that pop up in an Internet search or secondhand reports of "what the research says." Unfortunately, those who inform educators about research often have an incomplete understanding of the research literature themselves, are selectively reporting research findings to prove a point, or both.

Being confronted with contrasting findings in a research base seems particularly vexing to many practitioners. Contrasting findings can be found among high quality studies at times, but they are encountered with greater frequency when indiscriminately perusing the reams of readily accessible research findings from studies of both low and high quality or by learning about research secondhand (Bartels, 2003). Teachers who read or hear about studies reporting diametrically opposed findings may conclude that research is unreliable, can be manipulated easily, and is not to be trusted (Boardman, Arguelles, Vaughn, Hughes, & Klingner, 2005). Consequently, special education teachers may turn to more familiar approaches (e.g., their own experience, the experiences of others in similar situations, traditional practice) for determining what works. Paradoxically, then, the ease with which special educators can access reports of research may not have decreased the likelihood of Type I and Type II errors in teachers' decision-making. Instead, it may have reinforced educators' conventional reliance on personal experience, anecdotal information, and tradition as primary sources for determining what works. Special education leaders accessing the results of a more trustworthy, sophisticated, and user-friendly approach for determining what works (i.e., EBPs) may be a more fruitful approach to facilitate the implementation of effective practices than asking practitioners to critically examine research studies on their own.

Evidence-based Practices in Special Education

Following the lead of the medical profession in the 1990s (e.g., Sackett, Rosenberg, Gray, Haynes, & Richardson, 1996), professionals in a variety of fields, including education, have recently prioritized the implementation of EBPs (see Slavin, 2002, 2008). Conceptually, EBPs represent a systematic approach for examining the research literature across multiple studies to determine what works in such as way that minimizes Type I and, to a lesser degree, Type II errors. Generally speaking, EBPs are practices that are supported by a body of research studies that meets standards in four primary areas: research design, quantity, quality, and magnitude of effect (Cook, Tankersley, Cook, & Landrum, 2008; Cook et al., 2011).

Although evidence-based practice is sometimes used to refer broadly to an educational philosophy or approach that prominently features EBPs (Cook & Cook, in press), we use EBPs here specifically in reference to particular instructional practices supported by research that meets systematic criteria. Although a variety of different standards exist for determining EBPs in education, for our discussion we draw primarily on the work of Gersten et al. (2005) and Horner et al. (2005) who proposed the most widely applied set of standards for determining EBPs in special education (see Cook, Tankersley, & Landrum, 2009).

Research Design and Evidence-Based Practices

Most approaches for determining EBPs only consider research studies that utilize a research design from which causality can be inferred. For example, in special education, Gersten et al. (2005) and Horner et al. (2005) proposed that group experimental research (including true experiments and quasi-experiments) and single-subject research studies, respectively, should be considered when determining whether a practice causes changes in student outcomes. Although other types of research (e.g., correlational, qualitative) provide important information to special educators, they are not designed to meaningfully address the question of whether a practice works (e.g., Cook, Tankersley, Cook, & Landrum, 2008). By utilizing a control group and intra-individual comparison, for example, group experiments and single-subject research, respectively, control for Type I and Type II errors in ways that other research designs do not when determining which practices work.

Many of the apparently conflicting messages drawn from research may be due to studies utilizing different research designs. For example, it is possible that a qualitative study reports that a practice is perceived positively by teachers and administrators, that a correlational study shows that the same practice is used more frequently in high achieving schools, yet experimental research indicates that the practice does not cause improved student outcomes. At first blush, these findings may appear contradictory. Yet it is important to remember that educators can feel positively toward ineffective practices and that high achieving schools may sometimes use less than effective practices—which is why qualitative and correlational research are not used to identify EBPs. Using only group experimental and single-subject research studies to identify EBPs therefore reduces the likelihood of false positives and false negatives by relying solely on studies designed to determine meaningfully whether a practice works.

Research Quality and Evidence-based Practices

Of course, even if a study utilizes a research design from which causality can be inferred, when it is not conducted rigorously the odds of spurious findings increase. Although it is possible for low quality research to erroneously indicate that an effective practice did not work (Type II error), in general greater rigor is associated with lower effect sizes (Greenwood, 2009; Simmerman & Swanson, 2001)—suggesting that low quality studies are more likely to produce Type I errors (i.e., false positives). To guard against low quality studies being considered when determining EBPs, Gersten et al. (2005) and Horner et al. (2005) proposed lists of quality indicators for high quality group experimental and single-subject research studies, respectively.

Gersten et al. (2005) required that for a group experimental study to be considered in support of an EBP, it must meet at least 9 of 10 essential quality indicators (e.g., characteristics of students comparable across groups; adequate implementation fidelity documented; multiple outcome measures used, at least one of which is not closely aligned with intervention). Moreover, high quality group experimental studies must meet at least four of eight desirable quality indicators (e.g., attrition rates documented and comparable across groups, evidence of validity of outcome measures), whereas acceptable studies must meet only one desirable quality indicator. For single-subject studies to be considered when identifying EBPs, Horner et al. (2005) required that they meet all of 21 proposed quality indicators (e.g., adequate interrater reliability, adequate implementation fidelity, socially important outcome variable). By not considering studies that do not meet these multiple indicators of research quality, the process of determining EBPs relies solely on high quality studies that are relatively unlikely to reflect Type I or Type II error. See Gersten et al. and Horner et al. for more detailed discussions of quality indicators for group experimental and single-subject research, respectively, in special education.

Quantity of Research and Evidence-Based Practices

It is important to recognize that although well-designed and implemented group experimental and single-subject studies control for many prominent threats to validity, no study is perfect. For example, because of the complex nature of conducting research on real people in real schools, the findings of even high quality group experimental studies featuring random assignment, sometimes thought of as the gold standard in educational research (What Works Clearinghouse, 2003), can result in a Type I or Type II error. Furthermore, valid results of a study conducted in a particular setting with specific students may not generalize to other settings or populations. Deeming a practice as an EBP (or as a non-EBP) on the basis of only one study is, therefore, premature. Accordingly, Gersten et al. (2005) proposed that two high quality studies or four acceptable quality group experimental studies must support a practice for it to be considered an EBP in special education. Horner et al. (2005) recommended that for a practice to be considered an EBP on the basis of single-subject research, it must be supported by a minimum of five single-subject studies with at least 20 total participants.

Magnitude of Effect and Evidence-Based Practices

In addition to meeting standards related to research design, quality, and quantity of supporting studies, it is important that EBPs have a robust and meaningfully positive impact of student outcomes. In studies with a very large number of participants, small differences between groups can be statistically significant, leading to potential Type I errors in which a practice might be thought of as effective even though it is associated with relatively small gains in student outcomes that are not meaningful to educators. Accordingly, Gersten et al. (2005) recommended that for a practice to be evidence-based in special education on the basis of group experimental research, the weighted effect size across high quality and acceptable group experimental studies must be significantly greater than zero (i.e., zero is not within the 95% confidence interval for the weighted effect size). This standard further guards against Type I errors in instances of practices with conflicting research findings. For example, if a practice is supported by three group studies, but three other group studies show that the practice has a negative impact on student outcomes, the weighted effect size would likely not be significantly greater than zero.

For single-subject studies to count in support of an EBP in special education, a functional relationship must be demonstrated between the practice and positive changes in student outcomes (Horner et al., 2005). As opposed to group studies, in which magnitude of effect commonly is measured through statistical significance and effect sizes, robust effects are identified in single-subject research through the slightly more subjective process of visually inspecting graphs of student outcomes. Visual inspection criteria include the immediacy of change in student outcomes following the introduction and withdrawal of the practice, the proportion of data points that overlap in intervention and baseline phases, the extent of the change in student outcomes, and the consistency of data patterns across the different phases (e.g., baseline and intervention) (Horner et al., 2005).

Issues with Evidence-Based Practices in Special Education

In order to make sense of the complex and oftentimes confusing reality of classroom experiences, educational research applies systematic and logical guidelines to analyze observations of student performance in ways that minimize the likelihood of Type I and Type II errors. The process of identifying EBPs can be thought of as applying similar systematic guidelines and logic to analyze the potentially confusing array of findings from research studies in order to further reduce Type I and Type II errors (Cook et al., 2011). However, when working with practitioners, it is important that special education leaders do not give the false impression that using EBPs eliminates Type I and Type II errors. EBPs have important limitations that should be considered when engaging in evidence-based special education.

Although the time-consuming, multi-step, and rigorous process of identifying EBPs greatly minimizes the risk of Type I error, it does not eliminate that possibility (Chabris & Simons, 2010). Although it is highly unlikely that truly ineffective practices that do not work for large portions of the population will be identified as EBPs, it is important to recognize that no practice, not even an EBP, is guaranteed to work for every specific student. Indeed, because the social sciences, including educational research, deal with people (whose behavior is not perfectly predictable), causality in the educational research is probabilistic rather than absolute (Burns & Hoagwood, 2004). That is, when educational researchers say that a practice causes positive change in student outcomes, they do not mean that the outcomes of every student who receives the practice will improve inevitably. Rather, causality in educational research implies that an intervention is highly likely to bring about improved student outcomes.

Even the most effective practices will fail to positively impact a small proportion of students (e.g., Al Otaiba & Fuchs, 2006), who are often referred to as non-responders or treatment resisters. The possibility of an EBP not being effective for any individual student therefore cannot be eliminated completely. Accordingly, it is important that special education leaders encourage and facilitate the systematic monitoring of student progress, even when teachers implement EBPs, to determine whether an instructional practice is having the desired impact (Cook, Tankersley, & Harjusola-Webb, 2008). This recommendation is especially important for children with disabilities, whose learning characteristics and response to interventions may differ dramatically from what is expected (Greenwood, 2009).

Special education leaders should also take care not to assume that a practice is ineffective just because it has not been identified as an EBP (a Type II error). That a practice is not identified as an EBP does not necessarily mean that it has been shown conclusively by multiple, high quality research studies to have a negative effect or no effect on student outcomes. At least two other possibilities exist as to why a practice may not be identified as an EBP: (a) an evidence-based review has been conducted but insufficient high quality research exists to determine clearly whether the practice is evidence-based, (b) an evidence-based review has not yet been conducted on the practice. Given the considerable time and resources required for conducting an evidence-based review (e.g., Browder, Ahlgrim-Delzell, Spooner, Mims, & Baker, 2009, estimated that it took their team approximately 400 person hours to conduct their evidence-based review) and the relatively sparse base of high quality group experimental and single-subject research available on many practices in special education (e.g., Mastropieri et al., 2009; Seethaler & Fuchs, 2005), it appears that these reasons may explain why many seemingly effective practices are not classified as EBPs.

Thus, it is important for special education leaders to distinguish carefully between practices that have not yet been the subject of a complete evidence-based review, and those practices that are non-EBPs because they have been shown my multiple, high quality studies to not have a meaningfully positive effect on student outcomes. We recommend that special education leaders prioritize EBPs (see Table 16.1 for sources of EBPs in special education) in working with and training special education teachers. But for areas in which EBPs have not yet been identified, special education leaders should target promising practices (i.e., practices supported by some type of high quality research) (see Cook, Tankersley, & Harjusola-Webb, 2008).

Although EBPs have the potential to transform education and greatly improve student outcomes (Slavin, 2002), the increasing emphasis on EBPs has had little impact on classroom prac-

Table 16.1 Sources of Evidence-Based Practices (EBPs) in Special Education

Source	Description
Best Evidence Encyclopedia (BEE), Struggling Readers	The BEE, which identifies evidence-based programs in general education, applied its standards for EBPs to programs aimed at struggling readers (http://www.bestevidence.org/reading/strug/strug_read.htm)
Exceptional Children, 75(3)	This special issue contains five evidence-based reviews that applied Gersten et al.'s (2005) and Horner et al.'s (2005) standards for identifying EBPs in special education.
National Autism Center (NAC), National Standards Project	The NAC applied systematic standards to determine established (i.e., EBPs), emerging, unestablished, and ineffective/harmful practices for children with autism (http://www.nationalautismcenter.org/affiliates/reports.php)
National Center on Response to Intervention	Although the Center does not denote which practices are EBPs, it provides information on quality, design, effect size for each study reviewed, on the basis of which educators can determine which practices meet EBP standards (http://www.rti4success.org/chart/instructionTools/)
National Professional Development Center on Autism Spectrum Disorders	The Center identified 24 EBPs for students with autism spectrum disorder and includes links to briefs that include step-by-step directions for implementation (http://autismpdc.fpg.unc.edu/content/evidence-based-practices)
What Works Clearinghouse (WWC), Students with Learning Disabilities	The WWC, which identifies EBPs in general education, has begun to review practices specifically for students with learning disabilities (http://ies.ed.gov/ncee/wwc/reports/Topic.aspx?tid=19)
WWC, Early Childhood Education for Students with Disabilities	The WWC, which identifies EBPs in general education, has begun to review practices specifically for early childhood education for students with disabilities (http://ies.ed.gov/ncee/wwc/reports/topic.aspx?tid=22)

Note: Sources listed here applied systematic standards related to research design, quality of research, quantity of research, and magnitude of effect; or provided information along each of these dimensions.

tice or the outcomes of students with disabilities. Despite EBPs and research-based practices being emphasized in both the Individuals with Disabilities Education Act and the No Child Left Behind Act, many special educators continue to use practices unsupported by research (e.g., Burns & Ysseldyke, 2009; Jones, 2009). Identifying EBPs is, then, only a first step (i.e., necessary but not sufficient condition) in improving student outcomes. Without broad implementation, the potential benefits of EBPs will not be achieved (Cook et al., 2011). Leaders in special education will have to facilitate the application of EBPs in schools and classrooms.

Facilitating the Application of Evidence-Based Practices

"Research is not the real world" (Nelson et al., 2009, p. 28). This teacher's sentiment captures many educators' feelings regarding the irrelevance of research to their daily lives in the classroom (see Miller, Drill, & Behrstock, 2010). Furthermore, many teachers mistrust researchers and research findings (Bartels, 2003; Boardman et al., 2005; Hemsley-Brown & Sharp, 2003). After all, teachers may reason, researchers do not understand the daily realities and complexities in which I teach, and the environments and participants in studies differ meaningfully from my own classroom and students. Without efforts to increase the relevance and trustworthiness of EBPs and the research on which they are based to practitioners, it may not matter how many high quality studies are conducted, how many evidence-based reviews are completed, or how well EBPs control for Type I and Type II errors. Simply put, if teachers do not trust research, they are unlikely to use EBPs. Given the largely negative views that many practitioners appear to hold toward research, it appears that—as Timperley (2010) suggested—leaders in special education will need to play strategic roles in advancing the use of EBPs.

In their study of teachers implementing EBPs in the United Kingdom, Simons, Kushner, Jones, and James (2003) found that teachers typically did not generalize research findings to their own classrooms, but rather engaged in *situated generalization*. That is, teachers implemented instructional recommendations when they perceived a strong connection between them and their own situations. Generalization of instructional information becomes situated, and therefore credible, under two conditions: when (a) the situation (e.g., teaching environment, student characteristics) from which the instructional recommendation are derived clearly is recognized as connected and similar to the teacher's own situation and (b) the teacher has confidence and trust in the source of the recommendations (e.g., a trusted colleague).

Rather than value EBPs and research evidence, teachers tend to embrace practice-based evidence (i.e., evidence derived from practical experience, or craft wisdom)—likely because it meets the criteria for situated generalization. Although practice-based evidence may hold great appeal for practitioners, it is vulnerable to Type I and Type II errors—which created the need for EBPs in the first place. Thus, to make EBPs attractive to teachers, but to also protect against Type I and Type II errors, we propose that special education leaders work to merge EBPs and practice-based evidence. Toward that end, we briefly outline three ways that leaders in special education can utilize the concept of situated generalization to blend EBPs with practice-based evidence to create workable evidence-based special education: (a) generate local evidence supporting EBPs, (b) balance treatment fidelity with fit and flexibility, and (c) participate in use-inspired research.

Creating Local Evidence Supporting Evidence-Based Practices

Practice-based evidence holds considerable sway with practitioners, but relying solely on craft wisdom often ignores effective practices and may embrace practices that are ineffective (Kauffman, 2000). Special education leaders can both increase the appeal of EBPs and enhance the validity of practice-based evidence by creating localized evidence and support for EBPs. Perhaps the most direct way to create local evidence is piloting EBPs at local schools, documenting their positive impact on local students, and effectively disseminating this information to other local educators.

Special education leaders should first select an EBP that addresses important needs commonly faced by local teachers. Next, leaders should identify a small number of energetic, skilled, and trusted teachers with whom to work on initial implementation of the EBP. Confining initial involvement to a small group of expert teachers not only heightens the likelihood that the EBP will be implemented appropriately and effectively, but also increases the credence of the evidence generated from these initial efforts with other teachers. Through the process of implementing the EBP, the initial implementers create practice-based evidence to provide the basis for situated generalization. This practice-based evidence can take the form of stories and case studies (Nelson et al., 2009; Smith, Richards-Tutor, & Cook, 2010) that exemplify how the teachers successfully implemented the EBP and the impact that the practice had on their students. It is also important to collect objective data that is valued by local teachers (e.g., scores on curriculum-based assessments) to provide further, concrete evidence of the positive effect of the EBP on local students.

Although this type of evidence may not meet standards for rigorous scientific inquiry, it is likely to persuade other local practitioners because it meets the standards for situated generalization; that is, the information is from (a) a situation similar to that of the other teachers and (b) a trusted and capable source (Simons et al., 2003). Once teachers see that trusted colleagues can use an EBP successfully in classrooms and with students similar to their own, they are likely to expect it to work for them and implement it. And because the targeted practice is an EBP, special education leaders can be confident that they are promoting an effective practice.

Implementation Fidelity

For an EBP to be as effective in typical classrooms as it was shown to be in research studies, it appears logical that teachers must apply the practice in the same way it was in supporting research studies. Not surprisingly, a generally positive relationship has been documented between implementation fidelity and outcomes (e.g., Hagermoser Sanetti & Kratochwill, 2009). As such, when facilitating the implementation of an EBP, special education leaders should devote time and resources to ensure that practitioners demonstrate the ability to implement the critical elements of a practice as designed. Moreover, ongoing resources should be committed to systematically assessing practitioners' implementation fidelity over time. Doing so generates valuable feedback that identifies which critical elements of EBPs are not being implemented appropriately, which special education leaders can then use to guide ongoing training and supports.

In recent years, scholars have broadened their conceptualization of implementation fidelity beyond adhering to the critical elements of a practice. For example, Schulte, Easton, and Parker (2009) noted multiple dimensions of implementation fidelity in addition to adherence such as treatment exposure (i.e., number and length of intervention sessions), treatment quality or competence (i.e., quality or skill with which intervention is delivered), program differentiation (i.e., only planned elements of intervention were implemented, comparison condition differs meaningfully), participant exposure (i.e., amount of intervention received by participants), participant comprehension (i.e., degree to which participants understood intervention), and participant responsiveness (i.e., participant engagement with intervention). Thus, it is important that leaders in special education train and assess implementation fidelity across multiple dimensions.

However, researchers have begun to identify a curvilinear relation between treatment adherence and outcomes, whereby moderate treatment adherence is associated with the highest outcomes (Barber et al., 2006; Hogue et al., 2008). That low adherence is associated with low outcomes is hardly surprising, yet it may seem counterintuitive that the highest levels of adherence are not associated with the highest outcomes. Such findings are likely due to teachers needing to adapt practices, even EBPs, to their own environments, students, and personal strengths to maximize their effectiveness (McMaster et al., 2010). Demanding overly rigid adherence that negates the possibility of adaptation may, then, be counterproductive. Moreover, practitioners may be less willing to apply an EBP if they perceive that they must follow a prescribed, step-by-step procedure imposed by an outsider. As Simons et al. noted in regard to situated generalization, "teachers need to interpret and re-interpret what evidence means for them in the precise situation in which they are teaching" (2003, p. 361). Thus, special education leaders will need to walk a fine line between requiring faithful adherence to the core elements of EBPs yet allowing, even encouraging, teachers to adapt and situate EBPs appropriately—what Kendall, Gosch, Furr, and Sood (2008) termed *flexibility with fidelity*. We recommend that adaptation of EBPs be guided by special education leaders who are intimately familiar with a particular EBP and its implementation so that adaptation does not jeopardize the core features and effectiveness of the practice.

Use-Inspired Research

Researchers and practitioners tend to approach educational research from markedly different perspectives (Boardman et al., 2005; Nelson et al., 2009). Researchers predominantly value rigorous, experimental research, such as that used to identify EBPs; whereas teachers prioritize situated, local information (Alton-Lee, 2004; Boardman et al., 2005), which often takes the form of informal, even subjective, accounts of practice. Stokes (1997) described how these two perspectives on research have been viewed as polar opposites, with little common ground or room for compromise. Educational research, then, is often perceived as an "either/or" phenomenon—either rigorous or teacher-friendly, but not both. Stokes, however, recommended a far more interactive view of research, in which rigorous, evidence-based research is "inspired by considerations of use" (p. 74). Because most special education leaders work closely with practitioners in school settings yet are also trained in research and work with researchers, they are in an ideal position to broker meaningful communication between researchers and practitioners to facilitate use-inspired research.

Use-inspired research rejects the traditional, unidirectional flow of knowledge dissemination, in which the findings of rigorous research are handed down from researchers to practitioners (Stokes, 1997). Rather, it seeks to incorporate the perspectives of practitioners in the questions it asks and how research is conducted. For example, use-inspired research addresses questions valued by practitioners regarding the conditions under which practices work (e.g., where, for whom, under what conditions) (Shriver, 2007), not just whether a practice works generally. Moreover, typical teachers working in typical classroom are utilized as interventionists, research participants, or both. As such, these studies are likely to be perceived by teachers as relevant to their situations. Importantly, despite this practical orientation, use-inspired research is also scientifically rigorous. Rather than accepting the customary "either/or" view of educational research, use-inspired research represents a "both/ and" paradigm, in which education research is both scientifically rigorous and teacher friendly (i.e., situationally generalizable).

Leaders in special education can facilitate use-inspired research in at least two ways that both involve the establishment of mutually beneficial relationships between special education practitioners and researchers. First, special education leaders can pull teachers into the world of research by involving practitioners in research studies. Most educational researchers welcome the input, perspectives, and participation of local educators in framing and conducting their research. By explicating the benefits of research participation to practitioners and making the availability of research sites (e.g., schools, classrooms) known to researchers, special education leaders can expand the involvement of practitioners in all stages of researchers. Second, special education leaders can pull researchers into the world of teaching by having researchers provide training and support to make practitioners' data collection sufficiently rigorous to guard against common causes of Type I and Type II errors. For example, researchers can help teachers use valid single-subject research designs (e.g., reversal, multiple baseline; Kazdin, 2010) to reliably document the effect of a practice on the outcomes of individual students, small groups, or entire classes. Increasing the frequency and substance of interactions between practitioners and researchers in these ways has many advantages, including (a) improving the reliability of local, small-scale research; (b) making large-scale research easier to conduct, thereby increasing the number of existing studies (as is needed to meaningfully identify multiple EBPs); and (c) enhancing the situated generalization of large-scale research to its primary audience (i.e., practitioners).

Summary

Special education continues to be plagued by a gap between research and practice. Educators' customary sources for determining what works such as personal experience, anecdotal information, and tradition are vulnerable to both Type I (i.e., false positives) and Type II (i.e., false negatives) errors. Although scientific research presents a more reliable approach to determining what works in special education, special educators often are overwhelmed by the amount of research available; have neither the time nor training to meaningfully evaluate studies; examine studies individually; or receive inaccurate, second-hand reports of research findings. EBPs provide a systematic structure that special education leaders can use to determine what works by considering the research design, quality, quantity, and magnitude of effect of research studies. Although imbued with great potential to improve student outcomes, ongoing efforts to identify EBPs have not reduced significantly the research-to-practice gap. Disappointing implementation of EBPs may be due to practitioners' perceptions that research findings are irrelevant to their daily realities. We recommended three approaches that leaders in special education can use to increase the application of EBPs by enhancing their situated generalization: providing local evidence of EBPs' effectiveness, balancing flexibility and fidelity, and engaging in use-inspired research.

References

Al Otaiba, S., & Fuchs, D. (2006). Who are the young children for whom best practices in reading are ineffective? *Journal of Learning Disabilities, 39,* 414–431.

Alberto, P. A., & Troutman, A. C. (2008). *Applied behavior analysis for teachers* (8th ed.). Upper Saddle River, NJ: Merrill.

Alton-Lee, A. (2004). *Using best evidence syntheses to assist in making a bigger difference for diverse learners.* Auckland, NZ: New Zealand Ministry of Education. Retrieved from http://www.leadspace.govt.nz/leadership/leading_learning/synthesis.php

Barber, J. P., Gallop, R., Chris-Christophs, P., Frank, A., Thase, M. E., Weiss, R. D., & Gibbons, M. B. C. (2006). The role of therapist adherence, therapist competence, and alliance in predicting outcome of individual drug counseling: Results from the National Institute Drug Abuse Collaborative Cocaine Treatment Study. *Psychotherapy Research, 16,* 229–240.

Bartels, N. (2003). How teachers and researchers read academic articles. *Teacher and Teacher Education. 19,* 737–753.

Boardman, A. G., Arguelles, M. E., Vaughn, S., Hughes, M. T., & Klingner, J. (2005). Special education teachers' views of research-based practices. *Journal of Special Education, 39,* 168–180.

Browder, D., Ahlgrim-Delzell, L., Spooner, F., Mims, P. J., & Baker, J. N. (2009). Reviewing the evidence base for using time delay to teach picture and word recognition to students with severe developmental disabilities. *Exceptional Children, 75,* 343–364.

Burns, B. J., & Hoagwood, K. E. (2004). Evidence-based practice, part I: Research update. *Child and Adolescent Psychiatric Clinics of North America, 13,* xi–xiii.

Burns, M. K., & Ysseldyke, J. E. (2009). Reported prevalence of evidence-based instructional practices in special education. *Journal of Special Education, 43,* 3–11.

Carnine, D. (1997). Bridging the research-to-practice gap. *Exceptional Children, 63,* 513–521.

Chabris, C., & Simons, D. (2010). *The invisible gorilla and other ways our intuitions deceive us.* New York: Crown.

Cook, B. G., & Cook, S. C. (in press). Unraveling evidence-based practices in special education. *Journal of Special Education.*

Cook, B. G., & Schirmer, B. R. (Eds.). (2006). *What is special about special education: The role of evidence-based practices.* Austin, TX: PRO-ED.

Cook, B. G., Smith, G. J., & Tankersley, M. (2011). Evidence-based practices in education. In K. R. Harris. S. Graham, & T. Urdan (Eds.), *APA educational psychology handbook, volume 1* (pp. 495–528). Washington, DC: American Psychological Association.

Cook, B. G., Tankersley, M., Cook, L., & Landrum, T. J. (2008). Evidence-based practices in special education: Some practical considerations. *Intervention in School & Clinic, 44*(2), 69–75.

Cook, B. G., Tankersley, M., & Harjusola-Webb, S. (2008). Evidence-based practice and professional wisdom: Putting it all together. *Intervention in School & Clinic, 44,* 105–111.

Cook, B. G., Tankersley, M., & Landrum, T. J. (Eds.). (2009). Evidence-based practices for reading, math, writing, and behavior [special issue]. *Exceptional Children, 75*(3).

Cook, L., Cook, B. G., Landrum, T. J., & Tankersley, M. (2008). Examining the role of group experimental research in establishing evidenced-based practices. *Intervention in School & Clinic, 44*(2), 76–82.

Dammann, J. E., & Vaughn, S. (2001). Science and sanity in special education. *Behavioral Disorders, 27,* 21–29.

Gallagher, D. J. (2004). Educational research, philosophical orthodoxy, and unfulfilled promises: The quandary of traditional research in U.S. special education. In G. Thomas & R. Pring (Eds.), *Evidence-based practices in education* (pp. 119–132). Columbus, OH: Open University Press.

Gersten, R., Fuchs, L. S., Compton, D., Coyne, M., Greenwood, C., & Innocenti, M. S. (2005). Quality indicators for group experimental and quasi-experimental research in special education. *Exceptional Children, 71,* 149–164.

Greenwood, C. R. (2009). Treatment integrity: Revisiting some big ideas. *School Psychology Review, 38,* 547–553.

Hagermoser Sanetti, L. M., & Kratochwill, T. R. (2009). Toward developing a science of treatment integrity: Introduction to the special series. *School Psychology Review, 38,* 445–459.

Halberstadt, J., Winkielman, P., Niedenthal, P. M., & Dalle, N. (2009). Emotional conception: how embodied emotion concepts guide perception and facial action. *Psychological Science, 10,* 1254–1261.

Hemsley-Brown, J., & Sharp, C. (2003). The use of research to improve professional practice: A systematic review of the literature. *Oxford Review of Education, 29,* 449–470.

Hogue, A., Henderson, C. E., Dauber, S., Barajas, P. C., Fried, A., & Liddle, H. A. (2008). Treatment adherence, competence, and outcome in individual and family therapy for adolescent behavior problems. *Journal of Consulting and Clinical Psychology, 76,* 544–555.

Horner, R. H., Carr, E. G., Halle, J., McGee, G., Odom, S., & Wolery, M. (2005). The use of single-subject research to identify evidence-based practice in special education. *Exceptional Children, 71,* 165–179.

Jones, M. L. (2009). A study of novice special educators' views of evidence-based practices. *Teacher Education and Special Education, 32*(2), 101–120.

Kauffman, J. M. (2000). The special education story: Obituary, accident report, conversion experience, reincarnation, or none of the above. *Exceptionality, 8*(1), 61–71.

Kazdin, A. E. (2010). *Single-case research designs: Methods for clinical and applied settings.* New York: Oxford University Press.

Kendall, P. C., Gosch, E., Furr, J. M., & Sood, E. (2008). Flexibility with fidelity. *Journal of the American Academy of Child and Adolescent Psychiatry, 47,* 987–993.

Landrum, T. J., & Tankersley, M. (2004). Science in the schoolhouse: An uninvited guest. *Journal of Learning Disabilities, 37,* 207–212.

Lane, K. L., Bocian, K. M., MacMillan, D. L., & Gresham, F. M. (2004). Treatment integrity: An essential—but often forgotten—component of school-based interventions. *Preventing School Failure, 48*(3), 36–43.

Lassiter, G. D., Geers, A. L., Munhall, P. J., Ploutz-Snyder, R. J., & Breitenbecher, D. L. (2002). Illusory causation: Why it occurs. *Psychological Science, 13,* 299–305.

Maag, J. W. (2001). Rewarded by punishment: Reflections on the disuse of positive reinforcement in schools. *Exceptional Children, 67,* 173–186.

Mastropieri, M. A., Berkeley, A., McDuffie, K. A., Graff, H., Marshak, L., Conners, N. A., … Cuenca-Sanchez, Y. (2009). What is published in the field of special education? An analysis of 11 prominent journals. *Exceptional Children, 76,* 95–109.

McMaster, K. L., Fuchs, D., Saenz, L., Lemons, C., Kearns, D., Yen, L., … Fuchs, L. S. (2010). Scaling up PALS: The importance of implementing evidence-based practice with fidelity and flexibility. *New Times for DLD, 28*(1), 1–3. Retrieved from http://www.teachingld.org/pdf/NewTimes_ScalingUpPals2010.pdf

Miller, S., Drill, K., & Behrstock, E. (2010). Meeting teachers half way: Making educational research relevant to teachers. *Phi Delta Kappan, 97*(7), 31–34.

Mostert, M. P. (2010). Asserting the fanciful over the empirical [special issue]. *Exceptionality, 18*(1).

Most, S. B., Scholl, B. J., Clifford, E. R., & Simons, D. J. (2005). What you see is what you set: Sustained inattentional blindness and the capture of awareness. *Psychological Review, 112,* 217–242.

Nelson, S. R., Leffler, J. C., & Hansen, B. A. (2009). *Toward a research agenda for understanding and improving the use of research evidence*. Portland, OR: Northwest Regional Educational Laboratory. Retrieved from http://education-northwest.org/webfm_send/311

Sackett, D. L., Rosenberg, W. M., Gray, J. A., Haynes, R. B., & Richardson, W. S. (1996). Evidence based medicine: What it is and what it isn't. *British Medical Journal, 312*, 71–72.

Sagan, C. (1996). *The demon-haunted world: Science as a candle in the dark*. New York: Ballantine Books.

Schulte, A. C., Easton, J. E., & Parker, J. (2009). Advances in treatment integrity research: Multidisciplinary perspectives on the conceptuatlization, measurement, and enhancement, or treatment integrity. *School Psychology Review, 38*, 460–475.

Seethaler, P. M., & Fuchs, L. S. (2005). A drop in the bucket: Randomized controlled trials testing reading and math interventions. *Learning Disabilities Research & Practice, 20*(2), 98–102.

Shermer, M. (2002). *Why people believe weird things: Pseudoscience, superstition, and other confusions of our time*. New York: Holt.

Shermer, M. (2010). The pattern behind self-deception. Retrieved from http://www.ted.com/talks/michael_shermer_the_pattern_behind_self_deception.html

Shriver, M. D. (2007). Roles and responsibilities of researchers and practitioners for translating research to practice. *Journal of Evidence-Based Practices for Schools, 8*(1), 1–30.

Simmerman, S., & Swanson, H. L. (2001). Treatment outcomes for students with learning disabilities: How important are internal and external validity? *Journal of Learning Disabilities, 34*, 221–236.

Simons, D. J., & Chabris, C. F. (1999). Gorillas in our midst: Sustained inattentional blindness for dynamic events. *Perception, 28*, 1059–1074.

Simons, H., Kushner, S., Jones, K., & James, D. (2003). From evidence-based practice to practice-based evidence: The idea of situated generalization. *Research Papers in Education, 18*, 347–364.

Slavin, R. E. (2002). Evidence-based education policies: Transforming educational practice and research. *Educational Researcher, 31*(7), 15–21.

Slavin, R. E. (2008). What works? Issues in synthesizing educational program evaluations. *Educational Researcher, 37*(1), 5–14.

Smith, G. J., Richards-Tutor, C., & Cook, B. G. (2010). Using teacher narratives in the dissemination of research-based practices. *Intervention in School & Clinic, 46*, 67–70.

Snell, M. E. (2003). Applying research to practice: The more pervasive problem. *Research and Practice for Persons with Severe Disabilities, 28*, 143–147.

Stokes, D. E. (1997). *Pasteur's quadrant: Basic science and technological innovation*. Washington DC: Brookings Institution Press.

Timperley, H. (2010, February). *Using evidence in the classroom for professional learning*. Paper presented to the Ontario Education Research Symposium, Ottawa, Canada. Retrieved from http://educationalleaders.govt.nz/Pedagogy-and-assessment/Evidence-based-leadership/Data-gathering-and-analysis/Using-Evidence-in-the-Classroom

What Works Clearinghouse. (2003). Identifying and implementing educational practices supported by rigorous evidence: A user-friendly guide. Retrieved from http://ies.ed.gov/ncee/wwc/references/iDocViewer/Doc.aspx?docId=14&tocId=4

Whitson, J. A., & Galinsky, A. D. (2008). Lacking control increases illusory pattern perception. *Science, 322*, 115–117.

Ziffer, F. (2006). Educators ignore proven method of improving students' learning. *School Reform News*. Retrieved from http://www.heartland.org/policybot/results/19790/Educators_Ignore_Proven_Method_of_Improving_Students_Learning.html

17

School Leadership and School-Wide Positive Behavior Support[1]

George Sugai

UNIVERSITY OF CONNECTICUT

Breda V. O'Keeffe

UNIVERSITY OF UTAH

Robert H. Horner

UNIVERSITY OF OREGON

Timothy J. Lewis

UNIVERSITY OF MISSOURI

Many schools in the United States are struggling to meet public expectations with respect to academic achievement, high school graduation, character development, career and vocational preparation, and post secondary transition (National Center for Education Statistics, 2009a,b; Snyder, Tan, & Hoffman, 2006; Wagner, Newman, Cameto, & Levine, 2005; Zigmond, 2006). Fortunately, many of the instructional and behavioral technologies needed to address these expectations exist. For example, explicit instructional strategies for teaching reading and math, multiple opportunities for active academic engagement, active supervision and monitoring, direct social skills instruction, and adult mentoring have been established as important to maximizing academic and social success (Dixon, Carnine, Lee, Wallin, & Chard, 1998; Gersten et al., 2009; National Institute of Child Health and Human Development, 2000; Simonsen, Fairbanks, Briesch, Myers, & Sugai, 2008). For classroom and behavior management, prevention based approaches are recommended for establishing positive school culture and academic success over reactive disciplinary procedures (Biglan, 1995; Bradshaw, Koth, Thornton, & Leaf, 2009; Bradshaw, Mitchell, & Leaf, in press; Colvin, Kame'enui, & Sugai, 1993; Mayer, 1995).

Unfortunately, the infrastructure to take advantage of and maximize opportunities to implement these technologies seems to be difficult to establish. This implementation challenge is associated with a myriad of factors, for example, ineffective professional personnel development, insufficient funding, restrictive policies, competing initiatives, limited resource availability, etc. School leadership is often identified as important in addressing these challenges and meeting the expectations placed on schools (Louis, Leithwood, Wahlstrom, & Anderson, 2010).

In this chapter, the role of leadership and the implementation of prevention-based approaches, like school-wide positive behavior support (SWPBS), are highlighted. In particular, we provide a best-practices set of guidelines for school leaders that is based on the existing literature and the implementation needs of schools. Thus, the purpose of this chapter is to provide individuals in positions of school leadership with suggestions for how they might support the accurate and sustained implementation of SWPBS. To achieve this purpose, we describe (a) a sample of the literature on effective school leadership, (b) an overview of the elements that define the practices and systems of SWPBS, (c) a conceptual model and logic for the role of school leadership in SWPBS, and (d) a set of guidelines for promoting and assessing effective leadership skills.

Effective Leadership in Education

To determine what was known about effective leadership in education, we examined existing literature reviews, and primary empirical studies. This information is summarized in three sub-sections: (a) literature base, (b) implementation science, and (c) effective businesses.

Literature Base. In general, we discovered a literature base dominated by descriptive narratives and summaries highlighting perceived and reported qualities and traits of effective leaders. The primary support for this literature base was derived from surveys, case studies, and qualitative narratives (Day, 2000; Louis et al., 2010; Robinson, Llyod, & Rowe, 2008). The quantitative research literature on effective leaders in education is comprised primarily of correlational research that links characteristics of principals or district administrators to student outcomes (Cotton, 2003; Louis et al., 2010; Marzano, Waters, & McNulty, 2005; Richter, Lewis, & Hagar, in press; Robinson et al., 2008) Although these studies used a wide variety of methodologies, surveys of teachers or other administrators reporting on the administrators' leadership characteristics were used most often.

Student outcomes most frequently included scores on standardized tests. Narrative reviews of this literature reported mixed results with respect to determining a relationship between administrator behavior and student outcomes (Donmoyer, 1985; Hallinger, 2005; Hallinger & Heck, 1998; Witziers, Bosker, & Kruger, 2003). However, researchers conducting meta-analyses have found that administrator behavior typically has a small to moderate positive correlation with student outcomes (Marzano, et al., 2005; Robinson et al., 2008). Administrator influence on student outcomes is typically found to be indirect, in that administrators influence teacher behaviors and school climate, which, in turn, affect student outcomes (Leithwood, Louis, Anderson, & Wahlstrom, 2004; Leithwood & Mascall, 2008). Marzano and colleagues (2005) included 69 quantitative studies in their meta-analysis, and found that principal behaviors correlated positively with student outcomes (average $r = .25$).

Certain principal behaviors are reported as being correlated significantly with student outcomes (Cotton, 2003; Leithwood et al., 2004; Marzano et al., 2005; Robinson et al., 2008). Leithwood and colleagues (2004) organized these behaviors into three primary categories: (a) setting goals, (b) developing people, and (c) organizing the school. Marzano and colleagues (2005) identified 21 "responsibilities" of effective school leaders that correlated significantly with student outcomes, and that are closely related to those identified by Cotton (2003). We organized the responsibilities according to Leithwood and colleagues' categories (see Table 17.1). Average correlations between individual principal responsibilities and student outcomes ranged from .18 to .33.

Robinson et al. (2008) conducted a meta-analysis of correlational and experimental studies on different types of leadership in education. They separated "instructional leadership" studies (i.e., "including a learning climate free of disruption, a system of clear teaching objectives, and high teacher expectations for students," p. 638) from "transformational leadership" (i.e., the ability of leaders across many types of organizations to encourage employees to coordinate

Table 17.1 Summary of Principal Leadership Skills that Correlate Significantly with Student Outcomes

Leadership Behavior	Example	Average Correlation
Setting Goals[a]		
Monitoring/Evaluating[b]	Continually monitors the effectiveness of the school's curricular, instructional and assessment practices[b]	.27[b]
Change Agent	Systematically considers better ways of doing things	.25
Culture	Extends discussion of the purpose and mission of the school with staff	.25
Focus	Reminds faculty of the school goals at meetings	.24
Ideals/Beliefs	Demonstrates behaviors that are consistent with stated beliefs	.22
Developing People		
Situational Awareness	Anticipates potential problems in the school	.33
Flexibility	Is comfortable with making major changes in how things are done	.28
Outreach	Regularly sends a memo to superintendent with school accomplishments	.27
Input	Uses leadership teams in decision making	.25
Contingent Rewards	Recognizes and rewards individual effort and performance	.24
Intellectual Stimulation	Provides professional development based on effective schools research	.24
Communication	Is easily accessible to teachers	.23
Optimizer	Portrays a positive attitude about the ability of staff to accomplish goals	.20
Visibility	Makes daily visits to classrooms to interact with teachers and students	.20
Affirmation	Systematically and fairly recognizes and celebrates student and staff accomplishments	.19
Relationships	Greets teachers and asks how they are doing daily	.18
Organizing the School		
Discipline	Protects instructional time from interruptions	.27
Order	Provides and reinforces clear rules and procedures for staff and students	.25
Resources	Helps provide the necessary materials and staff development to enhance teaching	.25
Knowledge of Curriculum, Instruction, and Assessment	Reads research on effective instructional and assessment practices	.25
Involvement in Curriculum, Instruction, and Assessment	Helps teachers design curricular activities, instruction and assessment	.20

a Category headings adapted from Leithwood et al. (2004).
b Labels, examples, and correlations from Marzano, Waters, & McNulty (2005).

their efforts toward common goals, with added energy), and "other" studies. They found that "instructional leadership" behaviors had an average effect size of .42 on student outcomes (academic, social, and/or school engagement). "Other" types of leadership and "transformational leadership" had effect sizes of .30 and .11, respectively, on student outcomes. The authors suggest that instructional leadership may be more highly correlated with student outcomes because this leadership approach is more specific to schools and operationalized more clearly than transformational leadership approaches. Robinson and colleagues identified the following leadership behaviors as being moderately to strongly associated with more positive student social and academic outcomes: (a) establishing and clearly communicating strong academic goals, (b) structuring school routines to enable meeting these goals, (c) securing and allotting monetary and personnel resources to activities that support academic instruction, (d) involvement with teachers in making decisions about curriculum and instruction, (e) observing and providing formative and summative feedback to teachers on their instruction using "clear performance standards," (f) ensuring that the leaders and teachers use student-level data to inform instructional decisions, (g) actively participating in regular professional development with teachers, and (h) promoting a safe and supportive school environment by developing and enforcing clear behavioral expectations and helping resolve conflicts effectively. These behaviors are similar to the behaviors identified by Marzano and colleagues (2005), based on a somewhat different set of studies.

Little research has been conducted on the behaviors of district-level administrators (e.g., superintendents) that result in improved student outcomes (Lashley & Boscardin, 2003; Leithwood et al., 2004). However, Waters and Marzano's (2006) meta-analysis of 14 correlational studies revealed a significantly positive correlation between district leadership and student outcomes, $r = .24$. In addition, they identified five specific responsibilities that had significant correlations with student outcomes: "collaborative goal setting; non-negotiable goals for achievement and instruction; board alignment with and support of district goals; monitoring achievement and instruction goals; use of resources to support the goals for achievement and instruction" (pp. 3–4).

To conclude, one of the largest leadership survey studies was completed by Louis, Leithwood, Wahlstrom, and Anderson (2010). Using qualitative and quantitative results from direct observations in classrooms (312) and surveys and interviews with teachers (8391), administrators (471), and district (304) and state (124) administrative personnel from states (9), districts (43), and elementary, middle, and high schools (180), researchers examined generally what leadership practices directly and indirectly were reported as most affecting student learning. Their study was grounded in a conceptual framework (Figure 17.1) that considered student learning as a direct outcome of school conditions, teacher qualities and practices, and classroom conditions, which were facilitated by

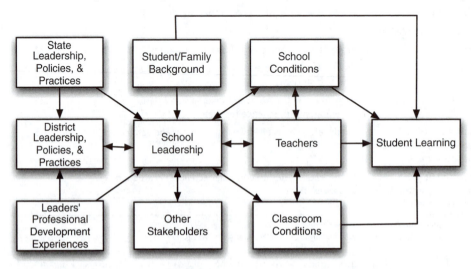

Figure 17.1 School leadership and contributing factors on student learning. Copied with permission from Louis, Leithwood, Wahlstrom, & Anderson (2010).

school leadership. Based on their review of the literature, these researchers concluded that school leadership was most directly affected by students, family, stakeholder, state and district leadership, and professional development experiences. In turn, school leaders affect student outcomes through reciprocal relationships with school and classroom conditions and teachers.

Louis and colleagues' (2010) conclusions from this large scale survey study confirmed and extended previous research on the relationship between school leadership and student learning that "leadership matters at all levels" (p. 283). Although their influence is manifested by how they relate to and guide school and classroom conditions and teacher practices, school leaders are essential and necessary to enhance student learning. More specifically, Louis and colleagues concluded the following:

1. "Principal—teacher relationships, district leaders' interactions with principals, and policy decisions at the state level all are intertwined in a complex and changing environment" (p. 282).
2. Schools that are characterized as having "shared leadership" between principals and teachers are also described as having strong working relationships and high student achievement. Shared leadership is achieved, in part, by specific tasks that are linked to clear goals and outcomes. Effective leaders also tend to retain and enhance their influence if shared leadership is associated with improved teacher and leadership efficacy.
3. The closer and more formal the interaction between principals and the classroom, the more collaborative the relationship the principal with teachers and district personnel.
4. Effective schools tend to have active professional communities that are supported by district leadership and facilitated by school leaders.
5. "Higher-performing schools generally ask for more input and engagement from a wider variety of stakeholders and provide more opportunities for influence by teacher teams, parents, and students" (p. 282).
6. High performing schools tend to have school leaders who set outcome goals and expectations that are higher than district minimums, and who promote the use of "multiple measures of student success" (p. 283).
7. District and school leaders look to state agencies as partners for general guidance regarding educational reform initiatives and policy. However, they also view translating these initiatives and policies into effective practice as what they do best as shared responsibilities with teachers.

Implementation Science.   From an organizational perspective, Fixsen, Naoom, Blase, Friedman, and Wallace (2005), at the National Implementation Research Network (www. nirn.org) and the State Implementation and Scale-up of Effective Practices Center (www. scalingup.org) provide useful information about how effective implementation science relates to effective school leadership. In brief, they emphasize that maximizing academic achievement and behavioral health outcomes of students are related to a school, district, and state department's established capacity to "carry out effective implementation, organizational change, and systems transformation strategies" (Fixsen & Blase, 2011). The implication is that school leadership must actively and systematically invest in establishing the capacities and structures that would enable sustained and scalable implementation of effective educational practices; thus, maximizing academic and social outcomes for students.

For the purposes of this chapter, the scaling up work by Fixsen and Blase (2011) provide four important leadership considerations. First, effective school leadership is grounded in the understanding that implementation of any educational practice is a multi-phase or -state process, and not achievable through a simple professional training event that occurs at the beginning of the school year, or on episodic inservice days. Instead, effective and durable adoption and use of an evidence-based practice occurs in phases (Fixsen et al., 2005):

Phase 1: Exploration and Adoption. Emphasis on adopting an innovation or practice that is based on a careful assessment of need, possible solution, resources, and commitment to proceed.

Phase 2: Installation. Emphasis on securing and organizing funding streams, personnel, political and policy supports, operating procedures, space and supply requirements, etc., that would support the early adopters and initial implementers.

Phase 3: Initial Implementation. Emphasis on change and adaptation that is required and associated with the initial implementation trial of a given practice or innovation.

Phase 4: Full Operation. Emphasis on directing resources and supports that enable full operation of an innovation or practice within an implementation setting or community.

Phase 5: Innovation. Emphasis on implementation with fidelity or accuracy, adaptations to local context, and evaluation of benefits to consumers.

Phase 6: Sustainability. Emphasis on establishing operation characteristics that occasion long-term implementation, continued effectiveness, and enhanced efficiency in the context of changing priorities, policy, and staffing.

Second, effective leadership is associated with a firm grounding in factors or drivers that facilitate movement through the implementation phases. Sugai, Horner, Fixsen, and Blase (2010) delineated nine such drivers: (a) policy (governance), (b) administrative (organizational), (c) coordination (procedural routines), (d) training (professional development), (e) coaching (facilitation), (f) evaluation (data-based decision making), (g) visibility (dissemination), (h) political support (administrative oversight), and (i) funding (fiscal support).

Third, effective leadership is linked to a systematic implementation process in which continuous regeneration is operationalized in a "Plan-Do-Study-Act" cycle (Fixsen et al., 2006; McIntosh, Horner, & Sugai, 2009; Sugai et al., 2010). Successful organizations have a formal and anticipatory implementation plan, implement in an intentional and overt manner, study the fidelity and outcomes of that implementation, and act based on those data to ensure increased efficiency, effectiveness, durability, and relevance.

Finally, given an implementation process (stages) and practices (drivers), effective leadership must involve informed decision making in which (a) policy enables practice implementation and (b) practice informs policy. Fixsen and colleagues (2005) emphasize that this process must be continuous (e.g., at least monthly) and formal (i.e., linked to regularly scheduled meetings and institutionalized by policy) so that relevance, effectiveness, accountability, and sustainability are maximized.

Effective Businesses.   Business and education have a number of common features that could guide school leaders to improve their effectiveness and productivity. Although the desired outcomes of schools may not be as tangible as the products and services of businesses and may be mandated rather than consumer-driven, they share common working considerations as exemplified in Table 17.2.

Given these similarities, additional guidance about effective school leadership might be gleaned from the business community. In 2009, for example, Buckingham and Coffman published a summary of two major research studies that were conducted by the Gallup Organization. In the first study, the focus was on answering the question "What do the most talented employees need from their workplace?" (p. 11). Based on their findings from the first question, the main question for the second study was "How do the world's greatest managers find, focus, and keep talented employees?" (p. 12). To answer these two questions, the Gallup Organization

Table 17.2 Comparison of Business and Education Features

Business	Education
• Equipment and materials	• Curriculum and supplies
• Workforce employees	• Teachers and assistants
• Supervisors and managers	• Principals and department chairs
• Cooperative executive officer	• Superintendent
• Board of directors	• Board of education
• Divisions and departments	• Grade levels and academic departments
• Research and development	• Professional development
• Consumers and customers	• Families, students, and communities

interviewed one million employees and 80,000 managers representing 400 successful companies. Although a variety of statistical tests were used, meta-analytic techniques were applied to summarize information collected across different performance measures used by different companies and examine commonalities between employee survey results and business performance measures. Four business outcomes were emphasized: "productivity, profit, retention, and customer service" (p. 31), which in schools are related to achievement, graduation, community and parental satisfaction.

As reported by Buckingham and Coffman (2009), the major finding from the first Gallup study was "Talented employees need great managers" (p. 11), and as a result, the second study attempted to identify the characteristics of "great managers." Overall, the Gallup Organization concluded that (a) the strength of the workplace is linked to the talent of its employees, (b) talented employees were most directly affected by their immediate managers or supervisors, and (c) effective managers acted in ways that facilitated effective performance from their employees.

> It's not that these employee-focused initiatives are unimportant. It's just that your immediate manager is more important. She defines and pervades your immediate work environment. If she sets clear expectations, knows you, trusts you, and invests in you, then you can forgive the company its lack of a profit-sharing program. But if your relationship with your manager is fractured, then no amount of in-chair massaging or company-sponsored dog walking will persuade you to stay and perform. It is better to work for a great manager in an old-fashioned company than for a terrible manager in a company offering an enlightened, employee-focused culture.
>
> *(p. 34)*

The major finding from the second Gallup research effort was that attracting and retaining the most talented employees was related to effective managers who acted in ways related to 12 core questions or elements:

1. Do I know what is expected of me at work?
2. Do I have the materials and equipment I need to do my work right?
3. At work do I have the opportunity to do what I do best every day?
4. In the last seven days, have I received recognition or praise for doing good work?
5. Does my supervisor, or someone at work, seem to care about me as a person?
6. Is there someone at work who encourages my development?
7. At work, do my opinions seem to count?
8. Does the mission/purpose of my company make me feel my job is important?
9. Are my co-workers committed to doing quality work?

10. Do I have a best friend at work?
11. In the last six months, has someone at work talked to me about my progress?
12. This last year, have I had opportunities at work to learn and grow? (p. 28)

Given the strength of these 12 elements, Buckingham and Coffman (2009) concluded:
To warrant positive answers to these questions from employees, managers must do four things well:

- When selecting someone, they select for talent ... not simply experience, intelligence, or determination.
- When setting expectations, they define the right outcomes ... not the right steps.
- When motivating someone, they focus on strengths ... not on weaknesses.
- When developing someone, they help him find the right fit ... not simply the next rung on the ladder. (p. 67)

In summary, although the quantitative literature on school leadership is primarily limited to correlational findings, summaries of that literature in combination with recommendations from implementation science and effective businesses provides information about what effective school leaders at the school and district level should do to lead their school organization to maximize the performance of teachers and academic achievement and social behavior of students. Effective leaders engage in actions or behaviors and establish working conditions that:

1. Emphasize setting clear goals;
2. Develop strength qualities of teachers;
3. Organize the operation of the school for success;
4. Consider the implementation phases, drivers, and processes associated with the utilization of an effective teaching practice;
5. Promote the strengths, talents, and capacities of their workers to achieve specific expectations and outcomes.
6. Monitor and measure the effects of their actions, decisions, and policies with relevant data.

Leadership and School-Wide Positive Behavior Support

Because successful academic achievement is such a prominent school priority, teachers, parents, and administrators emphasize the adoption and implementation of effective curricula and instructional techniques. In addition, these stakeholders know that positive, preventive, and safe classrooms and schools are important to maximize student engagement and to enable teachers to teach. Although effective classroom and school discipline practices have been promoted for many years, administrators generally have not formalized their adoption and sustained implementation, especially school-wide.

School-wide positive behavior support (SWPBS) (also referenced as positive behavioral interventions and supports or PBIS) is a framework or approach for enhancing the adoption and implementation of the organizational infrastructure that enables durable and accurate implementation of effective behavior and classroom management practices. In this section, we describe the defining features of SWPBS approach in the context of the important role of school leaders in its implementation.

SWPBS is defined as a behaviorally-based framework for enhancing the adoption and implementation of a continuum of evidence-based interventions to achieve academically and behaviorally important outcomes for all students (OSEP Center on Positive Behavioral Interventions and Supports, www.pbis.org, June 2010). As such, a number of important features characterize the SWPBS approach.

First, SWPBS is based on a prevention perspective in which desired social behavior expectations and routines are taught directly and formally, actively supervised, and positively reinforced. Students increase their use of more socially acceptable behaviors and skills because they are taught and encouraged, and students avoid acquiring and using inappropriate behaviors because more acceptable behaviors are more effective and relevant. Students who have more challenging problem behavior habits decrease their use of these behaviors because the peer and adult social cultures are no longer supportive of such behaviors (Walker et al., 1996).

Second, SWPBS practices are evidence-based and organized along a continuum of increasing intensity and specificity based on the unresponsiveness of student behavior to less specialized interventions. Evidence-based refers to the availability of empirical research that confirms and replicates the effectiveness of a behavioral intervention, that is, provides support or evidence for a causal or replicable relationship between a practice and a change in behavior. The SWPBS goal is to identify the smallest number of effective practices that can have the most socially and educational important outcome and effect. Evidence-based practices are organized into five main social behavior domains: (a) school-wide, which addresses all students, staff and families across all school settings; (b) classroom-wide, which considers those contexts in which teaching and learning are the priorities (academic success and engagement facilitate behavior success); (c) nonclassroom, which emphasizes settings in which academic instruction is not provided (e.g., cafeteria, hallways, buses, playgrounds, sporting events, assemblies and dances); (d) individual student, which supports students who do not benefit or respond to the general or basic teaching and social behavior practices; and (e) family, which considers how family and community can be actively engaged in the school culture and support their children's success at school. Horner, Sugai, and Anderson (2010) have summarized the evidence base for the practices of SWPBS.

Third, to improve the efficiency with which these interventions are selected and used, they are arranged in a continuum such that decision rules can be used to evaluate a student's behavior responsiveness to a given practice and to change that intervention. This continuum and its operation is also known as "response to intervention" (RTI; Bradley, Danielson, & Doolittle, 2007: Kame'enui, 2007). Like the general RTI framework, SWPBS emphasizes (a) data-based decision making and problem solving, (b) implementation fidelity, (c) continuum of evidence-based practices, (d) universal and regular screening for student responsiveness, (e) continuous progress monitoring, (f) prevention and early intervention, and (g) content expertise and fluency (Sugai et al., 2010).

Fourth, a systems approach or implementation process is emphasized in SWPBS. Although it would be relatively easy to focus on the features of effective practices, the SWPBS approach directs greater emphasis on the accuracy and process by which a practice is selected, initially implemented, sustained over time, scaled across new contexts, and regenerated or adapted to changing conditions. As such, SWPBS training is focused on school and district leadership teams who coordinate the implementation and establishes their capacities to implement the practice. The main outcome is school and district leadership "capacity" or the capability and competence to own the implementation of a practice, which requires more than just training. The OSEP Center on Positive Behavioral Interventions and Supports (PBIS) (2010) developed an "implementation blueprint" that emphasizes the establishment of a leadership or coordination team with four capacity building areas (training, coaching, evaluation, content expertise) and four operational priorities (funding, political support, visibility or marketing, policy).

Fifth, data-based decision making serves as the thread that holds together evidence-based practices, important learner outcomes, and implementation systems (Newton, Horner, Algozzine, Todd, & Algozzine, 2009). In SWPBS, data are used to (a) define a need or goal, (b) select an evidence-based practice that promises to achieve that need or goal, (c) measure the effectiveness and impact of the practice in meeting the need or goal, and (d) inform the systems that support the implementers' use of the practice.

Finally, SWPBS emphasizes the school leadership team as the primary implementation and coordination structure for transferring training content into a building-specific action plan. With membership from grade level, departments, special supports, classified staff, families, administration, etc., this team would develop and present a proposed implementation plan to the whole school staff. We would expect the training content and implementation plan to be more widely accepted if presented by school representatives who know the school culture. School leaders are particularly necessary members of this team because they are responsible for transferring policy into practice, and ensuring that practice represents policy.

In summary, when examined as a whole, SWPBS is a framework for organizing evidence-based practices into an integrated and logical continuum such that all students have maximum opportunity to experience academic and behavioral success. When the behaviors of some students are not responsive, then more specialized interventions are implemented. Establishing such a system requires (a) data processes that are sensitive to change, easy to use and measure important student outcomes, (b) the careful selection and accurate use of the best interventions, and (c) implementation teams that are responsive to the unique culture of each classroom and school. In addition, the practices and systems of SWPBS require school leaders that are active participants, models, and managers of the school as a whole.

Conceptual Model and Logic for School Leadership and SWPBS Implementation

Given the literature base for school leadership and the comprehensive nature of the practices and systems of SWPBS, any effort to guide school leaders should be based on a defendable and logical conceptual foundation. This foundation must be theoretically sound, empirically supported, educationally relevant, parsimonious in its explanations, and transferable into practice implementation. Given that SWPBS is directly grounded in a behavior analytic tradition, a similar logic is extended to our consideration of school leadership. In this section we describe the essential features of applied behavior analysis in relation to SWPBS, and then extend this logic to school leadership and SWPBS.

Applied Behavior Analysis. SWPBS is firmly rooted in a behavioral tradition, specifically, applied behavior analysis. Behaviorism is a theoretical position that emphasizes the importance of observable behavior and the relationship between behavior and the environmental conditions in which that behavior is observed. The influence of antecedent and especially consequence events or actions is important in describing, explaining, and affecting whether a behavior occurs. Early contributors to behaviorism include Ivan Pavlov, Edward Thorndike, John Watson, and B. F. Skinner, whose research contributed to a number of defining features or assumptions: (a) behavior is learned, (b) behavior is lawful, (c) behavior is manipulable, and (d) behavior is affected by environmental factors.

Behaviorism is a theoretical perspective with strong support from experimental research. In the 1950s and 1960s, the application of behavioral principles to describing and explaining human behavior resulted in an emphasis on the systemic study and improvement of socially important behavior. Researchers engaged in the experimental analysis of the variables that were associated with the occurrence of behavior and manipulated those variables to test and confirm functional relationships. In 1968, Donald Baer, Montrose Wolf, and Todd Risley wrote a seminal paper in the *Journal of Applied Behavior Analysis* that described the defining dimensions of applied behavior analysis: applied, behavioral, analytic, technological, conceptually systematic, effective, and generalizable.

Applied behavior analysis has a strong evidentiary base for understanding and improving the behavior of individuals, especially individuals with disabilities (Alberto & Troutman, 2009; Cooper, Heron, & Heward, 2007; Wolery, Bailey, & Sugai, 1988), and applications to the behavior of a wide range of individuals and situations have been documented. In the 1970s, increasing interest about more preventive and less aversive procedures resulted in the extension of applied behavior analysis into a perspective known as "positive behavior support." Antecedent-based interventions, quality of life indicators, and person-centered planning, for example, were emphasized (Carr et al., 2002; Sugai & Horner, 2002). Again, individuals with disabilities and their families were the main beneficiaries.

In the 1980s and 1990s, the need to improve the social behavior environments of classrooms and schools led to the extension of positive behavior support and applied behavior analysis principles and strategies to schools. The result was the establishment of the National Technical Assistance Center on Positive Behavioral Interventions and Supports (www.pbis.org) to disseminate to schools the most effective practices and systems for improving student social behavior. Because of the extended focus from individual students to classrooms and the whole school, the approach (as described above) became known as "school-wide positive behavior supports" (SWPBS) (Sugai et al., 2000; Sugai & Horner, 2002).

In this chapter, we further extend the behavioral and behavior analytic perspectives to describe what school leaders can do to improve the fidelity of implementation of SWPBS and to improve student outcomes and benefits. The conceptual logic (Figure 17.2) for this extension is represented by four guiding principles: (a) focus on principal and staff actions, (b) examine prior implementation learning history for patterns of variables that precede and follow behavior that have led to success or failure, (c) determine functional relationships between behavior and contextual and environmental variables, and (d) account for phase of learning of staff who are asked to implement new practices, and (e) evaluate student outcomes.

We acknowledge that the actions of school leaders are occasioned and motivated by a number of person-specific factors, for example, preservice training, teaching and leadership history, years of experience, skill or practice fluency, district and supervisor support, and individualized reinforcers or motivators. However, given our behavior analytic perspective, and focus on what school leaders can do to support the accurate and sustained implementation of SWPBS practices and systems, we emphasize the observable actions of school leaders as guided and influenced by the context in which they occur and are required. We also focus on the conditions under which school staff members are expected to respond to what school leaders do, in part to guide the most effective and efficient adaptations that school leaders can make.

This behaviorally based conceptual logic for school leadership emphasizes five key elements (Figure 17.2). The first is the *set of actions, behaviors, or activities* in which school leaders engage. In general, they fall into nine categories or areas summarized in Table 17.3.

Second, school leaders must be able to examine, understand, and adapt to the *context in which staff members must adopt and implement SWPBS practices*. Specifically, the learning history of staff members must be considered when selecting and engaging in leadership actions and behaviors. Every staff member has learning experiences and histories that are reflective of their culture, social development, professional training, language systems, and prior teaching experiences. Behavioral expressions of this learning history are affected by the immediate teaching and school conditions and environment, that is, the physical environment, student behaviors, curriculum and materials, colleague behaviors, policy and behavior expectations, leader actions and behaviors, family and community expectations and interactions.

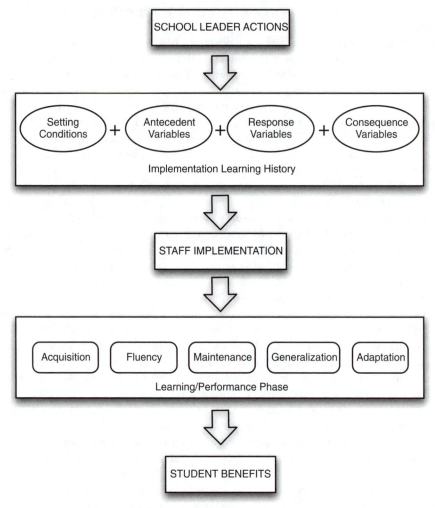

Figure 17.2 School leadership conceptual logic

Although school leaders may not have direct access to information about staff member learning histories and experiences, they can examine, arrange, and operate the teaching and learning conditions of classrooms and school. From our behavior analytic perspective, school leaders should consider their actions in the context of four main variables (Table 17.4): (a) setting, (b) antecedent, (c) response, and (d) consequence. School leaders can make better decisions and plans for their own actions and activities if they examine and understand the (a) setting and antecedent variables that might support and/or inhibit staff implementation, (b) history of existing (or missing) appropriate and inappropriate staff behaviors and practices, and (c) consequence variables that maintain or inhibit staff behaviors.

Third, staff responsiveness to school leadership supports and actions is functionally an examination of *implementation fidelity* or the degree to which implementation is accurate, fluent, durable, and associated with desired and maximum student outcomes (Hagermoser Sanetti, & Kratochwill, 2009). Thus, at minimum, school leaders should examine the relevance and effectiveness of their actions and behaviors against staff member implementation fidelity by addressing, for example, the following questions:

Table 17.3   School Leadership Actions in SWPBS

Area	SWPBS Example Actions
Policies and Procedures	• Write school policies that support practice • Model policy use
Curriculum, Initiatives, & Programs	• Identify & support selection of evidence based practices • Prevent selection & use of ineffective, inappropriate practices • Provide supports for high implementation fidelity
School Environment	• Actively supervise all school settings • Prepare, encourage, & support staff use of active supervision • Support selection & teaching of expected behaviors in each school setting
School Routines	• Establish, teach, monitor, & support typical school routines for students & staff • Actively participate in & supervise school routines
Management & Coordination	• Establish leadership team to advise school governance & operations • Develop organizational structure to coordinate school governance (e.g., teams/committees, meeting schedule) • Establish & lead staff meeting schedule • Work with leadership team to establish 3-5 year action plan for implementation of two to three initiatives/programs • Establish coaching or facilitation capacity to prompt & ensure implementation fidelity • Establish & utilize data system for monitoring implementation fidelity & student responsiveness • Establish professional development plan that is embedded within existing implementation & organizational routines & structures
Student Behavior	• Implement school-wide continuum of behavior support for encouraging expected behavior & preventing/reducing occurrences of rule-violating behavior • Actively supervise in all non-classroom settings on daily basis • Provide direct positive reinforcement to individual students, small groups of students, & whole school for demonstrations of expected behavior (e.g., daily, weekly, monthly, quarterly, etc.)
Staff Behavior	• Provide on-going and embedded professional development opportunities for SWPBS practices & systems • Provide regular prompts and/or precorrections for expected staff behavior • Actively supervise staff implementation of SWPBS practices • Regularly acknowledge staff individually, small group, or whole school for accurate & effective use of SWPBS practices • Report school-wide behavior data summaries to staff on at least monthly basis • Provide daily support for development & implementation of specialized behavior support for students with most unresponsive behaviors
District Leadership	• Report description & progress of 3-5 year action plan at least twice a year • Communicate at least monthly on implementation priorities, practice priorities, & data summaries • Communicate successes & accomplishments of staff & students at least monthly • Provide positive reinforcement at least monthly for district level support
Family and Community	• Report description & progress of 3-5 year action plan at least twice a year to stake holder groups • Include representatives in school-wide action planning & on school-wide leadership team • Include family emphasis in on-going SWPBS implementation practices & activities • Acknowledge family/ community at least monthly for support & participation in SWPBS implementation

Table 17.4 Implementation Variables that Leaders Should Consider in SWPBS

Implementation Variable	Description	Examples
Setting	Where staff members will be engaging in teaching & management actions & activities	• Classroom locations & access • Curriculum, supplies, materials, etc. • Classroom arrangements w/r to traffic patterns, furniture, etc. • Staff meeting • Professional development event • Other meeting, activity, etc.
Antecedent	What immediately precedes staff members' teaching & management actions & activities	• Student academic engagement & responding • Student appropriate & inappropriate behavior • Planned & unplanned activities • Adult interaction
Response	What staff have done & are expected to do	• Instructional practices • Classroom & behavior management practices • Other student &/or staff interactions
Consequence	What immediately follows staff members teaching & management actions & activities	• Same as antecedent variables above

1. Are staff members implementing the practice accurately as indicated by developer?
2. Are staff members implementing the practice at rates and with levels of consistency as indicated by developer?
3. Are staff members sustaining implementation of the practice with accuracy and fluency with appropriate and naturally available levels of support?
4. Are staff members making appropriate adjustments in the implementation of the practice based on student responsiveness and context variables to maintain or enhance learning outcomes?
5. Do staff have the resources, materials, supports, etc. to implement the practice over time with fidelity?
6. Do staff members receive regular, constructive feedback on their implementation fidelity and student outcomes?

Fourth, related to staff implementation fidelity, school leaders must shape their actions and behaviors with information about the *phase of staff learning* of a specific practice. Knowing the staff member's phase of learning gives school leaders the ability to determine what variable manipulation should be emphasized, that is, setting, antecedent, response, and/or consequence variables. School leaders should consider the five basic phases of learning in Table 17.5 (Sugai & Tindal, 1993; White & Haring, 1980; Wolery et al., 1988).

Ultimately, the impact of school leader actions is judged by the extent to which *students benefit* (academic achievement and social behavior competence) from the implementation actions of the staff. Effective school leaders evaluate their actions based on staff implementation fidelity, accomplishments and growth, indicated by academic achievement, social competence (peers and adults), rule following, etc. Thus, school leaders must invest in data systems that (a) give priority to data indicators that answer important learner questions, (b) enable efficient and doable data input and storage, (c) give automated visual summaries of data for direct and easy interpretation, and (d) enable data-based adjustments in practice implementation and supports.

Table 17.5 Five Phases of Learning

Phase	Description	Variable Emphasis
Acquisition	Accurate practice implementation	Setting, antecedent, response, & consequence
Fluency	Accurate & consistent practice implementation at appropriate rate or speed	Response & consequence
Maintenance	Accurate & fluent practice implementation over time & with reduced/removed training support	Consequence
Generalization	Accurate, fluent, & durable practice implementation across different & appropriate settings or contexts	Setting, antecedent & consequence
Adaptation	Adaptations of practice implementation to accommodate unique setting or context characteristics (e.g., language, culture, learning history)	Setting, antecedent, response, & consequence

Conclusion

Our purpose for this chapter was to provide school leaders with strategies to support the accurate and sustained implementation of school-wide frameworks, like SWPBS. To achieve this purpose, we described (a) a sample of the literature on effective school leadership, (b) an overview of the elements that define the practices and systems of SWPBS, (c) a conceptual model and logic for the role of school leadership in SWPBS, and (d) a set of guidelines for promoting and assessing effective leadership skills.

To reiterate, we acknowledge that the experimental research limits what we can recommend from an empirically-supported perspective; however, when the descriptive literature is combined with the suggestions from the implementation science and organizational-business world, some statements can be made about what school leaders might do to improve their effectiveness in maximizing student benefit. In fact, emerging research has documented value-added benefits from teachers' perspectives on the efficacy of principals' impact on social behavior and their overall satisfaction with principals and their jobs within SWPBS schools versus those not engaged in SWPBS (Richter et al., in press). To translate what we learned into a practical set of guidelines and strategies, we found it useful to link school leadership to the behavioral and behavior analytic foundations that define SWPBS.

We conclude this chapter with the following "big ideas" for school leaders and the implementation of evidence-based practices and systems, like SWPBS:

1. School leaders should consider that effective schools are like effective businesses in that they are characterized as having talented teachers (workers), who, in turn, are associated with talented Principals (immediate supervisors and managers).
2. School leaders are skilled instructional leaders who understand that student academic achievement is linked to (a) effective academic instruction, (b) high levels of academic engagement, and (c) safe and respectful classroom and school social cultures.
3. When making leadership decisions, school leaders should always consider whether and how students will benefit educationally.
4. School leaders affect student benefit through their ability and capacity to directly manage, lead, influence, and promote (a) high fidelity practice implementation by teachers, and (b) school and classroom conditions that support effective teaching and learning environments.

5. School leaders must carefully evaluate, translate, and prioritize the influence of (a) state and district policy and mandate, (b) their own professional preparation and development (learning history), (c) neighborhood and family characteristics, and (d) community stakeholders.
6. School leaders should establish a team-based, collaborative implementation approach that gives faculty members capacity for implementation success and authority, and maintains their roles, influence, and functioning as administrative leader.
7. School leaders consider schools as a whole from a "response-to-intervention" perspective: (a) universal screening, (b) continuous progress monitoring, (c) multi-tiered continuum of evidence based practices, (d) supports for high fidelity of implementation, (e) prevention and early intervention, (f) universal screening, and (g) team-based implementation coordination and leadership.
8. School leaders anticipate implementation and leadership challenges by (a) using student performance as an indicator of implementation fidelity or practice effectiveness, (b) intervening early to avoid having to implement reactive corrections, (c) building on or shaping aspects of successful implementation and student performance, and (d) providing recognition for effective teaching practice and successful student benefit.
9. School leaders should consider adult learning and systems change from the perspective of phases of (a) learning (i.e., acquisition, fluency, maintenance, generalization, and adaptation) and (b) implementation (i.e., exploration, installation, initial implementation, full operation, innovation, and sustainability).

School leaders should work closely with district leaders, school staff, and community stakeholders to (a) ensure a clear match between school needs and district initiatives, mandates, and policies, and (b) develop a doable school-wide action plan that is based on the top three school improvement needs and measurable outcome goals.

Note

1. The Center for *Positive Behavioral Interventions* & Supports is supported by a grant from the Office of Special Education Programs, US Department of Education (H326S980003). Opinions expressed herein do not necessarily reflect the position of the US Department of Education, and such endorsements should not be inferred.

References

Alberto, P. A., & Troutman, A. C. (2001). *Applied behavior analysis for teachers* (8th ed.). Englewood Cliffs, NJ: Merrill/Prentice-Hall.

Baer, D. M., Wolf, M. M., & Risley, T. R. (1968). Some current dimensions of applied behavior analysis. *Journal of Applied Behavior Analysis, 1,* 91–97.

Biglan, A. (1995). Translating what we know about the context of antisocial behavior in to a lower prevalence of such behavior. *Journal of Applied Behavior Analysis, 28,* 479–449.

Bradley, R., Danielson, L., & Doolittle, J. (2007). Responsiveness to intervention: 1997–2007. *Teaching Exceptional Children, 39*(5), 8–12.

Bradshaw, C., Koth, C., Thornton, L., & Leaf, P. (2009). Altering school climate through school-wide positive behavioral interventions and supports: Findings from a group-randomized effectiveness trial. *Prevention Science, 10,* 100–115.

Bradshaw, C., Mitchell, M., & Leaf, P. (in press). Examining the effects of school-wide positive behavioral interventions and supports on student outcomes: Results from a randomized controlled effectiveness trial in elementary schools. *Journal of Positive Behavior Interventions.*

Buckingham, M., & Coffman, C. (2009). *First, break all the rules: What the world's greatest managers do differently.* New York: Simon & Schuster.

Carr, E. G., Dunlap, G., Horner, R. H., Koegel, R. L., Turnbull, A. P., & Sailor, W. (2002). Positive behavior support: Evolution of an applied science. *Journal of Positive Behavior Interventions, 4,* 4–16.

Center on Positive Behavioral Interventions and Supports. (2010, June 1). What is school-wide positive behavioral interventions and supports? Retrieved from http://pbis.org/school/what_is_swpbs.aspx

Colvin, G., Kame'enui, E. J., & Sugai, G. (1993). School-wide and classroom management: Reconceptualizing the integration and management of students with behavior problems in general education. *Education and Treatment of Children, 16,* 361–381.

Cooper, J. O., Heron, T. E., & Heward, W. L. (2007). *Applied behavior analysis.* Upper Saddle River, NJ: Pearson/ Merrill-Prentice Hall.

Cotton, K. (2003). *Principals and student achievement: What the research says.* Alexandria, VA: Association for Supervision and Curriculum Development.

Day, C. (2000). Effective leadership and reflective practice. *Reflective Practice, 1*(1), 113–127.

Dixon, R. C., Carnine, D. W., Lee, D., Wallin, J., & Chard, D. (1998). *Report to the California State Board of Education and addendum to principal report: Review of high quality experimental mathematics research.* Eugene, OR: National Center to Improve the Tools of Educators, University of Oregon, Eugene.

Donmoyer, R. (1985). Cognitive anthropology and research on effective principals. *Educational Administration Quarterly, 22,* 31–57.

Fixsen, D. L., & Blase, K. A. (2011, January 17). About SISEP: Mission. Retrieved from http://sisep.fpg.unc.edu/ about-sisep

Fixsen, D. L., Naoom, S. F., Blase, K. A., Friedman, R. M., & Wallace, F. (2005). *Implementation research: A synthesis of the literature.* Tampa: University of South Florida, Louis de la Parte Florida Mental Health Institute, The National Implementation Research Network (FMHI Publication #231).

Gersten, R., Chard, D. J., Jayanthi, M., Baker, S. K., Morphy, P., & Flojo, J. (2009). Mathematics instruction for students with learning disabilities: A meta-analysis of instructional components. *Review of Educational Research, 79*(3), 1202–1242.

Hagermoser Sanetti, L. M., & Kratochwill, T. R. (2009). Toward developing a science of treatment integrity: Introduction to the special series. *School Psychology Review, 38,* 445–459.

Hallinger, P. (2005). Instructional leadership and the school principal: A passing fancy that refuses to fade away. *Leadership and Policy in Schools, 4*(3), 221–239.

Hallinger, P., & Heck, R. H. (1998) Exploring the principal's contribution to school effectiveness: 1980–1995. *School Effectiveness and School Improvement, 9,* 157–191.

Horner, R. H., Sugai, G., & Anderson, C. M. (2010). Examining the evidence base for school-wide positive behavior support. *Focus on Exceptionality, 42*(8), 1–14.

Kame'enui, E. J. (2007). A new paradigm: Responsiveness to intervention. *Teaching Exceptional Children, 39*(5), 6–7.

Lashley, C., & Boscardin, M. L. (2003). *Special education administration at a crossroads: Availability, licensure, and preparation of special education administrators.* (COPSSE Document No. IB-8). Gainesville: University of Florida, Center on Personnel Studies in Special Education.

Leithwood, K., Louis, K. S., Anderson, S., & Wahlstrom, K. (2004). *How leadership influences student learning: A review of research for the Learning from Leadership Project.* New York: Wallace Foundation.

Leithwood, K., & Mascall, B. (2008). Collective leadership effects on student achievement. *Educational Administration Quarterly, 44*(4), 529–561.

Louis, K. S., Leithwood, K., Wahlstrom, K. L., & Anderson, S. E. (2010). *Investigating the links to improved student learning: Final report of research findings.* Learning from Leadership Project. University of Minnesota Press.

Marzano, R., Waters, T., & McNulty, B. (2005). *School leadership that works: From research to results.* Alexandria, VA: Association for Supervision and Curriculum Development.

Mayer, G. (1995). Preventing antisocial behavior in the schools. *Journal of Applied Behavior Analysis, 28,* 467–478.

McIntosh, K., Horner, R. H., & Sugai, G. (2009). Sustainability of systems-level evidence-based practices in schools: Current knowledge and future directions. In W. Sailor, G. Dunlap, R. Horner, & G. Sugai (Eds.), *Handbook of positive behavior support* (pp. 327–352). New York: Springer.

Newton, J. S., Horner, R., Algozzine, B., Todd, A. W., & Algozzine, K. M. (2009). Using a problem-solving model for data-based decision making in schools. In W. Sailor, G. Dunlap, G. Sugai, & R. Horner (Eds.), *Handbook of positive behavior support* (pp. 551–580). New York: Springer.

National Center for Education Statistics (2009a). *The nation's report card: Mathematics 2009* (NCES 2010–451). Washington, DC: Institute of Education Sciences, U.S. Department of Education.

National Center for Education Statistics. (2009b).*The nation's report card: Reading 2009* (NCES 2010–458). Washington, DC: Institute of Education Sciences, U.S. Department of Education.

National Institute of Child Health and Human Development (NICHD). (2000). *Report of the National Reading Panel. Teaching children to read: An evidence-based assessment of the scientific research literature on reading and its implications for reading instruction: Reports of the subgroups* (NIH Publication No. 00-4754). Washington, DC: U.S. Government Printing Office.

Richter, M. M., Lewis, T. J., & Hagar, J. (in press). The relationship between principal leadership skills and school-wide positive behavior support: An exploratory study. *Journal of Positive Behavior Interventions*.

Robinson, V. M. J., Lloyd, C. A., & Rowe, K. J. (2008). The impact of leadership on student outcomes: An analysis of the differential effects of leadership types, *Educational Administration Quarterly, 44*, 635–674.

Simonsen, B., Fairbanks, S., Briesch, A., Myers, D., & Sugai, G. (2008). Evidence-based practices in classroom management: Considerations for research to practice. *Education and Treatment of Children, 31*(3), 351–380.

Snyder, T. D., Tan, A. G., & Hoffman, C. M. (2006). *Digest of education statistics, 2005.* Washington, DC: National Center for Education Statistics.

Sugai, G., & Horner, R. H. (2002). The evolution of discipline practices: School-wide positive behavior supports. *Child and Family Behavior Therapy, 24,* 23–50.

Sugai, G., Horner, R. H., Dunlap, G. Hieneman, M., Lewis, T. J., Nelson, C. M., et al. (2000). Applying positive behavioral support and functional behavioral assessment in schools. *Journal of Positive Behavioral Interventions, 2,* 131–143.

Sugai, G., & Horner, R. H., Fixsen, D., & Blase, K. (2010). Developing systems-level capacity for RtI implementation: Current efforts and future directions. In T. A. Glover & S. Vaughn (Eds.), *Response to intervention: Empowering all students to learn – A critical account of the science and practice* (pp. 286–309). New York: Guildford.

Sugai, G. M., & Tindal, G. (1993). *Effective school consultation: An interactive approach.* Pacific Grove, CA: Brooks/Cole.

Wagner, M., Newman, L., Cameto, R., & Levine, P. (2005). *Changes over time in the early postschool outcomes of youth with disabilities. A report of findings from the National Longitudinal Transition Study (NLTS) and the National Longitudinal Transition Study-2 (NLTS2).* Menlo Park, CA: SRI International.

Walker, H. M., Horner, R. H., Sugai, G., Bullis, M., Sprague, J. R., Bricker, D., & Kaufman, M. J. (1996). Integrated approaches to preventing antisocial behavior patterns among school-age children and youth. *Journal of Emotional and Behavioral Disorders, 4,* 193–256.

Waters, T., & Marzano, R. J. (2006, September). *School district leadership that works: The effect of the superintendent leadership on student achievement.* Denver, CO: Mid-continent Research for Education and Learning.

White, O. R., & Haring, N. G., (1980). *Precision teaching* (2nd ed.). Columbus, OH: Charles E. Merrill.

Witziers, B., Bosker, R. J., & Kruger, M. L. (2003). Educational leadership and student achievement: The illusive search for an association. *Educational Administration Quarterly, 39*(3), 398–425.

Wolery, M. R., Bailey, D. B., Jr., & Sugai, G. M. (1988). *Effective teaching: Principles and procedures of applied behavior analysis with exceptional students.* Boston, MA: Allyn & Bacon.

Zigmond, N. (2006). Twenty-four months after high school: Paths taken by youth diagnosed with severe emotional and behavioral disorders. *Journal of Emotional and Behavioral Disorders, 14*(2), 99–107.

18

Responsive Instructional Leadership for Early Intervention[1]

Patricia A. Snyder and Crystal D. Crowe

UNIVERSITY OF FLORIDA

Robert Crow

DEVELOPMENTAL BEHAVIOR ANALYSIS, GAINESVILLE, FL

The primary focus of this chapter is to extend discussion of instructional leadership and the evaluation of educational outcomes to early intervention and early childhood special education. We situate this discussion in the context of responsive instructional leadership. By *responsive*, we mean actions taken relative to internal or external situations or changes so the circumstances of the intervention program are maintained or improved. Responsive *instructional leadership* focuses on actions taken to improve or maintain instructional quality, instructional effectiveness, and to evaluate whether desired outcomes in early intervention and early childhood special education are being achieved.

We define early intervention and early childhood special education as systems of supports and services provided to young children birth through age 5 years with or at risk for disabilities, their families, and the personnel who interact with them. Early intervention supports and services are provided to eligible infants and toddlers (ages birth to 3) with or at risk for disabilities and their families under provisions associated with Part C of the Individuals with Disabilities Education Improvement Act (IDEA, 2004). Early childhood special education involves the provision of a free appropriate public education and related services for eligible preschool children (ages 3 through 5) under the Part B Section 619 provisions of the IDEA. Both Part C and Section 619 of IDEA were initially codified in federal statute in 1986 with the passage of Public Law 99-457. Most historical accounts of services and supports for young children with or at risk for disabilities birth through age 5 years, however, identify the emergence of an early intervention "field" in the 1960s (Snyder, McLaughlin, & Denney, 2011). In the remainder of the chapter, we use the term "early intervention" to refer to both the Part C and Section 619 programs of IDEA.

From 1968 through 1997, service delivery patterns and practices in early intervention were influenced significantly by model demonstration, outreach, research, state implementation, inservice training, and technical assistance projects funded under the Handicapped Children's Early Education Program (HCEEP), which later became the Early Education Program for Children with Disabilities (EEPCD). Over the almost 30 years the HCEEP/EEPCD programs existed, a variety of institutions and agencies were responsible for their administration. In their review of HCEEP/EEPCD programs, Garland and Linder (1988) noted that early intervention programs, like many educational and human service programs, existed in various contexts and did not suffer from a lack of management, but might have suffered from a lack of leadership. These authors acknowledged the field was "challenged anew by the opportunity of the Education of the Handicapped Act Amendments of 1986 (P.L. 99-457)" and needed "administrators who are able to go beyond management and are willing to make a commitment to leadership" (p. 6).

Contextual Features Relevant to Leadership for Early Intervention

In the 25 years since the passage of P.L. 99-457, the organizational, policy, and leadership contexts in which supports and services are provided to young children with or at risk for disabilities, their families, and the personnel who interact with them have further evolved. Similar to questions raised about the *specialness* of leadership in special education in relation to leadership in general education (e.g., Boscardin, 2007), questions might be raised about the *specialness* of leadership for early intervention in relationship to leadership for special education, general education, and early childhood education and care. We assert that several features of early intervention might have relevance for the *specialness* of leadership for the field (Crow & Snyder, 1998).

First, IDEA Part C and Section 619 statutes and implementing regulations focus on the provision of services and supports in natural and least restrictive environments, respectively. In addition to preschool supports and services being provided to children with disabilities and their families in elementary schools or school-based early learning programs, a range of community-based infant, toddler, and preschool early childhood education and care settings and environments (e.g., family home, park, playground, library) are instructional and learning contexts for early intervention. Ensuring instructional quality and instructional effectiveness in these diverse learning environments has implications for how responsive leadership is defined and operationalized.

Second, the significant and sustained focus on family-centered principles and practices in the field promotes ongoing interactions among practitioners and family members in home- and community-based settings, and the active involvement of families in the design, delivery, and evaluation of "instruction" or supports/interventions provided to children or families (Shelton, Jeppson, & Johnson, 1987; Trivette & Dunst, 2005; Turnbull, Turnbull, Erwin, Soodak, & Shogren, 2010). One document that serves as the roadmap for the design, delivery, and evaluation of early intervention supports and services is known as the individualized family service plan (IFSP), which highlights the central role of the family. Definitions and actions associated with instructional leadership in early intervention must accommodate family-centered principles and practices. This includes instructional leadership practices that are responsive to the diversity of children and families involved in early intervention.

Third, while some early intervention supports and services are instructional in focus, others are family-directed. Family-directed services include the provision of information, referral to community resources, coordination of services, or guiding and supporting family members to acquire and master strategies to promote child development and learning during typically occurring family activities or routines. "Instructional" leadership is more broadly defined and often is situated within an ecobehavioral framework. "Instruction" is provided not only to a child, but to parents, other family members, and members of the family's formal and informal support systems (Vincent, Salisbury, Strain, McCormick, & Tessier, 1990). Dimensions of instructional quality and instructional effectiveness vary based on the characteristics of the learner, the content of instruction, and the contexts in which instruction occurs. Responsive instructional leaders should be capable of supporting the application of appropriate interventions and making data-based decisions to promote quality and effectiveness related to identified outcomes.

Fourth, the accountability provisions of IDEA specify the desired child and family outcomes by which instructional leadership in early intervention will ultimately be evaluated (Early Childhood Outcomes Center, 2004). Since 2000, efforts have been underway within and across states to specify and measure the progress of eligible infants, toddlers, and preschoolers toward three generalized outcomes: (a) positive social-emotional skills, (b) acquisition and use of knowledge, and (c) use of appropriate behavior to meet needs (Early Childhood Outcomes Center, 2005). For families whose infants and toddlers are eligible for Part C of IDEA, states must also gather and report data related to three family outcomes: (a) families know their rights, (b) families effectively communicate their children's needs, and (c) families help their children develop and learn. Responsive instructional leaders in early intervention must focus efforts to ensure young children with disabilities and their families are receiving individualized "instructional" supports of sufficient form and intensity to (a) attain individual outcomes or goals and (b) ensure progress toward the identified accountability outcomes under IDEA.

Finally, early intervention programs funded under IDEA are considered one program "sector" under a broader array of programs supporting young children and their families (Snyder, Denney, Pasia, Rakap, & Crowe, 2011). Among the other early childhood program sectors are Early Head Start, Head Start, pre-K programs, early education and care programs, maternal and child health, family support, and mental health. The statutory and regulatory language of Part C and Section 619 programs under IDEA emphasizes natural and least restrictive environments and a primary goal of the field is focused on achieving meaningful inclusion (DEC/NAEYC, 2009). Supports and services for young children with disabilities and their families are increasingly situated within, not apart from, these other program sectors. Responsive instructional leaders must carry out their leadership actions within the cross-sector contexts in which early intervention occurs.

Taken together, these features of early intervention underscore the need for leaders to be broadly informed about early learning, education, and care for all children and families, including young children with or at risk for disabilities and their families. Early intervention leaders should be prepared to ensure instructional efforts are interdisciplinary and interagency. They should be equipped with general and specialized knowledge, skills, and dispositions so they can appropriately support the application of recommended practices in early intervention (Sandall, Hemmeter, Smith, & McLean, 2005) and developmentally appropriate practices in early childhood education and care (Copple & Bredekamp, 2009). Leaders in early intervention should act to implement a culture that uses data to inform collaborative decision-making and change (Harbin & Salisbury, 2005). As the integration of early childhood sectors occurs in support of inclusive practices, responsive instructional leaders will be needed to ensure the diverse characteristics, abilities, and needs of *all* young learners are met and desired outcomes are attained (Harbin & Salisbury, 2005; Snyder, 2006).

Conceptualizations of Leadership Relevant for Early Intervention

Given the features of early intervention described above, we define responsive instructional leadership in early intervention as actions taken to support the development and learning of young children with or at risk for disabilities and their families within inclusive or natural early learning contexts. Responsive instructional leadership actions involve an emphasis on "instructional" quality and "instructional" effectiveness. We propose three priorities for focused actions by responsive instructional leaders in early intervention: (a) guide the consistent implementation of theoretical frameworks that organize empirically based promotion, prevention, and intervention strategies (Snyder et al., 2011); (b) support the implementation of evidence-based, individualized "instruction" that is informed by recommended practices in early intervention (Sandall et al., 2005) and developmentally appropriate practices for young children (National Association for the Education of Young Children, 2009); and (c) use data-based decision making to support and improve instructional quality and effectiveness, and to evaluate whether desired child and family outcomes are being achieved. We emphasize that "instruction" in early intervention includes both instruction provided directly to children and instruction and supports made available to families, practitioners, and leaders across early childhood sectors. Broadly viewed, instructional leaders might include principals, program administrators, curriculum specialists, instructional coaches, teachers, practitioners, and family members. We primarily focus discussion in this chapter, however, on responsive leadership actions most likely taken by program administrators and practitioners who provide early intervention services and supports to young children and their families.

Several leadership models have influenced scholarship regarding leadership in general education and special education, and have affected the development of standards for leadership in special education (Boscardin, 2009; Boscardin, Mainzer, & Kealy 2011; CEC, 2003, 2009). Significant among these models are instructional leadership (e.g., Hallinger, 2003, 2005), transformational leadership (Leithwood, 2005; Leithwood, Tomlinson, & Genge, 1996), and transactional leadership (Bycio & Allen, 1995; Howell & Avolio, 1993). Although we use the term "responsive" to frame discussion about leadership in this chapter (cf. Boscardin, 2007; Crockett, 2002), we briefly review features of two models of leadership recognized as primary influences in educational leadership: instructional and transformational (Leithwood, 2005). This review highlights categories of leadership actions emanating from these two models that might be useful for characterizing responsive instructional leadership in operational terms for early intervention.

Instructional Leadership

Instructional leadership emerged as a predominant conceptual model in the 1980s, resulting from research identifying linkages among "top-down" leadership focused on curriculum and instruction and effective teaching and student achievement in elementary schools (Hallinger, 2003). Traditional instructional leadership models have focused on the role of the principal (as leader) in ensuring implementation of curriculum and instruction in schools. These models have described relationships among school goals, the principal's actions, and student achievement (Bamburg & Andrews, 1990). One conceptualization by Hallinger (2003) proposed three dimensions of the instructional leadership construct: (a) defining the school mission, (b) managing the instructional program, and (c) promoting positive school-learning climate. As shown in Table 18.1, 10 functions were associated with these three dimensions. In 2005, Hallinger offered a reconceptualization of instructional leadership, noting the contemporary emphasis on accountability had "reignited" interest in instructional leadership. He proposed seven reconceptualized functions of instructional leadership based on a review of 25 years of instructional leadership literature. These statements of functions are shown in Table 18.1 along with the previous 10 functions identified in 2003.

Transformational Leadership

According to Hallinger (2003) and Leithwood (2005), transformational leadership models initially focused on organizational leadership and were adapted for use in educational contexts in the 1990s. Transformational leadership emphasizes "fostering capacity development and higher levels of personal commitment to organizational goals on the part of leaders' colleagues" (Leithwood, 2005, p. 10).

The model of transformational leadership proposed by Leithwood and colleagues includes three broad categories of practice [comparable to the three dimensions in Hallinger's instructional leadership model] and what Leithwood and his colleagues (Leithwood, 2005; Leithwood et al., 1996) refer to as nine practices or dimensions [comparable to functions specified by Hallinger].

Table 18.1   Domains and Categories of Action Associated with Instructional Leadership and Transformational Leadership

Instructional Leadership Dimensions	Instructional Leadership Functions	Transformational Leadership Categories	Transformational Leadership Dimensions or Practices
Defining Mission	• Framing goals • Communicating goals • Creating shared sense of purpose, including clear goals focused on student learning*	Setting Directions	• Building school vision • Developing specific goals and priorities • Holding high performance expectations
Managing Instructional Programs	• Supervising and evaluating instruction • Coordinating curriculum • Monitoring student progress • Fostering continuous improvement through cyclical planning involving wide range of stakeholders* • Coordinating curriculum and monitoring student learning outcomes*	Developing People	• Providing intellectual stimulation • Offering individualized support • Modeling desirable professional practices and values
Promoting Positive School-Learning Climate	• "Protecting" instructional time • Promoting professional development • Maintaining high visibility • Providing incentives for teachers/practitioners • Providing incentives for learning • Developing a climate of high expectations and a culture aimed at innovation and improvement of teaching and learning* • Shaping the reward structure to reflect mission* • Organizing and monitoring a wide range of activities aimed at continuous development of staff* • Being a visible presence, modeling desired values of culture*	Redesigning the Organization	• Developing a collaborative school culture • Creating structures to foster participation in school decisions • Creating productive community relationships

Note: * = Reconceptualization of instructional leadership functions as noted by Hallinger (2005). Adapted from "Instructional Leadership and the School Principal: A Passing Fancy that Refuses to Fade Away," by P. Hallinger, 2005, *Leadership and Policy in Schools, 4*(1), pp 5 and 13. Copyright 2005 by Taylor & Francis, Inc. Adapted from *Educational Leadership: A Review of the Research*, by K. Leithwood, p. 10. Copyright 2004 by The Laboratory for Student Success, Mid-Atlantic Regional Educational Laboratory at Temple University Center for Research in Human Development and Education.

The three broad categories are (a) setting directions, (b) developing people, and (c) redesigning the organization. Table 18.1 shows the three broad categories and the nine associated practices characterizing transformational leadership alongside the comparable illustration of the domains and functions of instructional leadership.

Table 18.1 illustrates similarities and differences between instructional and transformational leadership with regard to dimensions/categories and practices/functions. For example, both models involve framing or developing goals. Instructional leadership focuses on promoting professional development, while transformational leadership emphasizes providing intellectual stimulation and offering individualized support. Instructional leadership primarily has been characterized as a "top-down" model; transformational leadership emphasizes a bottom-up approach to school improvement. In addition to these similarities and differences, Hallinger (2003) has identified other conceptual distinctions between these two leadership models. Although the dimensions/categories and practices/functions associated with instructional and transformational leadership are generally reflected in the leadership literature in early childhood and early intervention, explicit connections to these models have been limited (Muijs, Aubrey, Harris, & Briggs, 2004). Perhaps one reason for the lack of explicit connection is that the dimensions and practices associated with these two leadership models lack specificity about responsive actions leaders could take in relation to instructional quality and effectiveness beyond K–12 education contexts. These models describe leadership dimensions and actions that occur primarily in schools, likely reducing their perceived relevance for application in early intervention settings.

Responsive Leadership

Not readily apparent in either instructional or transformational leadership models are actions of a responsive nature to address instructional quality, instructional effectiveness, and evaluation of whether desired outcomes are achieved. To identify these actions, we reviewed Boscardin's (2007) conceptualization of "responsive leadership intervention." This conceptualization focuses on leadership actions that involve use of evidence-based leadership practices to design, implement, and evaluate leadership interventions designed to increase achievement for each student and for all students.

Boscardin (2007) identified relationships between responsive leadership interventions and the instructional framework of response-to-intervention (RTI). She noted that both responsive leadership interventions and the implementation of RTI should involve problem-solving actions. Among the problem-solving actions that could be associated with responsive leadership interventions would be gathering data, analyzing data, developing and implementing plans of action consistent with empirically supported practices, and evaluating outcomes and impacts. From a leadership perspective, this responsive leadership model is proposed to improve alignment between instructional frameworks and practices (i.e., RTI) with strategies used by administrative leadership for decision-making. This model of leadership would use evidence-based leadership practices to support the use of empirically supported instructional practices in classrooms. Frameworks similar to RTI and RTI frameworks appropriate for application in early childhood have been described in the literature (Snyder, McLaughlin, & Denney, 2011), suggesting the potential for using responsive leadership models and associated actions in early intervention.

Conceptualizing instructional leadership as *responsive* suggests individuals in decision-making roles would constructively *respond to* the presence of instruction-related opportunities and challenges occurring in a particular intervention context so instructional quality and effectiveness are enhanced. In a responsive model, leaders would focus efforts on accomplishing leadership processes (e.g., data-based decision making, problem solving, identifying needed implementation supports) and "incidental" leadership actions (e.g., modeling, coaching, and feedback) to support of the use of intervention practices. These responsive leadership practices would be validated and related to formative and summative data and used to inform ongoing "responsive" leadership actions. Boscardin (2007) noted the potential of responsive leadership actions when she stated, "Imagine administrative teams who are equipped to facilitate rapid, high quality, research-based leadership responses to guide and support all staff, with students becoming the beneficiaries of their administrative efforts" (p. 192).

The responsive leadership practices defined by Boscardin (2007) are characterized as "approaches that *promise* [emphasis added] better outcomes for students under certain cultural and ecological conditions" (p. 190). Similar to the dimensions/categories and practices/functions described in relation to instructional and transformational leadership, Boscardin offers general classes of behavior or actions that will likely need to be specified in functional terms for application in specific leadership contexts. For example, identifying responsive actions related to "use continuous progress monitoring of system-wide performance as a basis for decision-making about classroom and leadership practices" would need to be further specified and operationalized for specific practice contexts and for early intervention.

Review of Literature to Identify Responsive Instructional Leadership Actions

We conducted a review of literature to inform the identification of key features of a responsive instructional leadership framework for early intervention. The purpose of this review was (a) to expand functional understandings about instructional, transformational, and responsive leadership with reference to early intervention and early childhood education and care and (b) to compile reported leadership actions that might be useful for specifying categories of actions related to responsive instructional leadership in early intervention.

We examined the literature to identify categories of responsive instructional leadership actions that would apply to the direct intervention level and for leadership actions that reside between the direct and administrative levels. One procedure that has been used to identify sequences of performance in education and might be useful in specifying responsive actions that link direct intervention to administration is "backward mapping" (WestEd, 2002). Backward mapping involves identifying actions that occur in a proximal context (e.g., instructional practices of a teacher in a preschool classroom) and identifying factors that maintain or constrain these actions both in the proximal context as well as in distal contexts. Backward-mapping procedures might be useful as a process to explicate leadership actions ranging from the intervention level, through supportive levels, to administrative levels. To inform backward-mapping processes and to accumulate statements of leadership actions potentially useful for responsive instructional leaders, we reviewed literature related to early childhood/early intervention leadership practices and examined the 2009 CEC Standards for Administrators of Special Education for statements related to "responsiveness" in leadership and instructional leadership. From this review, we identified categories of action for responsive leadership with reference to early intervention to generate exemplars of how these categories might be useful to inform conceptual and operational definitions of responsive instructional leadership in early intervention.

Literature Review Processes

As a first stage, we conducted an electronic search of books and articles using a library catalog, databases in EBSCO Host, and three databases in Wilson Web (i.e., Education Full Text, Education Index Retro, and ERIC). Combinations of the following search terms were used: lead*, instruction, educational, teacher, administration, management, quality, organizational change, presc*, early childhood, special education, early intervention, and early education. The initial electronic search returned 30 books and 39 articles related specifically to early childhood or early intervention. After the initial search, we screened these articles and books for relevance to leadership in either early childhood or early intervention. Sources were retained if they discussed aspects of leadership for programs serving children birth through 5 years of age. Articles were retained only if published in peer-reviewed journals. After screening, we retained 22 books and 28 articles from the initial electronic search.

The second stage of the literature review involved a search of the reference lists of the articles and books retained from the original electronic search. As a result of this process, one additional book and five articles were included in the review for a total of 23 books and 33 articles. All articles and books were reviewed to determine if they were theoretical, research-based, or practice-based. In addition, we determined whether each publication included information on leadership, in general, or instructional leadership, specifically, and whether it addressed leadership within the context of early childhood general education and care (ECE) or early intervention.

Findings from the Literature Review

One book (Linder, 1983) and five articles (Fleming & Love, 2003; Lay-Dopyera & Dopyera, 1985; Marvin, LaCost, Grady, & Mooney, 2003; Swan, 1985; Wimpleberg, Abroms, Catardi, 1985) focused on early intervention. One of these articles was empirical, but focused on administrative actions rather than leadership (i.e., Marvin et al., 2003). The remaining 22 books and 28 articles focused on leadership in general early childhood education and care. Of these, 16 articles were empirical (i.e., Bloom, 1997; Bloom & Sheerer, 1992a,b; Catron & Groves, 1999; Couse & Russo, 2006; Curtis & Burton, 2009; Dana & Yendol-Hoppey, 2005; Hayden, 1997; Ho, 2005; Hujala, 2004; Larkin, 1999; Lunn & Bishop, 2002; Rodd, 1996, 1997; Ryan & Hornbeck, 2004; Woodrow & Busch, 2008). One article was a review of existing literature related to leadership in early childhood (i.e., Muijs, Aubrey, Harris, & Briggs, 2004), and one book contained a chapter based on empirical research (i.e., Waugh, Boyd, & Corrie, 2003). The empirical articles were largely descriptive or qualitative in nature, with only two articles describing quasi-experimental studies examining the effectiveness of leadership training in early childhood (Bloom & Sheerer, 1992a,b).

The majority of books focused broadly on managerial or administrative aspects of leadership in early childhood. From the 23 books and 33 articles, we selected 17 articles because they highlighted leadership actions similar to the dimensions/categories and functions/practices associated with instructional and transformational leadership models shown in Table 18.1 (i.e., Bloom & Sheerer, 1992a,b; Catron & Groves, 1999; Colmer, 2008; Freeman & Brown, 2000; Ho, 2005, 2010; Hujala, 2004; Kagan, 1994; Larkin, 1999; Lay-Dopyera & Dopyera, 1985; Lee, 2008; Lunn & Bishop, 2002; Rodd, 1996, 1997; Swan, 1985; Taba et al., 1999). Eight of the identified articles were research-based, five were theoretical, and the remaining four were practice-based descriptions or summaries or characterizations of leadership based on experiences. We labeled the leadership dimensions/categories or functions/practices described in these articles as "categories of action." These studies and associated categories of action are shown in Table 18.2.

For each article shown in Table 18.2, we list the prominent categories of actions noted in the article sorted under headings of the leadership model(s) with which we judged them to be most aligned. A total of 78 categories of leadership actions were sorted under three headings: categories of actions for instructional leadership ($n = 31$); categories of actions for transformational leadership ($n = 34$); and categories of actions for *both* transformational and instructional leadership ($n = 13$). Nine of the 17 articles specified leadership actions we judged to be associated with the two models.

Table 18.2 Statements Reflecting Categories of Action Specified in the Reviewed Articles Related to Instructional or Transformational Leadership Dimensions or Functions

Article Title	Author (Year of Publication)	Source of Knowledge	Actions for Instructional Leadership	Actions for Transformational Leadership	Actions for Both Leadership Models
Changing Organizations by Changing Individuals: A Model of Leadership Training	Bloom & Sheerer (1992a)	Research-based–Quasi-experimental Study	Train and supervise staff who work directly with children to support and advance program quality		
The Effect of Leadership Training on Child Care Program Quality	Bloom & Sheerer (1992b)	Research-based–Quasi-experimental	Train and supervise staff who work directly with children to support and advance program quality		
Teacher to Director: A Developmental Journey	Catron & Groves (1999)	Theory-based	Clearly articulate program philosophy and goals Maintain linkages between program activities and program goals and purposes Balance expertise in staff evaluation and problem-solving with establishing goals and activities for staff development Make programmatic decisions based on the needs of children, teachers, and families Manage, motivate, and maximize the potential of individual staff members	Involve staff members in setting program goals and objectives Support the development of individual staff members by using effective communication techniques and leadership skills to build a cohesive and committed team that sets common goals and works cooperatively	Model best practice in early childhood programming

(continued)

Table 18.2 Continued

Article Title	Author (Year of Publication)	Source of Knowledge	Actions for Instructional Leadership	Actions for Transformational Leadership	Actions for Both Leadership Models
Leading a Learning Organisation: Australian Early Years Centers as Learning Networks	Colmer (2008)	Practice-based	Move the organization toward goals associated with the program vision Make a strong commitment to professional development and support a range of professional development opportunities Promote change through continuous improvement	Develop and work toward a shared optimal vision Create a learning organization culture Engage staff as leaders Create an environment in which staff learning extends beyond professional development activities and is prolific in the program culture Support individual staff to achieve professional goals Invite creativity and innovation Foster a culture of reflection and evaluation Create distributed, shared, and participative leadership Promote the use of action research as a key research methodology Encourage strategic networking Create multidisciplinary teams and integrated services	
Evaluating the Child Care Director: The Collaborative Professional Assessment Process	Freeman & Brown (2000)	Practice-based	Use knowledge of child development and curriculum design to implement a high-quality program Create and maintain a nurturing program that responds to needs of children, parents, and employees	Offer insight and develop a vision	Set program goals

Title	Author	Type			
Teacher Participation in Curriculum and Pedagogical Decisions: Insights into Curriculum Leadership	Ho (2010)	Theory-based	Ensure that teachers are equipped with knowledge to make informed decisions regarding curriculum and pedagogy Build up leadership capacity for quality improvement	Be a curriculum leader rather than curriculum user Establish a collective culture Involve teachers in decision-making, particularly around curriculum and pedagogy Create a climate that is receptive to bottom-up management, collaboration, and collegiality	Hold high expectations
On Curriculum Change: The Developing Role of Preschool Heads in Hong Kong	Ho (2005)	Research-based—Case Study		Decentralize leadership and spread widely among the staff	Implement a collective reflective (action research) process that includes identification, classroom observations, management tasks, and construct feedback to support collaborative a team-based learning
Dimensions of Leadership in the Childcare Context	Hujala (2004)	Research-based—Focus groups	Clarify and advance the mission of the program Supervise education and care of children in accordance with the mission of the program Evaluate the basic functions of the program Be responsible for the program and decision making in it		Take care of well-being and human relations among personnel Support and motivate personnel Engage in cooperation and networking across ecological levels
Leadership: Re-thinking it—Making it Happen	Kagan (1994)	Theory-based		Promote shared leadership	
The Transition from Direct Caregiver to Administrator in Early Childhood Education	Larkin (1999)	Research-based—Multiple care study design		Encourage shared decision-making Nurture and support adults who are responsible for children	Influence others through modeling

(continued)

Table 18.2 Continued

Article Title	Author (Year of Publication)	Source of Knowledge	Actions for Instructional Leadership	Actions for Transformational Leadership	Actions for Both Leadership Models
ELP: Empowering the Leadership in Professional Development Communities	Lee (2008)	Practice-based		Engage in collaborative leadership Support opportunities for teacher leadership	
Administrative Leadership: Styles, Competencies, Repertoire	Lay-Dopyera & Dopyera (1985)	Theory-based	Make the program vision clear to others Make decisions about curriculum and instruction Devote time to the conduct and control of instruction	Hold a firm sense of the mission or vision Help teachers accomplish personal goals according to their unique needs	Emphasize achievement
Nursery Teachers as Leaders and Managers	Lunn & Bishop (2002)	Research-based—Life History Interview Approach	Remind team members of the vision Be a pedagogical leader	Build a culture based on caring and reciprocity Distribute leadership among staff Learn and reflect collectively	Support excellence in teaching and learning
Towards a Typology of Leadership for the Early Childhood Professional of the 21st Century	Rodd, (1996)	Research-based Structured Interviews	Encourage ongoing professional development for self and for staff Engage in continuous planning, informed decision making, and monitoring and evaluating	Have a vision to motivate and lead staff and parents toward it Engage in collaborative leadership Assist less-experienced staff	
Learning to be Leaders: Perceptions of Early Childhood Professionals about Leadership Roles and Responsibilities	Rodd, (1997)	Research-based Structured Interviews	Coordinate staff development Mentor new staff		Set program goals Act as a role model

| Implications of Current Research for the Administration and Leadership of Preschool Programs | Swan (1985) | Theory-based | Support implementation of curriculum and instruction
Adapt curricula to meet the unique needs of children with disabilities
Monitor and evaluate program implementation | Individualize training strategies to meet the needs of individual staff | |
| Lighting the Path: Developing Leadership in Early Education | Taba et al. (1999) | Practice-based | Effectively administer a program of personnel management and staff development | Develop and maintain and effective organization and view the organization as a system of components, including the environment, people, and culture | Plan and implement administrative systems that effectively carry out program missions, goals, and objectives |

Note: N = 17 articles.

Review of Advanced Standards for Special Education Administrators

In addition to the literature review described above, we examined the Council for Exceptional Children's Advanced Standards for Special Education Administrators (CEC, 2009) and Advanced Standards for Special Education Early Childhood Specialists in Early Childhood Special Education/Early Intervention Birth to Eight (CEC, 2009). These advanced standards include statements that inform categories of leadership actions for special education administrators and early childhood specialists. Both sets of standards have advanced core standards that are exactly the same and advanced standards that are specific to special education administrators or early childhood specialists. We chose to examine both the core and the specific standards given the focus in the present chapter on responsive instructional leadership in early intervention.

The CEC has systematically developed and periodically disseminated standards related to best practices of special education professionals. The current standards are described as "performance-based" (2009, p. xi) and developed as benchmarks for application in the preparation of special education personnel. These standards are expressed in terms of six content areas, with statements of advanced knowledge and skill sets organized under each area. The content areas are (a) leadership and policy, (b) program development and organization, (c) research and inquiry, (d) individual and program evaluation, (e) professional development and ethics, and (f) collaboration.

We examined the skill statements under each content area for special education administrators and early childhood specialists to determine if they met three criteria. First, the statement specifies *when* leadership actions should occur (e.g., chronology or at an opportunity or challenge). Second, the statement indicates a leadership action, expressed as a *verb*. Third, the statement specifies an *outcome* or *consequence* desired or expected from the action (e.g., solve a problem or improve instructional quality, effectiveness, or outcomes). We considered any skill statement meeting all three criteria to be a category of action compatible with responsive leadership. For skill statements that met these three criteria, we examined them further to determine whether the specified action was related to instructional quality or instructional effectiveness. The statements that met the latter criterion were categorized as actions aligned with responsive instructional leadership.

We evaluated 23 common core advanced skill statements, 25 skill statements for special education administrators, and 24 advanced skill statements for early childhood specialists.

Findings from the CEC Standards Review

Table 18.3 shows findings related to how many of the advanced core statements and the advanced statements for special education administrators or early childhood specialists met the three criteria related to responsive leadership or the four criteria related to responsive instructional leadership.

Across the 23 advanced core statements, only three statements met all three criteria for responsive leadership. These statements were associated with research and inquiry (2 statements) and collaboration (1 statement). One of the statements under research and inquiry met all four criteria: Evaluate and modify instructional practices in response to ongoing assessment. This is a category of action that aligns well with responsive instructional leadership.

For the advanced skill statements related to special education administrators, only two statements met all three criteria for responsive leadership. These statements were associated with research and inquiry and collaboration. There were no statements that met all four criteria for responsive instructional leadership. For the advanced skills statements related to early childhood specialists, only one statement met all three criteria for responsive leadership and it was associated with the collaboration content area. This same statement met all four criteria for responsive

Table 18.3 Number of Advanced Skill Statements by CEC Content Area that Met Criteria Related to Responsive Leadership or Responsive Instructional Leadership

Content Area	# Skill Statements	Responsive Leadership Criteria	Responsive Instructional Leadership Criteria				
		When	Verb	Outcome	All 3 Criteria	Instruction	All 4 Criteria
		Advanced Core Skill Statements for Administrators and Early Childhood Specialists					
Leadership and Policy	4	1	4	0	0	0	0
Program Development and Organization	4	0	4	2	0	4	0
Research and Inquiry	3	2	3	3	2	2	1
Individual and Program Evaluation	4	0	4	2	0	3	0
Professional Development and Ethical Practice	6	0	6	3	0	1	0
Collaboration	2	1	2	2	1	0	0
		Advanced Skill Statements for Special Education Administrators					
Leadership and Policy	5	1	5	2	0	0	0
Program Development and Organization	3	0	3	4	0	1	0
Research and Inquiry	3	1	3	3	1	2	0
Individual and Program Evaluation	4	2	4	2	0	3	0
Professional Development and Ethical Practice	2	1	2	1	0	1	0
Collaboration	8	3	7	7	1	2	0
		Advanced Skill Statements for Early Childhood Specialists					
Leadership and Policy	4	0	4	2	0	2	0
Program Development and Organization	8	1	8	4	0	5	0
Research and Inquiry	4	0	4	2	0	2	0
Individual and Program Evaluation	3	1	3	1	0	3	0
Professional Development and Ethical Practice	3	1	3	0	0	0	0
Collaboration	2	1	2	1	1	1	1

instructional leadership: Collaborate with stakeholders in developing and implementing positive behavior support plans to prevent and address challenging behavior.

Most statements (56 of 72) were not included in the tallies for responsive leadership or responsive instructional leadership because they did not specify sufficiently when a leadership action should occur. Several statements included the term "ongoing," which we coded as having met the "when" criteria. From the perspective of responsive leadership, the indication of when an action should be taken is crucial. This omission is not an indictment of the quality of the CEC standards because the statements were not developed using a particular model of leadership. Instead, the standards were intended as "benchmark" statements. Our post-hoc application of criteria was intended to inform the identification of categories of action related to responsive instructional leadership in early intervention.

Findings similar to those disclosed for the CEC Standards statements were obtained when we applied the three criteria for responsiveness to the statements of categories of actions reported in the literature and displayed in Table 18.2. That is, of the 78 of statements appearing in Table 18.2, none were judged to have all three criteria to be classified as related to responsive leadership. The term "instruction" appeared in only 3 of the 78 statements. Also similar to the skill statements in the CEC Standards, the descriptions of leadership actions located in the extant literature were phrased in relatively general terms, not expressed in operational or behavioral terms that might be desirable for observing, teaching, and evaluating actions of leaders. Our findings are similar to a review of the special education leadership and administrative literature completed by Crockett, Becker, and Quinn (2009).

Implications from the Literature Review and Review of CEC Standards

The findings from our review of the literature and examination of the CEC standards disclosed a list of general leadership actions not particularly descriptive of explicit practices associated with responsive instructional leadership. As Muijs and colleagues (2004) noted, much of the literature on leadership actions is based on anecdotal information and, in some cases, does not go beyond providing tips for leaders. Findings from our review of literature and the review conducted by Muijs et al. support the conclusion that the level of specificity related to leadership actions for early childhood or early intervention falls short of what is needed. Even less specificity is available in the extant literature about actions that relate to responsive instructional leadership for promoting instructional quality, instructional effectiveness, and achieving desired outcomes. Nonetheless, statements shown in Table 18.1 and Table 18.2 represent validated sets of descriptors, some of them suggestive of responsiveness in leadership actions. These statements are available for informing the development of more specific categories of action related to responsive instructional leadership within contemporary tiered instructional and support frameworks such as response-to-intervention (Snyder, McLaughlin, & Denney, 2011).

Organizational Behavior Management and Responsive Instructional Leadership

The development of increased precision about practices leaders would use to be responsive and to support instructional quality, instructional effectiveness, and achievement of desired outcomes might be informed by adopting relevant technology from other disciplines that address human performance in context. In particular, the discipline identified as organizational behavior management (OBM) addresses topics of human learning and performance within organizations (e.g., Crowell & Anderson, 1982a,b; Malott, 2003). OBM has been applied in developmental disabilities (e.g., Harchik & Campbell, 1998; Reid, 1998) and early intervention settings (Crow & Snyder, 1998). The principles and practices underlying organizational behavior management are those of applied behavior analysis (e.g., Baer, Wolf, & Risley, 1968). Applied behavior analysis is also a primary foundation for instructional practices in early intervention (e.g., Odom & Wolery, 2003; Strain et al., 1992). This common scientific foundation across organizational and early intervention instructional practices suggests the utility and compatibility of behavior analytic technology for examining and advancing responsive instructional leadership practices within early intervention programs.

Crow and Snyder (1998) discussed the use of applied behavior analytic principles and practices to achieve intended individual and organizational outcomes in early intervention settings. They described how these principles and practices have been validated in various organizational settings and suggested they be used to specify and measure responsive leadership actions within early intervention settings. Crow and Snyder presented results of a review of literature about specific OBM-related practices appearing over a 5-year period in all papers published in four journals prominent in the field of early intervention. The review was structured to determine whether four author-selected practices related to effective organizational behavior management (i.e., definition of staff performance, observation of their performance, occurrence of differential consequences for performance, and presentation of data regarding performance changes) were reported in the early intervention literature. Of the 565 articles published in the four journals across 5 years, only two articles (i.e., Bruder & Nikitas, 1992; Venn & Wolery, 1992) contained all four practices commonly associated with organizational behavior management.

For purposes of illustrating the four OBM procedural components noted above, we describe highlights of the Venn and Wolery (1992) study. This study focused on modifying instructional performance during diaper changing routines in an infant child care program. The desired instructional performance was to increase the quality of reciprocal interactions between practitioners and infants during diapering. This instructional performance would be consistent with embedded approaches to instruction in early intervention (Snyder et al., 2011). The authors defined the targeted performance skills as practitioners "looking, vocalizing, and touching" and playing "recognizable" games with the child during diapering (p. 306). Practitioners participating in the study were videotaped and scored for defined performances during baseline, training, and post-intervention conditions. After baseline, brief training followed by differential consequences related to targeted performance skills were provided for each teacher in a time-staggered experimental design. The primary consequence for practitioners after training and following their performance was interaction coaching that involved an instructor viewing taped sessions, then providing the teacher with corrective statements and praise. Results of the training intervention on practitioners' performance were provided in narratives and displayed graphically to show changes in performance related to experimental conditions.

To illustrate further the potential utility of the four OBM-related practices to contemporary responsive instructional leadership practices in early intervention, we offer the following exemplar. An initial skill standard for early intervention practitioners specified in the document *What Every Special Education Must Know* (CEC, 2009), is "embed learning opportunities in everyday routines, relationships, activities, and places" (p. 91). A responsive instructional leader observed a practitioner in her inclusive classroom for 30 minutes to determine whether the practitioner was implementing embedded instruction learning trials for a preschooler with disabilities during typically occurring activities and routines. She observed no instances of embedded instruction learning trials related to individualized goals specified on the individualized educational program.

To respond to these data, the leader subsequently scored three, 20 minute segments of video recorded over 2 days in the classroom. The instructional leader used a validated template to record the presence and accuracy of embedded instruction learning trials. Still not observing embedded instruction learning trials, the leader responded by providing instruction and coaching. The instructional leader and the teacher agreed on criteria for determining when the teacher was implementing embedded instruction learning trials frequently and accurately. In addition, they agreed the instructional leader would observe in the classroom for 15 minutes three times per week for 1 week and provide brief verbal and graphic feedback after the observation session.

After the first coaching observation session in which only one embedded instruction learning trial was observed, the leader reviewed the key components of embedded instruction learning trials, stressed the importance of these trials for ensuring individualized instruction, and engaged in problem-solving discussion with the teacher about her challenges and progress. Over the next two coaching sessions, the leader observed the teacher and modeled embedded instruction learning trials. Following the coaching sessions, two 20 minute video segments of teaching were taken when the leader was and was not in the classroom. The leader and the teacher scored the frequency and accuracy of the embedded instruction learning trials. Data showed the criteria for embedded instruction learning trials were reached. Descriptive feedback was provided to the teacher and the leader acknowledged her efforts to implement embedded learning trials. The leader showed the teacher how she had reached a benchmark associated with the CEC standards. The leader marked her calendar with prompts to score and provide periodic feedback to the teacher and the entire program staff about implementation of embedded instruction learning trials.

The Venn and Wolery (1992) study and the exemplar provided above serve to illustrate general "tools" of organizational behavior management and specific categories of action that might be associated with responsive instructional leadership to support instructional quality and instructional effectiveness. Taken together, our integrative review of the leadership literature, relevant CEC standards, and core components of OBM offer a framework for further defining and refining responsive instructional leadership for early intervention.

Future Directions: A Responsive Instructional Leadership Framework for Early Intervention

A framework for organizing research and development for responsive leadership in early intervention should guide the specification of priority categories of action. Categories of action associated with the framework might logically be organized under three areas: (a) actions to guide the implementation of practices congruent with contemporary frameworks for promotion, prevention, and intervention; (b) actions to support the implementation of evidence-based individualized "instruction" that is informed by recommended practices in early intervention and early childhood special education and developmentally appropriate practices for young children; and (c) actions to use data-based decision making to support and improve teaching and learning, and to evaluate whether desired child and family outcomes are being achieved.

Given the nature of the leadership actions described in the extant literature and in the CEC standards, we recommend principles and practices associated with organizational behavior management be used to specify in operational terms responsive instructional leadership practices. Using behavior analytic procedures, including task- and functional-analysis (e.g., Alberto & Troutman, 2012), leadership actions could be specified, and then examined for their empirical, functional, and social validities (e.g., Macmann et al., 1996). Relationships between these actions and their contributions to instructional quality, instruction effectiveness, and achievement of outcomes could also be identified.

Processes associated with specifying and validating responsive instructional leadership actions could be guided by an ecological perspective (see Figure 18.1). Responsive instructional leader-

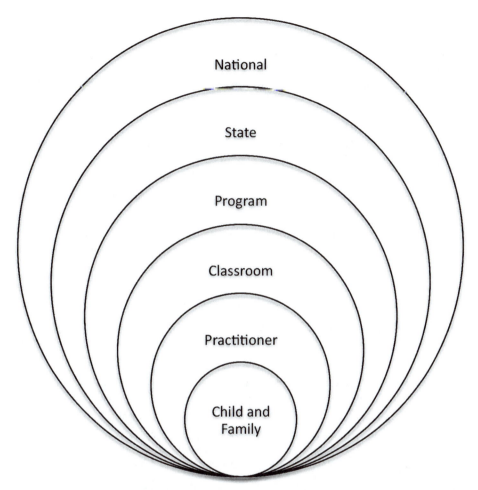

Figure 18.1   Ecological contexts for responsive instructional leadership in early intervention.

ship actions could be specified and validated within and across ecological contexts from proximal (e.g., child and family) to distal (e.g., program or state).

Taken together, these recommendations associated with refining responsive instructional leadership would result in the accumulation of specific leadership processes (e.g., protocols for training and evaluating implementation of recommended practices) and actions (e.g., using data-based decision making, observing for embedded instruction learning opportunities, and providing feedback). Although there are generally described categories of leadership action in the literature, few specific responsive instructional leadership practices have been specified for use in early intervention. The lack of a strong empirical foundation for leadership practices in early intervention has been acknowledged. Nevertheless, conceptual frameworks, recognized categories of actions, science-based principles, and preliminary demonstrations of responsive practices exist for meeting early intervention leadership challenges and responding to opportunities. Responsive instructional leadership to support implementation of recommended and developmentally appropriate practices should continue to be a research and development priority for the field.

Note

1   Preparation of this chapter was supported, in part, by a grant from the National Center for Special Education Research in the Institute of Education Sciences to the University of Florida (R324A070008). The opinions expressed are those of the authors, not the funding agency.

References

Alberto, P. A., & Troutman, A. C. (2012). *Applied behavior analysis for teachers* (9th ed.). Columbus, OH: Pearson.

Baer, D. B., Wolf, M. M., & Risley, T. R. (1968). Some current dimensions of applied behavior analysis. *Journal of Applied Behavior Analysis, 1,* 91–97.

Bamburg, J., &, Andrews, R. (1990). School goals, principals, and achievement. *School Effectiveness and School Improvement, 2,* 175–191.

Bloom, P. J. (1997). Navigating the rapids: Directors reflect on their career and professional development. *Young Children, 52*(7), 32–38.

Bloom, P. J., & Sheerer, M. (1992a). The effect of leadership training on child care program quality. *Early Childhood Research Quarterly, 7,* 579–594. doi: 10.1016/0885-2006(92)90112-C.

Bloom, P. J., & Sheerer, M. (1992b). Changing organizations by changing individuals: A model of leadership training. *Urban Review, 24,* 263–286.

Boscardin, M. L. (2007). What is special about special education administration? Considerations for school leadership. *Exceptionality, 15,* 189–200.

Boscardin, M. L. (2009). An integrated research-based approach to creating standards for special education leadership. *Journal of Special Education Leadership, 22,* 68–84.

Boscardin, M. L., Mainzer, R., & Kealy, M. V. (2011). Commentary: A response to "Preparing special education administrators for inclusion in diverse, standards-based contexts. *Teacher Education and Special Education, 34,* 71–78.

Bruder, M. B., & Nikitas, T. (1992). Changing the professional practices of early interventionists: An inservice model to meet the service needs of Public-Law 99-457. *Journal of Early Intervention, 16,* 173–180.

Bycio, P., & Allen, J. (1995). Further assessment of Bass's conceptualization of transactional and transformational leadership. *Journal of Applied Psychology, 80,* 468–478.

Catron, C. E., & Groves, M. M. (1999). Teacher to director: A developmental journey. *Early Childhood Education Journal, 26,* 183–188.

Copple, C., & Bredekamp, S. (2009). *Developmentally appropriate practice in early childhood programs serving children from birth through age 8* (3rd ed.). Washington, DC: National Association for the Education of Young Children.

Colmer, K. (2008). Leading a learning organisation: Australian early years centres as learning networks. *European Early Childhood Education Research Journal, 16,* 107–115.

Council for Exceptional Children (CEC). (2003). *What every special educator must know: Ethics, standards, and guidelines for special educators* (5th ed.). Arlington, VA: Author.

Council for Exceptional Children (CEC). (2009). *What every special educator must know: Ethics, standards, and guidelines for special educators* (6th ed.). Arlington, VA: Author.

Couse, L. J., & Russo, H. L. (2006). Service-learning: Mentoring leadership skills in the experienced teacher. *Mentoring & Tutoring: Partnership in Learning, 14,* 33–48.

Crockett, J. B. (2002). Special education's role in preparing responsive leaders for inclusive schools. *Remedial and Special Education, 23,* 157–168.

Crockett, J. B., Becker, M. K., & Quinn, D. (2009). Reviewing the knowledge base of special education leadership and administration. *Journal of Special Education Leadership, 22,* 55–67.

Crow, R., & Snyder, P. A. (1998). Organizational behavior management in early intervention: Status and implications for research and development. *Journal of Organizational Behavior Management, 18,* 131–156.

Crowell, C. R., & Anderson, C. D. (1982a). The scientific and methodological basis of a systematic approach to behavior management. *Journal of Organizational Behavior Management, 4,* 4–32.

Crowell, C. R., & Anderson, C. D. (1982b). Systematic behavior management: General program considerations. *Journal of Organizational Behavior Management, 4,* 129–163.

Curtis, L., & Burton, D. (2009). Naive change agent or canny political collaborator? The change in leadership role from nursery school to children's centre. *Education 3–13, 37*(3), 287–299.

Dana, N. F., & Yendol-Hoppey, D. (2005). Becoming an early childhood teacher leader and an advocate for social justice: A phenomenological interview study. *Journal of Early Childhood Teacher Education, 26*(3), 191–206.

DEC/NAEYC. (2009). *Early childhood inclusion: A joint position statement of the Division for Early Childhood (DEC) and the National Association for the Education of Young Children (NAEYC).* Chapel Hill: The University of North Carolina, FPG Child Development Institute.

Early Childhood Outcomes Center. (2004, April). *Considerations related to developing a system for measuring outcomes for young children with disabilities and their families.* Retrieved from http://www.fpg.unc.edu/~eco/pages/papers.cfm#SpanFOS

Early Childhood Outcomes Center. (2005, April). *Family and child outcomes for early intervention and early childhood special education.* Retrieved from http://www.the-eco-center.org

Fleming, J., & Love, M. (2003). A systemic change model for leadership, inclusion, and mentoring (SLIM). *Early Childhood Education Journal, 31,* 53–57.

Freeman, N. K., & Brown, M. H. (2000). Evaluating the child care director: The collaborative professional assessment process. *Young Children, 55*(5), 20–26.

Garland, C. W., & Linder, T. W. (1988). Administrative challenges in early intervention. In J. B. Jordan, J. J. Gallagher, P. L. Huntinger, & M. B. Karnes (Eds.), *Early childhood special education: Birth to three* (pp. 5–27). Reston, VA: Council for Exceptional Children.

Hallinger, P. (2003). Leading educational change: reflections on the practice of instructional and transformational leadership. *Cambridge Journal of Education, 33,* 329–351. doi: 10.1080/0305764032000122005.

Hallinger, P. (2005). Instructional leadership and the school principal: A passing fancy that refuses to fade away. *Leadership and Policy in Schools, 4*(1), 1–20.

Harbin, G., & Salisbury, C. (2005). Recommended practices: Policies, procedures, and systems change. In In S. Sandall, M. L. Hemmeter, B. J. Smith, & M .E. McLean (Eds.), *DEC recommended practices: A comprehensive guide for practical application* (pp. 165–188). Longmont, CO: Sopris West.

Harchik, A. E., & Campbell, A. R. (1998). Supporting people with developmental disabilities in their homes and communities: The role of organizational behavior management. *Journal of Organizational Behavior Management, 18,* 83–102.

Hayden, J. (1997). Directors of early childhood services: Experience, preparedness and selection. *Journal of Australian Research in Early Childhood, 1,* 49–67.

Ho, D. C. W. (2005). On curriculum change: The developing role of preschool heads in Hong Kong. *International Journal of Educational Management, 19,* 48–58.

Ho, D. C. W. (2010). Teacher participation in curriculum and pedagogical decisions: Insights into curriculum leadership. *Educational Management Administration and Leadership, 38,* 613–624.

Howell, J., & Avolio, B. (1993). Transformational leadership, transactional leadership, locus of control, and support. *Journal of Applied Psychology, 78,* 891–893.

Hujala, E. (2004). Dimensions of leadership in the childcare context. *Scandinavian Journal of Educational Research, 48*(1), 53–71.

Individuals with Disabilities Education Improvement Act of 2004, 20 U.S.C. § 1400 *et. seq.* (2004)(reauthorization of the Individuals with Disabilities Act of 1990)

Kagan, S. L. (1994). Leadership: Re-thinking it—Making it happen. *Young Children, 49*(5), 50–54.

Larkin, E. (1999). The transition from direct caregiver to administrator in early childhood education. *Child & Youth Care Forum, 28*(1), 21–32. doi: 10.1023/A:1021998501874.

Lay-Dopyera, M., & Dopyera, J. E. (1985). Administrative leadership: Styles, competencies, repertoire. *Topics in Early Childhood Special Education, 5*(1), 15–23. doi:10.1177/027112148500500103.

Lee, W. (2008). ELP: Empowering the leadership in professional development communities. *European Early Childhood Education Research Journal, 16,* 95–106.

Leithwood, K. (2005). *Educational leadership: A review of the research.* Philadelphia, PA: Temple University, Center for Research in Human Development and Education, Laboratory for Student Success.

Leithwood, K., Tomlinson, D., & Genge, M. (1996). Transformational school leadership. In K. Leithwood et al. (Eds.). *International handbook of educational leadership and administration* (pp. 785–840). Dordrecht, The Netherlands: Kluwer.

Linder, T. W. (1983). *Early childhood special education: Program development and administration.* Baltimore: Brookes.

Lunn, P., & Bishop, A. (2002). Nursery teachers as leaders and managers: A pedagogical and subsidiarity model of leadership. *Research in Education, (67),* 13–22.

Macmann, G. M., Barnett, D. W., Allen, S. J., Bramlett, R. K., Hall, J. D., & Ehrhardt, K. E. (1996). Problem-solving and intervention design: Guidelines for the evaluation of technical adequacy. *School Psychology Quarterly, 11,* 137–148.

Malott, M. E. (2003). *Paradox of organizational change: Engineering organizations with behavioral systems analysis.* Reno, NV: Context Press.

Marvin, C., LaCost, B., Grady, M., & Mooney, P. (2003). Administrative support and challenges in Nebraska public school early childhood programs: Preliminary study. *Topics in Early Childhood Special Education, 23,* 217–228.

Muijs, D., Aubrey, C., Harris, A., & Briggs, M. (2004). How do they manage? A review of the research on leadership in early childhood. *Journal of Early Childhood Research, 2*(2), 157–169.

National Association for the Education of Young Children. (2009). *Developmentally appropriate practice in early childhood programs serving children from birth through age 8* (Position statement). Retrieved from http://www.naeyc.org/files/naeyc/file/positions/position%20statement%20Web.pdf

Odom, S. L., & Wolery, M. (2003). A unified theory of practice in early intervention/early childhood special education: Evidence-based practice. *Journal of Special Education, 37,* 164–173.

Reid, D. H. (1998). Introduction. *Journal of Organizational Behavior Management, 18,* 1–5.

Rodd, J. (1996). Towards a typology of leadership for the early childhood professional of the 21st century. *Early Childhood Development and Care, 120,* 119–126.

Rodd, J. (1997). Learning to be leaders: Perceptions of early childhood professionals about leadership roles and responsibilities. *Early Years, 18,* 40–46.

Ryan, S., & Hornbeck, A. (2004). Mentoring for quality improvement: A case study of a mentor teacher in the reform process. *Journal of Research in Childhood Education, 19,* 79–96.

Sandall, S., Hemmeter, M. L., Smith, B. J., & McLean, M. E. (2005). *DEC recommended practices: A comprehensive guide for practical application in early intervention/early childhood special education.* Longmont, CO: Sopris West.

Shelton, T. L., Jeppson, E. S., & Johnson, B. H. (1987). *Family-centered care for children with special health care needs.* Washington, DC: Association for Care of Children's Health.

Snyder, P. (2006). Effects of evidence-based practice on research in early childhood. In V. Buysse & P. Wesley (Eds.), *Evidence-based practice in the early childhood field* (pp. 35–70). Washington, DC: Zero to Three.

Snyder, P., Denney, M., Pasia, C., Rakap, S., & Crowe, C. (2011). Professional development in early childhood intervention. In C. Groark (Series Ed.) & L. Kaczmarek (Vol. Ed.), *Early childhood intervention program policies for special needs children: Vol. 3. Emerging issues* (pp. 169–204). Santa Barbara, CA: Praeger/ABC-CLIO.

Snyder, P., McLaughlin, T., & Denney, M. (2011). Frameworks for guiding program focus and practices in early intervention. In J. M. Kauffman & D. P. Hallahan (Series Eds.) & M. Conroy (Section Ed.), *Handbook of special education: Section XII Early identification and intervention in exceptionality.* New York, NY: Routledge.

Strain, P. S., McConnell, S. R., Carta, J. J., Fowler, S. A., Neisworth, J. T., & Wolery, M. (1992). Behaviorism in early intervention. *Topics in Early Childhood Special Education, 12,* 121–141.

Swan, W. W. (1985). Implications of current research for the administration and leadership of preschool programs. *Topics in Early Childhood Special Education, 5*(1), 83–96. doi:10.1177/027112148500500108.

Taba, S., Castle, A., Vermeer, M., Hanchett, K., Flores, D., & Caulfield, R. (1999). Lighting the path: Developing leadership in early education. *Early Childhood Education Journal, 26*(3), 173–177.

Trivette, C. M., & Dunst, C. J. (2005). Recommended practices: Family-based practices. In S. Sandall, M. L. Hemmeter, B. J. Smith, & M. E. McLean (Eds.), *DEC recommended practices: A comprehensive guide for practical application* (pp. 107–126). Longmont, CO: Sopris West.

Turnbull, A., Turnbull, H. R., Erwin, E. J., & Soodak, L. C., & Shogren, K. A. (2010). *Families, professionals, and exceptionality: Positive outcomes through partnership and trust* (6th ed.). Upper Saddle River, NJ: Pearson/Merrill

Venn, M .L. & Wolery, M. (1992). Increasing day care staff members' interactions during caregiving routines. *Journal of Early Intervention, 16,* 304–319.

Vincent, L. J., Salisbury, C. L., Strain, P., McCormick, C., & Tessier, A. (1990). A behavioral-ecological approach to early intervention: Focus on cultural diversity. In S. J. Meisels & J. P. Shonkoff (Eds.), *Handbook of early childhood intervention* (pp. 173–195). New York, NY: Cambridge University Press.

Waugh, R. F., Boyd, G. S., & Corrie, L. F. (2003). Teacher leadership in early childhood education: A rasch measurement model analysis. In R. F. Waugh, & R. F. Waugh (Eds.), *On the forefront of educational psychology* (pp. 295–329). Hauppauge, NY: Nova Science.

WestEd. (2002). *The standards-based instructional planning process: Backwards mapping from standards to instruction* [Module 2]. Retrieved from http://www.calstate.edu/CAPP/

Wimpleberg, R., Abroms, K. I., & Catardi, C. L. (1985). Multiple models for administrator preparation in early childhood special education. *Topics in Early Childhood Special Education, 5* (1), 1–14.

Woodrow, C., & Busch, G. (2008). Repositioning early childhood leadership as action and activism. *European Early Childhood Education Research Journal, 16*(1), 83–93.

19

Leadership for Transition to Postsecondary Settings

David W. Test

UNIVERSITY OF NORTH CAROLINA AT CHARLOTTE

Valerie L. Mazzotti

WESTERN CAROLINA UNIVERSITY

April L. Mustian

ILLINOIS STATE UNIVERSITY

School life can be viewed as a series of transitions, from preschool to elementary school, elementary school to middle school, middle school to high school, and high school to postsecondary life. While all are important, the move from high school to adulthood may be the most critical one. Unfortunately, research has shown that since the 1980s, students with disabilities have consistently experienced poor post-school outcomes.

For example, in two of the initial studies reporting post-school outcome data for students with disabilities, first Hasazi, Gordon, and Roe (1985) reported data from 301 students from nine Vermont school districts indicating 55% were employed and only 67% of these individuals were employed full-time. Next, Wehman, Kregal, and Seyfarth (1985) reported data collected from 117 parents in four Virginia school districts. Their findings indicated that 78.6% of students were not employed, 12% were competitively employed, and 9.6% were in a sheltered workshop.

By the mid-1990s, data from the first National Longitudinal Transition Study (Blackorby & Wagner, 1996) indicated employment rates for students with disabilities lagged behind the rate of youth in general two years after graduation (46% vs. 59%). The same pattern was found for postsecondary education where 14% of students with disabilities and 53% of students without disabilities had attended some type of postsecondary education program.

Most recently, while data from Wave 4 of the National Longitudinal Transition Study 2 (Newman, Wagner, Cameto, & Knokey, 2009) indicated the transition outcomes gap is improving, students with disabilities continue to have poorer outcomes than students without disabilities. For example, 45% of youth with disabilities reported being enrolled in postsecondary education within four years of leaving high school, compared to 53% for youth in the general population ever having attended postsecondary school (Newman et al., 2009). In terms of postsecondary employment, 57% of students with disabilities were employed compared to 66% of youth in general.

One strategy for improving post-school outcomes for students with disabilities is to adopt what has been called transition-focused education (Kohler & Field, 2003). The goal of transition-focused education is to successfully prepare students for post-school life. It is guided by an individual student's stated post-school goals and "consists of academic, career, and extracurricular instruction and activities, delivered through a variety of instructional and transition approaches and services, depending on the local context and student's learning and support needs." (Kohler & Field, 2003, p.176). In order to understand the importance of a transition-focused education, it is necessary to provide a brief history of related special education and educational policies.

Transition focused education has an extensive history that dates back over 30 years. In the 1960s, cooperative work/study programs emerged, 1970s career education took focus, and finally, in the 1980's transition emerged and began to rapidly expand. It was not until 1980 that secondary transition was first recognized by Madeleine Will, the Director of the Office of Special Education and Rehabilitation Services (OSERS) as an important aspect of life for individuals with disabilities. In 1984, Will introduced a definition of transition and the Bridges Model, which included three bridges that represented transition from high school to post-school employment. Will (1984) defined transition as:

> An outcome-oriented process encompassing a broad array of services and experiences that lead to employment. Transition is a period that includes high school, the point of graduation, additional post-secondary education or adult services, and the initial years of employment. Transition is a bridge between the security and structure offered by the school and the opportunities and risks of adult life. Any bridge requires both a solid span and a secure foundation at either end. The transition for school to work and adult life requires sound preparation in the secondary school, adequate support at the point of school leaving, and secure opportunities and services, if needed, in adult situations.
>
> *(p. 2)*

The Bridges Model included: (a) No Special Services, which referred to services that were available to any person within the community (e.g., community college); (b) Time Limited Services, which referred to services that were specific for individuals with disabilities (e.g., vocational rehabilitation); and (c) Ongoing Services, which referred to services that would be available to an individual throughout an individuals life (e.g., supported employment). While Will's model was a step in the right direction, it focused specifically on post-school employment. Therefore, in 1985, the field of special education responded to Will's model by adding community adjustment (i.e., residential environment, social and interpersonal networks) recognizing that individuals with disabilities need more in post-school life than employment to be successful (Halpern, 1985).

In 1990, the Individuals with Disabilities Education Act (IDEA; P.L. 101-476) was signed into law and for the first time included a definition of transition services and inclusion of a transition component to the Individualized Education Program (IEP). IDEA 1990 mandated that students with disabilities have a transition component completed with the IEP no later than age 16. Additionally, by providing a definition of transition, the mandate described who should be involved in the transition planning process and stated that youth with disabilities be provided a coordinated set of services that linked the student with adult service providers in the community.

When IDEA was reauthorized in 1997, transition services were further strengthened. There were several changes to the law, which impacted the delivery of transition services for students with disabilities. Specifically, in IDEA 1997 transition services were broadened to include: (a) related services (e.g., speech-language, physical therapy, occupational therapy); (b) educational activities to help facilitate the transition into post-school employment and education; and (c) beginning no later than the student turning 14 years old, the IEP must include a statement of transition service needs related to the course of study. Finally, IDEA 1997 mandated that the IEP include a statement one year prior to the student reaching the age of majority indicating that the student was informed that rights would be transferred.

In 2004, IDEA was once again reauthorized and the mandates for transition services were further improved. First, the definition of transition services required services be designed "within a results oriented process" focusing on improving "the academic and functional achievement" of students with disabilities. Second, in an effort to improve vocational outcomes for students, vocational education was included as a transition service. Third, the law specifically stated that the goal of a student's secondary education is to prepare them for successful post-school employment, education, and independent living. Fourth, the mandate that transition services begin at the age of 14 was changed to age 16. Next, schools were required to include post-school goals for students with disabilities in the areas of employment, education, and when appropriate independent living. Finally, schools are required to provide students with a Summary of Performance at graduation from high school, which should include information related to academic and functional performance and recommendations for helping the student reach post-school goals.

To ensure states meet mandates of IDEA 2004, the Office of Special Education Programs (OSEP) with OSERS developed 20 SPP/APR performance indicators related to Part B (i.e., children with disabilities; age 3 to 22). Of these 20 indicators, four relate specifically to secondary transition for students with disabilities. The four indicators include: (a) Indicator 1, graduation rate improvement; (b) Indicator 2, decreasing drop-out rates; (c) Indicator 13, improving transition services; and (b) Indicator 14, improving post-school outcomes for students moving from secondary to postsecondary settings. Since Indicator 13 is the transition indicator, it is important to understand its relevance for state and local education agencies. Specifically, Indicator 13 states:

> Appropriate measurable postsecondary goals that are annually updated and based upon an age appropriate transition assessment, transition services, including courses of study, that will reasonably enable the student to meet those postsecondary goals, and annual IEP goals related to the student's transition services needs. There also must be evidence that the student was invited to the IEP Team meeting where transition services are to be discussed and evidence that, if appropriate, a representative of any participating agency was invited to the IEP Team meeting with the prior consent of the parent or student who has reached the age of majority.
>
> *(20 U.S.C. 1416[a][3][B]; OSEP, 2009).*

The National Secondary Transition Technical Assistance Center (NSTTAC; 2009) in coordination with OSEP developed an Indicator 13 checklist to help facilitate data collection on transition services. The checklist includes eight items and provides guidelines for teachers and schools in developing IEPs that meet the requirements of IDEA 2004 and the secondary transition needs of students with disabilities. IDEA (2004) mandates a student's IEP include (a) each of the eight items on the Indicator 13 checklist and (b) must be in effect beginning no later than the age of 16 or earlier based on state requirements or if the IEP team feels it is appropriate. The Indicator 13 checklist can be found at http://www.nsttac.org/content/nsttac_1_13_checklist.aspx.

While over the years IDEA has addressed transition-focused education to promote students with disabilities post-school success, there are several other major policies that have influenced transition into postsecondary education for students with disabilities. Beginning in the 1960s, the Vocational Education Act and Amendments (i.e., 1963, 1968, 1976) mandated states provide a minimum of 10% of state and local funds to provide vocational education for students with disabilities, which made vocational education an accessible option for these students (Test, Aspel,

& Everson, 2006). The School-to-Work Opportunities Act of 1994 mandated that secretaries of education and labor work together to improve the post-school outcomes of students with disabilities moving into postsecondary education, with the primary goal of infusing academic and vocational coursework in schools (Test et al., 2006). In 1984, the Carl D. Perkins Vocational Education Act was first passed to provide adults with disabilities the right to equal access to quality vocational education opportunities. Recently, this act was reauthorized in 2006, now known as the Carl D. Perkins Vocational and Technical Education Act, to provide an increased focus on academic achievement of career and technical education for all students, strengthen secondary and postsecondary education connections, and improve accountability at the state and local levels (United States Department of Education, 2010b). Finally, the Social Security Protection Act of 2003 removed barriers to allow individuals with disabilities in low-income situations to build assets in order to save money for things such as postsecondary education (Test et al., 2006).

For students with intellectual disabilities, the dream of going to college was recently improved when the Higher Education Opportunity Act (HEA; P.L. 110–315) was enacted on August 14, 2008. The law contained important new financial aid provisions, as well as creating a new model demonstration program designed to improve access to postsecondary education for students with intellectual disabilities. More information on this important opportunity can be found at http://www.thinkcollege.net.

Most recently, the call for all students to be "college and career ready" (Bill & Melinda Gates Foundation, 2009; United States Department of Education, 2010) has been at the forefront of the education reform movement and will have an effect on students with disabilities moving into postsecondary education settings. Currently, 46 states and 3 territories have adopted the Common Core State Standards developed by the National Governors Association, which are designed to prepare all students with real life skills and knowledge to prepare them for future college and careers (Common Core Standards Initiative, 2010). The idea behind developing Common Core State Standards comes from the recent P-16 Pipeline education reform initiative. The purpose of P-16 Pipeline initiative is to foster integration between early, elementary, middle, secondary, and postsecondary education to improve outcomes for all students. P-16 will allow for alignment of several education laws (i.e., IDEA, No Child Left Behind, Carl D. Perkins Vocational and Technical Education Act, HEA). It challenges states to develop comprehensive plans for education reform (National Governors Association, 2010).

Based on the P-16 Pipeline education reform initiative, the United States Department of Education has challenged states with Race to the Top. Race to the Top requires states to create a comprehensive plan for education reform to accelerate efforts towards a P-16 Pipeline. With Race to the Top, states are expected to make reforms in four key areas: (a) adopt standards and assessment that prepare all students for success in college and careers; (b) build data systems that measure student growth across the years to provide teachers and principals with information to improve instruction; (c) recruit, develop, reward, and retain effective teachers and principals in the most needed areas; and (d) improve the lowest performing schools (Achieve, 2010; United States Department of Education, 2010c). While these initiatives are just beginning, each will have meaning for students with disabilities as they move into postsecondary education settings.

As the field of special education moves forward, a transition-focused education program must use the most effective secondary transition practices derived from scientifically based research (U.S. Department of Education, 2010). Recently, the National Secondary Transition Technical Assistance Center (NSTTAC), funded by the U.S. Department of Education, Office of Special Education Programs, conducted a comprehensive set of literature reviews to identify (a) evidence-based classroom instructional practices (Test, Fowler, et al., 2009) based on rigorous experimental research (both group and single subject designs) and (b) evidence-based predictors of successful post-school outcomes (Test, Mazzotti, et al., 2009) based on rigorous correlational research. Together, these sets of evidence-based practices and predictors provide school leaders with the building blocks needed to construct a quality transition-focused education program.

Although secondary transition evidence-based practices and predictors have been identified, their adoption is inconsistent. One way to bridging the research-to-practice gap, is to provide school and district level administrators with the most current knowledge of "what works" in secondary transition for students with disabilities. Therefore, this chapter will summarize secondary transition evidence-based practices and predictors for students with disabilities and their use in schools. Finally, issues around providing transition-focused education within the context of school reform and improving school completion rates for students with disabilities will be discussed.

Evidence-Based Practices for Secondary Transition

In the first phase of NSTTAC's comprehensive literature review, evidence-based instructional practices for secondary students with disabilities were identified. To do this, NSTTAC used a systematic process for conducting the review. For a detailed description of the review process see Test, Fowler, et al. (2009).

Based on findings from the comprehensive review of experimental research studies, NSTTAC identified 61 evidence-based practices for secondary students with disabilities. Table 19.1 lists each evidence-based practice by the independent variable and provides a detailed description of each. Based on these descriptions, examples of how such practices can support student Individualized Education Program (IEP) goals and skill development are described in the following sections.

How to Implement Evidence-Based Practices

In order to understand how to effectively implement evidence-based practices, educators need to be aware of (a) how practices can be used in developing measurable annual IEP goals for students and (b) how practices can support student skill development.

Using Evidence-Based Practices to Support IEP Goals.　Using the evidence-based practice of computer-assisted instruction (CAI) as an illustration, as it has been shown to be an effective practice for teaching a variety of skills, two examples that incorporate CAI into IEP goals are:

- Given CAI on ordering at a restaurant, Isabel will order a meal in a fast-food restaurant with 100% accuracy by the end of the first school semester.
- Given CAI on grocery shopping, Jamarreo will read grocery aisle signs and locate specific grocery items with 90% accuracy for 3 consecutive weekly probes by spring of 2012.

Evidence-Based Practices Can Support Student Skill Development.　Once annual IEP goals are developed, an educator might search NSTTAC's Research to Practice Lesson Plan Starter Library for appropriate lesson plan starters (http://www.nsttac.org/ebp/ebp_main.aspx). For the IEP objectives written earlier, two lesson plan starters are available: (a) *Ordering in a Restaurant*, which can be used to teach restaurant ordering skills using CAI; and (b) *Teaching Grocery Shopping using Computer-Based Instruction*, which can be used to teach the specific grocery shopping skill to begin working toward an annual goal.

Table 19.1   Evidence-Based Practices

Category	Description of Practice	Evidence-Based Practices
Backward Chaining	Backward chaining is defined as a student performing the final behavior in a task analysis sequence and being reinforced once the task has been performed, at which time the next-to-last behavior is introduced to the student (Cooper, Heron, & Heward, 2007). Backward chaining has been used to teach first aid skills, grocery shopping skills, purchasing skills, and functional life skills to secondary students with disabilities. For example, Gast and Winterling (1992) used backward chaining to teach secondary students with disabilities first aid skills including treating cuts, burns, and insect bites.	• Using Backward Chaining to Teach Functional Life Skills
Computer-Assisted Instruction	Computer-assisted instruction (CAI) is defined as using a computer or some other type of technology (e.g., personal digital assistant, hypermedia systems) to improve students' skills, knowledge, and academic performance (Okolo, Bahr, & Rieth, 1993). CAI has been used to teach a variety of skills to secondary students with disabilities, including cooking skills, grocery shopping skills, employment skills, student involvement in the IEP, and other functional life skills. For example, Mechling (2004) used multimedia, computer-assisted instruction to teach grocery shopping skills to secondary students with mild to moderate intellectual disabilities.	• Using Computer-Assisted Instruction to Teach Cooking Skills • Using Computer-Assisted Instruction to Teach Grocery Shopping Skills • Using Computer-Assisted Instruction to Teach Employment Skills • Using Computer-Assisted Instruction to Teach Student Involvement in the IEP • Using Computer-Assisted Instruction to Teach Functional Life Skills
Community-Based Instruction	Community-based instruction (CBI) is defined as instruction of functional skills that takes place within the community where target skills can be practiced within a natural environment (Brown et al., 1983). CBI has been used to teach purchasing skills, grocery shopping skills, functional life skills, community integration skills, job specific skills, and communication skills. For example, Taylor, Collins, Schuster, and Kleinert (2002) used community-based instruction to teach secondary students with disabilities laundry skills.	• Using Community-Based Instruction to Teach Purchasing Skills • Using Community-Based Instruction to Teach Grocery Shopping Skills • Using Community-Based Instruction to Teach Communication Skills • Using Community-Based Instruction to Teach Job Specific Skills • Using Community Based Instruction to Teach Community Integration Skills
Constant Time Delay	Constant time delay (CTD) is defined as providing a student a fixed amount of time between instruction and giving a prompt in which the teacher initially presents multiple trials using a 0 sec delay followed by a simultaneous prompt condition using a fixed time delay (e.g., 3 sec or 5 sec; Cooper et al., 2007). CTD has been used to teach food preparation and cooking skills, purchasing skills, functional life skills, banking skills,	• Using Constant Time Delay to Teach Food Preparation and Cooking Skills • Using Constant Time Delay to Teach Purchasing Skills • Using Constant Time Delay to Teach Functional Life Skills • Using Constant Time Delay to Teach Banking Skills • Using Constant Time Delay to Teach Leisure Skills

Category	Description of Practice	Evidence-Based Practices
Constant Time Delay (*continued*)	leisure skills, communication skills, and applied math skills. For example, Bozkurt and Gursel (2005) used CTD to teach the cooking skills of making a drink and snack to secondary students with disabilities.	• Using Constant Time Delay to Teach Applied Math Skills • Using Constant Time Delay to Teach Communication Skills
Forward Chaining	Forward chaining is defined as teaching behaviors identified in a task analysis in their naturally occurring order. Reinforcement is delivered when the predetermined criterion for the first behavior in the sequence is achieved then the next step in the task analysis is taught (Cooper et al., 2007). Forward chaining is often used to teach functional life skills. For example, McDonnell and McFarland (1988) used forward chaining to teach secondary students with disabilities to use a washing machine and a laundry-mat soap dispenser.	• Using Forward Chaining to Teach Home Maintenance Skills
General Case Programming	General case programming is defined as a method for "training sufficient exemplars" by providing students with enough examples of a stimulus class in order for the student to perform the skill on any member of that stimulus class (Alberto & Troutman, 2009, p. 354). General case programming has been used to teach safety skills. For example, Horner, Jones, and Williams (1985) used general case programming to teach secondary students with disabilities how to cross the street.	• Using General Case Programming to Teach Safety Skills
"One More Than" Strategy	The "One More Than" strategy is defined as teaching students to pay one more dollar than requested (e.g., cost is $2.29, student would give $3.00; Denny & Test, 1995). The "One More Than" strategy has been used to teach counting money and purchasing skills. For example, Ayers, Langone, Boon, and Norman (2006) used the "One More Than" strategy in combination with CAI to teach students with intellectual disabilities to make purchases at a grocery store.	• Using the One More Than Strategy to Teach Counting Money • Using the One More Than Strategy to Teach Purchasing Skills
Parent Training Modules	Parent training modules are described as training packages in which a single topic or a small section of a broad topic is studied for a given period of time to parents (Morsink, 1988). Training modules have been used to teach parents about the transition planning process and how to be involved in the transition planning process. For example, Boone (1992) used training modules to teach parents the basic concept of transition planning, various transition components, and how to participate as a decision maker in the transition planning conference for their child.	• Using Training Modules to Promote Parent Involvement in the Transition Planning Process

(continued)

Table 19.1 Continued

Category	Description of Practice	Evidence-Based Practices
Progressive Time Delay	Progressive time delay is defined as gradually increasing the amount of time between instruction and giving a prompt during which the teacher initially begins with a 0 sec delay followed by a simultaneous prompt condition that gradually and systematically increases the time delay (e.g., 0 sec to 2 sec to 4 sec; Cooper et al., 2007). Progressive time delay has been used to teach functional life skills, purchasing skills, and safety skills. For example, McDonnell (1987) used progressive time delay to teach secondary students with disabilities to purchase snack foods.	• Using Progressive Time Delay to Teach Functional Life Skills • Using Progressive Time Delay to Teach Purchasing Skills • Using Progressive Time Delay to Teach Safety Skills
Published Curricula	Four published curricula have been identified as evidence-based practices for teaching students to participate in and lead IEP meetings, be involved in the transition planning process, and gain self-determination skills (Test et al., 2004). They are the Self-Advocacy Strategy (Van Reusen, Bos, & Shumaker, 1994), Self-Directed IEP (Martin et al., 2006), Whose Future is It Anyway? (Wehmeyer & Lawrence, 1995), and Check and Connect (Sinclair et al., 2005). For example, Martin et al. (2006) used the Self-Directed IEP to teach student participation in the IEP meeting.	• Using Self-Advocacy Strategy to teach student involvement in the IEP meeting • Using Self-Advocacy Strategy to Teach Student Participation in the IEP Meeting • Using the Self-Directed IEP to Teach Student Participation in the IEP Meeting • Using Whose Future Is It Anyway? to Teach Student Knowledge of Transition Planning • Using Whose Future Is It Anyway? to Teach Self-Determination Skills • Using Published Curricula to Teach Student Involvement in the IEP Meeting • Using Check and Connect to Promote Student Participation in the IEP Meeting
Response Prompting	Response prompting is defined as using stimuli that function as an extra cue or reminder for a desired behavior and is typically emitted in the form of verbal instructions, modeling, and/or physical guidance (Cooper et al., 2007). Response prompting has been used to teach a variety of skills, including purchasing, grocery shopping, home maintenance, laundry skills, cooking, food preparation, functional life skills, sight word reading, job specific skills, social skills, leisure skills, student involvement in the IEP, and completing a job application. For example, Alberto, Cihak, and Gamma (2005) used response prompting to teach making purchases with a debit card to secondary students with disabilities.	• Using Response Prompting to Teach Purchasing Skills • Using Response Prompting to Teach Grocery Shopping Skills • Using Response Prompting to Teach Home Maintenance Skills • Using Response Prompting to Teach Laundry Tasks • Using Response Prompting to Teach Food Preparation and Cooking Skills • Using Video Modeling to Teach Food Preparation and Cooking Skills • Using Response Prompting to Teach Employment Skills • Using Response Prompting to Teach Safety Skills • Using Response Prompting to Teach Functional Life Skills • Using Response Prompting to Teach Leisure Skills • Using Response Prompting to Teach Employment Skills • Using Mnemonics to Teach Completing a Job Application

Category	Description of Practice	Evidence-Based Practices
Self-Directed Learning Model of Instruction	The SDLMI is an instructional model that teaches students to become self-regulated learners in order to gain self-determination skills and includes three phases that provide students with opportunities to set a goal, develop a plan to address the goal, and evaluate changes to successfully meet the goal (Agran, Blanchard, & Wehmeyer, 2000). The SDLMI has been used to teach students to attain their educational goals. For example, Lee, Wehmeyer, Palmer, Soukup, and Little (2008) used the SDLMI to teach secondary students with disabilities to attain educational goals.	• Using the SDLMI to Teach Attaining Educational Goals
Self-Management	Self-management is defined as monitoring or evaluating personal behavior in order to change and control a subsequent behavior (Cooper et al., 2007). Self-management has been used to teach job specific skills, social skills, functional life skills, and self-determination skills. For example, Lamb, Bibby, and Wood (1997) used self-management to teach secondary students conversational skills.	• Using Self-Management Instruction to Teach Job Specific Skills • Using Self-Management to Teach Social Skills • Using Self-Monitoring to Teach Functional Life Skills
Simulation	Simulation is defined as using materials and situations in the classroom that approximate the natural environmental conditions where the behavior will be performed in the community (Bates, Cuvo, Miner, & Korebek, 2001). Simulation has been used to teach purchasing skills, banking skills, functional life skills, and social skills. For example, Cihak, Alberto, Kessler, and Taber (2004) used simulation to teach secondary students with disabilities to send a fax and collate a newsletter.	• Using Simulations to Teach Purchasing Skills • Using Simulations to Teach Banking Skills • Using Simulations to Teach Functional Life Skills • Using Simulations to Teach Social Skills
System of Least Prompts	System of least prompts, or least to most prompts, is defined as a method in which the teacher begins with the least obtrusive prompt giving the student the opportunity to perform the response with little assistance, followed by a gradually increasing the level of prompting based on the degree of assistance the student needs to emit the appropriate response (Cooper et al., 2007). Least-to-most prompting has been used to teach purchasing skills, grocery shopping skills, cooking skills, functional life skills, and specific job skills. For example, Taber, Alberto, Seltzer, and Hughes (2003) used least-to-most prompts to teach secondary students with disabilities to answer a phone call or using speed dial on a cell phone when lost.	• Using a System of Least-to-Most Prompts to Teach Purchasing Skills • Using System of Least-to-Most Prompts to Teach Grocery Shopping Skills • Using System of Least-to-Most Prompts to Teach Food Preparation and Cooking Skills • Using System of Least-to-Most Prompts to Teach Functional Life Skills • Using System of Least-to-Most Prompts to Teach Specific Job Skills • Using System of Least-to-Most Prompts to Teach Safety Skills

(continued)

345

Table 19.1   Continued

Category	Description of Practice	Evidence-Based Practices
System of Most Prompts	System of most prompts, or most-to-least prompts, is defined as a method in which the teacher begins with the most obtrusive prompt (e.g., physical guidance) guiding the student through the performance sequence and gradually decreases the level of prompting as training progresses (Cooper et al., 2007). Most-to-least prompting has been used to teach functional life skills. For example, Vandercook (1991) used most-to-least prompting to teach bowling and pinball skills to secondary students with disabilities.	• Using System of Most-to-Least Prompts to Teach Functional Life Skills
Total Task Training	Total task training is defined as training a student on each step of a task analysis during every instructional setting (Cooper et al., 2007). Total task training is often used to teach functional life skills. For example, McDonnell and Laughlin (1989) used total task training to teach purchasing skills to secondary students with disabilities.	• Using Total Task Training to Teach Functional Life Skills

Evidence-Based Academic Interventions

Mnemonic Strategies	Mnemonic strategies include memory-associative techniques, keyword mnemonic strategies, keyword-pegword, and reconstructive elaborations. Mnemonic strategies have been used to teach a variety of academic skills, including North American battles, vocabulary words and definitions, mineral hardness levels, science vocabulary, and state names and capitals. For example, Mastropieri, Scruggs, Bakken, and Brigham (1992) used a mnemonic strategy to teach secondary students with learning disabilities the names of states and corresponding capitals.	
Peer Assistance	Peer assistance involves having a student deliver academic instruction to another student and includes peer tutoring, cooperative learning, and peer instruction. Peer assistance has been used to teach math skills, conversational skills, academic tasks, specific writing strategies, social interaction, and the "Next Dollar" strategy. For example, Schloss, Kobza, and Alper (1997) used reciprocal peer tutoring to teach money skills using the "Next Dollar" strategy to secondary students with intellectual disabilities.	
Self-management Strategies	Self-management strategies involve self-monitoring, self-evaluation, self-instruction, goal-setting, and strategy instruction to allow students to monitor and assess academic and behavioral performance. Self-management strategies have been used to teach academic accuracy and productivity and appropriate behavior. For example, Carr and Punzo (1993) taught secondary students with emotional disturbance to self-monitor their behavior to improve academic accuracy and productivity.	
Technological Interventions	Technology interventions involve using some form of computer-assisted instruction to teach a variety of academic skills to students (NSTTAC, 2010). Technology interventions have been used to teach reading skills, math skills, health skills, increase active student engagement, and emotional recognition. For example, Calhoon, Fuchs, and Hamlett (2000) used computer-based test accommodations to teach secondary students with learning disabilities math skills.	
Visual Displays	Visual displays are representative tools used to facilitate learning and include graphic organizers, cognitive organizers, cognitive maps, structured overviews, tree diagrams, concept maps, and Thinking Maps. Visual displays have been used to teach reading comprehension and problem solving skills. For example, Boyle (2000) used a Venn diagram strategy to teach reading comprehension skills (i.e., literal, inferential, relational) to secondary students with mild disabilities.	

Evidence-based Academic Interventions for High School Students with Disabilities

While the evidence-based practices introduced above focus on teaching self-determination skills and functional life skills, NSTTAC has also identified evidence-based academic interventions for secondary students with disabilities. These practices include mnemonic strategies (Wolgemuth, Cobb, & Alwell, 2008), peer assistance (Winokur, Cobb, & Dugan, 2007), self-management strategies (Wolgemuth, Cobb, & Dugan, 2007), technological interventions (Dugan, Cobb, & Alwell, 2007), and visual displays (Wolgemuth, Trujillo, Cobb, & Alwell, 2008). These evidence-based academic interventions are described in more detail in Table 19.1.

Evidence-Based Predictors for Secondary Transition

For more than four decades, special education researchers have been conducting correlational studies to determine what in-school programs, services, instruction, and other factors in high school promote better post-school outcomes for students with disabilities. In an effort to synthesize high quality correlational research in secondary transition since 1985 to make recommendations for improving transition programming, Test, Mazzotti, et al. (2009) conducted a systematic literature review to determine what evidence-based predictors existed. As a result, 16 in-school predictors of post-school success were identified (see Table 19.2). Each predictor is described below with examples of how they can be implemented in schools.

Career Awareness

Career awareness refers to employment-related skills acquired by students often as a result of career or vocational instruction (i.e., vocational education) provided during high school tailored to prepare students with disabilities for future post-school employment. Career awareness skills may include job search skills, interview skills, and job-specific skills. For example, students in the specialized School to Work Transition Program who exited school with high career awareness skills or high job search skills had higher post-school employment (Benz, Yovanoff, & Doren, 1997).

Based on the literature, two recommendations for implementing career awareness in secondary transition programs are: (a) use a specific career awareness strategy, curriculum, or one or more of the evidence-base practices that were described earlier in this chapter; and (b) collect data on a standardized measure or assessment conducted with students prior to exiting high school to determine the level of career awareness skills gained during their secondary school experience.

Community Experiences

Within the secondary school setting, community experiences include community-based training, which is instruction in non-school, natural environments to teach students important skills, such as (a) mobility in the community and transportation skills, (b) daily living skills, (c) developing recreational and leisure skills, and (d) using workplace skills. White and Weiner (2004) found that community experiences that included instruction in social skill development, domestic skills, accessing public transportation, and on-the-job training correlated with higher post-school employment rates for students with disabilities. Additionally, students receiving curricular content that included community access were also more likely to be engaged in post-school education (Halpern, Yovanoff, Doren, & Benz, 1995). Based on the literature, it is recommended that secondary transition programs include community-based instruction for

Table 19.2   Evidence-Based In-School Predictors of Post-School Success

Predictor/Outcome	Education	Employment	Independent Living
Career Awareness	X	X	
Community Experiences		X	
Exit Exam Requirements/High School Diploma Status		X	
Inclusion in General Education	X	X	X
Interagency Collaboration	X	X	
Occupational Courses	X	X	
Paid Employment/ Work Experience	X	X	X
Parental Involvement		X	
Program of Study		X	
Self-Advocacy/Self-Determination	X	X	
Self-Care/Independent Living	X	X	X
Social Skills	X	X	
Student Support	X	X	X
Transition Program	X	X	
Vocational Education	X	X	
Work Study		X	

students with disabilities that includes specific skill instruction in (a) finance, (b) transportation, (c) social skills, (d) self–care, and (e) on–the–job training.

High School Diploma Status

Today's schools offer multiple diploma tracks (e.g., scholars diploma, traditional diploma, occupational diploma, standard diploma, alternative diploma) aligned with students' plans for entering post-school life. Heal and Rusch (1994) found students who had higher GPAs on academic activities and received a standard high school diploma had higher post-school engagement rates than their peers with lower GPAs who did not receive a traditional diploma. Based on the literature, two recommendations for implementing this predictor in secondary transition programs are: (a) examine specific data on the students with disabilities (e.g., diploma numbers, GPAs, courses passed) who exit school; and (b) revisit current graduation and school exit requirements for students with disabilities.

Inclusion in General Education

One of the strongest predictors of post-school success is inclusion in general education, which refers to the amount of time students with disabilities spend in courses with their peers without disabilities. While inclusion in general education can mean being a part of a general education elective course (e.g., physical education, art, music), federal initiatives (IDEA, 2004; NCLB, 2001) have placed more focus on inclusion of students with disabilities in core content areas (e.g., math, reading, science, social studies). Research indicates that inclusion in general education has been linked to improved post-school outcomes (e.g., Leonard, D'Allura, & Horowitz, 1999). For example, students who participated in regular academics were five times more likely to be enrolled in postsecondary education than their peers who were not taking regular academic courses (Baer et al., 2003). Simply put, students who participate more often in highly integrated, regular education classes with age-appropriate peers fare better in post-school life than those students who do not. Based on the literature, two recommendations for implementing inclusion in general education in secondary transition programs are: (a) although schools are required by IDEA (2004) offer the least restrictive environment for each child with a disability, inclusion in general education is not always considered as a viable option for students. Schools must shift current thinking to include access and inclusion in regular education as one, and perhaps the first, option on the service continuum; and (b) IEP teams should carefully consider on a case-by-case basis, the least restrictive environment for each student.

Independent Living Skills

Self-care and independent living skills are a result of specific instructional practices that emphasize life, employment, and occupational skill development for post-school success. Independent living skills instruction includes, but is not limited to: (a) leisure skills training, (b) social skills training, (c) self-care skills training, and (d) other adaptive behavior skills training.

Research suggests that students with high self-care and independent living skills experience positive post-school outcomes. For example, Blackorby, Hancock, and Siegel (1993) found that students with high self-care skills were more likely to be engaged in post-school education, employment, and independent living than those with low self-care skills. Additionally, students with high daily living skills were more likely to have a higher quality of life (i.e., independent living) and be engaged in post-school employment (Roessler, Brolin, & Johnson, 1990). Based on the literature, it is recommended that students with disabilities receive explicit instruction and training in leisure skills, self-care, social skills, and other adaptive behavior skills.

Interagency Collaboration

Interagency collaboration involves developing relationships among multiple parties during the transition process with the goal of working towards successful post-school outcomes for students with disabilities. Interagency collaboration may include participation during the transition planning process from (a) the student, (b) parents, (c) other family members, (d) special educators, (e) general educators, (f) vocational rehabilitation counselors, (g) independent living counselors, and/or (h) other adult service providers. Coordination and implementation of services with outside agencies has been linked to post-school success. Specifically, students receiving assistance from more community-based agencies (as compared to those receiving assistance from fewer) were more likely to be engaged in post-school employment and education (Bullis, Davis, Bull, & Johnson, 1995). Based on the literature, two recommendations for implementing interagency collaboration in secondary transition programs are: (a) actively include the student, parents, and those who can represent the various agencies, organizations, providers or others who can assist in providing support and/or services that are needed to accomplish the goals and objectives of the transition plan; and (b) use community mapping as a tool to increase interagency collaboration and better prepare students for life after high school. Community mapping is often a geographical or abstract mapping of assets or services within a target community.

Occupational Courses

Occupational coursework is often part of a modified curriculum or course of study for students with significant cognitive disabilities. Such coursework focuses on the acquisition of functional skills, independent living skills, and work readiness. Research indicates that students who participate in occupational coursework have higher post-school engagement rates. For example, students who participated in occupational coursework had higher postsecondary education engagement (Halpern et al., 1995) and postsecondary employment (Heal & Rusch, 1995) than those who received no instruction in occupational courses. Based on the literature, it is recommended that secondary transition programs include a course of study option that focuses on functional academics for students with significant cognitive disabilities.

Paid Employment/Work Experience

Experience gained through paid employment is another predictor of positive post-school success for students with disabilities. Paid employment and work experience means students with disabilities had a paying job during high school. Research has found students who worked for pay during school, especially in the last two years of high school, were more likely than those who did not to be engaged in post-school education and employment (e.g., Bullis et al., 1995; Doren & Benz, 1998). Additionally, students with paid jobs as a part of a specialized transition program (e.g., Benz, Lindstrom, & Yovanoff, 2000; Benz et al., 1997) were more likely than those without paid jobs to be engaged in post-school employment. Based on the literature, two recommendations for implementing paid employment/work experience in secondary transition programs are: (a) incorporate course-related paid work experiences, and (b) use specialized transition program models (e.g., Bridge's School-to-Work Program, Youth Transition Program) that contain or promote paid work components.

Parental Involvement

Parents play a critical role in their student's educational process during the transition years. Parental involvement means parents are active contributors in providing input during a student's transition years and the IEP and educational process overall. Students whose parents take a more active participatory role in the Individualized Education Program (IEP) process had better post-school outcomes than those whose parents were not as involved. For example, Fourqurean, Meisgeier, Swank, and Williams (1991) found that students with one or more parents who participated in more IEP meetings during the 11th- and 12th-grade years were more likely to be engaged in post-school employment. Based on the literature, two recommendations for implementing parental involvement in secondary transition programs are (a) elicit input from parents during the transition planning process and (b) maintain open and consistent lines of communication with parents regarding student progress and needs.

Program of Study

A high school program of study refers to courses of study available to students based on their post-school goals. Such programs of study include courses for students who plan to: (a) attend a 4-year college or university, (b) attend a junior college or technical program, and (c) enter the workforce. There is research evidence to suggest that students who participated in a program of study that included: (a) career major (i.e., sequence of courses based on occupational goal); (b) cooperative education (i.e., combines academic and vocational studies with a job in a related field); (c) school-sponsored enterprise (i.e., involves the production of goods or services by students for sale to or use by others); and (d) technical preparation (i.e., a planned program of study with a defined career focus that links secondary and post-secondary education) were 1.2 times more likely to be engaged in post-school employment than those students not involved in such a program of study (Shandra & Hogan, 2008). Based on the literature, three recommendations for implementing such a program of study in secondary transition programs are include: (a) a sequence of courses and services aimed at a specific postsecondary goal, (b) school-based or school-sponsored enterprise services as part of the program of study, and (c) transition services and stakeholder collaborations in support of such a program of study.

Self-Determination

Field, Martin, Miller, Ward, and Wehmeyer (1998) defined self-determination as: "a combination of skills, knowledge and beliefs" that help people "engage in goal-directed, self-regulated, autonomous behavior. Self-determination requires an understanding of one's strengths and limitations and a belief in oneself as capable and effective. When acting on the basis of these skills and attitudes, individuals have greater ability to take control of their lives and assume the role of successful adults in our society" (p. 2). Self-determination is comprised of many components, including choice-making, problem-solving, decision-making, goal-setting and attainment, self-regulation, self-awareness, self-efficacy, and self-advocacy. Research indicates that students who have higher self-determination skills were more likely to be engaged in post-school employment (Wehmeyer & Schwartz, 1997). Based on the literature, three recommendations for implementing self-determination instruction in secondary transition programs are: (a) provide explicit instruction using published self-determination curricula; (b) incorporate self-determination instructional strategies into general curriculum content (e.g., goal setting and attainment in reading fluency); and (c) involve students as active participants in the IEP process.

Social Skills

For many students social skills acquisition occurs naturally. Social competence allows students with disabilities to interact successfully with others both during school and beyond. Research indicates that students in the School to Work Transition Program who exited high school with high social skills were more likely to be engaged in post-school employment (Benz et al., 1997). Additionally, students with high social skills based on teacher ratings were more likely to have a higher quality of life (i.e., independent living) and be engaged in post-school employment (Roessler et al., 1990). Based on the literature, two recommendations for implementing social skills instruction in secondary transition programs are (a) implement explicit social skills training as part of a functional curriculum and (b) make use of peers and peer-mediated social skills instruction when there is limited instructional time available for traditional teacher-directed delivery.

Student Support

Student support may come from a variety of sources, including friends, family, teachers, and other integral people during high school. For example, research has shown that those students who feel they have been supported during school often fare well in post-school life. Specifically, students who had a support network (e.g., family, friends) to find a job were more likely than those who lacked such a support network to be engaged in post-school employment (Doren & Benz, 1998). Additionally, students who indicated high levels of satisfaction with the instruction and support received during high school were more likely than those who indicated otherwise to be engaged in post-school education (Halpern et al., 1995). Based on the literature, it is recommended that secondary transition programs include parents and other family members, in addition to the student, as active participants in the transition planning process.

Transition Program

A transition program is a comprehensive set of instruction and services implemented to allow students with disabilities to successfully work towards completing post-school goals in education, employment, or independent living. Research indicates that students who take part in specialized transition programs (e.g., Youth Transition Program) or transition programs comprised of specific types of services have positive post-school outcomes. For example, Benz et al. (2000) found that students who participated in the Youth Transition Program with four or more transition goals met were more likely to be engaged in post-school employment or education. Additionally, students who received transition planning services during the year prior to leaving school were more likely to be engaged in post-school education (Halpern et al., 1995). Even more recently, Repetto, Webb, Garvan, and Washington (2002) found that those students whose transition program characteristics included services and supports, such as (a) agency referrals, (b) case management, (c) community and family services, (d) interagency collaboration with multiple service providers (e.g., mental health, Easter Seals, vocational rehabilitation), and (e)social/leisure activities were more likely to be engaged in postsecondary education. Based on the literature, two recommendations for implementing specialized transition programs in secondary transition are: (a) deliver a specific transition strategy, curriculum or program (e.g., Youth Transition Program) for students with disabilities; and (b) include transition services and collaboration among stakeholders intended to help students with disabilities achieve their identified post-school goals

Vocational Education

Vocational education addresses strategies for choosing and preparing a career, skills and work habits that lead to success in future schooling and work, and skills such as interviewing, writing resumes, and completing applications that are needed for acceptance into college, or other post-secondary training or to the workforce. Research indicates that students who participated in vocational education were two times more likely to be engaged in full-time employment post-school (Baer et al., 2003). Harvey (2002) also found that students with vocational credits in high school were more likely to be engaged in post-school employment and education. Technology training also predicted post-school success for students with disabilities, in that students who received such training were more than twice as likely to be employed after high school (Leonard et al., 1999). Based on the literature, two recommendations for implementing vocational education in secondary transition programs are: (a) embed specific vocational courses or vocational education instruction within core curricula; and (b) increase the enrollment in, and support for, students with disabilities in vocational education courses within school programs.

Work Study

Work study is a program offered by most schools in which students spend a portion of their day taking traditional courses on the school's campus and the remaining part of the day at a job site working for pay or credit hours. Research has found that involvement in work study correlates with higher rates of post-school employment. For example, Baer et al. (2003) found that students who participated in work study were two times more likely to be engaged in full-time post-school employment than those who did not. Additionally, students who participated in the Bridges School to Work Program in their last year of high school and completed their internships were four times more likely to be employed post-school (Luecking & Fabian, 2000). Based on the literature, it is recommended secondary transition programs include a work study program for students with disabilities.

Implications and Recommendations

So far, this chapter has focused on providing school leaders information about evidence-based practices and predictors for secondary transition, as well as strategies for their use at classroom and school levels. The remainder of this chapter describes implications and recommendations for leaders in secondary transition and school reform and improving school completion rates.

Secondary Transition and School Reform

While it can appear that school reform has been constant in education, recently two similar schools of thought have achieved prominence. First, *Breaking Ranks II* (National Association of Secondary School Principals, 2004), outlined a process of change designed to ensure success for every high school student based on three core areas: (a) collaborative leadership, professional learning communities, and strategic data use; (b) personalizing the high school environment; and (c) student-centered curriculum, instruction, and assessment. Within these core areas were recommendations for a Personal Plan for Progress, real-life application of knowledge, relationships with individuals, organizations, and businesses, families as partners, and high schools coordinating delivery of physical and mental health and social services for youth.

These, as well as other recommendations are closely related to the 16 secondary transition evidence-based predictors (Test, Mazzotti, et al., 2009) described earlier in this chapter. As a result, secondary transition and the call for high school reform to make learning more student-centered are indeed compatible. In fact, the call for each student to have a Personal Plan for Progress, sometimes called an Individual Learning Plan, is similar to the IEP required for all students with disabilities. In addition, by having each high school student's post-school goals for education, employment, and independent living (if necessary) "drive" the content of the IEP, transition IEPs clearly meet the school reform recommendations for student-centered assessment, instruction, and curriculum.

More recently, the call for all students to be "college and career ready" (Bill & Melinda Gates Foundation, 2009; United States Department of Education, 2010) also aligns with the transition planning process and evidence-based predictors (Test, Mazzotti, et al., 2009). After all, the goal of any successful transition plan and program is to prepare each student with a disability to graduate from high school ready to take the next step towards college and a career. In fact, the dream of going to college was recently improved for students with intellectual disabilities when the Higher Education Opportunity Act (P.L. 110-315) was enacted on August 14, 2008. The law contained important new financial aid provisions, as well as creating a new model demonstration program designed to improve access to postsecondary education for students with intellectual disabilities.

Improving School Completion Rates

While school completion rates for students with disabilities appear to be improving, the 2007–2008 Individuals with Disabilities Education Act data (Data Accountability Center, 2010) indicated 59.3% of students with disabilities graduated with a diploma, 14.5% exited with a certificate, 1.5% aged out, and 24.7% dropped out. Hopefully, no one believes these numbers are acceptable, and therefore, strategies are needed to help improve school completion rates for students with disabilities. Fortunately, there are a number of resources available. First, the National High School Center (2010) has developed tools for collecting and using early warning data systems to identify students at-risk for dropping out. They recommend collecting data on school performance (i.e., freshman course failure, freshman GPA, credits earned) and attendance. Second, *Check and Connect* (Sinclair, Christenson, & Thurlow, 2005), a dropout prevention program for both students with and without disabilities, has been identified as a secondary transition evidence-based practice (Test, Fowler, et al., 2009). Finally, the National Dropout Center for Students with Disabilities has a searchable database of model dropout prevention programs on their Website at http://ndpcsd-eb.clemson.edu/modelprograms/index.php. Together, these resources provide an excellent starting point for school leaders who want to develop programs to increase school completion rates for students with disabilities, as well as all students.

In conclusion, secondary "transition is not just a program or a project or a set of activities that has a beginning and end. It is a vision and goal for unfolding the fullest possible potential for an individual and a systematic framework for planning to fulfill that potential" (Kochhar-Bryant & Bassett, 2002, p.19). This goal can be met for all students if school leaders adopt the concept of transition-focused education (Kohler & Field, 2003).

References

Achieve. (2010). *Race to the Top: Accelerating college and career readiness in states.* Retrieved from http://www.achieve.org/RacetotheTop

Agran, M., Blanchard, C., & Wehmeyer, M. L. (2000). Promoting transition goals and self-determination through student self-directed learning: The Self-Determined Learning Model of Instruction. *Education and Training in Mental Retardation and Developmental Disabilities, 35,* 351–364.

Alberto, P. A., Cihak, D. F., & Gamma, R. I. (2005). Use of static picture prompts versus video modeling during simulation instruction. *Research in Developmental Disabilities, 26,* 327–339.

Alberto, P. A., & Troutman, A. C. (2009). *Applied behavior analysis for teachers* (8th ed.). Upper Saddle River, NJ: Pearson Education.

Ayres, K. M., Langone, J., Boon, R. T., & Norman, A. (2006). Computer-based instruction for purchasing skills. *Education and Training in Developmental Disabilities, 41,* 253–263.

Baer, R. M., Flexer, R. W., Beck, S., Amstutz, N., Hoffman, L., Brothers, J., ... Zechman, C. (2003). A collaborative followup study on transition service utilization and post-school outcomes. *Career Development for Exceptional Individuals, 26,* 7–25.

Bates, P. E., Cuvo, T., Miner, C. A., & Korabek, C. A. (2001). A simulated and community-based instruction involving persons with mild and moderate mental retardation. *Research in Developmental Disabilities, 22,* 95–115.

Benz, M. R., Lindstrom, L., & Yovanoff, P. (2000). Improving graduation and employment outcomes of students with disabilities: Predictive factors and student perspectives. *Exceptional Children, 66,* 509–541.

Benz, M. R., Yovanoff, P., & Doren, B. (1997). School-to-work components that predict postschool success for students with and without disabilities. *Exceptional Children, 63,* 151–165.

Bill and Melinda Gates Foundation. (2009). *College-ready education plan.* Retrieved from http://www.gatesfoundation.org/college-ready-education/Pages/default.aspx

Blackorby, J., Hancock, G. R., & Siegel, S. (1993). *Human capital and structural explanations of post-school success for youth with disabilities: A latent variable exploration of the National Longitudinal Transition Study.* Menlo Park, CA: SRI International.

Blackorby, J., & Wagner, M. (1996). Longitudinal postschool outcomes of youth with disabilities: Findings from the National Longitudinal Transition Study. *Exceptional Children, 62,* 399–413.

Boone, R. (1992). Involving culturally diverse parents in transition planning. *Career Development for Exceptional Individuals, 15,* 205–221.

Bozkurt, F., & Gursel, O. (2005). Effectiveness of constant time delay on teaching snack and drink preparation skills to children with mental retardation. *Education & Training in Developmental Disabilities, 40,* 390–400.

Boyle, J. R. (2000). The effects of a Venn diagram strategy on the literal, inferential, and relational comprehension of students with mild disabilities. *Learning Disabilities: A Multidisciplinary Journal, 10,* 5–13.

Brown, L., Nisbet, J., Ford, A., Sweet, M., Shiraga, B., York, J., & Loomis, R. (1983). The critical need for nonschool instruction in educational programs for severely handicapped students. *Journal of the Association for Persons with Severe Handicaps, 8,* 71–77.

Bullis, M., Davis, C., Bull, B., & Johnson, B. (1995). Transition achievement among young adults with deafness: What variables relate to success? *Rehabilitation Counseling Bulletin, 39,* 130–150.

Calhoon, M. B., Fuchs, L. S., & Hamlett, C. L. (2000). Effects of computer-based test accommodations on mathematics performance assessments for secondary students with learning disabilities. *Learning Disability Quarterly, 23,* 271–282.

Carr, S. C., & Punzo, R. P. (1993). The effects of self-monitoring of academic accuracy and productivity on the performance of students with behavioral disorders. *Behavior Disorders, 18,* 241–250.

Cihak, D. F., Alberto, P. A., Kessler, K. B., & Taber, T. A. (2004). An investigation of instructional scheduling arrangements for community-based instruction. *Research in Developmental Disabilities: A Multidisciplinary Journal, 25,* 67–88.

Common Core State Standards Initiative. (2010). *Common Core State Standards.* Retrieved from http://www.corestandards.org/

Cooper, J. O., Heron, T. E., & Heward, W. L. (2007). *Applied behavior analysis* (2nd ed.). Upper Saddle River, NJ: Pearson.

Data Accountability Center. (2010). *Number of students ages 14 through 21 with disabilities served under IDEA, Part B, who exited school, by exit reason and state: Fall 2007–08*, http://www.ideadata.org/TABLES32ND/AR_4-1.htm

Denny, P. J., & Test, D. W. (1995). Using the one-more-than technique to teach money counting to individuals with moderate mental retardation: A systematic replication. *Education and Treatment of Children, 18,* 422–432.

Doren, B., & Benz, M. R. (1998). Employment inequality revisited: Predictors of better employment outcomes for young women with disabilities in transition. *The Journal of Special Education, 31,* 425–442.

Dugan, J. J., Cobb, R. B., & Alwell, M. (2007). *The effects of technology-based interventions on academic outcomes for youth with disabilities.* Ft. Collins: Colorado State University, School of Education.

Field, S., Martin, J., Miller, R., Ward, M., & Wehmeyer, M. (1998). *A practical guide to teaching self-determination.* Reston, VA: Council for Exceptional Children.

Fourqurean, J. M., Meisgeier, C., Swank, P. R., & Williams, R. E. (1991). Correlates of postsecondary employment outcomes for young adults with learning disabilities. *Journal of Learning Disabilities, 24,* 400–405.

Gast, D. L., & Winterling, V. (1992). Teaching first-aid skills to students with moderate handicaps in small group instruction. *Education & Treatment of Children, 15,* 101–125.

Halpern, A. (1985). Transition: A look at the foundations. *Exceptional Children, 51,* 479–486.

Halpern, A. S., Yovanoff, P., Doren, B., & Benz, M. R. (1995) Predicting participation in postsecondary education for school leavers with disabilities. *Exceptional Children, 62,* 151–164.

Harvey, M. W. (2002). Comparison and postsecondary transitional outcomes between students with and without disabilities by secondary vocational education participation: Findings from the National Education Longitudinal Study. *Career Development for Exceptional Individuals, 25,* 99–122.

Hasazi, S., Gordon, L., & Roe, C. (1985). Factors associated with the employment status of handicapped youth exiting high school from 1979–1983. *Exceptional Children, 51,* 455–469.

Heal, L. W., & Rusch, F. R. (1994). Prediction of residential independence of special education high school students. *Research in Developmental Disabilities, 15,* 223–243.

Heal, L. W., & Rusch, F. R. (1995). Predicting employment for students who leave special education high school programs. *Exceptional Children, 61,* 472–487.

Horner, R. H., Jones, D. N., & Williams, J. A. (1985). A functional approach to teaching generalized street crossing. *Journal of the Association for Persons with Severe Handicaps, 10,* 71–78.

Individuals with Disabilities Education Act of 1990, P. L. No. 101-476.

Individuals with Disabilities Education Act of 1997, P. L. No. 105-17.

Individuals with Disabilities Education Improvement Act of 2004, P. L. No. 108-446, 20 U.S.C.

Individuals with Disabilities Education Improvement Act of 2004, Public Law No. 108-446, 20 U. S. C. 1400, H. R. 1350.

Kochhar-Bryant, C. A., & Bassett, D. S. (2002). Challenge and promise in aligning transition and standards-based education. In C. A. Kochhar-Bryant & D. S. Bassett (Eds.), *Aligning transition and standards-based education: Issues and strategies* (pp. 1–24). Arlington, VA: Council for Exceptional Children.

Kohler, P. D., & Field, S. (2003). Transition-focused education: Foundation for the future. *Journal of Special Education, 37,* 174–183.

Lamb, S. J., Bibby, P. A., & Wood, D. J. (1997): Promoting the communication skills of children with moderate learning difficulties. *Child Language Teaching and Therapy, 13,* 261–278.

Lee S., Wehmeyer, M. L., Palmer, S. B., Soukup, J. H., & Little, T. D. (2008). Self-determination and access to the general curriculum. *Journal of Special Education, 42,* 91–107.

Leonard, R., D'Allura, T., & Horowitz, A. (1999). Factors associated with employment among persons who have a vision impairment: A follow-up of vocational placement referrals. *Journal of Vocational Rehabilitation, 12,* 33–43.

Luecking, R. G., & Fabian, E. S. (2000). Paid internships and employment success for youth in transition. *Career Development for Exceptional Individuals, 23,* 205–221.

Martin, J. E., Van Dycke, J. L., Christensen, W. R., Greene, B. A., Gardner, J. E., & Lovett, D. L. (2006). Increasing student participation in their transition IEP meetings: Establishing the *Self-Directed IEP* as an evidenced-based practice. *Exceptional Children, 72,* 299–316.

Mastropieri, M. A., Scruggs, T. E., Bakken, J. P., & Brigham, F. J. (1992). A complex mnemonic strategy for teaching states and their capitals: Comparing forward and backward associations. *Learning Disabilities Research & Practice, 7,* 96–103.

McDonnell, J. (1987). The effects of time delay and increasing prompt hierarchy strategies on the acquisition of purchasing skills by students with severe handicaps. *The Journal of the Association for Persons with Severe Handicaps, 12,* 227–236.

McDonnell, J., & Laughlin, B. (1989). A comparison of time delay and decreasing prompt hierarchy strategies in teaching banking skills to students with moderate handicaps. *Journal of Applied Behavior Analysis, 22,* 85–91.

McDonnell, J., & McFarland, S. (1988). A comparison of forward and concurrent chaining strategies in teaching laundromat skills to students with severe handicaps. *Research in Developmental Disabilities, 9,* 177–194.

Mechling, L. C. (2004). Effects of multimedia computer-based instruction on grocery shopping fluency. *Journal of Special Education Technology, 19,* 23–34.

Morsink, C. V. (1988). Preparing teachers as collaborators in special education. *The Clearing House: A Journal of Educational Strategies, Issues, and Ideas, 61,* 317–319.

National Association of Secondary School Principals. (2004). *Breaking ranks II: Strategies for leading high school reform.* Reston, VA: Author.

National Governors Association. (2010). *P-16 frequently asked questions.* Retrieved from http://www.nga.org/files/pdf/0506P16.FAQ.pdf

National High School Center. (2010). *Developing early warning systems to identify potential high school dropouts.* Retrieved from http://www.betterhighschools.org/topics/DropoutWarningSigns.asp

National Secondary Transition Technical Assistance Center (NSTTAC). (2008). *Ordering in a Restaurant.* Charlotte, NC: Author.

National Secondary Transition Technical Assistance Center (NSTTAC). (2009). *Indicator 13 checklist.* Retrieved from http://www.nsttac.org/content/nsttac-i-13-checklist

Newman, L., Wagner, M., Cameto, R., & Knokey, A.M. (2009). *The post-high school outcomes of youth with disabilities up to 4 years after high school. A report of findings from the national longitudinal transition study-2 (NLTS2) (NCSER 2009-3017).* Menlo Park, CA: SRI International. Retrieved from http://www.nlts2.org/reports/2009_04/nlts2_report_2009_04_complete.pdf

No Child Left Behind Act of 2001, Pub. L. No. 107-110, 115 Stat.1425 (2002).

Office of Special Education Programs (OSEP). (2009). Part B SPP/APR Indicator/measurement table. Retrieved from http://www2.ed.gov/policy/speced/guid/idea/bapr/2010/b2-1820-0624bmeastable111210.doc

Okolo, C. M, Bahr, C. M., & Rieth, H. J. (1993). A retrospective view of computer-based instruction. *Journal of Special Education Technology, 12*(1), 1–27.

Repetto, J. B., Webb, K. W., Garvan, C. W., & Washington, T. (2002). Connecting student outcomes with transition practices in Florida. *Career Development for Exceptional Individuals, 25,* 123–139.

Roessler, R. T., Brolin, D. E., & Johnson, J. M. (1990). Factors affecting employment success and quality. *Career Development for Exceptional Individuals, 13,* 95–107.

Schloss, P. J., Kobza, S. A., & Alper, S. (1997). The use of peer tutoring for the acquisition of functional math skills among students with moderate retardation. *Education and Treatment of Children, 20,* 189–208.

Shandra, C. L., & Hogan, D. P. (2008). School-to-work program participation and the post-high school employment of young adults with disabilities. *Journal of Vocational Rehabilitation, 29,* 117–130.

Sinclair, M. F., Christenson, S. L., & Thurlow, M. L. (2005). Promoting school completion of urban secondary youth with emotional or behavioral disabilities. *Exceptional Children, 71,* 465–482.

Taber, T. A., Alberto, P. A., Seltzer, A., & Hughes, M. (2003). Obtaining assistance when lost in the community using cell phones. *Research and Practice for Persons with Severe Disabilities, 28,* 105–116.

Taylor, P., Collins, B. C., Schuster, J. W., & Kleinert, H. (2002). Teaching laundry skills to high school students with disabilities: Generalization of targeted skills and nontargeted information. *Education and Training in Mental Retardation and Developmental Disabilities, 37,* 172–183.

Test, D. W., Aspel, N., & Everson, J. (2006). *Transition methods for youth with disabilities.* Columbus, OH: Merrill/Prentice Hall.

Test, D. W., Fowler, C. H., Richter, S. M., White, J., Mazzotti, V., Walker, A. R., … Kortering, L. (2009). Evidence-based practices in secondary transition. *Career Development for Exceptional Individuals, 32,* 115–128.

Test, D. W., Mason, C., Hughes, C., Konrad, M., Neale, M., & Wood, W. (2004). Student involvement in individualized education program meetings. *Exceptional Children, 70,* 391–412.

Test, D. W., Mazzotti, V. L., Mustian, A. L., Fowler, C. H., Kortering, L. J., & Kohler, P. H. (2009). Evidence-based secondary transition predictors for improving post-school outcomes for students with disabilities. *Career Development for Exceptional Individuals, 32,* 160–181.

U.S. Department of Education. (2010). *ESEA blueprint for reform.* Office of planning, Washington, DC: Office of Planning, Evaluation, and Policy Development.

Van Reusen, A. K., Bos, C., & Schumaker, J. B. (1994) *Self-advocacy strategy for education and transition planning.* Lawrence, KS: Edge Enterprises.

Vandercook, T. (1991). Leisure instruction outcomes: Criterion performance, positive interactions, and acceptance by typical high school peers. *The Journal of Special Education, 25,* 320–339.

Wehman, P., Kregal, J., & Seyfarth, J. (1985). Transition from school to work for individuals with severe handicaps: A follow-up study. *The Journal of the Association for Persons with Severe Handicaps, 10,* 132–136.

Wehmeyer, M., & Lawrence, M. (1995). *Whose future is it anyway?* Promoting student involvement in transition planning. *Career Development for Exceptional Individuals, 18,* 69–83.

Wehmeyer, M. L., & Schwartz, M. (1997). Self-determination and positive adult outcomes: A follow-up study of youth with mental retardation or learning disabilities. *Exceptional Children, 63,* 245–255.

White, J., & Weiner, J. S. (2004). Influence of least restrictive environment and community based training on integrated employment outcomes for transitioning students with severe disabilities. *Journal of Vocational Rehabilitation, 21,* 149–156.

Will, M. (1984, March–April). Bridges from school to working life. *Programs for the Handicapped.* Washington, DC: Clearinghouse on the Handicapped.

Winokur, M. A., Cobb, R. B., & Dugan, J. J. (2007*). Effects of academic peer assistance interventions on academic outcomes for youth with disabilities: A systematic review.* Ft. Collins: Colorado State University, School of Education.

Wolgemuth, J. R., Cobb, R. B., & Alwell, M. (2008). The effects of mnemonic interventions on academic outcomes for youth with disabilities: A systematic review. *Learning Disabilities Research, 23,* 1–10.

Wolgemuth, J. R., Cobb, R. B., & Dugan. J. J. (2007). *The effects of self-management interventions on academic outcomes for youth with disabilities.* Ft. Collins: Colorado State University, School of Education.

Wolgemuth, J. R., Trujillo, E., Cobb, R. B., & Alwell, M. (2008). *The effects of visual display interventions on academic outcomes for youth with disabilities: A systematic review.* What Works in Transition: Systematic Review Project. Colorado: Colorado State University.

Section V
Challenges for Educational Leaders
Introduction

Problems in complex organizations seldom have one "best solution." Instead, there are multiple imperfect solutions competing for attention and a few superior solutions lurking about somewhere—solutions that satisfy more preferences, increase the range of future options, allow the attainment of more common purposes, and avoid negative consequences. The better solutions are far more likely to be found if other people help you look.... As Aristotle said, "Feasts to which many contribute may excel those provided at one person's expense."

(Keohane, 2010, p. 60)

Contemporary educational leaders typically confront problems in the complex organization of schools that similarly have no one "best solution." As Keohane (2010) suggests, superior solutions lurk about somewhere, and we are optimistic that the authors who contributed to this volume will help us find them. In this last section of the book McLaughlin, Smith, and Wilkinson (Chapter 20) synthesize the critical research that informs leadership for special education from preschool through post-secondary transition and consider the challenges facing educational leaders. In doing so, they draw from the knowledge bases of both special education and educational leadership to help frame critical questions and point the way toward more effective and learner-centered inclusive leadership practices.

McLaughlin and her colleagues examine how the current educational policy context emphasizes the use of a rigorous curriculum with state imposed standards in the education of all students, including students with disabilities. Accordingly, the standards-based reform movement is seen as a way to promote educational equity and ensure that students reach, at minimum, state-defined levels of proficiency. However; there is some misalignment between the standards-based reform model and the principle of individualization in IDEA, yet the standards-based education movement has significant effects on students with disabilities. The biggest challenges concern the implications for leadership in reconciling the ambiguities between standards-based education and special education policies.

McLaughlin et al. capture the effects of various policies on the shaping of leadership for special education as they intertwine with educational policy and reform initiatives. As does Skrtic (Chapter 8), these authors challenge the contemporary interpretation of educational policies, interpretations that have made processes bureaucratic and moribund rather than inclusive and democratic while attempting to attain high levels of student achievement.

McLaughlin et al. emphasize that the misalignment between the standards-based reform model and the principle of individualization in IDEA needs to be resolved. Using evidence that supports and informs the utility of these reforms, these authors also consider greater levels of accountability so that students with disabilities not only have opportunities to learn in the contexts of general education schools and classrooms, but also to achieve the standards set for all students. The chapter concludes with a discussion of the implications for leadership in reconciling the ambiguities between standards-based education and special education policies as discussed throughout this volume.

References

Keohane, N. O. (2010). *Thinking about leadership*. Princeton, NJ: Princeton University Press.

20

Challenges for Leaders in the Not-So-New Era of Standards

Margaret J. McLaughlin

UNIVERSITY OF MARYLAND

Amy F. Smith

UNIVERSITY OF CALIFORNIA AT DAVIS

Tracy G. Wilkinson

UNIVERSITY OF MARYLAND

It is a well-established fact that over the past 40 years, individuals with higher levels of education have become the winners in the U.S. economy as measured by non-stagnant wages and greater job security (Elman & O'Rand, 2004). As the nation's economy became increasingly linked to the U.S. educational system, a spate of reforms, affecting all aspects of pre-k–20 education, have been initiated. The overriding goal of these reforms has focused on leveling the economic playing fields among our nation's children by attempting to reduce the contribution of a child's socio-economic and family background to his or her ultimate economic attainment. These reforms also shifted our view of what is fair and just from one that would distribute resources, such as funds, equally among children to one that endeavors to equitably distribute educational attainment and thus economic opportunity.

The Evolution of Today's Standards and Educational Policies

Most everyone cites the 1983 National Commission on Excellence in Education (NCEE) report, *A Nation at Risk*, as the genesis of the standards movement. While this was perhaps the most politically visible as well as alarming report, it was followed by a wave of others expressing concerns about the quality of education in the United States. For instance, an influential group were the governors, legislators and education policymakers who were members of a long-standing regional organization called the Southern Regional Education Board (SREB) which released 12 goals aimed at meeting or exceeding national standards for education by the year 2000 (Vinovskis, 1999). The SREB's Goals for Education: Challenge 2000 were comprehensive and addressed first grade readiness, decreasing school drop-out rates, regular assessment of postsecondary institution quality, and maintaining or increasing state funding for education (Vinovskis, 1999). The election of President George H.W. Bush in 1988, after a campaign in which both candidates made promises to reform education, set the stage for a historic meeting between Bush and the governors of all 50 states. The President's Education Summit, held in Charlottesville, Virginia, in September 1989, resulted in the development of six national education goals, including increasing the nation's high school graduation rate to 90% or better, assessing student performance in critical subjects at regular intervals and moving American students to the top achievers on international math and science assessments by the year 2000 (Bush, 1990).

These six goals were eventually incorporated into Goals 2000: Educate America Act (PL 103-227), which later was folded into the 1994 reauthorization of the 1965 Elementary and Secondary Education Act (ESEA, PL 103-382), Improving America's Schools Act. This legislation required that states to develop academic standards academic standards and assess the progress of their students toward meeting those standards (Geenen, Thurlow, & Ysseldyke, 1995). Further, states were to hold schools and local districts accountable for the levels of progress on state assessments achieved by students (McLaughlin & Thurlow, 2003). The changes made to the 1994 ESEA further evolved into the 2001 No Child Left Behind Act (PL 107-110) and foreshadowed changes made to the Individuals with Disabilities Education Act (IDEA) in the 1997 and 2004 amendments which will be discussed later in this chapter.

The Theory of Action Underlying Standards

The educational policies developed over the past 30 years are referred to as "standards-based" or "standards-driven" and have been criticized by educators as an idea that emerged from a business model that treats schools as factories and students like widgets. Key to understanding the intent of the standards movement is to understand how standards became linked to educational equity during the post *Brown v. Board of Education* decision. In 1966, the Equality of Educational Opportunity Study (EEOS) (Coleman et al., 1966), also known as the Coleman Study, was commissioned by the U.S. Department of Health, Education, and Welfare to assess the availability of educational opportunities available to children of different race, color, religion, and national origin. This study, conducted in response to provisions of the Civil Rights Act of 1964, was designed to assess the resource inequities across schools across the United States. The assumption underlying the study was that if students had access to schools with the same level of resources, including funding, facilities, teacher/pupil ratios, and curricular materials, they would have equal opportunity (Coleman, 1968; O'Neill, 1976). Thus, equity became linked to equality in funding, facilities, teachers and curriculum (O'Neill, 1976). The Coleman report documented wide disparities among schools in terms of funding and other critical educational resources, but it is probably best known for its conclusion that a child's economic status accounted for more of the variation in achievement than level of school resources. This conclusion began to shift thinking among progressive education policymakers from ensuring access to the same resources to beginning to focus on access to the same educational outcomes (Coleman, 1968).

The Role of Government in Education

A central tension in educational policy is the appropriate role of government or the state. For much of our country's history, policies have more or less been grounded in the belief that government should provide the opportunities for children to access a basic level of education if a child and his/her family desired (McLaughlin, 2010). However, following the Coleman Report and subsequent analyses and reanalysis, a new national focus on educational equity shifted toward measuring equity in terms of outcomes and began to redefine the role of government from passively providing resources to structuring or coercing school systems to ensure that they not only distributed resources equally, but were proactive in making sure that all students received the same or equivalent educational outcomes (McLaughlin, 2010; O'Neill, 1976). The thinking underlying the policy was the evidence that larger societal, economic and cultural forces limit students' educational outcomes and education must attempt to compensate for these factors (McLaughlin, 2010; O'Neill, 1976). From a resource perspective, this interpretation of educational equity became what Berne and Stiefel (1984) later defined as horizontal and vertical equity. Horizontal equity is interpreted as schools having equal or equivalent inputs such as funding or teacher/student ratios while vertical equity assumes that different or unequal inputs may be required to attain equal outcomes—in short that unequal students require unequal treatment (Berne & Stiefel, 1984). Further, the measure of equal treatment became the size of the gap in achievement between students with the most resources and those with the least, defined in terms of race and family income. The idea of equal outcomes requires standardization of outcomes and this notion of equity easily fused with the call for higher national standards and national competitiveness articulated in the reports of the early 1980s that were cited earlier in this chapter.

However, simply specifying universal standards is insufficient without a way to measure student attainment of those standards and a metric for determining equality. Thus, the need for universal assessments and benchmarks for measuring student progress became part of the standards movement. The third prong of the movement, accountability, combines both a business model of improvement with a civil rights notion of equity. The premise of the improvement cycle taken from a business model is that educational organizations such as schools and districts need clear goals and performance targets and information about student performance and if that information is fed back into the system schools will be able to detect educational problems and make appropriate changes in policies, practices, and instruction leading to improved student achievement (Hanushek & Raymond, 2002; Ladd, 2002; Mazzeo, 2002). An important part of the business model is the system of rewards and sanctions in which effective schools are provided with rewards and incentives and low-performing schools are subject to interventions designed to assist the schools in improving student learning (Hanushek & Raymond, 2002; Ladd, 2002).

The civil rights perspective centers on the role of government in this model, which believes that government must create and enforce policies that ensure educational equity, which is defined as equal outcomes. In order to implement the business/civil rights models of reform, policymakers must first reach a consensus on which subject matter content matters most and the levels of performance required of all students. Then, reliable and valid assessment tools must be used to measure student progress toward the standards. Presumably only then can incentives and sanctions truly work as the system requires valid and reliable information in order to design improvements.

The 2001 reauthorization of the ESEA, the No Child Left Behind Act defines current U.S. educational policy. The provisions of this law and its predecessor, the 1994 reauthorization of ESEA, have greatly changed the role of government in ensuring educational equity. States are required to establish rigorous academic and achievement standards, measure how students perform on the state assessments relative to the state standards, and hold school districts as well as individual schools accountable for meeting pre-specified levels of student performance on assessments as well as selected other indicators, such as attendance and graduation rates (Johnson, Thurlow, & Stout, 2007; Katsiyannis, Zhang, Ryan, & Jones, 2007). Accountability is based on both the aggregate performance of students as well as the disaggregated performance of specific student subgroups, including students with disabilities.

Students with Disabilities and the Standards Movement

Advocates for students with disabilities were aware early on that unless these children and youth were specifically addressed in emerging standards–based educational policies, they would be ignored and denied an opportunity to benefit from new programs and resources. These students were specifically noted in the Goals 2000 legislation but only to the extent that it was made clear that the provisions applied to this group of students. Recognizing that there were many answered questions regarding how students with disabilities could or should participate in standards, Goals 2000 contained a special provision that the National Academy of Sciences establish a committee to conduct a comprehensive study of the inclusion of students with disabilities in school reforms supported under the law (Sec. 1015). A report, *Educating One and All* (McDonnell, McLaughlin, & Morison, 1997) was issued with 12 recommendations based on two principles: "All students should have access to challenging standards and policymakers and educators should be held publicly accountable for every student's performance" (p. 9). The committee considered both principles to be consistent with the IDEA and the evolving federal legislation. The committee also recognized some of the most serious challenges to achieving the full inclusion in the standards-based reforms. Some of these were addressed in the 1997 amendments to the Individuals with Disabilities Education Act (IDEA) which added many new requirements that increased the inclusion and accountability of students with disabilities.

The 1997 reauthorization marked the first time that states were required to include students with disabilities in state and district-wide assessments (Zhang, Katsiyannis, & Kortering, 2007). These amendments state in section (612)(a)(17), paragraph (1)(A) that "children with disabilities are included in general State and district-wide assessment programs, with appropriate accommodations, where necessary." The amended law also required that state and local districts report the performance of students with disabilities on these assessments just as they report the performance of students without disabilities (IDEA 1997, Section 612(a)(17)(B)). The 1997 amendments included additional accountability provisions requiring states to develop alternate assessments for students with disabilities who are unable to participate in the general administration of state assessments, create performance goals and indicators for students with disabilities, and report progress toward meeting these goals to the public and the federal government (Kohl, McLaughlin, & Nagle, 2006; McLaughlin & Thurlow, 2003; Thurlow & Johnson, 2000). However, these amendments did not address how state standards or accountability systems were to explicitly apply to students with disabilities. This was remedied with the passage of No Child Left Behind wherein students with disabilities were addressed in statute and regulation as one of the subgroups required to meet specific achievement targets.

The requirements under NCLB are well known by now and include considerations of how students with disabilities are to participate in state assessments as well as in the central accountability mechanism, adequate yearly progress (AYP). In the years after NCLB was enacted, a trend of schools not making AYP solely because of the performance of students with disabilities began to develop (Center on Education Policy, CEP, 2009b). Because of this, the U.S. Department of Education (USDE) made the decision to change policies and allow exceptions for certain groups of students with disabilities in 2003 and 2005. The 2003 exception, often referred to as the 1% rule, allowed schools to test students with the most significant cognitive disabilities using alternate assessments tied to alternate standards, and school districts were allowed to count no more than 1% of the passing scores from these assessments toward their AYP calculations. A second exception was introduced in 2005, often referred to as the 2% rule, in which schools were allowed to test additional students other than those with significant cognitive disabilities using alternate assessments tied to modified standards. As with the previous exception, school districts were allowed to count no more than 2% of the passing scores on these assessments toward their AYP calculations (34 C.F.R Section 200). In 2007, additional regulations were introduced that gave states the option to offer an alternate assessment based on modified standards. This is not a requirement under NCLB, and as of late 2009, only eight states have developed and implemented this type of assessment (Albus, Lazarus, Thurlow, & Cormier, 2009). Of particular note, however, is that both alternate and modified assessments are to be aligned with a state's academic content standards. Thus, students with disabilities are required to have the opportunity to learn the same content as their peers without disabilities.

IDEA 2004. The 2004 reauthorization of IDEA continued to include amendments requiring states to include students with disabilities in state and district-wide assessments (Katsiyannis et al., 2007). Provisions were included to better align IDEA with NCLB. Under the 2004 reauthorization of IDEA, states and school districts must report the number of students with disabilities who participated in the regular administration of the state's assessment, the number utilizing reasonable accommodations during the administration of the assessment, and the numbers of students with disabilities participating in alternate assessments. The assessment results of all of these students must also be reported (IDEA 2004, Section 1412(16)(B)). Specific to standards are the inclusion of several new requirements for states, like establishing goals for the performance of students with disabilities that match with the state's definition of AYP and monitoring graduation and dropout rates (Katsiyannis et al., 2007). This alignment also included requirements for alternate assessments to be aligned with state academic achievement standards or alternate standards if a state has developed them under NCLB regulations. The alignment of IDEA with NCLB gives students with disabilities a better opportunity to access the same general curriculum as their peers and potentially improve outcomes for this group of students (Nolet & McLaughlin, 2005).

The Next Phase of the Standards Movement

For anyone who imagined that the standards movement would pass, it is not over. Several recent developments attest to this. These include a major step toward the standardization of standards. That is, instead of 50 plus sets of standards and assessments, the movement is toward one common set of state standards.

Common Core State Standards.

The Kindergarten-12 Common Core State Standards were introduced in June 2010 by the Council of Chief State School Officers (CCSSO) and the National Governors Association Center for Best Practices (NGA Center; Common Core State Standards Initiative, 2010b). The standards, which were developed by the two organizations after extensive feedback from various stakeholders in education, consist of expectations for students in all grade levels in the subject areas of English language arts and mathematics. These new standards build upon the college- and career-readiness standards, also developed by CCSSO and the NGA Center, and provide the research-based, more rigorous approach that the organizations believe will better prepare students for higher education and their careers. As of June 2010, 48 states, the District of Columbia, and two United States territories have stated that they plan to adopt the Common Core State Standards as their state academic standards.

The CCSSO and NGA Center believe that the Common Core State Standards give students with disabilities "an historic opportunity to improve access to rigorous academic content" (Common Core State Standards Initiative, 2010a, para. 2). The organizations recommend that schools provide additional supports to students with disabilities during instruction, including accommodations, assistive technology, and methods informed by the principles of Universal Design for Learning, so that access to the general curriculum and opportunities for success under the new standards can be maximized.

Common Assessments. Consistent with the model of standards driven reform, assessments of student performance must be aligned with the established standards. The Race to the Top Fund was introduced in 2009 as a competitive grant program funded by the American Recovery and Reinvestment Act of 2009 (ARRA) as a means to encourage educational reform by awarding states additional federal funding for developing plans to increase student achievement (Race to the Top Fund, 2010). One of the selection criteria upon which state applications are evaluated is development and implementation of "common, high-quality assessments" (p. 19507) as part of a multi-state consortium. Additionally, states that show evidence of participation in a consortium that includes more than half of the states in the country will receive the highest number of points possible for this criteria (34 C.F.R. Subtitle B, Chapter II, 2009). As of April 2010, 26 states had joined to form the Partnership for Assessment of Readiness for College and Careers (PARCC) consortium, which is focused on developing summative assessments, and 31 states in the SMARTER Balanced Assessment Consortium (SBAC), which is focused on formative assessments (Maryland State Department of Education, 2010; USDE, 2010). In September 2010, the U.S. Department of Education announced that, as part of the Race to the Top competition, it would award PARCC $170 million dollars and SBAC $160 million dollars to develop assessments for the states in their respective consortiums (USDE, 2010). The department expects the new assessments to be implemented during the 2014–15 school year, and both consortiums are taking steps to ensure that these assessments will be appropriate for students with disabilities.

Evolving Accountability. Despite the notion that student assessment should inform school improvement, assessments have been used primarily to comply with the accountability and reporting requirements of ESEA and IDEA and have come to be perceived as tools for imposing negative consequences (Data Quality Campaign, 2009). There are several reasons for this including the inadequacy of the assessments to provide the precision necessary to make changes at the classroom or school level. In addition, traditional approaches to student assessment largely consisted of a snapshot approach: assessments are administered at one point during a school year and the results may not even be available for use during the current year. Results are used only to determine how students, schools, and districts are performing at that point in time with a cohort of students referred to as the status approach (Data Quality Campaign, 2008). When used with specific performance targets such as those defined by AYP, the results are useful for determining whether students are proficient at that point in time. However, tracking individual student progress over time offers greater precision and some believe greater fairness to schools as it allows for schools to show growth, even if students fail to meet a preset target. In order to implement growth models, states must have student-based data systems that allow for longitudinal tracking of performance.

Longitudinal data systems which collect detailed information on students and staff that can be linked together overtime, providing a detailed description of an individual student's educational history from the onset of schooling through graduation, and even beyond high school into postsecondary education and employment. Longitudinal data systems have the potential to be a repository of data that can be used to follow students' progress as they move from grade to grade, to determine whether they are progressing toward college and career readiness, to identify students who are at risk for failure, to determine the value-added by specific schools and programs, to evaluate trends over time, and to identify consistently high performing schools (Achieve, Inc., 2006).

In contrast to the current accountability mechanisms required by NCLB which utilize snapshot data to determine whether a minimum number of students within states, school districts, and schools attain proficiency on annual assessments, longitudinal data systems allow for accountability based upon the "value added" by teachers (Harris, 2009). Although the standard based reforms and the accountability mechanisms in NCLB may be a promising policy for promoting student achievement, the multitude of factors that influence student achievement have been cited as a fundamental problem in holding schools accountable. In addition to schools, factors such as family and community demographics are strong predictors of student achievement. Consequently, non-school contributors are substantially reflected in current school performance measures, masking then genuine improvements in student achievement that should attributed to the school (Harris, 2009).

In response to the criticisms of the snapshot approach to accountability, a pilot program utilizing growth-based accountability models was announced by the U.S. Department of Education in 2005. Rather than relying on the traditional accountability approach where schools are held accountable for the number of students who are proficient on state exams in any given year, the growth models track individual student achievement from year to year and schools are given credit for improvements in student achievement overtime. In 2005–06, two states, Tennessee and North Carolina, received approval to participate in the pilot program and since then an additional 13 states received approval by the 2009–10 school year. Needless to say, the notion that different students can have different growth trajectories, while empirically validated, is not consistent with the concept of equity defined as equal outcomes.

Student-Level Accountability. Policies that have focused on measuring the aggregate performance of students at school and system levels have been the most predominant since the 1990s, but states and districts have also been increasing standards and accountability at the student-level, notably through new graduation requirements and exams. States began using exams to make decisions about graduation in the late 1960s and early 1970s (Johnson et al., 2007), but these tests were designed to make sure that all students achieved a basic level of education in core academic subjects. North Carolina, New York, and Florida were among the first states to administer minimum competency exams during the early years (CEP, 2009a). The use of these exams, which specifically tested literacy and numeracy skills, gained momentum in the 1970s and 1980s, and were relatively common in states in the early 1990s (Lerner, 1991).

The current national picture of student-level accountability has changed drastically. As of November 2009, 24 states required students to pass exit exams before they receive a high school diploma (CEP, 2009a). Sixteen of these states added this requirement within the last nine years (CEP, 2009a). Arkansas began withholding diplomas for students who did not pass the Arkansas Comprehensive Assessment Program in 2010, and in 2012, Oklahoma will no longer grant diplomas to students who do not pass the Oklahoma End-of-Instruction (EOI) Exams (CEP, 2009a). Of the 26 states that currently require or plan to implement exit exams as a requirement for graduation, 19 offer alternate pathways to graduation for general education students, and 22 states allow students with disabilities to pursue alternative methods. The requirements for students to demonstrate mastery of high school-level knowledge in an alternate manner vary widely from state to state, but alternative assessments, portfolio assessments, and waivers are popular options (CEP, 2009a).

Graduation Requirements and Students with Disabilities. As the minimum competency movement grew, so did the questions about including students with disabilities in the exams (Johnson et al., 2007). Without explicit federal policy, states were left to decide whether students with disabilities would be required to fulfill the test requirement. Some states chose to exclude students with disabilities from these tests altogether. Others decided to establish different standards for these students, modify the testing procedures, use a student's IEP as the standard for graduation, or allow no modifications at all (Wildemuth, 1983). While states are now required by law to include students with disabilities in statewide assessments, there is no federal policy that mandates specific graduation requirements. Accordingly, graduation requirements, including implementation of these requirements for students with disabilities, vary widely from state to state, and even between school districts within a given state (Johnson et al., 2007). Many states offered multiple diploma options tied to the different types of academic standards and performance on state assessments. Students with disabilities tended to be especially affected by this trend, as they could be awarded a certificate of attendance or other non-standard diploma when they are unable to meet traditional graduation requirements. These non-standard diplomas can lead to consequences after high school when students attempt to obtain a job or pursue further education (Johnson et al., 2007; Thurlow & Johnson, 2000). The use of such diplomas may be mitigated by recent changes in how states are to define and report graduation rates.

Standardizing Graduation Rates

While states have been increasing the requirements for obtaining a high school diploma, there has also been a movement to standardize how graduation rates are calculated. In 2005 the National Governors Association (NGA) convened a Task Force on State High School Graduation Data to make recommendations on how states could develop a graduation measure that was comparable across states and based on high quality data. The result was a recommendation, agreed to by all 50 governors, to calculate a high school graduation rate based on this formula:

$$\frac{\text{On-time graduates by year X}}{[(\text{first time 9th graders in year X-4}) + (\text{transfers in}) - (\text{transfers out})]} \text{ (NGA, 2005)}.$$

This graduation rate is applied to students who receive a standard diploma, not a certificate of completion or attendance or a General Educational Development (GED) certificate. Before a state can apply this formula it must have the ability to identify first time 9th graders, which generally implies that the state can track each student's enrollment and participation status from year to year.

On October 29, 2008, The U.S. Department of Education modified Section 200.19 of the Title I regulations of the Elementary and Secondary Education Act (ESEA), as amended by the No Child left Behind Act of 2001 (NCLB). The amendments change the "other academic indicators" that states use in defining "adequate yearly progress" including new requirements for calculating graduation rate, which is the other academic indicator for high school. The regulations require states to calculate graduation rates in a mandated uniform way referred to as the Adjusted Cohort Rate. This is defined in regulations as define the "four-year adjusted cohort graduation rate" as the number of students who graduate in four years with a regular high school diploma divided by the number of students who entered high school four years earlier (adjusting for transfers in and out, émigrés and deceased students. Students who graduate in four years include students who earn a regular high school diploma at the end of their fourth year; before the end of their fourth year; and, if a state chooses, during a summer session immediately following their fourth year (USDE, 2008). In order for a school or district to make AYP, it must meet or exceed the state's graduation rate goal or demonstrate continuous and substantial improvement from the prior year toward meeting that goal for each student subgroup, including those with disabilities. Each state must submit the following for peer review and approval by the U.S. Department of Education:

- A single graduation rate goal that represents the rate the state expects all high schools in the state to meet; and
- Annual graduation rate targets that reflect continuous and substantial improvement from the prior year toward meeting or exceeding that goal.

Graduation rates for each subgroup calculated as above will be reported as part of the AYP decisions beginning in school year 2011–12.

Teacher Policy.   Teachers are among the most important resources necessary for providing high-quality education for all students and increasing standards for teachers have been addressed in federal policy. Currently, NCLB and IDEA require teachers of core academic subjects to be "highly qualified," meaning they must hold a minimum of a bachelor's degree in the subject they teach or the credits equivalent to a major in the subject, have full state certification, and be able to demonstrate subject matter competency (Yell, 2006). However, research indicates that teacher's educational attainment, as well as other characteristic that are the bases for teacher compensation (e.g., experience) are weak predictors of teacher effectiveness (Hanushek, 1997). Consequently, accountability, as well as teacher compensation, based on teachers' impact on student achievement, has begun to gain momentum as a policy alternative for promoting teacher quality, and consequently student achievement. This approach to accountability and teacher compensation utilizes longitudinal data systems to determine the "value added" by teachers—their contribution to their students' achievement. As a result of this potential to use value added models to determine teachers' contributions to student achievement, there is renewed interest teacher merit pay policies, as well as using teacher value added as a component of teacher tenure decisions (Harris, 2009; Koedel & Betts, 2009).

Value-added accountability is viewed as a more effective and efficient way to improve teacher quality than current policies which reward teacher credentials and experience (Harris, 2009). Current policies emphasize educational attainment and experience (i.e., tenure) factors that have a weak relationship with teacher effectiveness (Hanushek, 1997); a value-added system shifts the focus away from credentials and experience toward student achievement. However, teacher merit pay based upon value-added models is not without limitations (Harris, 2009; Koedel & Betts, 2009). For example, one criticism of value-added models is the difficulty in isolating the value-added by individual teachers, separating it from other factors influencing student achievement including school administration, teamwork among teachers, and the cumulative nature of education (Harris, 2009). In addition, value-added models are often criticized for their reliance upon quantitative measures as these tend to be more reliable and stable over time compared to the less precise and qualitative measures of teacher performance (Gordon, Kane, & Staiger, 2006; Harris, 2009).

Summary

It is not an understatement that the scope and complexity of state and federal education policy have increased since the 1980s and continue to evolve. As policymakers and practitioners gained experience with some of the early standards driven initiatives, adjustments were inevitable. However, there has not been a retreat from the basic underlying goal of the reforms… educational equity defined as equal outcomes or closing the achievement gap for all students. However, two groups of students have proven to be particularly troublesome to accommodate within these reforms: English language learners and students with disabilities. Both of these student sub-groups pose unique issues to assessment policies; however there are deeper policy schisms for students with disabilities. In the following sections, we review what we know about progress students with disabilities have made under the standards-based reforms and consider how the interpretations of equity which undergird current policies can be reconciled with policies governing the education of students with disabilities.

Students with Disabilities and Standards: The Progress and the Challenges

Arguably there are various ways to assess what progress that has been made over the past two decades as students with disabilities moved from a simple notation in Goals 2000 to the current full inclusion in standards-based policies. One of the most important is to examine the progress made in closing the achievement gap between students with disabilities and other subgroups. This has been complicated by the changing state and federal policies that govern how students with disabilities were to be included in various reforms. For instance, as late as the mid-1990s it was common for states to have policies asserting that students with disabilities were to be included in their standards and assessment but at the same time allowing IEP teams to make decisions regarding if or how specific standards would be interpreted for an individual student (McLaughlin & Thurlow, 2003). Further, until the late 1990s, students with disabilities were routinely excluded from the National Assessment of Educational Progress (NAEP) and state and local assessments. Yet, the most recent NAEP data (NCES, 2009) indicate that the average fourth grade reading score for students with disabilities increased significantly from 1998 to 2009, however the mean scores have remained relatively flat since 2005 as has the gap of about 35 points between students with and without disabilities. For eighth grade reading, there has been no significant increase in average scores since 1998 and the gap has remained at about 36 points. The average mathematics score for students with disabilities in the 2009 NAEP assessment was higher than previous years and the gap between these students and those without disabilities was only 21 points. Eighth-grade math scores for students with disabilities were also higher than all previous years but there was a 58 point gap between the average score for students with and those without disabilities.

Aggregate information on the performance of students with disabilities on state assessments is difficult to obtain due, in part, to the variation among state standards, tests, and accommodation policies. McLaughlin, Krezmien, and Zablocki, (2009) analyzed 2005/06 school year assessment data compiled by the National Center on Educational Outcomes (NCEO) from state reports submitted to the U.S. Department of Education which used a common approach to classify students into three performance levels: basic, proficient, and advanced. The McLaughlin, et al. analyses of these data indicated that less than 40% of third grade students with disabilities scored at or above proficiency on state reading assessments and just over 40% scored at or above proficiency on state math assessments. The data also indicated a decreasing percentage of students scoring at or above proficiency as grade level increased.

There have been a number of limitations to assessing and reporting the performance of students with disabilities. These include issues with accommodation policies and test design (see for example, Cormier, Altman, Shyyan, & Thurlow, 2010). In addition, the population of students who receive special education changes from year to year, making it difficult to draw conclusions about changes in the aggregate achievement of students with disabilities over time. Individual students move in and out of the subgroup and the assumption is that the higher performing students will no longer receive special education and students with greater academic and functional learning needs will remain or enter. In addition, NAEP does not offer an alternate assessment and, therefore, some students with more severe disabilities are excluded. Consequently the NAEP data represent a higher functioning group of students than the national population of students with disabilities.

Educational Attainment and Economic Outcomes

Another way to judge the impact of reforms on students with disabilities is by examining educational attainment. Obtaining a high school diploma and a postsecondary degree or certificate has an important economic impact on individuals. Recent data from the Bureau of Labor Statistics (n.d.) indicate that among individuals ages 25 and over, the average weekly earnings of those with no high school diploma was about 47% less than individuals with high school diplomas and General Equivalency Degrees. While there is only about a 15% difference in average weekly wages between high school graduates and those with some college or an associate degree the wage gap only gets larger as individuals obtain more education (NCES, 2010).

There is a substantial body of research documenting the poor educational and post-school outcomes of students who have received special education (Blackorby & Wagner, 1996; Levine & Edgar, 1994; Newman, Wagner, Cameto, & Knokey, 2009; Wagner, Newman, Cameto, Garza, & Levine, 2005). For instance, the nationally representative National Longitudinal Transition Study-2 (NLTS2) which is following over 11,000 youth with disabilities has reported that 32% of students with disabilities in the sample who left high school in 2003 did not receive a diploma (Wagner et al., 2005). About 42% of these students had enrolled in some type of postsecondary education or training, compared to 51% of students in the general population (Wagner et al., 2005). Among the group enrolled, 6% had enrolled in business, vocational or technical schools, 13.1% in two-year colleges, and 7.6% in a four-year college or university. In comparison, 12% of the youth within the same age ranges in the general population were enrolled in two-year colleges and 28% in four-year institutions (Wagner et. al., 2005). However, in terms of employment, the NLTS2 found that about 40% of the youth in the sample who had left school were employed at the time of the first follow up, which was substantially below the 63% employment rate among students without disabilities in the same age group. However, employment varied by type of disability as well as by whether the student had received a high school diploma. A recent Current Population Survey (CPS), a monthly survey of households conducted by the Bureau of the Census, indicated a 72% employment rate for individuals without a disability ages 20 to 24 compared to 44% for the same aged individuals with a disability (U.S. Department of Labor, 2010). These employment outcomes have not improved significantly over time.

Yet, a 2001 report of the Urban Institute (Loprest & Maag, 2001) analyzed data from the Disability Supplement of the National Interview Survey to examine employment of persons with disabilities. They calculated that only 37% of the 16,000 working age persons reporting disabilities were working in 1994–95. While the main reason given for not working was lack of appropriate jobs (53%), 22% of the unemployed indicated lack of adequate training and skills as the reason they could not find a job. A separate survey of private and public sector employers (Bruyere, 2000) found that lack of experience (49%/53%) and lack of required skills/training (39%/45%) were the top barriers to employment and advancement of persons with disabilities.

Clearly, we know that education is a powerful mediator of adult income. Beyond the association with high school diplomas or postsecondary credentials, studies have found a significant positive association between reading assessment scores in adolescence and young adult outcomes, including educational attainment (Daniel et al., 2006; Lee, Daniels, Puig, Newgent, & Nam, 2008), employment (Caspi, Wright, Moffitt, & Silva, 1998) and wages (Neal & Johnson, 1996; Murnane, Willett, & Levy, 1995). For instance, Currie and Thomas (1999) found that both reading and math test scores at age 7 were significant predictors of future achievement at age 16 and labor market outcomes at age 23 and 33, even after controlling for demographic characteristics.

Researchers have similar findings with respect to mathematics. For instance, basic math skills, such as numeracy (i.e., number representation and ability to employ mathematical techniques), are associated with effective navigation of life events such as health care and making emergency medical decisions (Reyna & Brainard, 2007). Math course-taking has been shown to be associated with the likelihood of attaining a postsecondary degree and subsequent earnings (Rose & Betts, 2001). Using math course-taking data from the High School and Beyond Study (HSB), Rose and Betts found that in 1982 there was an earnings gap of $11,000 dollars between students whose highest level of math was vocational math versus students whose highest-level class was calculus.

Early acquisition of key educational skills gives the individual a relative advantage with cumulative returns in education (i.e., achievement in later grades, ultimate educational attainment and adult wages). Thus, decisions that restrict a student's opportunity to learn challenging subject matter content know to advantage them in the future are both inequitable and economically unsound. Yet, at the same time we must acknowledge that the data concerning students with disabilities, while indicating some progress toward increasing academic achievement and educational attainments, also suggest that the impacts on adult economic attainment are yet to be fully realized.

Some may argue that it is still too early to judge the impact of reforms on students with disabilities while others argue that the focus on closing the achievement gap between students with disabilities and other students is both unattainable, detracts from the necessity to provide more practical vocational and functional curricula which will improve their chances at being employed and thus conflicts with the basic guarantee to FAPE. This is the dilemma that will confront educational leaders as they are faced with implementing standards-driven policies within the context of special education policies.

The Challenge for Special Education Leaders

Among the first challenges that face special education leaders in today's educational context is communicating with practitioners and parents the intent and value of including students with disabilities in the standards, assessment and accountability while supporting them in developing processes and structures that permit individualized decision making. Leaders must help practitioners negotiate the tension between the guarantee to a Free and Appropriate Public Education (FAPE) that is the central entitlement within the IDEA and the requirement that students with disabilities be held to common standards. Since FAPE is defined through a student's IEP, which is determined by an IEP team, leaders need to provide guidance and support to these teams as they develop their understanding of how to reconcile traditional beliefs and practices with the notion of standards. The concept of "standardizing" special education has been problematic from the beginning of the standards movement (McDonnell et al., 1997). Leaders must be able to understand and communicate the important differences between the procedural and substantive components of an IEP. Procedures such as timelines, composition of the IEP team and similar policies representative the procedural rights accorded to students and their families and these must be standardized. The substantive component of the IEP refers to the educational benefit a child receives. Too often the sole focus for administrators is the procedural integrity of the IEPs and not its educational outcome. Standards-based IEPs have emerged in response to the need to focus on outcomes and educational progress.

Standards-Based IEPs

An IEP that is based on standards is one in which individual educational goals are directly linked to a state's grade level content standards and assessments (Nolet & McLaughlin, 2005; Holbrook, 2007). These IEPs are designed to allow each child to receive an individually designed plan of services and supports, but they are focused on moving the student toward attaining state-determined content and achievement standards (although for some students the achievement standards may not be the same as those used for regular students). These IEPs can seem counter to the principle of individualization and to subvert the procedural rights for determining what constitutes FAPE for a student. Yet, special educational leaders must understand that these IEPs can meet both the procedural standards as specified in the IDEA and provide real and meaningful educational benefit. The goal for leaders is to enable teachers, parents, and other practitioners to develop deep understanding of how to construct such IEPs. These must be implemented with integrity and with their intended goal of meaningful progress toward the standards.

From an equity perspective, the standards–driven IEPs can ensure access to the same curricula and opportunity to learn the content that has been established as necessary for all other students, but only when the focus is on benefit and not simply the procedures. Every educational leader is responsible for ensuring equity. On the other hand, this responsibility is quite tricky, because determining what a child needs to learn is bounded by the prevailing social, economic and political contexts which have defined various general education reforms over the years (Ladd, 2008) as well as movements in special education. The ways in which IEP teams have operated as well as the ways in which special educators have been trained to think about IEPs and individualized goal setting are being challenged by the standards movement. Leaders must understand that challenging traditional ways of thinking are not in and of themselves bad or illegal, but the question of educational benefit must be carefully considered. Thus, leaders must ensure that the progress of each and every student with an IEP is carefully monitored and that special education and related services and supports are flexible and responsive to changes in student progress.

Do We Have the Tools?

Perhaps the biggest challenge facing special education leaders today is how to responsibly enforce policies such as standard-driven IEPs if teachers do not have the tools to achieve the goals of higher levels of achievement. The practical reality is that the field of special education does not currently have the knowledge base needed to help all students with disabilities learn at the same pace and to same level established by the standards. McLaughlin et al. (2009) recently reviewed selected literature related to effective literacy and math instruction for students with high incidence disabilities. They concluded that while the field of special education has compiled a substantial base of research it is limited to very specific areas. For instance, we know a great deal about effective early reading instruction, but far less about developing reading comprehension or supporting the reading problems of older students. We know less about effective practices in mathematics instruction, particularly in higher level mathematics and mathematical reasoning. We have little empirical research on effective instructional practices that increase academic achievement among students with moderate to significant intellectual disabilities or for students with emotional and behavioral disorders. Finally, we have a limited number of interventions that have shown to be able to be scaled up and sustainable. We also have almost no research regarding curriculum policies and other school-level factors that might influence the achievement of students with disabilities (Wilson, Hoffman, & McLaughlin, 2009).

Leaders cannot wait until the knowledge base catches up with the policy expectations. They must accept the challenge of helping the front line professionals adjust their practices and build their competency and confidence in how to make possible the goal of equal educational opportunity for every student with a disability.

Summary

Special education is at a crossroads. In some respects, special educational leaders have been playing catch up with standards-based policies. While the general education community has been immersed in the standards movement and the arguments regarding the validity of the standards for almost two decades, special educators only began this process after major IDEA changes in 1997 and were only confronted with the full impact of the standards-based reforms after passage of NCLB in 2001. Special education leaders are still reconciling the policies of universal standards and accountability and the core goals of all disability policies which have been described by Silverstein (2000) as maximizing individualization, inclusion, self-determination, economic self-sufficiency, and independent living.

We are at a point where simply tweaking IEPs or attempting to align provisions of existing policies is insufficient. We must reexamine the core purposes of IDEA specifically within an environment in which students with disabilities are increasingly part of larger standards based policies. Current disability classification and eligibility requirements in the IDEA make no sense within a system that classifies students in terms of the standards (e.g., regular, modified, alternate) they are expected to achieve. We need also recognize that the lines between students with and without IEPs are blurring. Schools have substantial numbers of low achieving or struggling students who can and should benefit from additional specialized supports and services provided within the same curriculum and with the same performance expectations. At the same time we recognize that some students will require sustained specialized attention within our educational system. These students most likely will have IEPs and require some sort of special instructional strategies or other services that will necessitate additional educational resources and protections. Educational equity for both groups of students must be measured by progress toward valued and meaningful standards, and it is the responsibility of every educational leader to ensure that progress.

References

Achieve, Inc. (2006). *Creating a longitudinal data system: Using data to improve student achievement*. Retrieved from http://www.achieve.org/node/547

Albus, D., Lazarus, S. S., Thurlow, M. L., & Cormier, D. (2009). *Characteristics of states' alternate assessments based on modified academic achievement standards in 2008* (Synthesis Report 72). Minneapolis: University of Minnesota, National Center on Educational Outcomes.

Berne, R., & Stiefel, L. (1984). *The measurement of equity in school finance: Conceptual, methodological, and empirical dimensions*. Baltimore: Johns Hopkins University Press.

Blackorby, J., & Wagner, M. (1996). Longitudinal postschool outcomes of youth with disabilities: Findings from the National Longitudinal Transition Study. *Exceptional Children, 62*, 399–413.

Brown v. Board of Education, 347 U.S. 483 (1954).

Bruyere, S. M. (2000). *Disability employment policies and practices in private and federal sector organizations* (Technical Report). Ithaca, NY: Cornell University, Program on Employment and Disability, School of Industrial Labor Relations.

Bureau of Labor Statistics. (n.d.). *Labor force statistics from the Current Population Survey*. Retrieved November 16, 2010, from http://www.bls.gov/cps/home.htm

Bush, G. (1990). Address before a joint session of Congress on the State of the Union, January 31, 1990. *Weekly Compilation of Presidential Documents*. Washington, DC: National Archives and Record Administration.

Caspi, A., Wright, B. R. E., Moffitt, T. E., & Silva, P. A. (1998). Early failure in the labor market: Children and adolescent predictors of unemployment in the transition to adulthood. *American Sociological Review, 63*, 424–451.

Center on Education Policy. (2009a). *State high school exit exams: Trends in test programs, alternate pathways, and pass rates*. Washington, DC: Author.

Center on Education Policy. (2009b). *State test score trends through 2007–08, part 4: Has progress been made in raising achievement for students with disabilities?* Washington, DC: Author.

Coleman, J. (1968). The concept of equality of educational opportunity. *Harvard Educational Review, 38*(1), 7–22.

Coleman, J. S., Campbell, E. Q., Hobson, C. J., McPartland, J., Mood, A. M., Weinfield, F. D., & York, R. L. (1966). *Equality of Educational Opportunity Study (EEOS)*. Washington, DC: U.S. Department of Health, Education & Welfare, Office of Education/National Center for Education Statistics.

Common Core State Standards Initiative. (2010a). *Application to students with disabilities*. Retrieved June 3, 2010, from http://www.corestandards.org/assets/application-to-students-with-disabilities.pdf

Common Core State Standards Initiative. (2010b). *Introduction to the Common Core State Standards*. Retrieved June 3, 2010, from http://www.corestandards.org/assets/ccssi-introduction.pdf

Cormier, D. C., Altman, J. R., Shyyan, V., & Thurlow, M. L. (2010). A summary of the research on the effects of test accommodations: 2007–2008 (Technical Report 56). Minneapolis: University of Minnesota, National Center on Educational Outcomes. Retrieved from http://www.cehd.umn.edu/NCEO/OnlinePubs/Tech56/TechnicalReport56.pdf

Currie, J., & Thomas, D. (1999). *Early test scores, socioeconomic status and future outcomes.* National Bureau of Economic Research Working Paper No. 6943.

Daniel, S., Walsh, A., Goldston, D., Arnold, E., Reboussin, B., & Wood, F. (2006). Suicidality, school dropout, and reading problems among adolescents. *Journal of Learning Disabilities, 39*(6), 507–514.

Data Quality Campaign. (2008). *Tapping into the power of longitudinal data: A guide for school leaders.* Retrieved from http://www.dataqualitycampaign.org/files/publications-tapping_into_the_power_of_longitudinal_data-a_guide_for_school_leaders-010108.pdf

Data Quality Campaign. (2009). *The next step: Using longitudinal data systems to improve student success.* Retrieved from http://www.dataqualitycampaign.org/files/NextStep.pdf

Elman, C., & O'Rand, A. M. (2004). The race is to the swift: childhood adversity, adult education, and economic attainment. *American Journal of Sociology, 110,* 123–160.

Geenen, K., Thurlow, M. L., & Ysseldyke, J. E. (1995). A disability perspective on five years of education reform (Synthesis Report No. 22). Minneapolis: University of Minnesota, National Center on Educational Outcomes. Retrieved June 15, 2010, from http://education.umn.edu/NCEO/OnlinePubs/Synthesis22.html

Goals 2000: Educate America Act, Pub. L. No. 103-227 (1994). Retrieved June 15, 2010, from http://www2.ed.gov/legislation/GOALS2000/TheAct/index.html

Gordon, R., Kane, T. J., & Staiger, D. O. (2006). *Identifying effective teachers using performance on the job.* Retrieved from http://www.brookings.edu/~/media/Files/rc/papers/2006/04education_gordon/200604hamilton_1.pdf

Hanushek, E. (1997). Assessing the effects of school resources on student performance: An update. *Educational Evaluation and Policy Analysis, 19*(2), 141–164.

Hanushek, E. A., & Raymond, M. E. (2002). The confusing world of educational accountability. *National Tax Journal, LIV*(2), 365–384.

Harris, D. N. (2009). Would accountability based on teacher value added be smart policy? An examination of the statistical properties and policy alternative. *Education Finance and Policy, 4,* 319–350.

Holbrook, M. D. (2007, August). *Standards-based Individualized Education Program examples.* Alexandria, VA: National Association of State Directors of Special Education, Project Forum. Retrieved from http://www.nasdse.org/Portals/0/Standards-BasedIEPExamples.pdf

Improving America's Schools Act of 1994. Pub. L. No. 103-382.

Individuals with Disabilities Education Act Amendments of 1997, Pub. L. No. 105-17, §1400, 37 Stat. 111 (1997).

Johnson, D. R., Thurlow, M. L., & Stout, K. E. (2007). *Revisiting graduation requirements and diploma options for youth with disabilities: A national study* (Technical Report 49). Minneapolis: University of Minnesota, National Center on Education Outcomes.

Katsiyannis, A., Zhang, D., Ryan, J., & Jones, J. (2007). High-stakes testing and students with disabilities. *Journal of Disability Policy Studies, 18,* 160–167.

Koedel, C., & Betts, J. (2009). Value added to what? How a ceiling in the testing instrument influences value-added estimation. *Education Finance and Policy, 5,* 54–81.

Kohl, F .L., McLaughlin, M. J., & Nagle, K. (2006). Alternate achievement standards and assessments: A descriptive investigation of 16 states. *Exceptional Children, 73*(1), 107–122.

Ladd, H. F. (2002). School based accountability systems: The promise and the pitfalls. *New Tax Journal, 54*(2), 385–400.

Ladd, H. F. (2008). Reflections on equity, adequacy, and weighted student funding. *Education Finance and Policy, 3*(4), 402–423.

Lee, S., Daniels, M., Puig, A., Newgent, R., & Nam, S. (2008). A data-based model to predict postsecondary attainment of low-socioeconomic-status students. *Professional School Counseling, 11*(5), 306–316.

Lerner, B. (1991). Good news about American education. *Commentary, 91*(3), 19-25.

Levine, P., & Edgar, E. (1994). Respondent agreement in follow-up studies of graduates of special and regular education programs. *Exceptional Children, 60,* 334–343.

Loprest, P., & Maag, E. (2001). *Barriers and supports for work among adults with disabilities: Results from the NHIS-D.* Washington, DC: The Urban Institute.

Maryland State Department of Education. (2010). *Maryland Race to the Top application draft.* Retrieved from http://www2.ed.gov/programs/racetothetop/phase2-applications/maryland.pdf

Mazzeo, C. (2002). Frameworks of state assessment policy in historical perspective. *Teacher's College Record, 103*(3), 367–397.

McDonnell, L. M., McLaughlin, M. J., & Morison, P. (Eds.). (1997). *Educating one and all: Students with disabilities and standards-based reform.* Washington, DC: National Academy Press.

McLaughlin, M. J. (2010). Evolving interpretations of educational equity and students with disabilities. *Exceptional Children, 76*(3), 265–278.

McLaughlin, J. M., Krezmien, M., & Zablocki, M. (2009). Special education in the new millennium: Achieving educational equity for students with learning and behavioral disabilities. *Advances in Learning and Behavioral Disabilities, 22,* 1–31.

McLaughlin, M. J., & Thurlow, M. (2003). Educational accountability and students with disabilities: Issues and challenges. *Educational Policy, 17*(4), 431–451.

Murnane, R. J., Willett, J. B., & Levy, F. (1995). The growing importance of cognitive skills in wage determination. *Review of Economics and Statistics 78*(2), 251–66.

National Center for Education Statistics (NCES). (2009). *NAEP— 2009 Reading: Grade 4 National Results.* Retrieved from http://nationsreportcard.gov/reading_2009/nat_g4.asp?subtab_id=Tab_6&tab_id=tab1#tabsContainer

National Center for Education Statistics (NCES). (2010). *Digest of Education Statistics:2009.* Retrieved from http://nces.ed.gov/programs/digest/d08/tables/dt08_051.asp

National Governors Association. (2005). *Graduation counts: A report of the National Governors Association Task Force on state high school graduation data: Redesigning the American high school.* Washington, DC: Author. Retrieved from http://www.nga.org/Files/pdf/0507GRAD.PDF

Newman, L., Wagner, M., Cameto, R., & Knokey, A.-M. (2009). *The post-high school outcomes of youth with disabilities up to 4 years after high school. A report of findings from the National Longitudinal Transition Study-2 (NLTS2) (NCSER 2009-3017).* Menlo Park, CA: SRI International. Retrieved from http://www.nlts2.org/reports/2009_04/nlts2_report_2009_04_complete.pdf

No Child Left Behind Act of 2001, Pub. L. No. 107-110, 1001 et seq.

Nolet, V., & McLaughlin, M. J. (2005). *Accessing the general curriculum: Including students with disabilities in standards-based reform* (2nd ed.). Thousand Oaks, CA: Corwin Press.

Neal, D., & Johnson, W. (1996). The role of premarket factors in black-white wage difference. *Journal of Political Economy, 104*(5), 869–895.

O'Neill, O. (1976). Opportunities, equalities and education. *Theory and Decision, 7,* 275–295.

Race to the Top Fund, Final Rule, 34 CFR Subtitle B, Chapter II (November 2009). Retrieved June 2, 2010, from http://edocket.access.gpo.gov/2009/pdf/E9-27426.pdf

Race to the Top Fund; Notice Inviting Applications for New Awards for Fiscal Year (FY) 2010; Overview Information; Notice (April 2010). Retrieved June 2, 2010, from http://www2.ed.gov/legislation/FedRegister/announcements/2010-2/041410a.pdf

Reyna, V., & Brainard, C.J. (2007, March). The importance of mathematics in health and human judgment: Numeracy, risk communication, and medical decision making. *Learning & Individual Differences, 17*(2), 147–159.

Rose, H., & Betts, J. R. (2001). *Math matters: The links between high school curriculum, college graduation, and earnings.* San Francisco: Public Policy Institution of California. Retrieved from http://www.ppic.org/content/pubs/report/R_701JBR.pdf

Silverstein, R. (2000). *An overview of the disability policy framework: A guidepost for analyzing public policy.* Washington, DC: Center for the Study and Advancement of Disability Policy.

Thurlow, M., & Johnson, D. (2000). High-stakes testing of students with disabilities. *Journal of Teacher Education, 51,* 305–314.

U.S. Department of Education. (2008, October). *A uniform, comparable, graduation rate: How the final regulations for Title I hold schools, districts, and states accountable for improving graduation rates.* Retrieved from http://www2.ed.gov/policy/elsec/reg/proposal/uniform-grad-rate.html

U.S. Department of Education. (2010, September 2). *U.S. Secretary of Education Duncan announces winners of competition to improve student assessments.* Retrieved from http://www.ed.gov/news/press-releases/us-secretary-education-duncan-announces-winners-competition-improve-student-asse

U.S. Department of Labor. (2010). *Labor Force Statistics from the Current Population Survey: How the Government Measures Unemployment.* Retrieved from http://www.bls.gov/cps/cps_htgm.htm

Vinovskis, M. A. (1999). *The road to Charlottesville: The 1989 Education Summit.* Washington, DC: National Education Goals Panel.

Wagner, M., Newman, L., Cameto, R., Garza, N., & Levine, P. (2005). *After high school: A first look at the postschool experiences of youth with disabilities: A report from the National Longitudinal Transition Study-2 (NLTS-2).* Menlo Park, CA: SRI International.

Wildemuth, B. M. (1983). Minimum competency testing and the handicapped. *ERIC Digest* (ERIC Document Reproduction Service No. ED289886).

Wilson, M. G., Hoffman, A. V., & McLaughlin, M. J. (2009). Preparing youth with disabilities for college: How research can inform transition policy. *Focus on Exceptional Children, 41,* 1-12..

Yell, M. L. (2006). *The law and special education* (2nd ed). Upper Saddle River, NJ: Pearson Education.

Zhang, D., Katsiyannis, A., & Kortering, L. (2007). Performance on exit exams by students with disabilities: A four-year analysis. *Career Development for Exceptional Individuals, 30,* 48–57.

Index